W9-BFN-222

The Art of M&A
A Merger
Acquisition
Buyout Guide

The Art of M&A
A Merger
Acquisition
Buyout Guide

Stanley Foster Reed
and Lane and Edson, P.C.

Alexandra Reed Lajoux
Project Manager

DOW JONES-IRWIN
Homewood, Illinois 60430

Sponsoring editor: Jim Childs
Project editor: Joan Hopkins
Production manager: Bette Ittersagen
Jacket Designer: Sam Concialdi
Compositor: Publication Services, Inc.
Typeface: 11/13 Times Roman
Printer: The Maple-Vale Book Manufacturing Group

LIBRARY OF CONGRESS
Library of Congress Cataloging-in-Publication Data

Reed, Stanley Foster.
   The art of M&A.

   Includes index.
   1. Consolidation and merger of corporations.
I. Lane and Edson, P.C.   II. Title   III. Title: Art of
M and A.   IV. Art of M&A.
HD2746.5.R44   1989   658.1'6   88–25741
ISBN 1-55623-113-X

Printed in the United States of America
2 3 4 5 6 7 8 0 MV 5 4 3 2 1 0 9

CONTENTS

Bridge Loans. Equity Investment Funds. Seller
Takeback Financing. Registration Rights.
Intercreditor Issues. Subordination Issues.
Intercreditor Agreements.

The Non-Tax Factors. The Role of Tax Planning.
Definitions and Basic Tax Concepts, Taxation of
C Corporations, and Pass-Through Entities. Choice
of Entity. Asset Acquisition or Stock Acquisition.
Limitations on Loss Carryovers. Tax-Free and
Tax-Deferred Transactions. Structuring Taxable
Acquisitions. Disposition of Unwanted Assets.
Financing the Acquisition. Transaction Diagrams.

Introduction. Management Buyout Basics. Negotiating and Documenting an MBO. Legal Considerations
in MBOs. MBO Tax Considerations. Tax-Free Stock
Rollovers. Employment Agreements. Employee
Benefits in MBOs. Stockholders' Agreements.

Introduction. Financial Considerations in Evaluating the Target. Accounting for Mergers and Acquisitions. Carryover of Predecessor Cost in Leveraged
Buyouts. Involvement of Accountants in Mergers
and Acquisitions.

CHAPTER 8 Due Diligence Inquiry

Introduction. Getting Started. Buyer-Seller Relationship. Target Litigation Analysis. Environmental Exposure Analysis. Do-It-Yourself Due Diligence. Assessing Information. Duration of Due Diligence.

APPENDIX 8A Due Diligence Checklist

Documents. Market Studies/Reports on Company's Product. Key Information from the Company's Management. Key Information from Outside Sources.

APPENDIX 8B Sample Confidentiality Agreement

CHAPTER 9 Pension, Labor and Compensation Concerns

Introduction. Employee Benefit Plans. Determining Plan Assets and Liabilities and Their Effect on Company Books. Plan Split-Ups and Partial Terminations. Underfunded and Overfunded Plans. Employee Stock Ownerships Plans. ESOP Securities Issues. Using Non-ESOP Stock Plans. Problems in Acquisitions of Unionized Companies. Fringe Benefit Plans. Plans Holding Stock. Effect of Corporate Structure.

CHAPTER 10 Negotiating the Acquisition Agreement and the Letter of Intent

Introduction. Letter of Intent. The Acquisition Agreement. Component Parts of the Agreement. Introductory Material. Representations and Warranties. Covenants. Conditions to Closing. Indemnity Section. Acquisitions from an Affiliated Group. Transactions Involving Public Companies.

APPENDIX 10A Sample Letter of Intent

INTRODUCTION

Much can be and has been said about the broad economic, social, and business reasons for the mergers and acquisitions phenomenon. The widespread creation of conglomerate business ownership in the last several decades has prepared managers to treat businesses as articles of commerce not much different from the products these businesses sell. There is an ample supply of businesses for sale, thanks largely to conglomerates finding that the whole, for them, is less than the sum of its parts, and to a stock market that persists in undervaluing going concerns. Money is available to buyers, both directly and through lenders; perhaps because of lack of international lending opportunities or a disinclination to invest in the stock market, perhaps from the profits generated by high real rates of interest over the last eight years, or for a myriad of other reasons beyond our knowledge. The government regulatory atmosphere has been favorable, and the business climate, though still hesitant in the long wake of October 1987, largely confident.

The process of buying and selling operating businesses is now in full swing, and, feeding on itself, grows more active all the time. Increasing numbers of foreign investors seek acquisitions in the United States; lenders grow more sophisticated, and better able to carry out larger and more leveraged transactions; bidding becomes more intense as more potential buyers enter the market; acquisitions occur as defenses against being acquired.

As more and more businesses change hands, patterns of ownership, organization, and management are being reshaped. Companies are abruptly transferred out of the quiet (or at least the continuity) of family ownership or the backwater of a large corporate parent, and enter a new corporate life with the stimulus and burden of acquisition debt, or are trimmed and tailored to fit the needs of another enterprise. The changes are not always well planned, and can involve strain and human cost, but most of us are ready to believe that they tend to increase efficiency and redirect efforts into more productive and profitable directions. We also tend to think that there is a need, now being met through these changes, to bring ownership and management more closely into line with each other.

The M&A boom is a massive, complex, and important phenomenon, and any single observer, like one of the nine blind men of Hindustan confronting the elephant, can grasp only a part of it. Our part, in this book, is to look at the process of accomplishing an acquisition: how does it happen; who does what; what are the necessary parts and players; and how do they fit together? We leave to other observers both philosophic speculations about the broader significance or benefits of this process, and predictions of future trends in financing, government policy, or business climate that will continue to shape it. This is a book about the art of M&A, as practiced today.

Still, we are not modest about the importance of our part of the elephant. Anyone who wishes to understand the M&A phenomenon cannot stay in the lofty realms of social trends and macroeconomic factors. The mechanics of doing something greatly affects the end product. You must come down to the boiler room with us, watch the pistons pump up and down, and hear the clatter of the machinery.

In large part, the reason that companies are being bought and sold with great vigor today is that methods have been worked out that make it possible and profitable to do so. These methods evolve over time, making available new financing resources, accommodating new restrictions on takeovers or new sources of liability, whether environmental, labor related, or otherwise. They are shaped by basic cultural attitudes: a willingness to trust the representations of others or to bet on the entrepreneurial skill of a new CEO you've met only five times; a willingness to lend and to borrow even though repayment requires an improvement in performance over historical levels; an enormous attention to details, often highly technical and legalistic, of business relationships. They also depend on a highly developed technical support system for deal-doing that includes instant or overnight capacity to generate, revise, and communicate lengthy documents, and on access on very short notice to a wide variety of technical advice not just from lawyers and accountants, but also from environmental engineers, appraisers, actuaries, insurance specialists, and others.

Process shapes product, and the process this book describes has given rise to a profound reshaping of the way business is done in the United States today. We wrote this book to provide people actively engaged in the merger and acquisitions world with good nuts and bolts advice. We also recommend it to those who are trying to understand, direct, and shape this phenomenon, so that they will have a better understanding of how deals are done. The M&A process can and has been of great benefit to American business. This book will more than justify the effort that went into it if it enhances that benefit by causing more deals to be done *right*.

ACKNOWLEDGEMENTS

This book is the joint effort of an entrepreneur and a law firm, representing the intense experience of its many writers over a period reaching back as far as 1965, when Stanley Foster Reed founded *Mergers & Acquisitions*, the first journal to focus on corporate acquisitions, and 1977, when Stanley Foster Reed and Al Rappaport, Leonard Spacek Professor of Accounting at Northwestern University, launched "Merger Week," the annual M&A boot camp. Lane and Edson, P.C. has provided lead legal representation in dozens of major leveraged buyout transactions since the classic Gibson Greeting Cards acquisition in 1982.

The law firm of Lane and Edson, P.C. appears as author of this book because it would be impossible otherwise to list the authors or to properly express the collaborative effort that the firm's attorneys put into the final product. Obviously, any work of this kind cannot cover every legal issue that will arise in a particular transaction, and is no substitute for specific legal advice in each case. Although every effort has been made to achieve accuracy, the firm cannot guarantee precision in every detail, and much less in nuance and emphasis. Among the attorneys who made significant contributions to some or all of the chapters are the following:

Kenneth S. August	Richard L. Perkal
J. Goodwin Bennett	Eugene M. Propper
Matt E. Egger	Barry R. Schenof
Jack M. Feder	Harry K. Schwartz
Thomas C. Hipkins	Kenneth M. Socha
Glendon E. Johnson, Jr.	Abraham Sofer
Alicia M. Kershaw	Lorraine Sostowski
Michael J. Kliegman	Frederic J. Truslow
Mark Kotlarsky	Thomas E. Weil, Jr.
Bruce S. Lane	Justine E. Wilcox

In addition we wish to acknowlege the assistance of the following persons with respect to the following chapters.

Chapter One—Getting Started in Mergers and Acquisitions and *Chapter Two—Planning and Finding*: Robert Rock, MLR Enterprises, Philadelphia, PA; Robert F. Burgess, Jr., Reed Associates, McLean, VA; Edward A. Weihman, Managing Director, Chemical Bank, New York, NY; Malcolm Pfunder of Hopkins, Sutter, Hamel & Park, Washington, DC; Gerald Wetlaufer, Professor of Business Law, Indiana University, Bloomington, IN; Clive Chajet, Chairman, Lippincott and Margulies, New York, NY; and, Mark Feldman, Vice President and Director, Hay Management Consultants, San Francisco, CA.

Chapter Three—Valuation and Pricing: Al Rappaport, Richard Linhart, Vice President, Wesray Capital Corporation, New York, NY, and Mikel Dodd, Vice President, Bradley & Company, Washington, DC.

Chapter Six—Structuring Management Buyouts: E. Burke Ross, Jr., Vice President of Wesray Capital Corporation.

Chapter Seven—Financial and Accounting Considerations is the work of the Mergers & Acquisition Group of Arthur Young, Chicago, IL, under the direction of Harold Nidetz, Managing Director. Arthur Young is an international accounting firm with offices in major cities worldwide.

Chapter Eight—Due Diligence Inquiry: Dan L. Goldwasser.
Chapter Nine—Pension and Compensation Concerns: Jeffrey Gates, Director, Kelso & Company, New York, NY.

Chapter Twelve—Public Company Acquisitions: Robert D. Ferris, Senior Vice President, Doremus Public Relations, and James J. Hanks, Jr.

Chapter Thirteen—Special Topics Relating to Transactions with International Aspects: Van Kirk Reeves, Conseillier, Coudert Freres, Paris, and Douglas E. Rosenthal, Partner, Sutherland, Asbill and Brennan, Washington, DC.

In addition, the authors would like to express their appreciation to the editorial staff: project manager, Alexandra Reed Lajoux, former Editor of *Mergers & Acquisitions* magazine; legal researchers Robert X. Marcovici, Bonnie M. Clements, and Riccardo R. Trigona; index manager Diane M. Reitz; and editorial secretary Christine B. Lacey.

A final word: we want this guide to be the single most comprehensive treatment of the M&A/LBO field ever produced. As you encounter new questions in coming years, we hope you find the answers in this book. If not, give us a call. We will try to answer your question on the spot—and in the next edition.

Washington, D.C.   Stanley Foster Reed
July, 1988   and
                                          Lane and Edson, P.C.

CHAPTER 1

GETTING STARTED
IN MERGERS
AND ACQUISITIONS

"A little learning is a dangerous thing.
Drink deep or taste not the Pierian spring.
There shallow draughts intoxicate the brain
And drinking largely sobers us again."

—Alexander Pope

Perhaps nowhere does this maxim prove truer than in the merger, acquisition, and buyout area. The purchase or sale of a business enterprise is one of the most complex transactions a person or a firm can undertake. One cannot "skim the top" off a transaction with a little effort and expect cream—the best deals come from getting to the bottom of things.

To drink deep at this particular spring of knowledge, recognize first that there is an acquisition process with many crucial stages and many key players. To carry out any one stage well requires solid grounding in the entire process. In the spirit of Pope's caveat, this book sets forth the basic elements of the acquisition process as it is conducted today, reflecting the technical requirements, the negotiating points, the language, and the attitudes of those who actually do these deals.

Each of the players plays a different role, and so we have tried to reflect the differing perspectives of buyer vs. seller and the contrasting views of two main types of buyer: (a) the operator-buyer, who intends to build the company through supplementing or complementing existing operations (see Chapter 2, on Planning), and (b) the investor-buyer, usually involved in a leveraged buyout, who intends to operate the target as an

1

independent, nonintegrated entity in order to repay acquisition debt and eventually resell it or to go public (see Chapter 3 on Valuation and Pricing, and Chapter 4 on Financing).

But first, some general definitions for those without a background in the basics.

What is a merger?

A merger occurs when one corporation is combined with and disappears into the other. For instance, the Missouri Corporation, just like the river, "merges" and disappears corporately into the Mississippi Corporation. Mississippi is the "survivor." All mergers are "statutory mergers," and sometimes you hear that term, since all mergers occur as specific formal transactions in accordance with the laws or "statutes" of the states where they are incorporated. Generally, the only test of whether a merger has occurred is whether the filings that accomplish that formal combination have been made and officially recorded. The post-deal manner of operating or controlling the company has no bearing on whether or not a merger has occurred.

What is a corporate acquisition?

A corporate acquisition is the process by which the stock or assets of a corporation come to be owned by the buyer. The transaction may take the form of a purchase of stock, a purchase of assets, or a merger. In this book, we often refer to the acquired corporation as the "target" or the "company."

What's the difference between a merger and an acquisition?

Acquisition is the generic term used to describe the transfer of ownership. Merger is a narrow, technical term for a particular procedure that may or may not be part of an acquisition: You can do an acquisition followed by a merger (for example, Mississippi acquires all of Missouri's stock, then Missouri merges into Mississippi); you can do an acquisition by means of a merger (for example, Mississippi merges with Missouri, calling in Missouri stock and replacing it with Mississippi stock or cash); or you can do an acquisition in which no merger occurs (for example, Mississippi acquires Missouri's stock, and Missouri remains as a separate subsidiary of Mississippi; or Mississippi acquires all Missouri's assets, leaving Missouri as a shell corporation with its original stockholders unchanged).

What is a "short form" merger?

When all or substantially all of the stock of one of the merging corporations is owned by the other, a simplified, "short form" merger is generally permitted under state law without a vote of stockholders. Other than short form mergers, all mergers require an affirmative vote of stockholders of both corporations, and all sales of all or substantially all the assets of a corporation require the affirmative vote of the selling, but not the buying corporation's stockholders.

What is a "consolidation?"

Two or more existing corporations agree to "consolidate" and create a new corporation to absorb them. Just like the rivers that meet at Pittsburgh to form the Ohio river, the Monongahela Corporation and the Allegheny Corporation *consolidate* themselves into the Ohio Corporation. Monongahela and Allegheny are the constituents, and Ohio is the new or resulting corporation.

What is an amalgamation?

This is not a word of art in the United States. Any group of entities can associate together or "amalgamate" operationally but not corporately.

What is a leveraged buyout (LBO)?

A leveraged buyout is a transaction in which a company's capital stock or its assets are purchased with borrowed money, causing the company's new capital structure to be primarily debt. An acquisition of all of the stock, usually by a corporation created for that sole purpose, will be immediately followed by a merger of buyer and the target company, so that the assets of the acquired corporation become available to the buyer-borrower to secure the loan. Leveraged buyouts are a major focus of this book. To get acquainted with them, read particularly Chapter 3, the second half of which is devoted to the valuation and pricing of LBOs; Chapter 4, on financing of LBOs and the particular kinds of debt used; and Chapter 5, on tax and non-tax structuring of LBOs.

There are several types of leveraged buyouts:

- *Management leveraged buyouts* (MBOs), where a key ingredient is bringing in the existing management team as shareholders. (See Chapter 6, on Structuring Management Buyouts.)
- *Employee buyouts* (EBOs), where the employees, using funds from an Employee Stock Ownership Plan (ESOP), most of which will have been borrowed, buy out the owners. (See Chapter 9 on Pension, Labor, and Compensation Concerns.)
- *Restructurings*, in which a major part of the acquired assets are subsequently sold off to retire the debt. (See Chapter 4, on Financing Leveraged Buyouts.)

What is a recapitalization?

This is not an acquisition but can make a company look as if it had just gone through a leveraged buyout. A public company, principally for takeover defense, re-configures the right side of its balance sheet, adding more debt and reducing its equity through a buyback of its shares. (See Chapter 12, on Public Company Acquisitions.)

What is a hostile acquisition or takeover?

An acquisition not approved of or agreed to by the target's management or board of directors is considered "hostile." This book does not focus extensively on hostile transactions but does address some issues relating to them in Chapter 12 on Public Company Acquisitions.

Many books have been written on specific aspects of the acquisition process. Most have focused on the hostile takeover—the battle of Bendix and Martin-Marietta, among others—or the spectacular exploits of some raiders and speculators. Takeover defenses, the Hart-Scott-Rodino Act, and tender offer strategies have been well covered.

We have chosen a different focus. The great bulk of acquisitions are not hostile but are based on mutual interest, negotiation, and accommodation, carried on by practitioners who have built their knowledge from years of experience in doing deals. Most of that experience is in the basics—the issues that come up every time a company is bought and sold. Does it fit our operations? How much should I pay? Should I do a forward or a reverse merger? What sort of investigation should I make of the company? What should the obligations of the parties be under the acquisition agreement? What kind of financing should I obtain? How do I get it closed?

The objective of this book is to acquaint the specialist and the non-specialist alike with the basics of the negotiated acquisition, both the substance—the financial, legal, accounting, and business practice rules that govern deals done today—and something of the feel of the deal as well.

The chapters of the book follow the basic sequence of the acquisition process, from planning, finding, and pricing through financing, structuring, investigation, and negotiation of acquisition agreements to closing. Much of the content of these chapters is advanced and sophisticated material; it wouldn't be very useful if it weren't. Still, it has been designed to be accessible to the kind of person, like the authors, whose eyes glaze over at pages of dense and technical exposition. This book can be read straight through. Or it can be used as a reference for specific points at any or all stages in the merger process.

To find a particular piece of information in this book, use the index. If you have a name for the specific point—you want to know about "fraudulent conveyance" or the "Herfindahl-Hirschman Index"—look it up directly in the index. If the point has a number but not a name, e.g., "Section 338" or "Rule 10b-5," look it up under "Section" or "Rule" in the Index. If you want to understand better an area of the acquisition process, look up that area in the Index—for example, "financing"—and there you will find the entire structure of that area wherever it appears in the book. Run your eye down the headings until you see where to start reading.

Throughout the book, where legal cases contribute important authority to a point of law, we have provided a brief key word citation. For the complete citation—or to find all in one place the most important cases in this area—refer to the Table of Cases.

We can't claim completeness in all areas. The more we look into M&A, the more information, interrelationships, opportunities, and nuances we find that we haven't covered, or haven't covered fully. Perhaps that's what makes M&A an art, not a science. Drink deep.

CHAPTER 2

PLANNING AND FINDING

INTRODUCTION

This chapter addresses the first two stages in the merger/acquisition/buyout process—deciding what to buy and then finding it. In the first stages, the potential buyer determines the characteristics that it wants in a target. In the second stage, it seeks to identify specific targets that meet or approximate those criteria.

But buyers are of two different types: those who are looking to buy something to operate as part of a larger whole, and those who are looking strictly for an investment.

In the first case, the typical buyer is already a substantial operating company with one or several core businesses and wants to direct its acquisition efforts to strengthen, extend, and build its existing operations. Most of its analysis will be directed at selecting a target or targets with optimum interrelationships with the businesses it already has.

In the second case, the typical buyer is an investor—usually an investor group—who may not care at all about interrelationships. Its only concern is whether or not the target will generate the cash flow that will repay the purchase price and permit it, through dividends or subsequent resale, to turn a tidy or a massive profit on the transaction. Even if the investor/buyer owns many companies, it will want to minimize their interrelations so that each can be disposed of without affecting the others.

In a few words, buyers in the first category are primarily operationally driven while those in the second are primarily financially driven. There is a world of difference in their approaches to selecting a target.

This chapter focuses on the first type, the operator/buyer who, most likely, has institutionalized the strategic planning process. The investor/buyer, on the other hand, is likely to have a much narrower field of concern: price and its best friends, cash flow and financeability. He can buy and make good use of any company if the price is right and can be borrowed. His concerns and selection criteria are discussed in Chapters 3 and 4.

The portions of this chapter relating to finders and brokers and searching for specific targets should be of use to both the operating and the investing buyer. In fact, the investing buyer can probably benefit from a review of strategic planning considerations. After all, it's hard for him to price out an acquisition without either seeing the target's plans or creating a hypothetical one if he is prevented by law, timing, or resistance from seeing an existing one. And then, there's always the chance that the target doesn't even *have* a plan!

This chapter also addresses general government regulatory issues affecting acquisitions. Review of such limitations, particularly those relating to antitrust, should be performed as a part of the initial planning process, as it makes no sense for either an operating or an investing buyer to evaluate and search out a target which it is prohibited by law from acquiring.

Finally, the last section of the chapter covers post-acquisition planning, a key concern for all players—operators *and* investors. If you're buying management, but they don't agree with your plans for the company, you may be in trouble.

STRATEGIC PLANNING FOR OPERATING COMPANIES

Packaged strategic plans which categorized segmented operations in market-share/market-growth categories—and yielded classifications like "star" for high-growth/high-share, "dog" for low-growth/low-share, "cash cow" for high-share/low-growth, and "wildcat" for low-share/high-growth—were fine in the fifties and mid-sixties, but with the advent of cheap computing— especially the desk-top micro and seas of software—such simple abstractions have been supplanted by multi-variable analyses easily handled by even the simplest of desk-tops.

There are literally *hundreds* of variables that should be considered when contemplating a growth-by-acquisition strategy. Only the "systems approach" to strategic planning can encompass them all, isolate the key variables, and use them to develop plans that will work. (See Appendix B, Exhibit 4.)

How can strategic planning help the corporate merger/acquisition process?

Strategic planning is the process of identifying your corporate strengths and weaknesses and deciding what you intend to do about them: how you plan to exploit your strengths and to offset your weaknesses.

Having a plan of this sort in place greatly reduces the cost of analyzing specific acquisition opportunities—they either fit or they don't. A truly sophisticated strategy will even measure quantitatively how well or how poorly potential acquisitions fit and will rank them by degree of desirability.

One of the principal benefits of having a strategy for acquisitions is to prevent disastrous decisions by random "whyncha" processes. For example, the chairman or some influential board member of a cash-rich manufacturing company meets someone on a plane who says "Bowling is hot stuff, 'whyncha' buy some bowling alleys?" So in short order the company buys some bowling alleys, for which the company pays top dollar at the peak of the bowling boom—and it's trouble, trouble, trouble from there on out. They don't know the bowling business, and they paid too much even if they had!

Such decisions simply do not happen in companies where strategic thinking is ingrained in the board and in the executive team. Before deciding to enter a new area of business, strategic thinkers will make industry forecasts and study the "fit" with present operations. Because strategic planning requires choices, any opportunity—no matter how "hot"—will be forced to stand trial against other potential industry entries or internal expansions of present lines.

Strategic thinking, once installed, acts as a disciplinary force on everyone at the decisionmaking level. Instead of thousands of in-house and out-of-house ideas and acquisition suggestions coming up for detailed evaluation at great expense, any proposed area of entry can simply be matched against an agreed-upon set of criteria for the company's strategy. If it doesn't meet those criteria, it is turned down forthwith; little time or money is lost.

How can strategic planning help in divestiture?

In any multi-profit-center operation, strategic planning that does not automatically produce candidates for sell-off or shut-off is probably not truly strategic. It is necessary in any strategy to weigh what you *are* doing against what you *could* be doing with your resources. If the potential is greater in the new lines, then the old are converted to cash by selling them off, possibly at a premium to a firm where they "fit," and the cash is redeployed to new lines through internal or external development.

Are there various levels of strategy?

Yes. Strategies may be (and probably should always be) different at different levels in a corporation. The "six-level approach" is probably most suitable for the larger multi-companies and can be reduced to four or even three levels but probably not below that even for smaller companies.

What are the typical strategic planning levels?

Enterprise Strategy generally is developed at the board-of-director level. It asks and answers the question: "Why are we in this business (or these core businesses) anyway?" A strategy might develop at the enterprise level to expand the enterprise by making a major horizontal acquisition—perhaps some outfit three times as big—or a decision might be made to contract the enterprise by selling off major lines or to reallocate cash flows into entirely new lines totally unrelated to historic lines.

Two dramatic examples of this latter strategy in America are the complete conversion of Grace Lines—a 100-year-old shipping company—into a 100-division conglomerate under the leadership of Peter Grace, and the conversion of venerable American Can Company from a manufacturer of cans and paper cups into a financial services company under the guidance of Jerry Tsai.

Corporate Strategy the next level, deals with the allocation and reallocation of sector-level cash flows for reinvestment, for internal expansion, or for acquisition of new sector-level entries.

Sector Strategy calls for putting together those business units that have some common operating factors—technology, geography, distribution or market. Cash flows are redeployed to the more promising members of the group or are used to acquire additional business units that will complement or supplement present activities.

Business Unit Strategy deals with the reinvestment of a multi-product profit center's cash flows back into its present product lines or into new product lines by acquisition or start-up.

Product-Line Strategy deals with product life cycles—supplementing or replacing mature or aging products with new.

Functional Strategy, deals with alternate methods of manufacture—changing from aluminum die-casting to plastic injection molding for instance, or switching from wood to fiberglass or aluminum for a line of boats. It should also include plant relocation—looking for lower labor rates, cheaper rents, more employee amenities, proximity to raw materials, etc.

THE WHEEL OF OPPORTUNITY/FIT CHART APPROACH

What is the consensus planning model of growth by acquisition?

The original consensus model in M&A planning is the *Wheel of Opportunity/ Fit Chart Approach* ("WOFC"). (Note that WOFCs are made at *each* strategic level. Never try to mix them.)

How does the WOFC operate?

A Wheel of Opportunity/Fit Chart is a step-by-step method for creating a company "self-portrait" by answering the questions

1. What are our strengths and weaknesses?
2. What are our alternative opportunities for acquisitions and other changes?
3. What are our priorities for building on strengths and correcting weaknesses?
4. How do our opportunities fit with our priorities?

The WOFC system has been used by major U.S. and overseas firms from manufacturers to insurance companies, banks, and regional development authorities over the past two decades. Any business entity can make one and will profit by it. (A complete description of the process can be found in Stanley Foster Reed's three-part article in *Mergers & Acquisitions*, Vol.12, Nos. 2, 3 and 4 entitled "Corporate Growth by Strategic Planning.") Appendix A details the process.

The Process.   Having decided to construct a Wheel of Opportunity, the company or operating division assembles its top people. This group may include independent board members and outside consultants as well as officers—in fact, anyone who understands the operation's basic business and can be trusted with confidential corporate information.

In broadest outline, this group will develop (a) a list of possible alternative acquisitions, using a "Wheel of Opportunity" and (b) a set of criteria for selecting between these alternative acquisitions, based on a "Fit Chart." The alternative acquisitions on the Wheel are then scored against the Fit Chart criteria to determine which best meet the strategic needs of the company. (See Appendices A and B.)

Voting inputs will come from all participants, predominantly line chiefs, because they are responsible for profit-and-loss. Informational inputs will be provided by staff, who do not vote. In most companies, the CEO will have appointed someone to organize the WOFC sessions, to keep a record of the proceedings, and to make a summary which, with the help of the VP of Planning, will become the Strategic Plan. They will have selected the WOFC participants: usually, the CEO, the COO, the VP-Finance, the regional (or sector) operating heads, the VP for Marketing, and the VP for Planning (eight in all). Experience shows that eight to twelve participants is optimum: Fewer participants makes the results too sensitive to one person's vote; more makes the session drag on too long. The CEO often does not want to participate for fear his vote would influence the others. He should consent when he learns that most of his inputs will be anonymous.

Previous to the meeting, each of the participants has been given a pad of blank Opportunity Sheets and Strength and Weakness sheets evaluating the company, with instructions to fill them out and to get their principal employees to do likewise. (See Appendix A for examples.)

The sessions start with a review of the Strength and Weakness Sheets. Many are discarded outright, some are combined with others. Staff assistants make notes, and the final versions are typed up and redistributed as a package. It is important that each member of the group have the same understanding of the particular strength or weakness as the others. But no attempt should be made to *rate* them or relate any of them directly to any specific potential acquisition move at this stage.

Next, the Opportunity Sheets are reviewed and discussed at great length, again to make sure that each member of the group understands the nature of the potential entry. Only the most hare-brained schemes or suggestions are discarded. Again, staff assistants make notes, and the final versions are typed up and redistributed as a package.

A Wheel of Opportunity has six facets grouped into three modes. Each facet sets forth a different type of acquisition to be considered.

The Market Intensification Mode

- *Horizontal Integration*—acquiring a head-to-head competitor, someone who sells the same product or provides the same service that you do, to the same customer in your same geographic area.

- *Market Extension* — acquiring someone who sells the same product that you do to the same kind of customer in a geographic area you do not now serve.

The Vertical Integration Mode

- *Vertical Backward Integration* — acquiring a supplier.
- *Vertical Forward Integration* — acquiring a customer.

The Diversification Mode

- *Product Extension* — acquiring a producer of a new product or service that, in general, is sold to the same customers that you sell to.
- *Conglomerate or "Free-Form" Extension* — acquiring a producer of a new product or service in a geographic area not now served.

The primary purpose of the classification scheme is to make it possible to discover, through the device of the Fit Chart, not only which of the six particular *kinds* of entries score the highest, but which *modes* hold the most potential.

What is the key information needed to bring out the opportunities available in each category on the Wheel?

Step One. *Enter on the Opportunity Wheel the principal market (geographic) areas served by present product lines or services, usually noting growth in the market and the market share currently attained.*

Horizontal or Market Integration. The first facet that should be considered is Horizontal Integration. That's the interface with present competitors. For any principal line of endeavor, it is essential that growth in the marketplace and market penetration be known in order to develop a strategy. One of the major benefits of horizontal integration is the potential to reduce operating and financial costs associated with carrying of inventory.

Step Two. Enter all future potential markets for your present principal line or lines by logical geographic breakdowns. If known, enter growth rates for sales in that market.

Market Extension. This information identifies geographic areas not now significantly served and estimates the growth rate of demand for present products or services in those territories. Participants should enter market areas in whatever breakdowns make sense and estimate the growth rates according to their best judgment.

Horizontal or Market Integration plus Market Extension make up the Market Intensification Mode. In general, it is probably good policy to explore these two interfaces and this Mode thoroughly, for these are the low-risk interfaces, and this is the low-risk Mode.

Step Three. Lump all suppliers of each kind together and enter the percentage of your total annual purchases from each.

Backward Vertical Integration looks at what you buy. At this stage, rather than particular suppliers, you want to list the items or services you buy in significant quantities. These then are listed in natural groupings, and the percent of purchases in that industry is related to your total purchasing dollar.

The significance of making an entry into a supplier industry is primarily to reap the benefits that will be obtained from increased sales of the supplier if expansion takes place in the Market Intensification Mode. A company with a sales dollar composed of 20 percent costs of one service or commodity and which is contemplating *doubling* sales by the Market Intensification Mode should look early on to the profit potential that might be realized from a possible *doubling* of their purchases from any acquired supplier. There is sometimes more profit to be realized from this factor than from the reduction of inventories or the elimination of overhead in horizontal integrations. These are true "synergies."

Step Four. Lump all customers of each kind together and enter the percentage of total annual sales to each.

Forward Vertical Integration looks at those to whom your products or your services are sold. Again you are interested in the percentage of your total sales to each kind of industry.

Where there is a high level of technology, vertical integration can pay off in a consistently better product produced at lower and lower cost because manufacturing, parts and materials can be produced to exact tolerances—neither over-engineered, which cuts into profit margins, nor under-engineered, which creates assembly and service problems. Product planning, research and development, product engineering, and in some cases distribution and service functions are all aided by vertical integration. Inventory control in times of tight money, just-in-time (JIT) deliveries and reduction in sales costs are other factors that work in favor of vertical integration. And in times of shortages, owning its own supplier has saved many a company from failure.

A "Vertical ROI (Return on Investment) Analysis" is a device that will help decisionmaking as to which way to move—forward or backward—since there are vast differences in ROI *vertically* among industries which are generally driven by the number of competitors at each level of activity. (See Appendix B, Exhibit 4.)

Step Five. *Enter all possible new product or services extensions that might reasonably be considered to be logically related to present activity.*

Product or Service Extension has a natural appeal for most company executives contemplating "growth" because it involves doing new things. If properly controlled, it leads to impressive victories in the marketplace. But if composed of random "whyncha" entries, they can bring a company down.

Step Six. *Enter what appear to be the best of the Product or Service Extension candidates combined with the best Market Extension candidate areas for present lines.*

Free-Form Entry, the final sector of the Opportunity Wheel, is the sector posing the highest risk: It is the sector where one enters new services or industries in new geographic territories.

The group could simply randomize potential areas for entry. Manufacturing bicycles in China for a Chicago-based carbon-paper manufacturer shouldn't get through the Fit Chart, and it may as well be left out. (However, the utility of the Fit Chart can be demonstrated when a few such opportunities are injected and subsequently rejected when the entries are quantified. Better yet, run your losing acquisitions back through your Fit Chart and note how low the ratings are.) Rather than random entries, pick the most logical product extensions and combine with the most logical market extensions and enter in this final sector.

An Opportunity Wheel can be constructed in this manner for any company or operation doing anything anywhere. Next comes the Fit Chart, which will show how efficient these potential entries might be *relative to each other*.

Can the WOFC process be used to target sell-offs?

Yes, most certainly. The converse of the foregoing analysis is the sell-off decision, which can also be made using the Wheel of Opportunity and a Fit Chart. All present and potential product (or service) lines are put in their proper sector and, in effect, rated against each other. Candidates for sell-off are generated as it becomes obvious that a company is engaged in activities that do not "fit" with the rest of the company's present operations nor with its future, higher-ranked opportunities.

How does the Fit Chart operate?

There are three stages in developing and using a Fit Chart.

• The first is to identify the kinds of actions which can be taken to benefit the company. If these complement or offset its weaknesses, we call them "Complements"; if they reinforce, exploit, or supplement its strengths, we call them "Supplements."
• The second is to select out the principal Complements and Supplements and weight them according to their relative importance to each other.
• The third is to rank the previously identified acquisition

opportunities by their ability to maximize the desired complementary and supplementary effects.

What particular issues arise in identifying Complements and Supplements?

Normally, decisionmaking in this area is difficult because leaders of business enterprises are one of two types: those who are concerned with Complements ("We should get into something new") and those concerned with Supplements ("Where else can we apply our technology?").

Most programs of diversification take one approach or the other. Either they concentrate on exploitation of new and different opportunities *or* they concentrate on exploitation of known strengths. The basic concept of the Fit Chart, which has two sections, Complements *and* Supplements, is to form a strategy in both ways: What do we lack that can be filled by a new entry? And what strengths or assets, human and physical, do we have that are transferable to it? Anyone can find industry entries heavily weighted on one side or the other. But the trick is to find entries with high values on both sides—and, with work, they can always be found. And that's where the money is.

Why start with Complements?

No special reason. Do it either way. But prioritizing weakness analysis over strength analysis is probably better because people that are strength-sensitive generally have more energy and are more likely to power strategic planning sessions, and the human psyche dotes on strengths and tends to ignore weaknesses. So let's get in the weaknesses early on.

In generating Complements in a Fit Chart session, the idea is to pinpoint characteristics of businesses or industries that will compensate for a company's present weaknesses. Supplements are characteristics in a potential acquisition that exploit existing strengths—people, patents, knowledges, images, etc. The identified weak areas may be inherent in your industry or may be unique to your company. Either way, if you're going to expand by means of merger or acquisition, it makes sense to identify any existing problem areas.

How do you treat financial vs. operating variables?

We have discovered that, in first attempts, the Fit Chart should generally be confined to operating variables and the financial variables are impounded in the price. But if you feel confident, mix them.

What are some examples of Complements and Supplements?

In Appendix A, we have provided an extensive check list of possible Complements and Supplements (both operating and financial) that can help an executive team "think synergy."

Are there any general rules to guide the creation of Fit Chart Supplements and Complements?

Yes, here are a few guidelines:

• Don't overdo it with technology. It is a common notion that raising the level of technology will raise the return on capital. All it does is raise the risk. Probably a high-tech outfit should stay in high-tech, and it is debatable whether it can profit from switching from one high-tech field to another that's technologically unrelated.

• Financial variables always give trouble because some people believe that certain kinds of businesses are inherently more profitable than others. This is simply not true. Absent regulation, confiscatory taxation, duties, and the like, return on capital varies because risk varies. "High-margin" mining businesses at 65 percent gross profit go broke while the chain grocer gets rich at 10 percent. What's risky is for a low-margin operator to acquire a high-margin operator or vice versa because they won't have a philosophical "fit."

• Labor variables also give trouble. We know that many executives who went on the record in the first few moments of a Fit Chart session about "getting away from the union" after four days of self-analysis decided that, because they knew how to forestall a strike or how to take one comfortably, their ability to work in sensitive labor areas was, in fact, a major asset.

• Management variables also are troublesome. Only after a few days of self-analysis of past difficulties do people begin to see that many of their past acquisition or start-up failures were caused by poor management fit. For example, it may be that teaching an engineer to sell is simply easier than teaching a salesman engineering. Thus, there is more to fear along the production axis than along the marketing axis.

• Look for synergies. The conglomerate movement generated more jargon than profits with statements like: "We're not a conglomerate, we're a mutual fund that manages its own investments." That might fool the marketplace for a few quarters, but if there are no *operating* synergies, you don't have a viable enterprise. If there are no operating commonalities or cross benefits, the future losses will balance or exceed the present benefits every time. Further, one-time, or short-term tax benefits are eaten up by operating inefficiencies in short order. Tax-based deals without operating synergies are bound to fail eventually.

How do you weigh the relative importance of Complements and Supplements and narrow the list to the most important?

The WOFC methodology is no better than the process it uses to generate values that are used to rate potential entry. The one tested process is the Delphi process, introduced a little more than thirty years ago as a method of forecasting the future where there are many unknowns. The theory behind it is that the collective, intuitive judgments of a group of experts in an area with many unknowns (such as forecasting technological change) is probably superior to quantitative (and usually expensive) extrapolations of known trends.

In the Delphi process, a series of questions formulated by "monitors" are put to the "experts." Their answers are usually grouped into four quartiles of opinion. The opinions are separated in some fashion, usually numerically. The upper and lower quartiles are abstracted by the monitors and are sent back out to all participants with no identifications of whose opinions came from whom. The experts all read the abstractions and respond again, hopefully modifying their opinions in accordance with the perceived wisdom. These answers are again grouped, the upper and the lower quartiles again distributed (still without identification of the specific viewpoints of specific contributors), and the new, usually modified opinions or estimates are fed back to the monitors. The process goes on until some kind of a consensus is reached (or the monitors run out of time, money and/or patience).

As the WOFC process developed over the years, we found that it works best if each participant is allotted 1000 points to "play with," like the money that is handed out at the start of a game of Monopoly, representing the company's "stake" in the future. Each participant then "votes" his points among the variables—Complements and Supplements—under consideration, anonymously allocating them in accordance with his or her opinion as to the *relative* importance of each. (Theoretically, an individual could allocate all 1000 points to one variable, but no one ever has.) Without the point allocation system, talk is cheap. But when each participant is forced to "spend" his points, he has to decide on his priorities.

The anonymous allocations of each participant are tallied and summed up for each variable and averaged; these averages are then made known to the group generally by writing the number on a Fit Chart that has been chalk-lined on a blackboard. In the particular embodiment of the Delphi process that has developed in the WOFC process (called "Instant Delphi"), the persons giving the lowest and highest scores to each variable are now identified from the tally sheets and must defend their position. They may be joined by others in the low or the high quartile depending on how structured the inquiry system is. Each variable is discussed in an adversary fashion. The Chairman: "I think that 'Management Fit' line is for the birds. The bottom line is what counts, that's why I gave it zero." In opposition, the President, who spent 300 precious points on it, says "But, Hal, the last three companies we bought were run by people that you wouldn't even have to dinner—and we sold them all off at a loss!" It is not at all uncommon in the Delphi process to discover vast differences in opinion about basic operating and strategic philosophies right at the very top of the organization.

Generally, no abstracting monitor as in a full-scale Delphi is needed. If the lows wish to caucus and bring out a joint position, they are allowed to. The highs can do likewise. Middle-value people are not allowed to participate in the discussion because, in effect, they've not taken a position, have entered "chicken values," and soon learn that if they want to participate, they'd better take a stand. The lows and the highs battle it out verbally until debate is cut off by the facilitator. Thus, each variable is treated in discussion, after which the participants again spread their 1000 points. Variables not scoring an average of some minimum number of points are dropped from consideration unless some vehement argument should arise for their retention through another round. Generally, if a variable does not average 25 points, it is dropped from consideration.

The process continues for as many as five rounds. (There is no reason to believe that this is the optimum or the limit. However, experience shows that it is seldom necessary to go beyond the third round before consensus is reached or budgets or time runs out.) At the last round, the final cut-off figure for dropping variables is set (it might drop to 20 points), the points dropped are proportionately reallocated, and the final, average number per variable is then posted on the Fit Chart for all to see.

Exactly how is each opportunity ranked?

The easiest thing about the WOFC process is distributing the values to the acquisition opportunities. The final value ascribed to each variable represents the maximum score which any of the acquisitions being considered can achieve as to that variable. Most acquisitions would presumably achieve lower scores. For instance, say that "P/E Improvement," a common complementary variable, scored 200 points and the company conducting the analysis has a current P/E of 5. The acquisition opportunities are industries or companies with P/Es of 5, 10, 15, and 20. The vertical ratings would be zero for the entry with a P/E of 5, because it will do nothing for the P/E of the acquiring company; 200 for the entry having a P/E of 20, because it has the highest value; and the other potential entries are given proportionate scores—67 points for any 10 P/E entry, 133 for any 15 P/E entry, and proportionally for any other entries.

When all of the values have been distributed, they are summed across and rank-ordered.

How is a "Strategic Statement" developed?

A Strategic Statement is simply an abstraction of what we have learned from the WOFC process. A typical Strategic Statement appears in Appendix A.

IN-HOUSE SEARCH AND SCREEN

When does a search-and-screen program begin?

The search-and-screen program begins once the acquiring company has completed its strategic self-evaluation and has developed its acquisition strategy (i.e., search priorities from the Fit Chart) and search criteria (i.e., derived Complements and Supplements from the Fit Chart). The firm is now ready to begin identifying specific acquisition candidates. (The development of a company's acquisition strategy and criteria were outlined in the preceding sections on planning.)

Should it be centralized or de-centralized?

There are two ways to go about making acquisitions: 1) centralize the whole acquisition program at corporate headquarters, or 2) decentralize the search, screen and target identification, pricing, negotiation and closing process, within realizable guidelines, out to the various levels of the organization: Enterprise, Corporate, Sector, Business Unit, Product-line, and Functional.

The general trend in the United States is the decentralized form due to the deconglomeration movement. However, the general practice is that search and screen are decentralized while pricing and the deal structure are reserved to Corporate levels except for the largest of subsidiaries.

Who's responsible for search and screen?

At the Enterprise level it is usually the CEO that honchos a major program of diversification (though there is some present predilection to assign this to the non-CEO Chairman). At the Corporate Level a VP of Corporate Development coordinates the activity of Corporate, Sector, Business Unit, Product-line and Functional efforts. Each level usually has someone responsible for corporate development purposes which may or may not include the identification of acquisition candidates.

How long does a search and screen program last?

Depending on the scope of the program and how much in-house data is available on the subject, a search and screen program to produce a few viable targets takes a minimum of six months. At the end of six months, some target negotiations should be underway. However, don't be surprised if this process takes longer, since many candidates will not always be ready to sell at first. If the buyer is only interested in a few targets and those targets are not available, it could take years for the seed you planted to germinate in bona fide acquisition negotiations.

What are the primary steps in completing a full search and screen program?

The following list outlines the steps to be taken in a systems-based approach or opportunity-maker approach to the search and screen process: (See Exhibit 4 of Appendix B.)

- Develop general philosophies.
- Literature search/industry situation analysis.
- Develop target files.
- Screen targets.
- Contact principals.
- Obtain a price expression from seller.
- Negotiate preliminary price and terms.
- Engage in a due diligence process and business plan.
- Close the transaction.
- Develop a post-acquisition integration plan.

What are the primary means of a search-and-screen program?

There are two main types of buyers—opportunity-takers and opportunity-makers. Opportunity-*takers* are looking for investments at a favorable price. Their main line of defense against making an imprudent purchase is the care and completeness of their pricing and financing analysis. See Chapter 3, on Valuation and Pricing. The risk they run, particularly if they are not constrained by the need to borrow their purchase price against the target's assets and cash flow, is that in frustration they will eventually buy *something*—sometimes to their eventual sorrow. Opportunity-*makers* on the other hand narrow the scope of their search. They use strategic planning analysis to carefully examine their own strengths and weaknesses and then target entries that exploit their own strengths and offset their own weaknesses.

How does an opportunity-taker work?

The opportunity-taker establishes a network of brokers, financial intermediaries, investment bankers, finders, and the like to find companies that appear to be "bargains." The opportunity-taker approach tends to be random, unstructured, and unplanned, yet it is this flexibility that allows an opportunity-taker to seize opportunity when it presents itself. This approach tends to be more financially driven than operations driven.

How does an opportunity-maker operate?

Unlike the opportunity-taker, the opportunity-maker is probably searching for an acquisition with particular operational characteristics in one or two particular industries. This practitioner seeks to cherry-pick the proper industry player that best complements and/or supplements his current operations and overall long-range plans.

For example, if the opportunity-maker's core business is the distribution of industrial laboratory supplies, it may make strategic sense to vertically integrate backward into self-manufacturing of high-profit-margin items that the company currently distributes. By searching a number of publicly available data bases, the opportunity-maker can establish a set of criteria such as: product/market segment by S.I.C. code (Standard Industrial Classification code) within sales, net profit, and net worth ranges that will allow the searcher to create a list of target companies that fit the desired profile. Since the whole process is computer-driven, we call this the "high-tech opportunity-maker" approach. Standard & Poor's (Compustat) and Dun & Bradstreet both offer excellent data bases for this purpose.

As part of the high-tech approach, the opportunity-maker will expend considerable resources sifting through the literature—both published and nonpublished technical data bases and news reports for data to confirm or add to the results.

How should an effective literature search be conducted?

First, the researcher needs a clear understanding of the objective of the search. For example, when entering a new industry, an industry situation analysis is performed. This analysis determines an industry's pricing and profitability structure, growth, maturity, cyclicality, etc., and establishes a clear nomenclature so everyone is communicating properly.

Second, assemble a list of industry players. A list of competitors helps the researcher outline the competitive battlefield and yields points of reference.

Third, begin to collect industry data by contacting the industry trade associations, independent research firms who publish reports on specific industries, product/market segments and companies, and published data bases. With a specific literature search in mind, a researcher can pinpoint specific industry articles and reports by tapping into data bases such as Dialog and Nexus. These data bases contain hundreds of items that contain information on a particular subject matter—energy, mining, pharmaceuticals, etc.

Fourth, the researcher compiles a list of industry contacts to gain specific, first-hand insight into the industry's structure, trends, and key players involved. Usually, there are two or three people at either a university or a trade association, or acting as independent consultants, who know all that's worth knowing technically *or* economically about an industry or a significant segment of it.

Finally, the researcher is ready to tackle the nonpublished or field data area. Contact lists have been developed to conduct one-on-one interviews, to send out direct mail questionnaires, and to perform telephone surveys. One field-data gathering technique is attendance at industry trade shows. If the researcher is working under a healthy budget, trade shows are invaluable since the researcher is able to physically see the target products/services and talk directly with potential acquisition candidates. Also, since most trade shows attract industry gurus, it's possible to pick up rumors of industry divestitures. At the very least you have the opportunity to ask an industry representative if anyone is for sale or rumored for sale. It's also a grand opportunity to discover key executives who are looking to better themselves. And many an LBO/MBO has been started right on the exhibit floor.

How does the researcher compile a list of industry players?

First, contact the target industry's trade association(s) and obtain the membership directories. Second, refer to reference books such as *Thomas's Register* and trade periodical buyer's guides. These reference books normally group companies by the product or service sold. For example, the researcher looking for companies that manufacture fluid-bed dryers should start by referencing fluid-bed dryers in *Thomas's Register*. If the researcher wishes to be more specific and discover those manufacturers that produce fluid-bed dryers for the pharmaceutical industry, he or she would look under fluid-bed dryers in Pharmaceutical Technology's Annual Buyer's Guide.

And third, obtain prospectuses for special industry research reports by independent research firms. (These are listed and indexed by subject by Findex and are also on the Dialog database.) These prospectuses contain the study's table of contents, which usually discloses the names of key industry players. Also, both trade association and industry/company reports are invaluable information centers for industry data. Industry/company reports written by Frost & Sullivan, Business Communication Corporation, etc., normally cover an entire industry's structure or a particular product/market segment's structure. If you have significant funds to work with, it pays to purchase an industry report that addresses the issues you have outlined, but be sure it is current.

How does the researcher develop a contact list?

The researcher develops a contact list from trade articles and trade association information. In many cases, a trade association maintains a list of consultants who specialize in their industry. Also, list brokers, such as National Business Lists, may have special contact lists for your industry. Finally, depending on what type of expert you wish to contact, you will probably have to compile your own list of product end-users— for example, purchasing agents, plant managers, or engineers. These contacts can be identified in Standard & Poor's *Register*, Dun & Bradstreet's *Million Dollar Directory*, and *Corporate Affiliations*. But it usually takes hard, slogging telephone work to identify the key movers and shakers; i.e., the end-user rather than the order-placer.

What are the primary reference sources for industry information?

- Value Line Investment Survey
- Standard & Poor's Industry Survey
- U.S. Industrial Outlook
- Predicast's Basebook
- Predicast's Forecasts
- Standard & Poor's Statistical Service
- Annual Reports and 10Ks
- Stock Brokerage Research Reports
- Trade Associations
- U.S. Department of Commerce
- I.R.S.'s Corporation Sourcebook of Statistics of Income

- Census of Manufacturers, Retail Trade and Mineral Industries
- Independent Research Reports
- Trade Periodicals
- Local Newspapers
- Findex

How can a buyer find information on public companies?

There are many ways to find information on public companies. For public information the best sources are

- Value Line Investment Survey.
- Annual Reports, 10Ks, 10Qs, prospectuses, press releases, proxy statements, product literature, catalogues, company case studies and executive speeches.
- Standard & Poor's: *Register, Corporation Records, Industry Survey,* and *Stock Guide.*
- Directory of Corporate Affiliations - Who Owns Whom.
- Moody's: Industrial Manuals and Handbook of Common Stocks.

How can a buyer find information on private companies?

A good starting place is through Dun & Bradstreet's *Million Dollar Directory*, which is a combination of both public and private companies. But to get a more detailed report on a firm one can use Dun & Bradstreet's Quest—a subscription service either through a computer terminal or by mail.

If Dun & Bradstreet does not have the financial statements of a private company, it is extremely difficult to obtain the information without getting it directly from the company itself. However, many states, especially those with extractive activity, require both public and private businesses, whether corporate or unincorporated, to file annually the following kinds of information:

> Year of establishment, names of principal owners, key personnel, number of employees, annual sales, principal lines of business, plant size, import/export activity, extracted tonnages, types of computers used, etc.

Some states require much more information, compile it them-selves and sell the information to all comers. Certain private companies, such as Harris Publishing Company of Twinsburgh, Ohio, republish the state compendia (see above list) in book or directory form. They cover the states of Ohio, Pennsylvania, Michigan, Illinois, Indiana, West Virginia, Kentucky, and Missouri. Other regional firms of a like nature cover all the other states. (Harris sells their directories too. A complete set of such industrial directories was assembled by the publisher of *MERGERS & ACQUISITIONS* magazine when he established it in 1965. Using these names, created by law as opposed to optional (and often inaccurate) filings for credit purposes, M&A was an immediate success.) Washington Researchers Publishing specializes in teaching how to access public sources of information on private companies.

Often, private companies do not give their financials to Dun & Bradstreet, and many smaller public companies fail to update when they do. All information must be checked with the company itself. Normally, they will give some numbers, usually the number of employees. Thus, to get a ballpark figure for their annual sales volume, the buyer can apply a rule of thumb ratio (usually supplied by the trade association) of sales per employee, which is a good place to start. (Service company information is harder to come by than manufacturers as their trade organizations, if they exist, do not usually collect hard numbers.)

When conducting surveys, what is the best approach?

Superior results come from talking to users[1] over the telephone and going over a pre-prepared questionnaire with them. This aspect of the search sometimes can be subcontracted. Mailings do not work well because many users simply don't answer questionnaires. However, if the buyer can reach a potential target's personnel by phone, he should make them comfort-

---

[1] The word "user" is preferred over "purchaser" because many purchasing agents are simply "order placers" who take no part in a purchasing decision. However, the purchasing department can point you to the power.

able by telling them something that *they* don't know. They may then talk about their business.

It is important to realize that most users are fairly high up in their organization and they do not have a lot of time. Therefore, advance preparation is indispensable. One researcher asked a chief chemist what an "ion" was. End of conversation. Researchers must confine themselves to specific questions about specific topics about which they are reasonably knowledgeable.

The researcher must be aware of a fine ethical line in market research: how far can one go to extract information that is going to be "resold"? This is always a matter of judgment for the firm and the person making the survey. It is surprising how much information can be gleaned from a few telephone calls made by knowledgeable people to knowledgeable people— especially if they can *exchange* knowledge.

What are some of the mechanics and logistics of a survey?

The survey begins with a great number of telephone calls, and, depending on the cooperation of the individuals involved, it may take many hours per day before one gains a sense of the industry; so don't start with the target if you have one. Learn the industry on the peripherals.

The computer database searches—such as Dialog or Nexus— and literature searches can also be very time-consuming.

The cost involved can be significant. Telephone charges, travel, computer time, basic office personnel expenditures for any kind of a proper target search and identification program can run from the low to middle six figures to several millions. As a rule of thumb, it costs from $75,000 to $200,000 to bring a group of modest-sized target companies—$10 to $50 million in sales—to the point where a preliminary offer can be made. Megadeal searches start at the $200,000 level and can run into the low seven figures.

What information should be contained in a target's file?

Once the situation analysis and literature search are complete, the decision is made whether or not moving forward into this industry is actually desirable. If that decision is positive, the buyer puts together a *target profile* on each one of the acquisition candidates. This may entail a technology and manufacturing audit to make sure that their process will survive in the future. This is the very beginning of the buyer's "due diligence." (See Chapter 8.)

At this time the potential buyer must make a decision on buying one company versus another. Does it always come down to price?

If the buyer's team is using the "Fit Chart" or a similar approach, it should now run specific *company* targets through the Fit Chart and rate them against the buyer's specific strengths and weaknesses (Complements & Supplements). The first company may have a strong marketing force and weak technology, whereas the number five player has the opposite. That may lead a strong marketer to the decision to buy number five, believing that it can be inexpensively integrated into its own marketing and distribution channels. Other information relating to a particular target such as annual reports, 10Ks, Dun & Bradstreet credit reports, company fact books and product catalogues, press releases, print advertisements, published articles and executive speeches, and director and officer profiles should all be collected and placed in each acquisition target's file. Also, depending on how the researcher is cutting up the pie, it may be helpful to break down the industry by product/market segments and list the top five players in each product/market segment by market share. It is also important to itemize how each target's product is differentiated in any way from the competition and whether it enjoys any special "niche" advantages — either geographically, by industry, by age groups, etc.

Who should be contacted at the target company?

The principals of the targets selected are usually then contacted by telephone. In a wide-ranging search, the principals contacted may include the CEO, the CFO, or the COO. But directors, lawyers, accountants, their bankers — both commercial and investment — can all be contacted. Try to structure the conversations so as to avoid a direct turndown. Remember, you may only get one telephone call. Don't blow it.

If the acquisition proposal involves a relatively small subsidiary of any relatively large company, the contact person should be the senior vice president of corporate planning or corporate development—but *don't* call the division head unless it's public knowledge that it's on the block. And even then it's best to deal with planning at either the corporate, sector, or business unit level.

How should the conversation be structured?

Rather than inquiring of incumbent, non-owning management whether the company is "for sale," the caller should stress the potential for a mutually beneficial relationship. The company's non-owner management will be impressed with any expertise demonstrated by the buyer or the buyer's agent, and the caller's statement that the company contacted is one of the best in that industry—or can be made the best—is important.

The target profile will give the buyer more "information leverage" because the target will often know very little about the buyer. To set the management more at ease, the buyer or its agent should provide some useful information about itself to the target's management.

The ultimate goal of the initial conversation is to set up a meeting to further discuss a possible business combination. The business combination could be a merger, acquisition, or joint venture. No mention of price should be made at this stage of the process.

Where should buyer and target representatives meet at this early stage?

The parties have to agree on a mutually satisfactory meeting place. Visiting the target may start the rumor mill, and that can hurt a deal. On the other hand, the buyer can get a better feel for the target's operations and personnel if it's eyeballed.

An alternative would be a meeting at the offices of an investment banker or law firm or in neutral territory such as a large room at a hotel. Try not to meet in airline clubs, hotel lobbies, coffee shops or other public places—it starts the rumor mill going and can create competition for the target.

A good "cover" for eyeball meetings is the prospect of a joint venture or a supplier relationship. This plays very well where a company is not on the block. But be careful of any out-and-out prevarication.

Having agreed on a meeting place, it will benefit the buyer to try to obtain the target's financials prior to the meeting. (We assume you already have all of the sales literature, D&B reports, and, if it's a public company, 10Ks.) With such information in hand, an agenda for the meeting can be easily set, and it's important to have a written agenda at least for *your* side so that all of the important subjects are covered.

Also important is to recast the target's historical financials into more easily read form such as common-size, trended, and industry comparisons. When these are done, it is easy to compile a list of questions identifying the financial and operating anomalies for discussion. (See Appendix B, Exhibit 3 for example.)

What are "common-size, trended, and industry-comparison statements"?

Common-size and trended analyses are invaluable techniques for identifying problems and isolating areas for potential profit improvement. Instead of looking at absolute numbers, common-size and trended analyses point out the anomalies that may exist in a company's balance sheet or income statement. For instance, common-size financial statements utilize a common denominator such as net worth for balance sheets and net sales for operating statements, to point up change. Trended analyses use an appropriately selected base year or period that represents 100% for all items of the balance sheet and income statement. All dollar amounts for each item on the balance sheet and income statement in years subsequent to the base year are expressed as a percentage of the base year amounts—in the form of a business index. The anomalies become immediately apparent as areas for further investigation and become part of the meeting agenda.

For example, if accounts receivable and inventory combined accounted for 50% of total assets during the first year and increased to 62% the second year while sales only increased a meager 2%, this may lead one to believe that the company is selling to poorer quality customers. As a result, the buyer will want to double-check the collection period for accounts receivable, the adequacy of the firm's reserve for bad debts, and the inventory turnover.

What else can be accomplished at the first meeting with a target?

The meeting should give the buyer a sense of the company and its operations, whether there are any skeletons in the company's closets that may preclude a deal and whether the chemistry is right. The meeting should give the target a sense of the buyer and its management and the benefits of a business combination. There must be *reasons* for combining the companies corporately, operationally, or financially.

For public companies, it is good to have any financial write-ups—even if issued by a regional house. Also ask if they ever had a management consultant in. And ask to see the outside auditor's management reports if they have them.

If the parties' objectives and personalities seem to mesh, and more meetings take place, a deal is likely. It is important to follow up by telephone or letters to keep the target's interest alive and well and to answer any questions before they turn into problems.

Remember, most sellers and all buyers somewhere along the line get cold feet. So keep the deal going. It may not jell for months—or even years. But if it's right, it's right. So never give up on it. Never.

What is bundling?

Bundling describes non-diversifying growth—horizontal or vertical. After a buyer has bought a base firm, it can use that base firm as a "platform" for building a much larger business through "add-ons." (Note that concentration in a fractionated industry can be rewarding—the real estate agency, car rental, and brewery businesses are three recent examples where huge businesses, which benefit from national advertising, have been built by the coalescence of smaller units.)

The buyer may have the opportunity to integrate either vertically or horizontally or both. This decision may depend on antitrust issues. Horizontal integration tends to create significant economies of scale, which on a world base tends to make the company much more price-competitive. That is the principal reason why the antitrust division of the Justice Department tended recently to allow acquisitions which for years were challenged on antitrust grounds. Smaller companies simply do not have the capabilities or financial resources to compete on a world basis with these large integrated firms. Today federal antitrust actions have become less frequent because markets are now more global. The relevant market is no longer just the United States, but the whole world. Thus the possibility of building large units from smaller previously competing groups is much more likely in the '80s and '90s than it was in the '60s and '70s.

FINDERS AND BROKERS

Much of the foregoing describes in-house search processes, but even they use finders and brokers—especially the "opportunity-takers."

What's the difference between a "broker" and a "finder"?

A broker is an agent and thus a fiduciary with all that such term implies in law. Brokers represent only one side in a transaction. The rules governing their behavior have been established over the past five centuries by the common law—and many an M&A matchmaker has lost his fee because he was ignorant of these rules.

Finders, on the other hand, are not agents of or for anyone. Thus, they are not fiduciaries. They represent the deal rather than the parties. They can be paid by either party or by both parties even without the knowledge of the other.

Finders, however, must be careful not to negotiate, for it is the act of negotiation that takes them out of the finder class, creates an act of agency, places them squarely in the broker category which, depending on the locale, may require a license of some kind, and creates for them fiduciary responsibilities. Thus, they may lose their fee if they negotiate.

How is "negotiation" defined?

Generally, if the finder merely introduces the prospective purchasers and otherwise only acts to maintain contact between the parties to make the introduction effective, no negotiation on his part will be deemed to have taken place. If, however, the finder advises the purchaser on procedures and the desirability of the target or attempts to determine the sale price, the courts may infer that he "negotiated."

What is an "intermediary"?

People who are foggy about the distinction between brokers and finders try to solve their dilemma by billing themselves as "intermediaries." This straddling category can be risky because intermediaries are supposed to negotiate and a "negotiating intermediary" must be an agent of one party or the other in a contemplated transaction unless both sides have agreed— usually in writing—that the negotiation is in their common interest. If both buyer and seller do make such an agreement, then neither side has a fiduciary agent.

Are brokers and finders regulated and if so by whom?

In general, the act of brokering and finding is not regulated. But do not confuse the generic word "broker" with special kinds of brokerage activity such as "securities brokers," "commodity brokers," "real estate brokers," etc., who are supervised by various governmental and quasi-governmental bodies. This regulated brokerage activity includes "business opportunity brokers." Many states have passed laws regulating their activity or allow cities and counties to enact local ordinances to control such business opportunity, or "business chance" brokerage activity—usually through the act of examination, licensing, inspection of the broker's premises, etc. Lawyers, contrary to popular belief, are seldom excepted from the requirement to be licensed as a business opportunity broker.

No state has yet regulated the activity of the nonnegotiating finder with the possible exception of New York, which, in a long series of tortured court decisions and supporting legislation, says in effect that no finder can perform the act of finding *without* negotiating. Finders are, therefore, ipso facto agents and brokers involved in the transfer of property, and in order to comply with a specific provision of New York's Statute of Frauds, anyone dealing in the transfer of "property" must have an agreement in writing to collect a finder's or a broker's fee. Because Raytheon recently lost a court case on appeal for a substantial fee in their $800 million acquisition of Beech Aircraft, they successfully lobbied for passage of a bill in the Massachusetts legislature copying the New York law, but too late to help Raytheon. Other states have similar statutes of fraud but do not bar collection under general concepts of contract law such as "quantum meruit" where the services of the finder, in the absence of a writing, are valued so as not to unjustly enrich a buyer or seller from the services provided. In New York state, however, quantum meruit recovery not supported by a written contract is strictly barred.

What about fees?

There are numerous fee schedules, but an estimated 75% of all fees are based on the "M&A Formula," also referred to as "The Lehman Formula" or "The Wall Street Rule." This is a sliding scale–generally a 5-4-3-2-1 formula: 5% of the first $1 million, 4% of the second, 3% of the third, 2% of the fourth, and 1% of the balance. In larger transactions, the final 1% can continue to drop down to 0.5% or even 0.25% at the $50 million mark, the $100 million mark, etc. Generally, there is a "cap" put on the fee such as "no fee to exceed $1 million." Generally, in transactions above $100 million, the fee is usually negotiated. An $800 million transaction might call for a base fee in the $2–4 million range.

There is a tendency now, in dealing with finders especially—those who do not have the staff and resources to classify themselves as "investment bankers" and who in fact do not do extensive analysis or deal structuring—to arrive at a flat price for their services in a deal regardless of the price of the deal. This is often because determining the "price" in a complicated highly leveraged deal with equity kickers such as detachable warrants and rights, simultaneous spin-offs or spin-outs or sales of subsidiaries, can be very difficult and can lead to litigation. "If we do the deal you get $500K" might be the language that one hears today for a prospective $40 million deal—that works out to 1.25%. In such an arrangement, whether the buyer pays $30 million or $50 million, the finder gets his $500 thousand dollar fee for initiating the transaction.

Are "investment bankers" different from other brokers and finders?

Yes. While investment bankers often act as finders and are often retained as brokers to buy or sell whole companies or divisions, when they act as "bankers," they may do much more. They may render a "fairness opinion" or raise the funds to finance the deal. Lately, investment bankers even help finance deals either through funding "bridge loans" or by actually putting up some of the capital themselves. They then get a series of fees—finders', brokers', opinion, consulting, origination and underwriting fees and, if the securities are exchanged through their offices, a "security broker's fee." Together they are called "investment banking fees."

Do investment banking firms pay fees to finders for bringing them prospective deals?

Yes. Most investment banking firms will pay a finder's fee to someone who brings them a deal. Some firms, like Goldman Sachs, are on record as never paying such finders fees. But most successful firms are happy to pay in the area of 10% of their fees for a successful lead.

What is a "mere volunteer"?

Volunteers usually cannot collect finder's or broker's fees. A so-called "telephone book finder" for instance, one who sends out thousands of letters suggesting acquisition targets to major corporations and does little or nothing more, cannot collect a fee when one of the companies is actually acquired. He cannot prove he was the "procuring cause" of the transaction. Also, he hasn't been invited. Some degree of consent or invitation by a buyer or seller is necessary to establish a compensable finder relationship.

As a buyer, how can you protect yourself against claims for payment of unwarranted finders or brokers fees?

• Keep a log of inquiries, correspondence.
• Answer every unsolicited letter by rejecting offers of companies, and keep copies of all such correspondence. But be truthful. Don't say you're not interested if you are. It can cost you dearly.
• Keep your contacts up to date. Finder A refers your company to a business, then you drop the deal for six months, until Finder B "revives" your interest and you acquire. You may owe fees to both Finder A and Finder B.
• Find out whether your state regulates business opportunity brokers. If the broker is not licensed, you can defeat a finder's fee *if he negotiates*. But you must prove that he negotiated, and that is often hard to do.
• If you're in a state with a Statute of Frauds, the broker or finder may need a written agreement to collect a fee.
• Be aware that you may invite a possible RICO (Racketeering Influenced & Corrupt Organizations Act) claim and triple damages if you try to defraud the broker of a proper fee. Also, a broker or finder may be able to obtain punitive damages if you conspire to defraud him of a fee.

As a broker, how do I insure that I will be paid if I do a deal?

• Get a written agreement that includes specific language on the fee schedule, payment at closing, etc.
• Keep a log of conversations—especially telephone conversations. If you are out of the office when a client calls, make sure the date, time and message are recorded in writing. These "message logs" can be powerful evidence in some courts.
• Get the other side to agree (in writing if possible) that they won't close unless you get paid.
• Try to participate in all meetings of the principals.
• Get some paper on the record. Judges like to read *letters* from you to the buyer or target. So do juries. They both want you to *work* for a living since they do.
• Sue the second you're not paid. Don't wait, because they'll set someone else up, say he did the deal, pay him a fee and not you, and use it in court as a defense.

USING INTERMEDIARIES

If a broker advises a buyer about an opportunity that another broker closes, which broker should be paid?

Such contingencies should be spelled out in the broker/finder agreement. If they are not so defined, however, the second, successful intermediary, not the first, should be paid.

For example, suppose that the AB Waxworks is for sale and investment banker "A" tells John Smith about it. The seller wants $50 million dollars in cash. Mr. Smith offers him $40 million, is turned down and goes away.

Two weeks later another investment banker talks to John Smith and says, "By the way the AB Waxworks is for sale." John Smith says, "I know that, I was out there; the guy wants $50 million dollars and I offered him $40 million." Investment banker "B" says "Yes, but why don't you offer him $40 million dollars plus a royalty of 2% on sales for the next ten years, tax deductible to you. On $1 billion of sales over the next ten years, it *looks* like another $20 million. But the present value cost to you is only about $3 million." Smith makes the offer and AB Waxworks accepts it.

Who is entitled to the fee?

The first investment banker who originally showed AB Waxworks to Mr. Smith does not collect a fee because it's not the same deal. Somebody came along with a new idea as to how this could be accomplished; therefore, the second broker earned the fee.

There's an old common law principle cited in many court decisions in the real estate area that states: "It isn't the person who points out the tree that gets the apples, it's the person who shakes the tree."

Suppose the same situation occurs, but with a twist. An investment banker proposes a deal to Mr. Smith, who makes the offer, and the seller turns it down. Another broker comes along six months later. He brings Mr. Smith to the same company, making exactly the same offer he made before, and this time it is accepted.

Now the first investment banker *does* collect a fee in the absence of any agreement to the contrary, because it is the same deal. Mr. Smith may have created a legal obligation to pay the first person because he learned about the company from that person. Smith, however, should arrange that the fee be split.

ROLE OF INVESTMENT AND COMMERCIAL BANKS IN M&A

What is the difference between the M&A services offered by an investment bank and those offered by a commercial bank?

In today's increasingly competitive market for financial services, the differences in M&A services offered by investment banks and at least some commercial banks have narrowed considerably. As commercial banks' lending margins have shrunk, commercial banks have become more aggressive in their search for other kinds of income; they have targeted high-margined M&A advisory business, developing capabilities that in some cases rival those of some of the more prestigious investment banks. These capabilities include developing strategies for their clients with respect to acquisitions, recapitalizations, and leveraged buyouts and acting as dealer-manager in tender offers, as well as rendering fairness opinions.

The Glass-Steagall Act, however, prohibits commercial banks from underwriting corporate securities that may be issued in connection with these activities. Subsidiaries of commercial banks can, however, engage in underwriting activities.

Investment banks, meanwhile, have begun to invade some of the commercial banks' traditional territory by offering to commit their capital in the form of loans to their M&A clients to underwrite at least a portion of the cost of an acquisition, usually in the form of a bridge loan. It is not unusual for such institutions to share clients. For example, a Wall Street investment firm might act as an advisor to a company doing an acquisition. The Wall Street firm might then take its deal to a commercial bank to obtain an acquisition bridge loan and the long-term senior bank debt to refinance existing senior debt, later refinancing some or all of the bank debt with a private placement and/or underwriting of senior or subordinated public debt. See Chapters 3 and 4.

Is it illegal for a bank to fund one offeror for a company and to advise another, competing offeror?

No, it is not illegal; but many commercial and investment banks avoid such situations for fear of offending one or the other client or creating the impression of a conflict of interest. However, it is more common for commercial banks to offer financing for more than one offeror if an advisory role is involved. In this case a bank will attempt to erect a "Chinese Wall" between the different areas of the bank involved to avoid the possibility of a breach of confidence with respect to confidential information. While "tie-in" arrangements, where a client is given a loan only if the client buys the bank's advisory services, are illegal, some clients prefer to use a commercial bank or an investment bank as an advisor who is also willing to commit its capital in the form of a loan to facilitate an acquisition.

What is merchant banking?

Merchant banking describes a combination of advisory and investment banking services under which the commercial or investment bank uses its capital to assist the client in achieving his financial objective. The term often applies to services offered to new ventures and recapitalized companies. See Chapter 4, which extensively discusses bridge lending by investment bankers.

Are commercial banks involved in merchant banking?

Yes. Many commercial banks have venture capital groups which invest in both the equity and mezzanine securities in promising ventures, including start-up companies and leveraged buyouts. Commercial banks, in their role as investment bankers, are also increasingly becoming partners with their clients by purchasing both the equity and mezzanine securities of companies to whom they also provide senior debt.

GENERAL REGULATORY CONSIDERATIONS FOR BUYERS

What sorts of legal hurdles can be raised by an acquisition?

Depending on the facts and nature of the transaction, an acquisition may require compliance with federal, state or local statutes or regulations in a variety of areas, including laws with respect to antitrust, securities, employee benefits, bulk sales, foreign ownership, and the transfer of title to stock or assets. Some of these laws require only routine acts to achieve compliance, which can be attended to relatively late in the acquisition process. Other laws pose potential regulatory barriers that must be considered before proceeding with a given acquisition plan.

How does the purchaser determine what regulatory barriers may exist for a proposed transaction?

Unless the purchaser is a veteran in the relevant field of business it plans to enter, the purchaser must engage counsel familiar with the field and/or skilled in complex acquisitions.

Can the failure to identify and satisfy all regulatory requirements in a timely manner delay or kill the deal?

Yes. In some cases, one or both parties must obtain the consent or approval of the responsible agency before the transaction can be consummated. Failure to do so can result in penalties or rescission of the transaction.

What types of significant regulatory barriers are most often encountered in consummating an acquisition?

Antitrust. Certain business combinations require filings and clearances with the Federal Trade Commission (FTC) or Justice Department (DOJ) under the Hart-Scott-Rodino Act.

Regulated industries. The transfer of title to certain types of industrial or commercial assets may be subject to approval by the regulating agency, including

- Telecommunications facilities (Federal Communications Commission).
- Public Utilities (Public Utilities Holding Company Act, Federal Energy Regulatory Commission, state public utilities commissions).
- Airlines (Department of Transportation).
- Railroads (Interstate Commerce Commission).
- Shipping (Maritime Administration).
- Banks and other financial services institutions (The

Controller of the Currency, the Federal Reserve Board, FDIC, FSLIC, state agencies).
• Insurance companies (state regulatory agencies).

Contaminated real property.   Corporate acquisitions can trigger state law requirements relating to clean-up of sites contaminated by hazardous wastes. A buyer can also be hit under both federal and state law with clean-up costs even if he had no involvement in or knowledge of the pollution. (See Chapter 8, Due Diligence Inquiry; Environmental Exposure Analysis.)

Environmental operating permits.   Certain federal or state laws preclude the transfer by one party to another of environmental operating permits issued in the name of the first party.

Foreign ownership of U.S. assets.   Federal law prohibits or requires reporting of ownership of certain industrial or commercial assets by non-U.S. citizens or entities, including U.S. flag-registered vessels and aircraft, telecommunications facilities, newspapers, nuclear power plants, and certain defense industries. (See Chapter 13, International Transactions: Limitations on Foreign Ownership.)

U.S. ownership of foreign assets.   Many foreign governments regulate closely the ownership by non-citizens of domestic corporations or assets and require governmental approval of transfer of any such property to a non-citizen.

Some of those restrictions may apply to only a portion of the transaction. For example, where there are real property assets in several states, only one of which regulates the transfer of contaminated real property, the parties can structure the transaction to close on the unaffected assets in a timely manner, leaving the affected asset for subsequent transfer upon compliance with applicable law, or excluding it from the acquisition. Alternatively, if the principal purchaser cannot obtain regulatory consents for certain assets, the seller may consider a spin-off of those assets to another purchaser.

How can the parties assess the significance of regulatory barriers at the planning stage of an acquisition?

Interested parties should determine early on how likely it is that they will obtain the necessary consents, how long this will take, and how difficult and expensive it will be. When the procedures and the criteria for obtaining consents are well defined, this regulatory "audit" can be performed relatively quickly and reliably. Flexible or discretionary procedures and criteria for approvals can extend the time and increase the uncertainty of obtaining such approvals in a timely fashion. In general, especially where third party financing is involved, it may be not only imprudent but *impossible* to proceed with the affected part of the transaction prior to obtaining the necessary approval. Therefore, potential buyers and sellers should be sure at the initial planning stages to provide adequate time and resources for the regulatory compliance effort.

ANTITRUST CONSIDERATIONS FOR ACQUISITIONS

What general antitrust considerations should acquisition planners consider when contemplating an acquisition?

Antitrust practitioners divide corporate acquisitions into three types:

1. Vertical acquisitions—acquisition of suppliers or customers—that may foreclose markets to competitors;
2. Horizontal acquisitions—between competitors—which may give "monopoly" power or cause overconcentration; and
3. Conglomerate acquisitions—between firms in different fields—which might remove potential competition or discourage competition by others because of the financial or marketing strength of the resulting firm.

Section 7 of the Clayton Act prohibits a corporation from acquiring stock or assets of another corporation if the acquisition might "substantially lessen competition or to tend to create a monopoly" in any line of commerce in any section of the country.

A violation of Section 7 may give rise to an injunction against the acquisition, an order compelling divestiture of the property or other interests, or other remedies. Section 7 is enforced by the Antitrust Division of the U.S. Department of Justice and by the Federal Trade Commission.

In conjunction with the federal laws, there are state laws that can restrict mergers. Under federal law (the McCarran-Ferguson Act, 15 U.S.C. §1011f) states are given broad authority to regulate mergers involving insurance companies. There is similar authority in certain other areas in which the states have special regulatory jurisdiction, such as the wine and liquor businesses.

Mergers of companies with foreign operations or subsidiaries sometimes require review and approval by foreign governments. In addition, some foreign countries (most notably, Canada) have their own premerger notification programs which may have to be complied with. (See Chapter 13, International Transactions—Non-Tax Inbound Issues. Also, U.S. law governing foreign merger/acquisition activity of U.S. companies is covered there.)

HART-SCOTT-RODINO

How does the government gather information about proposed mergers and acquisitions?

The Hart-Scott-Rodino Antitrust Improvements Act of 1976 (the "HSR Act") provides that the parties to certain acquisition transactions must supply certain information about themselves to the Federal Trade Commission ("FTC") and the Antitrust Division of the Department of Justice before the merger is permitted to occur. The information supplied is used by these governmental agencies to determine whether the proposed transaction has certain anticompetitive effects which should be restricted before the transaction is completed. A mandatory "waiting period" follows the agencies' receipt of the HSR filings.

What mergers or acquisitions require premerger notification under the HSR Act?

Generally, all mergers and acquisitions which meet all of the following three criteria must be reported under the HSR Act and the related premerger notification rules:

- The transaction is between two persons with minimum sizes of $100 million and $10 million, respectively, in gross assets or, for manufacturing companies, annual sales;
- As a result of the transaction, the acquiring person will own either (a) more than $15 million of the acquired person's voting securities or assets or (b) 50% or more of the voting securities of a company that has consolidated annual sales or gross assets of $25 million or more; and
- One of the persons involved is engaged in United States commerce or in an activity affecting United States commerce.

The "persons" involved include not only the corporations involved, but also any other corporation which is under common control. "Control" for purposes of the HSR Act is defined as ownership of 50% or more of a company's voting securities or having the contractual power to designate a majority of a company's board of directors. Special control rules apply to partnerships and other unincorporated entities.

What information is required to be included in the premerger notification form?

The form requires a description of the parties and the proposed merger or acquisition, certain current financial information about the parties, and a breakdown of revenues of the parties according to the Standard Industrial Classification codes. This breakdown of revenues is used by the FTC and DOJ to determine whether the proposed combination of the businesses would result in an anticompetitive effect. The information filed is exempt from disclosure under the Freedom of Information

Act, and no such information may be made public except pursuant to administrative or judicial proceedings.

After the premerger notification form has been filed, how long must the parties wait before the merger or acquisition can be consummated?

Where the acquisition is being made by a cash tender offer, the parties must wait 15 days before the purchaser may accept shares for payment. In all other cases, the parties must wait 30 days before the transaction can be completed. If the acquisition raises antitrust concerns, the government may extend the waiting period by requesting additional information from the parties. In that case, the waiting period is extended for 20 days (10 days in the case of a cash tender offer) past the time when the additional information is provided.

The parties may request early termination of the waiting period. Where the acquisition raises no antitrust concerns, the government may grant the request, though doing so is within its discretion.

Are certain mergers and acquisitions exempt from the HSR Act?

Yes. Acquisitions made through newly formed corporate acquisition vehicles are frequently exempt from the reporting requirements of the HSR Act because the vehicle does not meet the "size of person" test, i.e., it does not have $10 million in gross assets or sales. This is true, however, only where no other person having $10 million in gross assets or annual sales owns 50% or more of the voting stock of the vehicle or has the contractual power to designate a majority of the vehicle's directors. If the vehicle is not controlled by another person, it will be the only company matched against the $10 million size of person test. If another company or person does control the vehicle, through either a 50% stock ownership or a contractual power to appoint a majority of its directors, that controlling person will be matched against this test. Special rules apply in determining control of partnerships and other unincorporated acquisition vehicles.

Special rules are also used to determine the "size" of a newly formed corporation, and care must be taken to avoid making contractual commitments for additional capital contributions or for guarantees of the new corporation's obligations until after the formation has been completed.

The assets of a newly formed acquisition vehicle that is not controlled by another person do not include the funds contributed to the vehicle or borrowed by the vehicle at the closing to complete the acquisition.

The HSR Act and FTC rules also provide numerous exemptions for special situations.

How can we tell whether a particular horizontal merger is likely to be challenged by the Department of Justice?

Current administration policy is set forth in the Department of Justice's 1984 Merger Guidelines. As in previous guidelines, horizontal mergers are assessed according to a sliding scale of permissiveness. Thus, the less concentrated the industry the larger the permissible merger. The index used to measure concentration, the Herfindahl-Hirschman Index (referred to as the HHI), sums the squares of the individual companies' market shares to measure both postmerger share and the growth in market share resulting from the transaction. Thus, for example, an industry of five firms having market shares of 30%, 25%, 20%, 15% and 10% respectively has an Index of $30^2 + 25^2 + 20^2 + 15^2 + 10^2$ or 2250. If the third and fifth firms merge, the resulting index is $30^2 + 25^2 + 30^2 + 15^2$, or 2650, and the increase in the Index would be 400.

An HHI analysis must be performed for each distinct "relevant market" in which both of the merging companies operate.

Specifically, the guidelines' policy is as follows:

"Unconcentrated industries" are those in which the postmerger HHI is below 1,000. This normally corresponds to an industry in which the largest four firms have 50% or less of the market. Historically, this description fits about 60% of U.S.

industries. In such industries, the Department is unlikely to challenge any merger.

Industries are "moderately concentrated" when the post-merger HHI falls in the range of 1,000 to 1,800. Included in this range are the roughly 25% of U.S. industries in which the four largest firms normally account for between 50% and 70% of the market. Within this range the Department will review other factors bearing upon the likelihood of collusion. Generally, within this range mergers that increase the HHI by more than 100 points are likely to be challenged. Thus, for example, the over-100 prohibited zone would be reached in such an industry by a merger of two firms each with a 7.1% market share, of a 10% firm with a 5% firm, a 25% firm with a 2% firm, and a 50% firm with a 1% firm.

Industries are "highly concentrated" when the postmerger HHI exceeds 1,800. This characterizes the 15% of U.S. industries in which the four-firm concentration ratio exceeds 70%. In such industries, a merger increasing the HHI by less than 50 points (less than 5% plus 5%, 10% plus 2.5%, etc.) is "unlikely" to be challenged. If the merger increases the HHI by between 50 and 100 points (again, a 100 point increase corresponds to 7.1% plus 7.1%, 10% plus 5%, 25% plus 2%, etc.), the merger may or may not be challenged. If the increase is above the 100 point threshold, a challenge is "likely."

Whatever the level of concentration, the Department will challenge those mergers that, by these criteria, are likely to create or enhance one-firm domination of a market. Thus a leading firm that accounts for 35% of the market and that is twice the size of its next largest competitor will normally not be allowed to acquire any firm accounting for 1% of that market.

In addition, analysis of horizontal merger is no longer governed by the single-minded focus on market concentration that has, in theory, been the rule since the Supreme Court's 1963 *Philadelphia National Bank* case. It considers instead other real-market factors including:

1. Ease of entry into the market (the easier it is for new firms to enter the market, the less the likelihood of challenge);

2. The availability of out-of-market substitutes (the more readily available, the less prospect of collusion);
3. The degree to which the merging firms confront one another within the relevant market (if they occupy separate sectors of the market, the merger is less a cause of concern than if they are head-to-head in the same corner);
4. The level of product homogeneity (the more homogeneous the product, the easier it is to collude);
5. The pace of technological change (the slower the rate of change, the more likely collusion);
6. The importance of nonprice terms (the more important they are, the harder it is to collude);
7. The degree to which firms have access to information concerning their competitors' transactions (the more information is available, the greater the likelihood of collusion);
8. The size and frequency of orders (the smaller and more frequent, the greater the likelihood of collusion);
9. Whether the industry is characterized either by a history of collusion or by patterns of pricing conduct that make collusion more likely (if it is, the likelihood of a challenge increases); and
10. Historical evidence of noncompetitive performance (challenge more likely).

Vertical and conglomerate mergers have only very rarely been challenged by the government since about 1981.

If the FTC and the Department of Justice either do not investigate a reportable transaction or allow it to proceed after investigation, can the transaction thereafter be challenged?

Technically, the government is not prevented from challenging any merger or acquisition at any time. But such challenges are almost unheard of where HSR filings have been made and the waiting period has been allowed to expire or has been terminated.

Does that mean that after the HSR waiting period the parties can be assured of being able to close their transaction?

In recent years mergers and acquisitions have occasionally been challenged by state attorneys general and by private parties. The law is unsettled as to whether, and under what circumstances, such challenges may be brought, but injunctions have been granted in private antitrust suits by targets of hostile takeovers and by competitors of one or both of the merging companies. Such an injunction has even been granted, in April 1988, despite a DOJ consent decree permitting the acquisition (*Beazer PLC*). These suits often fail because the challenging party cannot show that it will suffer "antitrust injury," but they can be disruptive nevertheless.

In addition, state attorneys general have recently become more active in reviewing proposed mergers, particularly in retailing industries, that may affect consumers within their states.

Is HSR reporting ever required for purchases of voting stock by anyone other than the principal parties to a transaction?

In March and April 1988 the FTC and the Justice Department obtained civil penalty consent judgments against several companies who were accused of buying stock through an investment banking company that allegedly acted as its "agent." These cases involved so-called "option agreements," under which the investment bank purchased stock but gave another company an "option" to "call" that stock and retained the right to "put" that stock to the other company. The enforcement agencies contended that the investment bank purchases conferred beneficial ownership of the stock on the companies holding the call rights, who were charged with failing to file HSR reports for such purchases.

CHANGING THE COMPANY NAME

Once you as a buyer or seller are certain that there are no antitrust or other regulatory obstacles to your planned transaction, the way is clear for actually doing the deal. But first, reflect on a few issues affecting life after the acquisition.

A name change should never be undertaken lightly, because a company's name lies at the core of its public image, and a company's image—the sum total of the perceptions of shareholders, the financial community, employees—is a key determinant of shareholder value. Still, this issue is fairly likely to arise when thinking through an acquisition, perhaps for both the buying corporation and the target.

Under what circumstances should a company's name be changed following an acquisition?

Sometimes an acquisition leads to a name change in the target because the old name was borrowed from the old parent and cannot be applied to an enterprise that has joined a different business group or gone off on its own. To take one of many examples, when Bell Atlantic Corp. acquired Greyhound Capital Corp. from its parent, Greyhound Corp., there was no way to put a bell on the greyhound, so it ended up as Bell Atlantic Systems Leasing. Aside from such issues, the only circumstance that justifies a name change is when the old name no longer communicates an accurate image of the company's mission and strategy. This sometimes occurs on the buyer level after a restructuring is undertaken to initiate and leverage new strategic initiatives. A good example is U.S. Steel, which diversified into many other businesses like Marathon Oil and Texas Gas. Despite the enormous equity in and prestige of the old name, management decided to change their corporate identity to USX, making U.S. Steel a division of the larger entity. A similar change occurred when United Aircraft changed its name to United Technologies.

Also consider a company name change when the effect of the merger or acquisition expands the scope of a company's operations beyond local markets. The First National Bank of Jackson, Mississippi, after acquiring banks throughout the state, changed its name to Trustmark.

Another sound reason for name change is when a company, despite acquisitions beyond its core business, is still identified with a particular consumer brand. Hart Schaffner & Marx, for example, acquired its way beyond men's clothing into diversified brands, retail stores, and international operations, and so renamed itself Hartmarx.

When is it appropriate to retain both names after a merger or acquisition to form a new identity for the corporation?

Both target and buyer names should be preserved when the equities of two merged companies' names on either a marketing or financial community level are so valuable or useful they should be preserved in the newly joined entity's identity. American/National Can Company, Prudential-Bache, RJR/Nabisco and WearEver-ProctorSilex, Inc. are examples of this particular identity strategy. However, this combination strategy does impose on the company the challenge of unifying all employees under a single banner with a shared vision. The advantages and disadvantages of dual identities should also be seriously considered in view of the newly-formed company's short and long-term goals. Carefully analyzing identity requirements can effectively reduce the possibility of confusion later on.

PRE-PLANNING OF POST-ACQUISITION INTEGRATION

Why is pre-acquisition planning of post-acquisition integration important?

According to McKinsey & Co., a worldwide management consulting firm, over two-thirds of the corporate diversification programs that it has examined have never earned what the buyer could have earned if it had invested the money in certificates of deposit. Other M&A experts believe that one-third of all corporate marriages are outright financial failures and three-fourths fail to fulfill the desired objectives.

Robert Duncan, a professor at Northwestern University's Kellogg Graduate School of Management, believes that most of these merger implementation programs fail because (1) no strategy to achieve synergy was developed; (2) the merger was hotly contested; (3) the parties then failed to *manage* the implementation transition; (4) failed to merge management skills; (5) failed to plan for organizational relationships such as integration mechanisms and rewards and incentives; and (6) lacked a supporting corporate culture. In a more macro sense many mergers and acquisitions have gone awry because the buyer ventured into an unknown industry, paid too high a price, forecasted too bullishly, and/or did not recognize the importance of the target's people.

Based on the aforementioned comments, the sixty-four (thousand or million) dollar question becomes "What did you think you could do for the acquired company that it wasn't able to do as a stand-alone?" "What makes the firms worth more together than they were apart?" "And how do you acquire a company, combine it with your present operations, and at the same time not upset the acquired firm's vitality that led you to buy it in the first place?" Obviously, it is these and other post-acquisition integration questions that need to be asked before an acquisition is made, because once a deal is done, it's done.

How much post-acquisition planning is normal?

It depends very much on the strategic level, the size of the acquisition, whether it is geographically dispersed or even internationally dispersed, and sometimes on what has been agreed to in the purchase agreement. Here are a few of the most common questions that must be answered.

As buyers, should we establish a merger transition team?

No matter what the size, yes. Nothing is worse than not knowing where to go for answers. J.B. Fuqua used to say that he'd fire the first person from headquarters who went into a newly acquired company and *told* in-place management what to do. *They* had transition processes. Acquiring management can jeopardize the post-acquisition integration process by precipitate action and underestimating the time, resources—internal and external—and management time required to ensure the new company's successful operation.

What creates the greatest post-acquisition stress—fear of change or fear of the unknown?

The latter. Usually the normal lines of communication are interrupted. People and their families live not only on money flows, but on information flows about what's going on. A new owner that doesn't create an information system to keep people informed—especially if there is a change in management as well as ownership—will be in for trouble. The rumor mill gets going and can play hell with morale.

How much integration should there be?

It depends on the plans. If it's to be sold off, the less the better. If it's a "keep," the maximum—but slowly, slowly.

How much press?

Generally, the maximum. But carefully, fully, and professionally. It's best to have it handled outside by professionals, and there are lots of experts around—especially for public companies.

What's the biggest cause of trouble?

Differing management styles. When a hands-on executive buys a company run by a skilled delegator, there's always trouble, and one of them—usually the acquired company's executive—has to leave. And that's too bad, because both styles work and make money for the stockholders. It will help if they both can find some other common interest like golf, or stamps, or *something*. Maybe even the stockholders!

What about executive compensation?

Hay Associates, the world's biggest executive compensation consulting firm, says that creating a compensation scheme that is internally fair and externally competitive for a new acquisition is a tough job and perhaps the most common cause of executive resignations. Here again, pre-acquisition executive compensation planning is a must. And explaining how executives are compensated must be the first order of post-acquisition business.

What about reporting? Isn't that a source of trouble?

It sure is. Entrepreneurs, used to running their own show, usually quit within months of selling out. Why? Because they don't like filling out 100 pages of figures per month. Figures they *know* don't matter. It is very hard for them to realize that the conversion from informal, shout-down-the-hall communication doesn't work when geographical space is interposed. The substitution of praise and promotion for invective and threat to galvanize action is often too much of a change. And the local language, both silent and spoken, replaced by standard corporatese, is lost in the wilderness of changeover. Any sensible buyer knows this about entrepreneurs and will see that the process is gradual and as painless as possible. But only the most enlightened buyers practice this gradualism and minimalism in corporate communications with their newly acquired operations.

How do you identify the decisionmaking hierarchy?

That is a problem. Research has shown that in hospitals, those with seniority dictate method. Newly hired M.D.s learn from 20-year veteran orderlies how to act in emergencies. Discovering the real rather than the ostensible decisionmaking process in any newly acquired operation is a problem for any buyer. The best way to discover it is to set up some kind of task-solving system and see who comes up with the solutions.

How do you cut down obstructionism and gain loyalty?

In *The Prince*, Machiavelli described how he ruled a newly conquered city: kill off or exile the leaders and promote every one else. You get rid of the troublemakers and gain loyalty this way. This time-honored practice was carried out in the Texas bank merger movement of the '60s and '70s, and the current results can be seen in the current collapse of the Texas banking system. Takeover tycoons flaunt their victories, use the spoils systems and carpetbagging, and really stick it to the "losers." The same ego that drives one to a financial victory is the same ego that creates vast operating problems. Only the "philosopher kings" can conquer corporately and reign for long, and they are few.

How about visits?

A *very* sensitive area. Certainly early visits should be scheduled, but then, there's nothing like the unexpected visit or two to keep everyone on their toes *all* the time. And in this day and age of EPA violations which are costing some buyers in the hundreds of millions of dollars to fix up previous violations, in environmentally sensitive industries, surprise visits should be a matter of course. But everyone there should know that it is company policy.

When should the merger transition and integration process begin?

It should begin almost when you sign a letter of intent and establish your initial agreement and begin your due diligence. You can, at the same time, be gathering data that will be useful in helping you facilitate the transition process and the ultimate integration (if you are going to full integration).

Is a company's size a factor in its ability to successfully avoid post-merger trauma?

Size shouldn't make a difference if, in fact, you have a carefully planned transition process. The key in every case between success and failure is whether you actively and aggressively initiate a planned transition and integration program.

What are the primary reasons why mergers and acquisitions fail to meet the goals and expectations of the acquiring companies?

A number of things occur—losses in market share, which occur in probably 90% of the acquired companies, not that they are unrecoverable; reduced efficiency and productivity; and loss of key personnel. Actually, poor transition planning is probably number one.

What if a buyer's goals or objectives are not realistic?

What is generally found is that the goal is attainable if the parent company is also willing to commit the resources to attain it. A company acquires another company with the notion of achieving some market advantage through some change in operations—that is a stated kind of reason. The inability to achieve such a goal occurs if, after the acquisition takes place, the parent has to allocate significant capital resources to accomplish the change but they're too debt-heavy to carry out the plan, and right away they're in trouble.

How soon should the acquiring company begin to affect changes within the acquired company?

A company has to react—in fact, act immediately—to reduce the depth and duration of any drop in efficiency and productivity. They also need to begin implementing whatever changes that are going to take place.

We recommend very strongly that a company act immediately to initiate any major changes. Why? Because the best time for change is when a major change—a merger or acquisition— has already taken place. And, please, don't issue a "no changes in personnel are contemplated" if, in fact, you *do* contemplate changes.

How should buyers treat their own management in the post-merger transition process?

In this period, when both companies are sizing each other up, and counterparts are looking at each other, the sensitive parent company is often paying so much attention to the newly-acquired company that they are ignoring the feelings of their own managers. We've seen companies going to the acquired company and saying, "Don't worry. If there is any consolidation, your job is secure." While they are saying that, the people back home, who know there is going to be some job consolidation and diminution, are taking that as a message that they are the ones who will probably be let go.

Anything else?

Remember that they're all *people*. And people are still children and react as such—especially when deep-pockets Daddy is around.

- So don't spoil them. You *must* be firm or you'll confuse them.
- Act quickly. Bad situations generally get worse, not better.
- Give out love and respect and you get it back. Give out mistrust and causticisms—especially in public meetings—and you get back hate, obfuscation, and, in extreme cases, sabotage.
- Know that mistakes are the inevitable result of the freedom that comes with independent entrepreneurial action. Mistakes are natural. But they are not *sins*. Cruel and unusual punishments are out. But some kind of corrective system which has a punishment component is as important as a reward system, so long as it is universally applied.
- And don't nag. If you have to repeat and repeat, it's more likely the corporate buyer's fault than the acquiree's.
- Remember that out-and-out lies are rare in our corporate culture but hyperbole is not. You must both learn to tell the difference in the new relationship.
- Don't let buyer or acquiree ever fall back on "We've been doing it that way successfully for 18 years." First, that's usually not true. Second, if they didn't change in 18 years there's something wrong. And, when you're wrong, for heaven's sake admit it, publicly.

Finally, remember that the greatest compliment people can pay you is to work for you. There is nothing wrong with thanking them for the compliment. Frequently.

CHAPTER 3

VALUATION AND PRICING

INTRODUCTION

No factor counts more than price in closing a transaction. Yet very few operating executives have any notion as to how much their or anyone else's companies are worth except from the stock tables. Very few know how to go about answering that question when they buy or sell.

To help get a grip on this key area, this chapter first focuses on valuation methods, and particularly on discounted cash flow (DCF) analysis, as set forth by Al Rappaport, the dean of DCF merger valuation. The second part of the chapter, prepared by Richard Linhart of Wesray Capital Corporation, applies DCF in a practical way to explain how leveraged buyouts are priced. Once the price has been arrived at, the final portion of the chapter describes how it is expressed in the pricing clauses of acquisition agreements.

Valuation is a highly specialized process. Specialists abound. There are people who value printing companies, while others concentrate on manufacturing, banks, and insurance companies. There are other firms who value engineering consulting firms, accounting firms, and law practices. There are rules of thumb for pricing restaurants, gas stations, grocery stores, and car washes. For example, some people say "Any tech-based company is worth at least its sales," or "I never pay more than 80% of net worth," or "The average company listed on the

New York Stock Exchange is worth at least 50% more than the current public value."

What is Discounted Cash Flow Value?

Regardless of all these rules of thumb, an elucidation of which is beyond the scope of this book, a company is worth only one value: the present value of all of its future cash flows discounted back to today at some rate proportional to the risk of actually realizing those cash flows. This discounted cash flow process has become the dominant valuation process in modern financial analysis.

Does top management know the DCF value of their companies?

Seldom, because to compute it requires long time horizons and some educated guesses about the future which managers are often reluctant to make. Outsiders are, however, not so reluctant, and those, along with the benefits of gaining control, are the reasons that very high premiums are often paid over market values for going companies.

Isn't this because the sum of the break-up values is greater than the market value?

Precisely. There is all too often no economic rationale for a conglomerate—the prefix "con" connoting some commonality. Most are agglomerates—an assortment of disparate operations, each paying a fee for what often proves to be headquarters hindrance rather than headquarters help. The benefits of association, the synergies, such as the evening out of cash flows in joining countercyclical operations, are often more than offset by headquarters stultification of the entrepreneurial process so necessary to successful growth.

The previous chapter's strategic planning process is essential to minimize such dissynergies. If they arise, however, the silver lining is that the component businesses are good candidates for divestment and acquisition, using the valuation and pricing principles that follow.

VALUATION METHODS*

What are the primary ways to assess the value of a company?

Traditionally, company value has been measured by accounting measures such as earnings, earnings per share (EPS), return on equity (ROE), and return on investment (ROI). For nearly two decades these numbers have had only limited use as a tool for valuation. The concept of "shareholder" value served to preempt the use of such measures for valuation purposes and to replace them with a discounted cash flow measure.

If accounting measures have only a limited use in valuation, why are they used?

Corporate financial reporting is regulated by the Financial Accounting Standards Board (FASB) and the Securities and Exchange Commission. The Securities Acts of 1933 and 1934 gave the SEC power to ensure "full and fair disclosure" by corporations issuing securities on an interstate basis.

Companies, on the other hand, have an incentive to *limit* reported information, particularly information about prospects for the future. This is because financial reports are publicly available and information provided to shareholders is also available to competitors, suppliers, customers, employees, the government, and others.

---

*The following material on Discounted Cash Flow (pages 65 through 81) was derived from Alfred Rappaport, *Creating Shareholder Value: The New Standard for Business Performance* (New York: The Free Press, 1987), with permission from the author and the publisher.

Therefore, compared to the internal information available to management, accounting information communicated externally necessarily represents "second-best" information.

Why is discounted cash flow used as a valuation approach?

The role of top management is to assess the relationship between today's investments and the magnitude and timing of future cash flows and not to be influenced by arbitrary accounting conventions that do not affect cash flow. Shareholder value is created by cash flow, not by accounting convention. By estimating the future cash flows associated with each potential investment, management can assess the economic value to the shareholder of alternate strategies generally at the business unit and corporate levels.

What are some of the current incentives for DCF valuation?

- The threat of corporate takeovers by those seeking undervalued or undermanaged assets;
- Increasing evidence that traditional accounting measures such as EPS and ROI are not reliably linked to increasing the value of the company's shares;
- Reporting of "returns to shareholders" along with other measures of performance in the business press such as *Fortune's* annual ranking of the 500 leading industrial firms; and
- A growing recognition that executives' long-term compensation needs to be more closely tied to total returns to shareholders.

How do earnings-related measures fall short of measuring value to shareholders?

- Alternative accounting methods may have been employed;

- Risk is excluded;
- Investment requirements are excluded;
- Dividend policy is not considered; and
- The time value of money is ignored.

What alternative accounting methods may be employed in earnings measures?

The earnings number may be computed using alternative and equally acceptable accounting methods. Prominent examples are the differences that arise from last-in, first-out (LIFO) and first-in, first-out (FIFO) approaches to computing cost of sales, various methods of computing depreciation, and purchase versus pooling-of-interests accounting for mergers and acquisitions.

The accountant's earnings figure results from attempts to match costs against revenues. This process involves allocating costs of assets, for example by depreciation, over their estimated useful life. Accounting allocations often differ among companies and for a particular company over time. Depreciation methods include the straight-line approach and accelerated depreciation methods such as sum-of-the-years' digits and double declining balance. All yield different earnings figures.

DCF AND RISK

Why and how does the DCF method include risk?

Risk must be taken into account in establishing the economic value of any asset. The level of risk is determined both by the nature of the firm's operations and by the relative proportions of debt and equity used to finance its investments. These two types of risk are commonly referred to as "business risk" and "financial risk," respectively. Earnings figures do not incorporate consideration of risk, but DCF does because DCF selects a discount rate that reflects risk.

Consider a business evaluating two competing strategies for its five-year plan. Management's earnings growth projections and probability estimates associated with each outcome are shown in Table 3–1.

The expected value or mean for each strategy is an earnings growth rate of 10 percent. The most likely value is also 10 percent in each case. The riskiness of the strategies is a function of the variability of the possible outcomes. The tighter the probability distribution, the less risky is the strategy. In this respect the two strategies are quite different. Note that the range of outcomes for Strategy A (6 to 14 percent) is wider than the range for Strategy B (8 to 12 percent). Further, the probabilities associated with the lowest and highest outcomes are higher for Strategy A, thereby contributing to even greater variability.

One summary measure of the dispersion of the probability distribution is the standard deviation. The standard deviation for Strategy A is 2.28 percent, and for Strategy B it is 0.90 percent. Strategy A, with a higher standard deviation, would be considered more risky than Strategy B. Using an earnings growth standard, management would be indifferent between these two strategies because the most likely forecast is a 10 percent rate in each case. Once risk is introduced into the analysis, Strategy B with its lower risk would be preferred over Strategy A.

TABLE 3-1
Sample Projections

	Strategy A		Strategy B
Probability	Earnings Growth Rate (%)	Probability	Earnings Growth Rate (%)
.10	6	.05	8
.25	8	.25	9
.30	10	.40	10
.25	12	.25	11
.10	14	.05	12

DCF AND DEBT

How does debt affect risk levels, and how does DCF reflect this?

When debt is introduced into the firm's capital structure, the rate of return required by investors incorporates not only a premium for business risk, but a premium for financial risk as well. As financial leverage is increased, the risk for shareholders likewise increases.

Consider a firm evaluating two alternative strategies for its initial capital structure—leverage and no leverage. The company requires $10 million in capital, and the initial price per share of common stock is $10. The leverage strategy calls for selling 500,000 shares and obtaining via debt an equal amount of capital, $5 million, at an after-tax cost of 8 percent, or $400,000. The no-leverage strategy simply involves the sale of one million shares at $10 per share.

Optimistic, most likely, and pessimistic scenarios for earnings levels appear in Table 3–2.

For the no-leverage strategy, the percent increase or decrease in operating earnings and EPS is identical, while for the leverage case, the change in EPS is greater than the

TABLE 3-2
Possible Scenarios

	Optimistic	Most Likely	Pessimistic
No-leverage strategy			
Operating earnings after taxes	$1,000,000	$ 800,000	$ 400,000
Shares outstanding	1,000,000	1,000,000	1,000,000
Earnings per share	1.00	0.80	0.40
Leverage strategy			
Operating earnings after taxes	1,000,000	800,000	400,000
Interest expense after taxes	400,000	400,000	400,000
Net income after taxes	600,000	400,000	0
Shares outstanding	500,000	500,000	500,000
Earnings per share	1.20	0.80	0.00

change in operating earnings. In the above example, a 25 percent increase in operating earnings, from $800,000 in the most likely case to $1 million in the optimistic case, results in an increase of 50 percent in EPS (from $0.80 to $1.20). The EPS range for the no-leverage case is $0.40–$1.00, while for the leverage strategy the range increases to $0.00–$1.20.

The increased variability and the greater danger of insolvency due to the introduction of leverage increases the financial risk to shareholders who will, in turn, demand higher rates of return as compensation. As long as the incremental earnings generated by debt financing exceed interest expense, debt financing will increase net income. But because debt also increases risk, the increase in earnings will increase the discount rate and may not necessarily lead to an increase in economic value calculated under DCF.

DCF AND WORKING CAPITAL

How do changes in working capital and fixed capital investment requirements affect company value, and how does DCF reflect this?

As a business grows, there will normally be an associated growth in its level of working capital—*accounts receivable, inventory,* and *accounts payable.*

An increase in *accounts receivable* between the beginning and end of the year means that the cash flow from sales is less than the revenue figure reflected in the income statement. Assume current year's sales are $10 million; receivables at the beginning of the year, $1 million; and year-end receivables $1.2 million. Cash flow from sales for the year is calculated as follows:

Beginning receivables	$ 1,000,000
Sales	10,000,000
Cash flow potential	11,000,000
Ending receivables	1,200,000
Cash flow realized	$ 9,800,000

Note that the $10 million sales figure does not represent the current period's cash generated. Instead, cash flow from sales is total sales less the $200,000 increase in accounts receivable. The $200,000 is not available to meet current cash commitments. For accounting purposes, revenue is recognized at the time goods or services are delivered. For purposes of economic valuation, recognition must await the receipt of cash. In brief, cash is received after revenue is recognized. Thus, for companies with expanding receivables, the sales figure on the income statement will overstate the current period's cash flow generated from sales.

Inventory investment is another important component of working capital that contributes to differences between earnings and the cash flow valuation approach. An increase in the level of inventory clearly involves cash payments for materials, labor, and overhead. For accrual accounting purposes the investment in additional inventory is, however, reflected as an asset on the balance sheet and is not included in the cost of sales figure appearing in the income statement. Therefore, for companies with expanding inventory levels, the cost of sales figure will understate the current period's cash outflow for inventory expenditures. In brief, for expanding firms, increases in accounts receivable and inventories will cause the earnings figure to be greater than cash flow.

The third major component of working capital, *accounts payable*, acts as a countervailing force. Accounts payable and accrued liabilities represent unpaid bills for items already included as expenses in the income statement or for increases in inventory reflected on the balance sheet. Thus, the cost of sales and selling, general, and administrative expense accounts in the income statement overstate the cash outflow by the amount of the related increase in payables. In other words, cash is disbursed after the expense is recognized.

When it comes to investment in *fixed assets*, we know that depreciable assets such as property, plant, and equipment are initially recorded at cost and included in the fixed asset section of the balance sheet. Accountants then allocate this cost over the estimated useful life of the asset through depreciation. They often stress that depreciation is a process of allocating original cost and not a process of valuation. Depreciation on fixed assets purchased during the current year as well as on those purchased in prior years is a deduction to arrive at net income. But while depreciation is an expense, it does not involve an outlay of cash. On the other hand, the earnings number will not include the capital expenditures made during the year. Thus, to move from earnings to cash flow, two adjustments are needed. First, the depreciation must be added back to earnings and second, capital expenditures must be deducted from earnings.

Incorporating the adjustments discussed in this section, cash flow from operations may be calculated as follows:

Cash flow from operations = Sales − Operating expenses including taxes + Depreciation and other non-cash items − Incremental working capital investment − Capital expenditures

Summing yields the net cash increment or decrement to be discounted to derive DCF value.

DCF AND DIVIDENDS

How do DCF and earnings measures compare when it comes to dividend policy?

The conflict between earnings and economic value can also be seen in the area of dividend policy. If the objective were to maximize earnings, one could argue persuasively that the company should never pay any dividends as long as it expected to achieve a positive return on new investment. But we know that if the company invested shareholders' funds at below the minimum acceptable market rate, the value of the company would decrease.

For example, suppose a company has a choice between paying a $1 million dividend and investing $1 million in additional inventory and thereby providing better service to its customers. The increase in net cash flow over the next five years resulting from the inventory investment is estimated to be $206,040 annually. For simplicity, assume that the annual earnings increase over the next five years was also projected to be $206,040.

From an earnings viewpoint, the dividend decrease looks very favorable because earnings would increase by $206,040 for each of the next five years. From an economic value standpoint, a very different conclusion emerges. The discounted cash flow rate of return on this investment is a modest 1 percent. If investors can invest in opportunities with similar risk at a yield of 15 percent, as soon as the market learns of management's intention to invest funds at substantially below this 15 percent opportunity investment rate, the market value of the stock can be expected to drop. Better pay the dividend.

How does DCF treat the time value of money ignored by earnings measures?

The economic value of an investment is the discounted value of the anticipated cash flows. Economic value calculations explicitly incorporate the idea that a dollar of cash received today is worth more than a dollar to be received a year from now because today's dollar can be invested to earn a return over the next year. The discount rate used to estimate economic value includes not only compensation for bearing risk but also compensation for expected rates of inflation.

DCF VS. ROI

How accurately does Return on Investment (ROI) reflect firm value?

The growing recognition that earnings increases are no guarantee of increases in shareholder value, particularly during inflationary periods, has led to the increasing popularity of accounting-based return on investment (ROI) and return on equity (ROE) as financial performance standards. However, taking an unreliable numerator (i.e., earnings) and relating it to an investment denominator generated by the same accounting process does not solve the problem.

Hurdle rates or minimum acceptable rates for ROI are often based on an estimate of the business unit's cost of capital or the corporate cost of capital. The assumption is that if ROI is greater than the cost of capital, then shareholder value will be created. The essential problem with this approach is that ROI is an accrual accounting return and is being compared to a cost of capital measure which is an economic return demanded by investors. Comparing one with the other is clearly an example of comparing apples with oranges.

The economic or discounted cash flow (DCF) one-year return for an investment is simply this year's cash flow plus the change in value over the year, divided by the value at the beginning of the year:

$$\text{DCF return} = \frac{\text{Cash flow} + (\text{Present value at end of year} - \text{Present value at beginning of year})}{\text{Present value at beginning of year}}$$

$$= \frac{\text{Cash flow} + \text{Change in present value}}{\text{Present value at beginning of year}}$$

The numerator of the DCF return (cash flow plus change in present value) is economic income. The change in the present value component of economic income is the net result of two factors. First, the present value one year from now excludes the current year's cash flow which will have already been received. Second, one year from now the cash flows for subsequent years will each be received one year sooner and thus increase in value. In brief, economic income for the year is derived by a comparison of cash flow projections at the beginning and at the end of the year.

Accounting or book income, in contrast, is calculated as follows:

Book income = Cash flow − Depreciation and
other noncash charges
+ Incremental investments in working capital
+ Capital expenditures

How do you compare DCF and ROI in a specific case?

The management of Noble Restaurant Inc. is considering acquiring a company with a purchase price of $1 million. Management forecasts operating results for a five-year period only, because it believes that in five years the facility will require substantial remodeling and much of the equipment will need to be replaced. Thus, management will be faced with another investment decision in five years that, in principle, will be much like today's decision of whether or not to open the restaurant. Projected cash flows for the next five years are $176,230, $250,000, $350,000, $400,000, and $400,000, respectively.

Assuming the cost of capital, which is reflected in the discount rate, is 15 percent, the net present value (NPV) of the investment is zero. That is, the present value of the cash flows discounted at 15 percent is equal to the $1 million investment:

$$
NPV = -1,000,000 + \frac{176,230}{1.15} + \frac{250,000}{(1.15)^2} + \frac{350,000}{(1.15)^3}
$$

$$
+ \frac{400,000}{(1.15)^4} + \frac{400,000}{(1.15)^5} = 0
$$

When the net present value of an investment is zero, the DCF rate of return is identical to the cost of capital or minimum acceptable rate of return.

While the restaurant investment is expected to yield an economic return of 15 percent, the ROI results are substantially different. ROI is computed as net income divided by total assets. ROI for this same investment progresses from a negative figure in the first year to 200 percent in the fifth year when the facilities are almost fully depreciated. Thus, ROI materially understates the economic rate of return in the first two years and significantly overstates returns for the last three years.

How does return on equity (ROE) work as a measure of value?

$$
ROE = \frac{Net\ income}{Book\ value\ of\ shareholders'\ equity}
$$

Whereas ROI relates net income to total assets, ROE employs shareholder equity as the denominator. ROI is the more commonly used measure at the business unit or sector level; ROE is the more popular measure at the corporate level. One of the principal reasons that management focuses on ROI rather than ROE at the business unit level is its reluctance to allocate debt to the individual units. The focus on ROE at the corporate level is often explained on the grounds that it is a measure of primary concern to investors.

Because ROE is so similar to ROI, it necessarily shares all the shortcomings of ROI enumerated earlier. In addition, ROE is particularly sensitive to leverage. Assuming that proceeds from debt financing can be invested at a rate of return greater than the borrowing rate, ROE will increase with greater amounts of leverage. ROE will, in fact, increase as more than optimal debt is issued and the value of the company decreases due to the increase in financial risk. Thus, once again we observe that an accounting-based performance measurement can conflict with the shareholder value criterion.

DCF AND SHAREHOLDER VALUE

How can managers estimate shareholder value?

The total economic value of an entity such as a company or business unit is the sum of the values of its debt and its equity. This value of the business is called "corporate value," and the value of the equity portion is called "shareholder value." In summary:

Corporate value = Debt + Shareholder value

The debt portion of corporate value includes the market value of debt, unfunded pension liabilities, and the market value of other claims such as preferred stock. Rearranging the above equation to solve for shareholder value:

Shareholder value = Corporate value − Debt

In order to determine shareholder value, one must first determine the value of the total firm or business unit, that is, corporate value. Corporate value, in turn, consists of two basic components:

1. The present value of cash flow from operations during the forecast period
2. "Residual value," which represents the present value of the business attributable to the period beyond the forecast period.

For a more precise estimation of corporate value, a third component must also be included: the current value of marketable securities and other investments that can be converted to cash and are not essential to operating the business. Neither these investments nor the income from them is included in cash flows from operations. Nonetheless, these investments clearly have value; thus, they need to be included in developing the corporate value estimate. Corporate value therefore has three components:

Corporate value = Present value of cash flow from operations during the forecast period + Residual value + Marketable securities

CALCULATING DCF

How is cash flow from operations calculated?

Cash flow from operations represents the difference between operating cash inflows and outflows. These cash flows are relevant for estimating corporate value because they represent the cash available to compensate debtholders and shareholders. Once the cash flow from operations is estimated for each year in the forecast period, these flows are then discounted back to the present. The cash flows are discounted by the cost of capital or the weighted average of the costs of debt and equity capital.

What is the appropriate rate for discounting the company's cash flow stream?

This rate would be the weighted average of the costs of debt and equity capital. For example, suppose a company's after-tax cost of debt is 6 percent and its estimated cost of equity 16 percent. Further, it plans to raise capital in the following proportion— 20 percent by way of debt and 80 percent by way of equity. It computes the cost of capital of 14 percent as follows:

	Weight (%)	Cost (%)	Weighted Cost (%)
Debt	20	6	1.2
Equity	80	16	12.8
Cost of capital			14.0

Measuring the cost of debt is a relatively straightforward matter once it is established that what is appropriate is the cost of new debt not the cost of previously outstanding debt. This is so because the economic desirability of a prospective investment depends upon future costs and not past or sunken costs. Since interest on debt is tax deductible, the rate of return that must be earned on debt-financed instruments is the after-tax cost of debt.

The second component of the cost of capital, the cost of equity, is more difficult to estimate. In contrast to the debt-financing case, where the firm contracts to pay a specific rate for the use of capital, there is no explicit agreement to pay common shareholders any particular rate of return. Nonetheless, there is some implicit rate of return required to attract investors to purchase the firm's stock and to induce shareholders to hold their shares. This rate is the relevant cost of equity capital. In assessing the company's cost of equity capital, or the minimum expected return that will induce investors to buy the company's shares, it is reasonable to assume that they will demand the risk-free rate as reflected in the current yields available in government securities, plus an additional return or equity risk premium for investing in the company's more risky shares.

Cost of equity = Risk-free rate + Equity risk premium

What is the "risk-free rate"?

Risk-free rate = "Real" interest rate + Expected inflation rate

What is the "equity risk premium"?

Risk premium = Expected return on Market − Risk-free rate

Does discounted cash flow for the forecast period account completely for a company's value?

No. Cash flow is usually forecast for a limited period of time; so there is a remaining or "residual" value to calculate.

This residual value often constitutes the largest portion of the value of the firm. For most businesses, only a small proportion of value can be reasonably attributed to its estimated cash flow for the next five or ten years.

However, while residual value is a significant component of corporate value, its size depends directly upon the assumptions made for the forecast period. Second, there is no unique formula for residual value. Its value depends on a careful assessment of the competitive position of the business at the end of the forecast period. There are several methods for estimating residual value that can be applied in different circumstances. For example, in the case of a harvesting strategy, liquidation value would most likely be the best estimate of residual value. By contrast, for the share-building case, a going concern measure, rather than a liquidation measure, would be relevant for estimating residual value.

How can residual value be calculated for a going concern?

The perpetuity method is particularly useful for valuing a wide range of going concerns. The perpetuity method is based on the assumption that a company that is able to generate returns above the cost of capital (i.e., achieve excess returns) will eventually attract competitors, whose entry into the business will drive returns down to the minimum acceptable or cost of capital rate. Specifically, the perpetuity method assumes that after the forecast period, the business will earn, on average, at a rate equal to the cost of capital on new investments. Another way of expressing this idea is to say that after the forecast period, the business will invest, on average, in strategies whose net present value is zero.

Once the rate of return has been driven down to the cost of capital rate, period-by-period differences in future cash flows do not alter the value of the business. Therefore, these future flows can be treated as if they were a "perpetuity" or an infinite stream of identical cash flows.

The present value of any perpetuity is simply the value of the expected annual cash flow divided by the rate of return:

$$\text{Present value of a perpetuity} = \frac{\text{Annual cash flow}}{\text{Rate of return}}$$

Using the perpetuity method, the present value (at the end of the forecast period) of a going concern is therefore calculated by dividing a "perpetuity cash flow" by the cost of capital:

$$\text{Residual value} = \frac{\text{Perpetuity cash flow}}{\text{Cost of capital}}$$

How can one estimate the value-creating potential of an acquisition to the buyer? What is an example of a perpetuity cash flow calculation?

A business in a mature industry generated $10 million in cash flow last year. If the company were to continue to generate $10 million annually—into "perpetuity"—and its cost of capital is 10 percent (10%), the value of the company would simply be equal to $100 million:

$$\frac{\text{Cash Flow}}{\text{Cost of capital}} = \frac{\$10 \text{ million}}{0.10} = \$100 \text{ million}$$

Valuing an acquisition requires that assessments be made of the stand-alone value of the target, the value of acquisition benefits, and the price required to gain control of the target. The respective roles of the above factors in the value creation framework can be gleaned from the following three fundamental equations.

$$\begin{array}{cc} \text{Value created by} \\ \text{acquisition} \end{array} = \begin{array}{c} \text{Value of} \\ \text{combined} \\ \text{company} \end{array} - \begin{array}{c} \text{Stand-alone} \\ \text{value of buyer} \\ \text{company pre-} \\ \text{acquisition} \end{array} - \begin{array}{c} \text{Stand-alone} \\ \text{value of} \\ \text{target} \end{array}$$

$$\begin{array}{c} \text{Maximum} \\ \text{acceptable} \\ \text{price to pay} \\ \text{to target} \end{array} = \begin{array}{c} \text{Stand-alone} \\ \text{value of} \\ \text{target} \end{array} + \begin{array}{c} \text{Value created by} \\ \text{acquisition} \end{array}$$

$$\begin{array}{c} \text{Value created} \\ \text{for buyer} \end{array} = \begin{array}{c} \text{Maximum acceptable} \\ \text{price to pay} \\ \text{for target} \end{array} - \begin{array}{c} \text{Price required} \\ \text{to gain control} \\ \text{of target} \end{array}$$

What is the stand-alone value to the buyer?

The "stand-alone" value to the buyer, whether of the pre-acquisition company or the target, is whatever value the buyer has determined as a result of shareholder value and/or other calculations.

What is the stand-alone value of the target to the seller?

The stand-alone value of the target to the seller would ordinarily be the seller's minimum acceptable, or floor, price because it usually has the option of continuing to operate the business. When the target company is publicly traded, market value is the best basis for establishing the seller's stand-alone value. To negotiate effectively, however, buyers need to recognize that the floor price depends on the seller's perceptions and not those of the buyer. The seller's floor price is determined by the attractiveness of his alternate opportunities.

PRICING ISSUES

The previous discussion was about value; we now move to price, the practical manifestation of value for a buyer and a seller. Very different prices may be offered for the same business by the buyer acquiring for the purpose of enhancing or supplementing existing operations (the "operating buyer") and the buyer acquiring in a leveraged buyout for investment and future resale (the "LBO buyer").

Typically the operating buyer has the cash available for an acquisition and is considering where to spend it. He is very conscious of synergies in combined operations and of competing opportunities for his resources. The time horizon of the operating buyer is probably relatively long-term, five years or more (although an important exception will arise if the acquisition is being considered as a defensive maneuver against a hostile takeover). Perhaps most important, the operating buyer is probably operating in an institutional, corporate framework in which full strategic planning is part of the intellectual culture.

For all these reasons, the process of strategic planning described in Chapter 2 should be followed, and the valuation analysis described above, building on a solid planning base, will lead through a "rational" process to a price based on value. If the seller is also an operating company, i.e., the transaction is a sale by one conglomerate of a division to another conglomerate, a reasonably consistent valuation process will probably have been followed, and a mutually satisfactory price should not be difficult to agree upon. The LBO buyer will probably undertake a different analysis in pricing an acquisition.

What are the characteristics of a typical LBO buyer?

The typical LBO buyer is usually a group (though it can be a single individual), perhaps organized in corporate or partnership form, which intends to finance the purchase price primarily through borrowing against the assets and cash flow of the target, providing a minimum of equity. They plan to pay down the debt through a combination of operating cash flow and, perhaps, some divestitures of operating divisions or assets. Once the debt is substantially reduced or eliminated, they will reap the benefits of their investment through dividends, public sale of stock, or sale of the company to another buyer (a conglomerate, another investor group, or the company's employee stock option plan). They probably rely on the existing management of the company to operate it without major changes in structure or personnel and may include key managers in the ownership group. While they may be simultaneously investing in other companies, they do not look for synergies between these other investments and the target; rather, their philosophy is "each tub on its own bottom." They prefer to keep their companies independent so that each can be operated and disposed of without affecting the others.

How does the LBO buyer price a potential acquisition?

Most experienced LBO buyers try to determine how much they must pay for a company and then analyze whether the deal works on this basis. In so doing, they look at a number of standard ratios that focus principally on the relationship of the gross unleveraged price to operating cash flow, operating income, or unleveraged book value. The ratios really only perform a support function. The business of finding, pursuing, negotiating, consummating, and overseeing LBOs is a practical business and, more than anything else, a people business. There is little reliance on theoretical financial models.

That seems to be a backward approach. Why is it done this way?

A key element of success in structuring and completing LBOs is creativity. If an LBO buyer tries to value a company in a vacuum, using the standard valuation techniques—earnings, cash flow, and book value multiples and discounted cash flow analyses —they will probably overlook the unusual elements that separate the truly successful LBOs from all others. If, however, the buyer has a target price that must be reached, the buyer will tend to push hard and be more creative in order to reach that target. It is basic human nature—people will perform better when they have a specific target. One of the great things about LBOs is that, if the deal works, it does not matter what conventions you have broken.

How do you decide if a deal works at a certain price?

That depends on the answer to two fundamental questions.

1. Can the deal be financed, given that only limited amounts of senior debt, subordinated debt, and equity are available for any company?
2. Can the company service the debt and still provide an attractive return to the equity holders?

Do you mean maximizing the return to the equity holders?

That is a part of it, but there is a lot more to it than that. Typically, the equity holders in an LBO will include two or three different types of investors, often with differing goals and objectives. They have differing risk return objectives and thus differing investment decisionmaking criteria.

The management team of the company is not only an equity investor but is also devoting its full time to running the business. Its equity stake, and the appreciation of the value of that stake, is an integral part of management's compensation. The potential value of that stake, when added to management's current compensation, must be competitive with other opportunities available to the individuals who form the management team.

The management team tends to have another important objective—to diversify the personal assets of its members. Typically, members of management do not have millions of dollars to invest. With their careers already tied to the company's future, individuals in senior management are often willing to give up some upside in dollars in order to retain personal assets outside of their investment in the company. In other words, not all investing managers are willing to "bet the farm," nor should they be expected to.

The LBO buyer who leads the deal also has several objectives. The sponsor must analyze an acquisition in terms of the opportunity cost of the time expended in pursuing, negotiating, closing, and subsequently overseeing the company. Regardless of the return on hard dollars invested, the sponsor must see a potential total dollar return that justifies the time investment.

An LBO firm must carefully consider risk. A passive investor can analyze investments in terms of risk and return and make a quantitative decision based on that investors' appetite for risk. An LBO firm with a good reputation has an important franchise to protect, a franchise that enables the firm to finance LBOs on an attractive basis. A successful LBO firm must look at every deal knowing that there is a lot more at risk than just its time and equity dollars. If the target eventually fails and a lender suffers a loss, it will adversely affect the firm's ability to attract and finance acquisitions in the future. Therefore, an LBO firm looks at risk not only in terms of its investment, but also in terms of the chance that a lender will suffer a loss. The potential profit on an acquisition must compensate a buyer for his time, his equity investment, and the risk to his business of financing an LBO.

Finally, there are the institutional equity investors. These are investors who are investors in LBO funds or investors who are given the right to buy equity as part of an agreement to lend senior or subordinated debt to the company. Investors in LBO funds, which many of the major LBO firms utilize today to finance deals, are looking for a pure financial return on their dollars, typically of 40% or more. Several LBO firms have delivered returns significantly higher than 40%. Lenders to the company sometimes seek equity participation in order to boost their blended returns to the mid to high teens in the case of senior lenders (typically banks) or the high teens or twenties in the case of subordinated lenders (usually insurance companies or junk bond buyers).

How do you decide whether a deal can be financed?

Financing LBOs is certainly more of an art than a science, but there are some useful guidelines. The first step is to gather some basic information about the company in order to begin formulating a financing plan. The key issues, on a broad level, include:

- What is the total financing required to close the acquisition and to finance future operations?

- What cash flow will the company generate that will be available to pay interest and principal?

The financing requirement is based, first on the purchase price and the need to refinance existing debt, and, second, on the company's ability to repay the loan out of its projected cash flow.

How do you project cash flow?

Projecting cash flow is the most difficult and usually most subjective part of doing a deal. It requires addressing a myriad of questions, including:

> What are the company's projections? Are they reasonable? Has the company been able to meet its projections in the past? What are the industry's prospects? How secure is the company's competitive position? Is it a cyclical business? Do the projections properly take this into account? What are the company's growth or expansion plans? What are the working capital and fixed asset requirements attendant to these plans? Is the business seasonal? What are the seasonal working capital needs? What events (such as strikes, currency fluctuations, foreign competition, loss of suppliers) could affect the projected results? Does the company have any excess assets or divisions that can or should be sold? What proceeds would these sales generate, and how long would it take to complete the sale? Are there any other potential sources of cash? What can go wrong in all this, and does the company have any contingency plans?

The above list is far from exhaustive, and it can take anywhere from a few hours to several weeks or months of due diligence to get a good feel for the cash flow. Once this has been done, the LBO buyer will be able to estimate reasonably the total financing needed at the closing date and prospectively for a five- to ten-year period thereafter.

What do you do with all this information?

Armed with these data, the buyer can begin to map out a financing plan. The boom in LBOs since the early 1980s has spawned a variety of debt instruments and financing sources, but generally all LBO debt can be classified as either senior debt or subordinated debt. See Chapter 4 for a fuller discussion of the different kinds of debt used in LBOs.

Most senior debt in LBOs is provided by banks and is either secured, meaning that specific assets or stock are legally pledged to secure the loan, or unsecured. Because senior debt is the cheapest source of financing, an acquiror should try to obtain the greatest amount of senior debt.

How does a senior lender decide how much to lend in an acquisition?

That depends on a number of factors, including the type of loan being obtained. Senior loans to LBOs generally defy strict classification, but can usually be divided into three groups— asset-based loans, cash flow loans, and bridge or interim loans.

In an asset-based loan, the bank is lending against specific assets or pools of assets and will decide how much to lend against each type of asset (the advance rate). For example, a bank may lend 80% against the book value of current accounts receivable, 60% against the book value of inventory in a warehouse, 30% against the book value of inventory in a retail store, and 50–75% against the fair market value of property, plant, and equipment.

In a cash flow loan, the bank is lending based on the company's ability to consistently generate cash flow from operations. On a cash flow loan, a bank will typically look for interest coverage (operating income divided by total interest expense) in the first year of at least 1.3 to 1.5 times and total repayment of the bank loan within 5–7 years. The bank may also seek to be covered on an asset basis within two to three years. An important factor in determining an acceptable coverage ratio is the degree of certainty of the projections. A lender may prefer 1.1% coverage with 95% probability to 1.5% coverage with 50% probability of achieving the projections.

A bridge or interim loan often contains elements of both asset-based and cash flow loans. Typically, it is used to finance the sales of assets or discrete businesses targeted for sale in the acquisition, and usually amounts to a percentage, between

50% and 100%, of the estimated net proceeds. The advance rate depends on the timing and certainty of the disposition and on the bank's degree of comfort with the value and marketability of the divested subsidiaries or assets. The loans are generally secured by the stock of subsidiaries or the assets targeted for sale. Loans that bridge to future subordinated debt financing, so-called junk bond bridge loans, are a different matter and are described in Chapter 4.

How do you decide which type of senior loan to borrow?

It depends on several factors, including the acquirer's plans for the company, the nature of its key businesses, and the composition of its assets. The primary goal, again, is to maximize the dollar amount of senior loans. A secondary goal is to obtain the lowest cost of funds. Certain types of companies, such as basic manufacturing companies and retailers, are rich in fixed assets, inventory, and receivables. If these assets are not already pledged to existing debt, an asset-based loan may yield the larger amount.

On the other hand, many businesses tend not to have large amounts of hard or tangible assets. This group usually includes companies in the fields of communications, high technology, and most service industries. For acquisitions of these types of companies, a cash flow loan will tend to yield the greater amount.

In LBOs where the acquirer anticipates realizing significant proceeds from the sale of assets or entire businesses within a relatively short period (up to two years) after the acquisition date, the acquirer should attempt to obtain a portion of the senior bank debt in the form of an interim or bridge loan tied to the realization of those proceeds.

What is the typical payment term of an LBO loan?

Bridge or interim facilities, which will be repaid upon the occurrence of specified events, can have a maturity in the range of six months to two years, depending on the expected timing of those events.

Revolver and term loans usually have terms of three to seven years. Revolver loans are often "evergreen" facilities, with no repayment schedule until final maturity, or sometimes one or two mandatory reductions over the life of the loan. Term loans generally mandate repayment schedules beginning immediately or certainly within one year of the acquisition closing date and specify a repayment schedule tied to the company's projections. Often, term loan repayment schedules are prorated over the life of the loan. Term loans may require both scheduled repayments and additional payments out of excess cash flow.

What is the role of junk bonds in an LBO?

Junk bonds, which are subordinated debt sold to institutional investors, play an integral role in the LBO business. Subordinated debt bridges the gap between what banks are willing to "pay" for companies and the equity that investors can and will contribute. (See Chapter 4, pages 157 through 162.)

The junk bond debt market is a relatively new market. More than any other factor, its tremendous growth in the past five years has fueled much of the LBO boom by allowing companies to be acquired for relatively small amounts of equity.

Compared to the market for senior debt, the junk bond market is less developed and much more volatile. In fact, after the October 19, 1987 stock market crash, the market for new junk bonds virtually dried up for two to three months and led to a temporary, but dramatic, slowdown in large LBO activity.

How do issuers of junk bonds decide how much to lend?

Junk bond lenders generally bear a significant portion of the risk in an LBO and are looking for a return to compensate them for their risk. Generally, the amount and terms of a subordinated loan or debt offering will reflect the risk/return relationship. Depending on the perceived riskiness of an acquisition, a junk bond lender will seek a return anywhere from a straight interest yield of 11–12% to a combined internal rate of return (IRR), factoring in equity participation, in the range of 25–30%. If risk is excessive, the lender will be unwilling to lend at any return.

In evaluating risk, junk bond buyers look to see (a) if the break-up value of the company exceeds the aggregate amount of senior and subordinate debt, and (b) whether cash flow from operations and asset sales are sufficient to meet senior and subordinated debt payment requirements.

How much equity should be invested in an LBO?

The amount of equity in an LBO is really a "plug" number—there should be enough equity to get the deal done and provide assurance for the company's success. Equity must fill the gap between the total debt financing obtained and the total funds required to consummate the acquisition. A minimum amount of equity contribution is necessary to assure solvency of the company (see Chapter 4, page 169); how much a lender will require depends on the lender's confidence in the company and the general business cycle.

Typically there is a complex interplay between the senior lenders, subordinated lenders, and equity investors in the financing of an LBO. The senior lenders seek to maximize the amounts of subordinated debt and equity, the subordinated lenders aim to maximize the amount of equity, and the equity investors try to minimize the amount of equity, maximize the senior debt, and bridge the gap with subordinated debt. It is occasionally said that 10% equity is a common starting point in the analysis, although 3–5% has often been achieved.

Every deal eventually comes down to the equity principal setting down all the facts (or his or her best estimate of the facts)—the terms and amounts of senior and subordinated debt and the required amount of equity—and deciding whether the potential returns to the equity justify the investment in time and dollars, and the risk.

In other words, you do your financial plan for a leveraged buyout before you price?

Exactly. Pricing is a function of financeability. The price will be equal to what the LBO buyer is able to borrow against the assets and cash flow of the target, plus a marginal amount of equity. The process is interactive. The buyer tries to ascertain what he or she must pay and to design a financial structure based on that price. As a result of these activities the buyer discovers whether he or she can meet the seller's price or at what level he or she can bid for the company.

How is this method of pricing consistent with the DCF analysis we went through earlier in this chapter?

It is entirely consistent and, in fact, directly applies DCF concepts. The LBO buyer simply sets out to accomplish in fact what the DCF analyst does in theory: extract in cash, through borrowings or equity investments, the present value of the target on a DCF basis, and use the proceeds to buy the target. The returns required by senior lenders, subordinated lenders, and equity investors represent, when blended, the required discount rate. The LBO buyer looks at the price and the amounts and costs of available financing. This allows him or her to determine what return remains for the equity investment. If it is sufficient to justify the risk, the deal works.

What is the role of various financial ratios and rules of thumb in valuing companies?

The financial ratios are important tools used to address the fundamental issues of financeability and return to the equity investors. The ratios provide quick ways to value businesses and to quantify prices and values in terms of easily understood figures. The ratios also facilitate easy comparisons of different divisions within a company, different companies within an industry, and different industries.

What is the most commonly used ratio?

The most common measurement of price or value relates the price paid, free of debt, to the free cash flow available to service debt. The exact calculation can vary depending on the nature of the company or industry. The numerator is the gross unleveraged purchase price, which is the price paid for the equity, plus any debt assumed, plus the fees and expenses of the acquisition. The denominator is the company's "free cash flow," that is, operating cash flow (operating income before deducting taxes, interest and depreciation) less the amount of capital expenditures required to maintain the company's current level of operations (the maintenance level).

For many manufacturing or industrial companies, the maintenance level of capital expenditures is approximately equal to depreciation, and operating income is therefore a good proxy for free cash flow. On the other hand, many service businesses—broadcasting, publishing, cable television, and others—require minimal amounts of maintenance level capital expenditures. For these companies, operating cash flow is a good proxy for free cash flow.

As an example of the calculation of this ratio, suppose that a manufacturing company had the following key characteristics:

Purchase price for equity	$100
Debt assumed	60
Cost of acquisition	8
Gross unleveraged purchase price	$168
Operating income	$30
Depreciation	10
Capital expenditures	10

The ratio would be defined as the operating income multiple, and would be calculated as follows:

$$\text{Operating income multiple} = \frac{100 + 60 + 8}{30} = \frac{168}{30} = 5.6 \times$$

(A common variant on this ratio compares free cash flow to annual interest expense. Obviously, 1:1 is a floor for this ratio, with 1.4:1 a more normal benchmark.)

Which year's financial statements should be used to calculate the free cash flow multiple?

Theoretically, you should be looking at free cash flow for the twelve-month period beginning on the acquisition closing date. This number will obviously be a forecast and should be viewed in light of historical results. Generally, and for purely psychological reasons, being relatively aggressive and optimistic people, investors tend to look at last year's numbers during difficult or depressed economic times and at next year's numbers during buoyant times.

The picture can cloud when a company is going through a major transition at the time the acquisition is closed, or will go through a major transition as a result of the acquisition. For example, suppose that a company is undergoing a major restructuring involving dramatic overhead reductions, the sale of an unprofitable business, and the absorption of a recently completed acquisition. Once the restructuring is completed, operating profit is expected to jump dramatically, giving rise to what is called a "hockey stick" projection: the line of the graph goes down a little, then turns and goes way up. Assume that actual and projected profit is as follows:

1987	$10
1988	$10
1989	$5
1990	$20

If the acquisition closes in the middle of 1989, the acquirer would look at 1990 earnings to calculate the free cash flow multiple, but had better know his or her lender well enough to be sure it will agree.

How do you apply the free cash flow ratio to acquisitions where several divestitures are envisioned?

In situations where an acquirer plans to divest one or more businesses, both the numerator and the denominator of the ratio must be adjusted. The gross purchase price should be reduced by the sum of the estimated net after-tax proceeds of the divestiture plus any debt to be assumed by buyers of divested operations. Operating income should be adjusted to reflect the pro forma operating income of the remaining operations.

What are the limitations of the free cash flow ratio?

The ratio fails to take into account a number of factors, including cyclicality and growth.

Cyclical companies tend not to make attractive LBO candidates because of the unpredictability of cash flow. When analyzing a cyclical business, it is important to determine the company's current stage in the economic cycle and factor the likelihood of a recession in the company's projections. Because of the volatility of earnings over the cycle, a free cash flow ratio based on just one year can be misleading, while a projection encompassing the entire business cycle will adjust properly. For further discussion of the kinds of companies suitable for LBOs, see Chapter 4, pages 108-109.

The free cash flow multiple does not adjust in any way for the growth of a company. Obviously, a company with $10 of operating income growing at 20% per year is worth more than a company with the same earnings growing at 5% per year. A pure multiple, whether of free cash flow, earnings, or any other financial statistic, does not indicate growth or the ultimate value of the company.

Growth prospects may, however, be reflected in the price to be paid for the company expressed as a multiple of free cash flow.

What rules of thumb does a lender use in considering how long the loan will be outstanding?

Lenders, particularly banks, like to see their loans retired and coverage improve reasonably rapidly. One common test is to see how much of the loan is projected to be paid off in five years. If substantially all the loan can be paid off in this time, the company has a good chance of getting through the early high-debt danger period successfully. Another test is to see how soon a 1.5:1 ratio can be reached between annual earnings and interest payments. Lenders can feel substantial confidence if this 50% cushion is projected to be achieved in 2 to 3 years, that being a period of time short enough to be somewhat reliably predictable by management. If projections don't indicate this point will be reached until the fifth or the seventh year, lenders may be much more dubious.

What are some other ratios used?

The other most commonly used ratio is the ratio of the purchase price to the book value of the company. The purchase price for the equity is the numerator and the book value of the equity is the denominator. However, the ratio is distorted if the acquired company is highly leveraged prior to the acquisition. In this case, both the numerator and denominator should be increased by the amount of existing debt.

For example, suppose a company has equity of $10 and existing debt of $50 and is acquired for $100. The standard calculation of purchase price to book value would be

$$\frac{100}{10} = 10 \times$$

However, if the ratio is adjusted for the debt, the book value multiple is

$$\frac{100 + 50}{10 + 50} = \frac{150}{60} = 2.5 \times$$

Book value multiples are most useful in valuing businesses in the manufacturing and financial sectors. These businesses tend to sell for 1.0–2.0 times book value, depending on several factors, particularly earnings and free cash flow.

At what prices have LBOs been done historically, expressed as a multiple of free cash flow?

Since 1980, prices have generally been increasing. In the early 1980s, companies were being priced at 3 to 4 times "free cash flow." By 1983, and in early 1984, most transactions were in the range of 4 to 5 times free cash flow. After 1985, as competition increased, transactions were being priced up to 6 or 7 times free cash flow. Such higher prices were made possible, in part, by a rising stock market and higher prices for equity in initial public offerings of LBO companies and by the greater availability of subordinated debt and junk bonds.

What effect do these price/cash flow multiples have on debt payout?

At 3 to 4 times free cash flow, a company can withstand a *decline* in operating cash flow and retire its debt within seven years. At 4 to 5 times free cash flow, a company can go a number of years with *flat* earnings and the equity will still appreciate in value. But at 6 to 7 times free cash flow, generally speaking, the company's earnings have to *increase* for the deal to make sense.

What is the utility of a debt-equity ratio?

A lot of people focus too much on capitalization ratios, the ratio of debt to equity. LBOs sometimes exhibit dramatic ratios of 100:1 or more, and these are taken as demonstrations that the company is overleveraged and will be in trouble after the closing. However, the ratio of debt to purchase price is not the real test. Much more important are the ratios of (a) debt to market value, which indicates the degree of solvency of the company, and (b) operating income to interest and principal payments, which measures the company's ability to service debt.

For example, suppose you can contract to purchase a broadcast company for $100, 10 times cash flow, and then before closing sell half of its stations for $65, 13 times cash flow, thereby effectively obtaining the remaining stations for 7 times cash flow, substantially below the prevailing market price. If your purchase price for the remaining stations was $35, of which you borrowed $34 and provided $1 of equity, but the stations are worth $50 on the closing day, it is more accurate to say your debt-equity ratio is 34:16 than 34:1.

Similarly, if the buyer is overpaying, a good debt-equity ratio won't make the deal successful. Suppose the target's cash flow will support $40 of debt, and it has been purchased for $60, of which $45 is debt and $15 is equity from a too-eager buyout fund. The capitalization ratio is a reasonable 3:1, but trouble is sure to come. Capitalization ratios work when the total value can be clearly determined by a smoothly functioning market which is reflected in the purchase price of the target. The valuation of companies is too complex and the market too imperfect to achieve that result with LBOs.

How useful are company projections in evaluating future cash flow prospects?

Extremely important. The LBO buyer is probably doing a management buyout, in the sense that pre-acquisition management will remain in place after the buyout and management stands to gain as stockholders or otherwise if the company prospers. Consequently, a cornerstone of the acquisition is a management team you can rely on, and the first step of reliance will be on their projections. After all, they know the business better than the buyer can hope to.

It is generally advisable for the buyer to begin by asking management to share their business plan projections of future economic performance, then ask for their past projections and compare them with how they actually did.

Generally speaking, the management team that can present a solid business plan and can give a crisp, precise, well-thought-out set of projections is going to be a winner. Losers are found in the team that fumbles around and says, "Gee, we don't do projections", or "We only do them once a year," or "We did them six months ago."

How do you avoid undue optimism in projections?

Two sets of projections should be considered, the "base case" and a "reasonable worst case." The base case tends to have some optimistic wishful thinking in it; the reasonable worst case is one that the chief executive officer believes he is 90% certain to reach. In large measure, the buyer's decision to pursue a deal and the amount of money he targets to borrow is dependent on that 90% case. If you rely on the reasonable worst case projection, everything need not fall exactly into place for a company to meet its debt obligations.

If base projections are far more optimistic than the reasonable worst case, be cautious. The company may have too high a level of volatility in its earnings to be a good LBO candidate.

When studying projections, the buyer should be sure to ask selling management why their company or division is for sale—is there something out there in the future that will cause this business not to earn as much money as it has been earning? Buyers should also focus on what effect the post-LBO company's leverage will have on its operations—for example, in obtaining trade credit.

EXPRESSING THE PURCHASE PRICE
IN THE ACQUISITION AGREEMENT

The form of the consideration to be paid can be almost as important to the buyer and seller as the amount that will be paid. The tax treatment of the purchase price is discussed in depth in Chapter 6, and a discussion of issues like subordination, escrows, and set-off are included in Chapters 4 and 10. Once the parties agree on the price, they must express it properly and concern themselves with the effect, if any, of a business's profits and losses, between signing and closing, on that price.

Once the purchase price is arrived at by buyer and seller, how is it set forth in the acquisition agreement?

The buyer and seller can agree that the price is a fixed amount or an amount determined by a formula. A fixed amount is specified as a total dollar amount, which may be payable in cash or a combination of cash and securities. The non-cash portion of the price will normally be in the form of subordinated promissory notes, preferred stock, or, if the buyer is a publicly held company, common stock of the buyer. It is less common for the seller to retain a common stock interest in the acquired company.

Where the price is determined by a formula, it is commonly based on book value, or stockholders' equity from a balance sheet prepared as of the closing date, plus or minus a dollar amount.

Under another variation, a fixed price is established, and the buyer receives a credit against the price for any earnings, or is required to pay an increased amount equal to the losses realized by the business, after a specified date. This can be expressed as an adjustment for changes in working capital, i.e., the difference between (a) cash and other current assets and (b) current liabilities of the company on the closing date.

How is a book value formula price implemented?

Typically, the acquisition agreement provides that the buyer will purchase the company by paying the estimated book value at closing, plus or minus x, and that an adjustment is made after the closing when a precise book value figure has been determined.

How do these provisions work?

The seller typically delivers an estimated closing balance sheet five business days prior to the closing together with supporting documentation. The parties agree on, and close on the basis of, the estimated balance sheet. Subsequent to the closing, the seller prepares the balance sheet as of the closing date, which is usually the end of an accounting period. The actual closing balance sheet (ABS) is compared to the estimated closing balance sheet (EBS). If the ABS shows a higher book value than the EBS, the buyer pays the seller the difference. If such value is lower, the seller pays the buyer.

Are accountants used in this process?

Absolutely. The seller's accounting firm will often audit the closing balance sheet. The buyer's accountants then review the audit. If the parties and the accountants differ on the correct presentation of the balance sheet, buyer and seller (or their accountants) may turn to a third accounting firm to resolve any differences.

Such review procedures vary from the simple to the exceedingly complex. The agreement often provides that if the final balance sheet varies by more than a specified percentage (often 10%), then the challenging parties' fees are paid. If they do not vary materially, the challenger may be required to pay the fees of the prevailing party.

Because of the different results which can be obtained while complying with generally accepted accounting principles, some agreements provide that the net effect of any challenge to seller's balance sheet presentation must be more than a specified dollar amount to require an adjustment.

What other issues arise in such provisions?

In addition to specifying that such balance sheets are prepared in accordance with GAAP, the parties should specify which inventory valuation is used. Taxes may also be important in determining book value. It is also wise to state that the balance sheet should not reflect any liability that arises solely from the sale of the business.

What other arrangements are used in pricing?

Some deals provide that the acquisition is treated as effective on a specific date. After that date, the profits and losses of the business are for the buyer's account. This period is sometimes called the interim or stub period. Typically, gains decrease (and losses increase) a fixed purchase price. As with adjustments to book value, rather than waiting for the final results, closings are often made on the basis of an estimate and adjusted when the actual results are determined.

Such provisions require that even more care be given to requiring that the business be operated in the ordinary course if the period between the benchmark date and the closing date could be lengthy. The buyer's best protection is having or putting a person at the company's offices monitoring the results of the business.

To measure profit and loss, the parties must define precisely what they intend. For example, "net income" may be calculated without deduction for administrative charges and interest expense. Net income should not be reduced by non-recurring expenses incurred in connection with the transaction, such as legal and accounting fees.

Sophisticated sellers may credit the buyer with the earnings but offset against them interest at a fixed rate (e.g., 10%) on the purchase price during the interim period.

When is it appropriate to use a formula rather than a fixed price provision in the acquisition agreement?

If a substantial period of time is to pass between signing the acquisition agreement and closing, the buyer will want protection against changes in the value of the target during the interim. Book value changes over a relatively short period of time probably result from changes in current assets and liabilities, particularly if, as it should, the acquisition agreement bars the seller in the interim from selling fixed assets, or otherwise operating, other than in the ordinary course of business. Therefore, a book value formula provides this protection while the addition or, less likely these days, the subtraction of a fixed dollar amount from book value corrects for whatever differences exist between book value and real value.

The variant method of setting a fixed price and then providing a working capital or earnings adjustment to the price may have the advantage for both buyer and seller of reducing the amount of variation possible between estimated and final price, and focusing more sharply on those aspects of company performance which the adjustment is intended to cover.

The variant method thus reduces the difficulty of that critical moment in the process that arises when the seller presents the buyer, on the eve of the closing, with the estimated balance sheet book value number. The appearance of this number at the last moment is an invitation for further negotiations, not only on price but also other issues that both parties have been identifying as loose ends since the acquisition agreement was signed. A party nervous about closing would prefer the price issues raised by this number to be as small as possible.

What issues arise where the price is determined by reference to the seller's or buyer's stock price?

The parties could agree that the value of a share is equal to the market price on the day the deal is struck. Because the market price can be higher or lower on the closing date, the parties may agree to use the market price on the closing date. Typically they use an average price and place a maximum and minimum on the purchase price. For example, the buyer may agree to purchase all outstanding stock at the 20-day average closing market price for the stock. The parties will then set limits, or a collar, on the total consideration. For example, if a stock's average price is $30 prior to signing, the parties may agree that regardless of the actual average before closing, the price per share will be no lower than $25 or higher than $32. The collar can also regulate the maximum and minimum number of the buyer's shares that the buyer must deliver to selling stockholders.

Is there any other approach that should be considered?

Underwriters have "market outs" in their underwriting agreements which are essentially stock purchase agreements. Such provisions permit underwriters to terminate their commitment to buy shares if trading on stock exchanges is halted, if the U.S. is at war, or if other adverse market conditions exist. Subsequent to the October 1987 stock market crash, tender offers, and even some other agreements, excuse non-performance where indexes like the Dow Jones or S&P 500 have declined 25% or more. Sellers theoretically could seek such rights but rarely do because they don't want the buyer to request reciprocal rights to walk from the deal if such adverse events occur.

In transactions involving public companies, how can buyers use a combination of cash and securities?

Some transactions are structured, usually for tax reasons, to provide for fixed percentages of cash and stock. For example, the buyer might offer $20,000,000 and 2,000,000 shares of buyer's stock to holders of the 2,000,000 shares of a public company. The agreement can allocate such cash and securities proportionally —$10 and 1 share for each share of the public company. Alternatively, stockholders of the public company may have the option to elect between all cash and all securities or any combination. If too many stockholders elect cash, they may be forced to take some stock as well. Such provisions are often referred to as a "cramdown," because of their coercive nature. As an alternative, to avoid a cramdown, certain large insider stockholders may agree separately to take a combination of cash and securities so that other, smaller holders can elect to be paid all cash. See Chapter 12 on Public Company Acquisitions.

What is an "earn-out?"

An "earn-out" is a method of compensating a seller based on the future earnings of a company. It is the contingent portion of the purchase price. A common type of earn-out provides for additional payments to a seller if the earnings exceed agreed-upon levels. Another type of earn-out may provide that certain debt given to the seller as part of the acquisition price is paid out of earnings exceeding agreed levels.

Earn-outs require consideration of various factors: the type of contingent payment (cash or stock), the measurement of performance (operating income, cash flow, net income or other), the measurement period, maximum limits, if any, and the timing of payments.

Why would the parties use an earn-out?

The parties may disagree on the value of the business because they have different opinions about the profitability of the company in the next few years. Often the buyer is relying on the seller's projections of future cash flow in setting his price. The buyer and seller may disagree on the seller's ability to realize the projected results. A buyer will be willing to pay a higher price for greater cash flow if, and only if, the projected cash flow is realized. An earn-out permits the buyer to pay a reasonable price plus a premium when the cash flow is realized and allows the seller to realize the full value of his business if it is as profitable as represented.

Why are earn-outs not more common?

Sellers or buyers may not want an earn-out. This is particularly the case when a conglomerate seller is selling a division or subsidiary to an LBO buyer. The buyer wants, and may need, the upside potential of cash flow for his lenders, while the seller has probably decided that the target no longer fits its corporate plan, and is not interested in retaining an earn-out which is a distraction from its main strategic concerns.

Sellers may also be able to command their asking price without taking any of the consideration in the form of an earn-out or other contingent consideration. In the alternative, the seller may not do an explicit earn-out, but may structure the purchase price to include other types of contingent consideration which have much the same effect, such as subordinated debt, preferred stock, or warrants. See Chapter 4, "Financing the Leveraged Buyout," pages 168-172. Earn-outs are also difficult to administer.

Why are earn-outs difficult to administer?

A typical earn-out might provide that the seller will receive an additional payment in each of the first three years after the sale provided that in such year the acquired company realizes operating income of over $1,000,000.

While simple in concept, this raises a number of definitional problems. The buyer and seller must agree on the definition of operating income. The buyer will want to be sure that such income comes from continuing operations and not extraordinary or non-recurring events. Furthermore, the earn-out may require that the acquired company be operated separately, and consistently with past practice. If the buyer wants to combine certain of its operations or modify them, such changes will be difficult to factor into the levels of earnings to be achieved, particularly if they are not decided upon until after the sale.

What concerns will the seller have in an earn-out?

The seller is interested in assuring that changes in the operation of the company after the sale do not affect the company's ability to attain the earnings. The seller may thus seek agreements that goodwill will be ignored in making the calculations and that the company will continue to be operated in a fashion consistent with past practice and will not be charged a new administrative overhead expense. The seller may also focus on depreciation, interest charges, and intercompany transactions with the buyer's company.

The seller will want to receive credit for target's post acquisition results, even if the $1,000,000 level in the example is not achieved. If in the first three years the company earns, respectively, $800,000, $1,000,000 and $1,200,000, the seller will feel entitled to receive the total contingent payment, even though operating income did not exceed $1,000,000 in the first year. The parties may agree on a sliding scale or averaging approach and a maximum payment.

The seller will also focus on when it receives a contingent payment—after each year or at the end of the period, say, three years. The buyer must now consider whether this will trigger any obligation to refund a payment for year one if the results in years two and three are substandard.

Ultimately, no legal agreement can provide complete protection for both parties in drafting earn-outs. Buyer and seller must either rely on provisions expressed in terms of the intent or good faith of the parties or their reasonable business judgments. By the time buyer and seller have gone through a turbulent acquisition closing with each other, they may find little comfort in such arrangements. Many proposed earn-outs are bought-out as the closing approaches.

Are there tax and accounting considerations with earn-outs?

Earn-outs can spread out income in taxable transactions for sellers with resulting tax benefits. To have a tax-free reorganization, contingent shares must be issued within five years of the closing. The buyer may also obtain a tax deduction where the earn-out is paid as compensation under an employment agreement.

CHAPTER 4

FINANCING THE LEVERAGED BUYOUT

INTRODUCTION

The difference between an acquisition and a leveraged acquisition is, of course, financing; typically a large amount of it. The main objective of the leveraged buyout maestro is to finance as large a part of the cost of an acquisition as possible by borrowing against the assets and the cash flow of the acquired company. Through careful structuring of financing, LBO players can reduce their equity investment to 5% or less of the acquisition price. LBOs seem to defy conventional buy-sell wisdom. How, one may ask, can the buyer borrow against the assets of the acquired company when it is a different entity and needs the money as a precondition to the acquisition? If a person wants to buy stock in IBM, IBM won't finance it. Why is a leveraged buyout different?

To answer such practical questions, this chapter will begin with an introduction to the basic issues of financing the highly leveraged transaction, and then guide the reader through the actual financing process typically used in successful LBOs. The focus is on financing for buyouts of privately held companies; financing for a publicly held company being taken private is often different and is described in Chapter 12. Some of the principles described here are also applicable to less leveraged acquisitions, but we will not take pains to point out such broad applications. It is not nearly as difficult to borrow just a little money.

How can a buyer finance the acquisition with the target's assets and revenues?

The typical leveraged acquisition is not simply a stock purchase, though it often starts as one. A key structuring objective is to cause the assets and revenues of the acquired company to be located in the buyer-borrower. This can be achieved in three different ways:

- The buyer can acquire the assets and business of the target;
- The buyer can acquire the stock of the target and immediately thereafter merge with the target (the question which entity survives the merger is important for tax and, occasionally, other reasons, and is dealt with in Chapter 5);
- Skipping the stock acquisition stage, the buyer and the target can simply merge directly.

If the buyer and target merge, a problem of timing arises at the closing: payment for the stock purchased by the buyer must be made before the merger places the assets of the acquired company in the buyer's possession, but the loan to the buyer cannot be funded until the merger is consummated. To resolve this problem, the parties to the closing agree that all transactions will be treated as occurring simultaneously or, for the sticklers, that the seller of the stock will get a promissory note which is repaid minutes later when the merger documents are filed. Sometimes lenders prefer to have both the buyer and the target named as borrowers on the acquisition loan. Tax or contract compliance questions may be raised by these timing issues (see Chapter 5), and they should be thought through carefully.

Why would a buyer want to do a highly leveraged buyout? Doesn't this leave the acquired business in a very exposed position?

A high degree of leverage allows a buyer with limited resources to own a company, and in particular lets a management group take over its business. It also permits an investor the possibility of an enormous equity upside return. To gain these benefits requires incurring substantial risk, and is therefore not recommended for those who feel very uncomfortable with substantial degrees of financial exposure for their companies. (We are not contemplating here personal exposure of individual buyers through guarantees, which presents an even higher level of risk.) The conventional business wisdom looks with alarm at the prospect of imposing large amounts of debt upon a company. In fact, however, one of the reasons leveraged buyouts have been so successful is that having a large amount of debt on the balance sheet provides tremendous "survival" incentive for managers to perform efficiently. Management focuses on making the core business profitable, minimizing the use of capital and maximizing cash flow, rather than on building corporate empires. By contrast, managements of companies with relatively small amounts of debt and disproportionately large cash flow may become complacent and even spendthrift, pursuing, for example, nonstrategic diversification programs that they could not afford if they had a heavy debt to service.

Of course, if the buyer plans to impose a heavy financial leverage on a company, he must be sure the company can bear it and must minimize operating risks.

What kinds of businesses lend themselves to financial leverage?

Look for businesses that generate cash flow on a steady basis. High growth is not an objective; more probably, suitable targets will show moderate growth. Producers of basic products or services in stable markets are the best LBO prototype. Start-up situations and highly cyclical companies should be avoided. So should companies whose success is highly dependent on forces beyond the control of management. Oil and gas deals that depend on fuel prices are thus not suitable, as contrasted to oil pipeline or trucking companies, which receive a steady, stable payment for transportation charges and do not speculate on oil prices.

In any industry, stable management offers an important element of reassurance. A team that works well together and has been through several business cycles can be better relied upon to provide the stable conservative projections necessary to evaluate whether the debt can be paid.

Leveraged buyout candidates should be at the far end of the spectrum from venture capital operations, which are typically predominantly equity financed.

With the burdens of debt comes an important advantage for the leveraged buyer, however: a real outside check on the accuracy of his economic analysis. You can all too easily convince yourself that Acme Widgets is the greatest buy of the century. If a lender is willing to follow you, you gain significant and reliable reassurance that your calculations were sound, and the deal will work well for everyone.

But isn't it true that the higher the leverage, the greater the risk that the buyer may lose his equity contribution?

True enough, but consider these corollaries: First, the smaller the equity contribution, the higher the return on equity if the acquired company does well. Second, the smaller the equity contribution, the smaller the loss to the buyer if the acquired company fails.

MINIMIZING BORROWING

A buyer's first thought in financial planning should be a very simple one: the less I have to lay out at closing, the less I have to borrow.

The financing needs to be met at the closing can be calculated as follows:

- The purchase price of the stock or assets of the acquired company;
- Plus any existing debt that must be refinanced at closing;
- Plus any working capital needs of the acquired company (these amounts need not actually be borrowed, but the credit line must be large enough to cover them);
- Plus costs of the acquisition; and
- Less any proceeds from partial divestitures of the acquired business or cash or cash equivalents found in the business.

(Seller takeback financing also reduces the closing payment, but is analyzed here as part of the borrowing program because of the many interconnections between it and other financing layers.)

The next step in our analysis is thus to explore how to minimize each of the principal elements of this closing payment.

How can the buyer minimize the purchase price?

A buyer need not necessarily offer the highest price in order to gain the LBO contract. He should also offer the seller non-cash incentives for the deal, such as:

- We can close faster;
- We have a good track record in obtaining financing and closing similar transactions;
- We can offer a substantial deposit on signing the acquisition agreement; and
- We can work well with you (the seller) and your management.

One of the most delicate questions of LBO judgment is whether to obtain a lower price by assuming substantially greater risks or accepting significant defects in the target. Such risks or defects can loom very large in the eye of the acquisition lenders, and the timing of negotiations does not always permit them to be checked out with a lender before signing the contract. A cardinal rule is: negotiate and sign *fast* when the price is right. Still, some of the most spectacularly successful deals have been achieved when a buyer has been able to discern that management and a lender could live with something the seller thought was a major problem.

Because management is crucial to the successful repayment of the company's debt, the seller's attitude toward management of the company should be watched closely. Close relations with and incentives for management are likely to be an important part of the financial plan; management may be receiving shares in the company, favorable employment contracts, profit sharing plans, and the like. If the seller is interested in assuring that the departing management is well treated, these arrangements may favorably dispose a seller toward the buyer. If, however, as is all too often the case, the officers of the seller negotiating the transaction have previously developed an adversary, supervisory relationship with the target, benefits offered management may tend to excite jealousies, and the less said about them the better. Issues particularly affecting management buyouts are covered in Chapter 6, "Structuring Management Buyouts."

Can you select what you acquire?

It is desirable for a buyer to be as selective as possible about what he acquires, though often difficult to achieve. The seller may be packaging some dogs together with some strong operations; therefore, the buyer should consider "gaming" the offer out from the seller's point of view and making a counter proposal. Crucial for such selection is knowing the seller's business better than he does—not impossible if the seller is a large conglomerate of which the target is a small part, and management is the buyer or is already on the buyer's side. The offer of sale may include several businesses, some of which are easier to finance than others, or assets used in part by several business operations. The buyer may have a choice, for example, between buying a building or a computer system, or merely renting it. Sometimes a deal can be changed to the buyer's advantage after the main price and other negotiations have been completed. The seller may then be receptive to either including or excluding what appear to be minor ancillary facilities as a last step to signing. To encourage the seller, the buyer may guarantee the resale price of unwanted assets or share any losses realized on their disposal. Taking or not taking these "minor" assets may become the key to cash flow in the critical first two years after the buyout.

How can a buyer keep existing debt in place?

Review carefully the existing debt of the target and determine whether prepayment is necessary or can be avoided. The acquisition may entitle the lender to prepayment, perhaps at a premium. In some cases where prepayment is not required, existing debt should be prepaid because of high interest rates or burdensome covenants. Preservation of existing debt may require changing the structure of the acquisition, because leases, loan agreements, or indentures, are more likely to prohibit a sale of the debtor's assets without the lender's consent than they are to prohibit a change of control of the debtor or a merger in which the debtor survives. A common legal issue that arises in such cases is whether the merger of the debtor into another corporation constitutes a transfer of ownership requiring the lender's consent. In most cases it is possible to conclude that the merger is not a transfer to another entity, because the original debtor continues as part of the surviving entity, although the conclusion varies according to state law.

It can be quite difficult to keep existing debt in place in a restructuring or spin-off acquisition if the target is subject to covenants, common in unsecured and secured borrowings of publicly held corporations, requiring lender's consent to the sale of all or substantially all its assets. Restrictions on sale of assets provide important protection to a lender who otherwise cannot prevent major changes in the structure of operations of its debtor, and courts have interpreted them liberally in favor of lenders. Any sale of more than 25% of the assets raises questions, particularly if the assets being sold constitute the major revenue producing operations of the historical core business.

Indentures for unsecured borrowings also typically contain covenants prohibiting the imposition of liens on assets of the debtor and may prohibit more than one class of debt or interlayering (e.g., both senior and subordinated debt). Thus, the financing for a company with this kind of existing debt must be done on an unsecured basis and without recourse to some of the techniques for layering of debt which are discussed later in this chapter. Debt of this kind is deceptively simple. It may first appear that the lack of elaborate and specific covenants such as those contained in the typical secured loan offers many opportunities to substantially restructure the company without the lenders' consent. It is likely to turn out, however, as the buyer analyzes the loan agreement, that the broad prohibitions on sale or encumbrance of assets or on the making of payments of or similar to dividends, defeat most financing plans. Just as the technically tight, detailed loan agreement encourages and legitimizes the use of loopholes based on technicalities, so the broadly written loan agreement makes lawyers and other technicians less willing to rely on highly refined justifications for arrangements that may violate the spirit of the existing debt agreement.

What particular issues arise with respect to existing working capital debt?

Working capital debt of the target before the acquisition is likely to appear in any of at least four forms:

- A secured revolving credit loan from an outside lender;
- A parent's intercompany transfers, either with or without interest;
- Bank letters of credit or guarantees to secure purchases from suppliers, principally for foreign sourcing; or
- More or less generous payment terms from suppliers.

The first three kinds of debt will almost certainly have to be refinanced at the acquisition closing. A secured revolver, or even an unsecured one, will inevitably tie up assets and stand in the way of any plans for secured acquisition financing, and the parent/seller does not want to retain what are probably short-term, rather informal financial arrangements of an in-house nature. There may, however, be some room for a buyer to argue for at least some short-term financing through a seller takeback of existing intra-company loans.

A senior revolving credit acquisition lender often provides letter of credit financing after the acquisition and will probably insist upon doing this financing as part of the deal. Sometimes this can be trouble, because a letter of credit lender should be familiar with the target's business operations, and while the new acquisition lender is learning the ropes, there can be awkward slip-ups in a sensitive area. One possible solution is to explore including the existing letter of credit lender in the lending group where its expertise will be accessible.

It usually should not be a problem to retain existing relationships and favorable terms with suppliers. They will probably be relieved to find that the buyer doesn't plan to close the business or move it elsewhere. In some cases, suppliers have relied on the presence of a deep pocket parent company as added security, and may be looking for special assurances difficult for the post-acquisition company to provide. In other cases, it is possible to structure the acquisition so that a subsidiary that purchases on trade credit has a better debt to equity ratio than its parent and can retain favorable trade terms.

What should be done if existing debt includes tax exempt industrial development bonds?

Tax exempt industrial development bonds give the borrower the advantage of low interest rates but also carry disadvantages: they encumber assets better used to support new borrowings, and may carry with them old parent company guarantees that must be lifted as a condition of the acquisition. Often these bonds can be "defeased" under the terms of their trust indentures: that is, high quality obligations (usually issued or guaranteed by the United States government) can be deposited with the trustee bank for the bond issue in an amount high enough to retire the bonds over their term through scheduled payments on the obligations. If the interest rate on the bonds is low enough, the amount of obligations required to defease them may be less than their face amount, and, once the bonds are defeased, their covenants and liens cease to have any effect. Note, however, that the defeasance of high interest rate bonds, such as those common in the late '70's and early '80's, is expensive, and the defeasance of variable rate bonds is impossible because they lack a predictable interest rate for which a sufficient sum certain can be set aside. In addition, tax problems can arise: are the earnings on the defeasance fund taxable, and does the defeasance give rise to discharge of indebtedness income for the borrower?

Tax exempt bond issues are likely to be complex, and any transactions involving them may require special attention from the bank serving as bond trustee and the issuer's original bond counsel. Such issues involve a two-step process: the funds are borrowed by a governmental body, then reloaned to the target to build a facility or used to construct a facility which is leased to the target, normally but not necessarily on terms which permit a purchase for a nominal price at the end of the lease term. Check with a tax expert for hidden problems.

Can a buyer always finance all or part of a transaction through partial divestments or spin-offs?

Not necessarily. This is possible only when the business acquired consists of separate components or has excess real estate or other assets. The buyer must balance financial and operational considerations; there should always be a good business reason for the divestment. Consider selling off those portions of the business which are separable from the part you are most interested in. As indicated earlier, not all businesses generate the cash flow or have the stability necessary for highly leveraged transactions, yet many cash-rich buyers are available for such businesses. A solid domestic smokestack business with valuable assets, itself highly suitable for leveraged financing, may have a subsidiary with foreign manufacturing and distribution operations, a separate retail division, and a large timberland holding. The foreign operations, which are accessible to a whole new set of possible buyers, the retail division, which would function better as part of another company's nationwide chain, and the timberland, which does not generate cash flow, are divestiture candidates.

Many buyout transactions are undertaken in order to divest assets at a profit. These transactions are better called restructurings or break-ups. For example, the recent acquisition of Beatrice Foods by KKR resulted in the disbanding of its senior management and the sale of most of its assets. This is an entirely different kind of transaction from a management leveraged buyout, where the core business is highly leveraged, but preserved, and management takes an ownership interest and remains as a team.

There is a question of timing here; it is not advisable to start beating the bushes for a purchaser of the Buggy Whip Division until you have a signed contract for the purchase of General Buggies Company as a whole. Once the contract is signed, time may be short to complete the spin-off before your closing date, but assuring that the spin-off sale closes in timely fashion can be crucial. It is not uncommon to have an escrow closing of the spin-off sale in advance to minimize the risk of last minute hold-ups. Even if the spin-off sale does not close simultaneously with the main acquisition, the presence of the spin-off acquisition agreement may make possible a bridge loan to be taken out at the spin-off closing.

What cash can a buyer find in the company?

Identify and take into account the cash and cash equivalents held by the acquired company. You need not borrow the dollar you spend to buy cash. Cash can be found on the balance sheet, as well as in more unusual places. Does the acquired company have a law suit pending against a third party that can be settled quickly and profitably? Does it have excess funded reserves? Is its employee benefit plan over-funded, and if so, can it be terminated or restructured? Can its pension plan acquire any of the company assets? Typically, pension plans can invest a portion of their assets in real estate of a diversified nature, including real estate acquired from the company. Has the company been acquiring marketable stock or debt of unrelated companies? Does it have a valuable art collection that can be cashed in at the next Sotheby's auction? Keep track of changes in the company's cash position between signing the acquisition agreement and closing. The terms of the acquisition agreement can either assure that the buyer retains cash at the closing, or that all cash goes to the seller. See Chapter 3, pages 98 –101.

STRUCTURE OF THE FINANCING

After minimizing the need to borrow, the next step is to organize and orchestrate the borrowing program. The art of structuring a financing is to allocate the revenues and assets of the acquired company to lenders in a manner which:

- Maximizes the amount loaned by the most senior and highly secured and thus lowest interest rate lenders;

- Leaves sufficient cash flow to support, if needed, a layer of subordinated, higher interest rate "mezzanine" debt, as well as any seller take-back financing;
- Provides for adequate working capital and is consistent with seasonal variations and foreseeable one-time bulges or dips in cash flow;
- Permits the separate leveraging of distinct assets that can be more advantageously set aside for specialized lenders, such as sale-leasebacks of office buildings or manufacturing facilities;
- Accommodates both good news and bad—that is, permits debt prepayment without penalty if revenues permit and permits non-payment and non-enforcement of subordinated debt if revenues are insufficient; and
- Avoids and, where necessary, resolves conflicts between lenders.

Customarily these results are achieved through layering of debt.

What types of debt are typically used in a leveraged buyout?

Although sometimes only one secured lender is needed, or, in the case of a very simple strong cash flow business, only a single unsecured lender, multiple tiers of lenders are normally necessary for large transactions. The multi-lender leveraged buyouts may include several or all of the following layers of debt, in rough order of seniority:

1. *Senior revolving debt*, secured by a first lien on current assets (inventory and accounts receivable), a first or second lien on fixed assets (property, plant and equipment, or PPE), liens on intangibles, and, perhaps, a pledge of stock of the acquired company or its subsidiaries. This debt typically provides a part of the acquisition financing and working capital, including letter of credit financing, and is generally provided by commercial banks or similar institutional lenders.

2. *Senior term debt*, secured by a first lien on fixed assets, a first or second lien on current assets, and liens on intangibles and stock of the company and subsidiaries, to provide acquisition financing. Sometimes—but not very frequently—this debt

is subordinated to the senior revolving debt. It is normally provided by commercial banks in conjunction with senior revolving debt, or by similar commercial lenders or insurance companies.

3. *Senior subordinated debt*, known as *mezzanine debt*, or, in its less secure manifestations, *junk bonds*, unsecured or secured by junior liens on the assets securing the senior debt, used for acquisition financing. It is mainly placed by investment bankers, the principal purchasers being insurance companies, pension and investment funds, and financial institutions.

4. *Sale leasebacks or other special financing arrangements*, for specific facilities or equipment. These arrangements may range from installment purchases of office copiers or long-term computer lease-purchases, to sales of the target's real estate to an independent investment partnership, which then net leases such real estate to the target.

5. *Seller's subordinated note*, secured or unsecured, perhaps convertible to stock.

6. *Seller's preferred stock*, perhaps exchangeable for a subordinated note, usually appearing as an alternative to item 5.

7. *Preferred or common stock sold to an independent third party*, perhaps a leveraged buyout investment fund or one of the lenders.

8. *Common stock sold to the buyer or its principals, key managers and employees.*

9. *Warrants or options* to acquire common stock granted to any of the parties providing financing, or to the seller. These do not provide financing directly, but provide inducements to other financing participants.

We will discuss senior debt from both banking and insurance companies, junk bonds, leveraged buyout investment funds, and seller takeback financing in greater detail later in this chapter. First, however, we should consider how much debt can be obtained at each of these layers.

How is the amount of the different layers of debt determined?

The initial decision is, of course, the lender's. Based on the analyses discussed below and in Chapter 3 (see pp. 87-90), the lender for each layer of the financing will indicate to the buyer a range or approximation of the amount it is prepared to lend. If several alternative lenders are being pursued for any layer, there will be choices to be made, based largely on amount, interest rate and pay back period, but also on ability to perform. A basic objective is to maximize senior debt, which bears the lowest interest rate. At the same time, senior debt also requires relatively favorable coverage ratios; therefore, there will be excess cash flow left over after servicing senior debt to support junk bonds or other mezzanine debt. After mezzanine debt is covered, something should still remain to persuade the seller that his takeback financing has a reasonable chance of payment.

The process is not exact. Each lender evaluates the cash flow and assets of the target differently, and uses a different formula for setting the loan amount. While the term lender may be willing to lend $10 more if the revolving lender lends $8 less, the buyer may be reluctant to explore that possibility for fear that the term lender had not previously focused on the exact amount being loaned by the revolving lender, and a second review by the term lender's credit committee could result in a decision not to make the loan at all.

When resources and time permit, the best course of action for a buyer will probably be to obtain bids from several lenders on each layer. Then select, at the moment when lenders' commitment letters are about to be signed, the optimum combination and present it to each approved lender as a *fait accompli*, burning no bridges to the unsuccessful lenders until the package has been accepted by all the intended players. In this way, commitments can be entered into with the optimum combination of lenders. The competitive nature of the process will discourage objections by the lender fortunate enough to be selected. In addition, lenders tend to leave to the later stages of the closing a full investigation of the other lenders' terms, by which time they may be less likely to rethink the terms of *their* loan.

How does a senior lender decide how much to lend in an acquisition?

A number of considerations are key to a bank's lending decision:

- Liquidation value of the collateral;

- Credibility of the borrower's financial projections;
- Whether the borrower's projections show enough cash flow to service the debt (including junior debt);
- Whether proposed asset liquidations are likely to take place in time and in sufficient amount to amortize the term debt (or reduce the revolver commitment);
- Potential company profitability and industry prospects;
- The amount of junior debt (and capacity of the junior creditor to assist the borrower with additional funds in a workout scenario); and
- The amount of equity.

What is commercial paper and can it be used to finance LBOs?

Commercial paper sometimes appears as a part of a buyout, but only as an element of working capital financing. Commercial paper refers to very short term (usually six months or less), low interest rate notes, or paper, sold to large corporations and institutions. It needs to be highly secure, and thus is usually backed by a take-out commitment from the senior lender, and can be thought of as part of the revolving credit financing. Sales of commercial paper are usually done under an exemption from securities registration requirements which requires that the proceeds be used for working capital. It is rarely important in LBO acquisition financing.

What considerations arise in sale-leasebacks?

A part of the financing package may be the sale of the target's real estate to a third party, which then net leases such real estate to the company. To prepare for a sale-leaseback, a detailed appraisal, an as-built survey, and title insurance of the real estate must be ordered, preferably at least six weeks in advance of closing. The other loan documents must be drafted to permit the sale-leaseback. The sale-leaseback may be financed by a mortgage loan. The lease and the mortgage loan documents must clarify that the borrower/tenant continues to own, and the senior lender continues to enjoy a first and prior lien upon, all equipment and fixtures used in borrower's/tenant's business.

SENIOR DEBT

Ideally, the senior lender should be brought into the transaction as early as possible, and thus one of the first steps a buyer takes is to prepare his presentation of the deal to lenders. Many lenders are reluctant to review a proposed acquisition unless they already have a formal or informal agreement to go through with the transaction, or at least to cover their costs and, perhaps, a fee. Thus, the presentation is quickly followed by a commitment letter.

The senior lender's loan will usually represent the single largest amount of the cash to be raised for the transaction. If the senior lender is not willing to finance, the deal cannot be done. For that reason, the buyer must be sure to make a correct judgment about the financeability of the transaction before he incurs the considerable expense of negotiating an acquisition agreement.

What form does senior debt take?

Typically, senior debt is part term loan and part revolving loan, with the term loan used to finance the purchase price, and the revolving loan used to provide working capital (although a portion of the revolving loan is often used to finance the purchase price as well). Usually senior debt is provided by banks or their affiliates, and thus we often use the term "bank" to refer to a senior lender.

What is demand lending?

It is becoming more and more common for senior debt to be provided by banks in a demand format quite different from traditional local bank financing that relied primarily on the personal guarantees of the business owner, had a fixed term and limited covenants, and kept its nose out of the borrower's business. By contrast, demand lending gives the initial impression to a borrower of being intrusive and one-sided: the bank may have the right to call the loan at any time, make revolving loan advances only at its discretion, require all business receipts to be applied immediately to repayment, and have a bristling array of protective covenants which require bank consent for almost any action not in the ordinary course of business. The appropriate trade-offs for these provisions are absence of personal guarantees and a willingness to lend relatively large amounts.

Because this style of lending is unfamiliar to many borrowers and lenders, the logic of the trade-offs may not be observed: the bank may require a demand loan and guarantees as well, or the borrower may seek a high loan limit but refuse to consider demand repayment. Borrower and bank need to clearly understand their relationship from the start. Success depends on both players recognizing that it will be an intimate one involving cooperation and mutual dependency.

Can lenders be arbitrary?

No. A borrower can take considerable comfort in the principle of "commercial reasonableness" that binds lenders, and should thus understand that many of the rights the bank obtains on paper it cannot exercise in practice. A number of cases have held that if a bank makes a loan on terms which give it extensive power over a company's financial affairs, it cannot use that power arbitrarily, and may in fact be liable for consequential damages if the company is put out of business or otherwise damaged because of an unreasonable refusal to lend. See *Irving Trust*.

PRESENTATION AND COMMITMENT LETTER

How is an LBO transaction presented to prospective lenders?

The normal medium of the LBO transaction is the so-called "Bank Book," a brief narrative description of the proposed transaction and the target company. The Bank Book indicates what financing structure is contemplated and includes projections of earnings sufficient to cover working capital needs and amortize debt, along with a balance sheet setting forth the pledgeable assets. (Since the balance sheet will typically reflect assets on a GAAP basis, an appraisal of actual market and/or liquidation value, if available, may be attached or referenced.)

What happens after the "Bank Book" is presented to a lender?

If the loan officer believes that the bank may be willing to make a loan that meets the dollar amount and general terms requested by the buyer, he will seek to obtain as much information as possible about the company from the buyer. This information will include 10-Ks and 10-Qs if the target is a public company, and audited financials or tax returns if it is not. The loan officer will also send out a team of reviewers to visit the company facilities and interview its management, and will obtain an internal or outside appraisal of the assets. This review can take from half a week to a month or more. Banks are aware that they are in a competitive business and generally move quickly, particularly if the loan is being simultaneously considered by several of them.

The loan officer will then prepare a write-up recommending the proposed loan, and present it to the bank's credit committee. The committee may endorse the recommendation as made, approve it with changes (presumably acceptable to the buyer), or turn it down. If the proposal is approved, the bank will prepare a commitment letter (sometimes with the assistance of its counsel, but often not) setting forth the bank's binding commitment to make the loan. This letter thereafter becomes the officer's governing document in future negotiations.

What does the commitment letter contain?

Apart from the bare essentials (the amount of the loan, how much will be term and how much revolver, the maturity of the term loan and amortization provisions, and interest rates), the

commitment letter will also set forth the bank's proposals on:
- fees to be paid to the bank (see p. 133);
- voluntary prepayment rights and penalties under the term loan;
- what collateral is required; whether any other lender may take a junior lien on any collateral on which the bank has a senior lien; and whether the bank is to receive a junior lien on any other collateral subject to another lender's senior lien;
- how the funds are to be used;
- the amount of subordinated debt and equity which may be required as a condition to the making of the senior loan; and
- payment of the bank's expenses (see p. 134).

The commitment may also set forth in some detail lists of covenants, default triggers, reporting requirements, and conditions to closing, including legal opinions to be furnished by counsel to the borrowers; it also usually contemplates additional closing conditions and covenants which may be imposed by the bank as the closing process evolves. The commitment letter will also contain an expiration date, typically a very early one. For example, it may provide that the offer to make the loan will expire in 24 hours if not accepted in writing by the borrower, or it may allow as much as two weeks.

The commitment letter, if it provides for a revolving line of credit (usually called a "revolver"), will generally state both the maximum amount which may be borrowed under the line (the "cap") and a potentially lower amount which the bank would actually lend, expressed as a percentage of the value, from time to time, of the collateral pledged to secure the revolver. This lower amount is called the "borrowing base." The difference between the amount actually borrowed on the revolver at any time and the amount that could be borrowed (i.e., the lower of the cap or the borrowing base) is called "availability."

How is the borrowing base determined?

If receivables are pledged, the commitment letter may distinguish between "eligible receivables" and other "receivables."

Both are subject to the bank's lien, but only the former may be used to enhance the amount of availability, i.e., may constitute assets against which borrowings may be made.

In a typical situation, "eligible receivables" will be those which are not more than 90 days old or past due, have been created in the normal course of business, arise from bona fide sales of goods or services to financially sound parties unrelated to the borrower or its affiliates, and are not subject to offset, counterclaim, or other dispute. The bank will lend up to a specified percentage (typically 70–90%) of eligible receivables. This percentage is known as the "advance rate." Thus, notwithstanding the maximum amount of the line theoretically available to the borrower, revolving loans outstanding may not at any time exceed that stated percentage of eligible receivables, determined monthly, or even weekly.

Inventory is also usually used as collateral. To be eligible, inventory will generally have to be of the kind normally sold by the borrower (if the borrower is in the business of selling goods), and will be limited to finished goods boxed and ready for sale, not located in the hands of a retail store or in transit. In such circumstances an advance rate of 50% is not uncommon. In addition, in some circumstances banks will lend against work in process or raw materials. However, a rather low advance rate—perhaps 15%—will be applied against such unfinished goods, because of the problem a bank would experience in attempting to liquidate the collateral. The bank may also impose an "inventory sublimit"—an absolute dollar ceiling on the amount of inventory-based loans.

What does this method of determining the amount of the loan imply for company operations?

It is important to have accurately calculated the need for working capital at the time the loan is committed for, and then to operate within the ceiling and borrowing formulas imposed by the revolving loan. A heavy penalty falls on the manager who allows inventory to build up, and a lesser but still significant penalty falls on the one who fails to collect receivables promptly. Only 50 or 60 cents can be borrowed for every dollar tied up in finished inventory, and every dollar of uncollected receivables costs the company 10 to 30 cents of inaccessible revenues. Financing practices of the pre-acquisition company may have been much looser, particularly if it was part of a well-heeled conglomerate or run as a family business, and untried chief financial officers can get in trouble very quickly after the closing if they don't understand the business implications of their loan terms.

Are the terms of the commitment letter negotiable?

The best, and often the only, time to negotiate is when early drafts of the commitment letter are circulated or when the loan officer sends the buyer an initial proposal letter, before credit committee approval. Buyers should be careful to involve their lawyers and other advisors at that stage, and not wait until later to get into details. Be sure you understand the lender's procedures. The proposal letter may be the only opportunity to negotiate a document in advance; sometimes commitment letters only appear after the credit committee has met. Afterwards, expectations of the lender become set, and the loan officer will find it awkward to resubmit the proposed loan to the credit committee. The borrower typically does not know how much latitude the loan officer has to modify the commitment without returning to the credit committee. Because time is of the essence in the typical LBO, and a new credit action can result in delay, it is also frequently not in the interest of the borrower to return to the credit committee.

Once the commitment letter is signed, how long will the commitment remain open?

The lender's commitment to make a loan will typically provide that definitive documentation must be negotiated, prepared, and signed by a certain date. Sometimes the time allowed is quite short: 30 or 45 days. Sometimes closing on the LBO will be protracted because of the need to obtain administrative consents, such as FCC consents to change of ownership of television stations. In such cases, the termination date of the commitment must be pushed back to allow reasonable time to accomplish all of the actions necessary to effect the closing of the acquisition.

FRAUDULENT CONVEYANCE

Lenders worry about "fraudulent conveyances" in LBOs. Why?

A bank which lends money to finance the acquisition of a business needs to be assured that, in the event of a bankruptcy of that business, its lien on the assets will secure the loan and the note given by the acquired company will be enforceable. However, if the pledge of assets and the giving of the note are determined to be "fraudulent conveyances or transfers" under the Federal Bankruptcy Code, or under comparable state law (either the Uniform Fraudulent Conveyance Act or the Uniform Fraudulent Transfer Act, as the case may be), the lien will be set aside and voided, and even the note can be rendered worthless.

Can a pledge of collateral, or a note or guaranty, be a "fraudulent conveyance" even though there is no intent to defraud anyone?

Yes. Both the Bankruptcy Code and comparable provisions of state law permit the voiding of a lien or obligation as "fraudulent" without the requirement of malign intent. These laws may, in effect, be utilized to protect the interests of general creditors of acquired companies where the transactions financed by the banks have the effect of depriving the acquired company of the means to pay its debts to its general creditors, whether those transactions are actually intended to do so or not.

Is there a special risk of creating an unintended "fraudulent conveyance" in an LBO loan, as opposed to an ordinary corporate loan?

Yes. Under Section 548 of the Bankruptcy Code and comparable provisions of state law, a lien given by the acquired company on its assets, or the note secured by that lien, will be deemed "fraudulent" if the company receives less than "reasonably equivalent value" in exchange, *and* one of the following three conditions exists: (1) the company was "insolvent" at the time of such transfer, or became "insolvent" as a result of the transfer; (2) the company was left with "unreasonably small capital" as a result of the transfer; or (3) the company incurred or intended to incur debts beyond its ability to pay.

In an LBO loan, no matter how the transaction is structured (whether as a cash merger, stock purchase, or asset purchase), most of what the bank lends winds up not in the hands of the acquired company, but rather, in the pockets of the sellers. On the date after closing, the acquired company is, by definition, "highly leveraged." It has a great deal of new debt, and liens on all its assets, but a large portion of the money raised by such debt (which the company is required to repay) has gone to the previous stockholders. It is not hard to see why an unsecured creditor of the company, viewing the new debt obligations of the company and the encumbrance of its assets, would complain that the company (as opposed to its former owners) did not receive "reasonably equivalent value" in the transaction.

Assuming that the lack of "reasonably equivalent value" may be a problem in all LBO loans, can't the problem be solved by showing that none of the other three conditions that would trigger a "fraudulent conveyance" exist?

It can, if each of the three conditions can be shown not to exist, but that is more difficult to do in the typical LBO than may appear. Of the three conditions, (1) "insolvency," (2) "unreasonably small capital," and (3) "ability to pay debts," the last two are relatively easier to overcome. To the extent that the company and the bank can demonstrate, through well crafted, reasonable projections, that the company will have sufficient revenues, and borrowing capacity, to meet its reasonably anticipated obligations (including servicing the acquisition debt), it should be possible to establish that the company's capital, although small, is adequate, and that the company will be able to pay its debts. Solvency, however, is another matter.

Why is it difficult to show that an acquired company is "solvent" for fraudulent conveyance purposes?

Because the definition of "solvency" as used in the Bankruptcy Code and state counterpart legislation is different from that used under generally accepted accounting principles. Under GAAP, there are a number of different tests which can be used to prove the solvency of a company. Solvency under GAAP can mean having sufficient assets to pay its debts as they mature, or having book assets which are greater than book liabilities. In the typical LBO, at least one of the tests for GAAP solvency can usually be met. But for fraudulent conveyance purposes, a company is solvent only if the "fair, salable value" of its assets is greater than its probable liabilities. The inquiry is not limited to GAAP balance sheet liabilities. All liabilities, contingent as well as direct, must be considered. Assets will be valued at their worth upon disposal; perhaps in a liquidation mode, rather than book.

Why is the "fair, salable value" test a problem for LBO loans?

In the early days of LBOs, companies were generally sold at prices that reflected the actual cash value of hard collateral—plant, machinery, and equipment—rather than a relatively high multiple of earnings. As the LBO field became more crowded and stock market multipliers increased as well, prices were bid up, with the result that *pro forma* balance sheets for acquired companies began to reflect more and more goodwill. In addition, companies with relatively little in the way of hard assets, such as advertising agencies, came into play. Although such deals could be financed on the basis of their cash flow performance and projections, they would typically flunk the GAAP balance sheet test for solvency with the acquisition debt loaded on. Although they might be able to meet an alternative GAAP test based on capacity to service debt, they would inevitably lack hard assets having "fair, salable value" at least equal to their direct and contingent liabilities.

Is the "fraudulent conveyance" problem inescapable for all LBOs?

Each sophisticated lender who is willing to make an LBO loan has made a bottom-line decision that it can live with the risk of unclear law in this area. The leading case on the subject, *Gleneagles*, actually involved intentional misconduct, although the court's reasoning in that case cast a cloud over innocent LBOs as well. A number of commentators, supported by some court decisions (*Kupetz, Credit Managers*), have argued that the "fraudulent conveyance" doctrine should not be employed as a blunt instrument against LBOs. While it is not possible yet to say how the law will develop, a reasonable compromise might be that creditors who predate the acquisition and did not consent to it should receive protection that realistic standards for solvency are met at the time of the acquisition, while subsequent creditors who knew or could have known of the terms of the acquisition loan and its security arrangements should not be entitled to the benefit of fraudulent conveyance laws.

Are there structural arrangements in LBOs which can trigger fraudulent conveyance problems?

Yes. In addition to the issue of lack of "reasonably equivalent value" to the company, lenders and borrowers can get into trouble in transactions involving multicompany groups. These problems are not unique to LBOs, but they can occur in such transactions. Typically they occur when collateral is provided by a subsidiary to secure a borrowing by its parent ("upstreaming") or when collateral is provided by one subsidiary to secure a borrowing by a sister subsidiary ("cross-streaming"). Similarly, upstream and cross-stream guaranties can run afoul of the fraudulent conveyance prohibitions. By contrast, guaranties and pledges by a parent to support a borrowing by its subsidiary ("downstreaming") do not present fraudulent conveyance problems.

Why are "upstreaming" and "cross-streaming" bad?

Because the donor entity—the one providing the collateral or the guaranty—is not getting "reasonably equivalent value," which is going instead to its affiliate. Thus, one of the triggers (although not the only one) for fraudulent conveyance is tripped. In addition, each subsidiary is typically asked to guarantee all the senior debt of its parent; yet the assets of the subsidiary represent only a fraction of the total acquisition. The result is that each subsidiary, taken by itself, cannot repay the full acquisition debt, and may be rendered insolvent if the guarantee is called against it alone. This illogical result would be avoided if the test of solvency took into account that all the subsidiaries would share in meeting the guarantee obligation. While some cases give support for this conclusion, the law is unfortunately not clear enough to eliminate the risk.

Are there ways to solve "upstreaming" and "cross-streaming" problems?

Yes. If the transaction passes each of the three additional tests—(1) no "insolvency," (2) not "unreasonably small capital," and (3) "ability to pay debts"—there is no fraudulent conveyance. However, to guard against the risk that one of the tests is flunked, two kinds of additional solutions can be explored: (A) merging the entity providing the collateral or guaranty with the borrower before the acquisition is consummated, or (B) dividing up the loan into two or more distinct credit facilities, each collateralized by (and commensurate with) the collateral provided by each borrower. Care should be taken, if the latter course is used, to avoid having the loan proceeds simply pass through one of the borrowers into the hands of another borrower or affiliated entity. The loan proceeds can be used to pay off bona fide intercorporate debt, but if the cash flow among the borrowing entities indicate that the separate loans are shams, the transaction runs the risk of being "collapsed" in a bankruptcy proceeding. In such a case, the liens and guaranties could be voided.

Are "upstream" or "cross-stream" guaranties which are limited to the net worth of the guarantor fraudulent conveyances?

Limiting the guaranty (and the lien collateralizing it) to the amount of the guarantor's net worth at the time of delivery of the guaranty should provide an ingenious way to assure that the guarantor is not rendered insolvent by delivery of the guarantee, and consequently should eliminate any fraudulent conveyance problem. However, the guarantor must have the requisite "net worth" in the bankruptcy sense, and not just GAAP net worth, in addition to being able to pay its debts and not having unreasonably small capital. Net worth guarantees have yet to be tested in a bankruptcy proceeding, and although they appear conceptually sound, there are no certain predictions on what the courts will say.

Will accounting firms give solvency opinions?

No. Such opinions were given from time to time in the past to provide reassurance to lenders. After adverse outcomes on some such opinions in early 1988, the American Institute of Certified Public Accountants (AICPA) prohibited all accounting firms from rendering solvency letters, and they are unlikely to reappear soon. Some appraisers or valuation consultants will give such opinions, however.

Will law firms give opinions that fraudulent conveyance laws have not been violated?

Almost never. Law firms generally refuse to give fraudulent conveyance opinions, largely because they cannot evaluate the question of solvency, and because lawyers have traditionally refused to predict what actions a bankruptcy court may take under a set of unforeseeable circumstances. While lenders usually understand and accept this reluctance, sometimes some skirmishing occurs at the closing on this point.

OTHER PRINCIPAL ISSUES IN SENIOR LOAN AGREEMENTS

What fees are typically charged by the bank?

Bank fees for lending services tend to be as various as the ingenuity of lenders can devise, and as high as borrowers can accept. In some cases, the lender may charge a fee upon the delivery of the commitment letter signed by the bank (the "commitment letter fee") and a second commitment letter fee upon its execution by the borrower. Both such fees will probably be nonrefundable, but may be credited against a third due from the borrower at closing on the loan (the "closing fee").

If the loan has been syndicated, the bank may charge an agency or management fee for its services in putting together the syndicate. This will typically be an ongoing fee (as opposed to the one-time commitment letter and closing fees), payable quarterly or monthly at a percentage of the total facility (1/4% per annum is not uncommon).

The total amount of fees charged by a bank at the closing ranges between 1 and 2 1/2%. The percentage depends on the speed demanded of the bank, the complexity of the transaction, the size of the banking group (the more lenders there are, the more expensive it is), and the degree of risk. A short-term bridge loan will probably involve a higher front-end fee than a long-term facility, since the bank has less opportunity to earn profit by way of interest over the life of the loan. Usually the New York money center banks charge fees at the higher end of this range.

In addition to the front-end fees, there will usually be a commitment fee or facility fee (typically, 1/2%) on the amount from time to time undrawn and available under the revolver.

If the borrower will need letters of credit, the bank will typically assess a letter of credit fee (typically 1% to 1.5% per annum) on the amount committed under a standby or commercial letter of credit.

Finally, the bank will often seek early termination fees on the unpaid balance of the term portion of the financing. These are intended to compensate the bank for economic losses it may suffer if the borrower terminates the term loan prior to its maturity because of a cheaper financing source, thus depriving the bank of the anticipated profit on the loan for the balance of the term. These fees may step down in amount the longer the term loan is outstanding. It is usually possible to get the bank to drop these termination fees, or at least limit them to terminations occurring in the first year or two. This is worth spending some chips to achieve. If the company does well, the buyer will probably want to refinance the senior loan as quickly as possible to escape a whole panoply of burdensome covenants, and these fees are likely to be a problem.

What bank expenses is the borrower required to pay?

Typically, whether the loan is made or not, the commitment letter will require that the borrower be liable for all of the lender's out-of-pocket expenses and obligations for fees and disbursements of the bank's outside counsel. This provision is not negotiable; banks never expect to pay their own counsel for work done in connection with a loan. Such fees are always assessed against the borrower or, if the loan does not close, the intended borrower.

What interest rates do banks charge for LBO loans?

Typically, a bank will charge 1 1/2% to 2% over the "prime rate" or "base rate." Contrary to popular belief, "prime" does not necessarily mean the lowest rate a bank charges its customers, as the loan agreement will often admit. Rather, the prime or base rate will be whatever the lending bank says it is, from time to time.

Are reference rates other than "prime" ever used in floating rate loans?

Yes, and the loan agreement may permit the borrower to switch back and forth. A common alternative is LIBOR, the London interbank rate. LIBOR, which is sometimes referred to as a "Eurodollar Rate," is typically calculated as the rate the lender would have realized on deposits in dollars with a "first-class" bank in the London interbank market (see Chapter 13). Another reference rate frequently used is the "Federal Funds Effective Rate." This rate may be based on the weighted average of rates on overnight Federal funds transactions with members of the Federal Reserve System arranged by Federal funds brokers, as published by the Federal Reserve Bank of New York, or as an average of quotes from a specified number of Federal funds brokers "of recognized standing" selected by the bank.

The amount of the premium charged by the bank above the reference rate will depend on which reference rate is used, and the present and anticipated differentials between the bank's own "prime" and the alternative third party reference rate or rates; premiums are generally about 100 basis points greater for Eurodollar Rate loans than they are for prime rate loans. This is largely, but not completely, offset by the fact that LIBOR is usually a lower rate than prime; the net effect of selecting LIBOR is probably to increase rates about 25 to 50 basis points. LIBOR is more responsive to interest rate changes and will move more quickly. A change in prime represents a significant political decision for a bank, and thus changes in prime come less frequently and in bigger steps.

Are there problems in having more than one lender participate in a loan?

Frequently LBO loans are made by groups of banks, or "syndicates. " In some cases the banks involved in making the loan will all be parties to the loan agreement, with one of their number designated as the "agent bank." In other cases, only one bank will sign the loan agreement, but it will sell off participation interests to other banks. While the number of participants in a loan makes no difference to the borrower from a legal standpoint, the practical implications of having to deal with multiple lenders can be serious and troublesome.

Because of the high degree of leverage involved, LBO lenders tend to limit their risks by imposing an intrusive array of covenants—negative and affirmative, financial and operational—upon the borrower. These covenants are designed to assure that the business will be conducted as represented to the bankers and in accordance with the financial projections submitted to the bankers by the borrower. Any deviation, any change in the manner of operation of the business, any bad financial development, is likely to trigger a default. Because it is not always possible for a buyer to foresee all future developments in the way the business will be conducted, it is generally not possible, even in the absence of bad financial news, to operate at all times within the requirements imposed by the loan covenants. Hence, the borrower will generally find it necessary, from time to time, to go back to his lenders to have certain covenants waived or amended. If only one lender is involved, the process can be relatively simple. If the consent of a dozen or more is involved, the process can be expensive, time consuming, and painful.

Do all the members of a lending group have to approve every waiver and amendment?

Generally, no. But the provisions which relate to interbank matters, such as the percentage of lenders needed to grant waivers, are generally contained in a document (sometimes called the "Participation Agreement") to which the borrower is not a party, and, frequently, which it may not even be allowed to see. Although lender approval arrangements are various, it is not unusual for them to provide that certain changes in the loan (such as changes in interest rates, due date, principal amount) are so fundamental that all lenders must consent, whereas others can be approved by banks holding at least a 51%

interest (or 66 2/3% interest) in all loans outstanding or lending commitments.

What is a "negative pledge" covenant, and why do lenders seek them?

A "negative pledge" is an undertaking by the borrower not to pledge to someone else, assets which may be subject to the bank's lien, or to no lien. It is generally used to bar junior liens on collateral that is subject to the bank's senior lien. Although in theory the rights of a junior lienholder should not impinge on the senior lender's rights in the collateral, in practice lenders strongly prefer not to be accountable to a second lienholder with regard to their stewardship over the collateral on which they have a first lien. A junior lienholder is, in the eyes of a senior lender, someone who can second guess your actions in realizing upon the collateral, and sue you if you slip up, or even if you don't.

What kinds of problems are most likely to be encountered in attempting to perfect liens on the collateral?

- Prior unsatisfied liens may be discovered. (For this reason, as well as for general due diligence considerations (see Chapter 8), it is prudent to begin a lien search as promptly as possible in all jurisdictions in which record filings may have been made affecting the collateral.)
- Liens on patents, trademarks and trade names, and copyright assignments require special federal filings, which may be time consuming, and require the services of specialized counsel.
- Collateral assignments of government contracts and receivables from the U.S. Government require federal approval, a potentially time-consuming process.
- Uniform Commercial Code filings giving notice to the world of security interests must be made at state and, sometimes, local government offices where the target and its assets are located. Filing requirements in Puerto Rico

and Louisiana, the two non–UCC jurisdictions in the United States, are markedly different from, as well as more elaborate than, filing requirements in other United States jurisdictions. Local counsel should be contacted early and will play key roles.

- Security interests in real estate and fixtures require separate documentation and recordation in the localities and states in which they are located. Lenders will often require title insurance and surveys, both of which involve considerable lead time.
- Lenders will often want local counsel opinions as to perfection and priority of liens, the obtaining of which can be a major logistical task (see Chapter 11).

For interest rate and fee calculations, bankers typically treat the year as having only 360 days. Why?

Because it produces a slight increase in yield over the stipulated rate or fee. This practice has acquired the status of a convention, and is not generally subject to negotiation.

What are "default rates"?

Loan agreements typically provide for an increase in interest rates in the event of default, or at the time of acceleration of the loan. A premium of 2% or 3% above the rate normally in effect is not uncommon. A borrower should try to have a default rate go into effect only after the lender makes a formal declaration of default, since minor technical defaults are all too easy to stumble into and should not be a source of profit to the lender.

Why are mandatory prepayment obligations imposed by lenders?

The use of mandatory prepayment requirements will reflect the bank's perception of the transaction. In some transactions the lender is anxious to recoup and redeploy its money as swiftly as possible. This desire, and the anticipated availability of cash derived from cash flow projections, will tend to drive in the direction of an aggressive amortization schedule on term debt. (In some cases borrowers may also be asked to "amortize" revolving lines of credit as well, by accepting scheduled reductions in availability over a period of time and making any principal payments required by such reductions.) In addition, amortization payments may be scheduled to match the buyer's plans for selling off assets or terminating pension plans, in effect forcing the buyer to honor his promises to break up and sell off parts of the acquired business or to terminate such pension plans as represented to the bank. Finally, the loan agreement may require that all or a portion of excess cash flow be paid down to reduce senior term debt. Although the bank may permit distributions of dividends to stockholders of an S corporation for the purpose of paying federal, state, and local income taxes on income of the company, and the retention of some earnings for capital expenditures, it may also require that everything left over after junior debt is paid be used to pay off any outstanding balance on the term loan.

Why do banks insist on applying prepayments first to the last installments due (in inverse order) rather than the other way around?

Banks reverse the order of LBO loan payments in order to keep the flow of cash coming into the bank, and get the loan paid off as swiftly as possible. If borrowers could prepay the next payments due they would, in effect, be buying themselves a payment holiday. Sometimes prepayments may result from sale of income producing assets (or the bank's application of casualty insurance proceeds to prepay principal in lieu of making such proceeds available to the borrower) which reduce the subsequent capacity of the borrower to pay debt service. In such cases the loan should be recast to proportionately reduce the combined total of subsequent interest and principal payments.

Can a letter of credit facility be combined with an LBO loan?

Yes. If the business uses letters of credit in its ongoing operations (for purposes such as assuring payment for raw materials or foreign-sourced goods), it can generally obtain a commitment from the lenders to provide such letters of credit up to a stipulated aggregate amount. The letter of credit facility will typically be carved out of the revolving line of credit, will be collateralized by the same collateral which secures the revolver, and will have the effect of limiting availability under the revolver to the extent of the aggregate letter of credit commitment. Draws on letters of credit will be treated, in such circumstances, as draws on the revolver. Separate fees (frequently ranging from 1% to 1.5% per annum) will be charged by the lenders for standby letters of credit outstanding from time to time.

Sometimes companies have a practice of issuing a large letter of credit for all shipments in a certain period, then securing specific orders as they arise. In such cases, it may be possible to limit availability by the amount of claims that can be or have been made against the letter of credit for specific orders and not by the larger unused balance of the letter of credit.

LBO loan agreements typically contain a lengthy list of conditions to closing. Are there any which are likely to be particularly troublesome?

Although points of sharpest contention vary from transaction to transaction, there are some which crop up regularly. They include:

• Requirements regarding perfection and priority of security interests in collateral. If, for example, first liens are to be given to the lenders on inventory in various jurisdictions: FIRST, lien searches have to be completed and reports received and reviewed (there are professional companies which can be hired to conduct computerized searches of liens on record in any state or county office); SECOND, documents terminating old liens have to be prepared, signed, and sent for filing; and THIRD, documents perfecting new liens have to be prepared, signed, and sent for filing. Once all that has been done, filing must be coordinated in each of the jurisdictions so that it occurs contemporaneously with the funding of the new loan and the payoff of the old loan. In a complex, multijurisdictional transaction, such coordination, if it is to be done successfully, requires a combination of monumental effort and plain old good luck. Not infrequently, lenders have some flexibility about the filing of termination statements in connection with the old loan being discharged and will allow a reasonable period after closing for this to be accomplished.

• Counsel opinions. Few deals crater over the failure of counsel for the borrower to deliver required opinions, but it is not unheard of for a closing to be delayed while final points in the opinions are negotiated between counsel for the bank and the borrower. Problems typically occur in local counsel opinions and relate to the validity of the bank's lien in a particular jurisdiction. There is no magic solution, but early involvement of local counsel for the borrower is always a good idea.

• Auditors' opinions. Especially since the AICPA banned "comfort letters" in early 1988, auditors are becoming increasingly reluctant to opine as to the solvency of borrowers, an opinion which banks have often requested as a way of limiting their fraudulent conveyance risk. Comfort letters were statements by auditors as to the solvency of their client made without an actual audit. Similarly, auditors may be reluctant to address the reliability of financial projections provided by the borrower to the bank. The best advice is to determine at an early stage what the auditors will, and will not, agree to say in writing at the closing.

• Governmental consents and approvals. In certain transactions, approval of a governmental entity is a central element in the transaction. For example, a sale of a television station cannot be effected without requisite FCC approvals. The timing of such approvals, even if they are reasonably assured, is outside the power of the parties, and the failure of a governmental agency to act when expected can wreak havoc on the schedule for closing an LBO.

• Material litigation and adverse changes affecting the company. The filing of a major lawsuit which, if successful, could seriously harm the company's business can block a loan closing and halt the acquisition unless counsel can persuade both the buyer and the bank that the suit is frivolous or unlikely to succeed, or that its consequences would not be material to the company or its operations. Similarly, bad economic news can cause either the buyer or the bank to halt the process, resulting either in a negotiated price reduction or a termination.

Are there continuing conditions which apply to subsequent draws on the revolving line of credit?

Yes. In most loan agreements, the bank's obligation to honor subsequent draws upon the revolver is subject to a variety of conditions. Chief among them is reaffirmation by the borrower that the original warranties and representations made in the loan agreement are still true (including those stating that there have been no material adverse changes in the business since a date generally preceding the closing date) and a requirement that no covenant default exists. If the foregoing conditions are not met, the bank is not required to lend.

What purposes do the representations and warranties in the loan agreement serve?

The representations and warranties are intended to assure the lender that all of the information provided to it, upon which the credit decision was based, is correct. They constitute, in effect, a checklist of potential problem areas as to which the borrower is required to state that no problem exists, or to spell out (by way of exceptions or exhibits) what the problem is. Thus, typical warranties will state that:

- The financial statements of the borrower which have been submitted to the bank are correct (while it is comforting to have this conclusion backed by an auditor's certification, usually the auditor's report is laced with qualifications);
- There are no liens on the borrower's assets, except as disclosed to the bank or permitted pursuant to the loan agreement;

- The transactions contemplated will not conflict with laws or any contracts to which the borrower is a party or by which it is bound (the so called "non-contravention" representation);
- There are no lawsuits pending or threatened against the borrower which are likely to have a material adverse effect on it if decided against the borrower, except as disclosed to the bank;
- The loan will not violate the "margin rules";
- The borrower has no ERISA exposure;
- The borrower is not a regulated Public Utility Holding Company or investment company (since, if it were, various governmental orders would be required);
- The borrower is "solvent" (so as to mitigate concerns about fraudulent conveyance risks);
- The borrower's assets (and principal office) are located in the places specified (since this information is needed to assure that perfection of security interests in the collateral is effected by filing notices in the correct jurisdictions).

What happens if a representation is wrong?

A breached representation can have two practical consequences for a borrower: (1) if such a breach occurs, the bank may refuse to make a requested advance, either at or after the closing, and (2) breach of a representation or warranty can trigger a default under the loan agreement. The first consequence—bank refusal to fund—should not be surprising. The truth and accuracy of the representations is typically a condition to the initial loan made at the time the loan agreement is signed, and also to any subsequent draws on the revolving line of credit.

If, for example, the borrower has warranted in the loan agreement that it has no significant environmental problems, and subsequently it is discovered that it has been guilty of illegal dumping of hazardous wastes, the bank will probably have the right under the loan agreement to shut off further draws on the line of credit. Such a decision could be catastrophic for a company precluded from financing itself from cash flow because its loan agreement also provides for the "lock boxing" of revenues and mandatory paydown—i.e., a requirement that they be deposited in a lock box under the lender's control, and used to pay off bank debt.

The second consequence—a default under the loan agreement—triggers the remedies a lender generally has under a loan agreement, one of which is the right to "accelerate" the loan, i.e., to declare all monies loaned immediately due and payable, even though the amounts due under the term portion may not be otherwise due for several years, and the revolver may not expire until the end of the current year.

The right to accelerate is, in a practical sense, the right to trigger the bankruptcy of the borrower, and for that reason is unlikely to be exercised except in those cases where a lender determines that its interests will be better protected by putting the borrower in bankruptcy than through other means. Since bankruptcy is viewed by most secured lenders as risky, slow, and a last resort (and potentially liability producing for the bank), a breached warranty is generally unlikely to bring the house down. But unless the breach is waived by the lender, its existence in effect turns what was originally conceived of as a term loan into a demand loan, callable by the bank at any time. Frequently, highly leveraged transactions result in the bank having a demand loan even in the absence of a default, so going into default does not make matters much worse; also, some lenders and their counsel try to negotiate loan agreements which are so tight that the company is arguably in default from the moment the agreement is entered into. Banks also impose default rates of interest in some cases, so that the cost of borrowing can go up on a warranty breach. This is a more effective sanction for the bank, provided the company's fiscal health is not endangered.

Covenants in LBO loan agreements frequently appear more intrusive than those in most commercial loan agreements. Why?

Because in a typical leveraged acquisition the lenders are significantly more at risk than they are in a normal business loan.

Both from a balance sheet standpoint (because of the absence of a substantial equity "pad" under the senior debt) and an operating standpoint (because of the burden debt service will place on the borrower's cash flow), the lender is likely to view itself as significantly exposed. Lenders attempt to address this problem by imposing covenants on the borrower to achieve the following five results: FIRST, to obligate the borrower, by express contractual provision, to operate the acquired business in accordance with the business plan submitted to and approved by the bank; SECOND, to provide early warning of divergence from the business plan or of economic bad news; THIRD, to protect the collateral; FOURTH, to prevent the leakage of money and property out of the borrower, whether as "management fees" or other payments to related parties, costs of new acquisitions, capital expenditures or simply as dividends; and FIFTH, to enable the bank to exercise its remedies at as early a stage as possible if things go awry, by exercising its right to declare a default as a result of a covenant breach.

What are the covenants a borrower is most likely to be confronted with from the standpoint of:

Compliance with the Business Plan?

- To use the proceeds of the loan only for the stipulated purposes;
- To engage only in the kinds of business contemplated by the lenders;
- To refrain from merging or selling all or substantially all of its assets, or any portion thereof in excess of a specified value, without the bank's consent;
- To limit capital expenditures, lease payments, borrowings, and investments in affiliates and third parties to agreed amounts;
- To prevent change in ownership or control of borrower without lenders' consent;
- To bar acquisitions of other businesses; and

- To make changes in the acquisition agreement, subordinated debt instruments, or other material documents.

Providing Early Warning of Economic Trouble?

- To remain in compliance with financial covenants (discussed below);
- To provide periodic (monthly, quarterly, annual) financial reports, with annual reports to be audited;
- To give prompt notice of any material adverse development affecting the operations of the business;
- To provide revised and updated projections, on at least an annual basis, prior to the commencement of each new fiscal year; and
- To permit visits and inspections by bank representatives.

Protecting the Collateral?

- To keep the business and property adequately insured;
- To limit sales of property to merchandise sold in the ordinary course of business;
- To require property to be kept free of liens (a "negative pledge");
- To bar leases of property by the borrower; and
- To provide key man life insurance for principal executives of the borrower.

Preventing Leakage out of the Borrower?

- To cap executive compensation and management fees;
- To limit, or often prohibit (at least for a specific time period, or until specified financial tests are satisfied), dividends and other distributions to equity holders;
- To prohibit transactions with affiliates, except as expressly agreed upon and except for those provided on an "arm's length" basis for services definitely required by the borrower; and
- To lend money or guarantee the obligations of other parties.

*What kinds of financial covenants are likely
to be imposed?*

The borrower may be required to maintain stipulated ratios for:

- interest coverage (earnings before interest and taxes to interest expense);
- debt to net worth;
- current assets to current liabilities; or
- fixed charges to net income (or cash flow).

In addition, the borrower may be required to attain stipulated minimum goals for:

- net worth, and
- cash flow;

and not to exceed stipulated maximum limits for:

- capital expenditures, and
- total debt.

The financial covenants lenders are most concerned with relate to the company's cash generation and cash distribution. Lenders are vitally concerned about monitoring the company's ability to service current and future obligations to the lender. Thus, in general, they want to limit "unnecessary" cash outflows such as dividends, excessive capital expenditures, and future payment obligations (i.e., additional debt) until their claims are satisfied. In addition, lenders want sufficient advance information about the company's cash inflow relative to debt service requirements. If this ratio starts to deteriorate and approach default levels, the lender will increase monitoring activity and notify management of relevant default consequences.

How do lenders determine financial covenant levels?

Lenders use information provided by the borrower and their own lending experience to set financial covenant levels. The projected financial statements serve as the basic data for establishing covenant levels. Since financial covenants are usually designed as early warning devices, lenders want covenants that are good indicators of debt service capability. Contrary to popular belief, lenders do not want financial covenants as high as possible. What they try to achieve is an effective filter system, identifying problem loans that merit special attention. If covenants are too high, the lender may waste valuable administrative time on a relatively low-risk situation.

For example, assume a senior lender provides $2,000,000 at 12% fixed interest to be paid over 5 years. The company's projected cash flow and debt service requirements appear in Table 4–1.

The projected coverage ratio is calculated by dividing projected cash flow by total debt service.

Given this data, the lender will make a judgment about the projected volatility of the company's cash flow. Assuming the company's prospects satisfy the senior lender's loan committee, a projected coverage ratio covenant must be determined. The level selected will probably be a simple discount on expected performance that still provides the lender with reasonable security. Once the company is out of the woods, the lender should be comfortable and should not keep increasing the level of required performance even if the projections indicate that it can be achieved.

The covenant level will probably rise over time to reflect the lender's desire to see the company's cash flow continue to

TABLE 4-1

Sample Company's Projected Cash Flow and Debt Service Requirements (in thousands of dollars)

Year	1	2	3	4	5
Loan Balance at 1/1	2,000	1,700	1,250	800	350
Interest	240	204	150	96	42
Principal Payments	300	450	450	450	350
Total Debt Service	540	654	600	546	392
Projected Cash Flow	1,000	1,200	1,400	1,600	1,800
Projected Coverage Ratio	1.85	1.83	2.33	2.93	4.59

TABLE 4-2
Sample Covenant (in thousands of dollars)

Year	1	2	3	4	5
Covenant Ratio	1.4	1.4	1.8	2.1	2.5
Minimum Cash Flow (covenant ratio times debt service)	756	915.6	1,080	1,146.6	980

increase. A sample covenant and the resulting minimum cash flow to prevent default appear in Table 4–2.

The covenant levels shown above require the company to sustain cash flow levels that provide the lender with an adequate cushion, and still require the company to increase cash flow each year until the last, when the lender's risk has been significantly reduced.

Borrowers are faced with an interesting dilemma when presenting a prospective lender with the target company's projected financial performance. A borrower may be motivated to make the target's future performance look good in order to obtain the loan. However, these same projections will form the basis for the lender's financial covenants. If the projected performance was inflated, the company could continually be in default on the loan agreement. On the other hand, if the borrower downplays the future performance of the target company to avoid this possibility, he runs the risk of making the loan relatively unattractive to the lender. Ultimately, both sides benefit the most when forecasts are submitted that genuinely reflect the buyer's expectations for the target.

When are financial covenants usually negotiated?

Very late in the process, usually just before closing. The buyer prefers to get the commitment for the loan before negotiating these provisions in detail. Often the most reliable financial projections become available only at the last moment, and they provide the base for the covenants. Sometimes the bank sets the covenants too tight at the closing, and the negotiating process continues through the initial months of the loan in the form of waivers. This should be avoided if possible.

What events typically trigger default?

- Payment defaults (failure to pay interest, principal, or fees when due, or in the case of interest and fees, sometimes within a stipulated grace period—see below);
- Breach of a representation or warranty (sometimes subject to the qualification that the breach be material—see below);
- Breach of covenant (sometimes subject to a right to cure certain breaches within a specified cure period, and/or to the qualification that the breach be "material" or have a "material adverse effect" on the borrower);
- Cross default provisions (which result in a default in the loan agreement being triggered by a default in another loan document, such as a security agreement, or in another unrelated but material agreement to which the borrower is a party, such as a subordinated debt instrument. Typically, for a cross default to be triggered, the default in the other instrument must be "mature;" i.e., all cure periods must have expired and the other lender must have the right to accelerate. In addition, defaults on other debts below a specified dollar threshold may be carved out so as not to trigger a cross default in the loan agreement);
- Insolvency or voluntary bankruptcy; or involuntary bankruptcy, if not discharged by the borrower within a stipulated period (typically 60 days);
- An adverse final court judgment above a stipulated dollar amount which is not discharged or stayed on appeal within a prescribed period;
- The imposition of a lien (other than a lien permitted pursuant to the loan agreement) on assets of the borrower;
- The happening of an event triggering ERISA liability in excess of a stipulated amount; and
- The death of the chief executive officer or an individual

guarantor or other termination of the employment of certain specified managerial employees.

What techniques can be used to take some of the "bite" out of default provisions?

There are basically two default softeners: the use of "grace" or "cure" provisions, and the concept of "materiality."

A "grace period" is a period of time, following the due date for the making of a payment, during which payment may be made and default avoided. It is rare, but not without precedent, for a grace period to be accorded to a principal repayment obligation. More common are grace periods for interest payments or fees. Five days grace beyond the due date is not uncommon; sometimes ten or even fifteen days may be granted. "Cure" periods apply to defaults triggered by covenant breaches. Generally the lender will attempt to limit their application to those covenants that are manifestly susceptible of cure (the duty to submit financial reports at specified dates) but deny them for covenants designed to provide early warning of trouble (breach of financial ratios). Sometimes the cure period will not begin to run until the lender has given the borrower notice of a failure to perform; in other cases, the cure period will begin to run when the borrower should have performed, whether the lender knew of the borrower's failure or not. Cure periods vary greatly from transaction to transaction, and from provision to provision. However, 5-day, 10-day, and 30-day cure periods are seen from time to time, and sometimes the concept of counting only "business days" is used to extend the period by excluding Saturdays, Sundays, and nationally-recognized holidays.

The concept of "materiality" is more commonly applied in the case of defaults triggered by warranty breaches. The borrower will assert that default should not be triggered if a representation turns out to be untrue, but the effect of such inaccuracy is not materially adverse to the borrower or the collateral, or to the lender's position. The concept of a cure right for misrepresentations is not at all common, but is not illogical in many cases. In some cases, where the loan agreement does not afford the borrower the right to cure a breached covenant, it is sometimes provided that such a breach will nevertheless not trigger a default if the effect is not material and adverse.

INSURANCE COMPANY FINANCING

For many years, insurance companies have provided senior fixed-term financing—both secured and unsecured—for terms of up to 10, 12, or 15 years through "private placements." If a company's capital requirements are sufficiently great, one or more additional insurance companies may participate in the transaction as co-lenders. Frequently these groups are assembled by investment bankers. Because the behavior and practices of insurance company lenders differ somewhat from banks, they deserve special attention.

What kind of financing is usually available from insurance companies?

Loans may be secured, unsecured, or a combination of each. All, or any portion, may be senior debt, the remainder being subordinated debt generally bearing a greater rate of interest. Rates are usually fixed for the term of these financings.

Does it make a difference which insurance companies are solicited?

It may, for several reasons. While lending terms tend to be somewhat standardized, certain companies will lend into a riskier credit, with a rate premium and perhaps a somewhat more onerous set of covenants, although most won't. In addition, over the years several life insurance companies and their counsel have devised and perfected lengthy, onerous forms of Note Purchase Agreements (essentially the equivalent of a loan agreement), with which many borrowers became disenchanted, taking their business elsewhere. Since then, in an effort to regain the lost business, at least one company has developed a new, streamlined, and more readable form of agreement which is definitely preferable to its predecessors, from the borrower's point of view. It may be appropriate to agree in advance of documentation that a streamlined form of agreement will be utilized.

If insurance companies are a source of long-term funds required to close an acquisition, is timing critical?

Insurance companies are generally more bureaucratic than banks, and decisionmaking often seems to take longer. In-house counsel can, in some cases, march to a different drummer delaying legal responses, but their input is required notwithstanding the presence of an outside law firm.

Although substantial acquisitions have been closed with insurance company funds, delays can be expected to occur. Often, if time is of the essence, it is prudent to arrange for a bridge lender to fund initially and be taken out within a period of several months by an insurance company private placement. The bridge lender could even be the bank providing the revolving financing. Even this solution can be difficult to achieve, however, since the principal terms of the takeout financing must be negotiated in advance with the insurance company, and often between it and a senior lender, to be sure the takeout financing can be closed in the future.

How are insurance company private placements generally negotiated?

The deal is negotiated and, frequently, put in the form of a "term sheet" which is "circled" (approved) by each insurance company, or alternatively, commitment letters may be issued, particularly if sufficient pressure is placed on the lenders by borrower or its counsel.

Once a term sheet or commitment letter is agreed to, the lead lender (usually the insurance company taking the largest percentage of the total loan) will have its outside counsel prepare a first draft of the Note Purchase Agreement; such counsel generally acts for the entire lending group, although with varying degrees of authority and effectiveness. The other participants (and their in-house counsel) will generally review this draft before it is forwarded to the borrower and its counsel. The content of this Agreement has the potential to change significantly for the worse—from the borrower's perspective—as it progresses through successive drafts, as in-house counsel for each participant gets additional bites at the apple. A strong lead lender, however, is likely to be able to prevent this from occurring.

How should the borrower or its counsel respond if, during the negotiation of a Note Purchase Agreement, a representative of the insurance company should suggest that an issue being negotiated be dropped, and that, instead, a waiver be obtained by the borrower at a later date if necessary?

These agreements should be negotiated as fully as possible prior to closing. Although subsequent waivers are obtainable, a borrower should not be surprised if some payment is required to be made in connection with the waiver, particularly if interest rates have risen significantly since the funding of the transaction. Even when rates have not risen, some companies have been known to impose fees when waiver requests are made, frequently in order to compensate for their staff time spent in evaluating the requests; of course, the cost of any outside counsel will be the responsibility of the borrower. Furthermore, waivers are generally more readily obtainable from banks, less so from insurance companies. One should act accordingly in negotiating the initial insurance company documentation.

Is it possible to provide for optional prepayments without incurring significant prepayment premiums?

Yes. Generally, prepayment provisions in Note Purchase Agreements have followed a formula which allows for optional annual prepayments in any year in the amount of any specified annual mandatory prepayments, without additional charge. If, however, the loan is to be prepaid in any given year by an amount in excess of this permitted optional prepayment, a percentage premium would be applied to this excess, with the amount of this percentage declining annually, reaching zero within a year before maturity. The applicable percentage would then be multiplied by the amount prepaid in excess of any permitted optional prepayment, and the resulting product is the dollar amount that must be paid, in addition to the outstanding principal balance, in order to prepay the principal indebtedness evidenced by the Note Purchase Agreement or an appropriate portion. These percentages can start out in the vicinity of 9 1/2%, scaling down as maturity approaches.

Recently, many life insurance companies have become gun-shy of the fixed premium method for prepayments and are moving toward what is known as a "make-whole" arrangement. This consists of a formula which pays to the lender the net present value of the lost return during each year that the notes issued under the Note Purchase Agreement would have been outstanding, compared to a theoretical reinvestment at an agreed formula rate.

Are other prohibitions on prepayment found in insurance company financings?

Yes. Prepayment is usually prohibited if the source of funds for such prepayment is borrowings, or proceeds from the sale of preferred stock, having a lower after-tax interest cost to the company than the company's after-tax cost of interest at the rate payable under the insurance company's notes.

Is there any way to structure the borrowing in order to reduce the amount of prepayment premiums?

Yes. If a portion of the amount borrowed is at a variable rate tied to prime or Eurodollar rates, prepayment premiums on that portion can be avoided.

Do insurance companies provide revolving loans, take-out commitments or other forms of guarantees?

Insurance companies don't do revolving loans. For this reason, they are not suitable for working capital lending. Insurance companies are not organized for the continuous financial monitoring required for revolving lending. Also, unless operating as a surety, insurance companies do not give guarantees. They may not make a loan unless it would be prudent at the time made. Thus, they may not give enforceable commitments to take out or back another lender if the borrower gets into trouble.

What material covenants would you expect to find in a more streamlined insurance company Note Purchase Agreement?

- Typical financial reporting covenants, including requirements for a statement of the principal financial officer of the company setting forth computations pertaining to compliance with financial covenants (including long- and short-term debt incurrence, secured debt incurrence, and the making of restricted payments);
- Maintenance of corporate existence, payment of taxes and compliance with statutes, regulations and orders of governmental bodies pertaining to environmental and occupational safety and health standards, or even broader governmental statutes and regulations with a materiality standard;
- Maintenance of specified types of insurance;
- Restrictions on debt incurrence (including limits on short-term debt and long-term debt, each of which may be restricted to specified dollar amounts or by formulas relating to consolidated tangible net worth and consolidated net earnings available for fixed charges);
- Restrictions on encumbrances, sale and leasebacks, and payment of restricted payments;
- Maintenance of financial condition—minimum amount of

consolidated tangible net worth, minimum ratio of consolidated net tangible assets to consolidated debt, minimum current ratio, maximum long-term rentals, restriction on subsidiary stock dispositions, and issuance of shares by subsidiaries;
- Limitations on amounts of annual capital expenditures; and
- Restrictions on mergers and consolidations affecting the company and subsidiaries, and disposition of company or subsidiary assets.

JUNK BONDS

What are junk bonds?

Junk bonds are medium- to long-term obligations (10–15 years) of the target that (1) are subordinated to its senior debt, (2) are normally unsecured, and (3) bear high interest rates (13–17%). Their rather inelegant name comes from the fact that they are riskier than senior debt; but they generally deserve a better label, and are thus called by some underwriters "high-yield securities." They are normally not prepayable for an initial period (3–5 years), and thereafter only prepayable at a premium. The main purpose of junk bonds is to provide mezzanine financing for acquisition transactions, filling in the gap between senior secured debt, which pays a lower interest rate, and the seller's take-back financing or the buyer's equity financing, which is the last to be paid back. There is sometimes more than one layer of junk debt—one being senior subordinated and the other junior subordinated debt.

To whom and how are junk bonds sold?

They are commonly sold to large financial institutions—insurance companies, pension funds, mutual funds, including overseas investors—usually in blocks of $500,000 or more—and are primarily for the sophisticated investor. Often, but not necessarily, the offerings are registered under the federal securities laws to increase their marketability and are sold in a package with warrants to acquire common stock in the target. If they are privately placed, they often carry registration rights that will enable the holders to require the borrower to register the debt for sale in a public offering. See the discussion of registration rights at pages 172–181. Drexel Burnham Lambert Inc. was the first investment banker to sell junk bonds in large scale, and it still dominates the market, though Merrill Lynch, Shearson Lehman Hutton, First Boston, and it some others now participate substantially.

How do the warrants relate to the junk bonds?

The junk bonds offer some of the same high risk/high reward characteristics of equity, and it is a natural combination to offer them together with an "equity kicker" in the form of warrants. Warrants are rights to buy stock from the company at a specified price for a future period of time. Frequently, the institutions buying the bonds sell the warrants (sometimes back to the underwriter), thereby obtaining the junk bonds at a discount. See the discussion of junk bond yield in Chapter 3, page 89.

What is a bond indenture?

The indenture is the basic agreement setting forth the terms of the junk bonds and is entered into between the borrower and a bank, acting as trustee for the bond holders. It serves the same function as the credit or loan agreement executed with the senior secured lender and the note purchase agreement executed with an institutional mezzanine lender. The indenture contains the covenants, events of default, and other material terms of the transaction, including the various responsibilities and rights of the issuer, trustee, and bondholders. If the bonds are issued or subsequently sold pursuant to a public offering, the indenture must qualify under the Trust Indenture Act of 1939. Much of the boilerplate in the indenture is derived from requirements under that law.

The principal objectives of the covenants are to prevent disposition of the assets of the borrower (unless the sale proceeds are reinvested in assets used in the same business by the borrower or used to pay off the junk bonds or senior debt), to assure that if any merger, consolidation, or change of the borrower occurs, the successor entity is obligated to repay the bonds on the same terms and is in as strong or stronger a financial position after the transaction as before, to limit the creation of additional debt and liens (particularly secured debt senior to the bonds), to limit payments of dividends and distributions to stockholders ("restricted payments"), and to restrict transactions with affiliates.

What covenants do junk bonds normally contain?

Compared to senior debt agreements, unsecured junk bond indentures are simpler, fitting the classic bond indenture mold. Unlike senior debt instruments, which provide for total information flow to lenders, hair-trigger default provisions, and, in theory, extensive second guessing and approval of management decisions, bond indentures tend to rely more on the borrower's good judgment and the value of the company as a going concern, and limit themselves to protecting against major restructurings or asset transfers or increases in amounts of senior or secured debt. This difference in approach reflects the longer term nature of such debt and the impracticality of obtaining consents from a large, diverse group of public bondholders. In the very rare case that the junk bonds are secured, however, a more elaborate set of covenants relating to the protection of collateral will be included.

Generally, borrowers should try to limit the financial covenants in junk bond issues to "incurrence" tests rather than "maintenance" tests. In other words, the covenants should not require that any specified level of financial health be maintained, and should be breached only by a voluntary act, such as (these are the four normal circumstances) paying a prohibited dividend, incurring prohibited debt, merging or combining with another company or selling assets unless certain tests are met, or dealing with affiliates other than at arms-length. These covenants will often closely restrict operating subsidiaries of the borrower to assure that all debt is incurred on the same corporate level.

In many transactions the covenants go much further. They may include detailed financial maintenance covenants relating to net worth, current ratios, interest coverage and the like, limitations on investments, and application of asset sale proceeds.

Which bond covenants are particularly subject to negotiation?

The following key issues should be focused on in the indenture:

1. *Restrictions on Mergers and Asset Sales.* There are a variety of such restrictions. The most onerous require that the surviving entity in the merger or the purchaser of all or substantially all the assets have a net worth not lower than the borrower had before the merger and that the fixed charge coverage ratios (generally the ratio of debt payments to cash flow [pre-debt service]) equal a certain percentage of the ratio that pertained before the merger. The effect of this type of provision is to preclude a sale of the business in a leveraged buyout that will cause a material increase in total debt of the company after the merger. The borrower thus has fewer means available to him for disposing of the business.

Some indentures require the borrower to offer to prepay junior debt from asset sale proceeds that are not used to prepay senior debt. (It must be an "offer" because the debt is usually not prepayable without the consent of the lender.) Senior lenders object to this provision because they believe that it may be necessary for the proceeds to be left in the business, particularly if there is trouble and the asset sale was used to gain needed liquidity for the business. The dispute can usually be solved by allowing, until the senior lender is paid in full, a limited amount of such proceeds to be left in the business before a prepayment offer must be made.

A borrower should always check in advance to learn what the investment banker's standard format is (best done by reviewing indentures from previous transactions). Once you've locked in with an investment banker, you'll hear over and over again that it can't market the debt without the restrictions it is used to. Be prepared with examples of other junk debt with less onerous provisions. If you have any specific plans to sell off assets, be sure they don't violate this provision.

2. *Debt Incurrence.* Many junk bond indentures have very tight restrictions on debt incurrence by the issuer. The simplest form of restriction is that the issuer cannot issue "sandwich debt" or "interlayer debt"; that is, debt subordinated to the senior debt but senior to the junk debt. This restriction allows the issuer to borrow as much senior debt or debt junior to the junk debt as the lenders are willing to lend. The holders of the junk debt are relying on the limitations senior lenders will place on the amount of senior debt that can be incurred.

Other types of restrictions limit the incurrence of debt to a percentage of the original amount of debt or require the achievement of certain financial ratios before incurring additional debt. The ratios, and any particular provisions necessary for a particular business plan, are all subject to negotiation with the lender. The senior lender will want the borrower to be able to incur new senior debt somewhat in excess of the unpaid amount of the existing senior debt in order to permit minor workout arrangements and to finance some expansion.

3. *Restrictions on Prepayments.* Most junk bonds preclude prepayments for several (often, five) years, and thereafter may permit prepayments only on payment of substantial premiums. This restriction is not as troublesome if the covenants in respect of mergers and debt incurrence are not too strict. A long non-prepayment period means that the issuer can't rid itself of the debt, except through defeasance of the bonds, if the covenants become too burdensome.

4. *Subordination Provisions.* See pages 185 to 195.

5. *Restricted Payments.* These restrictions prohibit dividends and other distributions as well as stock redemptions unless specified conditions are satisfied. The conditions usually prevent payments until a specified minimum net worth level has been attained, and thereafter payments may not exceed a certain percentage (25–50%) of accumulated net income.

Be careful of this provision because it may have the effect of precluding a sale of the company through a leveraged buyout unless the junk bonds are also prepaid. Such a buyout normally requires the borrower, or a successor obligor under the junk bond indenture, to borrow the acquisition debt and pay the proceeds to the target's shareholders. Such payments probably constitute a restricted payment that may not be made unless the tests are satisfied (and in most such cases they won't be). Even if all the other tests for the merger are satisfied (e.g., net worth, coverage ratios), this test may present another and often insurmountable hurdle.

But won't it be possible to just waive these covenants if they prove to be too restrictive?

No. It very likely will be either impossible or very expensive to prepay the junk bonds because of prepayment restrictions and penalties. In addition, unlike the case of senior lenders, it is often impossible or, at the least, very difficult to obtain waivers of covenants from a multitude of public bondholders. Therefore, the restrictions contained in the junk bond indenture should be something the borrower can live with for a long time. Special care must be taken to assure that the covenants fit the long-term plans of the company in respect of acquisitions, dispositions of assets, expansions, etc. Once the covenants are in place, you'll have to live with them pretty much unmodified.

BRIDGE LOANS

Underwriters will sometimes offer a buyer immediate short-term financing for an acquisition in exchange for the right to replace that financing with a later junk bond issue. Junk bond bridge lending began as a marketing device for underwriters trying to break into the market dominated by Drexel. Drexel's practice had been to issue "highly confident" letters stating that they had reviewed a transaction and were sure that they could place the financing. Bridge loan financing gained popularity initially in 1986, during the year-end rush to beat the new tax law deadline, and thereafter prior to the October 1987 stock market drop because it met the needs of buyers for immediate funding in situations in which a rapid private placement of junk bond debt was not possible and there was not time before the acquisition closing for the lengthy process of registering the bonds for public sale.

The risk in bridge lending is that the market will go sour before the loan is repaid and the bonds are sold, which in fact happened in October 1987. For a three-month period following the crash, interest rates rose to over 17%, and many deals could not be financed. Nevertheless, the market recovered thereafter, and bridge loans are still being made. (We just address junk bond bridge loans here; elsewhere [Chapter 3, page 87, and Chapter 4, page 116] we cover bridge lending pending a planned disposition of assets.)

What should be the interest rate on the bridge loan?

The interest rate on the bridge loan, being short-term financing, should initially be 5% to 8% over the treasury or federal funds rate, lower than the expected rate on the junk bonds that will be sold to repay the bridge loan. This rate should rise by 1/2% or more per annum if the underwriter cannot refinance the bridge loan in a three to six month period. The increasing interest rate compensates the underwriter for the bridge financing risk, as does a warrant for a small amount (normally 3–5%) of the common stock of the target. The underwriter will also receive substantial fees: commonly 1% upon execution of a commitment letter for the bridge loan, and another 1% or more when the loan is funded.

What issues arise in the negotiation of a bridge loan/junk bond financing?

The bridge lender is most concerned about assuring that it will be able to market the refinancing debt, that is, the junk debt that will be used to repay its loan. Thus, it will seek to clarify in advance any potential issue that could arise with the borrower or with other lenders. The bridge lender will also seek utmost flexibility in the terms of the refinancing debt that it can offer (e.g., interest rate and equity kickers such as warrants) and will further require that the borrower use its best efforts to get the offering done as soon as possible. The bridge lender's prime concern is to get its debt refinanced, and it will seek to build into the contract strong incentives to motivate the borrower toward that end.

The borrower on the other hand wants to be sure, if possible, that its permanent mezzanine debt is borrowed on terms it can repay. The borrower should seek to place limits on the terms of the refinancing debt and also to assure that the bridge lender's debt will roll over into longer term debt if the refinancing debt can't be placed.

These general concerns are reflected in the following specific points of negotiation:

1. *The term of the bridge loan.* In many cases, the bridge loan falls due at the end of a fixed period, usually 3–9 months. If the refinancing debt is not placed by then, the bridge loan is in default. The senior lenders are often unwilling to accept this risk, and the borrower should be concerned as well. The refinancing debt may not be marketable on reasonable terms even though the company is doing extremely well; the problem may simply be a failure of the markets (e.g., the post-October 1987 period) or in the marketing efforts of the bridge lender. The other parties will have made financial commitments based on the confidence level of the investment banker that the refinancing debt would be available.

For the foregoing reasons, the bridge lender can often be persuaded (particularly in a competitive environment) to commit to a longer term investment if the refinancing debt doesn't get placed. This takes the form of either a "rollover" provision where the terms of the note change after the maturity date and it becomes long-term subordinated debt with covenants and other provisions, similar to subordinated junk debt. Another technique is to cast the original bridge note as a long-term note that the borrower is obligated to prepay with the proceeds of refinancing debt or other cash proceeds such as equity offerings. In either case, the extended bridge note will have higher than normal, or increasing, interest rates to encourage refinancing of the bridge debt at the earliest possible time.

2. *The terms of the refinancing debt.* The borrower should obtain reasonable limits on the terms of refinancing debt that it will be obligated to accept. The usual formulation is something like "at prevailing market rates and terms," subject to limitations on the interest rate, the term, scheduled principal payments and the amount of equity that the purchasers of the refinancing debt will be entitled to receive. The borrower may seek a limitation on the amount of cash interest payable annually or, alternatively, on the average yield on the instrument, though it is difficult to bar access of the bridge lender to takeout financing even if there has been a major interest rate move in the market. The senior lender also will be interested in assuring that the terms of the refinancing debt don't violate its expectations about coverage ratios and limits on other indebtedness.

3. *The covenants and events of default, of the bridge loan.* The senior lender and the borrower will generally try to make the bridge loan covenants, events of default, and subordination provisions similar to the refinancing debt that will take out the bridge loan. They resist, often successfully, attempts by the bridge lender to make the bridge loan agreement a tighter, restrictive document or to have the bridge lender ride on the covenants of the senior lender. Avoidance of overly tight default triggers is especially important where the obligation of the bridge lender to sell the refinancing debt is conditioned on absence of a default under the bridge note. The tighter the covenants, the greater the risk of a default that could prevent the rollover into the longer term note and thus could put the company into a financial crisis soon after the acquisition.

EQUITY INVESTMENT FUNDS

An equity investment fund is a type of financing vehicle often used to provide the mezzanine level of financing in a management buyout or business recapitalization. The investment fund raises equity capital from private investors and uses the capital to make equity and subordinated debt investments in a portfolio of companies that are in need of mezzanine financing. In return for their capital, investors in an investment fund typically receive income from the debt the fund provides to its portfolio of companies and the potential for capital appreciation from the fund's equity investments.

How are investment funds structured?

Generally, investment funds are organized as limited partnerships. The interests in the partnerships are considered securities under federal and state securities laws and, consequently, are offered and sold in a registered public offering or in reliance on an exemption from the registration requirements.

Most commonly the investment funds have been marketed to a limited number of sophisticated, wealthy individuals, institutions, and pension funds in a private placement offering. Proceeds of the offering are used by the investment fund to acquire common equity, preferred stock, and subordinated debt in a series of management buyouts.

How do the fund investors share in the benefits of the investment?

Fund investors do not directly own any stock or other interests in the company to be acquired. Instead, each participant, or investor, in an investment fund contributes capital to each acquisition vehicle formed and will become a limited partner in the acquisition vehicle, receiving a return on investment in accordance with the partnership agreement. For example, in two private funds sponsored by Forstmann Little & Co. and Kohlberg Kravis Roberts & Co., respectively, the general partner receives 20% of the realized profits from the investments made by the fund, and the remaining balance is distributed to the limited partners. In certain public funds, income and gain may be distributed 99% to the limited partners and 1% to the general partner until the limited partners have received distributions of an amount equal to a 10% cumulative annual return on their capital contributions. Thereafter, the general partner is permitted to take a larger share of the profits.

Are the acquisitions in which the fund will invest identified in advance?

No. Investment funds are typically structured as "blind pools," meaning that the portfolio of companies in which a fund will invest will not be identified or known at the time each investor purchases his interest in the fund. The general partner of the fund will have complete discretion in selecting the companies in which the fund will invest. Generally, the funds do not invest in companies where management is opposed to the acquisition. Private investment funds are often structured so that each investor enters into a commitment, for an average period of 5–6 years, to make a capital contribution upon the request of the general partner. The commitment is usually quite large, ranging from $5,000,000 to $10,000,000; however, investors have control over and use of their capital until it is actually invested in a particular acquisition vehicle upon request of the general partner.

What other investments do funds make besides mezzanine and equity financing?

Occasionally, an investment fund will provide bridge financing rather than mezzanine financing. Bridge financing is provided for a short term, typically nine months or less, to supply funds during the interim period before permanent financing is arranged. After the bridge loan is repaid, the fund remains with an equity interest in the acquired company and can roll the loan proceeds over into another acquisition.

In addition, investment funds may be structured to allow the fund to use its capital to finance a friendly tender offer for stock of a publicly held company whereby 51% of the stock is acquired in the tender offer and the remaining stock is acquired in a cash merger. This structure permits leveraged purchases of public companies, despite the margin requirements that prohibit acquisition financing secured by more than 50% of the value of the securities acquired. The initial 51% of the stock acquired in the tender offer is financed half by borrowings and half by equity from the fund. When the cash merger occurs, the additional financing can be supported by the assets of the target, and all or a part of the initial equity investment can be repaid. See Chapter 12 on Public Companies.

What regulatory controls are imposed on investment funds?

The principal regulatory control is the Investment Company Act of 1940, a particularly complex statute that is for experts only. It is likely to apply to any investment fund that raises money from the public and uses the proceeds primarily to acquire securities of other companies, other than operating subsidiaries held and managed in a classic holding company manner. The Act prohibits dealing with affiliates, requires a primarily equity-based capital structure, and imposes various public reporting and fiduciary obligations on the fund's principals. To avoid the effect of the Act, most leveraged buyout funds raise their capital from private placements.

A word of warning: Anyone who is in the business of buying companies, holding them short term (particularly under two years) and selling them, while not actively engaging in their day to day management, and who uses the proceeds of publicly held junk bonds for financing, should check to be sure he is not subject to regulation under the Investment Company Act. Problems can arise even if no investment fund is involved.

SELLER TAKEBACK FINANCING

Many leveraged acquisitions involve some takeback by the seller of debt or stock. This is particularly likely to occur if the seller is a major corporation divesting a minor operation. If debt is taken back, it may be accompanied by warrants. A seller takeback is not always possible. In particular, it may be necessary to pay stockholders of publicly held companies the acquisition price entirely in cash because of the delays and disclosures involved in offering them debt or other securities which require a prospectus registered under the United States security laws.

Why do sellers consider takeback financing?

Sellers are generally reluctant to take back stock or debt which is junior to all other debt. Still, a seller benefits from such subordinated financing by receiving an increased purchase price, at least nominally, and obtaining an equity kicker or its equivalent. The seller may well be aware, and should be prepared to face the fact, that the note or stock will only realize full value if the acquired company prospers, and that there is a real risk that this part of the purchase price will never be paid.

By the same token, however, the upside potential that the seller can realize if the transaction is successful can be much greater than it could receive if no part of its purchase price was contingent or exposed. There may also be cosmetic advantages to both buyer and seller in achieving a higher nominal price for the target company, even though a portion of that price is paid in a note or preferred stock with a market value and a book value below face. Thus, for example, if the seller has announced that he will not let his company go for less than $100 million, but has overestimated its value, he may eventually be pleased to settle for $60 million cash and a $40 million 10-year subordinated note at 4% interest. The note will go onto the seller's books at a substantial discount. (The amount of the discount will be useful for the buyer to discover if he later wishes to negotiate prepayment of the note in connection with a restructuring or a workout.)

What are the relative advantages of subordinated debt and preferred stock?

Preferred stock has the advantage of increasing the equity line on the balance sheet, and thus helps protect the highly leveraged company from insolvency and makes it more attractive to senior and junk bond lenders. Remember that an insolvent corporation cannot transfer its property to anyone else without receiving full consideration. To do otherwise is to defraud its creditors—i.e., to deprive them of access to its assets. (See pages 127 to 133.) Thus, if solvency is an issue, the seller and lenders may feel more comfortable in including some preferred stock on the balance sheet.

Subordinated debt offers considerable advantages to the seller, however. Payments are due whether or not there are corporate earnings, unless otherwise restricted by subordination provisions. Negotiators may have been told to sever completely the seller's connection with the company. Taking back a note bespeaks a greater degree of separation, and greater apparent certainty that the amounts due will be paid. The seller may intend to sell the paper it takes back and can get more for a note than it could get for preferred stock. The seller may be able to obtain security interests in the acquired company's assets, junior of course to the liens of the acquisition lenders, but no such security interest accompanies preferred stock.

From the buyer's point of view, a note has the major advantage of generating deductible interest payments rather than non-deductible dividends. Preferred stock has the important disadvantage of preventing a buyer from electing pass-through tax status as an S Corporation. For both reasons, be sure that if a note does emerge, it is not subject to reclassification as equity by the Internal Revenue Service. Seller preferred stock can also have other adverse tax consequences. (See Chapter 5, pages 291 to 292, 299 to 302, 304-305 and 321-327.)

Absent unusual circumstances, if the buyer can persuade the senior and junk bond lenders to accept a seller's subordinated note rather than preferred stock, the seller should have no objections. If not, the lenders and seller may accept preferred stock convertible into a note at buyer's option once the company achieves a certain net worth or cash flow level. As a last resort, the buyer may persuade the seller, 6 months or a year after closing when debt has been somewhat reduced, to convert his preferred stock into a note.

How can a seller obtain an equity kicker in the company it is selling?

Sometimes, as mentioned before, a takeback note has the same effect as an equity kicker because it serves to inflate the sales price beyond the company's real present worth, and can only be paid if the company has good future earnings. It is also quite possible for the seller simply to retain common stock in the acquired company. In the alternative, the seller can obtain participating preferred stock, in which dividend payments are determined as a percentage of earnings or as a percentage of dividend payments made to common stockholders, and in which the redemption price of the preferred rises with the value of the company. Some of these choices have tax significance. See Chapter 5, pages 327 to 331.

What is the role of warrants?

One increasingly popular alternative to preferred or common stock is a warrant to acquire common stock at some time in the future. This has the double advantage for the buyer of not making the seller a common stockholder entitled to receive information and participate in stockholders' meetings during the immediate post-acquisition period, and of not adversely affecting the target's eligibility for S Corporation status. S Corporations may not have more than 35 stockholders, and, with minor exceptions, all stockholders must be individuals. Thus, a corporate seller cannot remain as a stockholder of an S Corporation, but can remain as a warrant holder. It is important, however, that the warrants not be immediately exercisable, since their exercise will cause a loss of S Corporation status. Thus certain "triggers" are established as preconditions to their exercise. These are basically events which entitle the stockholder investors to extract value from their stock: a public sale of stock, a sale of substantially all the stock or assets, or a change of control of the target. Once one of these events occurs, S Corporation status is likely to be lost anyway, and it is logical to let the warrant holder cash in and get the benefit of equity ownership.

What are generally the key terms found in warrants?

Key provisions will address: how many shares can be acquired upon exercise of the warrant; the amount of the "exercise price" (the amount to be paid to acquire the shares); the period of time during which exercise may occur (which, to prevent interference with any future sale of the company, should not extend beyond the date of any such sale); any restrictions on transfer of the warrant; and any rights, discussed more extensively below, when the warrant holder may have to register his shares or participate in registrations by the company for a public stock offering under the securities laws. There are also lengthy and technical provisions providing for adjustment in the number of shares for which the warrant can be exercised to prevent dilution if there are stock splits or dividends or if shares are sold to others at less than full value.

Does the seller ever receive security as a subordinated lender?

Occasionally, but not typically. The seller may take a subordinated note either on an unsecured basis or with security. Security interests strengthen a seller's bargaining power with senior lenders in the event of bankruptcy or refinancing. The collateral gives the seller a right to foreclose, as well as a seat at the bankruptcy table, even if under the subordination provisions he has no immediate right to payment. Possession of a security interest also gives the subordinated lender leverage to effect a refinancing.

REGISTRATION RIGHTS

What are registration rights?

Registration rights are rights given to an owner of debt or equity securities (a) to require the issuer of the securities to register such securities for public sale under federal and state securities laws, or (b) to participate in any such public sale initiated by the issuer or another security holder. They are key provisions of warrants, preferred stock and privately placed subordinated debt issues, and thus deserve special attention here. They also appear in stockholders' agreements and agreements with management. (See Chapter 6, "Structuring Management Buyouts").

Why do security holders want registration rights?

Debt or equity privately placed in connection with an acquisition usually cannot be resold freely to the public. Any such resale must either be made by another private placement or otherwise pursuant to an exemption from the applicable registration provisions of federal and state securities laws, or must comply with the holding period and other limitations of Rule 144 of the Securities Act of 1933, which restricts the amounts of "control," restricted or unregistered securities that can be sold at any one time and the manner in which those securities may be sold. These restrictions are more than just an administrative nuisance and, because of the decrease in the liquidity of the investment represented by such securities, may reduce substantially their market value. In order to minimize the effect of these restrictions, holders of acquisition debt or equity, particularly holders of privately placed junk bonds, preferred stock, warrants for common stock, or common stock, are usually interested in obtaining from the buyer a promise to include the securities in a registration statement under the Securities Act of 1933 at the securityholders' request.

Note that registration is not an all-or-nothing process: each registration statement relates only to a particular, specified number of shares or amount of debt obligations of a particular type, and thus some securities of a company may be freely available for sale while others, even if otherwise identical, may still be restricted. In order to protect a securityholder, it is not enough to require that securities of the *kind* of security held by him be registered; rather, his particular securities must be registered.

Why wouldn't the buyer automatically grant registration rights?

There are considerable costs to the company in granting registration rights. The registration process involves substantial expense for preparation of the registration statement, including the fees of accountants, attorneys, and financial printers. These costs usually amount to several hundred thousand dollars. In addition, the registration process is an arduous one for the issuing company and its officers and directors, and requires company employees to spend a significant amount of time and attention that would otherwise be focused on management of the company and its business. Perhaps most important of all, the buyer wants to control when and if the company goes public. The exercise of registration rights may cause the company to become a "reporting company" under the Securities Act of 1934, necessitating the filing of periodic reporting documents with the Securities and Exchange Commission (SEC) and resulting in additional expenses. Through the registration process, the target subjects itself to various potential liabilities as well as a host of regulations under federal and state securities laws. If the registration rights relate to common or preferred stock, the buyer will, futhermore, not want to go to the public market until its acquisition debt has been paid down and it is sure that the offering will be a success.

What are "demand" registration rights?

"Demand" registration rights entitle a holder of securities of a company to cause the company to register all or a part of such securities for resale by the securityholder. Usually the company is required to effect such registration promptly upon demand of the securityholder, or within some other reasonable time frame.

What are "piggyback" registration rights?

"Piggyback" registration rights entitle a securityholder to cause the company to include all or a part of his securities in a registration of the same or other classes of securities of the company undertaken other than at the request of the securityholder. Piggyback registration rights might allow a lender holding warrants, for example, to have the shares of common stock for which his warrants can be exercised included in a registration of common stock or subordinated debt of the company that was undertaken by the company with a view towards raising additional capital. Piggyback registration rights generally are not exercisable, however, at times when the registration is of securities to be issued in connection with an acquisition or exchange offer, or securities to be issued pursuant to employee benefit plans, such as employee stock ownership plans.

How many times should securityholders be entitled to exercise their registration rights?

Generally, the number of registration rights that securityholders receive is a function of the relative bargaining powers of the buyer-borrower and its securityholders. It is fairly common for lenders with common stock warrants or privately placed junk bonds to receive one or two demand registration rights. It is often the case, however, that for demand registration rights other than the first demand, certain other terms and conditions of the registration rights, such as payment of expenses and limitations on the number of shares allowed to be included become more restrictive with respect to the securityholder and more favorable to the borrower.

A greater or unlimited number of piggyback registration rights are often granted to securityholders, with the primary limitations being those upon the time during which such rights are exercisable and the amount of securities that the securityholder can include in the registration.

What time restrictions should apply to demand registration rights?

The company's desire for a period of stability after the acquisition must be balanced against the selling securityholder's desire for liquidity. Therefore, demand registration rights usually will not be exercisable for some fixed period of time, often several years, after the acquisition. In addition, demand registration rights are often not exercisable until after the company has conducted its own initial public offering of its common stock. In this manner the company can control the key decision whether and when to go public. Sometimes, if the company has not gone public before a certain extended deadline, perhaps the date on which warrants will expire, the securityholder can compel registration.

Registration rights should not be exercisable during a stated period, usually six to nine months, following a prior registration of securities by the company, in order to avoid an "overhang" problem—that marketing of the prior offering will be hurt by the large volume of additional securities entitled to go to market in the near future.

Securities are sometimes registered by a company for a sale to take place at a future time but as to which the exact date and terms of the sale are not yet determined. Such a registration is referred to as a "shelf registration," because the securities are put on the shelf for later sale, but with most of the work on the registration process already done. Demand registration rights usually do not entitle a securityholder to demand registration of his securities in a shelf registration until after the company has already effected such a shelf registration of its securities, if at all.

What about timing for piggyback registration rights?

Piggyback registration rights raise additional timing issues, since they may be exercisable upon a registration by the company of securities of a type other than the securities to which the rights attach. A holder of common stock, for example, could require inclusion of some or all of his shares in a registration statement that covers debt securities of the company. In the acquisition context, in which the company's ability to sell debt securities during the first months or years after the acquisition may be crucial, care must be taken that piggyback rights do not create competition for the company's own offering. It is thus normal for piggyback registration rights to be restricted only to registrations of equity securities for several years after the acquisition.

When do registration rights terminate?

The exact termination date for registration rights is a matter for negotiation, but it is common for such rights to terminate when the securities of the issuing company are widely held, when the securityholders could otherwise make use of the existing market for such securities to sell their shares without significant limitations, or when a securityholder has sold, or has had the opportunity through piggyback rights to sell, a specified percentage of securities held by him.

What is the minimum aggregate amount of securities required in order to initiate a demand registration?

Registration rights agreements usually provide that the holders of a certain percentage, often as high as a majority, of the securities must join together in order to exercise their demand registration rights. The obvious concern here is that the company will be forced to undertake the expensive and time consuming process of registration for relatively small amounts of securities. The company also wishes to be able to forestall an offering if it can persuade a substantial number of securityholders that one would be inadvisable at any time.

In addition, a threshold dollar amount must be reached before the offering will be large enough to be marketed efficiently by underwriters. For this reason, demand registration rights are usually not exercisable unless the aggregate offering price (or market price, if a market exists for such securities) of the securities to be registered exceeds a certain threshold amount, which may be $5 million or more.

What amount of securities may each securityholder include on a demand or piggyback basis in any particular registration statement?

This issue arises when the number of securities sought to be included in the registration is so great that the underwriter cannot place such a large number of securities at a suitable price. Registration rights agreements usually provide that the underwriter is the final arbiter of the question of just how many securities may be included in the registration statement. In such a case, an orderly system for priorities with respect to inclusion of securities in the registration statement must be spelled out in the registration rights agreement. If the registration is being carried out pursuant to a demand registration right, those making the demand usually have priority. Securityholders with piggyback registration rights often have the next priority, the includable shares being allocated among them on a pro rata basis, depending on the relative bargaining positions of the securityholders. In demand registrations the company is often the last one that is able to participate, and thus may be unable to sell for its own account.

These priorities usually change, however, with respect to registrations of securities initiated by the company in which securityholders are exercising piggyback rights. If the registration involves an underwritten distribution of securities, then the priorities will generally be as follows: first, securities that the company proposes to sell for its own account (this is important in order to permit the company to raise needed capital), and second, shares of selling securityholders, who may be either members of the investor/management control group or outside securityholders exercising piggyback registration rights. Such selling shareholders will generally participate pro rata according to the relative numbers of shares held by them or the relative number of shares sought to be included in the registration statement by them, although it is a matter of negotiation between the control group and those with piggyback rights as to whether those with piggyback rights will have priority over the control group.

Who pays the expenses of registration?

The company generally pays the expenses of registering securities pursuant to demand registration rights. This is true at least with respect to the first demand registration right exercised by a securityholder. These expenses include expenses such as SEC filing fees, accountants, attorneys' fees, and expenses of financial printers. The securityholders including securities in the registration statement will, if such shares are sold by an underwriter, have to pay underwriters' and broker dealers' commissions from the sale of their shares, as well as applicable stock transfer fees. An open item for negotiation is the payment of any applicable fees and expenses relating to the sale of securities under various state securities laws (the "blue sky" fees). Responsibility for payment of expenses of registering securities pursuant to exercises of demand registration rights other than the first such exercise are often the subject of negotiation and may be payable in whole or in part by the securityholder demanding registration, in order to put some limitation on the exercise of such subsequent demand rights. Sometimes state blue sky commissioners will insist that selling stockholders pay a pro rata share of expenses, particularly if they feel that insiders would otherwise get a free ride, and such a possibility should be provided for in the registration rights provision.

Expenses incurred in registering securities included in a registration pursuant to the exercise of piggyback rights are usually relatively small and are usually, except for underwriters' and brokers' commissions, paid by the company.

What indemnification will a securityholder seek in negotiating a registration rights agreement?

Registration rights agreements, because of the potential liabilities involved under federal and state securities laws, generally provide that the company will indemnify the securityholders including their shares in a registration statement, against liabilities arising through any misstatement or omission of a material fact in the registration statement and the prospectus. This indemnification should not, however, include statements supplied by the selling securityholders themselves for inclusion in the registration statement or prospectus. A mirror image of this indemnification should be included in the registration rights agreement to provide for indemnification of the company by the securityholders including securities in the registration statement with respect to the information provided by them. The SEC and several court decisions have maintained that indemnification against liabilities under federal and state securities laws are against public policy and therefore unenforceable. In the event that such indemnification is unenforceable, "contribution" (that is, a right to require pro-rata sharing of liabilities) between the company and the securityholders may be allowed, however, and is customarily included in the registration rights agreement as an alternative to indemnification.

Who picks the underwriter?

The company. This is customary even in demand registrations, although sometimes an institutional securityholder will try to get this right.

What special problems arise with respect to registration rights of debt securities and preferred stock?

The company and the debt holders may have planned from the start to sell the debt publicly, in which case the initial placement is really a bridge loan pending the registration, and the registration rights provisions serve to lay out the next stage in the proposed financing sequence. In the alternative, the debt holders may plan to continue to hold the debt, but with a shelf registration in place so as to be able to sell publicly at any time. Under either circumstance, the registration rights provision presents no problems, and the subordinated debt should be issued from the start in a publicly held junk bond format with appropriate covenants and other indenture provisions.

Sometimes, however, the mezzanine debt has been structured to be privately held. The covenants may be tight, so that the company knows that it can only operate on the basis of repeated requests for waivers. This is particularly likely to occur if the subordinated debt holder has also taken a substantial equity position in the company and plans to operate effectively as a business partner of the company. Under such circumstances, the loan agreement with the subordinated debt holder will have to be completely rewritten before a public registration can occur. It will be necessary either to negotiate in advance and include in the registration rights provisions an entire alternate indenture, or have a brief, more informal understanding that registration of the debt can occur provided that the loan covenants are adjusted to a conventional format for a public issue and, perhaps, that the company has otherwise issued some class of publicly held securities.

Preferred stock raises some of the same issues, since a private placement of preferred stock may contain provisions, such as special exchange or redemption rights, not suitable for publicly held preferred. In addition, demand or piggyback registration rights create marketing problems when they compel the simultaneous offering of different classes of securities, particularly at the time of an initial public offering of common stock. The company should consider offering the preferred stock holder a right to redeem preferred stock from a specified percentage of the proceeds of the common stock offering in lieu of granting preferred stock registration rights. In the alternative, a demand preferred stock registration should not be permitted until a reasonable time (120–180 days) following an initial public offering of common stock, and no piggyback rights should arise on such initial public offering or thereafter without the approval of the common stock underwriter.

INTERCREDITOR ISSUES

What are "intercreditor issues?"

Intercreditor issues are legal and business conflicts arising between lenders. The major areas of difference relate to (1) subordination provisions and (2) rights to collateral.

Do not underestimate the importance of these issues. Intercreditor issues can give rise to serious negotiating problems and can even imperil the deal itself. Unlike buyers and sellers, both of whom usually have a strong stake in achieving a closing and therefore considerable negotiating flexibility, lenders may feel less impelled to close the deal and may condition their participation on compliance with a rather narrow and specific set of security and return criteria.

Once misunderstandings or conflicts arise as to who is to get what collateral or how subordinated the junior debt will be, they are often very difficult to resolve. For example, if two lenders' negotiators have sold the deal to their loan committees on mutually inconsistent bases, misunderstandings can take weeks to straighten out. Competitor banks or insurance companies, rather than focusing on closing the deal, may try to settle old scores, prove their negotiating skills, win points with their superiors or meet the not-always-appropriate standards of their lending manuals. Nothing can be more alarming and frustrating for buyer and seller than watching lenders' loan officers or counsel come to loggerheads over major or even minor points where neither lender has much incentive or institutional flexibility to accommodate or withdraw gracefully. The situation becomes worse when each lender is not a single entity but a syndicate of banks or insurance companies. For these reasons, transactions should be structured and planned to minimize and resolve intercreditor conflicts as rapidly and as early on in the process as possible.

Why doesn't the buyer simply make clear to each lender from the start which security rights and priorities each will have?

Most intercreditor problems arise when two creditors are negotiating subordination rights or rights over collateral and encounter an issue that has not been raised and resolved as part of their respective loan commitments. Consequently, solution number one is to identify as fully as possible at the commitment stage which priorities, assets, or kinds of assets will be allocated to each lender. Some areas are clear and well accepted: revolving lenders get a first lien on current assets; term lenders get a first position in property, plant, and equipment. Less clear is who gets the first position in intangibles, other than those (such as patents) necessary to use a particular piece of equipment, or licenses necessary to sell inventory, which go with the tangible assets to which they relate.

The buyer may, however, choose to keep this point unclear as a matter of negotiating tactics—he may not want to deprive one lender of a particular piece of collateral unless he is sure that another lender will insist on getting it. The lender may be more easily persuaded to get along without the additional collateral once its loan officers are fully involved and appraisals and due diligence have been satisfactorily completed. The buyer may also be trying to keep some assets unencumbered.

Or the buyer may simply miss the point. There is likely to be a lot of time pressure at the stage at which loan commitments are being negotiated, and the buyer may have landed the target by promising to close in two weeks. Furthermore, even if all the major terms can be worked out between the parties, the commitment letter won't cover minor issues, such as how much time the term lender will give the revolving credit lender to complete processing of or remove the inventory (revolving credit collateral) from the premises before being free to close down and sell the plant (term lender collateral). Even these questions can be troublesome sources of delay or conflict at the late hours of the closing.

How can such intercreditor problems be avoided?

There are two cardinal rules to follow in minimizing intercreditor issues. (1) Try to resolve the major issues in advance while there is still competition between potential lenders and before substantial commitment fees are paid. (2) The borrower should try for as long as possible to negotiate the issues via "shuttle diplomacy" between the lenders and not permit direct negotiation between the lenders.

How do you identify and solve intercreditor issues early in the process?

Prior to signing the commitment letter, the borrower should seek to obtain from each potential lender copies of its most recent *executed* (as opposed to draft) intercreditor documents. The executed documents will reflect concessions that the drafts will not. The documents should be compared to see which senior and junior lender has the most reasonable provisions, and these should be used as the basis for negotiating with all of the lenders. A comparison of the junior and senior documents will reveal the areas most likely to create material conflicts, i.e., those that could imperil the deal, as opposed to those that are susceptible to easy resolution in the course of negotiations.

If the borrower has decided which junior lender it will use and is choosing among competing senior lenders, it is often useful to present the typical language that the junior lender has agreed to in respect of the major intercreditor issues for review by the potential senior lenders. Before the commitment is made final, the borrower should seek senior lender approval of the most important parts of the typical junior lender language. The same process works in reverse if the senior lender has been chosen and there are several potential junior lenders.

Once the conflict areas are identified, the borrower must make a judgment about whether the differences are so great that the issues must be resolved at this stage of the negotiation. This would be the case, for example, where one lender requires provisions that are novel or likely to be provocative. Where subordinated debt is to be sold in a public offering, investment bankers will often insist on subordination provisions which, they assert, the market expects and demands. If the investment banker is making a bridge loan which depends for its takeout upon having easily marketable junk debt, it will be particularly insistent on the inclusion of these basic provisions in the junk debt. If the senior lender expects substantially different provisions, you are in for big problems. Iron them out at this stage, while you still have time to get a new lender if necessary.

Nothing helps more on such a negotiation than having an in-depth knowledge of the current practices in the market place. It's always easier to decide to postpone resolving an issue if you know you can make the argument later to your senior lender that all or most other lenders give in on this point.

Remember that you are engaged in a balancing act between the desire to resolve intercreditor issues early and the other more crucial economic terms of the loans, such as interest rate, fees, term, and prepayment schedule. It is foolish to press hard unnecessarily on intercreditor issues before you have commitments on the basic terms of the loan, when the result could be adverse trade-offs on material terms. On the other hand, great economic terms are only meaningful if the deal actually closes.

Should lenders work out intercreditor questions between themselves?

Typically, no—at least not in the initial stages of negotiation. Especially early on, the buyer should try to avoid having the lenders communicate directly with each other about these issues. He will have much more control over the negotiating process if, like Henry Kissinger shuttling between Cairo, Damascus, and Jerusalem, he filters the proposals of each party. More important, there is a much better chance of reaching agreement if the buyer can formulate a compromise position and sell it to each party. This is especially true because the intercreditor meetings can involve a cast of thousands—each tier of lenders, the borrower, and sometimes trustees and their respective counsel, each of whom brings its own group of partners and associates. It is far harder to achieve major concessions in such a crowded environment with everyone's ego on display. If you're forced to agree to direct intercreditor negotiation, try to minimize the size of the meeting.

By the late stages of negotiating the loan agreements and the intercreditor agreement the lenders are more likely to come into direct contact, and, if the transaction is well advanced and the personalities and relationships of the lenders are suitable, the final minor issues can often be resolved most efficiently directly between them. Even then, however, the buyer should be ready to continue the shuttle diplomacy process right up to the end if any of the lenders or their counsel are difficult or the negotiating atmosphere is tense.

The one exception to the no early direct negotiations rule can arise when the lenders involved have worked together successfully in prior deals and agreed precedents exist between them for resolving intercreditor issues. If one lender says, when you mention the identity of the other, "Oh, is Jim doing it? We'll use the Amalgamated format," you can relax a little. But still keep a close eye on them.

SUBORDINATION ISSUES

What are subordination provisions?

Subordination provisions basically determine who among the lenders gets paid first if the borrower has insufficient money to pay all of the lenders. The subordinated lender (often referred to as the "junior lender") is the one who gets paid after the lender to which it is subordinated (the "senior lender"). A distinction is commonly made between "substantive" subordination provisions (i.e., who gets paid first in the event of trouble?), and "procedural" subordination provisions (i.e., when and how can the subordinated lender proceed against the borrower if there is a default in the subordinated loan?). Priority of payment under subordination provisions is different from lien priority, which relates only to the question of which lender has first access to proceeds of sale or foreclosure on the particular asset covered by the lien.

What are the principal subordination provisions?

1. In the event of any insolvency or bankruptcy proceeding, the junior lender agrees that the senior lender will be paid in full before the junior lender receives any payment.

2. Payments of the junior debt are prohibited if the senior debt is in default. Sometimes only defaults in payment (or certain major financial covenants of senior debt) will block payments of junior debt, or blockage will only occur, as to certain categories of default, for a limited period (see p. 189). Since any major default in the senior debt can lead to an acceleration of the debt, in theory the senior lender can convert any major covenant default into a payment default, if necessary, to prevent payment of junior debt. Senior lenders do not want, however, to be forced into taking the extreme step of acceleration, which can quickly lead to bankruptcy. Much negotiation of subordination provisions arises from the senior lender's desire to keep the junior lender from (a) being paid even if the senior debt is not accelerated, and (b) being able to force the senior lender to accelerate.

3. The junior lender agrees to hold in trust for, and pay over to, the senior lender, any amount received by the junior lender not in accordance with the subordination provisions. This clause, known as a "hold and pay" provision, gives the senior lender a direct right to recover from the junior lender without going through the borrower.

What issues arise in negotiating substantive subordination provisions?

1. *Principal Payments on Junior Debt.* The financing is almost always arranged so that no principal payments are scheduled to be made on junior debt until after the final maturity date on the senior debt. The senior loan agreement normally prohibits payments of junior debt ahead of schedule. A common exception to this rule is that senior lenders will often permit prepayment of junior debt with the proceeds of equity offerings or other junior debt. Also, the borrower is often allowed to prepay the junior debt to the extent it could otherwise make dividend or similar payments to shareholders. Where there are notes to the seller, the parties are sometimes able to negotiate financial tests that, if satisfied, will permit principal payments on the notes. This is especially true where the note involves contingent payments to the seller.

2. *Priority of Ancillary Obligations to the Senior Lender.* The senior lender will often seek (and get) the right to have all of its penalties, fees, and expenses of collection paid before the junior lender gets any payments. If there is conflict with the junior lender over this point, it can usually be resolved by setting a cap on the fees.

3. *Priority of Refinancings of Senior Debt.* A very important clause for the borrower in a typical subordination agreement is one which provides that the junior lender continues to be junior to any refinancing or refunding of the acquisition debt. Refinancing eventually occurs in at least half of all leveraged buyouts, and borrowers want to be sure they can replace a senior lender with another one on more favorable terms. They don't want such a transaction to become an opportunity for the seller or any other junior lender to make trouble. This provision is more often an issue with sellers in seller takeback financings than it is with junior institutional lenders, who tend to accept rather broad definitions of senior debt. Senior debt is usually defined in junk bond subordination provisions as any debt for borrowed money that is not expressly made subordinated to the junior loan. Seller subordinated debt is more likely to define senior debt in terms of specific debt instruments, and any refinancings or refundings thereof. Sellers sometimes exclude from the definition of senior debt any debt owed to the buyer or its shareholders.

Both seller and junk bond subordination provisions often will limit the amount of debt to which the junior loan is subordinated to a fixed amount, say 125% to 150% of the senior debt on the original date of borrowing. This limitation is designed to prevent the junior lender from being buried under a growing burden of senior debt that could substantially reduce its chances of getting paid.

4. *Priority of Trade Debt.* This issue, again, is particularly likely to arise with sellers. Trade debt is particularly important in buyouts because in a typical LBO the buyer is purchasing a company that has been under the credit umbrella of its parent. Company management has never worried about its trade credit security because everybody knew that it was a subsidiary of a great big parent with all the money in the world, and now it has become a separate, heavily leveraged company on its own. All parties should consider at an early stage the impact that the acquisition will have on all the target's suppliers. It may be necessary in order to preserve supplier relationships that the seller be willing to remain below the suppliers in loan priority. The senior lender may insist on this feature in order to assure that the company can retain its suppliers if financial storm clouds start to gather.

What issues arise in negotiating procedural subordination provisions?

These tend to be particularly difficult. They can best be divided into "blockage" and "suspension" provisions.

What is "blockage?"

The blockage provisions are those parts of the subordination agreement that prevent the borrower from making payments to the junior lenders under certain circumstances. Seller subordinated notes frequently provide that if there is any default of any kind to a senior lender, no payments may be made on the seller note. In the case of institutional and junk bond lenders, payments on the junior debt are usually barred indefinitely when there is a payment default on the senior loan, and for a limited period of time (anywhere from 90 to 270 days, but usually around 180 days) when a non-payment default exists, unless the senior lender accelerates its debt, in which case the blockage continues. Such periods of blockage are often available only once each year.

The fact that a payment is blocked does *not* mean that there is no default under the junior loan. The blockage provisions do not *by themselves* prevent the junior lender from declaring a default, accelerating its loan, and, if appropriate, forcing an involuntary bankruptcy on the borrower, although the "suspension provisions" discussed below may. Such provisions are merely an agreement between the lenders and the company that no matter what action the junior lender takes, during the blockage period the company may not make the proscribed payments.

Because a blocked payment will constitute a default on the junior debt and entitle the junior lender to accelerate the loan, unless prevented by the suspension provisions, a senior lender is likely to waive its right to blockage unless the company is in serious trouble.

What are the "suspension" provisions?

These are the parts of the subordination agreement that limit a junior lender's rights to take enforcement actions if there is a default on the junior loan. These provisions are prevalent in privately placed subordinated debt. Enforcement actions include suing the borrower, accelerating the loan, and declaring the entire amount due or putting the borrower into bankruptcy. Depending upon the type of loan these rights may be severely restricted until the senior debt is paid in full or for a significant length of time, or they may be subject to few or no restrictions.

The suspension provisions are also important where both

lenders have security interests in the same collateral (i.e., a senior and junior lien on fixed assets). In such a case it is not uncommon for the junior lender to be required to refrain from taking any action against the collateral until the earliest to occur of: the expiration of a fixed period of time, acceleration of the loan by the senior lender, or the full payment of the senior lender.

What rights do the senior and junior lenders want to have if the borrower defaults?

The senior lender wants to be as certain as possible that its superior position is meaningful in a practical sense. It wants no money leaving the corporation if there is any default on its loan, and it wants to control the timing, pace, and final resolution of any workout including possible asset sales or restructuring of the business. For that reason it wants to restrict the junior lender to relatively few events of default (generally only those that are a signal of substantial financial difficulties, e.g., a payment default on the junior loan or acceleration of other significant debt) so that the junior lender will have fewer opportunities to force the borrower into a workout, or worse, bankruptcy. If there are fewer possible events of default under the junior loan, a senior lender may be able to keep the junior lender on the sidelines by keeping the interest payments on the junior debt current while it arranges a workout with the borrower. Once there is actually a default on the junior loan, the senior lender seeks the suspension provisions to forestall efforts by the junior lender to sue the borrower, accelerate the maturity of the junior loan or throw the borrower into bankruptcy. The effect of all these provisions is to reduce the negotiating leverage of the junior lender.

The junior lender wants to minimize the time it is not participating in the workout and the ability of the senior lender to work out matters with the borrower without its consent or, at least, participation. It basically wants a "seat at the table" of any workout as soon as possible. It also wishes to keep the blockage periods as short as possible and minimize suspension provisions so that it can pressure the senior lender not to block payments on the junior debt. To gain negotiating leverage, the junior lender will also seek to structure the subordination provisions so that once there is a default it can threaten to accelerate its loan and bring down the financial house of cards. In actuality, however, the junior lender is unlikely to accelerate, since it would probably have more to lose than the senior lender in a bankruptcy.

The borrower is trapped in the middle. He is mainly concerned with not letting these issues kill the deal. He also has a strong interest in having the subordination provisions not create a situation where he will have little or no time or leverage to work out problems with the senior lenders before financial Armageddon arrives. He does not favor an unrestrained senior lender who can sell off all the assets and close down the business to pay its own loan off rather than live with an extended workout that offers a better chance for ultimate survival of the borrower. He particularly wants to be sure that the seller will be tied down without the ability to compel action by the institutional lenders, both senior and junk bonds. A deeply subordinated seller is more likely to accept 10¢ on the dollar and go away—often a key step in a workout if the borrower's stockholders are to have any incentive to make the additional effort and investment necessary to save the company.

What does the senior lender require with respect to defaults on the junior loan?

A basic objective of the senior lender is to eliminate or at least minimize opportunities for the junior lender to declare a default. Thus, the senior lender will be likely to strongly oppose a "crossdefault" provision in favor of the junior lender, i.e., that any default under the senior loan is a default under the junior loan. If such a provision is given, it should at least be narrowed to certain specific senior loan defaults and should provide that any waiver by the senior lender or cure of the default terminates the default and rescinds any resulting acceleration on the junior loan as well. The senior lender will also wish to be sure that any default on the junior loan is a default on the senior loan, that is, have a cross-default provision running in its favor, so that the junior lender is never in a position to take enforcement action against the borrower at a time when the senior lender cannot. The senior lender should not object, however, to a "cross-acceleration" clause permitting the junior lender to declare a default and accelerate its loan if the senior lender accelerates the senior loan.

Are subordination provisions generally the same for all junior loans?

Definitely not. First, the subordination provisions and all other intercreditor issues are the subject of negotiation and rarely are two deals exactly the same. Second, the subordination provisions vary greatly depending upon the type of junior lender, and whether the junior debt is privately placed or sold in a public offering. The range of subordination (from most deeply subordinated to least) is seller's notes, institutional mezzanine lenders and other privately placed funded debt, and public junk bonds.

Typical provisions for public junk debt, for privately placed institutional debt, and for seller paper are set forth in an appendix at the end of this chapter. Note that there are almost no suspension provisions in the case of public debt and very extensive ones for seller debt.

The case of public debt is worth special note because of its prevalence in today's transactions. In almost all cases you will end up with provisions close to these. If a senior lender has plans to deviate from the current norms for blockage periods or other customary provisions, you will run into serious problems in getting a bridge loan from an investment banker. The areas where negotiations do occur are typically (1) the number of days in a blockage period (120–180 days seems most customary at this time) and the number of blockage periods which can occur in any 365-day period; (2) notice periods before the junior loan can be accelerated; and (3) rescission of acceleration by the junior lender resulting from cross acceleration provisions if the other lender has rescinded its acceleration.

For how long is the subordinated debt subordinated?

Usually the junior debt is subordinated throughout its term or until the senior debt, including refinancings, is paid in full.

Is preferred stock subordinate to all debt?

Preferred stock is subordinated in liquidation to all debt. But preferred stock is a creature of contract between the company and its preferred stockholders, and if it is to be subject to payment restrictions imposed by lenders, the company's articles of incorporation should specifically say so.

In what agreement do subordination terms appear?

Very often, subordination provisions are found in the junior debt instrument itself, but in many cases the lenders prefer to have a separate subordination agreement. This is especially true where the junior lender doesn't want some or all of the subordination provisions to apply after the particular senior loan has been repaid. The borrower must be careful here because if the subordination provisions fall away, the borrower may have a hard time refinancing its senior loan. As discussed above, it is customary to expect and get continuing subordination of some kind on the part of the junior lenders.

How are subordination issues affected by corporate structure?

Corporate structure has a powerful effect on relative rights and priorities of lenders, and sometimes is deliberately taken advantage of to keep intercreditor relationships, and thus problems, to a minimum, or to enhance one lender's position against another's. An over-simplified example will illustrate how this works. Suppose the target is a retail company in the form of a parent corporation with a principal operating subsidiary. The revolving credit and term lender could lend to the operating subsidiary, secured by its current and fixed assets, except the stores. The stores could be financed through loans to a separate partnership which owns them and leases them to the subsidiary. The subsidiary can obtain its working capital by selling certain categories of its accounts receivable to a separate corporation, which would finance the purchase with notes secured by the accounts. The mezzanine debt could be loaned to the parent corporation. The result is shown in Figure 4–1.

Because each lender lends to a different entity, there is minimum contact between lenders and their security rights, and relative priorities are determined by the assets and corporate structure of their respective borrowers. The revolving credit and term lender to Corporation B is in the senior position, except that its rights do not extend to the stores, which are owned by Partnership D, nor accounts receivable, which are sold to Corporation C. Proceeds from the sale of accounts receivable are used to pay down both the revolving and term loan, to pay rent on the stores, and, after these needs are met, can be paid out as dividends to Corporation A, which then can pay the mezzanine debt. To the extent that the revolving loan is paid down, Corporation B gains working capital financing through its ability to borrow again under the revolver, assuming sufficient availability. Because no dividends will be paid if Corporation B's revenues cannot cover its debts to the revolving and term lender and Partnership D, the mezzanine debt is auto-

FIGURE 4-1
Subordination and Corporate Structure

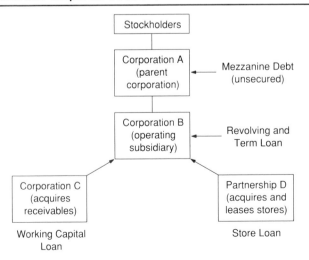

matically subordinated to both the revolving and term lender and Partnership D. Such a structure makes the relationships between lenders clear from the start and minimizes opportunity for conflict between them.

This method of structuring priorities can, at least in theory, give one lender a very strong advantage over another in bankruptcy. (We say "in theory" because no one can predict the behavior of a bankruptcy judge, who has ample power to disregard corporate layers and combine bankruptcy proceedings of different corporations so as to sweep away even the most elegant structural devices.) If, in our example, Corporation B goes bankrupt, the revolving and term lender is its sole creditor, other than trade credit and, but only to the extent of overdue rent, Partnership D. The revolving and term lender can thus control the bankruptcy proceeding without even giving the mezzanine lender a place at the creditor's table. For that reason, the mezzanine debt, which is unsecured, is even more deeply subordinated than it would be if all loans were made to the same entity but subject to the subordination provisions discussed earlier in this chapter. Junior lenders may, consequently, object strongly to being required to lend at the parent level if the senior debt is at the operating level.

Lending at different levels can also present state tax problems. Some states do not permit consolidation of parent and subsidiary tax returns. Consequently, in those states, the deductions derived by Corporation A from interest payments on the mezzanine debt cannot be netted against the operating income received by Corporation B. In addition, care must be taken to be sure that loan agreements and corporate laws permit the necessary dividends to be paid so that funds can flow as required between the different corporations. See also Chapter 5, pages 225–226.

INTERCREDITOR AGREEMENTS

What is an intercreditor agreement?

This is an agreement among lenders to a particular borrower to which the borrower may or may not be a party. It governs, among other things, the priority rights of lenders in collateral and proceeds of collateral, and sets forth which lender or group of lenders shall have the right to make decisions about collateral. It is normally drafted by the most senior lender.

What issues are most likely to come up in negotiations of an intercreditor agreement?

1. *Issues of equal or fair treatment.* When one lender has a first priority in some assets and another lender in other assets, each should have parallel rights as to priority, initiation of foreclosure proceedings, exercise of other remedies, payment for related expenses, and the like. A senior lender may seek to write in overbearing provisions with respect to junior liens. It may, for example, try to grant itself the right to foreclose on or sell collateral whether or not at market price. Such provisions should be avoided because they are probably not enforceable and raise the hackles of junior lenders.

Preserving the form of equal treatment between lenders can be very important. In one situation where the term and revolving lenders had been at each other's throats and the intercreditor agreement was expected to be very difficult to negotiate, no problem arose because despite great differences in the quality and amount of the collateral, the lawyer for the senior lender was careful to keep the clauses of the intercreditor agreement in strict parallel—for every grant of a right to the revolving lender there was a similar (if less valuable) grant for the term lender.

2. *Rights of one lender to amend its loan agreement without the consent of another lender.* It is not uncommon for a junior lender to be barred from shortening amortization schedules or the weighted average life of a financing, since senior lenders will not want subordinated lenders paid off while senior debt is still outstanding. Nor will one lender permit another lender to increase interest rates or rate formulas without its consent, because these terms may affect the company's ability to service all of its debt. However, a borrower should be able to agree with any one lender to ease terms of payment or to amend covenants or waive defaults without involving other lenders. Subordinated lenders frequently require that the borrower may not enter into

amendments to its loan agreement that materially adversely affect the junior lender. This is a vague provision that will tend to make the senior lender cautious but leaves leeway for the run-of-the-mill adjustments and corrections that normally are needed in a loan agreement after the closing. It often provides a reasonable compromise.

3. *Changes in status between lenders.* Sometimes one lender is prepared to take a lower priority against another only for a limited period of time or until some external event occurs. If one lender ceases to be secured, another lender may also be willing to release its security. If a senior lender agrees to extend the term of its loan past a certain date, the subordinate lender may demand the right to gain equal seniority, i.e., to become "pari passu."

4. *Allocation of shared rights over collateral.* If an intangible right, such as a patent or copyright, is needed for realization of value for assets pledged to two different lenders, or if exercise of its rights by one lender blocks another lender's rights (as, for example, if the term lender's right to foreclose on a factory building blocks the revolving lender's right to remove or complete processing of inventory), these matters should be covered.

5. *Voting rights of creditors and other rights in bankruptcy.* Senior lenders try very hard to have control of creditors committees in bankruptcy. Although such rights may not be enforceable, they may seek to require junior creditors to waive contests of bankruptcy plans, marshalling questions and issues of interpretation of the intercreditor agreement.

APPENDIX 4A

SUBORDINATION PROVISIONS OF PUBLICLY ISSUED NOTES

SUBORDINATION

Section 1.1. Agreement to Subordinate. The Company agrees, and the holders of the Subordinated Notes by accepting the Subordinated Notes agree, that the Indebtedness evidenced by the

Subordinated Notes is subordinated in right of payment, to the extent and in the manner provided in this Article, to the prior payment in full of all Senior Debt of the Company and that the subordination is for the benefit of the holders of Senior Debt of the Company, but the Subordinated Notes shall in all respects rank *pari passu* with all other Subordinated Debt of the Company.

Section 1.2. Default on Senior Debt of the Company. No direct or indirect payment by the Company of principal of or interest on the Subordinated Notes whether pursuant to the terms of the Subordinated Notes or upon acceleration or otherwise shall be made if, at the time of such payment there exists a default in the payment of all or any portion of principal of or interest on any Senior Debt of the Company (and the Trustee has received written notice thereof), and such default shall not have been cured or waived. In addition, during the continuance of any other event of default with respect to such Senior Debt pursuant to which the maturity thereof may be accelerated, upon the receipt by the Trustee of written notice from the holders of Senior Debt, no such payment may be made by the Company upon or in respect of the Subordinated Notes for a period of [180] days from the date of receipt of such notice; *provided, however,* that the holders of Senior Debt may give only [one] such notice in any 360 day period, and *provided, further,* that this provision shall not prevent the payment of an installment of principal of or interest on the Subordinated Notes for more than [180] days.

Section 1.3. Liquidation, Dissolution, Bankruptcy. Upon any distribution of the assets of the Company in any dissolution, winding-up, liquidation, or reorganization of the Company (whether voluntary or involuntary and whether in bankruptcy, insolvency, or receivership proceeding or upon an assignment for the benefit of creditors or any marshalling of the assets and liabilities of the Company or otherwise):

1. holders of Senior Debt of the Company shall be entitled to receive payment in full on the Senior Debt of the Company before the holders of the Subordinated Notes shall be entitled to receive any payment of principal of, or premium, if any, or interest on the Subordinated Notes; and

2. until the Senior Debt of the Company is paid in full, any distribution to which the holders of the Subordinated Notes would be entitled but for this Article shall be made to holders of Senior Debt of the Company as their interests may appear.

Consolidation or merger of the Company with the sale, conveyance or lease of all or substantially all of its property to another corporation upon the terms and conditions otherwise permitted in this Agreement shall not be deemed a dissolution, winding up, liquidation or reorganization for purposes of this Article.

Section 1.4. When Distribution Must Be Paid Over. If distributions are made to the holders of the Subordinated Notes that because of this Article should not have been made, the holders of the Subordinated Notes who received the distribution shall hold it in trust for the benefit of the holders of Senior Debt of the Company and pay it over to them as their interests may appear.

Section 1.5. Subrogation. After all Senior Debt of the Company is paid in full and until the Subordinated Notes are paid in full, the holders of the Subordinated Notes shall be subrogated to the rights of holders of Senior Debt of the Company to receive distributions applicable to Senior Debt of the Company. A distribution made under this Article to holders of Senior Debt of the Company which otherwise would have been made to the holders of the Subordinated Notes is not, as between the Company and the holder of the Subordinated Notes, a payment by the Company on Senior Debt of the Company.

Section 1.6. Relative Rights. This Article defines the relative rights of the holders of the Subordinated Notes and holders of Senior Debt of the Company. Nothing in this Agreement shall:

1. impair, as between the Company and the holders of the Subordinated Notes, the obligation of the Company, which is absolute and unconditional, to pay principal of, premium, if any, and interest on the Subordinated Notes in accordance with their terms; or
2. prevent the holders of the Subordinated Note, from exercising their available remedies upon a Default, subject to the rights of holders of Senior Debt of the Company to receive any distribution otherwise payable to the holder of the Subordinated Notes.

Section 1.7. Subordination May Not Be Impaired By Company. No right of any holder of Senior Debt of the Company to enforce the subordination of the Subordinated Notes shall be impaired by any act or failure to act on the part of the Company or its failure to comply with this Agreement.

Section 1.8. Modification of Terms of Senior Debt. Any renewal or extension of the time of payment of any Senior Debt or the exercise by the holders of Senior Debt of any of their rights under any instrument creating or evidencing Senior Debt, including without limitation the waiver of any default thereunder, may be made or done without notice to or assent from the holders of Subordinated Notes or the Trustee.

No compromise, alteration, amendment, modification, extension, renewal or other change of, or waiver, consent or other action in respect of, any liability or obligation under or in respect of, any Senior Debt or of any of the terms, covenants or conditions of any indenture or other instrument under which any Senior Debt is outstanding, shall in any way alter or affect any of the provisions of this Article or of the Subordinated Notes relating to the subordination thereof.

Section 1.9. Reliance by Holders of Senior Debt on Subordination Provisions. The holders of the Subordinated Notes by accepting the Subordinated Notes acknowledge and agree that the foregoing subordination provisions are, and are intended to be, an inducement and a consideration to each holder of any Senior Debt, whether such Senior Debt was created or acquired before or after the issuance of the Subordinated Notes, to acquire and continue to hold, or to continue to hold, such Senior Debt and such holder of Senior Debt shall be deemed conclusively to have relied on such subordination provisions in acquiring and continuing to hold, or in continuing to hold, such Senior Debt.

Section 1.10. This Article Not To Prevent Events of Default. The failure to make a payment pursuant to the Subordinated Notes by reason of any provision in this Article shall not be construed as preventing the occurrence of a Default or an Event of Default. Nothing in this Article shall have any effect on the right of the holders of the Subordinated Notes to accelerate the maturity of the Subordinated Notes.

Section 1.11. Definition of Senior Debt. "*Senior Debt*" means the principal of, premium, if any, and interest on, (1) all indebtedness incurred, assumed, or guaranteed by the Company, either before or after the date hereof, which is evidenced by an instrument of indebtedness or reflected on the accounting records of the Company as a payable (excluding any debt which by the terms of the instrument creating or evidencing the same is not superior in right of payment to the Subordinated Notes) including as Senior Debt (a) any amount payable with respect to any lease, conditional sale or installment sale agreement or other financing instrument, or agreement which in accordance with generally accepted accounting principles is, at the date hereof or at the time the lease, conditional sale or installment sale agreement, or other financing instrument or agreement is entered into, assumed, or guaranteed by the Company, required to be reflected as a liability on the face of the balance sheet of the Company; (b) all borrowings under any lines of credit, revolving credit agreements or promissory notes from a bank or other financial renewals or extensions of any of the foregoing, (c) any amounts payable in respect of any interest rate exchange agreement, currency exchange agreement or similar agreement and (d) any subordinated indebtness of a corporation merged with or into or acquired by the Company and (2) any renewals or extensions or refunding of any such Senior Debt or evidences of indebtedness issued in exchange for such Senior Debt.

APPENDIX 4B

SUBORDINATION PROVISIONS OF PRIVATELY PLACED INSTITUTIONAL NOTES

Section 1.1. Agreement to Subordinate. The Subordinated Notes shall be subordinated to Senior Debt to the extent set forth in this Article, and the Subordinated Notes shall not be subordinated to any debt of the Company other than Senior Debt.

Section 1.2. Default on Senior Debt of the Company. In the event of a default in any payment of interest or principal in respect of any Senior Debt, whether at the stated maturity, by acceleration or otherwise, then no payment shall be made on account of principal of or interest or premium, if any, on the Subordinated Notes until such default shall have been cured or waived.

Section 1.3. Liquidation, Dissolution, Bankruptcy. In the event of (i) any insolvency, bankruptcy, liquidation, reorganization or other similar proceedings or any receivership proceedings in connection therewith, relative to the Company or its assets, or (ii) any proceedings for voluntary liquidation, dissolution or other winding-up of the Company, whether or not involving insolvency or bankruptcy proceedings, then all principal of and interest (including post petition interest), fees (commitment or other), expenses and premium, if any, then due and payable on all Senior Debt shall first be paid in full, or such payment shall have been duly provided for in the manner set forth in the proviso to the next sentence, before any further payment on account of principal or interest, or premium, if any, is made upon the Subordinated Notes. In any of the proceedings referred to above, any payment or distribution of any kind or character, whether in cash, property, stock or obligations, which may be payable or deliverable in respect of the Subordinated Notes shall be paid or delivered directly to the holders of the Senior Debt (or to a banking institution selected by the court or Person making the payment or delivery as designated by any holder of Senior Debt) for application in payment thereof, unless and until all Senior Debt shall have been paid in full, *provided, however*, that in the event that payment or delivery of such cash, property, stock or obligations to the holders of the Subordinated Notes is authorized by a final non-appealable order or decree which takes into account the subordination of the Subordinated Notes to Senior Debt, and made by a court of competent jurisdiction in a reorganization proceedings under any applicable bankruptcy or reorganization law, no payment or delivery of such cash, property, stock or obligations payable or deliverable with respect to the Subordinated Notes shall be made to the holders of Senior Debt. Anything in this Article to the contrary notwithstanding, no payment or delivery shall be made to holders of stock or obligations which are issued pursuant to reorganization, dissolution or liquidation proceedings, or upon any merger, consolidation, sale, lease, transfer or other disposal not prohibited by the provisions of this Agreement, by the Company, as reorganized, or by the corporation succeeding to the Company or acquiring its property and assets, if such stock or obligations are subordinate and junior at least to the extent provided in this Article to the payment of all Senior Debt then outstanding and to payment of any stock or obligations which are issued in exchange or substitution for any Senior Debt then outstanding.

Section 1.4. When Distribution Must Be Paid Over. In the event that the holder of any Subordinated Note shall receive any payment, property, stock or obligations in respect of such Subordinated Note which such holder is not entitled to receive under the provisions of this Article, such holder will hold any amount so received in trust for the holders of Senior Debt and will forthwith turn over such payment to the holders of Senior Debt in the form received to be applied on Senior Debt. In the event of any liquidation, dissolution or other winding up of the Company, or in the event of any receivership, insolvency, bankruptcy, assignment for the benefit of creditors, reorganization or arrangement with creditors, whether or not pursuant to bankruptcy laws, sale of all or substantially all of the assets or any other marshalling of the assets and liabilities of the Company, holders of Subordinated Notes will at the request of holders of Senior Debt file any claim or other instrument of similar character necessary to enforce the obligations of the Company in respect of the Subordinated Notes.

Section 1.5. Subrogation. Upon payment in full of all Senior Debt the holders of the Subordinated Notes shall be subrogated to the rights of the holders of Senior Debt to receive payments of distributions of assets of the Company applicable to Senior Debt until the principal of the premium, if any, and interest on the Subordinated Notes shall have been paid in full, and, for the purposes of such subrogation, no payments to the holders of Senior Debt of any cash, property, stock or obligations which the holders of Subordinated Debt would be entitled to receive except for the provisions of this Article shall, as between the Company and its creditors (other than the holders of Senior Debt) and the holders of the Subordinated Notes, be deemed to be a payment by the Company to or on account of Senior Debt.

Section 1.6. Relative Rights. The provisions of this Article are for the purpose of defining the relative rights of the holders of Senior Debt on the one hand, and the holders of the Subordinated Notes on the other hand, against the Company and its property and nothing herein shall impair, as between the Company and the holders of the Subordinated Notes, the obligation of the Company, which is unconditional and absolute, to pay to the holders thereof the full amount of the principal thereof, and premium, if any, and interest thereon, in accordance with the terms thereof and the provisions hereof, and to comply with all of its covenants and agreements contained herein; nor shall anything herein prevent the holder of any Subordinated Notes from exercising all remedies otherwise permitted by applicable law or hereunder upon Default hereunder or under any Subordinated Note, subject to the rights, if any, under this Article of holders of Senior Debt to receive cash, property, stock or obligations otherwise payable or deliverable to the holders of the Subordinated Notes and subject to the limitations on remedies contained in sections 1.5 and 1.9.

Section 1.7. Subordination May Not be Impaired by Company. No present or future holder of any Senior Debt shall be prejudiced in the right to enforce the subordination of the Subordinated Notes by any act or failure to act on the part of the Company.

Section 1.8. Modification of Terms of Senior Debt. Each holder of Subordinated Notes consents that, without the necessity of any reservation of rights against such holder of Subordinated Notes, and without notice to or further assent by such holder of Subordinated Notes, (a) any demand for payment of any Senior Debt may be rescinded in whole or in part and any Senior Debt may be continued, and the Senior Debt, or the liability of the Company or any other Person upon or for any part thereof, or any collateral security or guaranty therefor or right of offset with respect thereto, and any Senior Debt, may, from time to time, in whole or in part, be renewed, extended, modified, accelerated, compromised, waived, surrendered, or released and (b) any document or instrument evidencing or governing the terms of any Senior Debt or any collateral security documents or guaranties or documents in connection therewith may be amended, modified, supplemented or terminated, in whole or part, as the holders of Senior Debt may deem advisable from time to time, and any collateral security at any time held by such holder or any collateral agent for the benefit of such holders for the payment of any of the Senior Debt may be sold, exchanged, waived, surrendered, or released, in each case all without notice to or further assent by the holders of Subordinated Notes which will remain bound under this Agreement, and all without impairing, abridging, releasing or affecting the subordination provided for herein, notwithstanding any such renewal, extension, modification, acceleration, compromise, amendment, supplement, termination, sale, exchange, waiver, surrender or release. Each holder of Subordinated Notes waives any and all notice of the creating, renewal, extension, or accrual of any of the Senior Debt and notice of or proof of reliance by any holders of Senior Debt upon this Agreement, and the Senior Debt shall conclusively be deemed to have been created, contracted or incurred in reliance upon this Agreement, and all dealings between the Company and the holders of Senior Debt shall be deemed to have been consummated in reliance upon this Agreement. Each holder of Subordinated Notes acknowledges and agrees that the lenders in any refinancing have relied upon the subordination provided for herein in entering into such refinancing and in making funds available to the Company thereunder. Each holder of Subordinated Notes waives notice of or proof of reliance on this Agreement and protest, demand for payment and notice of default.

Section 1.9. Limitations on Rights of Subordinated Noteholders to Accelerate. The right of the holders of Subordinated Notes to declare the Subordinated Notes to be immediately due and payable pursuant to this Agreement upon the occurrence and continuance of an Event of Default under this Agreement shall be subject to the following:

1. if such Event of Default shall arise solely out of a default in specified financial covenants, then such holders may only so declare the Subordinated Notes due and payable if the holder of any Senior Debt shall have declared to be due and payable any obligations of the Company in respect of Senior Debt by reason of a default in respect thereof;

2. if such Event of Default shall arise out of a failure to make payments on the senior debt then such holder may not so declare the Subordinated Notes due and payable until the earliest to occur of (a) the continuance of such Event of Default for 180 consecutive days, (b) the day upon which the next payment is actually made of principal of or interest on any Senior Debt, or (c) the day upon which holders of Senior Debt declare to be due and payable before its normal maturity any obligations of the Company in respect of Senior Debt.

Section 1.10. Definition of Senior Debt. "Senior Debt" means Debt which is not by its terms expressly subordinated in right of payment to other Debt.

"Debt" of any Person means (i) all indebtedness of such Person for borrowed money or for the deferred purchase price of property, (ii) all obligations under leases which shall have been or should be, in accordance with GAAP (as defined herein), recorded as capital leases in respect of which such Person is liable as lessee, (iii) all indebtedness referred to in clause (i) or (ii) above secured by (or for which the holder of such indebtedness has an existing right, contingent or otherwise, to be secured by) any lien, security interest or other charge or encumbrance upon or in property (including, without limitation, accounts and contract rights) owned by such

Person, (iv) all indebtedness referred to in clause (i) or (ii) above guaranteed directly or indirectly in any manner by such Person, or in effect guaranteed directly or indirectly by such Person through an agreement to pay or purchase such indebtedness or to advance or supply funds for the payment or purchase of such indebtedness, or to otherwise assure a creditor against loss, and (v) liabilities in respect of unfunded vested benefits under Plans and withdrawal liability incurred under ERISA by such Person or by such Person as a member of the Controlled Group to any Multiemployer Plan, *provided* that Debt shall not include trade and other accounts payable in the ordinary course of business in accordance with customary trade terms and which are not overdue for a period of more than 60 days, or, if overdue for a period of more than 60 days, as to which a dispute exists and adequate reserves in accordance with GAAP have been established on the books of such Person.

APPENDIX 4C

SUBORDINATION PROVISIONS OF SELLER NOTES

SUBORDINATION

Section 1.1. Agreement to Subordinate. The obligations of the Company in respect of the principal of and interest on the Subordinated Notes shall be subordinate and junior in right of payment, to the extent and in the manner set forth in this Article, to any indebtedness of the Company in respect of Senior Debt.

Section 1.2. Default on Senior Debt of the Company. No payment of principal of or interest or distribution of any kind on the Subordinated Notes shall be made at any time when a default has occurred and is continuing under any Senior Debt, and, if any such payment or distribution is made, then the holder of the Subordinated Notes will hold the same in trust and pay it over to the holders of the Senior Debt.

Section 1.3. Liquidation, Dissolution, Bankruptcy

(a) In the event of any insolvency or bankruptcy proceedings, and any receivership, liquidation, reorganization, arrangement, readjustment, composition or other similar proceedings in connection therewith, relative to the Company or to its creditors, as such, or to its property, or in the event of any proceedings for voluntary liquidation, dissolution or other winding-up of the Company, whether or not involving insolvency or bankruptcy, or in the event of any assignment by the Company for the benefit of creditors or in the event of any other marshalling of the assets of the Company, then the holders of Senior Debt shall be entitled to receive payment in full of all principal, premium, interest, fees and charges on all Senior Debt (including interest thereon accruing after the commencement of any such proceedings) before the holder of the Subordinated Notes is entitled to receive any payment on account of principal or interest upon the Subordinated Notes, and to that end the holders of Senior Debt shall be entitled to receive for application in payment thereof any payment or distribution of any kind or character, whether in cash or property or securities, which may be payable or deliverable in any such proceedings in respect of the Subordinated Notes.

(b) In the event that the Subordinated Notes are declared due and payable before their expressed maturity because of the occurrence of an Event of Default (under circumstances when the provisions of the foregoing clause (1) shall not be applicable), the holders of the Senior Debt outstanding at the time the Subordinated Notes so become due and payable because of such occurrence of such Event of Default shall be entitled to receive payment in full of all principal of, and premium, interest, fees and charges on, all Senior Debt before the holder of the Subordinated Notes is entitled to receive any payment on account of the principal of, or the interest on, the Subordinated Notes.

Section 1.4. Relative Rights and Subrogation.

The provisions of this Article shall not alter or affect, as between the Company and the holder of the Subordinated Notes, the obligations of the Company to pay in full the principal of and interest on the Subordinated Notes, which obligations are absolute and unconditional. In the event that by virtue of this Article any amounts paid or payable to the holder of the Subordinated Notes in respect of the Subordinated Notes shall instead be paid to the holders of Senior Debt, the holder of the Subordinated Notes shall to this extent be subrogated to the rights of such holders; provided, however, that no such rights of subrogation shall be asserted against the Company until the Senior Debt has been paid in full.

Section 1.5. Subordination May Not be Impaired by Company. No present or future holder of Senior Debt shall be prejudiced in his right to enforce the subordination of the Subordinated Notes by any act or failure to act on the part of the Company. This subordination of the Subordinated Notes, and the rights of the holders of Senior Debt with respect thereto, shall not be affected by any amendment or other modification of any Senior Debt or any exercise or nonexercise of any right, power or remedy with respect thereto.

Section 1.6. Modification of Terms of Senior Debt. The holders of Senior Debt may, at any time, in their discretion, renew or extend the time of payment of Senior Debt so held or exercise any of their rights under the Senior Debt including, without limitation, the waiver of defaults thereunder and the amendment of any of the terms or provisions thereof (or any notice evidencing or creating the same), all without notice to or assent from the holder of the Subordinated Notes. No compromise, alteration, amendment, modification, extension, renewal or other change of, or waiver, consent or other action in respect of any liability or obligation under or in respect of, any terms, covenants or conditions of the Senior Debt (or any instrument evidencing or creating the same) and no release of property subject to the lien of the Senior Debt (or any instrument evidencing or creating the same), whether or not such release is in accordance with the provisions of the Senior Debt (or any instrument evidencing or creating the same), shall in any way alter or affect any of the provisions of the Subordinated Notes.

Section 1.7. Restrictions on Holders of Subordinated Notes

(a) The terms of the Subordinated Notes shall not be modified without the prior written consent of the holders of the Senior Debt.

(b) The holder of the Subordinated Notes shall not take any action against the Company with respect to any Event of Default until and unless (i) any event described in Section1.3(a) has occurred, or (ii) a holder of Senior Debt shall have accelerated payment of any Senior Debt obligation of the Company, or (iii) the Senior Debt shall have been paid in full.

(c) The holder of the Subordinated Notes shall provide to the Company, at any time and from time to time, at the Company's request and at no expense to the holder of the Subordinated Notes, a written acknowledgment by the holder of the Subordinated Notes addressed to any holder of Senior Debt to the effect that such holder is a holder of Senior Debt, provided that prior to furnishing such acknowledgment, the holder of the Subordinated Notes shall have received from the Company such information as the holder of the Subordinated Notes shall reasonably request demonstrating to the holder of Subordinated Notes reasonable satisfaction that such holder is a holder of Senior Debt.

Section 1.8. Definition of Senior Debt. "Senior Debt" means (i) any indebtedness of the Company in respect of a certain Revolving Credit and Security Agreement between the Company and [the specific Lender], including any advances or readvances under refunding or refinancings with the same or other lenders of the aforementioned loan agreement, (ii) [specific existing long-term indebtedness of the Company] and (iii) all trade debt of the Company.

CHAPTER 5

STRUCTURING (TAX/NON-TAX)

THE NON-TAX FACTORS

Introduction

The structuring of the transaction—the determination of what form it will take—is often the most challenging aspect of any acquisition. The range of available forms (asset sales, stock transfers, mergers of a variety of types, tender offers, etc.) and the variety of relevant factors, ranging from tax consequences to securities law and accounting issues, provides fertile ground for the imaginative planning needed to coordinate what are often conflicting goals. Added to this hodgepodge are the concerns of lenders for assuring valid security interests in assets of the target. This chapter is devoted to analyzing the tax and certain other considerations that determine what the most efficient or desirable form of the transaction will be. Issues relating to accounting are covered in Chapter 7, and issues unique to the public company arena in Chapter 12.

Although the first part of this chapter will discuss non-tax factors, it is important to recognize that in most cases where the parties have a choice about the structure, the tax considerations will be paramount. This is especially true since the Tax Reform Act of 1986 greatly increased the cost of a sale of assets by a corporation. See pages 245–246.

Do not skip this section on taxes simply because of a fear that it is too arcane or complex. The tax section is designed to accommodate both the neophyte and the person who wants greater depth. Anyone who wants to understand the merger business must have at least a basic understanding of the impact of the tax laws on the structure and economics of an acquisition. *If you want a primer on the basics only, read only those questions marked by an asterisk.* You will be amazed at how much can be learned by the nontax specialist and how much help that learning can be in anticipating or solving problems. You also won't be impressed or confused when people start throwing around terms like "Let's just do a Section 338(h)(10)," "This is a killer after the repeal of General Utilities," or "Section 279 will kill this financing scheme," or "S corporation is our best hope here." Instead, if you choose to, you'll respond in kind with relish and leave others confused or impressed. Yes, you will still need a tax expert, but at least you won't waste the first half hour of each conversation having the basics explained to you. These days, the half hours tend to get expensive.

What are the various forms that a transaction can take?

There are three general forms used for the acquisition of a business: (1) a purchase of the assets of the business; (2) a purchase of the stock of the target owning the assets; (3) a statutory merger of the buyer (or an affiliate) with the target. It is possible to combine several forms so that, for example, some assets of the business are purchased separately from the acquisition of the stock of the company that owns the rest of the assets, and a merger occurs immediately thereafter between the buyer and the acquired company. Or a transaction may involve the purchase of assets of one corporation and the stock of another, where both corporations are owned by the same seller.

What happens in an asset transaction?

The target transfers all of the assets used in the business that is the subject of the sale, including real estate, equipment, and inventory, as well as "intangible" assets like accounts receivable, contract rights, leases, patents, trademarks, etc. These may be all or only part of the assets owned by the selling company. The target executes the specific kinds of documents need-ed to transfer the specific assets, e.g., deeds, bills of sale, assignment.

The buyer also will assume those liabilities that are agreed to. As a general rule, any liabilities not assumed by the buyer remain as liabilities of the target.

When is an asset transaction appropriate?

Many times, the choice of an asset transaction is dictated by the fact that the sale involves only one part of the business owned by the selling corporation. This is true, for example, when the sale involves only one or more divisions of a corporation.

The major advantages of an asset transaction are (1) where the seller will realize taxable gain from the sale (i.e., the tax basis of the assets in the acquired company is lower than the purchase price), the buyer generally will obtain significant tax savings from structuring the transaction as an asset deal and thus stepping up the asset basis to the purchase price. Conversely, if the seller will realize a tax loss, the buyer is generally better off inheriting the tax history of the business by doing a stock transaction, and thus keeping the old high basis. Unfortunately, the opposite effects obtain for the seller. See pages 254–276 for an explanation of these results. (2) In an asset sale, as a legal matter, the buyer generally only assumes the liabilities that it specifically agrees to assume. The exceptions to this rule are discussed below.

Will the buyer be able to avoid all liabilities that it doesn't expressly assume?

The general rule is yes, but there are several exceptions.

In certain jurisdictions, most notably California, the courts have required the buyer of a manufacturing business to assume the tort liabilities for faulty products manufactured by the seller when it controlled the business.

There is also the bulk sales law, explained in greater detail below, which is found in the Uniform Commercial Code, and which is applicable in one form or another in all jurisdictions in the U.S. (except Louisiana). If the parties fail to comply with that law, and there is no available exemption, the buyer can be held liable for certain liabilities of the seller.

Under certain state statutes, if the transaction constitutes what is known as a "fraudulent conveyance," the assets acquired by the buyer can be reached by creditors of the seller. Such statutes do not require actual fraud but can be applicable where the purchase price is not deemed fair consideration and the seller is left insolvent or without sufficient capital to meet its debts. See Chapter 4, pages 127–133.

In certain jurisdictions, if a buyer buys an entire business and the shareholders of the seller become the shareholders of the buyer, there is a doctrine known as the "de facto merger doctrine" that treats the transaction as a merger. In a merger transaction, the buyer takes on all of the seller's liabilities. The de facto merger doctrine is generally not applicable in Delaware, the state where many corporations are incorporated.

A buyer can not usually terminate a union collective bargaining contract by doing an asset sale and not assuming the liabilities under the contract. See Chapter 9, pages 484–529.

What are the disadvantages of an asset sale?

First and foremost is the additional tax cost of doing an asset transaction in many cases after the Tax Reform Act of 1986 (see pages 244–246).

Second, an asset transaction is usually more time consuming and significantly more costly than the alternatives. An asset transaction requires a legal transfer of each asset. Real estate transfers are often subject to significant state and local transfer and recordation taxes. Such transfers may also motivate local tax assessors to increase the assessment of the property and thereby significantly increase the real estate tax burden on the company. If the property is spread over numerous jurisdictions, different forms may be required for each jurisdiction.

Third, many intangible assets and leases may not be assignable without the consent of the other party to the transaction. Assuming the other party is willing to consent (and it isn't always willing), you can expect the other party to exact a price for its consent. This can be especially true where the seller has leases that provide for rent that is below the then prevailing rental rates. It is possible that consent may then be obtained only by agreeing to significant rent increases. The same is true of other types of contracts with terms that are favorable for the target. The loan agreements of the target must also be carefully reviewed to assure that the asset transaction will not trigger default provisions.

Many businesses have local licenses needed to operate their business, and a change of ownership may involve lengthy hearings or other administrative delays as well as a risk of losing the license. Similarly, many businesses are grandfathered, and thus exempt, from the need to make costly improvements to their property required for new property under local fire codes or rules relating to access for the handicapped. The asset transfer can require the implementation of costly improvement programs to conform to such rules.

For these reasons, if an asset transfer is proposed, it is necessary to conduct an in-depth review of all of the legal arrangements of the business to determine whether an asset deal is feasible. If problems are discovered, the parties will have to negotiate about who should have to bear the costs, such as the costs of obtaining consent. Usually, the buyer prevails because the purchase price is premised upon certain cash flows. To the extent that rents or other fees are materially increased, the value of the company is affected.

Finally, the asset transaction may require compliance with, or the risks of failing to comply with, the Bulk Sales Law (see below).

What is the Bulk Sales Law and what effect does it have on asset transactions?

The Bulk Sales Law, subject to variations among states, requires the purchaser of a major part of the material, supplies, merchandise, or other inventory of a seller whose principal business is the sale of merchandise from inventory to give at least 10 days advance notice of the sale to each creditor of the seller. The notice must identify the seller and the buyer and contain a statement whether the debts of the seller will be paid as they fall due. If orderly payment will not be made, further information must be disclosed. In addition, 20 states impose upon the buyer the duty to ensure that the seller applies the consideration received in exchange for the transfer to existing debts and the obligation to hold in escrow an amount sufficient to pay any disputed debts.

Although the requirements of the law are straightforward, its applicability to particular sellers and to particular transactions is ambiguous. For example, notice to creditors is required when more than 50 percent of the inventory stockpiled by an "enterprise" whose principal business is the sale of merchandise from stock is sold as a unit. The failure of the statute to define the term "enterprise" has resulted in uneven application of its provisions, particularly with regard to sales of inventory by diversified, multi-location, and inter-state businesses, because a determination whether the sale meets the "major part" test established by the Bulk Sales Law depends upon the meaning given the term "enterprise." These ambiguities take on prime importance when considered in conjunction with the fact that the parties to a transaction most often wish to avoid compliance with the Bulk Sales Law, particularly the requirements that the purchaser oversee application of the proceeds of the sale and hold in escrow a fund to pay disputed debts.

The parties may escape compliance by structuring the transaction to fall within an exception to the law, allowing the parties to substitute a public notice of the sale for full compliance with the statute. The most often employed exception permits public notice of a transfer to a purchaser who undertakes to pay all disclosed debts of the seller.

If an exception to compliance is not available, the buyer may elect to incorporate into the purchase agreement an indemnity by the seller against claims arising under the Bulk Sales Law. However, this approach may be opposed by the purchaser's secured lenders, whose prime concern is the quality of the security interest in the purchased inventory to be granted by the buyer. In view of the fact that noncompliance with the Bulk Sales Law gives a creditor of the seller whose debt is not timely paid, a claim against the transferred assets superior to the acquisition lender's security interest, a lender may require a particularly strong indemnity from the seller. However, a lender's decision to permit noncompliance with the Bulk Sales Law is most often the result of a business decision that the financial health of the seller and the short statute of limitations for claims under the law make claims against the transferred assets unlikely. Care should be taken to resolve Bulk Sales Law issues as part of the acquisition agreement in advance of closing so that compliance with the law or the exceptions does not delay the transaction.

Are any stockholder approvals required for an asset transaction?

Yes. Under Delaware law, for example, a sale of all or substantially all of the assets requires the approval of persons holding more than 50% of the stock entitled to vote.

Does an asset transaction always involve a cash payment to the seller?

The payment for the assets can be made in any form acceptable to the seller, including the stock of the buyer.

What happens in a "stock" transaction?

The seller transfers its shares in the target to the buyer in exchange for an agreed upon payment. Although the buyer occasionally will buy less than all of the stock in a public company (through a tender offer), it is rare for this to occur in purchases of private corporations, and typically only occurs when some previous stockholder who will be active as a manager of the post-acquisition company retains a stock interest.

When is a stock transaction appropriate?

A stock transaction is appropriate whenever the tax costs or other problems of doing an asset transaction make the asset transaction undesirable. Because of recent tax reforms, asset transfers will occur far less frequently than was the case before in any substantial transaction; they simply produce too onerous a tax cost on the transaction. Apart from tax considerations, a stock deal may be necessary if the transfer of assets would require unobtainable or costly consents or where the size of the company makes an asset deal too inconvenient, time consuming, or costly.

The sellers frequently prefer a stock deal because the buyer will take the corporation's business subject to all of its liabilities. This often is not as big an advantage as it appears, because the buyer will usually seek to be indemnified against any undisclosed liabilities.

Will a stock deal always avoid the problem of obtaining third party consents that often arise in an asset transaction?

No. The pertinent documents must be carefully reviewed for "change of control" provisions. Many recently drafted leases, for example, require consent if there is a change in the control of the tenant. Other contracts or local permits or leases may have similar requirements.

What are the disadvantages of a stock deal?

First, it may be more difficult to consummate the transaction if there are a number of stockholders. Assuming that the buyer wants to acquire 100% of the company, it must enter into a contract with each of the selling stockholders, and any one of them might refuse to enter into the transaction or might refuse to close. The entire deal may hinge on one stockholder. As will be shown below, the parties can achieve the same result as a stock transfer through a merger transaction and avoid the need for 100% agreement among the stockholders. See page 220.

Also, the stock transaction may result in tax disadvantages after the acquisition that can only be avoided by choosing an asset transaction. Under Section 338 of the Internal Revenue

Code, however, it is possible to have most stock transactions treated as asset acquisitions for federal income tax purposes. Thus, the tax benefits can be achieved while avoiding the non-tax pitfalls of an asset transaction. See pages 258–259.

What happens in a merger transaction, and what are the differences between a "reverse merger," a "forward merger," and a "subsidiary merger"?

A merger is a transaction in which one corporation is legally absorbed into another, and the surviving corporation succeeds to all of the assets or liabilities of the absorbed corporation. There are no separate transfers for the assets or liabilities; the entire transfer occurs by operation of law when the certificate of merger is filed with the appropriate authorities of the state.

In a reverse merger the buyer is absorbed by the target. The shareholders of the buyer get stock in the target, and the shareholders of the target receive the consideration agreed to. For example, in an all cash deal, the shareholders of the target will exchange their shares in the target for cash. At the end of the day, the old shareholders of the target are no longer shareholders, and the shareholders of the buyer own the target. For federal tax purposes, a reverse merger is often treated essentially like a stock deal.

In a forward merger, the target merges into the buyer, and the target shareholders exchange their stock for the agreed upon purchase price. When the dust settles, the buyer has succeeded to all the assets and liabilities of the target. For federal income tax purposes, such a transaction is treated as if the target sold its assets for the purchase price and liquidated and distributed the sales proceeds to the target's shareholders as a liquidation distribution.

Although both forms of merger convey the assets in the same simple manner, the forward merger, in which the assets end up in another corporate shell, in certain jurisdictions may violate lease and other contract restrictions the same way a direct asset transfer does. Both the law of the jurisdiction that governs the agreements and the agreements themselves must be checked in such a case. It is rare for a reverse merger to violate the agreements of the target unless the agreement requires consent for a change of control of the target or there are net worth tests which must be met by the survivor of the merger. Similarly, in some jurisdictions, recordation taxes may be due after a forward merger when the buyer seeks to record the deeds in its name to reflect the merger.

A "subsidiary merger" is simply a merger where the buyer corporation incorporates an acquisition subsidiary which merges with the target. In a reverse subsidiary merger, the acquisition subsidiary merges into the target; in a forward subsidiary merger, the target is merged into the acquisition subsidiary. Various forms of reverse, forward, and subsidiary mergers are presented in Exhibits 5.3 through 5.7 on pages 342–344.

What steps must be taken to effect a merger?

Generally, the board of directors of each corporation that is a party to the merger adopts a resolution approving an agreement of merger and the shareholders owning a majority of the stock must approve the transaction. In some cases the corporate charter may require a higher percentage for shareholder approval. The merger becomes effective upon the filing of a certificate of merger. Under Delaware law the approval of the surviving corporation's stockholders will not be necessary if its certificate of incorporation will not be amended by the merger and if the shares of the survivor issued to the sellers comprise less than 20% of the outstanding shares of the survivor.

The agreement between buyer and seller in the case of a merger is essentially the same as in a stock or asset deal, except that the means of transferring the business is the statutory merger as opposed to a stock or asset transfer. (See Chapter 10, "Negotiating the Acquisition Agreement and the Letter of Intent," for a discussion of a typical merger/acquisition agreement.)

What are the advantages of using a merger?

The merger method has many of the advantages of a stock deal: it is simple and will generally avoid the problems of an asset transaction. This is particularly true of a reverse subsidiary merger. Since the advent of the Section 338 election for tax purposes, using a reverse merger to avoid asset transfer problems will not preclude taking advantage of the tax benefits of an asset deal. If certain conditions are met, the Internal Revenue Code allows the taxpayer that uses a reverse merger to elect to treat the transaction as an asset deal. See pages 258–261 for a discussion of the rules and for the consequences of a Section 338 election.

A merger agreement, unlike a stock deal, is executed only with the target company and generally must be approved by a majority or some specified super majority percentage of the stockholders. Thus, the deal does not depend upon reaching an agreement with each stockholder or upon each stockholder consummating the transaction. The stockholders who dissent from the transaction are forced to go along as a matter of law. They do have certain dissenter's rights, however, that purport to assure that the minority's economic rights are protected. See pages 222–223.

Under what circumstances is a stock acquisition combined with a merger?

In certain cases a stock deal is combined with a merger transaction. The first step is an acquisition of part of the stock (usually at least a majority) of the target; the second step is a merger with the target.

Two-step transactions are useful if the buyers wish to pay a majority stockholder a premium for his control block, a premium that generally is permissible under most state laws. The buyer would buy that stock separately and then in a second step vote the majority stock to approve a merger transaction. The balance of the stock owned by the selling shareholders would be exchanged in the merger for a lesser purchase price that reflects the absence of a control premium. (Federal law may prevent this for publicly held targets. See Chapter 12.)

Another use for two-step transactions arises where part of the consideration consists of notes or preferred stock in the survivor and there is a desire to limit the persons to whom the noncash payments are to be made. The first step would consist of a stock deal with certain of the stockholders where the consideration includes notes, etc., and the second step would be an all-cash merger. This may be important, for example, if there are many individual shareholders and the distribution of the securities to all of them would constitute a public offering that would require the filing of a registration statement under the securities laws. See pages 227–231 for the role of securities laws in structuring the transactions. This also may be useful where certain of the sellers want to encourage a positive vote of the stockholders by absorbing the risk of holding notes or equity in the target and allowing the other stockholders to receive the full purchase price in cash.

Two-step transactions are very common in public company acquisitions where the first step is the acquisition of a control block through a tender offer which is followed by a second step merger in which the minority is bought out. See Chapters 12.

When is a "subsidiary merger" desirable?

A merger generally must be approved by the stockholders of each corporation that is a party to the merger, but this requirement does not apply to a merger of a subsidiary into its 90% or more parent. Where the acquiring corporation is a public corporation, it is generally not desirable to have to obtain from the acquiring corporation's stockholders consent to the transaction (because of the expense, delays, and inconvenience of filing the necessary proxy statement with the SEC under the securities laws and conducting a shareholder's meeting). The acquiring entity will use a subsidiary merger because then only the board of directors, and not the shareholders, of the acquiring entity must approve the transaction on behalf of the acquiring entity.

After a subsidiary merger, the buyer owns the target's business in a subsidiary. This has the effect of keeping the businesses legally separate and not subjecting the assets of the parent to the liabilities of the acquired business. The shareholders of the target must of course consent to the merger.

What are dissenters' rights, and are they available only as a result of a merger?

The answer depends upon state law and varies from state to state. The state of incorporation of the target will govern the dissenters' rights. In most jurisdictions, a dissenting stockholder from a merger transaction approved by the necessary percentage of stockholders of the target has the right to have his stock appraised by a court and to have the surviving corporation pay that value in cash for its shares in lieu of the consideration agreed to in the approved merger. The law thus assures the minority shareholders that they cannot be forced to accept a deal that does not reflect the fair value of the stock. Procedures outlined in the state statutes must be carefully followed by the dissenters if their rights are to be preserved.

Under Delaware law, the appraisal rights are not available if the shares that are subject to the appraisal rights are listed on a national securities exchange or are held of record by more than 2,000 stockholders.

Are dissenters' rights available only for merger transactions?

No. Under Delaware law a corporation can allow the dissenters' rights to apply to asset sale transactions and other transactions that require an amendment to the certificate of incorporation. Many other states require this result. An example of such a transaction would be a "reverse split," where the certificate of incorporation is amended to reduce the outstanding shares by converting them into a smaller number of shares. For example, through an amendment to the certificate of incorporation, each 500 shares of common stock could be mandatorily converted into a single share. Each shareholder would exchange his shares for new shares at the prescribed ratio. Cash will typically be issued in lieu of fractional shares, so that a person with 750 shares would receive one new share and cash equal to the value of the 250 shares (which otherwise would have been exchanged for one half of a new share). If the certificate of incorporation so provides, the shareholders receiving cash in lieu of fractional shares can have a right to dissent and require appraisal of their shares.

Why would a corporation give such rights to dissenters voluntarily?

Giving these rights may make sense when there is a concern that the dissenters might try to enjoin the transaction. Assuming the parties are dealing fairly, the availability of the appraisal right should greatly reduce the possibility of a successful action for an injunction, since the dissenter, as an alternative, may receive the value of his or her stock interest, and the courts are reluctant in such a case to permit other remedies (particularly under Delaware law).

Are dissenters' rights significant to a transaction?

They can be. Where the parties propose to treat a transaction as a pooling rather than as a purchase (see pages 403–413), there are strict limitations on the amount of cash consideration that can be paid. There are also similar restrictions on cash payments in certain types of tax-free reorganizations. (See pages 283–284.) As a result, it is not uncommon to provide as a condition to closing that no more than a limited percentage of the stockholders shall have applied for dissenters' rights. A similar concern arises in a highly leveraged transaction. The lenders are concerned if there are significant numbers of dissenters because of the risk that the cash outlay for the transaction could be materially increased if the appraisal value is much greater than the agreed upon merger price, or if the agreed upon merger price is to be paid partially in notes while dissenters will receive all cash.

Notwithstanding the availability of the dissenters' rights, they do not usually cause a problem in an arm's length transaction between buyer and seller because it is unlikely that a court will find a higher value than the agreed upon purchase price. There is a greater risk, and hence a need for greater care, in a management buyout where corporate insiders will own the surviving corporation because such a transaction is more susceptible to a challenge that the price isn't fair. (See Chapter 6.)

What is the most typical form for a leveraged buyout?

The buyer usually incorporates an acquisition corporation solely for the purpose of merging with the target. Usually the acquisition corporation does a reverse merger into the target. If the buyer wants a holding company structure, i.e., wants the target to be a subsidiary of a holding company, it forms a holding company with an acquisition corporation subsidiary. After the merger, the holding company will own all of the stock of the target, and the buyer owns all the stock of the holding company.

Why do mergers seem to be the most common form of transfer these days? Does it have anything to do with the lenders in leveraged buyouts?

The practical benefits described above, plus the practical necessity of using mergers as part of most public deals (due to the number of shareholders and the tax and logistical problems associated with asset deals in large corporations), make mergers the star of today's acquisition stage. But there is another very important reason.

The discussion of financing in Chapter 4 shows that in leveraged transactions there is almost always a layer of senior secured debt. The senior lender wants security interests in the assets of the target and usually prefers to lend directly to the entity that will own the assets. In a stock deal, the buyer ends up owning stock of the target. If the senior lender lends to the buyer, it will obtain a security interest in the stock of the target. As a practical matter, that means that all of the creditors of the target, including trade creditors and persons who prevail in lawsuits against the target and then become what are called "judgment creditors" of the target, will get paid before the lenders if the target goes bankrupt. This is so because, after foreclosing on the stock of the target, the lender stands in the shoes of an equity owner and is not a direct creditor of the target. Of course, the lender could obtain a secured guaranty by the target of the buyer's acquisition debt, but the resulting debt and security interests may be very susceptible to being voided as a "fraudulent conveyance." See pages 127–133 for a discussion of "fraudulent conveyances." The best format from the secured lender's point of view is a merger in which the lender lends to the surviving corporation and obtains a security interest in the assets of that corporation; the loan proceeds are being used to satisfy the obligation to pay off the stockholders of the target.

Does the lender always prefer a merger format involving a direct loan to the target? Don't lenders sometimes prefer loans to a holding company that owns the target?

In certain cases the real value of the company lies in a sale of the business as a going concern and not in a piecemeal transaction. This is true where the business depends upon a valuable license, e.g., a TV station, or where there are relatively few assets producing substantial earnings (an "earnings-based deal"). Also in certain cases the target may own a number of operating subsidiaries, and it may not be advisable to merge all of the subsidiaries up into a single entity, e.g., because of the need to keep the litigation or other potential liabilities of each subsidiary separated. This is especially true where the subsidiaries are engaged in activities that are prone to substantial litigation or environmental liabilities, e.g., amusement parks, chemical manufacturing, etc. With separate subsidiaries, an extraordinary loss by one entity generally won't taint the operations of the other subsidiaries.

In such cases the senior lender may prefer to have a transaction structured in a holding company arrangement. In such a structure, the senior lender lends to a corporation (the holding company) that acquires the stock of the target. The senior lender obtains a senior security interest in the stock of the target, and if there are loan defaults the lender can foreclose and sell the stock to obtain proceeds to have its debt repaid. For this structure to succeed, all the layers of financing must be made at the holding company level. If the junior lenders were to lend directly to the target, they would in effect become senior to the senior lender. This is so because the senior lender's rights would be limited to becoming a stockholder of the target by foreclosing on its security interest in the stock. Unlike the junior lender, it would have no direct claim as a creditor of the target. In a workout or bankruptcy of the target, the junior lenders would get paid before the senior lenders who are trapped up in the holding company.

In a holding company structure, the senior lender will often ask for a secured guarantee from the target, notwithstanding the fraudulent conveyance risks. (See pages 130–132.) It can be expected that the junior lenders will ask for a backup guarantee in such a case. Otherwise the senior lender could theoretically proceed directly against the target, and the junior lender, trapped at the holding company level with no direct claim against the target, would have no vote as a creditor in a financial workout of the target. This adds a layer of complexity to the intercreditor negotiations, a factor a buyer never relishes, but generally is not problematic. However, where the junior loan is debt sold in a public offering, and where there are several subsidiaries, each guarantor subsidiary will be viewed as a separate issuer, for Securities Act purposes, which greatly complicates, and increases the cost of, compliance with the securities laws when the debt is sold. Although complicated, the public issuance of such debt would not be precluded under such circumstances. (See also Chapter 4, pages 193–195.)

If a holding company structure is desirable, must it be accomplished by the buyer doing a stock acquisition of the target?

No. A corporate buyer can incorporate a subsidiary and use it to merge with the target (a "subsidiary merger"). After the merger (whether it is a reverse merger or a forward merger) the buyer winds up owning the stock of the target or a corporation that has succeeded to its assets. This structure enables the buyer to get into the preferred holding company format while availing itself of the benefits of doing the acquisition as a merger.

A "subsidiary merger" is also often used in connection with a Section 338 election. In order to make the election the buyer must be a corporation. The buyer sets up the subsidiary and causes it to merge into the target (a "reverse subsidiary merger") which for tax purposes is treated as a stock deal.

Are there any other lender concerns that impact on structure?

When the target is part of a consolidated group of corporations, and the senior lender wants a security interest in all of the assets of each member of the group, it may be desirable to include in the structuring plans a merger of all of the entities into a single corporation to which the lender will lend the acquisition funds and from which it will obtain the security interests in all of the assets. The lenders will greatly prefer this type of loan to a loan to the target guaranteed on a secured basis by each of the subsidiaries. Such guarantees are susceptible to attack as fraudulent conveyances which would cause the lender's security interest to be voided as against other creditors of the subsidiary even if the rest of the transaction withstands such an attack.

The preferred approach is to have the consolidating merger occur immediately before the actual acquisition merger. Alternatively, the acquisition merger agreement can provide that the target shareholders will receive a demand note of the target in exchange for their stock as part of the merger. Immediately after the acquisition merger, as a result of which the buyer owns the target, all the subsidiaries of the target can be merged up into the target. The lender would lend to the target and obtain a security interest in the assets of the target (now including the assets of the entire consolidated group).

The parties must consider the fact that eliminating the group through the upstream mergers may create some of the same problems as an asset transfer or otherwise may be undesirable if there is a strong need to operate the subsidiaries as separate legal entities, e.g., because of liability fears.

What is the role of federal securities laws in acquisition structuring?

The securities laws tend to have their greatest impact when the target is a public company. The securities law and other consideration in such transactions are considered at length in Chapter 12.

The securities laws also impact upon the structure of corporate acquisitions of private companies. When a buyer issues consideration other than cash, say, notes or stock, or where the merger agreement provides that the stockholders of the target will receive notes, stock, or warrants in exchange for their stock, the noncash consideration is almost certainly a security for federal and state securities law purposes.

When the sellers receive securities in connection with a merger, or a sale of assets (where the securities will be distributed to the stockholders of the seller) requiring approval of the target stockholders, Rule 145 under the Securities Act provides that the transaction is an offer to sell the securities. If the offer constitutes a "public offering", the transaction may not take place unless there is a registration statement that has been declared effective under the Securities Act. These rules would apply, for example, (1) where a buyer uses a reverse merger and where the target survives as a subsidiary of the buyer, and the target stockholders get notes or preferred stock or warrants of the target or of the buyer (if the buyer is a corporation), or (2) where the buyer sets up a corporation that buys the stock of the target in exchange for cash and notes or other securities of the corporation.

There is nothing at all wrong with doing a transaction involving a public offering of this type, but the parties have to be aware of the expense and delays involved. The registration statement must be prepared and filed with the SEC. Assuming adequate audited financial statements are readily available (at least three years of balance sheets and two years of income statements), and often they are not, it will take several weeks to prepare an adequate registration statement for filing with the SEC, and it will take 45–60 days for the SEC to complete its review. The process is not cheap. Also, after the offering, the entity which issued the stock will be a company that is "public," and it may be required to file regular reports under the Securities and Exchange Act of 1934. The hassles and expense should be avoided if they can be. Where possible, the transaction should be structured as a "private placement" rather than a public offering.

The concept of private placement is discussed in the next

question, but one key test of whether there is a public offering is the number of offerees. One useful technique for reducing the number of people who will receive the security is to do a reverse stock split before the merger occurs. (See pages 222–223 for a description of how such a procedure works). If cash is paid in lieu of fractional shares, the reverse stock split will reduce the number of shareholders who, in the merger, would receive securities. The reduction of the shareholders through the split to a few wealthy individuals or substantial corporations may permit the offering to be treated as a private placement.

Private Placement

What is a private placement?

A private placement is a transaction in which securities are offered and sold in reliance on an exemption from the registration requirements under federal and state securities laws. Typically, the entity selling its securities (i.e., the "issuer") will rely on the exemption from registration provided by Section 4(2) of Regulation D of the Securities Act of 1933. If an exemption for the transaction is not available, the issuer will be required to "register" the offering under federal and state securities laws.

The registration procedure requires the preparation and filing of documents that provide detailed information about the issuer, the offering, and the securities being sold. Such offering materials must be submitted for review and comment by the Securities and Exchange Commission and comparable state regulatory authorities, and must be declared "effective" before securities may be sold publicly.

What are the requirements for a private placement?

In contrast with a registered offering of securities, or a "public offering", a private placement may only be directed to certain select types of investors and generally, to a limited number of such investors. In addition, the securities purchased are subject to resale restrictions and, consequently, are relatively illiquid in comparison with publicly registered securities. In a Section 4(2) transaction, the investors must have a demonstrable relationship with the issuer so as to have access to information substantially equivalent to that which would be provided in a registration statement in a public offering. In general, each investor should be sophisticated regarding financial and investment matters and should have sufficient wealth to afford a long-term investment in the securities without need for liquidity.

Historically, the rule of thumb as to the number of investors permitted to participate in a 4(2) transaction was 25 or fewer. This purportedly insured the private nature of the transaction and, thereby, the validity of the exemption from registration under the securities laws. It also came to be accepted that a more flexible rule should be available for sophisticated "institutional investors" such as insurance companies, pension funds and mutual funds.

Regulation D was enacted in 1982 to provide more certainty that the exemption from registration would be available. Regulation D consists of a series of rules regarding required disclosures, the manner of offering of the securities, and the number and types of investors to whom the securities may be sold. To the extent the private placement is made in substantial compliance with Regulation D, the issuer can be confident that the transaction is exempt from registration.

A brief notice of sale on federal Form D must be filed with the Securities and Exchange Commission for informational purposes. There is, however, no federal review or comment process for a Regulation D private placement.

Regulation D broadened the availability of the exemption from registration by permitting up to 35 nonaccredited investors to participate in a Regulation D private placement and an unlimited number of "accredited" investors. An "accredited investor" is defined under Regulation D to include wealthy individuals, entities with substantial net worth, certain of the traditional "institutional" investors as well as executive officers and directors of the issuer. Anyone who does not fit within the definition of "accredited" is considered nonaccredited.

In transactions where up to 35 nonaccredited investors purchase securities in an unregistered offering, Regulation D requires that information similar to that provided in a registration statement be provided in a disclosure statement (a "private placement memorandum") to all investors in the Regulation D offering. To the extent, however, that the issuer directs offers to only "accredited" investors, there are no express disclosure requirements under Regulation D.

THE ROLE OF TAX PLANNING

Introduction

Effective tax planning for a change in ownership of a corporate business is crucial. The potentially high tax costs of acquiring, operating, and selling a corporation or its assets mean that proficient tax planning can make or break a deal. Governments—federal, state, local and, on occasion, foreign—are silent partners in every business venture, and their share of profits may exceed that of the owners. Comprehensive acquisition-to-disposition tax planning should be given the same priority, attention, and degree of expertise as the negotiations with the opposing party and lenders.

A discussion of all tax matters relevant to an acquisition, divestiture, or reorganization is beyond the scope of this work. The federal income tax laws are far too complicated to be distilled and succinctly presented in a relatively brief presentation. Instead, this chapter sets forth the most basic tax concepts and the most common issues that arise in mergers, acquisitions, divestitures, and reorganizations. The following discussion is nothing more than a primer on certain tax concepts for persons with a basic understanding of the federal income tax laws; it is no substitute for the professional advice necessary for effective tax planning.

Tax Goals and Issues

What are the principal goals of tax planning for a merger, acquisition, or divestiture?

From the purchaser's point of view, the principal goal of tax planning is to minimize, on a present value basis, the total tax costs of acquiring, operating, and selling the target corporation or its assets. Pre-acquisition tax planning decisions may significantly affect the taxation of the target's post-acquisition operations and disposition. In addition, effective tax planning provides various safeguards to protect the parties from the risks of potential changes in circumstance or the tax laws. Moreover, the purchaser should consider the tax costs of the transaction to the seller. In the increasingly competitive acquisition market, the ability to minimize the tax costs to the seller may determine the successful bidder.

From the seller's point of view, the principal goal of tax planning is to maximize, on a present value basis, the after-tax proceeds from the sale of the target corporation or its assets. This tax planning includes, among other things, devising the target's structure prior to its acquisition, developing techniques to provide tax benefits to a potential buyer at little or no tax cost to the seller, and structuring the receipt of tax-deferred consideration from the buyer.

Are the tax planning goals of the buyer generally consistent with those of the seller?

Generally, no. More often than not, the most advantageous tax plan for the buyer is the least advantageous plan for the seller. For example, the tax benefit of a high basis in the assets of the target corporation may be available to the purchaser only at a significant tax cost to the seller. As a practical matter, the immediate and prospective tax costs of a transaction are likely to affect the price that a seller is willing to accept or that a buyer is willing to offer. Generally, the parties will structure the transaction to minimize the aggregate tax costs of the seller and buyer, and allocate the tax burden between them through an adjustment in price.

At what stage of the transaction should a tax adviser be consulted?

A tax adviser should be consulted as soon as the seller or buyer gives serious consideration to the disposition or acquisition of the target company. In any event, the advice of a tax practitioner is essential prior to earnest negotiations. If the tax structure and, therefore, the tax costs of the deal are not established, an agreement on price between the parties will likely be either tentative or regrettable. Where "negotiations" are being conducted by competitive bids, early tax analysis and structuring may be decisive in producing, and living with, a winning bid.

*What tax issues typically arise in a divestiture or acquisition?

There is no definitive checklist of tax issues that may arise in every acquisition or divestiture. The specific tax considerations for a transaction depend upon the facts and circumstances of that particular deal. Certain tax issues, however, many of which are interrelated, are far more common than others. Several of these are identified here and addressed in more detail in the balance of the chapter.

One of the initial questions to be resolved in many acquisitions is the so-called choice of entity issue: whether the operating entity will be a C corporation, an S corporation, or a general or limited partnership.

A related issue concerns the basic structure of the transaction: whether the transfer is effected as a stock acquisition or as an asset acquisition. The optimal structure is generally that which maximizes the aggregate tax benefits and minimizes the aggregate tax costs of the transaction to the target corporation, the seller, and the buyer.

The tax implications of the financing arrangement must be analyzed. Two key issues are the debt/equity distinction and the effect of the original issue discount rules.

The issue of management participation and compensation should be addressed. Top-level managers of the target may be invited to purchase stock, or they may be granted stock options, stock appreciation rights, bonuses, or some other form of incentive compensation. Different structures of management participation may create vastly different tax results. These considerations are dealt with in Chapter 6.

Tax advisers should examine the tax effects that the proposed structure will have on the post-acquisition operations of the target company. Consideration should generally be given to, for example, net operating loss and credit carrybacks and carryforwards; the alternative minimum tax; foreign tax credits; earnings and profits; depreciation; planned asset dispositions; elections of taxable year and accounting methods; integration of the target's accounting methods into the buyer's existing operations; and the interrelationships among the differing tax systems of the United States and other countries in which the target does business.

Tax advisers should also give attention to the effects of state tax laws, the tax consequences of future distributions of the target's earnings, and the ultimate disposition of the target corporation or its assets. These issues and all others should be analyzed with an eye on pending tax legislation and revisited whenever tax law developments require.

Does the Internal Revenue Service play a direct role in the consummation of business acquisitions?

Unlike certain transactions regulated by the Interstate Commerce Commission, the Federal Communications Commission, or the Federal Trade Commission, one is not required to obtain advance approval from the Internal Revenue Service before consummating an acquisition, divestiture, or reorganization. Ordinarily, the IRS will not have occasion to review a transaction, unless and until an agent audits the tax return of one of the participants.

An important and often useful exception to this rule is that the parties to a transaction can often obtain a private letter ruling issued by the National Office of the IRS. The ruling will state the agency's position with respect to the issues raised. Private letter rulings are binding upon the IRS, to the extent that the transaction actually consummated by the taxpayer conforms to that described in the letter ruling. Although timing or other considerations may ultimately prevent one from obtaining a private letter ruling, this avenue should be kept in mind at all times.

What role do state and local taxes play in structuring mergers and acquisitions?

For a number of reasons, state and local taxes generally play a secondary role in planning acquisitions and divestitures. First, most state income tax systems are based largely on the federal system, particularly in terms of determinations of what is taxable, to whom, when, and in what amount. Second, where a target corporation operates in a number of states, it could be inordinately difficult to take account in basic structural planning of the interaction of the various state tax systems. On the other hand, serious and embarrassing mistakes have been made by tax planners who ignored the state tax consequences. Although a detailed discussion of state income tax consequences deserves a book on its own, several extremely important state tax issues will be mentioned throughout the following discussion.

Beyond income taxes, there are numerous taxes imposed by states and localities that may impact an acquisition, usually in the form of increased costs rather than structural prohibitions or incentives as to structure. For example, where assets are being acquired in connection with an overall business acquisition, the transaction is usually exempt from a state's sales tax. This should not be taken for granted, however, and it is crucial that the availability of such an exemption be confirmed. Where real estate is being transferred, there will often be unavoidable real property gain, transfer, or deed recordation taxes. Perhaps the most notorious of the real property gain and transfer taxes worth mentioning specifically are those imposed by New York State and New York City, respectively, upon certain sales of real estate and of controlling interests in entities holding real estate.

Certain types of state and local taxes that one would not associate directly with an acquisition can be significantly affected by an acquisition or by the particular structure of the acquisition. For example, a state's real property and personal property taxes are based upon an assessment of the value of the property owned by a taxpayer. Often, a transfer of ownership of the property will either by operation of law or as a matter of practice trigger a reassessment of the value of the property.

DEFINITIONS AND BASIC TAX CONCEPTS, TAXATION OF C CORPORATIONS, AND PASS-THROUGH ENTITIES

In order to understand the major tax issues in structuring acquisitions, one must first become familiar with a number of fundamental concepts and terms in the taxation of business entities and their owners. Without this basic information, it will be virtually impossible to appreciate the tax planning issues involved in even the simplest of acquisitions. Equipped with this information, the reader will have gone a long way to understanding the core issues at stake in tax structuring.

Definitions and Basic Tax Concepts

What is basis?

A taxpayer's basis in an asset is the value at which the taxpayer carries the asset on its tax balance sheet. An asset's basis is initially its historical cost to the taxpayer, and the initial basis is subsequently adjusted for receipts, losses, allowances for depreciation, expenditures, and other items chargeable against or allocable to the asset. The taxpayer's initial basis, as increased by capital expenditures and decreased by depreciation, amortization, and other charges, is the taxpayer's "adjusted basis" in the asset. Upon the sale or exchange of the asset, gain or loss for tax purposes is measured by the difference between the amount realized for the asset and its adjusted basis. The basis of the asset represents, in effect, the amount at which the cost of the asset may be recovered free of tax through depreciation deductions and adjustments to gain or loss upon disposition.

What is ACRS?

In 1981, Congress replaced the traditional rules for tax depreciation with the Accelerated Cost Recovery System (ACRS). The principal change brought about by ACRS was the institution of accelerated, short-life depreciation as a norm, designed to promote capital investment and growth in the economy. Under ACRS, each asset is assigned a specific recovery period, and the cost of the asset is written off or "recovered" according to a predetermined rate over the recovery period of the asset.

In 1986, Congress substantially modified ACRS. The modified system works in essentially the same manner as the ACRS, the principal difference being that the revised system is less generous with respect to certain assets. One type of property that suffered was real estate; the recovery period for nonresidential real property, for example, was extended from 19 years to 31.5 years.

What are the Original Issue Discount (OID) rules?

In recent years, Congress and the Treasury Department have enacted an extensive set of rules and regulations designed to ensure that taxpayers properly account for the interest component of deferred payments. While these rules are broadly categorized under the title original issue discount, or OID, they include rules governing the characterization of a payment as interest or principal, rules requiring the recognition of or "imputing" interest income and deductions to the lender and borrower, rules setting forth the treatment of related party transactions involving below-market financing, and rules concerning market discount and premium. The OID rules are discussed in greater detail later in conjunction with the discussion of financing the acquisition.

What is a distribution?

A corporate distribution means an actual or constructive transfer of cash or other property (with certain exceptions) by a corporation to a shareholder acting in the capacity of a shareholder. For tax purposes, a transfer of property to a shareholder acting in the capacity of an employee or lender, for example, is not a corporate distribution.

What is a liquidation?

The status of liquidation exists when the corporation ceases to be a going concern, and its activities are merely for the purpose of winding up its affairs, paying its debts, and distributing its remaining assets to its shareholders in complete cancellation or redemption of all of its stock. A liquidation for tax purposes may be completed prior to the actual dissolution of the corporation under state law.

What is a liquidating distribution?

A liquidating distribution is generally one (or one of a series) made by a liquidating corporation in accordance with a plan of complete liquidation.

What is a nonliquidating distribution?

A nonliquidating distribution is any distribution by a corporation to a shareholder that is not a liquidating distribution. A nonliquidating distribution is generally, but not always, either a dividend or a distribution in redemption of some, but not all, of the corporation's outstanding stock.

What are earnings and profits?

The term "earnings and profits" is a term of art in the Internal Revenue Code (the "Code"). The amount of a corporation's earnings and profits is roughly equivalent to a corporation's net income and retained earnings for financial reporting purposes, as distinguished from current or accumulated taxable income. The primary purpose of the earnings and profits concept is to measure the capacity of a corporation to distribute a taxable dividend. Certain nonliquidating distributions are treated as dividends to the extent of a corporation's current and accumulated earnings and profits.

What is an affiliated group of corporations?

An affiliated group of corporations consists of two or more "member" corporations where the "parent" corporation owns, directly or indirectly, 80 percent or more of the stock of each of the "subsidiary" corporations. More precisely, the parent corporation must generally own 80 percent of the voting power and equity value of at least one of the subsidiary corporations; and the 80% of voting power and equity value of each member corporation (except the parent corporation) must be owned by other members of the group. Certain corporations, such as foreign corporations, are not permitted to be members of an affiliated group.

What is a consolidated federal income tax return?

An affiliated group of corporations has the privilege of making a single federal income tax return in lieu of a separate return for each member of the group. That single return is referred to as a consolidated return.

Not all states allow an affiliated group of corporations to file a combined (consolidated) tax return. Some states do not allow combined returns at all, while others allow them only in limited circumstances.

What are the advantages of filing consolidated federal income tax returns?

The basic principle of the consolidated return provisions is that the members of the affiliated group are treated as a single "entity" whose tax is based upon the aggregate profits and losses of the individual members, disregarding or "eliminating" the profits and losses arising from transactions between members of the group. The principal advantages of a consolidated return are that (i) losses incurred by one member of the group may be used to offset the taxable income of another member; (ii) the tax consequences of many intragroup transactions are either deferred or wholly eliminated; and (iii) earnings of the subsidiary corporations are reflected in the parent's basis in the stock of the subsidiary, so that such earnings are not taxed again on the sale of such stock by the parent. Many tax planning opportunities exist with respect to consolidated return groups.

Obviously, the advantages of combined (consolidated) tax returns are not available with respect to state income taxes, if the state requires the members of the group to file separate returns. As a result, a group may suffer an overall tax loss and still owe state taxes, intergroup transactions may be taxed, and a subsidiary's earnings may be taxed several times.

What is a tax year?

Every entity and individual that is required to file a tax return must do so on the basis of an annual accounting period. For individuals the annual accounting period is almost always the calendar year. For other entities, however, the tax accounting period may be either a calendar year or a fiscal year ending on the last day of a month other than December. An entity's tax year need not coincide with its fiscal year for purposes of financial accounting. Extensive rules govern the selection of tax years other than calendar years by C corporations, S corporations, partnerships, and trusts, which are designed largely to curb abuses.

Can tax savings be obtained through proper selection of a tax year?

Although in many cases, particularly with respect to pass-through entities, there is ultimately little flexibility regarding the choice of a tax year, there are opportunities for tax savings in this area. For example, the ACRS rules provide that personal property is deemed placed in service at the mid-point of a taxable year, under the half-year convention. Thus, if Corporation X purchases assets in January of year 1 and selects a calendar tax year, it will derive only one-half year's ACRS deduction for its first year (as the assets are deemed to be placed in service on July 1). Because C corporations not included in a consolidated return are permitted to choose any tax year they wish,

Corporation X may elect a fiscal tax year ending on January 31. As a result, the half-year convention will be applied only with respect to its initial short year ending on January 31 of year 1, and it can begin to take a full year's ACRS deduction for its tax year beginning February 1.

Where the target is initially a C corporation that the buyer wishes to convert to an S corporation, substantial tax savings can be obtained through tax-year planning. The goal of such planning is to arrange for the S election to be effective as soon after the acquisition as possible. In such cases, an S election will often not be available until the beginning of the target's second taxable year after the acquisition. Because very substantial tax savings can result from an early S election, it is extremely useful to arrange for the target to initially adopt a fiscal year ending shortly after the acquisition date.

Taxation of Corporations and Shareholders

What is the federal income tax rate structure?

The Tax Reform Act of 1986 revised the federal income tax rate structure in three significant respects. First, the maximum corporate and individual tax rates were reduced to 34 percent and 28 percent, respectively. Second, for the first time in decades, the maximum tax rate on corporate income was set at a level in excess of the maximum tax rate on individual income. And third, the preferential tax rate for capital gains was abolished. These changes significantly affect the traditional tax strategies for certain acquisitions and divestitures, particularly the choice of entity issue.

Is the distinction between capital gains and ordinary income still relevant in tax planning?

Yes. Congress explicitly retained the myriad rules and complexities in the Internal Revenue Code (the "Code") pertaining to capital gains and losses. This was done with the expectation that, at some point in the future, Congress may reintroduce the capital gains preference. In fact, in the Tax Reform Act of 1986, Congress lengthened the holding period for long-term capital gains from six months to one year. More important for tax planning is that the Code retains various limitations on the use of capital losses to offset ordinary income. Thus, attention still must be paid to the characterization of income or loss as capital or ordinary, and to the determination of the holding period of capital assets as short-term or long-term.

*What is the significance of the relationship between the corporate and individual tax rates?

Until recent years, corporations were used to accumulate profits because the tax rate on the income of corporations was less than the tax rate on the income of individuals. Moreover, a shareholder's tax on the sale or liquidation of his interest in the corporation was determined at preferential capital gains rates. The Tax Reform Act of 1986 decidedly changed this tax strategy by reducing the maximum individual tax rate to a level below the maximum corporate tax rate and by eliminating the capital gains preference. Moreover, the Tax Reform Act of 1986 repealed most methods by which taxpayers could avoid the double tax on corporate earnings. As a result, the accumulation of profits in corporations will generally be more costly than accumulating profits in pass-through entities.

*Are the earnings of a corporation also taxed to the shareholders of the corporation?

The Code sets forth a dual system of taxation with respect to the earnings of corporations. Under this system, a corporation is taxed as a separate entity, unaffected by the characteristics of its shareholders; the corporation's shareholders are also subject to tax on the income from the corporation, if and when corporate earnings are distributed to them.

What are the practical consequences of the dual system of corporate taxation?

The primary consequence of the dual system of taxation is that corporate earnings are generally subject to double tax—first at the corporate level and again at the shareholder level—and the effective rate of this double tax may be significant. Assume, for example, that both the corporation and its shareholders are in the 40 percent combined federal and state tax brackets. If the corporation earns $100, it will pay $40 in tax and retain $60. If these $60 are then distributed by the corporation to its shareholders, they will pay tax of 40 percent of $60, or $24, and retain only $36. The net result is a combined 64 percent tax on corporate earnings. The shareholder-level tax may be deferred but not eliminated in situations where the corporation retains its earnings: The shareholders will effectively pay a second level of tax when they sell their interests in the corporation. As can be seen from this example, double taxation may substantially reduce the value of a trade or business in the hands of a corporation.

Does this mean that if a C corporation has corporate shareholders, its earnings will be subject to triple taxation?

Generally, no. The Code contains various provisions intended to eliminate triple taxation. Where the shareholder corporation (the "parent") and the distributing corporation (the "subsidiary") are members of the same affiliated group, the parent corporation is generally entitled to a deduction for 100 percent of the amount of the dividends received from the subsidiary. The 100 percent deduction or its equivalent is one of the benefits of filing a consolidated federal income tax return; and the deduction is available to nonconsolidating members of affiliated groups where they so elect.

Generally, if the shareholder corporation is not affiliated with the distributing corporation, some earnings will be subject to triple taxation. A corporation owning between 20 and 80 percent of the stock of another corporation may exclude from its income 80 percent of dividends received; where the distributee owns less than 20 percent of the stock of the distributing corporation, the exclusion is limited to 70 percent of the dividend. Finally, because a combined (consolidated) state tax return may be unavailable and because some states tax dividends received by a corporation, a triple (or more) state income tax is a real possibility.

How can leverage reduce the effects of double taxation?

Leverage is a self-help approach to the elimination of double taxation of corporations. A leveraged target is a corporation whose capital structure is tilted toward debt instead of equity. Capitalization with debt is relevant to double taxation because interest paid or accrued is deductible by the corporation in the computation of taxable income, while distributions with respect to its stock are not. As a result, corporate earnings distributed to lenders as interest payments will escape the corporate level tax. Thus, leverage can substantially reduce or virtually eliminate, at least temporarily, the tax detriment of double taxation.

It is very important to remember, however, that the Internal Revenue Service may take the position that a purported debt is actually equity, thus eliminating the benefit of leverage. The debt-versus-equity issue is one of the most important tax issues of acquisition financing; it will be discussed later in this chapter.

What is the alternative minimum tax, or AMT?

Over the years Congress has been concerned that certain high-income individuals and corporations were paying little or no tax. The alternative minimum tax was enacted in 1969 to ensure that taxpayers could not exploit various deductions and preferences to the point that the tax imposed upon their economic income was inordinately low.

Under the Tax Reform Act of 1986, Congress amended the minimum tax provisions and created a rather severe regime of alternative minimum tax, particularly for corporations. The alternative minimum tax for both individuals and corporations is determined by computing taxable income under the regular method (with certain adjustments), and adding back certain deductions or "preferences" to obtain alternative minimum taxable income. To this amount is applied the alternative minimum tax rate of 21 percent for individuals or 20 percent for corporations. The taxpayer is required to pay the greater of the regular tax or the alternative minimum tax.

A new preference item was added in the Tax Reform Act of 1986 that will increase uncertainty and complexity in the taxation of corporations—the so-called book income preference. The book income preference adds to the alternative minimum taxable income of a corporation an amount equal to one-half the difference between its alternative minimum taxable income and the net income as reported for financial accounting purposes. Because the book income preference applies only with respect to the corporate AMT and not the individual AMT, it can be a significant impetus to utilize a pass-through entity for engaging in business transactions. Additionally, corporations disposing of businesses must take into account the book income preference in determining the tax costs of transactions that are ordinarily nontaxable, but are reportable in financial income.

*What is the "General Utilities" rule?

Under the dual system of taxation, corporate earnings from the sale of appreciated property are taxed twice, first to the corporation when the sale occurs, then to the shareholders upon the distribution of the net proceeds. A long-standing exception to this system was the so-called *General Utilities* rule, named after a 1935 Supreme Court decision, that permitted nonrecognition of gain to corporations upon certain distributions to shareholders of appreciated property. Subsequently, the rule was codified to include both liquidating and nonliquidating distributions of appreciated property by a corporation to its shareholders, as well as certain sales of appreciated property made during the course of a complete liquidation ("liquidating sales"). Not only did the rule permit appreciated property to escape corporate tax, but it also allowed the transferee to obtain a basis in the property equal to its fair market value. The term "*General Utilities* rule" was used in the broad sense to refer to the right by which appreciated property could be removed from corporate solution, and its basis stepped-up to fair market value, without the imposition of corporate tax.

The breadth of the *General Utilities* rule was narrowed over the years, both statutorily and judicially. In the Tax Reform Act of 1986, Congress repealed the rule entirely, with certain temporary exceptions for small corporations.

What is the significance of the repeal of the "General Utilities" rule?

The repeal of the rule of *General Utilities* increases the tax costs, or reduces the tax benefits allowed under prior law, of acquiring and disposing of appreciated corporate assets. Specifically, the change in law has substantially narrowed the circumstances in which an acquisition or divestiture will be structured as an asset purchase, and will increase the prevalence of stock transactions. Additionally, the repeal of the *General Utilities* rule places greater emphasis upon the use of pass-through entities wherever possible.

What are the tax consequences to corporations of distributions of property to their shareholders?

The taxation of corporate distributions involves myriad complex rules, many with exceptions and qualifications. In general, however, the tax consequences to corporations of distributions of property depend upon (i) whether the property distributed is cash or property other than cash; (ii) whether the recipient shareholder is an affiliated corporation; and (iii) whether the distribution is a liquidating or nonliquidating distribution.

Distributions of cash, both liquidating and nonliquidating, generally have no tax consequence to the distributing corporation, except that the amount distributed reduces the corporation's earnings and profits.

Distributions of appreciated property, both liquidating and nonliquidating, generally trigger the recognition of gain to the distributing corporation to the extent of the appreciation in the asset. The recognition of such gain is deferred, however, if the distributee shareholder is an affiliated corporation that files a consolidated return with the distributing corporation. And no gain is recognized if the distribution is a liquidating distribution to a corporation that owns more than 80 percent of the vote and value of the equity of the distributor corporation. Nonliquidating distributions of appreciated property are not deductible to the distributing corporation, but, like distributions of cash, such amounts reduce its earnings and profits.

The rules governing distributions of depreciated property (i.e., property with a tax basis exceeding its fair market value) are generally similar to those applicable to distributions of appreciated property, except that no loss is recognized on nonliquidating distributions of depreciated property.

What are the tax consequences to a shareholder of nonliquidating distributions that are not in redemption of all or a portion of his stock?

The tax consequences to a shareholder of the receipt of a nonliquidating distribution, which is not in redemption of stock, depends upon whether the corporation has current or accumulated earnings and profits. Such distributions to shareholders are treated as dividend income to the extent of the distributing corporation's current and accumulated earnings and profits. Nonliquidating distributions in excess of such earnings are treated as a tax-free recovery of capital to the extent of the shareholder's basis in his stock. Once a shareholder's invested capital or stock basis has been recovered, further distributions are taxed as gain (usually capital).

What are the tax consequences to a shareholder of nonliquidating distributions made in redemption of all or a portion of his outstanding stock?

A "bona fide" redemption—one that is treated as a redemption for tax purposes—is a transaction in which the corporation distributes money or property to a shareholder in exchange for some or all of the shareholder's stock. The shareholder is treated just as if he sold his stock to an unrelated party: he recognizes gain or loss based upon the difference between the amount realized on the sale and the basis of the stock redeemed.

Where substantially less than all of a shareholder's interest in the corporation is redeemed, the "redemption" may not differ significantly from a dividend. For example, where a corporation purports to redeem the same percentage of each shareholder's outstanding stock, the distribution is the economic equivalent of a dividend because the redemption neither decreases nor increases the interest in the corporation of any shareholder.

The rules governing redemptions are found in Section 302 of the Code. The primary function of Section 302 is to distinguish between an actual redemption and a disguised dividend. The essential distinction between a bona fide redemption and a dividend distribution is whether the shareholder has suffered a meaningful reduction in his interest in the corporation.

What are the tax consequences to a shareholder of liquidating distributions?

A shareholder who surrenders stock in exchange for property distributed by a corporation in complete liquidation generally recognizes capital gain or loss to the extent of the difference between the fair market value of the property received and the shareholder's basis in the stock. Under a special provision, however, no gain or loss is recognized by corporate shareholders that own 80 percent or more of the vote and value of the liquidating corporation.

CHOICE OF ENTITY

What types of entities may operate the business of an acquired company?

Three types of entities may be used to acquire and operate the business of the target: regular or C corporations, S corporations, and partnerships, either general or limited.

What are the primary differences among the three types of business entities?

A regular or C corporation is a separate taxpaying entity. Therefore, its earnings are taxed to the corporation when earned and again to its shareholders upon distribution. Partnerships and S corporations, in contrast, are generally not separate taxpaying entities. The earnings of partnerships and S corporations are taxed directly to the partners or shareholders, whether or not distributed or otherwise made available to such persons. Moreover, partnerships and S corporations may generally distribute their earnings to the equity owners free of tax. Because S corporations and partnerships are generally exempt from tax, but pass the tax liability with respect to such earnings directly through to their owners, these entities are commonly referred to as "pass-through entities."

What is a C Corporation?

A C corporation is defined in the Internal Revenue Code as any corporation that is not an S corporation. The term "C corporation" as used in this chapter, however, excludes corporations granted special tax status under the Code, such as, for example, life insurance corporations, regulated investment companies (mutual funds), or corporations qualifying as real estate investment trusts (REITs).

What is an S corporation?

An S corporation is simply a regular corporation that meets certain requirements and elects to be taxed under Subchapter S of the Code. Originally called a "small business corporation," the S corporation was designed to permit small, closely held businesses to be conducted in the corporate form, while continuing to be taxed generally as if operated as a partnership or an aggregation of individuals. As it happens, the eligibility requirements under Subchapter S, keyed to the criterion of simplicity, impose no limitation on the actual size of the business enterprise.

It should be noted that not all states recognize the S corporation. For those that do not, the corporation pays state income taxes as if it were a C corporation. For those states that do recognize S corporations, both resident and nonresident shareholders of the state where the corporation does business must file returns and pay taxes to that state. In such cases, a shareholder's state of residence will usually (but not always) provide a credit against its own tax.

What is a partnership for tax purposes?

Except under rare circumstances, a partnership for tax purposes must be a bona fide general or limited partnership under applicable state law. Because of the great similarities of limited partnerships to corporations, it is not sufficient that the organization be a state law partnership to ensure that it will not be treated as a corporation for tax purposes. The tax rules regarding the classification of limited partnerships are arcane, with the results turning upon some fine and arbitrary distinctions. It is an area in which there is strong disagreement among even the most experienced and distinguished tax practitioners as to where the line is drawn between a limited partnership and an association of individuals taxed as a corporation. Most importantly, where the entity is a limited partnership with a corporate general partner, great care must be taken to ensure partnership characterization.

Taxation of Pass-Through Entities

*What are the pass-through entities?

There are three types of pass-through entities: (1) an S corporation, (2) a partnership, both general and limited, and (3) a C corporation that files a consolidated income tax return with its corporate "parent." The earnings of an S corporation, with certain exceptions, are subject to taxation only at the shareholder level. The earnings of a partnership are also subject to a single tax, but only to the extent that such earnings are allocated to noncorporate partners (unless the partner is an S corporation). Partnership earnings that are allocated to corporate partners are subject to double taxation, just as though the income were earned directly by the corporations. The earnings of all C corporations are subject to double tax, but the consolidated return provisions generally permit the earnings of subsidiary members of the consolidated return group to be taxed to the ultimate parent with the imposition of only one level of tax. In that sense, the subsidiary corporation is treated as a pass-through entity with respect to its parent corporation.

*Should a pass-through entity be used to operate the business of the target company whenever possible?

Absolutely. The aggregate of the two levels of tax imposed upon the earnings of regular or C corporations is almost always greater, often substantially greater, than the income tax imposed upon the earnings of an S corporation or a partnership. Where the purchaser and the target corporation are members of the same affiliated group after the acquisition, the tax imposed upon the earnings of the target under the consolidated return provisions will generally be less than the tax imposed upon the target and its shareholders under the separate return method.

*What are the basic principles of pass-through taxation?

There are four basic mechanisms for pass-through taxation applicable to S corporations, partnerships, and subsidiary members of consolidated return groups. These are the provisions concerning the pass-through of income and loss, the adjustments to basis, the treatment of distributions, and the loss limitations. The first three sets of rules basically ensure that only one level of tax is imposed upon the earnings of pass-through entities; the last set of rules is designed to limit abusive or artificial tax benefits.

Under the pass-through provisions, the income or loss of the pass-through entity, and the resulting tax consequences, are allocated to the shareholders or partners of the entity. Thus, the tax liability with respect to the income of S corporations and partnerships is imposed directly upon the shareholders and partners; the tax liability with respect to the income of each member of a consolidated return group is the responsibility of all members of the group. Partners and S corporation shareholders are taxed on the earnings of the pass-through entity whether or not the earnings are distributed or made available to such persons. For example, if individual A owns all the stock of an S corporation T, and T has $100 of net earnings in 1988, the $100 of corporate earnings is included in the income of A whether or not the earnings are distributed by T to A.

Second, the owners of a pass-through entity—the partners of a partnership, the shareholders of an S corporation, and the parent of the consolidated subsidiary—increase or decrease the basis of their interest in the pass-through entity to the extent of the income or loss of the entity recognized by such persons. The consequence of the basis adjustment rules is that the income or loss of the pass-through entity is not included in the income or loss of the shareholder or partner again upon distribution or, in the absence of a distribution, upon the sale or exchange of his interest in the entity. In the example above, if A's basis in his T stock is $200 at the beginning of T's 1988 taxable year, A would increase his basis in his T stock from $200 to $300 by reason of including in his income the $100 of T's 1988 earnings.

Third, the distribution rules, in conjunction with the basis adjustment rules, allow earnings to be distributed from the pass-through entity to its owners free of tax. For partnerships and S corporations, the tax-free distribution is limited to the extent of the partner's or shareholder's basis of his or her interest in the entity, and the amount distributed reduces the basis of the recipient's interest in the pass-through entity. In the example above, T could distribute up to $300 to A at the end of its 1988 year without the imposition of tax, but A's basis in his T stock would be reduced by the amount distributed. For consolidated subsidiaries, distributions likewise reduce basis but may be made without a tax to the parent even when the basis has been reduced to zero. These excess distributions create an excess loss account, which must be taken into income at a later time.

Fourth, there are various loss limitation rules that impose a ceiling on the amount of pass-through losses that a partner or shareholder can recognize with respect to his or her interest in the pass-through entity. Generally, such limitations do not apply in a consolidated return. Under the facts in the example above, the aggregate losses that A may recognize with respect to his T stock is limited to his basis in such stock.

*What are the principal loss limitation rules applicable to the owners of pass-through entities?

There are three principal limitations on the deductibility of losses generated by pass-through entities: the basis limitation rules, the at-risk rules, and the passive loss rules. There are exceptions and limitations with respect to the application of each set of rules; and none of the limitations generally applies to the parent corporation with respect to its consolidated subsidiary, unless the parent corporation is closely held.

The basis rules generally limit the deductibility of pass-through losses to the basis of the interest in the entity held by the partner or shareholder.

The at-risk rules generally limit the extent to which a pass-through loss can be recognized by a taxpayer to the amount that the taxpayer has put at economic risk.

The passive loss rules limit the extent to which losses from passive activities may be offset against active income—generally salary and active trade or business income—or against portfolio income—interest, dividends, etc. These rules were designed to prohibit the use of tax-shelter deductions.

It is important to remember that the loss limitation rules have little applicability to widely held C corporations.

ASSET ACQUISITION OR STOCK ACQUISITION

Probably the most fundamental tax issue to be dealt with by buyers and sellers is whether to structure a transaction as a stock acquisition or an asset acquisition. As will be seen, these terms have a unique significance in tax terminology, and actually refer only to two different sets of tax consequences for the parties. As we proceed, the reader should begin to think in terms of carryover basis/stock acquisitions and cost basis/asset acquisitions.

In later sections we will deal separately with the actual structuring of the transaction to achieve asset sale versus stock sale treatment for tax purposes, as well as the issues to be considered in structuring transactions for tax-free or tax-deferred treatment for the seller. In this section, however, these questions are put aside in favor of the fundamental questions as to the benefits and costs of a carryover basis/stock acquisition or a cost basis/asset acquisition. The acquisition structures discussed here are presented in diagram form on pages 341–348.

General Concepts

How does an asset acquisition differ from a stock acquisition?

The primary distinction between an asset acquisition and a stock acquisition concerns the purchaser's basis in the assets acquired. When a purchaser directly acquires the assets of a target corporation in a transaction in which the target is subject to tax on the sale or exchange of the assets, the basis of the assets to the purchaser is their cost ("cost basis"). When a purchaser indirectly acquires the assets of a target corporation through the acquisition of stock, the basis of the assets in the possession of the target corporation is generally not affected ("carryover basis"—the basis of an asset in the target corporation "carries over" on the change of stock ownership).

With the exception of a stock acquisition governed by the

provisions of Section 338, which is discussed below, the acquisition of all or part of the stock of a target corporation does not alter the bases of the assets owned by the corporation. And with the exception of an asset acquisition governed by the tax-free reorganization provisions, which are discussed below, the acquisition of the assets of the target will produce a cost basis to the purchaser. A cost basis transaction is, therefore, often referred to as an "asset acquisition"; and a carryover basis transaction is often referred to as a "stock acquisition." The term "cost basis transaction" will be used interchangeably in this chapter with the term "asset acquisition," as will the terms "carryover basis transaction" and "stock acquisition." Moreover, neither term—asset acquisition or stock acquisition—necessarily reflects the actual structure of the transaction.

Are there any other significant tax differences between an asset or cost basis transaction and a stock or carryover basis transaction?

Yes. In carryover basis transactions, the purchaser acquires (or the target retains), by operation of law, the target corporation's tax attributes—net operating loss carryovers, business credit carryovers, earnings and profits, accounting methods, and others—each of which may be either beneficial or detrimental to the purchaser. The most beneficial tax attributes, however, are generally subject to various limitations that are triggered upon a significant change of stock ownership of the target corporation. In all cost basis transactions, the purchaser acquires the target corporation's assets without the target's tax attributes.

Do the tax considerations determine whether the acquisition of the target corporation is structured as an asset acquisition or a stock acquisition?

Not necessarily. In certain circumstances, the parties do not have the prerogative to choose between asset and stock transactions. Where the purchaser is acquiring a division of a target corporation or otherwise acquiring less than all of the assets of a corporation, for example, a stock acquisition may not be possible. Actual asset acquisitions (as opposed to constructive asset acquisitions under the Section 338 election procedure) may not be practical where the transfer of such assets requires the consent of lessors, creditors, or other interested third parties. There are numerous other situations where the structure of the transaction is determined primarily by non-tax considerations.

*What types of transactions are stock or carryover basis transactions?

There are several types of stock or carryover basis transactions. The direct purchase of the target corporation stock in exchange for cash and debt is the most straightforward stock acquisition. The merger of the acquiring corporation into the target corporation—a reverse merger—where the shareholders of the target corporation relinquish their shares in exchange for cash or debt in a fully taxable transaction is treated, for tax purposes, as a sale of stock. The acquisition of the stock or assets of the target corporation in a transaction free of tax to its exchanging shareholders, which generally involves the reorganization provisions of the Internal Revenue Code, is a carryover basis or stock acquisition. As a general rule, a stock or carryover basis acquisition includes any transaction where the stock or assets of the target corporation are acquired by the purchaser, and the bases of the assets of the target are not increased or decreased on the change of ownership. There are other, less common "stock" transactions in which the purchaser may obtain a carryover basis in the assets of the target corporation.

*What types of transactions are asset or cost basis transactions?

There are several types of asset or cost basis transactions. The direct purchase of the assets from the target corporation in exchange for cash or indebtedness is the quintessential asset acquisition. The statutory merger of the target corporation into an acquiring corporation—a forward cash merger—where the shareholders of the target corporation exchange their shares for cash or other property in a fully taxable transaction is treated, for tax purposes, as an asset acquisition. In certain circumstances, a corporation may acquire the stock of the target corporation and elect under Section 338 of the Code to treat the stock acquisition, for tax purposes, as an asset acquisition. There are other, less common, transactions in which the purchaser obtains a cost basis in the assets of the target corporation. As a general rule, an asset or cost basis acquisition includes any transaction where the pre-acquisition gains and losses inherent in the assets acquired are triggered and recognized by the target corporation.

Does a purchaser always have a cost basis in property acquired in an asset acquisition?

Not necessarily. A purchaser will generally have a carryover basis in the assets acquired from a target corporation in a tax-free transaction or in a merger of the target corporation into the purchaser pursuant to the tax-free reorganization provisions of the Code. As a general rule, the basis of an asset is not increased or decreased where the asset is acquired from the target corporation in a nontaxable transaction (see discussion below).

What is a forward cash merger?

A forward cash merger is the statutory merger of the target corporation into the acquiring corporation, where the acquiring corporation is the survivor and the shareholders of the target corporation receive cash or debt in a fully taxable exchange for their target corporation stock. For tax purposes, the transaction is treated as the sale by the target corporation of its assets, followed by the liquidation of the target and the distribution of the sales proceeds to its former shareholders. Tax is imposed upon both the target corporation (on gain realized in the deemed asset sale) and upon its shareholders (on gain realized on the receipt of consideration in exchange for the target stock).

What is a Section 338 election?

Section 338 creates a fictional transaction relevant only for tax purposes. A Section 338 election is a procedure by which a corporate purchaser may treat a stock acquisition as an asset acquisition. The election is available only where, among other things, the purchasing corporation acquires at least 80 percent of the stock of the target corporation. Where the requirements are satisfied and the election is made, the target is treated or "deemed" (i) as having sold all of its assets in a single, taxable transaction at the close of the date on which the purchasing corporation acquires the stock of the target corporation, and (ii) as a new corporation that purchased all of the assets of the target at the beginning of the following day. The deemed sales price is approximately equal to the fair market value of the assets of the target, determined by the sum of the purchase price of the target corporation stock and the liabilities of the target, including the tax liability on the deemed asset sale.

It is unclear whether every state allows a Section 338 election to be made for state income tax purposes. It is possible that a transaction will be treated as an asset acquisition for federal income tax purposes, but as a stock acquisition for state tax purposes.

Who is liable for the tax on the deemed sale of assets pursuant to a Section 338 election?

The target corporation is deemed to sell its assets pursuant to a Section 338 election, and the target is liable for the tax arising from the sale. Since the purchaser becomes the sole or primary shareholder of the target, the economic burden of the tax will fall on the purchaser, and not the selling shareholders of the target corporation stock. In effect, the purchaser pays a corporate tax to have the transaction treated as an asset or cost basis transaction. The only exception to this rule—that the tax burden of the Section 338 election falls on the purchaser—is where the purchaser and the seller make an election under Section 338(h)(10) of the Code.

What is the practical consequence of a Section 338 election, and under what circumstances is the election generally advisable?

A Section 338 election triggers taxable gain recognition to the target corporation on the deemed sale of its assets. Moreover, the selling shareholders are taxed on any gain realized on the actual sale of the target corporation stock. The incremental tax costs to the target and its shareholders attributable to a Section 338 election are generally substantially greater than the present value of tax benefits to be realized through the increase in the basis of the assets of the target corporation. Because of the substantial tax costs that generally arise from a Section 338 election, it is seldom made in practice.

There are two situations in which a Section 338 election is advisable. The first is where the gain recognized on the deemed sale of target assets is offset, in whole or in substantial part, by net operating losses; and the increase in the basis of the target corporation's assets is more valuable to the purchaser than the carryover of the target's net operating losses. The second situation in which a Section 338 election is advisable is where the purchaser and seller jointly make an election under Section 338(h)(10), thereby avoiding the tax otherwise imposed on the sellers of the target corporation stock.

What is a Section 338(h)(10) election?

Section 338(h)(10) also creates a fictional transaction for tax purposes. Section 338(h)(10) provides that if the target corporation is a member of an affiliated group of corporations that files a consolidated income tax return, and the purchaser makes a Section 338 election with respect to the acquisition of the stock of the target corporation, then the purchaser and seller may jointly elect to treat the target corporation as a member of the selling consolidated group with respect to the deemed asset sale. The primary tax benefit of a Section 338(h)(10) election is that no gain will be recognized on the actual sale of the stock of the target corporation by the consolidated group in which the selling shareholder and the target were members.

There are four basic consequences to a Section 338(h)(10) election. First, the target corporation is treated as having sold all of its assets in a single, taxable transaction. Second, the gain or loss on the deemed sale of the target's assets is reported in the consolidated tax return for the affiliated group that includes the target corporation and the corporations that sold the target stock to the purchaser. Third, the target corporation is treated as having been liquidated tax-free after the deemed asset sale, so that its tax attributes carry over into the affiliated, selling shareholder corporation. And fourth, the affiliated selling corporation does not recognize gain or loss on the sale of the stock of the target corporation. One purpose behind Section 338(h)(10) is to ameliorate the otherwise harsh tax result of triple taxation—once to the target corporation on the deemed asset sale, once to the shareholders of the target corporation on the sale of the target stock, and again to the shareholders of the selling corporation on the ultimate receipt of the sales proceeds.

In addition to the general uncertainty of the availability of a Section 338 election for state income tax purposes, it is unclear what the practical consequences of a Section 338(h)(10) election are in the case of a corporation not filing a combined (consolidated) state income tax return.

Under what circumstances is an election under Section 338(h)(10) advisable?

A Section 338(h)(10) election is typically made where the purchaser and the seller determine that the transaction should be treated as a cost basis/asset acquisition, but, for reasons of convenience or necessity, prefer to effectuate the transaction through the sale of the target corporation stock instead of through the actual sale of its assets or a forward cash merger. It is important to note that a Section 338/338(h)(10) election is generally advisable in all situations where it is available, whether or not a Section 338 election without a Section

338(h)(10) election is otherwise appropriate. An exception to this rule is the situation where the tax to the selling consolidated group on the deemed asset sale by the target corporation substantially exceeds the tax to the selling group on the actual sale of the target corporation stock. Even there, the potential tax benefits to the purchaser may substantially outweigh the additional tax costs to the seller.

Basis Considerations of the Purchaser

What is the significance to the purchaser of the basis of the assets in the target corporation?

The basis of the assets in a target corporation may have a significant and continuing effect on the tax liabilities and, therefore, the cash flow of either the purchaser or the target corporation. The basis of an asset represents the extent to which the asset may be depreciated or amortized (if at all), thereby generating noncash reductions of taxable income. Basis also represents the extent to which the consideration received in a taxable sale or exchange of an asset may be received by the seller free of tax.

What is the prospective cost basis of an asset to the purchaser?

The prospective cost basis of an asset to the purchaser is the price that it will pay for the asset, directly or indirectly, which is presumed to be its fair market value.

What is the prospective carryover basis of an asset to the purchaser?

The prospective carryover basis of an asset to the purchaser is simply the "adjusted basis" of the asset in the possession of the target corporation prior to its acquisition. The adjusted basis of an asset is generally its historical or initial cost, reduced or "adjusted" by subsequent depreciation or amortization deductions.

*What is meant by "stepped-up" basis?

Where the basis of an asset is increased from the target corporation's low, historical cost, depreciated, or amortized basis to a basis determined by a purchaser's cost or fair market value, the basis of the asset is said to have been "stepped-up." The term may refer, however, to any transaction in which the basis of an asset is increased. In most asset or cost basis transactions, the basis of the assets of the target corporation is stepped-up to the purchaser's cost. An acquisition in which the basis of the assets of the target corporation is increased is referred to as a "step-up" transaction.

*Is it more beneficial to the purchaser that the acquisition of the target corporation be structured — either as a cost basis transaction or as a carryover basis transaction — to provide the highest basis in the assets of the target corporation?

Generally, yes. High tax basis in an asset is always more beneficial to its owner than low basis. The higher the basis, the greater the depreciation or amortization deductions (if allowable); and the less the gain (or the greater the loss) on the subsequent disposition of the asset. An increase in these deductions and losses will reduce the tax liabilities of the purchaser or the target corporation during the holding period of the assets, thereby increasing after-tax cash flow. For the same reasons, a high basis in the target corporation's assets will enhance their value to a potential carryover basis purchaser.

The acquisition of a target corporation should generally be structured to maximize the basis of the assets of the target corporation. If a purchaser's prospective cost basis in the assets of the target corporation exceed its prospective carryover basis, an asset acquisition or "step-up" transaction is generally more beneficial to the purchaser than a stock acquisition; if a purchaser's prospective carryover basis exceeds its prospective cost basis in the assets of the target corporation, a stock acquisition is generally more beneficial to the purchaser than an asset or cost basis acquisition.

The primary exception to this general rule is the situation where (i) in a carryover basis transaction the purchaser would acquire beneficial tax attributes—net operating losses, tax credits, or accounting methods—and (ii) the value of such tax attributes to the purchaser exceeds the value of the stepped-up basis in the target's assets that would have obtained in a cost basis transaction.

*Will a purchaser's cost basis in an asset generally be greater than its carryover basis?

Yes. Where an asset has appreciated in value, or where the economic depreciation of an asset is less than the depreciation or amortization deductions allowed for tax purposes, a purchaser's prospective cost basis in the asset will exceed its prospective carryover basis. The depreciation and amortization deductions allowed for tax purposes for most types of property are designed to exceed the actual economic depreciation of the property. As a result, the fair market value of most assets, which represents the prospective cost basis of the asset to a purchaser, generally exceeds adjusted tax basis. The aggregate difference between the purchaser's prospective cost and carryover bases of the target corporation's assets is often substantial.

*Will a purchaser generally receive greater tax benefits by acquiring a target corporation through a cost basis transaction than through a carryover basis transaction?

Yes. A purchaser will generally acquire a higher basis in the assets of the target corporation through a cost basis transaction than through a carryover basis transaction because the cost or fair market value of the target's assets is generally greater than the adjusted basis of the assets prior to the acquisition. In that circumstance, a cost basis transaction will "step-up" the basis of the assets of the target corporation. The amount of the increase in basis—the excess of cost basis over carryover basis—is referred to as the "step-up amount."

*Do all asset or cost basis transactions step-up the bases
of the target corporation's assets?*

No. Where the purchase price of the assets of the target corporation, which is presumed to equal their fair market value, is less than the carryover basis of the assets, a cost basis or asset transaction will result in a net reduction of basis. The amount of the reduction in basis represents the taxable loss recognized by the target corporation on the sale or exchange of its assets. In situations where the prospective carryover basis of the target's assets exceeds the prospective cost basis, then, subject to the value or liability of the target corporation's tax attributes, the transaction should generally be structured as a carryover basis or stock acquisition.

*What is the value to the purchaser of the increase
in the basis of the assets of the target corporation
by the "step-up amount"?*

The tax benefits of the basis step-up amount are essentially two-fold. First, the purchaser or the target corporation may significantly enhance after-tax cash flow from operations of the target assets through the depreciation or amortization of the step-up amount. In a highly leveraged acquisition, this increased cash flow may be quite important, especially during the early years after the acquisition. The value of this aspect of the step-up amount is equal to the present value of the tax savings attributable to the increased depreciation or amortization deductions. The other principal benefit of the step-up amount is the reduction in tax upon the ultimate disposition of the target's assets. The present value of this aspect of the basis step-up amount varies inversely with the expected holding period of the assets.

*How does one quantify the tax benefits of a basis
step-up amount?*

It is often difficult to quantify the tax benefits that may be obtained by stepping-up the bases of the assets of the target corporation. While there is unquestionably some benefit in virtually all step-up transactions, the decision whether to seek a cost, rather than a carryover, basis in the target's assets requires a specific comparison of the expected tax benefits and the cost of such benefits. Ultimately, the value of a basis step-up depends on many factors, including, among other things, depreciation methods and recovery periods, the economic life of the target's assets, and whether the target will be operated as a pass-through entity. Often, only a sophisticated computer analysis can properly evaluate the various scenarios and relevant factors to estimate the net value of the tax benefits of a basis step-up.

In determining the benefits and detriments of a cost basis versus a carryover basis acquisition, attention must be paid not only to an asset's eligibility for depreciation or amortization deductions, but also to the depreciation method and recovery period of the property. It is not uncommon to find an asset (most notably, real estate) which, even with the target's lower carryover basis, is entitled to more generous depreciation deductions in the early years after an acquisition than it would obtain under the different depreciation rules applicable to a buyer obtaining a higher cost basis in the property.

What are the practical tax consequences to the purchaser of a carryover basis transaction?

The difference between the carryover basis of an asset (which is its adjusted, pre-acquisition basis) and the cost basis of the asset (which is generally its fair market value) represents its "built-in gain" or "built-in loss" that would be includible in income or loss if the property were immediately sold by the target or the purchaser in a taxable transaction. When a purchaser acquires an asset with a carryover basis and built-in gain—which is the excess of fair market value over carryover basis—the purchaser essentially acquires the asset with a potential tax liability. The tax liability will accrue when the property is sold or exchanged, unless it depreciates in value prior to its disposition. The amount of the built-in gain in a depreciable or amortizable asset also represents the depreciation or amortization deductions that the purchaser essentially forfeits by reason of acquiring the asset in a carryover basis, instead of a cost basis, transaction.

The converse applies in those situations where an asset is acquired by a purchaser with a carryover basis and a built-in loss—which is an excess of carryover basis over fair market value. The built-in loss may generate tax benefits to the purchaser in the form of a taxable loss on the sale of the asset as well as depreciation or amortization deductions that would not have been available to the purchaser had the asset been acquired in a cost basis transaction.

In what circumstances are carryover basis transactions more beneficial to a purchaser, from a tax standpoint, than cost basis transactions?

There are two situations where a carryover basis or stock transaction may be more beneficial to the purchaser than a cost basis or asset acquisition. The first is where the carryover basis of the target corporation's assets to the purchaser exceeds their cost basis. This excess represents potential tax benefits to the purchaser—noncash depreciation deductions or taxable losses—without a corresponding economic loss. That is, the tax deductions or losses from owning the assets may exceed the price paid for such assets. The second is where the target corporation possesses valuable tax attributes—net operating loss carryovers, business tax credit carryovers, or accounting methods, for example—that would inure to the benefit of the purchaser. Situations where carryover basis transactions are preferable to the purchaser than cost basis transactions, however, are more the exception than the rule.

LIMITATIONS ON LOSS CARRYOVERS

What are loss carryovers and carrybacks?

If a taxpayer has an excess of tax deductions over its taxable income in a given year, this excess becomes a net operating loss of that taxpayer. Section 172 of the Code allows that taxpayer to use its net operating loss (NOL) to offset taxable income in subsequent years—a carryover or carryforward—or to offset taxable income in earlier years—a carryback. For most taxpayers, an NOL may be carried back for up to three taxable years and may be carried forward for up to fifteen years.

Under other provisions of the Code, certain tax losses or tax credits that are unusable in a given year may be carried forward or carried back to other tax years. Examples of such deductions or credits are capital losses, excess foreign tax credits, and investment credits. Generally, those provisions of the Code that impose additional limitations on a company's ability to utilize NOL carryovers apply as well to these other items. For purposes of simplicity, all of these items tend to be grouped together with loss carryovers; this is a practice that we will follow in the discussion here.

Generally speaking, each state has its own NOL carryback and carryforward rules, which may not necessarily match the federal rules. Therefore, a target may have different amounts of available federal and state NOLs.

What role do loss carryovers play in mergers and acquisitions?

Obviously, an entity that has a generous amount of loss carryovers will have much greater flexibility in planning both acquisitions and dispositions. Nevertheless, the reporting of taxable transactions must often reflect a tax expense for financial accounting purposes notwithstanding the availability of net operating loss deductions to eliminate an actual tax liability. Recognizing this, as well as the fact that NOL carryovers, like everything else in life, are finite, tax advisers to companies with even very substantial NOL carryovers still prefer to minimize taxable income.

As we said earlier, a potential advantage in carryover basis acquisitions—both taxable stock purchases and tax-free reorganizations—is the carryover of basis and of favorable tax attributes in the hands of the buyer. To the extent that a buyer can acquire a target corporation and retain favorable NOL carryovers, it can increase the after-tax cash flow generated by the activities of the target and, to some extent, utilize those losses to offset tax liability generated by the buyer's own operations.

Over the course of many years, culminating in the tax legislation enacted in 1986 and 1987, Congress and the IRS have imposed various limitations on the use of loss carryovers by persons other than those who owned the entity at the time that the loss was generated. Because these rules have achieved a level of complexity that is extreme even by the standard of the tax laws generally, we will discuss only some of the highlights of those rules.

What kinds of limitations are imposed on the use of loss carryovers?

We have already discussed briefly the basic limitations on loss carryovers set forth in Section 172: namely, they are limited to the taxpayer that generated them and expire at the end of 15 years. Two exceptions to the rule that the losses may only be used by the taxpayer that generated them are for the inheritance of tax attributes by an acquiring corporation in a tax-free reorganization and the ability of an affiliated group of corporations to file a consolidated tax return determined as if the group were a single taxpayer. There are several limitations contained in the consolidated return regulations on the ability to use loss carryovers of members of the group. The one limitation that we will mention here is the Separate Return Limitation Year, or SRLY, limitation. In general, the SRLY rules limit an affiliated group's use of loss carryovers from a subsidiary's separate return years to the amount of taxable income generated by that subsidiary. What this is intended to do is to prevent a group from acquiring a corporation with loss carryovers and using those carryovers to offset taxable income generated by other members of the group.

The broadest provision of the tax laws governing the acquisition of loss companies is Section 269 of the Code. Section 269 gives the IRS authority to disallow any deduction if it finds that a person has acquired control of a corporation, or the assets of a corporation in a carryover basis transaction, with the principal purpose for the acquisition being the evasion or avoidance of federal income tax. For this purpose, control generally means 50 percent of the voting power or value of the stock of a corporation. The classic case for applying Section 269 is one where a profitable corporation acquires another corporation that has substantial net operating loss carryovers and very little else, and is able to use those losses to offset its income, for example, by contributing some of its own income producing assets to the newly acquired entity. Section 269 has been held to apply as well, however, to the acquisition by a loss corporation of another corporation that is producing taxable income, where the loss corporation would not otherwise have taxable income with which to utilize its losses. The outcome of the litigated cases depends for the most part upon there being a presence or absence of apparently bona fide business reasons for the acquisition. To the extent that a taxpayer can show that there were good business reasons for the acquisition, then Section 269 will not usually be applied, even though the presence of NOLs in the target entered into the price discussions.

Despite the existence and looming presence of Section 269 as an IRS weapon against blatant tax avoidance, Congress long ago enacted other provisions designed to provide a more objective and certain set of limitations on the use of loss carryovers following corporate acquisitions. As set forth in Code Sections 382 and 384, enacted in 1986 and 1987, these rules are among the most comprehensive and complex in the tax laws.

What are the Section 382 rules?

The essential model that underlies Section 382 is that a new owner of a loss corporation should not be permitted to utilize NOL carryovers of the loss corporation any more quickly than the loss corporation would have in the hands of its former owners. This is put into effect by building into the statute an irrebuttable presumption that the loss corporation would have generated a rate of return on its equity value equal to the prevailing interest rate on long-term U.S. Government obligations, discounted as if the return were free of federal income taxes. Thus, if a loss corporation undergoes an ownership change as defined in the statute, its loss carryovers may be used by it or its successor in any given year only to the extent of the Section 382 Limitation for that year. The Section 382 Limitation is equal to the value of the stock (including pure preferred) of the loss corporation immediately prior to the ownership change multiplied by the Long-Term Tax-Exempt Rate prevailing at the time of the ownership change. For example, if all the stock of Loss Corporation, having NOL carryovers of $10 million, were purchased for the sum of $10 million, at a time when the Long-Term Tax-Exempt Rate was 7.5%, the $10 million of NOLs could only be used to offset taxable income of $750,000 in any one year. To the extent that there was not sufficient income in a year to fully utilize this Section 382 Limitation loss amount, the unused amount would carry over to the following year.

Three particulars of Section 382 should be mentioned here. First, the Section 382 limitations apply not only with respect to net operating loss carryovers of the loss corporation, but apply as well to "built-in losses" of the loss corporation. Generally, built-in losses are present to the extent that a corporation has assets with tax bases that are higher than their fair market values. In the eyes of Congress, there is no difference of substance between net operating losses on the one hand, which represent tax losses that have previously accrued and been realized, and built-in losses on the other hand, which have previously accrued but have not yet been realized. In this connection, depreciation deductions of assets with built-in losses will be subject to the Section 382 rules to the extent of the built-in losses. Section 382 will apply to these built-in losses, however, only if the corporation has a net unrealized built-in loss when its assets are looked at in the aggregate.

The second rule that should be mentioned is one that pertains very specifically to leveraged buyouts of loss corporations. In determining the value of a loss corporation's stock for purposes of computing the Section 382 Limitation, the value of the stock is reduced by the amount of debt imposed upon the target in order to finance the acquisition. Although at the time of this writing we have only a broad statement of intent from Congress, and must, therefore, await more detail from it or the IRS, it seems reasonably clear that this rule was intended to apply to debt incurred by the target itself as well as debt incurred by a holding company whose sole asset is the target. What is not clear is whether the IRS will apply this rule in the case of an acquiring entity that has other operations and subsidiaries and incurs debt directly or indirectly to finance the acquisition of a loss corporation. In operation, this rule effectively means that a highly leveraged acquisition of a loss corporation will generally result in the forfeiture of its NOL carryovers.

An important exception to the Section 382 limitations is that there will be no limitation on the use of a target's losses to offset gain recognized by the target itself on the sale of its assets or the making of a Section 338 election, to the extent it has substantial unrecognized built-in gains in its assets. Thus, where a target has substantial loss carryovers, it will often be advantageous to purchase assets or make a Section 338 election, especially if the target is being acquired in a highly leveraged transaction.

What are the Section 384 Limitations?

Section 384 concerns itself with corporations having loss carryovers that acquire other corporations that generate taxable gains. Specifically, Section 384 imposes limitations upon a loss corporation's ability to offset its losses against taxable gains recognized by subsidiaries that it acquires and with which it files a consolidated tax return. These limitations apply as well where the loss corporation acquires the gain assets from another corporation in a tax-free reorganization or liquidation that results in a carryover of basis. As in the case of Section 382, loss carryovers of the acquiring corporation include unrealized built-in losses.

Basis Considerations of the Target Corporation and Its Shareholders

What are the tax consequences of a cost basis or asset acquisition to the target corporation?

The general rule is that the basis of an asset in the possession of a target corporation may not be stepped-up to cost or fair market value without the recognition of taxable gain to such corporation. In a cost basis transaction, the target will generally be subject to an immediate tax on an amount equal to the aggregate step-up in the bases of the assets. In addition, the sale or exchange of an asset may trigger the recapture of investment or business tax credits previously taken by the target on the acquisition of the asset.

*What are the tax consequences of a cost basis or asset acquisition to the shareholders of the target corporation?

The shareholders of the target will be subject to tax upon the receipt of the asset sales proceeds (net of the corporate level tax) from the target corporation, whether the proceeds are distributed in the form of a dividend, in redemption of the shareholders' target stock, or in complete liquidation of the target corporation. If the asset sales proceeds are retained by the target corporation, then the value of those proceeds are indirectly taxed to the shareholders upon the sale or exchange of the stock of the target corporation. Although the proceeds of the sale of the target corporation assets may be distributed to certain corporate shareholders with little or no tax imposed, those proceeds will ultimately be taxed when distributed up the chain of ownership to noncorporate shareholders. The shareholders of the target corporation are generally subject to a double tax on a cost basis transaction: they bear the economic burden of the tax imposed on the asset sale by the target corporation, and they are subject to tax again either upon the receipt of distributions from the target, or upon the sale or exchange of their target stock.

*In what circumstances will a target corporation and its shareholders be subject to double tax on a cost basis or asset acquisition?

The target corporation and its shareholders will typically be subject to double tax where: (i) the target corporation sells, or is deemed for tax purposes to sell, its assets to the purchaser in a taxable transaction; (ii) the shareholders of the target corporation will ultimately receive the proceeds of the sale, either directly or indirectly through the sale of their stock in the target corporation; and (iii) the receipt of the proceeds by the shareholders of the target corporation will be taxable to such shareholders. The cost basis transaction in these circumstances causes the proceeds of the sale to be taxed twice, first to the target corporation and again to its shareholders. There are several significant exceptions to this general rule, and these are identified below.

*What are the tax consequences of a stock or carryover basis transaction to the target corporation and its shareholders?

There is generally only one level of tax imposed in a carryover basis or stock transaction, and that tax is imposed on the shareholders of the target corporation. The target corporation realizes neither gain nor loss in a stock or carryover basis transaction because its assets are not actually or constructively sold in a taxable sale or exchange. Rather, the shareholders of a target corporation are taxed on the gain recognized on the sale of their target corporation stock.

There are numerous exceptions to the general rule that only one level of tax is imposed in stock or carryover basis transactions. The most common exception is those situations where a selling shareholder of the target corporation stock is a C corporation: the proceeds from the sale of the target stock by a corporate shareholder will likely be taxed again upon their ultimate distribution to noncorporate shareholders.

Putting It All Together: Asset or Stock?

*Do the tax benefits to the purchaser in an asset or cost basis acquisition exceed the tax costs to the target corporation and its shareholders?

Generally, no. The tax benefits to the purchaser arising from the basis step-up amount are realized over time through depreciation and amortization deductions, or upon the taxable disposition of the assets. The immediate tax cost to the target corporation and its shareholders on the basis step-up amount is generally greater than the present value of the tax benefits to the purchaser. Unless the present value of the tax benefits to the purchaser exceeds the aggregate tax costs to the target corporation and its shareholders, there is little or no justification for a cost basis or asset acquisition transaction instead of a carryover basis or stock acquisition.

*Does the double tax burden to the target corporation and its shareholders in a cost basis acquisition mean that stock transactions are more prevalent than asset acquisitions?

Yes. The tax bite in a double tax situation may be substantial. The shareholders of a target corporation generally have a significant tax incentive to avoid the double tax by selling the stock of the target corporation instead of having the target corporation sell its assets. The purchaser's insistence on an asset transaction will likely be met with a demand for a higher purchase price, thereby shifting the cost of all or a substantial part of the additional tax burden to the buyer. The higher purchase price, however, will likely create both further tax liability to the target corporation and additional financing needs for the buyer. As a result, stock acquisitions, where attainable, are the rule rather than the exception.

*What are the circumstances in which a cost basis or asset acquisition transaction is justifiable for tax purposes?

An asset or cost basis transaction is generally advisable for tax purposes in situations where the double tax burden to the seller can be partially or wholly avoided, and in situations where double tax is inevitable regardless of the structure.

There is one circumstance where the immediate tax to the target corporation on the asset basis step-up transaction can be obviated in whole or in part. Target corporations that have current or carryover net operating or capital losses can often use such losses to offset or "shelter" the gain realized on the asset basis step-up transaction. In the best of circumstances, the entire gain on the asset sale can be offset by such losses or deductions. The cost of this benefit, however, is the reduction of the target corporation's net operating loss carryovers that may have otherwise been available to shelter income in future years.

Cost basis or asset acquisitions may also be preferable to carryover or stock acquisitions where the proceeds of the sale will ultimately be taxed twice regardless of the structure of the transaction. This circumstance typically exists where the target corporation is a subsidiary member of a consolidated return group, and the selling consolidated group will recognize approximately the same taxable gain on the sale of the assets of the target as it would recognize on the sale of the stock of the target. Under the consolidated return rules, the asset sales proceeds received by the target corporation may be distributed free of tax to its corporate shareholders who are members of the selling consolidated group. Double tax will be effectively imposed, however, on the distribution of the sales proceeds by the target corporation to its minority shareholders that are not members of the selling consolidated group. A cost-basis transaction may be effected by an actual asset transfer or by a constructive asset transfer pursuant to an election under Section 338.

Can the double tax be avoided where the target is an S corporation or a partnership?

Generally, yes. In the case of a target that is an S corporation or a partnership, the tax pass-through and basis adjustment rules generally operate to allow the seller to escape with approximately the same net tax cost on an asset sale as on the sale of stock or partnership interests. It is important to note, however, that these basis adjustment rules may not operate perfectly or properly in all cases. For example, taxpayers are generally not permitted to offset ordinary income against capital loss; and the presence in an S corporation target of assets with substantial depreciation recapture or other similar ordinary income items can thwart the operation of the pass-through benefit. Moreover, where the S corporation shareholders wish to utilize installment sale treatment, an asset sale may not be as beneficial to the sellers as a stock transaction.

Can a seller avoid the double tax by converting the target to a pass-through entity immediately prior to a sale?

No. The principal pass-through benefits to members of a consolidated return group, to shareholders of an S corporation, and to the partners of a partnership are achieved only on a going forward basis. A corporation, for example, can convert to a partnership only by undergoing a taxable liquidation. Where a C corporation target converts to S corporation status, a special corporate level tax will be imposed upon the sale or exchange of the assets of the target corporation to the extent of the built-in gain in its assets as of the time of the conversion.

Are there any other situations in which the purchaser can acquire a step-up in the basis of the assets of the target corporation, but where the target and its shareholders are subject to a single level of tax?

Yes. The discussion above describes the most common situations in which an asset basis step-up can be achieved with a single level of tax. Other strategies are available in particular factual circumstances, and still others will be developed by astute tax practitioners. It is beyond the scope of this work to delve into those areas.

TAX-FREE AND TAX-DEFERRED TRANSACTIONS

In this section, we focus principally, although not exclusively, upon the seller and investigate various aspects of providing tax-deferred or tax-free consideration in the transaction. Although from a tax standpoint we focus on the treatment to the seller, it is important to remember that such transactions often carry benefits to a buyer by allowing it to finance an acquisition with its own stock or subordinated debt issued to a seller. We will also discuss the impact of tax-free transactions on the overall stock acquisition versus asset acquisition decision.

Deferral Concepts

How does deferred consideration reduce the seller's tax costs?

The simplest way to reduce the seller's tax bill is to postpone the recognition of gain. This may be accomplished in a tax-free or partially tax-free acquisition or via the installment sale route. For example, suppose corporation S wants to sell the stock of its subsidiary T for $100 and its basis in the stock of T is $0. Instead, P agrees to accept $80 in cash and $20 in preferred stock of T. If this transaction qualifies as a partially tax-free recapitalization (as it should), P will not recognize $20 in gain on the receipt of the preferred stock. Rather, P will be taxed when P sells the preferred stock. Similarly, if P accepts $80 in cash and a $20 debenture, P will not recognize gain until the principal amount of the debenture is paid.

In effect, the deferral of the payment of tax on the receipt of the preferred stock or the debenture permits P to reinvest $20 of the consideration received undiminished by taxes. In contrast, if the transaction were immediately taxable in full, P would have available for reinvestment only the after-tax residue of $20—say, $15. Thus, deferral allows P to invest, temporarily, an extra $5 throughout the period of the deferral.

Installment Sales

*What is an installment sale?

An installment sale is a disposition of property (by a person who is not a "dealer" in such property) where at least one payment is to be received after the close of the taxable year in which the sale occurs. Basically, an installment sale is a sale or exchange for a promissory note or other debt instrument of the buyer. In the case of an installment sale, the gain on the sale is recognized, pro-rata, whenever principal payments on the note are received, or if earlier, upon a disposition of the installment obligation. For example, if A sells property to B for a note with a principal amount of $100 and A's basis in the property was $60, A realizes a gain of $40. Since the ratio of the gain recognized ($40) to the total amount realized ($100) is 40%, this percentage of each principal payment received by A will be treated as taxable gain. The other 60% will be treated as a nontaxable return of capital.

Installment treatment is only available with respect to a debt obligation of the buyer itself, as opposed to even a related third party issuer. An obligation of the buyer will not qualify if it is payable on demand, or, generally, if it is in registered form and/or designed to be publicly traded.

Note, however, that an installment obligation may be guaranteed by a third party, and may even be secured by a standby letter of credit. In contrast, installment obligations secured by cash or cash equivalents, such as certificates of deposit or U.S. Treasury instruments, do not qualify.

What kinds of transactions are eligible for installment sale treatment?

The installment method is generally available for sales of any property other than installment obligations held by a seller, and other than inventory and property sold by dealers in the subject property. Subject to certain exceptions, installment treatment is generally available to a shareholder who sells his stock or to a corporation or other entity that sells its assets. Under a provision added in 1986, installment treatment is not available for sales of stock or securities that are traded on an established securities market. Although the provision is not entirely clear on this point, installment treatment appears not to be available in an acquisition of a publicly held target—even though its stock will be "privately held" upon the consummation of the transaction.

Where a transaction is structured to achieve asset sale treatment rather than stock sale treatment for tax purposes, the application of the installment sale rules becomes more problematical. For one thing, the gain recognized to a target corporation as a result of an election under Section 338 or Section 338(h)(10) is not eligible for installment treatment. In addition to the limitation on installment treatment for inventory, certain additional limitations apply to asset sales. Any portion of a seller's or a target's gain that is subject to depreciation recapture is not eligible for installment treatment. Further, under legislation enacted in 1987, where real estate is sold by a non-dealer for an installment obligation, the seller must pay the IRS interest on the deferred tax liability resulting from the installment method. Where assets of a target include real estate, therefore, a portion of any purchase money obligation would ordinarily be subject to this rule.

Where a C corporation sells its assets for an installment note and distributes the note to its shareholders in liquidation, the installment gain will be fully triggered as a result of the liquidating distribution of the note. In such a case, only the shareholder level gain may be reported under the installment method. Where the target is an S corporation, the results of such a transaction are more complex and, at the time of this writing, technically unclear. As stated in the 1986 Tax Act, the installment rules require immediate gain recognition to the S corporation upon liquidation, just as in the case of a C corporation; such a rule effectively denies any benefit from installment treatment to owners of an S corporation. Under so-called technical correction legislation now pending in Congress, the S corporation would be able to defer the gain recognized on the asset sale so as to provide the shareholders with the full benefits of installment treatment. Finally, if the S corporation was formerly a C corporation, special planning issues are likely to be presented in an asset sale involving installment debt.

What role do the original issue discount rules play in installment sale transactions?

The original issue discount (OID) rules, in effect, require that installment debt provide for an interest rate equivalent to the rate the United States Treasury pays on loans of similar maturity (the "applicable federal rate"). If this interest rate is not provided, the debt instrument will be recharacterized to constitute an obligation in a lower principal amount with sufficient interest accruing thereon to carry the adequate interest rate.

For example, if a seller accepts a three year, no-interest note with a face amount of $10,000, and the "applicable federal rate" is 8%, the note will be deemed to be a three-year, 8% note with a principal amount of $7,938. As a result, the seller will be deemed to receive, and the buyer will be deemed to pay, $635 of interest during the first year, $686 of interest during the second year, and $741 of interest and $7,938 of principal during the third year. For the seller, $2,062 of potential capital gain is converted into ordinary interest income; in addition, because the OID rules require the interest to be reported on an economic accrual basis, the recharacterized portion will be reported over the term of the note, rather than at maturity. For the buyer, although it will take the purchased stock or assets with a lower basis ($7,938 rather than $10,000), it will have converted the forfeited basis into deductible interest.

This does not mean that the seller does not obtain a deferral advantage from the installment sale; the deferral of tax still exists with respect to the gain inherent in the principal amount. If, in the above example, the note provided for a principal of $7,938 with simple interest of 8% payable annually, the seller would be much better off than if he obtained $7,938 in cash and used the net after-tax proceeds to purchase a three-year certificate of deposit paying 8%. The reason is that in an all-cash sale, the seller is left with only the after-tax proceeds to invest at an 8% return, whereas in the installment sale the pre-tax sale proceeds are fully invested for the 8% return. In short, particularly where the buyer needs to finance its acquisition with borrowed funds from some source, there is a tax advantage in having the seller be that source.

The OID rules will be further discussed in the financing discussion later in the chapter.

Tax-Free Transactions

What kinds of transactions may qualify for tax-free treatment?

Every transaction involving an exchange of property is taxable unless otherwise specified in the Code. Thus, corporate acquisitions are generally taxable to the seller of stock or assets.

However, several types of acquisition transactions may be tax-free to the seller, but only to the extent the seller receives stock in the acquiring corporation (or in certain corporations closely affiliated with the acquiring corporation).

In general, tax-free acquisitions fall into three categories: statutory mergers, exchanges of stock for stock, and exchanges of assets for stock. Except for the Section 351 transaction discussed later, all of the available tax-free acquisition transactions are provided under Section 368 of the Code. In all, considering the various permutations of its provisions, Section 368 ultimately sets forth more than a dozen different varieties of acquisition reorganizations. The most commonly used forms of reorganizations, the "A," "hybrid A," "B," "C," and "D" reorganizations, appear in diagram form on pages 344–346.

What are the tax consequences of a typical tax-free reorganization?

In the classic tax-free acquisition, individual A owns all of the stock of Mom and Pop Grocery, Inc. ("Grocery"), which is acquired by Supermarkets, Inc. ("Supermarkets"). In the transaction, A surrenders to Supermarkets all of his stock in Grocery solely in exchange for voting stock of Supermarkets. This is a fully tax-free "B" reorganization, in which A recognizes no immediate gain or loss.

The corollaries to tax-free treatment here as elsewhere are carryover and substituted basis and holding period. In other words, A obtains a basis in his Supermarkets stock equal to his basis in the Grocery stock surrendered (substituted basis), and continues his old holding period in the stock. Similarly, Supermarkets takes a basis in the Grocery stock acquired equal to A's basis (carryover basis) and also picks up A's holding period.

What are the advantages of tax-free transactions to sellers and buyers?

By participating in a tax-free transaction, the seller is provided the opportunity to exchange stock in the target for stock of the buyer without the immediate recognition of gain. Because the seller will have a basis in the buyer's stock that is the same as his old basis in the target stock (a "substituted basis"), tax is only deferred until the target stock is ultimately sold. Where the target is closely held and the buyer is publicly held, the seller may obtain greatly enhanced liquidity without a current tax.

Additionally, although death and taxes are both said to be inevitable, a seller participating in a tax-free transaction may utilize the former to avoid the latter. Under a long-standing but controversial rule in the Code, an individual's estate and beneficiaries take a new, fair market value basis in the decedent's properties at his death. Thus, a seller may avoid the payment of any tax on the buyer's stock received in exchange for his old target stock by holding this new stock until his death.

For the buyer, there are two principal advantages to a tax-free acquisition. First, where the buyer is able to use its stock in the transaction, the target can be acquired without the incurrence of significant debt. Where equity financing in general is attractive from a buyer's point of view, it will often make sense to do so in a business acquisition. Second, although subject to certain limitations, the target's tax attributes (including net operating loss carryovers) will remain usable after the acquisition.

What types of tax-free transactions are provided in the Code?

Except for the Section 351 transaction discussed later, all of the available tax-free acquisition transactions are those qualifying as tax-free reorganizations under Section 368 of the Code.

The Reorganization Provisions

*What requirements must be met by all acquisition reorganizations?

Because of the way Section 368 has evolved over the years, it now constitutes a somewhat arbitrary patchwork of formal requirements. While it is not efficient or useful for anyone other than a tax specialist to be even conversant with the various requirements, it is well to know that there is likely to be within Section 368 a transaction that fits within the framework of a buyer's and seller's desires.

All acquisition reorganizations must meet three non-statutory requirements. First, the reorganization must have a business purpose. Second, the acquiring corporation must satisfy the continuity of business enterprise requirement, involving the continuation of a significant business of the target or the use of a significant portion of the target's business assets. The third requirement, probably the most burdensome, is the continuity of interest requirement.

*What is the continuity of interest requirement?

As noted above, tax-free treatment is generally only available to a target's stockholders to the extent they either retain their target stock or exchange it for stock in the acquiring entity or group. Continuity of interest requires that this qualifying stock consideration constitute a substantial portion of the total consideration received by the target shareholders in the overall transaction. For this purpose, a substantial portion is at least 40%; if a private ruling from the Internal Revenue Service is desired, the stock consideration must be at least 50% of the total.

It must be emphasized that this continuity of interest requirement is not merely necessary for a given shareholder to receive tax-free treatment. Rather, it is a prerequisite to the entire transaction's qualifying as a "reorganization," and thus, for *any* of the stock consideration received by target shareholders to be eligible for tax-free treatment.

What is the tax treatment of "boot" issued in a reorganization?

As we have indicated, a transaction may qualify as a reorganization even though the target shareholders receive nonqualifying consideration in addition to stock in the acquiring company. In the jargon of tax practitioners, such nonqualifying consideration received in a tax-free reorganization is called "boot." Except in the rare instance where boot consists of appreciated property of the target or the acquiring corporation, the issuance of boot in a reorganization will not have an adverse tax effect on either the target or the acquiring corporation, provided the boot is distributed to the shareholders or creditors of the target. Generally, where appreciated property is used by the acquiring corporation or is distributed by the target corporation in a reorganization, gain will be recognized to it on the appreciation.

Shareholders of a target who receive boot in a reorganization will recognize gain on their target stock to the extent of the boot received, subject to potential dividend characterization as explained below. What is important to note here is that the gain is not merely prorated among the shares of target stock surrendered in the exchange. Rather, all gain realized by a shareholder on the overall transaction is recognized to the extent he receives boot.

To illustrate, assume shareholder A owns 100 shares of target stock with a basis of $40 and a value of $100. In a reorganization, A surrenders his 100 shares of target stock for 50 shares of stock in Acquirer corporation and $50 in cash. If A had sold his target stock for $100 in a taxable transaction, recognizing as capital gain the excess of the $100 realized over his $40 basis in his stock, one could say that 60% ($60/$100) of the proceeds was taxable gain. If, as in our example, 50% of the consideration is tax-free and 50% is boot, one might think that the boot would only be taxable to the extent of 60%. The rule, however, is that the entire amount of gain of $60 is recognized to the extent of the $50 of boot received. Thus, A will recognize $50 of gain on the reorganization, not 60% of $50, or $30.

The boot rules also provide that if the exchange of target stock for stock in the acquiring corporation and boot has the effect of the distribution of a dividend, then the gain recognized under the rules discussed above will be treated not as capital gain but as dividend income to the shareholder. The question of how one determines whether this dividend equivalence exists has been a subject of much controversy in the courts for a number of years and, in fact, is finally scheduled for decision by the United States Supreme Court in the near future. While this issue is of relatively little significance under the current tax rates, it may again become important if and when Congress reinstates a preferential tax rate for capital gains.

Do the reorganization rules permit an exchange of target common for preferred stock in the acquiring corporation?

Except for certain kinds of reorganizations that explicitly require that the consideration consist solely of voting stock, nonvoting preferred stock will be qualifying consideration in tax-free reorganizations.

Do the reorganization rules permit a tax-free exchange of debt securities?

Generally, debt securities (i.e., medium and long term balloon notes, debentures, and bonds) may be received in tax-free reorganizations only to the extent they are exchanged for debt securities of the target. Note, however, that even where gain is recognized on the receipt of a debt instrument, installment sale reporting is usually available.

Does reorganization status have consequences for the target corporation as well as its shareholders?

Definitely. As to any of the transactions that are treated as asset acquisitions for tax purposes, i.e., statutory mergers and actual asset transfers, the transaction will be treated as *fully taxable* to the target corporation as well as its shareholders, unless the transaction qualifies as a reorganization. Thus, to ensure tax-free treatment, the continuity of interest requirement must be met, in addition to the various other reorganization requirements of the statute, regulations, and case law.

Is it possible to effect a tax-free exchange of stock without meeting the continuity of interest requirement?

There are two types of transactions that can achieve this result, the Section 351 transaction (described below) and the "E" reorganization or recapitalization. Regarding the latter, the Internal Revenue Service has declared that the continuity of interest requirement does not apply to an E reorganization. This means that where a buyer acquires the stock of a target, the target's shareholders may achieve tax-free treatment by exchanging some or all of their stock for new common or preferred stock in the target, simultaneously with or immediately prior to the sale of the controlling interest to the buyer. For example, a target shareholder holding $100 of target stock may exchange 10% of that stock for $10 of target preferred and sell the remaining 90% to the buyer for $90, and only be taxed on the latter exchange.

The National Starch Transaction

What is a Section 351 transaction?

Section 351 of the Code provides nonrecognition treatment on the transfer of property to a corporation by one or more parties in exchange for stock or stock and securities of the transferee corporation, provided the transferors possess 80% control of the transferee corporation immediately after the transaction. Although designed for the initial incorporation of a previously unincorporated business, Section 351 can be utilized as an alternative to the reorganization provisions in order to allow nonrecognition of gain to some of the target shareholders.

What is the National Starch transaction?

The so-called National Starch transaction (so named for an acquisition technique utilized by the company in 1978) involves the joint transfer of cash by the buyer and target stock by one or more target shareholders to a newly-formed corporation (Newco) under Section 351, in exchange for target common and preferred stock, respectively. Newco then utilizes the cash to purchase the remaining target stock. Because the initial transfer of target stock and cash to Newco qualified under Section 351, no gain is recognized to the target shareholders on the receipt of the Newco preferred stock. A diagram of this transaction appears in Exhibit 5–14 (Page 348).

Generally, there are no significant tax reasons favoring the use of a National Starch transaction as against a recapitalization. The principal difference between the two is that in the recapitalization, the target stockholders will end up holding minority interests in the target itself, while in the Section 351 transaction a newly formed holding company that acquires the target will be issuing the preferred stock or minority stock to the target shareholders.

From a tax standpoint, where the buyer is issuing debt as well as stock, more favorable treatment may be obtained by utilizing Section 351 as opposed to installment sale treatment in conjunction with a recapitalization of the target. Assume, for example, that individual A owns 100 shares of target stock with a basis of $40 and a fair market value of $100. In either a recapitalization or a National Starch transaction, A exchanges his target stock for $50 of preferred stock and $50 of debt securities due in 10 years. If the transaction is a recapitalization, the boot rules discussed above dictate that A's realized gain of $60 be recognized to the extent of the $50 boot received. Under the installment sale provisions, however, this $50 gain need not be reported by A until principal is paid on the debt security. Contrast this with the Section 351 treatment of a debt security. Because the security is not boot under Section 351, but is technically entitled to nonrecognition treatment along with the stock, A takes a basis in the debt security equal to a ratable portion of his $40 basis in the target stock surrendered. Taking, therefore, a $20 basis in the debt security, A will recognize only $30 upon the later retirement or sale of the debt security for $50 in cash.

An additional benefit in utilizing the Section 351 nonrecognition provisions instead of the installment sale rules to effectuate tax deferral on receipt of a debt instrument involves the differing treatment of the two upon the death of the holder. Upon the death of a holder of an installment obligation, including one issued as boot in a reorganization, the previously untaxed income will be accelerated and taxed to his estate. In stark contrast, where a selling target shareholder dies holding a debt instrument received in a tax-free transaction under Section 351, there will be no tax at all and the estate will receive a new basis in the obligation equal to its fair market value. Of course, in either event the debt instrument will be included in the gross estate for estate tax purposes.

The Role of Spin-offs

What is a tax-free spin-off?

In addition to the acquisition reorganizations provided under Section 368, the tax law provides for a corporation to "spin off" the stock of its corporate subsidiary to its shareholders in a tax-free transaction under Section 355 of the Code. This transaction is diagrammed in Exhibit 5-11. As is discussed elsewhere in this chapter, a tax-free spin-off may sometimes be an acquisition to a taxable divestiture or sale of a corporate subsidiary. In the context of acquisition transactions, the spin-off may be useful where a parent corporation is itself being acquired in a tax-free reorganization, and the acquiring corporation does not wish to own the stock of the subsidiary. Because of the complex legal requirements for qualification under Section 355, the tax-free spin-off is generally not feasible where the target or distributing corporation is to be acquired in a taxable, rather than a tax-free, transaction.

When a spin-off is done on a non–prorata basis—i.e., one group of the original stockholders ends up holding one portion of the corporate assets, and another group the rest—this is known as a "split-up" or "split-off." It nevertheless still can qualify as tax-free under Section 355. This transaction is diagrammed in Exhibit 5-12 (p. 347).

STRUCTURING TAXABLE ACQUISITIONS

Introduction

We now revisit some of the issues addressed earlier in the chapter with a view to putting together the actual structure for the acquisition. In particular, we will focus here upon taxable transactions, i.e., those not seeking to qualify for tax-free treatment.

Where we have previously described in general the benefits of pass-through entities, we now look to determine which, if any, will be most advantageous or feasible. Next, having discussed the issues involved in choosing whether a carryover basis or cost basis acquisition is appropriate, we now address the question of how a taxable acquisition may be structured to achieve the desired result.

Choosing the Entity

What is the most tax efficient structure to acquire or operate a target's business?

If practicable, not even a single level of corporate tax should be paid on income generated by the target's business. For this reason, a pass-through entity owned by individuals should be the structure wherever possible. With respect to an acquisition of assets by individuals, this means that the acquisition vehicle would be either a partnership (presumably limited) or an S corporation. In the case of a stock acquisition by individuals, the target generally should be operated as an S corporation.

Where the buyer is a C corporation, the target business, whether acquired through an asset or stock purchase, should be operated as a division of the buyer or through a separate company included in the buyer's consolidated return. In either case, the income of the target will be subject to only one level of corporate tax prior to dividend distributions from the buyer to its shareholders.

Under what circumstances may a consolidated return be filed?

In order for two or more corporations to file a consolidated return, they must constitute an "affiliated group" for tax purposes. Although subject to numerous qualifications and complications, an affiliated group is essentially a chain of corporations in which a common parent owns at least 80% of the voting power and at least 80% of the value of the stock of the other members of the group. In the case of the parent's ownership of at least one first-tier subsidiary, this 80% stock ownership must be direct; as to all other members of the group, the 80% ownership may be through combined holdings of other members of the corporate group. Nonvoting preferred stock that does not share in corporate growth and that does not have a significant discounted issue price relative to its liquidation value—so-called "pure preferred"—is not taken into account as stock for purposes of the affiliation rules. Thus, ordinarily, a parent may file a consolidated return with a subsidiary in which it owns at least 80% of the common stock, even though one or more series of pure preferred stock may be held by third parties.

Generally, only ordinary domestic corporations are includible in the affiliated group eligible to file a consolidated return. Foreign corporations, tax-exempt corporations, regulated investment companies, and various other types of corporations subject to special tax rules are not includible. Special rules are set forth for the filing of consolidated returns by insurance companies.

Where preferred stock in the target is issued to the seller in connection with an acquisition, care must be taken to ensure that the seller's ownership of this preferred stock will not thwart the buyer's intention to file a consolidated return. Probably the most subtle pitfall in this regard is where the seller is issued preferred stock in the target which, because of the speculative nature of the target's ability to fund the preferred dividend and liquidation rights, has an initial value (and hence, issue price) that is substantially lower than its liquidation value. In this instance, the preferred may not be excludible in judging affiliated group status as between the buyer and the target.

In addition, a similar risk of disaffiliation may be present where the seller or other parties (for example, holders of mezzanine debt) are issued warrants to acquire stock in the target. Congress has authorized the Treasury Department to set forth circumstances under which the existence of warrants or other options to acquire stock in a subsidiary will be taken into account in determining 80% stock ownership for purposes of the affiliation requirement. Until regulations are issued (and perhaps even after the regulations are issued), there will remain a possibility that the issuance to third parties of rights to acquire more than 20% of the outstanding stock of a subsidiary might result in disaffiliation, and should, therefore, be avoided.

*When should an S corporation be considered?

Typically, an S corporation should be considered where the target is, or can become, a free-standing domestic operating corporation owned by 35 or fewer U.S. individual shareholders. Because the S corporation requirements are designed to ensure that such entities will have relatively simple structures, they are not inherently user-friendly vehicles for larger, complex operations. Nevertheless, because there is not a limit on the size of the business that may be conducted in an S corporation, it is often possible to plan around obstacles to qualification under subchapter S and to utilize this immensely favorable tax entity.

Briefly, an S corporation may not: (i) have more than 35 shareholders; (ii) have as a shareholder any person (other than an estate and a very limited class of trust) who is not an individual; (iii) have a nonresident alien as a shareholder; (iv) have more than one class of stock; (v) be a member of an affiliated group with other corporations; or (vi) be a bank, thrift, insurance company, or certain other types of business entity.

Probably the most significant of the above provisions in their impact on business acquisitions are the prohibitions on noncorporate shareholders, more than one class of stock, and membership in an affiliated group. Where an S corporation is utilized, it is impossible to utilize preferred stock financing or to have a corporate seller take back any equity at all. Assuming that subordinated debt is a feasible alternative from the point of view of the company's overall debt structure, one may substitute subordinated debt, even a convertible subordinated debt, for preferred stock without running afoul of the above rules. Additionally, one could issue subordinated debt with warrants that are only exercisable under certain specified conditions, so as not to permit the exercise thereof to disqualify the corporation from S status. It should be noted, however, that where an S corporation is utilized, the typical debt/equity recharacterization problem takes on a heightened significance, because a recharacterization of purported debt as equity may cause the corporation to be disqualified from S corporation status.

Because an S corporation cannot be a member of an affiliated group with other corporations, it cannot own an 80% or greater interest in a subsidiary, regardless of whether it files or would be permitted to file a consolidated return with the subsidiary. Thus, where a target's business operations are conducted through one or more operating subsidiaries, converting the target to an S corporation would not be possible. In such cases, consideration should be given to whether the subsidiaries' operations could be conducted directly as nonincorporated divisions of the target rather than in corporate subsidiaries.

Where the operations of a domestic target and its subsidiaries can be conducted in a single domestic entity, consolidation can be achieved through liquidation or merger, so as to permit the operating entity to become an S corporation. Alternatively, where the existing subsidiary structure is desirable or necessary, but the subsidiaries are of relatively little significance in terms of their earnings, disaffiliation should be considered. Disaffiliation might also be considered where there are foreign subsidiaries, as their income cannot, ordinarily, be consolidated with that of the domestic parent. Generally, disaffiliation can be brought about with relatively little cost in money or inconvenience, mainly by causing the subsidiary to issue a high vote, low value stock to one or more shareholders of the parent company.

*When should a partnership be considered?

The partnership is an alternative to the S corporation, with several notable advantages. First, it is always available without restriction as to the structure or composition of the target's ownership; therefore, it can be used when the S corporation is unavailable for technical reasons. In addition, the partnership is unique in enabling the partners to receive distributions of loan proceeds free of tax. Finally, if the target is expected to generate tax losses, a partnership is better suited than an S corporation to pass these losses through to the owners. The latter two advantages result from the fact that partners, unlike S corporation shareholders, may generally include liabilities of the partnership in their basis in the partnership.

Unfortunately, the partnership also has its own limitations and disadvantages. One limitation of the partnership structure is that, as a practical matter, the only way that individual buyers can convert a target from a corporation to a partnership is to liquidate it, and therefore, such acquisitions will be taxed as asset acquisitions with the resulting tax costs discussed earlier. Second, a number of potentially burdensome requirements must be complied with to ensure that a partnership is treated as such for tax purposes. Third, many simple corporate structuring and financing issues, such as the issuance and exercise of warrants or the incurring of debt, can be rendered a great deal more complicated. Fourth, because of the treatment of publicly traded partnerships as corporations, a subsequent public offering will raise special issues. Finally, one still encounters resistance from lenders and underwriters where a borrowing business entity is a partnership or group of partnerships. All of these considerations, as well as other legal and business issues, must be weighed to determine whether the partnership form of acquisition is appropriate.

Planning for Cost versus Carryover Basis

In addition to the choice of entity, what major structural issue should be considered?

From a tax standpoint, probably the most important issue is whether the buyer should seek to obtain a cost basis or a carryover basis in the assets of the target. Because of the potential for obtaining either of these results regardless of whether assets or stock are actually acquired, the determinations of the tax goal and the actual structure may initially be made on a separate basis.

We have already discussed earlier in the chapter what issues must be considered in determining whether to seek a cost basis. In order to make even a preliminary determination as to whether a cost basis acquisition is desirable or feasible, the buyer must obtain and evaluate information about the asset makeup and structure of the target's business, as well as information about special circumstances on the seller side that would allow for a cost basis acquisition. With respect to the desirability of obtaining a cost basis, and the potential justification of an enhanced purchase price, the principal focus will be on assets in the target that can be written up and then depreciated on an accelerated basis.

Consideration should also be given at this point to the buyer's likely disposition of the target, or parts thereof. For example, the benefit of a basis step-up may be greater where the buyer intends to dispose of portions of the target in the relatively near future, or to turn a fairly quick profit on the entire target business. On the other hand, if the intention of the buyer is to either integrate the target into an existing business for the indefinite future or to ultimately take the target public, a basis step-up may be less valuable.

With respect to the feasibility of obtaining a cost basis, the buyer must begin with the general rule that the benefits to the buyer of a basis step-up will not be sufficient to justify the increase in cost over a stock purchase if there is a full double tax on the seller side. Therefore, it will only be advantageous to the buyer to undertake a cost basis acquisition where circumstances on the seller's side may serve to diminish or eliminate the double tax. The list of such circumstances includes: a seller and target filing a consolidated return, a target that is an S corporation or partnership, and a target that has net operating loss carryovers.

What are the mechanics of achieving a cost or carryover basis?

In a taxable acquisition, carryover basis can only be achieved through a stock acquisition. For federal tax purposes, however, stock may be acquired in two ways: first, through a direct purchase of seller's stock; and second, through a reverse cash merger.

As indicated earlier, a cost basis can be achieved by purchasing either assets or stock from the seller. As in the case of a stock purchase, the tax law permits an asset purchase to be effected in two ways: first, through a direct purchase of the seller's assets; and second, through a forward cash merger. In the context of a stock acquisition, a cost basis can be achieved by making an election under Section 338 of the Code.

Is it possible to obtain a cost basis in some of the assets of the target and a carryover basis in other assets?

Generally, this is a result that Congress and the Internal Revenue Service have sought to prevent, and at this effort they have been for the most part successful. Thus, Section 338 of the Code provides that where a buyer makes a qualified stock purchase of more than one corporation affiliated with the target ("target affiliate"), it may not make a Section 338 election with respect to one of those corporations without automatically making a Section 338 election with respect to all of them. This rule is commonly called the stock consistency rule under Section 338.

That Section also provides an extremely stringent asset consistency rule. Under the asset consistency rule, where a target is purchased in a qualified stock purchase, and no Section 338 election is made, the buyer runs a risk of having a deemed Section 338 election thrust upon it in the event that it purchases an asset from the target or from a target affiliate in a so-called tainted asset acquisition. Tainted asset acquisitions generally include any transaction, other than those in the ordinary course of business, by which the buyer or the target obtains a cost basis in an asset of the target or a target affiliate. Notwithstanding these and other rules, it is sometimes possible to obtain a cost basis in some of the assets associated with the target's business without purchasing all of the target's assets or making a Section 338 election.

When a buyer purchases stock of the target and does not wish to step up the basis in all of its assets, can it protect itself against inadvertently violating the asset consistency rules?

Recognizing that a buyer might well engage in a tainted asset acquisition without intending to circumvent the consistency rules, the regulations under Section 338 provide that a taxpayer may avoid a deemed Section 338 election by filing a protective carryover basis election. Stated simply, the effect of such an election is to cause assets acquired in a tainted asset acquisition to be taken by the buyer with a carryover basis, rather than a cost basis. A protective carryover basis election should be filed following any stock acquisition that *might* be treated as a qualified stock purchase for Section 338 purposes, where (as in most cases) the effect of a Section 338 election would be detrimental.

Cash Mergers

*What are the differences in the tax treatment of forward and reverse cash mergers?

As indicated earlier in this chapter, a cash merger may be treated as either a stock acquisition or an asset acquisition depending upon whether it is a reverse merger or a forward merger. A forward cash merger, which is treated as an asset acquisition for tax purposes, involves a merger of the target corporation either into the buyer itself or into a corporate subsidiary of the buyer. The reason this is called a forward merger is that it is moving in the direction that the overall acquisition is taking, i.e., from the selling side to the buying side. It is treated for tax purposes as a sale by the target corporation of its assets followed by a taxable liquidation, resulting (because of the repeal of *General Utilities*) in two levels of tax on the transaction.

A reverse merger, or more accurately, a reverse subsidiary merger, is one in which the buyer, wishing to buy stock in the target, causes its newly-formed subsidiary to merge into the target. In the merger, the buyer exchanges its stock in the subsidiary for stock in the target, and the seller exchanges its stock in the target for the consideration issued in the merger. A reverse subsidiary merger is treated as a stock purchase for tax purposes because it ordinarily involves a newly formed subsidiary of the buyer whose existence is ignored for tax purposes. Note that the "buyer" in such a case may be a group of individuals or other entities, who will be treated as purchasing the stock of the target.

As discussed earlier, there are often non-tax reasons for effectuating a purchase of target stock via a reverse subsidiary merger, rather than through a direct acquisition of the stock. One reason may be that the target has numerous shareholders, and the merger is a convenient way of bringing about a transfer of the target shares. Additionally, where the transaction is a leveraged buyout, financed through debt borrowed against the assets or business of the target, the financing can be put in place in the merging subsidiary and the loans can be closed simultaneously with the merger.

The statutory merger is among the most beneficial and efficient legal devices in the acquisition area, but for the same reasons, it is also inherently perilous. The principal danger of the merger lies in the simplicity and ease by which many millions of dollars of assets may be transferred in a taxable transaction—in effect, by the simple push of a button. As we said before, a forward cash merger, unlike a reverse cash merger, is treated as a taxable sale and liquidation by the target. The greatest care must be taken to make sure that where a reverse merger/stock acquisition is intended, a forward merger is not inadvertently executed. In addition, where a forward merger is executed, it must be determined whether the assets of the target include one or more domestic or foreign subsidiaries. If so, a deemed Section 338 election with respect to those subsidiaries may result, unless a protective carryover basis election is made.

Are there any tax differences between a forward cash merger and an actual asset sale?

One tax difference between a forward cash merger and an actual asset sale should be noted. As has been mentioned, a forward cash merger is treated for federal income tax purposes as a sale of assets followed by a liquidation of the target. In an actual sale of assets by the target followed by a liquidation, the shareholders of the target will bear the burden of both the corporate level tax and their own shareholder level tax on liquidation; there is generally no liability on the purchaser because it has paid full value for the assets of the target. In contrast, although a forward cash merger is treated for federal income tax purposes as a sale/liquidation, the surviving corporation assumes the tax liabilities of the target along with all other liabilities by operation of state law. Therefore, unless provision to the contrary is made in the merger agreement, the merger consideration paid out to the target shareholders is likely to be free and clear of any liability for the target's tax on the liquidation. In this respect, a forward merger may result in the same economic burden on the buyer as a Section 338 election.

Among other cost savings and efficiencies, state real property and other transfer taxes are often reduced or eliminated by effecting an asset transfer through a statutory merger.

Obtaining a Cost Basis in Stock Purchases

What are the structural requirements for a Section 338 transaction?

The requirements for a regular Section 338 election and a Section 338(h)(10) election are the same, except for the additional requirement in the latter case that the target be a subsidiary member of an affiliated group filing a consolidated federal income tax return. Unless the target has substantial net operating loss or other favorable tax carryovers, it is unlikely that a buyer would wish to file a regular Section 338 election. As noted earlier, however, Section 338(h)(10) acquisitions should be considered far more frequently.

The central requirement for a Section 338 election is that the purchasing corporation (recall that the buyer must be a corporation) acquire the stock of the target corporation in a "qualified stock purchase." Generally, this means that the buyer must purchase at least 80% of the outstanding stock of the target in a taxable transaction, or a series of taxable transactions, within a single 12 month period. If a transaction was even partially subject to nonrecognition, the stock so acquired will generally not be considered to have been "purchased." The 80% ownership requirement for purposes of Section 338 is identical to that required for the filing of a consolidated tax return. Therefore, the buyer must purchase at least 80% of the voting power and at least 80% of the value of all of the target stock, with the exception only of pure preferred.

To the extent that the buyer acquires less than 100% of all of the outstanding stock of the target, the purchase price paid for the acquired stock is "grossed up" to determine the resulting value of the entire target enterprise, and this grossed-up amount will be used to determine the deemed sale price for purposes of Section 338. Notwithstanding the 80% purchase requirement, the buyer will have a good qualified stock purchase where the overwhelming majority of the consideration is supplied by the target itself, or from loans secured by the assets of the target; such payments by the target are treated as redemptions for tax purposes.

May a Section 338 election be made where a seller takes back stock in the purchasing corporation?

As a general matter, whenever a seller takes back any equity interest in the buyer, the target, or their affiliates, careful examination is required to determine whether the acquisition may be either wholly or partially tax-free. As noted above, if the transaction even partially qualified for tax-free treatment, it will probably be disqualified from the stock "purchase" requirement of Section 338. Indeed, even where from the seller's perspective the transaction ends up being wholly taxable, the transaction may fall within the terms of certain nonrecognition-type provisions which may preclude Section 338 qualification. Aside from the more obvious categories of tax-free reorganization, the transaction may fall within the terms of Section 304 or Section 351 of the Code, and thereby risk disqualification under Section 338.

What is Section 304 of the Code?

Section 304 of the Code was enacted many years ago to address a tax avoidance technique involving the sale of stock in one related corporation to another related corporation, in which a common shareholder could withdraw cash or property from his corporations while retaining undiminished ownership. The classic case involves individual A who owns all of the stock of corporations X and Y, and who sells some or all of his X stock to Y for cash. In such a case, Section 304 recharacterizes the transaction and treats it as a dividend from Y accompanied by a nontaxable contribution of X stock to Y, instead of merely a sale of X stock that would qualify as capital gain.

The reach of Section 304 goes far beyond the above example, and the statute encompasses any situation in which there is direct or indirect "control" by the selling shareholder of the stock of both the buying corporation and the target corporation. Control is defined here as 50% of the voting power or 50% of the value of a corporation's stock (including pure preferred); control of the buyer acquired in the transaction itself is included.

Where the buyer is a preexisting operating or holding company that is well capitalized, it will be very unusual for Section 304 to be an issue. The reason for this is that any equity issued to the seller in the transaction will not be such as to place it anywhere near the 50% level. Where, however, the target is acquired in a leveraged buyout, and the value of the common stock of both the target and the newly-formed purchasing corporation, on a book value basis, is fairly negligible, even a relatively small amount of preferred stock in the purchasing corporation issued to the seller may cause its ownership of the buyer to exceed the 50% mark in terms of value. In such a case, Section 304 would come into play.

When Section 304 applies, it treats the proceeds received by the selling shareholders as proceeds of a stock redemption. A determination must then be made, under the Section 302 redemption rules discussed earlier, as to whether this redemption should be treated as a sale of stock or as a dividend.

Section 304 undermines the treatment of a stock purchase under Section 338 in its characterization of the purchaser's receipt of the target shares. As amended in the Tax Reform Act of 1986, Section 304 will cause the purchaser to take a carryover basis, and thus prevent a qualified stock purchase, only where and to the extent that a seller receives dividend treatment on its deemed redemption. In the typical case, where a seller receives a large amount of cash and a small amount of preferred stock in the purchasing corporation, the seller should obtain sale, rather than dividend, treatment, and thus not be disqualified under Section 338. However, there are many reasons for uncertainty on this point, and if faced with the need to resolve this Section 304/302 issue, one should probably seek a ruling from the Internal Revenue Service.

Note that Section 304 will apply not only to the case where a single seller is in a 50% control relationship to the target and the buyer after the sale, but also where a group of sellers together have the requisite control relationship to the entities. Where, however, a majority of the shareholders of the target receive solely cash or debt and do not receive stock in the purchasing corporation, so that the shareholders who receive stock own, as a group, less than 50% of the stock of either the purchasing corporation or the target corporation, Section 304 will not apply and the transaction may qualify as a purchase under Section 338.

Where, instead of taking back preferred stock in the purchasing corporation, the seller takes back or retains preferred stock in the target itself, Section 304 will not apply. However, as noted earlier, the retention of this preferred stock may interfere with the 80% purchase requirement of Section 338 to the extent that the retained preferred has a value in excess of 20% of the aggregate stock value in the target, and has an issue price substantially below its redemption and liquidation value.

How may preferred stock be issued to the seller without falling under Section 304?

One way of avoiding these problems is to issue the seller a subordinated debenture or other long-term debt instrument, rather than stock. In such a case, unless the debt has peculiar features involving a high risk of recharacterization as equity, Section 304 and the 80% affiliation problems can be clearly avoided.

Where financing for a transaction requires that the seller receive equity rather than debt, an alternative approach may be in order. In such a case, it might be worthwhile to seek out a third party preferred stock investor, whose interest could be superior to that of the seller. By thus increasing the amount of stock value not held by the seller, Section 304 can be avoided.

How can Section 351 prevent a qualified stock purchase?

Section 351 of the Code is designed to provide nonrecognition treatment to one or more persons who transfer property (including cash) to a corporation in exchange for substantially all of the corporation's stock. Where the purchasing corporation is a newly formed entity, there is some risk that everyone who receives stock in the entity in connection with transactions that were firmly contemplated at the time of its incorporation will be treated as a transferor receiving nonrecognition treatment under Section 351.

The facts in this regard can vary significantly. On the one hand, where a group of investors forms a corporation to negotiate for and ultimately acquire another corporation, and the purchasing corporation has been fully capitalized prior to the commencement of negotiations with the target and its shareholders, any stock ultimately received by the target shareholders should probably not be treated in connection with the initial incorporation of the purchaser. On the other hand, where a group of individuals contemplating an acquisition negotiates with the shareholders of the target prior to the incorporation or even the capitalization of the purchasing corporation, the risk that stock in the purchaser ultimately issued to the target shareholders will be treated under Section 351 is very high. As will be discussed at greater length elsewhere, the latter situation may often arise where there are existing shareholders of the target who are members of a management group participating in a leveraged buyout.

As was the case with Section 304, where more than 20% of the stock of the target is received, or is treated as received, by the purchasing corporation in a Section 351 transaction, the qualified stock purchase under Section 338 will fail.

After a Section 338 acquisition, must the purchaser retain the target as a subsidiary?

The purchasing corporation is permitted to liquidate the target in a tax-free liquidation as soon after the qualified stock purchase as it wishes. Such a liquidation may be effected by way of a statutory merger.

May the purchasing corporation instead merge down into the target after a Section 338 acquisition?

From a practical standpoint, it is usually far easier to merge a recently-formed purchaser down into the target than to merge the target up into the purchaser. Although most tax practitioners agree that such a so-called downstream merger should be as benign as the upstream merger in terms of Section 338, they also agree that it is not, and that this difference in form does make all the difference in the world. Where a newly-formed purchasing corporation acquires the stock of the target and then merges down into the target, it is likely that the IRS will disregard the existence of the purchasing corporation for tax purposes. If the corporation is held by individuals, there will not be a qualified stock purchase by a corporate purchaser.

Thus, where the purchasing corporation has been recently formed, a merger of the purchasing corporation down into the target shortly after a qualified stock purchase should not be undertaken where a Section 338 election is desired. One exception to this rule is that such a downstream merger may be effected where the purchasing corporation is itself owned by another corporation that can stand as a qualified corporate purchaser for purposes of Section 338 in the event that the existence and actions of the purchasing corporation itself are ignored for tax purposes.

May the purchaser elect S corporation status in conjunction with a Section 338 acquisition?

Although the state of the law is somewhat unclear, it is likely that an S corporation cannot be a qualified purchaser in a Section 338 transaction. Similarly, it is unlikely that a liquidation into an S corporation parent may qualify as a tax-free subsidiary liquidation. Thus, initially, the purchasing corporation should be a regular C corporation. Immediately following the qualified stock purchase of the target, it should be merged up into the purchasing corporation. Assuming it otherwise meets all of the prerequisites, the purchaser may elect S corporation status effective at the beginning of its first taxable year immediately following the acquisition. The period of time between the acquisition date and the beginning of the purchaser's next tax year can be reduced to less than one month by the simple expedient of the purchaser's adopting as its initial tax year a fiscal year ending on the last day of the month in which the acquisition occurs. Thus, for example, if an acquisition takes place on January 15, 1989, the recently formed purchasing corporation will elect a January 31 tax year, and will elect S corporation status effective the first day of its second tax year, February 1, 1989. Once the purchaser is an S corporation, it will ordinarily be required to adopt a calendar year.

Given these various pitfalls in achieving a Section 338 acquisition, may all of these problems be avoided by doing a forward cash merger or other taxable asset acquisition?

Generally speaking, it is much easier from a tax standpoint to achieve a cost basis purchase by doing a direct asset acquisition, including the use of a forward cash merger. However, in some respects, the same problems loom where the target shareholders will be receiving preferred stock in the acquiring corporation. In such a case, there exists a risk of treatment quite similar to that under Section 304, namely, the "D" reorganization.

The "D" reorganization is a peculiar breed of Section 368 reorganization, diagrammed on page 346, in which the law is unclear enough to allow for a strong possibility that even though the conventional continuity of interest tests for reorganizations would be failed, all that is required to achieve reorganization status (and, therefore, carryover basis) is that one or more target shareholders receive stock in the acquiring corporation with a value equal to at least 50% of the outstanding value of all stock in the acquiring corporation (including pure preferred). As was the case in Section 304, this is a likely result where the acquisition is highly leveraged and the target shareholders receive preferred stock. Although many tax practitioners believe that the continuity of interest requirement should apply to a "D" reorganization above and beyond this 50% requirement, there is no law on point and one must proceed warily.

Allocation of Purchase Price

How are purchase price allocations made for tax purposes?

Although businesses are usually bought and sold on a lump-sum basis, for tax purposes each such transaction is broken down into a purchase and sale of the individual assets, both tangible and intangible. There is no specific requirement under the tax laws that a buyer and seller allocate the lump-sum purchase price in the same manner. Because each party has tended to take positions most favorable to it, allocation issues have been litigated by the IRS fairly often over the years. At the same time, courts and, to a lesser extent, the IRS have tended to defer to allocations of purchase price that have been agreed upon in writing between a buyer and seller in an arm's-length transaction.

Traditionally, there has been a tax tension between buyers and sellers, with sellers seeking to maximize capital gain and minimize ordinary income, and buyers seeking to maximize allocations to assets that would yield depreciation and other deductions. It has been largely because of this tax tension that courts have been so willing to defer to allocations agreed upon between the parties.

For many years, buyers and sellers have negotiated over the allocation of amounts as between a payment for goodwill of a business and a payment to the seller as consideration for his entering into a covenant not to compete. This issue presents a classic example of tax tension because these items, while difficult to distinguish factually, have dramatically different tax consequences for buyer and seller. Specifically, a sale of goodwill will be treated as capital gain to the seller and not amortizable to the buyer, while a covenant not to compete will generate ordinary income to the seller and ordinary deductions to the buyer.

By eliminating the tax rate differential between ordinary income and capital gains, the Tax Reform Act of 1986 has likewise eliminated the tax tension from the goodwill/noncompete allocation issue. Nevertheless, it can be expected that both the IRS and the courts will take several years to change the course of tax examination and litigation to the point that agreements between buyer and seller on these issues will be completely ignored. In this as in other cases, it is probably more important now than ever that buyers and sellers agree upon some written allocation of the purchase price in a manner that will yield the maximum tax savings to the parties.

Beyond the question of a written purchase price allocation, buyers have become increasingly creative in identifying intangible assets among the items purchased that, while resembling nonamortizable goodwill, can be shown to have a limited life and therefore may be amortized for tax purposes. The IRS has consistently objected to such creativity and has insisted that these are merely artificial means of redesignating goodwill. One asset of such a nature that has been litigated quite a bit in recent years is a "core deposit" base of a bank or thrift institution. Although eventually deleted from the Tax Reform Act of 1987, a provision was contained in the House Bill under which any amount paid to acquire customer base, market share, or any renewing or similar intangible item would be treated as paid for nonamortizable intangible property. Although such a provision may well surface in future legislation, and in any event is likely to be argued by the IRS, the search for such amortizable and tangible assets should continue to occupy the attention of buyers.

Are there any rules governing the allocation of purchase price?

Under the Tax Reform Act of 1986, a purchase price paid for assets, or deemed paid for assets as a result of a Section 338 election, must be allocated in accordance with the provisions of the regulations under Section 338. Those regulations require a tiered allocation of purchase price, resulting in the use of what is called the residual method of valuing goodwill. The regulations require all assets of the target to be divided into four classes. Class I assets include cash, bank demand deposits, and similar cash equivalent assets. Class II assets are certificates of deposit, U.S. Government securities, readily marketable stock or securities, foreign currency, and other readily marketable assets. Class III assets include all other assets except goodwill and going concern value. Class IV assets are goodwill and going concern value.

Under the regulations, the total purchase price is first allocated to Class I assets on the basis of their face amounts. The remaining amount of the purchase price is allocated first among Class II assets in proportion to their relative fair market values, then among Class III assets in proportion to their relative fair market values. Finally, any remaining purchase price is allocated to goodwill and going concern value.

Thus, it is not left to the taxpayer to obtain an appraisal that values goodwill explicitly at a conservative amount; rather, any remaining purchase price after allocation among Classes I–III is automatically allocated to goodwill. The buyer can ultimately seek to minimize the allocation to goodwill by substantiating a liberal valuation of Class III assets with independent appraisals or a written allocation agreement with the seller. Once again, to the extent that the overall purchase price can be reduced by allocating payments to a covenant not to compete or other arrangements with the seller, there will be that much less residue of purchase price to be allocated to Class IV.

DISPOSITION OF UNWANTED ASSETS

Introduction

Regardless of whether a buyer is planning an asset acquisition or a stock acquisition of the target, it often must deal with the task of disposing of certain assets in the target that it either cannot or does not wish to retain. Most commonly, this occurs in larger leveraged buyouts where a buyer's financing plan depends upon its ability to divest significant portions of the target's holdings to pay down debt shortly after an acquisition. In fact, the assets disposed of may be the jewels hidden on the balance sheet of the target. In such cases, it is certainly a misnomer to speak of "unwanted assets," and it would be more appropriate to simply speak in terms of early dispositions of the target's assets.

In other circumstances, the buyer does not expect to obtain value for itself from disposing of a piece of the target at a premium, and might well prefer that the seller retain this "unwanted" portion of the target's business. Similarly, the seller itself may wish to sell only certain portions of the target's operations to the buyer, perhaps preferring to sell other portions to third parties or even retaining a certain piece for various reasons of its own.

As will be seen, the most problematic, but unfortunately, the most common, of the above situations is that in which a buyer wishes to purchase the stock of the target (with a corresponding carryover basis in the target's assets) and engage in early dispositions of the target's assets. Where the buyer either is able to arrange a cost basis acquisition, or is able to have the seller divest the target of the unwanted assets prior to the acquisition, tax planning can produce more favorable results.

Planning Goals

Can an acquisition be structured to reduce the tax costs of early asset dispositions?

Although Congress and the IRS have been quite active within recent years in curtailing or foreclosing many planning devices, it is still extremely important for a buyer to structure its acquisition with a view to minimizing the tax costs of expected asset dispositions.

What are the principal planning goals in early asset dispositions?

It will be helpful to illustrate the "unwanted assets" problem with a simple factual scenario that will be referred to in the discussion that follows. Purchaser corporation P wishes to acquire target corporation T from selling corporation S in a leveraged buyout for $100. The operations of T consist of two divisions, T1 and T2. The purchase price for the T stock has been financed largely through borrowed funds. S has a tax basis in its T stock of $20, and T has a tax basis in the T1 and T2 assets of $0. To pay down acquisition debt, P must dispose of the T2 division to a third party shortly after the acquisition of T. Although the two divisions of T are of approximately equal value, P believes that it will be able to sell the T2 division alone for $60.

The principal goal of tax planning for the disposition of unwanted divisions or assets has been to put into practice the following intuitive judgment: if P has purchased all of T for $100, it should be able to dispose of all of T immediately thereafter for $100 and recognize no taxable gain. What should follow is that if P disposes of the T2 division, constituting one-half of the value of T, for $50, then no gain should be recognized there as well.

As a general matter, whether or not this intuitive proposition will be true depends upon whether P has purchased the assets of T or the stock of T. As explained earlier, where P, directly or through a subsidiary, purchases the assets of T for $100, or makes a Section 338 election, it will obtain a cost basis in all of the T assets, and will recognize no gain if it disposes of some or all of those assets for an amount equal to their cost. However, where P purchases the stock of T, and no Section 338 election is made, T retains a carryover basis in its assets, and P will have to incur a tax on T's $50 of "built-in gain" upon a disposition of the T2 division.

The general rule, the integrity of which Congress seems

obsessed with maintaining, is that the assets of T may not be disposed of by T without the recognition of a tax on the appreciation in those assets, notwithstanding that a buyer may have obtained a cost basis in the *stock* of T. The most direct and sure means of eliminating a second tax on built-in gain inside a target will be to obtain a cost basis in the target's assets through a direct asset acquisition, forward cash merger, or Section 338 transaction. When one seeks to avoid the built-in gain tax through other means, one enters the thicket of recent tax legislation, and the risks of failure are usually high.

Is the situation any different where T1 and T2 are corporate subsidiaries of T?

Although many tax professionals, academicians, and even IRS officials believe that P should be able to arrange to dispose of the stock of subsidiaries of T without incurring a built-in gain tax, this view has now been defeated in the Congress. Thus, the general rule holds true for T's corporate subsidiaries as well as its directly owned divisions, that a cost basis obtained by P in the stock of T cannot be used to offset gain realized on a disposition of a subsidiary of T.

The Mirror Family

What is a mirror subsidiary transaction?

The mirror subsidiary technique is a structure for acquiring stock of a target and obtaining a pro rata cost basis in the stock of subsidiaries holding the respective divisions of the target. This technique was used with some frequency in the mid-1980's, was placed into considerable question beginning in 1987 as a result of the Tax Reform Act of 1986, and has been unambiguously rendered ineffective by the Revenue Act of 1987. Although it now may be of only historical interest, it is worth illustrating how the basic technique worked.

Working with the example set forth earlier, P sets up its acquisition structure for T in the following manner. P obtains $100 through debt and/or equity financing, and contributes $50 to each of two newly formed subsidiaries, Mirror 1 and Mirror 2 (the "Mirror Subsidiaries"). Mirror 1 and Mirror 2 each purchase 50% of the T stock from S for $50. At this point, P, Mirror 1, Mirror 2, and T are affiliated corporations and elect to file a consolidated tax return. T then liquidates and distributes the T1 division assets to Mirror 1 and the T2 division assets to Mirror 2. P will then sell the stock of Mirror 2 to a buyer for $60.

The mirror technique involves two essential tax ingredients. First, by contributing a proportionate amount of the total acquisition cost to a Mirror Subsidiary, P indirectly obtains a cost basis in each piece of T's operations. Second, the liquidation of T into the Mirror Subsidiaries must be tax-free. As explained earlier, corporate liquidations ordinarily are taxable both to the shareholders and to the liquidating corporation, and the shareholders take a stepped-up basis in the assets of the liquidating corporation. Where a subsidiary corporation liquidates into its 80% corporate parent, no gain or loss is recognized to either the liquidating subsidiary or the parent corporation. In the above example, neither Mirror 1 nor Mirror 2 was an 80% parent of T. However, under the consolidated return regulations, 80% stock ownership of a member of the group (T) is attributed to each member of the group (Mirror 1 and Mirror 2) for purposes of various provisions of the Code.

Where the mirror transaction worked (as it clearly did prior to the Tax Reform Act of 1986), the assets of the target passed tax-free and with a carryover basis into the hands of the Mirror Subsidiaries. There would then be no tax on built-in gain upon a disposition of a Mirror Subsidiary. To the extent that P could sell the stock of a Mirror Subsidiary for an amount greater than its basis, as it does in the above example, this amount would be subject to tax. In the above example, T has a $50 basis in the stock of Mirror 2, and sells it for $60, resulting in $10 of taxable gain.

When the Tax Reform Act of 1986 was passed, the staff of the congressional committees cast into doubt whether the consolidated return regulations could be used to avoid a full recognition of tax to T upon its liquidation into the Mirror Subsidiaries. As a result, use of the mirror technique became extremely controversial and relatively rare during 1987. In the Revenue Act of 1987, which was passed at the end of 1987, the issue was clarified prospectively, and the mirror subsidiary technique was eliminated. Although the full and precise consequences of a liquidation of T into the Mirror Subsidiaries is not yet clear, at the very least, the entire $60 gain with respect to the T2 division will be recognized, and probably the gain with respect to the T1 division as well.

What other types of transactions may be utilized to avoid a tax on built-in gain?

With the doubt cast upon the mirror transaction at the end of 1986, tax planners focused extensively upon alternative techniques for disposing of unwanted assets following corporate acquisitions. Such transactions included the use of Section 304 in order to move the stock of "wanted" subsidiaries to affiliates of the purchasing corporation and permit the sale of the target and its "unwanted assets" at little or no gain; the use of a Section 355 spin-off to remove a subsidiary from a target corporation; and the use of the consolidated return investment adjustment rules in the infamous "son of mirrors" device.

For several reasons, it would not be instructive to go into detail on these transactions. First, at least with respect to transactions relying upon Sections 304 and 355, they were available only in limited circumstances. More important, Congress foreclosed the use of such transactions in large part in the Revenue Act of 1987. As to the son of mirrors transaction, the IRS announced in early January 1987 that it would amend the consolidated return regulations so as to eliminate the technique, and that such regulations would be retroactive to the date of the announcement. Nevertheless, because the investment adjustment rules used in the son of mirror transaction may still retain some viability in certain important cases, it is useful to have some understanding of what that transaction involved.

How did the son of mirrors technique operate?

Returning to our example of P and T, assume that P has purchased the stock of T for $100, and P and T commence filing a consolidated tax return. Assume also that T1, instead of being a directly held division, is a wholly owned subsidiary of T. As before, P wishes to sell the T2 division and retain the T1 division. Unfortunately, P cannot merely cause T to sell the T2 division. An immediate sale of T2 will cause a T level tax, as T has a $0 basis in the T2 assets. A liquidation of T will not help, because this would cause P's $100 basis in T to disappear, and P would take a carryover basis of $0 from T.

To circumvent this problem, P executes a son of mirrors transaction as follows. T distributes the stock of T1 to P as a dividend. P then sells the stock of T to a third party for $60.

Under the consolidated return rules, the dividend of the T1 stock to P is not taxable to P, but T recognizes a gain on the distribution equal to the difference between the fair market value of the T1 stock ($50) and T's basis in the stock of T1 ($0). This $50 gain is not immediately taxed to T, but is deferred until either T or T1 leaves the consolidated return group.

At this point, the key to the technique comes into play. Under the consolidated return rules, when a subsidiary engages in a transaction that increases or decreases its earnings and profits, this produces a like effect on the earnings and profits of its parent corporation in the group, and also produces a like effect upon the parent's basis in the stock of that subsidiary. These are called the investment adjustment rules in the consolidated return regulations. In the example, the $50 of gain recognized by T, and taxed to the consolidated group, increases T's earnings and profits and P's basis in its T stock by $50. The distribution of a $50 dividend reduces earnings and profits and in turn P's basis in the T stock.

Thus, P's basis in its T stock will remain at $100, even though the value of the T stock has been reduced by $50 as a result of the distribution of the T1 stock. When P then sells the stock of T (consisting solely of the T2 division) for $60, it will recognize a capital loss of $40. Reducing the $50 capital gain incurred as a result of the distribution of the T1 stock by the $40 capital loss resulting from the sale of the T stock, the P consolidated group will end up with a capital gain of only $10.

Would the transaction have worked as well with T1 as a division rather than a subsidiary?

Actually, it was the fear that son of mirrors could succeed with T1 as a division rather than a subsidiary that brought on prompt and direct action by the IRS. If successful, this transaction would have permitted P not only to have disposed of an unwanted T subsidiary without a tax on the built-in gain, but would have permitted it to obtain a cost basis in the T1 assets as well. Even those who had argued that the regular mirror transaction should be permitted did not believe that P should be able to obtain a cost basis in any of the T assets without somebody's paying a tax on the sale of those assets.

In fact, many tax practitioners did not believe that the son of mirrors transaction could succeed in stepping up the basis of target assets (as opposed to the stock of target subsidiaries) without violating the Section 338 consistency rules. In short, they pointed out that a dividend distribution of T1 assets to P would be a tainted asset acquisition under the Section 338 rules; this would result in either a deemed Section 338 election for the entire target group or in a carryover basis in all of the assets, including those of the T1 division. (See p. 295.)

How did the IRS stop the son of mirrors transaction?

On January 6, 1987, the IRS published Notice 87-14. The Notice announced that the IRS would amend the consolidated return regulations to deny P an increase in the basis of T's stock as a result of T's recognition of gains that were "built-in" at the time the stock of T was acquired by P. Although it may be a long time before such regulations are promulgated, the Notice has had a significant chilling effect on tax planning because it states that the new regulations will apply retroactively to stock in T that is acquired after January 6, 1987.

Remaining Options

Does this mean that the investment adjustment rules can no longer be used for unwanted asset dispositions?

Notice 87-14 did not go that far. Generally, to the extent that a consolidated group has assets in which gain has accrued in the hands of that group (as opposed to some predecessor), the investment adjustment rules remain unaffected by the Notice, and presumably, by whatever regulations will eventually be issued.

What this means in practice is that the investment adjustment rules will not be usable by buyers in arranging transactions in their own consolidated groups, but the rules will be usable in arranging transactions within sellers' consolidated groups prior to the purchase of a target.

Thus, where corporation S owns the stock of T, with divisions T1 and T2, S continues to be able to effectively eliminate a double tax upon stock sales of one division to one party and another division to another party. Using the earlier figures, assume that S wishes to sell T1 to buyer 1 for $50 and T2 to buyer 2 for $50. Since S has a $20 basis in the stock of T, it expects to recognize a total gain of only $80, just as if it had sold T in a single transaction. S first causes T to sell the T1 division to buyer 1 for $50, distributing the proceeds up to S. The S group will recognize $50 of taxable gain on the sale of T1. After taking account of the gain and distribution of proceeds, S will be left holding T stock with a basis of $20 and a fair market value of $50. S will then recognize $30 gain on the sale of T (holding only the T2 division) to buyer 2, leaving a total gain for both sales of $80.

There are numerous possible variations upon the above facts, all utilizing the investment adjustment rules to prevent the taxation of gain inside the target. In most cases, the seller will not be lining up separate buyers for the two divisions; rather, a single buyer considering the purchase of the entire target will be the party focusing upon a breakup of 'he target. With early, cooperative discussions between buyer and seller, the investment adjustment rules can still be used in such situations. Subject to some important caveats, including the Section 338 consistency rules, it is even possible to have different affiliates of the buyer purchase T1 and T2 from the selling group. It is important to note that as the involvement of the buyer in such transactions by the selling group increases, so does the possibility that the IRS may be successful in attributing those transactions to the buyer, thus eliminating the benefit of the investment adjustments. Note, also, that business problems can arise if the buyer reveals to the seller plans for subsequent profitable spin-offs.

Under what circumstances will the IRS permit the removal of unwanted assets prior to an acquisition of the target?

As a general matter, where a spin-off is followed by a sale by the shareholder of the stock of either the distributing corporation or the spun-off subsidiary, the spin-off is likely to violate the requirements of Section 355. One important exception to this rule is that a target corporation is permitted to spin-off a subsidiary to the target's shareholders prior to an acquisition of the target in a Section 368 tax-free reorganization. Where the shareholder of the target is a corporation, it is probable that the IRS would permit a significant amount of cash to be issued in the transaction along with qualifying stock consideration. Where the shareholders of the target are individuals, one should expect not to be permitted to utilize much cash in the transaction.

FINANCING THE ACQUISITION

Unlike many other aspects of structuring acquisitions, decisions as to the method of financing the transaction are most often made without much consideration of tax benefits or detriments. Such issues as security interests, priority among creditors, term of loan or investment, and type and amount of lender or investor compensation are of such direct importance to lenders and other investors that the role of the tax adviser will be largely to analyze and explain the tax consequences of the financing methods chosen, to suggest ways of minimizing or eliminating tax problems that may result from the chosen plan, and to adapt the overall acquisition structure to the financing plan that has been chosen. The issues to be considered in financing an acquisition apart from the tax considerations described here, as well as the typical forms and layers of financing in various acquisitions, are discussed in Chapter 4.

There are many ways of financing business acquisitions, including the use of an acquiring company's own working capital. In the discussion of tax issues, as in the broader discussion of financing in Chapter 4, our chief topic will be financing pertaining directly to a particular acquisition transaction, as opposed to financing for the general needs of a business. Most of the issues, both tax and non-tax, that are encountered in financing leveraged buyouts will be encountered as well in all financing transactions, but are merely more sharply focused in the context of leveraged buyouts.

In the discussion of the tax aspects of financing acquisitions, it will be useful to bear in mind a spectrum of financial instruments ranging from straight debt held by third parties at one end and common stock at the other. To emphasize the vertical nature of the relationship among these different instruments, it might be useful to visualize a layer cake, with the safest financing—straight secured debt—as the top layer, and the riskiest and potentially most rewarding investment—common stock—as the bottom layer. Between the secured debt and the common stock, one may often encounter third party unsecured debt, debt with equity features, purchase money notes, preferred stock held by institutional investors, preferred stock held by a seller, warrants and options, and special classes of common stock.

There are special tax issues accompanying the use of these various forms of financing. We will begin by discussing the most ubiquitous tax issue in financing, original issue discount. As we move away from straight debt and into financial instruments with greater risk and reward, we will encounter the amorphous, but extremely important, issue of characterizing instruments as debt or equity. We will then move down to the special uses for preferred stock in financing acquisitions, and to the potential uses for special purpose common or "alphabet" stock. Finally, we will discuss ESOP financing and examine some special financing issues for S corporations and partnerships.

Original Issue Discount (OID) Considerations

What tax issues should be analyzed in structuring straight debt financing?

Generally, straight debt is an unconditional obligation to repay principal and interest, has a fixed maturity date not too far removed, is not convertible, and has no attached warrants, options, or stock. A straight debt instrument ordinarily does not include interest that is contingent on profits or other factors, but may provide for a reasonable variable interest rate. It will not have a principal that is subject to contingencies.

In short, straight debt is an instrument without significant equity features. Straight debt instruments are generally classified as debt for tax purposes. Accrued interest on a straight debt instrument is deductible by the borrower and taxable to the lender. As a practical matter, the only tax issue in straight debt financing is the computation of the accrued interest.

The Code and proposed regulations contain an extremely complex set of comprehensive rules regarding interest accruals. The details of these original issue discount (OID) rules are well beyond the scope of this discussion. It suffices to say that the original issue discount rules generally require that interest must accrue whether or not a payment of interest is made. Thus, interest may be taxed, or deducted, before or after interest is paid. For example, assume that a $1,000,000, 10-percent, 15-year instrument allows the borrower to defer the payment of the first year's interest until maturity. This deferred interest is added to the principal and will accrue interest at the same rate of 10 percent. If the borrower defers its 1988 interest payment, the OID rules require the borrower to deduct in 1988, and the lender to include in its 1988 taxable income, $100,000 of accrued but unpaid interest.

Ordinarily, this result should please the borrower, but not the lender. A lender would prefer not to pay tax 15 years prior to the receipt of cash. On the other hand, tax-exempt lenders, such as pension funds and (under certain circumstances) foreign entities, often are willing to allow the borrower to create tax deductions not requiring current cash outlays. In spite of the tax benefits to the borrower, however, the use of OID financing in leveraged buyouts tends to result more from the borrower's cash flow restrictions than from aggressive tax planning. For this reason, the amount of interest expense deducted by the borrower will likely reflect a premium rate charged by the lenders.

Are there any special reporting requirements for OID?

When a publicly offered debt instrument is issued with original issue discount, the Code and regulations require specific disclosure of the OID information on the instrument itself or accompanying the instrument, as well as the filing of a special OID information return with the Internal Revenue Service. For instruments that are not publicly offered, there are less stringent disclosure requirements, and a filing with the IRS is not required.

How is OID dealt with when debt is issued as part of an investment unit?

As is the case with financial accounting treatment, the tax rules require that a lump sum paid for an investment unit consisting of a debt instrument and a warrant (or any other property) be allocated between the two based on their relative values. The amount allocated to the debt instrument will be its issue price, upon which a determination will be made as to whether there is original issue discount. For example, if $1,000 is paid for an investment unit consisting of a $1,000 face amount debenture and a warrant, and the debenture is worth $900 and the warrant is worth $100, then the debenture will have an issue price of $900 and a redemption value of $1,000, resulting in $100 of original issue discount. This $100 of OID will be taken into account by the holder as interest income and by the issuer as interest expense on an economic accrual basis over the term of the loan. The holder will take a $100 cost basis in the warrant.

Where either the debt instrument or the warrant is publicly traded at the time of issuance, that value must be used to determine to what extent the issue price of the unit must be allocated. Where neither piece of the investment unit is publicly traded, the proposed regulations permit the issuer and the holder to make a reasonable allocation, based upon the interest rate on the debt instrument as compared to the interest rates on similar debt of that issuer or others in the same business. As a practical matter, as long as the warrant is not "in the money," and the interest rate on the debt instrument is reasonably high, the parties can generally choose to allocate little or no value to the warrant, and thus eliminate OID on the debt instrument.

What are the special OID considerations in using purchase money notes?

Purchase money notes are notes of the target or the acquiring entity which are given to the seller as a part of the target's total purchase price. Ordinarily, purchase money notes carry a fairly low rate of unconditional interest. The notes will usually be subordinated to all third party debt of the issuer, to a degree that may render the repayment of principal and interest a subject of speculative risk. For this reason, purchase money notes may be susceptible to recharacterization as equity. The preceding discussion of the debt/equity issue, therefore, is particularly relevant to the structuring of purchase money debt.

Purchase money notes are subject to the original issue discount rules, including those pertaining to instruments issued for property. Under these rules, virtually all purchase money obligations must provide for an interest rate at least equal to the rate mandated by the Code (the "Applicable Federal Rate"). If interest accrues at a lower rate, the Code requires that the principal amount of the note be reduced, for tax purposes, and the interest rate be increased. The result is that the buyer and the seller will account for more interest and less principal than provided for under the terms of the note.

For example, assume that the seller accepts a $1,000,000, 6%, 5-year note. If the Applicable Federal Rate is 9%, compounded annually, the note will be treated, for tax purposes, as a 9% note with a principal amount of $883,311. As a result, the seller will have less of the immediate capital gain, but more interest income during the next 5 years. The target, on the other hand, will obtain additional interest deductions, but, in an asset acquisition, lose some of the basis step-up. The original issue discount rules govern the computations of interest accrual on the recharacterized loan.

Debt vs. Equity and Hybrid Instruments

What are the tax consequences if debt with equity features is recharacterized as equity?

The crucial tax issue in the case of debt with significant equity features is the determination of whether, for tax purposes, a purported debt instrument is debt or equity. The consequences of recharacterization of purported debt into equity may be quite severe. First, interest payments with respect to recharacterized debt will be treated not as interest but as distributions to a shareholder and, thus, will not be deductible. Repayment of debt principal is tax-free to the debt holder, but if treated as a redemption of stock, it may be taxed as a dividend.

Second, the recharacterization may destroy the pass-through status of the issuer. When debt is recharacterized as equity, it is ordinarily expected to be treated as a kind of preferred stock. Because an S corporation may not have two classes of stock, a recharacterization of debt into equity can create a second class of stock invalidating the S election and causing a corporate level tax. If the issuer is a member of a consolidated group, the recharacterized debt will most likely be treated as preferred stock that is not "pure preferred" stock. As such, the company may be disaffiliated from the consolidated group if, after taking into account the newly recharacterized stock, the members of the consolidated group own less than 80 percent of the company's stock.

A recharacterization of debt into equity raises a somewhat different concern in the case of the debt of a partnership. Debts of a limited partnership for which no general or limited partner is personally liable (nonrecourse debts) increase the basis of the limited partners in the partnership. A recharacterization will not convert a partnership into a tax paying entity, but the lender will become a partner, and the entire amount of the recharacterized debt will be allocated to increase only the lender's basis in its recharacterized debt of the partnership. As a result of the reduction in their own bases, the other partners may encounter unexpected tax results. For example, cash distributions in excess of their recharacterized bases will produce income, and, if the partnership generates a taxable loss, some or all of the loss may have to be allocated to the lender-partner.

Third, a recharacterization of debt into equity may completely change the structure of the deal. For example, the recharacterization may invalidate a Section 338 election, because for a valid election the buyer and the target must be affiliated at the time of the election. If the recharacterization of a purported debt into equity disaffiliates the buyer and the target, the election is invalid. In the case of purchase money notes, the conversion of debt into stock consideration may convert a taxable acquisition into a tax-free reorganization.

Finally, a recharacterization of debt held by foreign investors may be an especially difficult event. It is relatively easy to structure a debt to allow a foreign investor to receive interest free of United States tax. If the debt is recharacterized, however, a payment of purported interest will be treated as a dividend. Dividends received by foreign taxpayers are subject to United States tax at either the 30 percent regular withholding rate or at a lower withholding rate provided for in a treaty. Where a foreign investor asks for and obtains an indemnification for United States taxes, the incidence of tax will fall on the issuer and, indirectly, its shareholders.

How is debt distinguished from equity for tax purposes?

What can only please cynics and critics of the tax system is that a question of such overwhelming importance is one that uniquely defies a certain response. There simply do not exist in the tax law specific, objective criteria to determine whether a given instrument should be treated as debt or equity. The debt/equity characterization issue has produced an abundance of tax litigation, with a resulting body of case law in which there are very few common principles. The judicial response in defining debt and equity has much in common with its response in defining an obscenity under the First Amendment; that is, it has been unable to enunciate a complete definition, but knows it when it sees it.

In 1969, Congress enacted Section 385 of the Code authorizing the IRS to issue regulations regarding the debt versus equity issue. Eleven years later, the IRS promulgated the first version of the Section 385 Regulations. These regulations were twice rewritten, and finally withdrawn in 1983. There is a widespread belief that the IRS will not issue a new version of the Section 385 Regulations in the foreseeable future.

Since the failure of the Section 385 approach, tax advisers have dealt with the issue through a combination of: looking to the criteria set forth in the defunct Section 385 Regulations; studying court cases and IRS rulings for the most commonly cited criteria, the most commonly determinative criteria, and the fact patterns that most commonly are associated with recharacterization; determining what types of arrangements have received acquiescent treatment by the IRS; and finally, simply keeping track of what most other tax advisers—through blind faith or otherwise—are recommending.

Despite this introduction, a few useful generalizations can be made. Virtually all of the litigation and activity by the IRS has been in the recharacterization of purported debt as equity. Notwithstanding the close similarity between a preferred stock with strong redemption protection for the preferred stock with strong redemption protection for the holder and a debt instrument, it is very safe to say that recharacterization is not a problem when one is dealing with a purported equity instrument.

In examining a purported debt instrument, the courts look for objective indicia that the parties intended a true debtor-creditor relationship. In particular, they have placed great weight on whether the instrument represents an unconditional promise to pay a sum certain at a definite time. Other significant factors that are considered include: whether the loan was made by shareholders of the borrower, the borrower's debt-to-equity ratio, whether the loan is subordinated to the third-party creditors, and whether it has a market rate of interest.

Until the IRS signals a newly aggressive stance, the view of most tax advisers is that debt issued to third-party investors for cash is not likely to be recharacterized as equity, even though the debt may be subordinated to senior debt, convertible into common stock, or part of a capital structure involving a high ratio of debt to equity. This will at least be true where the instrument contains the common indicia of indebtedness, i.e., a certain maturity date that is neither unduly remote nor contingent, a reasonable interest rate, and creditor's rights upon default. Note, however, that even if the above criteria are met, the IRS is likely to argue for equity characterization if the conversion features of the instrument are such as to make it economically inevitable from inception that the instrument will be converted into stock. This was the case regarding certain adjustable rate convertible notes that were issued in the early 1980s.

Will the characterization of debt be followed for state income tax purposes?

Generally, the states apply the federal tax criteria for treating an instrument as debt or equity, although a state court or administrative body will be the tribunal that makes the determination.

In planning a debt structure for a leveraged acquisition, it is important to focus upon the state *income tax considerations* as well. The most troublesome issue in this regard is likely to occur in cases where the target's operations are to be held in an affiliated group of corporations filing a consolidated federal income tax return. In such a case, the acquisition debt will often be issued by the parent.

For federal income tax purposes, the group is treated as a single taxpayer, in which the parent's interest deductions offset the operating income of the subsidiaries. But from the point of view of the various states in which the subsidiaries do business, there is no consolidation with the parent; therefore, the parent's interest payments, even though funded by cash flow from the subsidiary, will not reduce the subsidiary's state income tax liability.

In such cases, it will ordinarily be important, where feasible, to pass the parent's interest deductions directly down to the subsidiaries by their assuming portions of the parent's indebtedness directly, or indirectly via bona fide intercorporate indebtedness owed to the parent by the respective subsidiaries. Great care must be taken to avoid adverse tax treatment to the parent in its own state of residency or under the federal tax laws as a result of such restructuring.

Are there any special debt/equity rules for S corporations?

As noted before, where the issuer is an S corporation, a recharacterization of debt into equity carries the especially unbearable result of disqualifying the issuer from S corporation status. For this reason, Subchapter S of the Code provides a "straight debt" safe harbor, under which a purported debt instrument that meets the requirements for straight debt will not be treated as a second class stock that would disqualify the corporation from S status. The straight debt safe harbor does not, however, insulate the issuer from a recharacterization of the instrument as equity for all other tax purposes. However, as a practical matter, the IRS may be less likely to challenge the debt treatment of an instrument that meets the safe harbor requirements under Subchapter S.

For purposes of the safe harbor, "straight debt" means any written unconditional promise to pay on demand or on a specified date a sum certain in money, provided the interest rate and payment dates are not contingent on profits, the borrower's discretion, or similar factors; the debt is not convertible into stock; and the creditor is an individual or entity permitted to own stock in an S corporation.

What is Section 279?

In 1969, Congress not only was concerned about debt/equity issues generally, but was particularly concerned about the use of hybrid debt instruments in mergers and acquisitions. As a result, Congress added to the Internal Revenue Code Section 279, the provisions of which remain in full force today. Section 279 disallows interest deductions to a corporation in excess of $5 million a year, on debt that is used to finance an acquisition, to the extent that the company's interest deductions are attributable to "corporate acquisition indebtedness."

Corporate acquisition indebtedness is defined as debt incurred by a corporation to acquire either stock in another corporation or at least two-thirds of the assets of another corporation, if the debt meets certain specific subordination tests, is convertible into stock or is issued as part of an investment unit, and the issuing corporation has a high debt-to-equity ratio as specifically set forth in the statute and regulations.

Because its effects are direct and harsh, Section 279 must be considered in evaluating any debt instrument used in connection with a corporate acquisition, or a refunding of such a debt instrument. Furthermore, it is usually through some technical loophole that major corporate acquisitions do not run afoul of Section 279. For this reason, corporate counsel to issuers, lenders, and underwriters must be sure that tax counsel is consulted as to even seemingly minor changes in the terms of a debt instrument or the acquisition structure.

Even when an instrument meets all other tests under Section 279, that Section will not apply in the case of indebtedness incurred by a target corporation itself to finance the acquisition or redemption of its own stock. This is a loophole that benefits not only corporations undergoing recapitalization transactions, but also unrelated buyers engaging in leveraged buyouts of the target. Because the IRS treats funds obtained from borrowing against the assets of the target as if they were paid out by the target itself, leveraged stock acquisitions in which loans are secured by the target's assets or otherwise owed by the target itself immediately following the acquisition will not be subject to Section 279. It should be noted that the version of the Revenue Act of 1987 that was passed by the House of Representatives had contained a provision, new Section 279A, to close this loophole by extending interest disallowance rules to debt incurred by a corporation to redeem its own stock. This provision was dropped in the final House-Senate Conference Agreement. Such a provision could always resurface, however, the next time new tax revenues must be raised.

Financing with Preferred Stock

From a tax standpoint, when might preferred stock be more advantageous than subordinated debt?

Practically speaking, there may be very little difference between a subordinated debt instrument and a preferred stock. Thus far, we have approached the debt/equity issue from the standpoint of seeking the former and avoiding the latter. As noted, there are some situations, such as elections under Subchapter S, where the use of preferred stock is entirely out of the question. There are other situations, for example, where the target is to be included in a consolidated return, where the issuance of certain types of preferred stock may preclude its inclusion in the return.

On the other hand, there are numerous situations in which preferred stock financing is not only desirable from a financial standpoint, because lenders wish to see shareholders' equity on the balance sheet, but because preferred stock may better serve the particular tax needs of the parties than any sort of debt instrument would.

The most common tax reason for using preferred stock over debt is to enable an acquisition to qualify as a tax-free reorganization. As we discussed earlier, shareholders can obtain tax-free treatment on the receipt of nonvoting, redeemable preferred stock, and such stock will qualify in satisfying the continuity of interest requirement. More generally, preferred stock can be used to provide tax-free treatment to a target's shareholders, while still effectively converting their interest to that of a passive investor or lender.

When an issuer is not in need of additional interest deductions (for example, when it expects to generate or otherwise have available net operating losses), there may be no tax imperative to use debt, and preferred stock may be a sensible alternative. Where this will have benefits to the issuer beyond the enhancement of its balance sheet is where the preferred stock can be sold to corporate investors that can take advantage of the dividends received deduction. Although dividends are not deductible to the issuer, the corporate holder may exclude from its taxable income 70% of the dividends received. As a result, the tax rate of a corporate preferred stock investor on dividend income will be only 30% of its regular tax rate. Therefore, the issuer should be able to sell the preferred stock with a lower dividend rate than the interest rate on a comparable debt instrument.

The value of the dividends received deduction can best be illustrated in the preferred stock financing technique sometimes used by thrift institutions with net operating losses. This technique essentially involves the issuance by a finance subsidiary, holding nothing but secure, government-guaranteed assets, of a money market rate preferred stock to corporate investors. Because the preferred stock qualifies as "pure preferred," the issuer is able to file a consolidated return with its thrift or thrift holding company parent. In short, although the finance subsidiary's assets generate sufficient cash flow and earnings and profits to permit the payment of dividends, little or no taxes are paid because of the net operating losses of the consolidated group. The issuing group is able to pay a lower rate than on comparable borrowings.

Do the OID rules apply to preferred stock?

While the OID rules per se apply only to debt instruments and not, therefore, to preferred stock, there is a separate, more arcane set of rules under Section 305 of the Code that applies to preferred stock.

Section 305 of the Code governs the treatment of stock splits and stock dividends involving both common and preferred stock. The chief purpose of the complex regulations under Section 305 is to determine whether certain apparently innocuous transactions involving a corporation's own stock should be treated as taxable dividends to its shareholders. One simple example of the Section 305 rules is that a pro rata distribution of common stock on common stock is tax-free to the recipients; where, on the other hand, some common shareholders receive cash or property, or are even given the option to receive cash or property, in lieu of new common stock, the entire distribution of new common stock will be a taxable dividend.

Unlike a distribution on common stock, any distribution of stock on preferred stock is per se a taxable dividend to the preferred stockholder. For this reason, a payment-in-kind, or PIK preferred, in which dividends may be paid in additional shares of preferred stock, will result in taxable dividend income to the holder to the extent that new shares of preferred stock are received, even though no cash dividend is paid. In this respect, the treatment of a preferred holder is very similar to the treatment of the holder of a PIK debt (in which interest may be paid in additional debt instruments) or other OID instruments. The underlying principle in the case of Section 305 is that the holder receives a dividend to the extent its preferred claim on earnings and on redemption proceeds is enhanced.

What is probably most analogous to OID is a provision in the Section 305 regulations requiring that redemption premiums be taxed as dividends to the holders of preferred stock during the period preceding the actual redemption. Specifically, if a corporation issues preferred stock that is redeemable (at the option of the holder or the corporation) after a specified period of time at a price higher than its issue price, the holder will be treated as receiving dividends in the amount of this redemption premium ratably over the years between issuance and permissible redemption.

There are two exceptions to this rule. There will not be an

imputed dividend where (1) the redemption premium is a "reasonable" redemption premium in the nature of a penalty for a premature redemption, as compared with prevailing premiums for similar instruments, or (2) the preferred stock is redeemable immediately, rather than only after a specified period of time. The latter exception is one that has been only unofficially sanctioned by the IRS, and upon which tax advisers rely somewhat warily.

Is there a way to obtain the tax benefit of interest deductions while using preferred stock to strengthen the balance sheet of a target?

Restrictions imposed by senior and mezzanine lenders may require that a subordinated level of capital be in the form of preferred stock rather than subordinated debt. Where the target is not a pass-through entity, there may be insufficient leveraging to eliminate all tax at the corporate level. Assuming that the preferred stock investors are not corporations relying on the tax benefit of the dividends received deduction, one way of effectively converting nondeductible dividend obligations on the preferred stock into deductible interest obligations is to convert equity into debt via a new holding company.

In such a transaction, all of the common and preferred stock of the target is issued to a new holding company, which issues all of its common stock to those who would otherwise own the common of the target directly. In addition, the holding company issues subordinated debt to the preferred investors, in the same amounts and on essentially the same terms as the target's preferred stock. All rights negotiated with the preferred/subordinated debt investors will be mirrored in the terms of the preferred stock obligations running from the target to the holding company. Because the target and the holding company will file a consolidated tax return, interest deductions with respect to the subordinated debt of the holding company will be used to offset taxable income generated by the target. The funding of these interest payments, through dividend distributions from the target to the holding company, will not be taxable to either corporation.

What is Section 306 stock?

Section 306 of the Code contains rules that may be a pitfall for investors in preferred stock. That provision is designed to prevent the avoidance of dividend treatment through the issuance of preferred stock. More specifically, if a corporation distributes preferred stock on a tax-free basis under various circumstances, that preferred stock will be characterized as Section 306 stock, and as a result, a shareholder may have ordinary income treatment upon a subsequent sale or redemption of the stock. The reason that this section focuses on preferred stock is that Congress believed that a common stockholder could break off a piece of the company in the form of preferred stock, convert that stock into cash, and still retain an undiminished share in the growth of the company.

Where preferred stock is acquired for cash, the holder need not be concerned about Section 306. It is also very unlikely to arise in a case where a seller retains preferred stock and sells its common stock to a buyer.

Alphabet Stock

What role can special class or "alphabet" stock play in tax planning?

Special class or alphabet stock financing is a device that tax planners have thought about a good deal in the past few years, but have rarely acted upon. Special class stock is a variation upon series class stocks that have been used by mutual funds for many years, but was first used for a standard business organization when General Motors acquired Electronic Data Systems Corporation in 1984. GM again used the device a year later when it acquired Hughes Aircraft Company. The reason that the special class stock is sometimes referred to as alphabet stock is that in those two acquisitions GM issued a new class E and class H stock, respectively.

The chief goal in devising a special class of stock is to inject into the stock special rights, or at least strong expectations, indicating that holders will actually own not an undivided share, but only a particular piece, of the issuer. Specifically, in the case of GM there was a strong, non–tax-motivated desire for holders of class E stock to perceive themselves as owning an interest only in GM's EDS unit, rather than the automobile business, and for the holders of class H stock to regard themselves as owners of the Hughes Aircraft unit rather than the automobile business. The tax planning challenge is to foster such a market perception while maintaining that for tax purposes the various classes of stock are merely classes of stock of General Motors, rather than of a particular subsidiary.

In fact, from a state law standpoint, the class E and class H stocks are stocks of General Motors, and are ultimately subject to all of the vicissitudes of GM's automobile business. Both voting rights and rights to share in assets on liquidation pertain to the entire GM enterprise, just as in the case of its regular common stock. GM's stock in its EDS and Hughes subsidiaries is subject to the claims of its general creditors. Even as to dividends, state law restrictions on the payment of dividends on each of the classes of stock will look to the current and retained earnings of GM more or less in the aggregate.

The ability to cause the class E and class H stocks to behave as if they were direct shares in EDS and Hughes is based upon a combination of certain legal restrictions as to the payment of dividends on the various classes of stock as well as certain announced dividend policies of GM. As to the legal restrictions on the payment of dividends, each class of stock is assigned a separate earnings pool, consisting of paid-in capital and surplus and retained earnings attributable to a particular business, and the payment of dividends on that class of stock is limited to that pool. Thus, for example, holders of class E stock are ostensibly assured that if EDS prospers and Hughes or the automotive business does poorly, they will not have to share the wealth with holders of class H and regular common stock. What is perhaps more important, however, is that GM maintains a stated policy of making dividend distributions of a certain percentage of the earnings of EDS or Hughes to the holders of class E or class H stock. Without such an assurance, and without a great deal of credibility behind that assurance, the holders of special class stock would have no protection from the company's utilizing earnings generated by a particular segment to reinvest in the growth or maintenance of another segment, without a distribution of the earnings to the shareholders.

If a company is in a position, as is GM, to ensure the integrity of the special classes of stock, the non-tax financing benefits can be enormous. In the case of GM, the ability to offer a class of GM stock to employees of EDS whose performance would track the performance of the EDS unit may have been crucial in maintaining the highly skilled and motivated work force of EDS in the acquisition. Additionally, if GM wishes to raise capital in the equity markets for use in the Hughes or EDS division, it can do so by selling a special class of stock with a price-to-earnings ratio unencumbered by the modest valuation placed by the market on the automobile business.

Of course, the most direct method of accomplishing these non-tax objectives would be to simply utilize stock in an EDS or Hughes subsidiary. There are several important tax reasons why the use of a subsidiary's stock would be far less advantageous than the use of a special stock of the parent. One, unlike the case where stock is issued in the subsidiary directly, a parent can issue an unlimited amount of special class stock without sacrificing its ability to file a consolidated tax return with the subsidiary. Second, while a parent must recognize taxable gain (or loss) on the sale of subsidiary stock, or on the distribution of subsidiary stock to its shareholders, no gain or loss is recognized by the parent corporation on the sale or distribution of its own stock. Third, while a distribution of subsidiary stock to shareholders of the parent will usually be a taxable dividend to the shareholders, a distribution of the parent's own stock will ordinarily be received by them on a tax-free basis.

Although neither the IRS nor a court has ruled upon the issue, GM's class E and class H stocks will probably qualify as stock in GM for tax purposes. Nonetheless, potential issuers of alphabet stock should appreciate that this method of financing is subject to the risk that the IRS might argue that the alphabet stock is not stock in the parent corporation for tax purposes. To the extent that the legal rights of the holders of a particular class are restricted even more than in the case of GM to the assets and earnings of a single segment of the parent's operations, the likelihood of an IRS challenge will be greater.

Can special class stock be used as a substitute for disposing of unwanted assets?

Theoretically, a buyer could acquire a target and, instead of disposing of unwanted assets, cause the target to issue a new special class of stock with rights restricted to the unwanted asset or business. If this could be done successfully, the buyer would have accomplished the great elusive goal, which is to convert the target's ownership of the unwanted asset into cash, without the recognition of any gain.

For example, assume that the target owns a trademark worth $10 million that is not integral to the target's business and is not likely to appreciate significantly in the coming years. Because the trademark will expire at the end of a fixed period of time, there will be no residual value in the asset thereafter, and, therefore, the asset can be valued strictly in terms of a predictable and finite stream of income. The target has a zero basis in the trademark, and would therefore recognize $10 million of gain upon a sale. Upon advice of its tax counsel, the target makes a public or private offering of $10 million of a new class T stock. The holders of the class T stock are entitled to receive dividends equal to 100% of the revenue generated by the trademark.

If the form of the transaction is respected, the issuing company will receive $10 million tax-free and, also, will retain control over the trademark. This latter point may be relevant where the target wishes to keep the trademark out of the hands of its competitors.

The IRS could be expected to challenge this transaction. High on its list of arguments would be that the target had actually sold the trademark itself, and that in any event, the holders of class T stock could not in any meaningful sense be considered "stockholders" in T. Even before reaching that point, however, potential investors in the class T stock would have very serious reservations about such an investment. Assuming the target was acquired in a leveraged buyout and that the main purpose for the disposition of the trademark was to pay down debt, it would be virtually impossible to assure the class T investors that the trademark's cash flow would be devoted strictly to the payment of their dividends. From the point of view of the target's lenders, this trademark and its cash flow would remain as an asset of the target subject to their claims as creditors. If, on the other hand, some arrangement could be made to remove this asset from the claims of the target's creditors, then the IRS would have little trouble in arguing successfully that the asset had been truly divested by the target.

To conclude, the potential uses for special class or alphabet stock are thus far largely untapped, and tax planners as well as business planners should consider such a possibility where appropriate. Realistically, however, the use of such stock may turn out to be far more limited than imaginations may suggest.

The Leveraged ESOP

Can an ESOP be used to provide favorable financing in a leveraged buyout?

As described in Chapter 9, an Employee Stock Ownership Plan, or ESOP, is a type of qualified employee benefit plan that invests primarily in stock of the employer. In order to encourage the use of ESOPs, Congress has provided a variety of special tax benefits both to stockholders who sell their stock to an ESOP and to lenders providing financing for so-called leveraged ESOPs. Shareholders who sell their stock to an ESOP may qualify for tax-free rollover treatment under Section 1042 of the Code. Briefly, that section permits the shareholder to defer the payment of a capital gain tax upon the sale of his stock, provided he or she reinvests the sale proceeds in stock of another active business corporation within one year after the sale. Additionally, where the selling shareholder is an estate, or other entity holding the employer's stock at the time of the decedent's death, as much as one half of the proceeds of the sale of the stock to an ESOP may be deducted from the gross estate for federal estate tax purposes.

There are two tax benefits provided to a company that sets up a leveraged ESOP. First, all payments of both interest and principal on loans incurred by an ESOP to purchase employer stock are deductible to the company. Additionally, qualified lenders on ESOP loans are permitted to exclude 50% of the interest received on such loans. Such a tax exclusion for the lender may be expected to provide a strong incentive to make loans available for ESOP financing on favorable terms.

With such clear tax incentives, the ESOP should be considered in many contexts in mergers and acquisitions. Provided an investor group is willing to share the ultimate economic benefits of a target with the employees, at least to the extent of the 30% interest in the company required by the tax laws, the leveraged ESOP may be a viable alternative to other means of financing a leveraged buyout.

Special Issues for Pass-Through Entities

Can equity in an S corporation be offered to corporate investors?

As we have said, a corporation will be disqualified under Subchapter S if it either has more than one class of stock or has any shareholder that is a corporation, partnership, or other non-qualifying entity. In a world where lenders and institutional investors are increasingly insistent upon receiving some kind of equity kicker in addition to a more conventional, albeit generous, fixed return, it is necessary to adapt the S corporation to equity participation by non-individuals. The way in which the need to issue equity to such entities has been reconciled with the S corporation rules is through the issuance of warrants, other options, or convertible debt.

The IRS has a longstanding position distinguishing between rights in stock presently outstanding and rights to buy stock in the future represented by warrants or other options. In effect, the mere fact that a party holds a warrant to buy shares of some new class of stock, or that a corporation holds a warrant to buy shares of common stock, will not disqualify the issuer from S corporation status unless and until those warrants are exercised. What often occurs is that a corporation acquired in a leveraged buyout by a group of individuals will elect S corporation status and will remain an S corporation until the company is either sold or taken public. At such time, corporate warrant holders may exercise their warrants; disqualification from S corporation status, at that point a matter of indifference, will occur.

The basis for the IRS's liberal position is that S corporation principles are not violated where a warrant holder possesses no present rights to vote or to receive distributions of current earnings. So long as the warrant holder is truly content to allow such rights to reside solely in the common shareholders until the warrant is exercised, all should be well for tax purposes. Problems arise, however, when a warrant holder pushes closer to current enjoyment of these enumerated rights. For example, it may wish to have the right to name a member of the board of directors. Because the IRS regards the right to elect directors as the touchstone of voting rights, this is particularly dangerous.

Another possibility is that a warrant holder may negotiate to be compensated for dividends it would have received had it been a shareholder at the time dividends were actually distributed. Although in many leveraged buyouts this may be an academic issue because of severe restrictions on dividend distributions in loan agreements, it certainly can and does arise. From the standpoint of preserving S corporation status, such desires on the part of a warrant holder should be strongly resisted. Because the benefits to the common stockholders of preserving S corporation status will far outweigh the current benefits of receiving dividend distributions, it would even be worthwhile for them to agree not to receive such distributions. Of course, both loan and warrant agreements should in any event permit distributions to the stockholders to pay taxes on account of the income of the S corporation.

What other questions should be considered in fashioning S corporation warrants?

A different, and more subtle, issue from that described in the preceding paragraphs involves the issue price of the warrant. Outside the S corporation context, the IRS has suggested that ownership of a warrant is distinguished from stock ownership in a corporation by the fact that a stockholder has already invested its capital in the corporation, while a warrant holder has paid a relatively small sum for the right to lock in a price at which it might in the future invest capital in the corporation. To illustrate this concept, if a corporate investor were to pay $95 for the right to purchase 100 shares of stock in the S corporation for $5, and the stock's original issue price to the common shareholders was $1 per share, the warrant might be regarded as a sham in that the corporate investor would have already invested substantially all of the capital necessary to make it a full stockholder. What this means from a practical standpoint is that a comparison should be made between the amount paid for a warrant and the exercise price. At the very least, the parties should make sure that the amount paid for the warrant does not exceed the exercise price.

As explained earlier, where a warrant is issued to a lender as part of an investment unit, the issue price of the debt instrument and the amount paid for the warrant must be determined by allocating the single amount paid for the unit between the two according to their relative values. Although it is often possible to allocate a minimal amount of the purchase price to the warrant, where the issuer is an S corporation it may be worthwhile to attempt to realistically determine the warrant's value relative to its issue price, in order to evaluate the risk of recharacterization of the warrant as a class of stock.

Where an investor holds a warrant or option in an S corporation that generates tax losses, a fairly unique problem can arise. Unlike a C corporation, the S corporation will not have a net operating loss carryover of its own. Instead, its losses are passed through to the shareholders each year, and these losses will only be usable by those individuals, either on a current basis to offset taxable income from other sources or, as is more likely, only to offset taxable income passed through to them from the S corporation. Regardless of whether or not the losses are usable by the shareholders, they will not be available to the corporation as carryovers when it becomes a C corporation. To this extent, the C corporation (and, correspondingly, its future shareholders and even creditors) will have lost the benefit of this "asset."

Because the loss of S corporation status will generally be accompanied by a public stock offering or other event favorable to the creditors, it may be only the warrant holder that sees some unfairness in this arrangement. The only direct solution that we have seen involves an agreement between the shareholders and the warrant holder requiring some kind of cash compensation to the warrant holder to account for this fact. Because you have a possibility that there will be no real benefit to the shareholders for the pass-through of the losses—as a result of basis, at risk, and passive loss limitations—and the detriment to the warrant holder as a future stockholder is only indirect and impossible to quantify, such agreements tend to involve more trouble than they are worth. On the other hand, if this is what it takes to allow a transaction to proceed on a pass-through entity basis, it is probably worth putting up with.

What are the special issues in partnership financing?

The important overall problem in partnership financing is that most of the parties involved in large-scale business lending have little experience or familiarity with the partnership format. This problem pervades all aspects of the financing, not merely tax. As a result of this lack of familiarity, and a concern about either ignorance or legal restrictions hampering institutional investments, a partnership will often use a corporate finance subsidiary when it issues mezzanine debt. The way this will work is that the finance subsidiary will issue the debt, and its partnership parent will unconditionally guarantee that debt. A prospectus describing the debt issue will make little pretense that there is any substance whatsoever to this arrangement, and it will probably refer to the partnership parent as the "company."

For tax purposes, there is strong authority for ignoring the role of the finance subsidiary and treating the debt as if it were issued by the partnership directly. Such a conclusion is based upon the doctrine that the tax treatment of a transaction will be governed by its substance rather than its form. In structuring such arrangements, however, tax advisers should ensure that the arrangements will work even if the form is respected. As such, the main goal is to prevent any possibility that the finance subsidiary, which is a C corporation, will end up with interest deductions offsetting 100% of any income that it might be deemed to receive.

There are in fact numerous tax issues that are unique to the financing of partnership operations, many of which directly affect the partners in the partnership rather than the lenders. These concerns relate to the determination of the partners' basis in the partnership as well as to the allocation and utilization of deductions. Careful tax planning, in light of the partners' objectives, should be able to mitigate these concerns. One example of such a concern is where tax planners seek to ensure that the form of the indebtedness of a limited partnership is such as to allow the limited partners to be allocated their pro rata share of basis attributable to such debt. This will often involve simply making sure that the loan documents indicate that the lender will not have recourse to the assets of the general partner, but only to the assets of the limited partnership itself. Further, if the loan were guaranteed by any partner, or were made by a party related to a partner in the partnership, special problems would arise.

A key difference between a partnership and an S corporation is that although both are pass-through tax entities, the partnership is a more complete pass-through entity. With respect to such transactions as the issuance of its stock or debt, the S corporation is treated in exactly the same way as a C corporation: such events are not taxable transactions to it. Likewise, no taxable event is recognized to an S corporation when its warrants are issued or exercised. In contrast, most transactions undertaken by a partnership are viewed for tax purposes as if they were undertaken by the partners themselves. If one seeks in this context to treat the partnership solely as an entity apart from its partners, and thus avoid thrusting tax issues upon them, one will likely find that the business arrangement will be undermined. Thus, what is in the corporate context a most straightforward and simple transaction, the issuance and exercise of a warrant to buy a stated percentage of the outstanding stock of the corporation, becomes a far more complex and challenging transaction to structure and analyze when it involves an interest in a partnership.

TRANSACTION DIAGRAMS

The following diagrams attempt to illustrate graphically many of the transactions discussed in this book. In each diagram, an SH represents a shareholder, a square is a corporation, and a circle represents corporate assets. Vertical and diagonal lines indicate the ownership of stock or assets and arrows represent the flow of cash, assets, stock, etc.

EXHIBIT 5-1
Stock Purchase

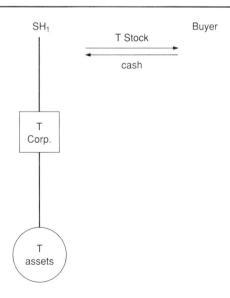

1. SH_1 owns 100% of the stock of T.
2. Buyer purchases 100% of the stock of T in exchange for cash.

EXHIBIT 5-2
Asset Purchase

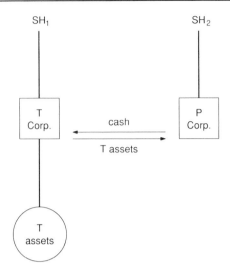

1. SH₁ owns 100% of the stock of T; SH₂ owns 100% of the stock of P.
2. P purchases all assets of T in exchange for cash.

EXHIBIT 5-3
Taxable Forward Merger

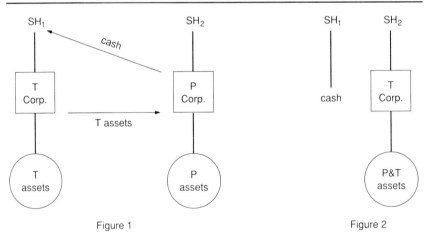

Figure 1   Figure 2

1. SH₁ owns 100% of the stock of T; SH₂ owns 100% of the stock of P.
2. T is merged into P: T's assets are transferred to P, the stock of T is cancelled, and the existence of T is terminated.
3. P transfers cash to SH₁.

EXHIBIT 5-4
Taxable Reverse Merger

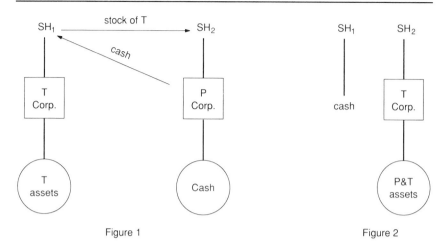

Figure 1   Figure 2

1. SH$_1$ owns 100% of the stock of T; SH$_2$ owns 100% of the stock of P.
2. P is merged into T: The stock of P is cancelled, and the corporate existence of P is terminated.
3. By the terms of the merger agreement, SH$_1$ receives cash of P, and SH$_2$ receives the stock of T.

EXHIBIT 5-5
Taxable Forward Subsidiary Merger

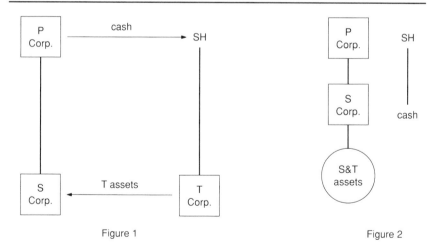

Figure 1   Figure 2

1. Corporation P owns 100% of the stock of S; SH owns 100% of the stock of T.
2. T is merged into S, by the terms of the merger agreement, T's assets are transferred to P, the stock of T is cancelled, and P transfers cash to SH.

EXHIBIT 5-6
Tax-Free Forward Merger ("A" reorganization)

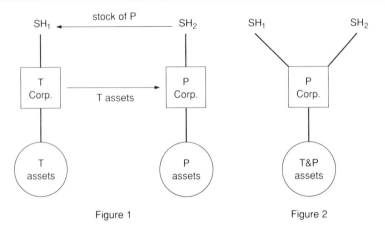

Figure 1   Figure 2

1. SH₁ owns 100% of the stock of T; SH₂ owns 100% of the stock of P.
2. T merges into P: T's assets are transferred to P and the stock of T is cancelled.
3. SH₂ transfers a portion of the stock of P to SH₂.
4. Both SH₁ and SH₂ are now shareholders of P.

EXHIBIT 5-7
Tax-Free Forward Triangular Merger
(A Hybrid "A" Reorganization—section 368 (a)(2)(D)

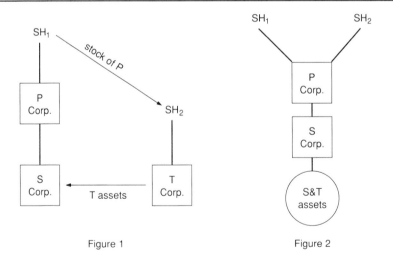

Figure 1   Figure 2

1. SH₁ owns 100% of the stock of P; P owns 100% of the stock of S.
2. SH₂ owns 100% of the stock of T.
3. T merges into S: T's assets are transferred to S and the stock of T is cancelled.
4. SH₁ transfers a portion of the stock of P to SH₂.

344

EXHIBIT 5-8

Tax-Free Acquisition of Stock for Voting Stock

("B" Reorganization)

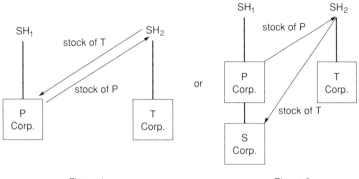

Figure 1   Figure 2

"B" Reorganization (Figure 1)
1. SH_1 owns 100% of the stock of P, SH_2 owns 100% of the stock of T.
2. SH_2 transfers all of the stock of T to P.
3. In exchange for its stock of T, SH_2 receives shares of the stock of P.

Triangular "B" Reorganization (Figure 2)
1. In a triangular "B" reorganization, P owns 100% of the stock of S.
2. SH_2 transfers all of the stock of T to S.
3. In exchange for its stock of T, SH_2 receives shares of the stock of P.

EXHIBIT 5-9

Acquisition of Property for Voting Stock

(A "C" Reorganization)

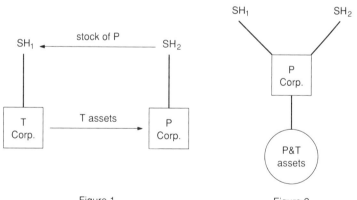

Figure 1   Figure 2

1. SH_1 owns 100% of the stock of T.
2. SH_2 owns 100% of the stock of P.
3. T transfers its assets to P.
4. SH_2 transfers a portion of the stock of P
   to SH_1 and T is liquidated.

345

EXHIBIT 5-10
Acquisition of Property for Voting Stock (A "D" Reorganization)

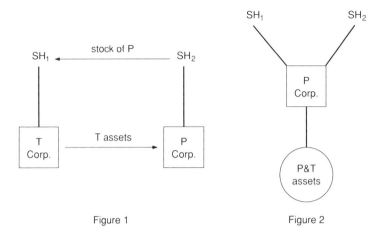

Figure 1   Figure 2

1. The value of T is greater than the value of P
2. SH_1 owns 100% of the stock of T.
3. SH_2 owns 100% of the stock of P.
4. T transfers its assets to P, and T is liquidated.
5. SH_2 transfers a portion (more than 50%) of the P stock to SH_1.

EXHIBIT 5-11
Spin-Offs

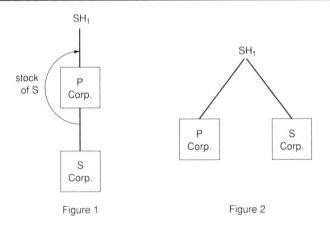

Figure 1   Figure 2

1. SH_1 owns 100% of the stock of P.
2. P owns 100% of the stock of S.
3. P distributes (spins off) the stock of S.

346

EXHIBIT 5-12
Split-Offs

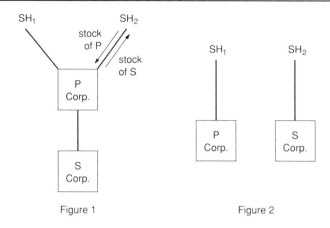

Figure 1   Figure 2

1. SH₁ and SH₂ own together 100% of the stock of P.
2. SH₂ surrenders its stock of P.
3. In exchange, P distributes the stock of S to P.

EXHIBIT 5-13
Split-Ups

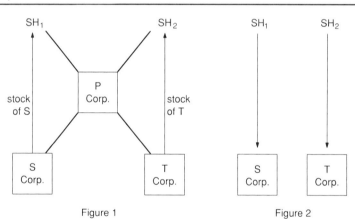

Figure 1   Figure 2

1. SH₁ and SH₂ together own 100% of the stock of P.
2. P owns 100% of the stocks of S and T.
3. P is liquidated.
4. SH₁ receives 100% of the stock of S, and SH₂ receives
   100% of the stock of T.

347

EXHIBIT 5-14

National Starch Transaction (A Section 351 Acquisition)

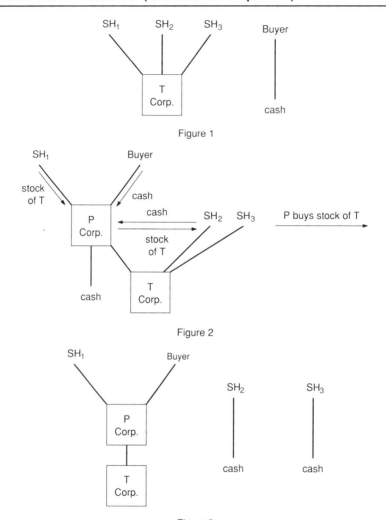

Figure 1

Figure 2

Figure 3

1. SH_1, SH_2, and SH_3 together own 100% of the stock of T.
2. Buyer and SH_1 incorporate P: Buyer transfers cash to P;
   SH_1 transfers its stock of T. Buyer and SH_1 receive the stock of P.
3. P buys the stock of T from SH_2 and SH_3 in exchange for cash.

348

CHAPTER 6

STRUCTURING MANAGEMENT BUYOUTS

INTRODUCTION

Management buyouts are the "fair-haired boys" of the merger and acquisition business. While the spectacle of corporate raiders, hostile takeovers, and enormous debt burdens worries the public, the idea of managers or a company's employees recapturing their company from the bureaucratic clutches of a conglomerate is appealing. Here is a step toward individual initiative, the little man reasserting control against the faceless corporation.

There is some truth in this image. Many companies have prospered under the direct control of their managers, and great opportunity awaits the manager who has the vision to put together a buyout (or is lucky enough to be in the right place at the right time when one happens).

In many respects, management buyouts (MBOs) are simply special types of leveraged buyouts, and the discussion in this book relating to LBOs should be read by anyone interested in MBOs. In particular, the pricing discussion of Chapter 3, the financing analysis of Chapter 4, the tax and non-tax structural discussion of Chapter 5, and the use of Employee Stock Ownership Plans (ESOPs) described in Chapter 9 are directly applicable to MBOs and will not be repeated here.

The purpose of this chapter is to focus on aspects unique to MBOs, including the circumstances in which they may arise, the relationship between management and financial buyout firms which commonly act as their advisors, special tax considerations, particularly affecting management compensation, and special considerations for employee benefits and stock ownership.

MANAGEMENT BUYOUT BASICS

What is a management buyout?

A management buyout is a transaction in which a company, or subsidiary or division, is acquired by a new company in which management of the acquired business holds a significant, if not controlling, equity stake.

Under what circumstances might the opportunity arise for management to engage in a buyout?

A company may be up for sale, or the owner may be persuaded to sell it, for many different reasons. The owners of a family business may want to retire; a public company may be going private to avoid a takeover; a conglomerate owner may be selling a subsidiary or division to raise cash for another acquisition or to reduce debt. Managers may initiate the sale. Management may be bitten by the entrepreneurial bug. There may be disagreement among managers or stockholders, offering management a chance to solve the problem by buying out the other group.

Management may have noticed that its public company would be better off private. Public companies have reporting and disclosure obligations which can increase expenses and which can provide helpful business information to competitors. The need for public companies to report increasing quarterly and annual earnings may conflict with a company's needs to reinvest its earnings in certain activities, such as research and development, to achieve long-term growth.

In other cases, the company may be auctioned. In that case, other companies, LBO firms, and management may all be competing to purchase the company. This, as discussed later, is often a difficult situation for management.

One general rule to remember is that leveraged buyouts depend for their success on taking advantage of one or several special features of a business or a situation which can be translated into financing opportunities. These opportunities can crop up anywhere. Thus, the first step in determining whether favorable circumstances exist for an MBO is a full and open-minded analysis of the financial condition, need and internal politics of the company to see what opportunities may exist.

How can management discover if the company can be bought out?

There is so much buyout business being done today in corporate America that any responsible executive in a top position can ask the owners, as a matter of course, whether the entity is or might be for sale. If the answer is that it's "a keep," simply ask to be informed any time that it does come up for sale.

If the answer is a qualified "no" or even "well, everything is for sale at a price," it could be a start. After all, every senior executive has a right to know who he *might* be working for, and this can lead into a discussion with the owners about the expected price, how far they've advanced with negotiations, etc.

Is there any chance that an executive could be fired for bringing up the question?

It's possible, but it seems to be more a matter of personal relationships than procedures. Any executive who could be fired for inquiring as to whether or not the operation is for sale is probably on the way out anyway. Those who ask this question are confronting the difference between being an employee and being an entrepreneur. This is the kind of risk they had better be prepared to run if they are planning to take over. Note that many managers can see the advantages and the opportunities of a buyout but do not really want the independence, the responsibility, and the risk of running their own business. If the managerial group does not have a leader or partner who is prepared to take on this role, it should be very reluctant to proceed.

What about "office politics"?

There are pecking orders in all societies. If an MBO is in the offing, the selection of who is and who is not invited to join the group can be a source of difficulty. In family situations, where one faction wants to buy out the company and exclude others, bitter litigation can result, especially if the price is low. For these reasons, any officer investigating the possibility of a buyout should think through very carefully who he talks to in the management group from the earliest stages.

Is the MBO sometimes not management's initiative?

In some cases the buyout may be forced upon management. The owner may decide to sell, determine that management is the buyer who can be caused to give him the best price, and order them to buy, perhaps taking advantage of the tax advantages of an Employee Stock Ownership Plan. (See Chapter 9, Pension and Compensation Concerns.) Situations of excess owner dominance over management can generate trouble after the closing, usually because the selling owner set the price too high.

An investor group engaged in doing LBOs often, as part of the standard method of operations, includes management in the ownership group and relies heavily on it to make the acquisition a success. Although management in such cases does not initiate the transaction, it stands to gain from the transaction and tends to respond very well to the challenge.

What are the principal risks in initiating an MBO?

Attempting a buyout without reasonable assurance of financing the buyout or winning the bid can result in putting the company "in play" or up for sale prematurely. Members of management could lose their jobs or independence if the company is acquired by another concern.

Is there a risk of violating the legal duties an officer has to the company?

Officers proposing an MBO of a publicly held company have an inherent conflict of interest. This is particularly true for officers who are also directors. They want to buy the company at the lowest possible price, but their duty to the stockholders is to obtain the highest possible price. In practice, the board of directors or its independent committee assumes the duty of negotiating the best price and terms, or at least approving the deal. The conflict is less acute if the target is a subsidiary or division because management of the parent company can protect the company's interests.

How do MBO risks and opportunities differ between publicly and privately held companies?

For management to make a preemptive bid for the stock of their publicly held company is to invite disaster. All too often the initial management bid simply establishes a floor value for the company, and a bigger, better capitalized operation later wins the bidding war at a 50% higher price. How management fares after that is anyone's guess, but they certainly didn't start out on the right foot with the winning side.

The opportunities are much better when management can tie up a control block of stock at the start, or attempt a buyout of a closely held private corporation or a division of a conglomerate. In both cases, management has the great advantage of being able to negotiate directly with the owners, rather than with representatives of public stockholders who must permit a competitive bidding process to develop. Management must still be able to meet the market price but has a better chance of fending off or co-opting unwanted competition and can use its insider advantages.

What advantages does management have in undertaking an LBO?

Management is often the first to know that the business is for sale. Management also has access to, or can develop most accurately, the information required to determine the buyout price. Management can affect the price by initiating a buyout at a time when the business is not performing at its optimal level. Management can also initiate the MBO when the company's stock is trading at low levels on a comparative basis or just before the business is about to emerge from a difficult period, such as an economic recession.

Management is often critical to the success—even survival—of a company, particularly in high-technology or service companies such as computer software companies or advertising agencies. If the owner does not agree to sell the company, key members of management can leave the company and join a competitor or start a new, competing business. Every seller realizes that much of the value of a business is the knowledge and expertise of its managers and that the best price for the business can be obtained only if management is preserved. This is particularly true if the company is in trouble.

For these reasons, investment firms have a natural interest in becoming partners with management. They need a quality team that has experience operating the company through several economic cycles. Lack of such operating expertise can be the reason for a deal to fail, as did the Ponderosa Restaurant buyout in March, 1988. Performance projections and the ability to meet them are paramount in determining what the purchase price should be and whether the new company can obtain the necessary financing and then repay the debt incurred in the transaction (the Ponderosa problem). Managers have the advantage of knowing which expenses can be reduced to increase cash flow. They may be able to determine better than an outsider whether any debt is assumable in the transaction. At some time, managers have longed to eliminate certain promotional or other expenses which were incurred under the orders of corporate headquarters. Other times corporate headquarters may have restrained the managers in taking steps that could increase revenue.

Management usually has the good will of the company's board of directors. Managers may be personally acquainted with major stockholders and thus better able to negotiate with them to purchase their holdings. Such purchases are often referred to as "lock-ups." Many stockholders are more comfortable negotiating with their managers than with Wall Street professionals.

What other reasons are there for management's participation in such transactions?

Partners, promoters, and lenders want management to be involved because (1) they want to see that management is willing to risk its money in the company and (2) management's investment acts as a deterrent to, or "golden handcuff" on, management's premature abandonment of the company. A potential buyer wants management as its ally in part to deny management's support to its competition.

Should management have a partner or adviser, such as an investment banking firm or a leveraged buyout firm?

A professional partner or adviser can help immensely with the pricing, financing, and consummation of a management buyout. Although managers are typically experts in managing the marketing and manufacture of the product, they frequently lack significant experience in acquiring and financing businesses. This is particularly true if the company has previously been part of a large conglomerate in which, as is usually the case, the subsidiaries or divisions did not deal with outside lenders or raise debt or equity in the public capital markets. They probably have had no experience in valuing or pricing a business, particularly when, as described in Chapter 3, pricing should be done on the basis of a plan for financing the acquisition.

Moreover, investment banking firms and leveraged buyout firms sometimes can negotiate with owners and directors in a manner which managers cannot because of their need to preserve their existing working relationships. Such partners add credibility to management's proposal to buy the company. They are experienced in structuring such transactions and have access to financing, including funds designed to invest exclusively in MBOs and LBOs as purchasers of debt or preferred stock. They are also experienced in arriving at an appropriate purchase price, marketing the MBO to banks and other lenders, preparing the financing books and projections essential to obtaining financing from banks and financial institutions and doing related tax planning.

Should a top executive—especially a CEO—proceed secretly to meet with financial people, perhaps even disclose "inside" or non-public information, and try to structure a deal that way?

It seems that many deals start in exactly that fashion. If a reasonably large financial house is approached, they'll simply take over the deal and, using publicly available information, make some kind of an offer—usually a low-ball opening offer and disclose that they have talked to management—generally without disclosing that they were *solicited* by management.

But the minute that the offer comes in, the company is "in play" and must permit competing bids to protect the stockholders.

What other approaches are there?

An approach to the outside counsel might work, but his first loyalties are to the company, and he should, and probably will, report the inquiry. Accountants generally do not get involved with buyouts in the early stages and might oppose the move for fear of losing the account. The same with the bankers *unless* the company is in trouble, and then you have a friend.

One way to get the ball rolling might be to employ a third party to contact the owners, or the outside or inside counsel. An attorney might be employed to make a confidential disclosure to outside counsel. A local finder might be employed to simply call up the company and state that he has a potential buyer. He is under no obligation to disclose the name or even the nature of the potential buyer. (In fact, such a finder should sign a non-disclosure agreement, also called a "confidentiality agreement" that he will not disclose the names of the buying group nor "shop" the deal to anyone else.)

The test of what is and is not suitable behavior is whether the action is in the stockholders' interest or not. The outside counsel, the accountant, the banker, while employed, engaged or retained by management, should be reminded that they owe their first duty to the stockholders and not to management, and if it is in the stockholders' interest to explore a possible buyout without disclosing that it is an inside group that is interested, then they should keep the confidence. But it's a touchy area.

How can principals in an MBO ensure management motivation?

Management receives a carrot and a stick: substantial appreciation in value of their stock holdings if they succeed and a substantial amount of debt on the balance sheet to keep them running until it is repaid. For these reasons, the first few years after an MBO are often remembered by top company officers as the most exciting and stimulating of their work lives. Many managers are surprised at how an MBO focuses their attention on increasing revenues and reducing expenses and increases their devotion to a company's success.

Does an MBO create any special personnel needs for the target?

Yes. Most non-publicly held MBOs involve a division or subsidiary of a conglomerate which has operated as a distinct unit in all respects except financially. It almost certainly lacks a chief financial officer experienced in administering a complex series of loan agreements and probably has an inexperienced accounting staff. A necessary and often painful step that often must be taken immediately is to replace or fortify the CFO.

In addition, the high prices being paid in acquisitions are likely to require that the free cash flows of the company increase, and that hard personnel choices be made throughout the organization. The division's or subsidiary's greatest opportunity may be to expand its sales. A new sales-oriented president or a new "vice president—sales" may be the key ingredient for successful post-acquisition operations. Remember, life will not get easier after the buyout.

NEGOTIATING AND DOCUMENTING AN MBO

What is the course of negotiation between a management group and an outside financial or investor group?

The typical MBO involving an outside financial partner requires at least three separate but coordinated negotiations: (1) the negotiation between management and the financial partner as to the nature of their relationship, (2) the acquisition negotiation between a team consisting of management and the financial partner on one side, and the seller on the other, and (3) the negotiation with lenders, in which the financial partner usually plays the lead role but management participates because of its knowledge of the business and its financing needs and management's desire to remain involved. The second and third negotiations are the subjects of Chapters 10 and 4.

Because both the second and third negotiations demand close coordination between management and the financial partner and a considerable amount of mutual trust, the first negotiation should, to the extent possible, be completed successfully at the earliest possible stage. This usually does not happen. MBOs, like most LBOs, normally take place under acute time pressure, and management and the financial partner have probably only just met for the sole purpose of doing the acquisition. The issues between them are difficult and go to basic questions of allocation of benefits and burdens and management self-esteem. It is often difficult for management to accept how much equity the financiers receive when they don't even know how to run the company. Therefore, it is likely that management and the financial partner are working out their relationship at the same time that they negotiate with the seller and the lenders. To some extent, this is unavoidable, even with ample time and advance contact, because the terms negotiated with the seller or the obligations imposed by a lender cannot be entirely foreseen and will involve changes in the allocations of responsibilities or benefits between the acquirors. It may even be beneficial, as during the course of negotiations both management and the financial partner begin to appreciate how essential the other is to accomplish the transaction.

The first step is reaching an understanding of the terms of management and the financial partner's relationship. While this is often an oral agreement, occasionally management and its financial partner may enter into a written preincorporation agreement or prenuptial agreement.

What issues should the preincorporation agreement address?

(a) The terms on which the acquisition will be conducted: that each party will bear its own expenses or how they will be shared; that neither will be liable to the other if the transition is not consummated; that neither will negotiate with another party; that information about the other will be kept confidential; that each will use its reasonable efforts to accomplish the acquisition; the responsibilities that each party will have in negotiating the acquisition (i.e., the financial party will probably commit to obtain financing on a best efforts or reasonable efforts basis).

(b) The share each party will have in the ownership of the acquired company.

(c) The voting power or veto power each party will have over the business operations of the acquired company and over sale or refinancing of the company.

(d) The makeup of the board of directors.

Are there any provisions a preincorporation agreement should not contain?

The lender, as part of its due diligence, may well insist upon seeing a written preincorporation agreement. Therefore, leave out of it anything not for the lender's eyes, such as contingency plans specifying which of the parties will provide personal guarantees for the loan, if necessary.

How is a manager-investor understanding expressed if there is no preincorporation agreement?

These arrangements are then handled as a matter of oral understanding and custom which ultimately, after the acquisition, may be reduced to writing in various agreements such as employment, consulting, and stockholder agreements, and in the target's articles of incorporation and bylaws. Informal agreements are often indicators of a more healthy and successful relationship between the management and the investor group, since the key element in any event is trust and cooperation, and trying to put everything in writing is a great way to get into arguments.

In a typical leveraged buyout, what levels of equity does management hold?

Without a partner, management may own all of the equity. In a typical management LBO, key management will often receive between 10 to 25 percent of the equity, though a chief executive officer who controls the deal can sometimes achieve a 50–50 or better deal for management with his financial partner. Equity percentages are good reflections of the relative negotiating strength of the parties and of which of the two parties brought the deal to the other. Such stakes will be reduced or diluted by equity, or equity equivalents like warrants or convertible securities, issued to a seller or to a financial institution.

What are typical allocations of control over corporate decisions?

Again, allocations vary greatly according to which party controls the deal, how badly they need each other, and how much they trust each other. Discussions tend to reflect a basic division of interest: management tends to think in terms of preservation, expansion, and meeting operating needs of the company, while the financial partner tends to think of satisfying a lender in order to achieve the acquisition and, thereafter, realizing value by payment of dividends, sale of stock, or divestitures.

Management will presumably make ordinary course of business decisions, subject to the board of directors, which may be equally divided between the parties, include independent third-party directors, or be proportionate to stockholdings. If management has less than 50% of the stock, it may have the protection of a supermajority provision for stockholder votes affecting major transactions, such as sale of the company, public issuances of stock, or refinancings. If the financial partner does not have a majority of the stock, it may insist on the ability to sell its interest or take the company public after a certain period of time.

How many members of management are typically included in a management LBO?

Key management can range from as few as one or two managers to over 20 people. The numbers may be limited because of securities law limitations on purchasers in a Regulation D private offering (35 unaccredited investors) or tax limitations on the number of shareholders in an S corporation (35 individuals, no corporations).

How can the value of management be "locked in"— for example, if key people leave or die?

Two very important factors in a management LBO are:

- employment contracts with key personnel for three- or five-year terms; and
- key-man life insurance

Compensation and equity participations can be structured through employment and stockholder agreements so that key managers have everything to gain and nothing to lose by staying; therefore, the risk of voluntary departure can be minimized. These agreements are discussed later in this chapter.

Key-man life insurance should always be part of any MBO planning. No group of financial wizards will substitute for a strong CEO who knows his business, particularly if the plan is to place the company deeply into debt to finance the acquisition. Lenders will frequently require life insurance on the chief executive and perhaps one or two others; even if they don't, any financial group working with management should require it. One of the authors of this book was advising a purchaser some years ago and noticed at the closing, that the CEO was smoking and coughing very heavily. He insisted successfully that the closing not occur without a key-man life insurance binder in the amount of the acquisition loan. One week after the closing, the CEO dropped dead.

LEGAL CONSIDERATIONS IN MBOs

Must interested officers or directors take a leave of absence from the company when they are part of a proposed MBO?

No. An officer or director can continue to perform his or her duties while attempting an MBO. Great pressure falls on an employee who must both operate the business and participate in the MBO as a principal. However, unless he engages in malfeasance or performs his duties in a grossly negligent manner, the officer or director can continue to work for the company. Usually the company cannot afford to lose the services of the employee during the several months an MBO transaction can take to close.

Can directors respond favorably to a proposal for an MBO without violating their duty of loyalty?

Once a company has been put up for sale, it is the duty of the directors to ensure that shareholders obtain the best possible price for their stock (*Edelman*). Directors who also are officers of the company may decide to structure their own competitive bid for the company, tender their own shares to the management-sponsored offering group, and receive the resulting benefits, all without breaching the directors' fiduciary duty to the shareholders. However, when structuring their own bid, the board must still foster competition in the bidding process. When board members take measures that are intended to halt the bidding process, they may be sued for those actions.

In *Edelman*, the board members of Fruehauf Corp. attempted to thwart a hostile takeover attempt by the Edelman Group by formulating a management buyout of the company with Merrill Lynch. A special committee of Fruehauf's outside directors approved the buyout. The court held that even though the MBO had been approved by the outside directors, the transaction was invalid. Though they had fully disclosed the transaction, the outside directors had still breached their duty of loyalty to the shareholders. They did not treat the Fruehauf managers and the Edelman Group equally, but instead accepted the management proposal without giving the Edelman Group an opportunity to bid further. They simply "rubber stamped" the MBO proposal. See also the discussion of the *Van Gorkom* case in Chapter 12, pages 744-745.

What fiduciary duties does the company's board of directors have in reviewing an MBO?

When management proposes an MBO, the company's board of directors has a fiduciary duty to its stockholders to review the fairness of the proposed transaction. It must remain impartial in considering factors such as the adequacy of the price, whether the price is to be paid in cash or a combination of cash and securities, and the likelihood of the purchaser's successfully financing the MBO. The board of directors should have an independent committee of the board of directors review the transaction. The independent committee may decide to retain independent legal counsel to review the offer and negotiate the agreement. The board and independent committee usually seek a fairness opinion with respect to the offer price from an investment banking firm. (See Chapter 12, "Public Company Acquisitions.")

Is there an insider trading risk in MBOs of public companies?

Yes. Managers may have inside information about the company, and purchasing securities while in possession of such information is illegal. Trading while knowing that a proposal has been made but not publicly announced can also be illegal.

Under the short-swing profit trading rules (Section 16(b) of the Securities Exchange Act), officers and directors forfeit profits on purchases of securities where a sale takes place within six months of the purchase. Therefore, an officer and director will not want to purchase securities of a public company in contemplation of an MBO because his or her securities will usually be sold within the six-month period.

Are there other securities law considerations in MBOs?

Yes. Management should be alert to the consequences of formation of a group which collectively owns more than 5% of the equity securities of a public company. The formation of such a group requires disclosure under the Williams Act of the existence of the group and the purposes of the group and its intent to acquire the company. Disclosure is made on a Schedule 13D.

A summary of securities law considerations is found in Chapter 12, "Public Company Acquisitions." Some principal points are: where public stockholders' consent to the transaction is required, the company must issue a proxy statement which makes disclosures about the transaction. If stockholders will receive securities (such as preferred stock or subordinated notes or debentures) in the transaction, the company must have an effective registration statement under the Securities Act of 1933, unless an exemption is available. In a proxy statement or tender offer materials, management must consider disclosing its projections for the company's earnings and any other material information on the company's future prospects. A stockholder is entitled under securities laws to have all material information necessary to evaluate the desirability of receiving cash and securities for his equity against the desirability of retaining his equity for future capital appreciation and dividend income. An MBO is also a going private transaction under Rule 13e-3 of the Securities and Exchange Commission, the initiative for the acquisition is taken by an LBO group or other investor, and management does not make any agreement with respect to its own equity interest until after the acquisition is complete. Rule 13e-3 requires special disclosures relating to the fairness of the transaction.

As with any transaction involving a public company, the company will be required to consider when to disclose management's offer to purchase the company. A leak or premature disclosure may cost management the deal.

How is an MBO typically structured?

For a complete discussion of structuring, see Chapter 5. In brief, management, together with any financial partner, typically forms a new company to acquire the target business. The acquiring company may acquire all the assets of the target company, or all stock of the target company, or merge with the target company. Often management forms a holding company, and its subsidiary engages in a forward or reverse merger with the target company. If management owns stock, it can either have the acquiring company repurchase its existing shares or contribute its equity in the target business to the acquiring company. These methods have different tax consequences, discussed below.

Should the transaction be structured as a tender offer, a merger or a stock purchase?

A tender offer is the fastest method to purchase a majority of a public company's stock. However, tender offers have certain disadvantages. Tender offers may require the expenditure of money prior to gaining access to the target company's cash flow, and without any assurance of ever tapping it. The margin rules of the Federal Reserve Board (Regulations G and U) restrict a purchaser from borrowing more than half of the purchase price against the pledge of publicly traded securities. (See Chapter 12, "Public Company Acquisitions.") Because the margin rules complicate financing, acquisitions of public companies are often done as mergers or use unsecured financing.

The transaction is usually structured as a merger. A merger usually requires approval of the stockholders of both corporations in non-cash transactions and of the non-surviving corporation in cash transactions. A merger transaction involving a public company will require the filing of proxy materials with the Securities and Exchange Commission and a registration statement complying with federal and state securities laws where securities are to be issued. A stock purchase can be done where ownership of the target's shares are concentrated in the hands of a few persons, but typically must be consummated contemporaneously with a merger to obtain the required financing.

Can an MBO be structured as an ESOP transaction?

Yes. An ESOP (Employee Stock Ownership Plan) is a pension plan which owns company stock and in which all or most employees participate. An ESOP buyout is one in which an ESOP is the sole or a principal purchaser of its company's stock. Senior management can own stock in addition to the stock owned through the ESOP. The ESOP purchase of the stock is financed by a loan, either directly to the ESOP or through the company. The loan is almost always backed by the company's assets. Interest payments to the ESOP lender are given favorable tax treatment and therefore can be obtained at below market rates, lowering the company's interest expense. Loan repayments are treated for tax purposes as contributions to a pension plan and are deductible in full, in effect making principal repayments deductible as well as interest. Thus, the ESOP is a powerful and efficient financing tool. However, because the ESOP is a tax-qualified pension plan subject to ERISA and the Code, there are limits on the size of the ESOP and the extent to which it may benefit senior management. An ESOP's advantages, disadvantages, structure, and legal constraints are discussed in detail in Chapter 9, "Pension, Labor, and Compensation Concerns."

MBO TAX CONSIDERATIONS

What special tax issues ordinarily arise in a management buyout?

For the most part, a management buyout raises the same tax issues as any other leveraged buyout. In addition, there are a few categories of issues that pertain specifically to acquisitions with equity participation by management. These issues relate primarily to the manner in which management's investment will be paid for or financed, and generally involve questions of whether significant amounts of compensation income will be deemed to be received by management. Where members of management already own stock or stock rights in a target, special care must be taken in structuring the transaction to allow a tax-free conversion of these existing equity rights.

A discussion of management equity participation in a buyout inevitably leads to a broader discussion of executive compensation. Here, we will focus primarily on management's direct equity participation in an acquisition. It is worth noting, however, that to the extent management does obtain a direct ownership interest in the company, many of the conventional devices employed by large companies to motivate and reward management such as bonus plans and stock option plans may become less important.

A management buyout will likely require a greater cash investment than most of the management participants will have available from personal resources. Unless the management pays for the stock, in cash, at fair market value, there may be taxable income to the employee when he obtains stock. The employee and the corporation will have some control over when the taxable income is treated as being received. Their interests may differ. The tax consequences of the alternative ways of making this investment are governed by the basic rules under Section 83 of the Code.

What is the basic rule for taxation of an employee who receives or purchases stock in an MBO?

As a general rule, under Section 83 an employee receives taxable compensation to the extent that the value of any property received from the employer exceeds the amount the employee pays for that property. To the extent that the employee has taxable income, the employer is entitled to a deduction and is required to withhold tax on the same basis as if regular salary were paid. These rules apply whether the employee is receiving stock or other kinds of property. If an employee has not paid full value for the stock and is thus taxed on the receipt of the stock, the employee will obtain a basis in the stock equal to the amount actually paid for it, plus the amount of taxable income recognized. If an employee has paid full value for the stock, the employee will have a basis in the stock equal to his cost and will have no compensation income. In either case, when the employee later sells the stock, the employee will have capital gain or loss measured by the difference between the sale proceeds and the basis in the stock.

There is an important exception to the general rule. If the stock is not substantially vested in the employee, there is no tax to the employee and no deduction to the employer until such time as the stock does become substantially vested. Stock is substantially vested if it either is not subject to a "substantial risk of forfeiture" or is transferable by the employee. When the risk of forfeiture or the restriction on transferability lapses, rendering the property substantially vested, the employee will be required to pay tax on the excess of the stock's value *at the time the property vests* over the amount paid for the stock. This rule will apply even if the employee originally paid full value for the stock, and cannot be avoided unless the employee otherwise elects under Section 83(b), as described below.

To illustrate these rules, assume that a management employee will acquire 100 shares of company stock from the company in the MBO. The employee buys the stock for $100, which is the full fair market value of the stock. If the stock is then fully vested and transferable, the employee recognizes no taxable income. If, two years later, the stock is worth $150, there will be no impact on the employee; only if the stock is actually sold for $150 will the employee have $50 in long-term capital gain. The company will have no deduction. But if the employee acquires the stock subject to a substantial risk of forfeiture which does not lapse for a two-year period, the result is different. There is still no income at the outset. Two years later, when the stock is worth $150, the risk of forfeiture lapses. The employee must then recognize taxable income of $50 (which is the difference between the $150 fair market value of the stock at that time and the $100 paid for the stock two years earlier), even if the employee has not sold the stock and has no cash proceeds to pay the tax. At that time, the company is entitled to a $50 deduction.

What is a "substantial risk of forfeiture"?

Many typical "golden handcuff" techniques create a substantial risk of forfeiture and can therefore undermine the tax plans. The receipt of stock is subject to a substantial risk of forfeiture if the employee will be required to return the stock upon the happening of a particular event, or the failure to satisfy some condition. The typical example of a substantial risk of forfeiture is a provision requiring that the employee return the stock to the company in the event that he terminates his employment with the company within a certain period after the receipt of the stock. There is not, however, a substantial risk of forfeiture where the company is required to pay the employee full value for the stock upon a termination of employment. A requirement that the employee return the stock unless certain earnings goals are met is also a substantial risk of forfeiture. Where the event that will produce a forfeiture is peculiarly within the control of the employee, such as his dismissal for cause or his taking a job with a competitor of the company, there will not be a substantial risk of forfeiture. Under a special rule in the statute, if the sale of the stock could subject the employee to a suit under Section 16(b) of the Securities Exchange Act of 1934, which makes profits on sales in a six-month period illegal, the employee's rights in the property are considered subject to a substantial risk of forfeiture. Consequently, when the six month period ends, the employee's interest vests and the employee becomes subject to tax on any increase in value of the stock over what he paid for it.

If the employee sells his stock before the risk of forfeiture lapses, he will have taxable income equal to the excess of the amount realized on the sale over the amount paid for the stock. The employer can take a deduction in this amount.

Will receipt of stock by a management investor always be treated as receipt of stock by an employee?

Technically, Section 83 only applies to the receipt of stock or other property by an employee if he receives it in connection with the performance of services. This includes past, present, and future services. In some circumstances, a reasonably strong case can be made that the employees are not receiving stock in connection with the performance of services, but are receiving stock on the same basis and in the same context as other members of an investor group. In spite of this commonsense analysis, most tax advisers recommend that planning in this area proceed on the assumption that the IRS will apply Section 83 in determining the tax consequences to members of an investor group who are employees of the company.

May employees elect to recognize any taxable income currently?

If an employee receives stock that is substantially nonvested, he may elect under Section 83(b) to take any gain into income at the time of receipt of the stock. He will recognize compensation income in the amount of the excess, if any, of the stock's value over the amount paid for it. The employer receives a deduction at that time, equal to any compensation income recognized. The election must be made, no later than 30 days after the receipt of the stock, by filing a form with the IRS Service Center at which the employee files his tax returns. The employee must also file a copy of the election with his tax return. The IRS is quite strict in applying the 30-day filing deadline, and one should not expect any flexibility on this point. Additionally, once such an election is made, it may not be revoked.

Note that a Section 83(b) election may be made even where the effect of making the election will be to recognize no income because at the time the stock was issued there was no spread between its value and the amount paid. Thus, such an election can be useful for an employee who does pay full value at a time when the prospects for subsequent appreciation in the stock are significant. The employee described above, with $100 in forfeitable stock, could have filed an 83(b) election, recognized a gain of zero, and avoided the $50 gain when the risk of forfeiture lapsed.

Where management is purchasing stock in an acquiring entity or in a target that is the subject of a leveraged buyout at or before the acquisition closing and at the same price as other investors, it can usually be comfortably argued that the amount paid for the stock at the inception of the transaction is equal to its fair market value. In such a case, there will be no compensation income to the management participants under Section 83, provided that either the stock is substantially vested or the management participants file Section 83(b) elections.

If the employee's stock purchase is financed with a note, is Section 83 income avoided?

Management rarely has enough cash to buy as large an equity interest as they would like. The stock acquisition of management is usually financed by the company, the investor partner or a third party. A promissory note from the employee will be treated as a bona fide payment for the stock in an amount equal to the face amount of the note, provided it meets two important requirements. First, the note should provide for adequate stated interest at least equal to the Applicable Federal Rate. Second, the note should be with recourse to the employee.

As explained in the foregoing chapter, the original issue discount rules provide that if property is purchased for a note that does not provide for an adequate stated interest rate, the note will be recharacterized so as to impute an adequate interest rate, and thereby reduce the principal. This reduction in principal will be taken into account in determining how much the employee paid for the stock and thus how much Section 83 income must be recognized. In order to have an adequate stated interest rate, the note must provide for interest at no lesser rate than the Applicable Federal Rate as published monthly by the IRS. The Applicable Federal Rate is determined by reference to U.S. obligations of comparable maturities. Over the term of the note, the employee will obtain interest deductions for the OID amount, subject to complicated interest deductibility restrictions enacted in 1986.

The problem that arises from using a nonrecourse note is far more serious. The regulations under Section 83 make it clear that if an employee purchases stock with a nonrecourse note that is secured solely by the purchased stock, he will be treated as having been given an option by the company to purchase stock for the amount of the note, and to exercise the option only when the note is repaid. When an employee receives a non-qualified stock option, unless the option is actively traded on an established market, the employee will not be treated as having received anything from the company until the option is exercised. At that time, he will have compensation income under Section 83 equal to the excess over the amount paid of the stock's fair market value *at the time of exercise* (that is, at the time he pays off the loan). If the stock appreciates substantially, this could be a very large amount, taxed at ordinary income, not capital gains rates. (While there is not presently a lower rate for capital gains, there is a substantial possibility that the rate differential will be reinstated at some time in the future.)

When should the employee be treated as receiving income?

The employee's principal objective is to make sure that whatever event will trigger income to the employee will also cause the employee to have converted his stock investment into cash. Suppose an employee buys 100 shares of company stock for $100, which is its fair market value at that time. To assure that he will not later be taxed on appreciation in the stock on the basis of a claim that his interest has not yet vested, he files a Section 83(b) election. Thereafter, he sells his stock for $500. Traditionally, the main planning goal would be to ensure that the $400 of appreciation would be taxed at favorable capital gains rates. Now that capital gains and ordinary income rates are the same, however, the employee will be largely indifferent as to whether the $400 gain is taxed as capital gain or as ordinary compensation income, so long as he is not taxed until he sells the stock. It appears that he has achieved his objective.

On the other hand, the company's tax planning objectives may have not been well served. There is no benefit to the company as a result of the employee's recognition of $400 of capital gain upon the sale of the stock. Where, however, the employee is able to defer the triggering of Section 83 until he sells the stock, the company will obtain a deduction in the amount of $400. The value of this deduction will be very significant for any company which is a C corporation. The employee is taxed at 28%; the employer deducts at 34%.

In some cases, the tax problem can be solved by a company commitment to pay the employee a bonus sufficient to cover the employee's tax. The bonus is deductible to the company, of course, at rates currently higher than those paid by the employee. The combination of tax bonus plus Section 83 deduction may be better for the employer than the employer's making an 83(b) election, and the employee will be indifferent, since his tax is paid by the employer.

Are there additional adverse consequences to an employee who purchases stock with a nonrecourse note when the employer is an S corporation or a partnership?

As explained above, where the employee purchases stock with a nonrecourse note secured solely by the stock, he will be treated as holding only a non-qualified option to buy stock. As such, he is not treated as owning any of the stock for tax purposes. This will have a dramatic effect where the company is a pass-through entity, either an S corporation or a partnership. For each tax year before the note is paid, all of the income or loss of the entity will be passed through to all other shareholders or partners, excluding the employee. The resulting distortions will be permanent and will almost always work to the disadvantage of the employee.

Assume that an employee has purchased with a note and is therefore treated as having an option to purchase 10% of the stock of an S corporation for $100. In each of the next two years, the company generates aggregate taxable income of $1000, and distributes $350 to the shareholders (including the employee) to reimburse them for federal and state income taxes. At the end of year 2, the employee completes the purchase and sells his stock for $300. Because his basis is $100, he recognizes a short-term capital gain of $200. If the employee had been treated as a stockholder in the company, his basis in his company stock would have been increased by $65 (10% of the company's undistributed taxable income) for each taxable year in which he held company stock. Upon the sale of his company stock for $300 after year 2, he would have recognized only $70 long-term capital gain, i.e. $300 proceeds realized, less $230 basis. This adverse consequence is somewhat offset by the fact that he was not taxed on the company income during prior years.

What happens when management borrows from third-party investors rather than from the company itself?

Where stock of the company or a nonrecourse loan to buy stock in the company is made available to an employee from a party that is a shareholder in the company, the Section 83 rules are clear that the employee will suffer the identical income tax results as if the stock or loan were made available directly from the company itself. As to the shareholder who makes the stock or loan available to the employee, any value transferred to the employee thereby is treated as having been contributed to the company by the shareholder on a tax-free basis. The only benefit obtained by the shareholder will be an increase in his basis in his stock of the company.

If a nonrecourse loan to purchase stock in the company is made available to an employee not by another investor, but by an unrelated party that does not itself own stock directly in the company, the situation is somewhat less clear. The application of Section 83 by the IRS to such arrangements is rendered more difficult as the relationship between the lender and the company or its shareholders becomes more attenuated. Nevertheless, such arrangements still present a substantial risk that the desired goals will not be achieved. Particularly, there remains good reason to fear that the IRS may successfully argue that the employee has not purchased stock at the initial price and does not even own the stock for tax purposes until the nonrecourse debt is repaid.

Can some of the employee's assets be protected from the recourse loan?

Typically, even in the most highly leveraged transactions, the amount of money required for management to purchase their shares cannot be repaid if the buyout does not succeed, without having a fairly severe impact on the lifestyle of the employee. Given a high level of confidence in the venture, and a relatively low stock purchase price, a management participant should be willing to risk his capital in a meaningful way, albeit not with personal bankruptcy as the consequence. In such cases, it might be worthwhile to consider a loan that is with recourse to the borrowing employee, but which specifically excludes recourse with respect to certain of his assets—for example, his house.

Although there is no authority on this question, one would have to stretch the Section 83 regulations very substantially to treat such partially nonrecourse loans as non-qualified options. As long as the debt, and the personal liability of the employee thereon, is bona fide and real, it should probably be respected as such for tax purposes.

What other techniques provide management with full equity rights at a lower cost than the cost to third-party investors?

The most direct and effective means of reducing the cost of management stock relative to that purchased by other investors is through some multi-class arrangement. There are numerous variations on this theme. Here is an example of the most straightforward: Assume that a leveraged buyout is to be capitalized with $5 million in common equity, and that third-party investors are willing to put up this entire sum. The third-party investors could be given a preferred stock with a liquidation preference of $5 million and some reasonable preferred dividend rights. For a relatively nominal sum, both the third-party investors and management would purchase all of the common shares of the company.

By providing the third-party investors with preferential rights equal to virtually the entire shareholders' equity of the corporation, the book value, and arguably the fair market value of the common stock, will be nominal.

There are two problems with this arrangement. First, the IRS can argue that the preferred stock was in fact worth less than $5 million and that in any event the common stock was worth more than the nominal value ascribed to it because of the very low risk-to-reward ratio of the investment. Second, having more than one class of stock will prevent the company from electing to be an S corporation. Where S corporation status is desired, the purchase price of the common stock can be reduced by having third-party investors purchase deeply subordinated debt instruments in addition to their common stock.

TAX-FREE STOCK ROLLOVERS

If management already owns stock, how can management convert their existing stock ownership into stock in the buyer on a tax-free basis?

There are several tax-free ways in which management (as well as other shareholders) of a target may exchange their existing equity in the target for a participating interest in the acquiring company in a leveraged buyout. Depending upon the other structural goals and requirements, a tax-free rollover may occur in the context of a recapitalization of the target, some other tax-free reorganization, or a "Section 351 National Starch" transaction. All of these are discussed in some detail in Chapter 5.

Achieving a tax-free rollover of management's equity can adversely impact other aspects of the tax structuring of the transaction. Most notably, if the management buyout is intended to be treated for tax purposes as a cost-basis asset acquisition, overlapping ownership between the target and the buyer may thwart such a characterization. A discussion of these problems in the broader context of tax structuring may be found in Chapter 5.

If cash is received as part of the exchange, how is it treated?

Because leveraged buyouts involve a very significant reduction in the value of the target's equity through increased debt financing, a target shareholder who wishes to retain an equity interest will either realize a significant increase in his percentage ownership of the outstanding stock or receive cash or other non-equity consideration in addition to his stock. In the latter case, management's tax advisers must analyze the facts to ensure that the receipt of non-stock consideration will be treated as capital gain rather than a dividend to the participant. The significance of this characterization remains even though the tax rates for ordinary income and capital gains are presently the same. One key difference between a dividend and capital gain is that under the latter characterization the shareholder will be permitted to reduce his taxable income by his basis in the stock.

Do the same rules apply where management owns nonqualified options or substantially nonvested stock?

No. In the case of both nonqualified options and stock subject to a substantial risk of forfeiture, for which a Section 83(b) election has not been made, the exchange of the option or restricted stock for stock in the buyer that is not subject to a substantial risk of forfeiture will give rise to compensation income under Section 83 in an amount equal to the value of the target stock involved. If the employee holds restricted stock for which he has made a Section 83(b) election, he will be eligible for tax-free treatment.

EMPLOYMENT AGREEMENTS

In addition to equity, what other benefits are typically made available to management?

Prior to trying to sell a division or subsidiary to a third party or to managers, a seller may ask its managers to sign employment agreements. Usually, the officers have not previously had a written contract. Such agreements keep managers with the company while the business is being offered for sale. Company officers involved in buyouts often enter into employment agreements that provide for compensation at levels varying with responsibility and experience. Typically, three to five of the company's most senior officers, including the chief executive officer, chief operating officer, and chief financial officer, can reasonably expect to enter into such agreements. All officers may participate in employee benefit plans, such as stock option plans and pension plans.

Should an MBO manager enter into an employment agreement?

Generally, managers should accept such agreements, as they often offer protection against termination by a new owner. On the other hand, managers should be wary of signing off on broad "covenants not to compete" preventing them from working with competitors. If an employee must agree to such provisions, which is likely given the strong interest the company will have in protecting its business, he or she will want to be compensated during the non-compete period and will want to limit the period, for example, to one year, and perhaps limit the territory affected.

After purchasing the business, key members of management will want to have new employment agreements replacing those entered into before the sale of the business. Such an agreement will at the least provide a term, a specified salary and non-competition provisions. Management's partner or its bank lenders will usually also want key management to have such agreements.

What provisions relating to non-competition normally appear in employment agreements?

Such agreements prohibit an employee from:

- Competing with the employer by participating in a competing business or aiding a competitor;
- Disclosing confidential information; and
- Owning equity in a competitor (other than insubstantial interests—less than 5–10%) of publicly held companies.

Will courts enforce covenants not to compete?

Courts will enforce the restrictions of covenants not to compete that are reasonable in duration and territory. In general, however, courts are very reluctant to prevent employees from earning their livelihood in their chosen profession, and so tend to favor employees in their decisions.

What are the typical terms of a post-buyout employment agreement with managers involved in an MBO?

An employment agreement should specify the term of employment, the amount of compensation and bonuses, and the conditions under which an executive can be terminated.

Employment agreements can be for a fixed term of years or can be extended from year to year under an "evergreen" provision unless one party gives notice to the contrary to the other within a limited period before the start of each year.

The agreement will specify a base salary. The agreement can provide that the salary can be increased by specified increments or by an adjustment such as a rise in the Consumer Price Index. The agreement may also require that the executive receive a percentage of the excess of the company's pre-tax earnings or net income over projected levels of earnings or income. The agreement might also incorporate an existing bonus plan, as well as special pensions or stock plans, and might guarantee specific benefit levels.

The employer will have the right to terminate the employee for just cause, which usually includes at minimum willful misconduct or gross negligence in the course of employment, fraud in the course of employment, or the conviction of a crime. Just cause may include other matters, but the employee's interest is in limiting the bases for termination for just cause. If the employer has the right to terminate an employee without just cause, the employee is usually compensated by receiving his base salary through the end of the term in a lump sum or periodic payments, or by receiving payments in addition to his or her base salary. If the employee gets a new job, his salary may or may not reduce the amount which must be paid under these provisions by the terminating employer.

The agreement protects the employer and the employee if the employee is disabled for a continuous period of time. If an employee is disabled or dies, the employee or his estate may be entitled to receive benefits after disability or death.

What other provisions may be included in an employment agreement?

Other employment agreement provisions may stipulate that:

- The executive work in a specified city and not be required to relocate;
- The executive receive a company car;
- The company pay for country club memberships and other expenses; and

• Other special benefits, such as guaranteed vacation leave policies, the right to run for public office, etc.

An employee may also negotiate for a deferred compensation agreement. Deferring income can have financial and tax benefits to individuals. The employee may be able to negotiate funded deferred compensation, with amounts payable out of insurance or a special trust.

What are the benefits and detriments of a severance agreement?

Occasionally, an employee who is not offered an employment agreement or is resistant to entering into an employment agreement will enter into a severance agreement instead. The severance agreement, sometimes called a "golden parachute," will provide that the employee receive two or three times his annual salary if he is terminated. These rights may be terminated after an acquisition or change in control in the company, but the employee may be entitled to receive the severance benefit if he chooses to leave under such circumstances. Such agreements are more prevalent in public companies than the private companies that emerge from an MBO. Golden parachutes are often found in employment contracts as well.

Such agreements protect employees by discouraging arbitrary termination that would trigger substantial payments to the employee. On the other hand, such agreements can harm the employer by giving the employee a strong incentive to become uncooperative and even disruptive in order to cause termination and trigger the severance payment. It is not uncommon for management to be asked to give up or scale back its golden parachute protections as part of the price for participating in an MBO.

Golden parachutes can have significant tax consequences to the employer.

What are the tax penalties for golden parachute payments?

In 1984, concerned about certain tactics utilized by companies to fight hostile takeovers, Congress enacted the golden parachute rules taxing excess parachute payments. Under the legislation, as amended in 1986, if a corporation makes an "excess parachute payment" to an employee, the payment may not be deducted by the corporation, and the employee will be subject to a 20% nondeductible excise tax on the excess parachute payment in addition to any regular income tax he pays on it.

The definition of an excess parachute payment is complex. Generally an excess parachute payment is made to a high-level management employee, is exceptional in relation to the employee's previous compensation, and is contingent upon a change of control of the company. The definition is broad enough to include circumstances in which a friendly buyer enters into a compensation arrangement with the employee. Management equity participation which results in taxable compensation under Section 83 will be taken into account along with all other compensation under the golden parachute rules, and thus may be subject to additional tax as an excess parachute payment. As such, the Section 83 issues discussed above should be given extra careful attention.

EMPLOYEE BENEFITS IN MBOs

What other benefits should management bargain for?

Management will want to retain at least the same life and health insurance benefits after the MBO as they had before, and continuous benefit coverage before and after the transaction. Management will also desire continued retirement benefits. After an MBO, the new company may try to reduce its pension expense by adopting new plans or by changing to a defined contribution plan from a defined benefit plan. Management may be able to continue its higher coverage with a new qualified plan. (See Chapter 9, "Pension, Labor, and Compensation Concerns.") Managers may also be entitled to benefits, such as bonus, deferred compensation, severance pay, vacation, and pension benefits under the sellers' plans. Payment of these benefits should be negotiated with care. The employee usually wants control of the money but may want to avoid current tax.

What kinds of bonus plans are there?

Management may also create and participate in new bonus plans after the buyout. Companies after MBOs or LBOs often provide incentives to managers through bonus plans. Such plans may provide for additional cash payments equal to a percentage of salary if the company's net pre-tax income exceeds specified levels. These levels are often the same approximate levels projected by a company in its financing projections. They may be fixed or change from year to year. The benefits may be available for a small group or hundreds of employees. (If for a large group, these plans are subject to ERISA.)

What are nonqualified stock option plans?

Companies often offer senior employees participation in nonqualified stock option plans. Under such plans, employees are granted an option to purchase shares at a specified price. Typically the price is the fair market value on the date of grant, and the option can be exercised beginning on the date of grant or some delayed date and prior to the tenth anniversary of grant. Such plans may permit aggregate purchases of as much as 5% to 10% of a company's stock. (There is no limit on the percentage of stock which can be provided by an option.) The employee pays a tax at the time of exercise, equal to the excess of the stock value over the exercise price. The employer takes a deduction equal to the income recognized by the employee. Tax can be deferred if the stock acquired is forfeitable (see section 83 discussion above). Some companies pay a tax bonus to employees to pay the tax. IRS and SEC also permit the tax to be paid with some of the stock acquired. Nonqualified plans are very flexible, but for public companies they are subject to SEC Rule 16h-3, which requires *inter alia* a written plan, shareholder approval, and a stated limit on shares subject to options. Consider including provisions which accelerate the exercise of options when there is a tender offer or merger involving the issuing company.

What are incentive stock options?

Incentive or qualified stock options (ISOs) are defined in Section 422A of the Internal Revenue Code. Prior to the Tax Reform Act of 1986, ISOs were very popular in executive compensation plans because they allowed an employee both great flexibility in choosing when to cash out and, thus, trigger an income tax, and to have the entire benefit taxed at favorable capital gains rates. Now, these considerations may weigh more in favor of non-qualified options.

In general, an employee is not subject to taxation at either the time of the grant or the exercise of an ISO. Instead, the employee only pays a tax when the stock is sold. The employee is taxed on the entire amount of proceeds less the amount paid for the exercise of the ISO. If the employee holds the shares for at least two years after the ISO was granted and one year after the ISO was exercised, the entire amount of any sale proceeds (less the amount he paid for the stock) will be taxable as capital gains. The company does not receive any tax deduction. If the holding periods are not satisfied, the employee's gain will be ordinary income and the company will receive a corresponding deduction.

An important attribute of ISOs is that the spread between the fair market value of the stock at the time of exercise and the exercise price is a preference item for purposes of the individual alternative minimum tax. Because this spread may be very substantial in a given tax year relative to the employee's other sources of income, and because the alternative minimum tax rate of 21% is exceedingly close to the regular tax rate of 28%, this issue can be important.

There are numerous requirements that must be satisfied for a stock option plan to qualify as an ISO plan. SEC Rule 16b-3 also applies. One such requirement, which may render ISOs less attractive in management buyouts, is that the option price may not be less than the fair market value of the stock at the time the option was granted. If ISOs are granted to employees of 10% of employer stock, the exercise price must be 110% of the fair market value and the option may not be exercisable for five years. Additionally, there are relatively low limits on the amount of ISOs that any employee may be granted in a given year ($100,000 worth of stock exercisable in any one year).

Which plan to choose?

After the Tax Reform Act of 1986, capital gains and ordinary income are taxed at the same rate, eliminating the main incentive for ISO plans. Therefore right now, non-qualified plans can offer tax benefits to the corporation without a detrimental effect on the employees, especially if a tax bonus is offered. Nevertheless, there may be reasons for setting up or continuing such plans. If a target company has an existing ISO plan and existing management effectively enjoys current equity rights through such plan, it may be desirable to retain these rights and avoid taxable cashouts of ISOs to management. Through careful planning, rights under the ISO plan can be rolled over into the post-acquisition company on a tax-free basis. Alternatively, ISOs may be exercised and the stock may be rolled over on a tax-free basis.

Are stock appreciation rights and phantom stock useful in management buyouts?

Stock appreciation rights and phantom stock are contractual rights between a company and certain employees that culminate in cash (or possibly stock) payments to the employees determined as if the employees had owned stock in the company during a given period.

Phantom stock will typically be "issued" to an employee by a company under an arrangement that calls for a cash payment to the employee in "redemption" of his phantom stock at some particular point in time, for example upon his leaving the company. Stock appreciation rights (SARs) are similar contractual arrangements between the company and the employee under which the employee receives an amount equal to the spread between the fair market value of an agreed-upon number of shares of the company's stock at the time of exercise and the value of the shares at the time the plan was established. In each case, the IRS has been quite liberal both in not treating the employee as actually owning the stock in the company, and in allowing the deferral of any compensation income until a payment is actually made under the plan. At the latter time, the company receives a corresponding deduction. (Income will be recognized if there is a cap on the SAR or phantom value and the cap is reached.)

Typically, SARs and phantom stock are not used at the outset of management buyouts. Instead, management will take a direct equity interest in a company. On the other hand, there is good reason to look closely at such devices, particularly for the purpose of involving larger numbers of employees at lower levels in a buyout, while also allowing the company what may be a generous tax deduction at such time as the investors, managers, and other employees are in a position to cash in.

STOCKHOLDERS' AGREEMENTS

At or shortly following the acquisition closing, it is usually advisable for the acquirers to enter into a stockholders' agreement. If the post-acquisition entity is a partnership, the partnership agreement will contain comparable provisions.

What are the main reasons for the buyers of a business to enter into a stockholders' agreement?

To the extent that they have not already done so in a preincorporation agreement, a stockholders' agreement will allow the buyers:

- To obtain advance commitments for additional equity or debt;
- To exercise control over who the owners of the business will be; and
- To specify their respective legal rights over the governance of the business.

Why might the buyers want to exercise control over who the owners of the business will be?

Presumably, one of the main reasons the buyers completed the transaction was their particular individual and collective strengths. They wanted to be in business *together* rather than with other persons or entities. In an MBO (with or without an outside investor group), equity ownership by the persons who will be running the business is a key ingredient to the future success of the enterprise. Therefore, especially in the early period following the acquisition closing, the buyers will want to limit the ownership of the business to those who are active employees or members of the initial investor group. Moreover, the acquisition lenders will have similar concerns and usually will require that the equity ownership of management and the initial investor group be maintained at certain levels for so long as their loans are outstanding.

What are some of the typical ways to limit the equity ownership of the target?

The stockholders' agreement will contain so-called "restrictions on transferability," which are limitations on the persons or entities to whom the stockholders may transfer their stock, the time periods during which the stock may be transferred, or the manner in which the stock may be transferred. For example, the stockholders may agree that, in order to give themselves an opportunity to put the business on a solid footing, for a specified period of time, usually from one to five years after the closing, no stockholder will be allowed to transfer stock to anyone other than to an affiliate in the case of a corporate stockholder or to a spouse or child in the case of a stockholder who is a natural person. Management stockholders may even be locked in for a longer period, perhaps as long as they continue to be employed by the corporation. Conversely, in the case of a management stockholder, the stockholders' agreement may also provide that upon termination of his or her employment, the corporation or the other stockholders will have the option to purchase the terminated employee's stock. One benefit of a provision like this is that the purchased stock could then be sold to another employee of the corporation, including the terminated employee's replacement, enhancing his or her incentive to perform well. Another benefit is that the stock need not remain in the hands of a fired or otherwise disgruntled former employee.

Are such restrictions on transferability legally enforceable?

Generally speaking, yes, assuming that there is a valid business purpose for the restriction, the restriction is reasonably related to a business purpose, and that no stockholder has been induced by deception or forced into agreeing to the restriction. However, the more expansive the restriction, the greater the risk that a court will find the restriction to be an "unlawful restraint on the alienation of property." In addition, under the laws of most states, the existence of transfer restrictions must be noted in the form of a legend on the stock certificate in order for those restrictions to be enforceable against third-party transferees who have no knowledge of their existence.

Are there any other ownership restrictions that management may want to have in a stockholders' agreement?

Where management is in a minority position vis a vis the other stockholders, it may want some protection against dilution of its interest, or some influence over when, and to whom, additional stock may be issued.

Through the stockholders' agreement, management could be given an option to purchase such additional stock, or a proportion thereof, for the same price and terms on which they would otherwise be sold to a third person or entity. It could also be given certain consensual rights over the issuance of such additional stock (see discussion below).

How may a stockholders' agreement create the framework by which the corporation will be governed?

The stockholders' agreement may contain provisions (i) whereby the stockholders commit themselves in advance to vote their shares to maintain a certain governing structure, (ii) which require that certain matters normally within the province of the Board of Directors or the President shall be regulated by the stockholders, or (iii) which require that, under certain circumstances, normal majority rule by the Board or the stockholders, as applicable, will not be sufficient.

An example of the first type of provision is where the stockholders agree that they will exercise their power to adopt and amend the corporation's bylaws to maintain a Board of Directors of a particular number and that they will vote to elect as directors representatives nominated by various groups of stockholders. In the case of a typical MBO in which the majority of stock is held by an investor group, the stockholders' agreement would provide that the stockholders will at all times vote their shares so as to maintain a Board of Directors of, say, five members, three of whom shall be nominated by the investor group and two of whom shall be nominated by the management group.

An example of the second type of provision is where the parties agree that the stockholders must approve the dismissal of certain executive officers, or any contracts with affiliates of the corporation, or the issuance of stock—activities which are usually handled by the Board of Directors.

An example of the third type of provision is where the stockholders agree that the corporation cannot engage in certain major transactions, such as a merger or a sale of substantially all the assets of the corporation, without the approval of all of the stockholders or some greater proportion of the stockholders than the proportion required under the applicable state corporation statute.

In most, if not all states, it will also be necessary for the second and third types of provisions to be stated in the certificate of incorporation or bylaws of the corporation. For example, Delaware Code Sections 141 and 216 provide, respectively, (i) that the business and affairs of every Delaware corporation shall be managed by its Board of Directors unless the corporation's certificate of incorporation provides otherwise, and (ii) that unless the corporation's certificate of incorporation or bylaws provide otherwise, all matters, other than election of directors, subject to stockholder approval shall be approved by majority vote, and in the case of the election of directors, by plurality vote. In this case the stockholders' agreement should also provide that the stockholders will vote their shares to adopt and maintain these types of provisions as part of the company's certificate of incorporation or bylaws, as applicable.

For how long are voting agreements enforceable?

This matter is governed by the corporation statutes of the state in which the company is incorporated. In Delaware, for example, such agreements are valid for only ten years, but at any time within two years prior to expiration of a voting agreement, the stockholders may extend such agreement for as many additional periods, each not exceeding ten years, as they desire. It is possible, however, through the use of devices such as irrevocable proxies, to lock in stockholder votes for a longer period than that permitted for voting agreements.

What kinds of additional financial commitments are usually found in stockholders' agreements?

Since in most cases, especially LBOs, the buyers do not intend to make further equity contributions to the corporation, the stockholders' agreement usually does not contain any provision for additional capital calls. However, where the corporation is in a volatile industry, or where the acquisition is highly leveraged, serious consideration should be given to requiring the stockholders to commit themselves to contributing additional equity to, making loans to, or extending personal guarantees on behalf of the corporation. In addition to the conditions under which such a commitment will be triggered, the extent to which any group of stockholders, e.g., the investor group, will assist the other stockholders in obtaining the funds to meet their commitment should also be incorporated in the stockholders' agreement.

What are some of the exit strategies typically embodied in a stockholders' agreement?

The following are the major kinds of provisions relating to opportunities for the stockholders to liquidate their investment:

1. Voting provisions pursuant to which the stockholders agree to vote their shares in favor of any arms-length merger or asset sale recommended by a certain group of stockholders (e.g., the investor stockholder group) or a certain percentage of all the stockholders;
2. The right to sell stock to any third-party person or entity, subject to the right of the corporation or the other stockholders to purchase the stock for the same terms offered by the third.party (a "right of first refusal");
3. The right of any stockholder to sell stock to any other stockholder;
4. The right of a stockholder to "tag along" with other stockholders, i.e., to require a third-party offeror to purchase a pro rata portion of each stockholder's stock rather than purchase the same number of shares from the original offeree;
5. The right of any stockholder or group of stockholders to "force along" the other stockholders, i.e., to sell their shares to a third-party offeror;
6. The right of a stockholder or his or her heirs to sell his or her stock to the corporation in the event of death, disability, or termination of employment; and
7. The right of a stockholder to require the corporation to register his or her shares in a public offering.

Are any of the foregoing rights particularly important to management owning a minority interest in the corporation?

Yes, the so-called "tag along" right and the right to sell stock upon termination of employment, including death and disability, are especially important to management.

Without the "tag along" right, management holding a minority interest in the corporation can be frozen into the corporation since it is unlikely that a third party would be interested in purchasing a minority interest in a closely held corporation, especially if such stock is subject to significant transfer restrictions. Moreover, management could be left with a new investor group with objectionable business goals or interpersonal style.

Without the right to sell his or her stock upon termination of employment, what may be the largest asset of a management stockholder, or his or her heirs, would be illiquid at a time when liquidity is needed most.

At what point should "tag along" rights be triggered?

From a minority interest management's point of view, the trigger should be as low as possible. The general principle is that, since the parties are partners and management is devoting its full-time efforts to enhancing the value of the corporation, the investor group should not be allowed to liquidate a substantial portion of its investment in the corporation without giving management the opportunity to do the same. A trigger in the range of 10% to 15% would be excellent for management; anything over 40% would be unacceptable.

How does this trigger work?

It can work in several ways. One way is if a third party offers to purchase more than, say, 15% of the stock held by the investor group, management will have the right to sell the proportion of its shares equal to the proportion of investor group shares to be sold to the third-party offeror. Another way is that once the investor group has liquidated a certain portion of its investment, say, 15%, it cannot sell another share without offering management the opportunity to participate in the sale on a pro rata basis. If the trigger threshold is low, this latter type of trigger is preferable from management's point of view since it prevents the investor group from "trickling out" of the corporation.

From management's point of view, what are the important negotiation points of a "buy/sell" arrangement upon termination of employment?

The following are crucial:

1. *Mandatory v. optional requirement.* Management wants a mandatory obligation or, preferably, a "put," particularly in the case of death or disability;

2. *Price.* Management wants fair market value, preferably at all times, but at least in the case of death, disability, retirement, or termination without cause;

3. *Determination of Price.* Management at least wants an opportunity to get an independent appraisal at the time a buyback is triggered;

4. *Payment Terms.* Management wants the pay-out period to be as short as possible, preferably in cash at the closing (particularly in case of death or disability); and

5. *Security for payment.* Unless premium payments would cripple the company, where the buyout price is significant or where acquisition loan agreements have low caps on the amount of non-insured buy-backs the corporation can make, management wants the corporation to purchase life insurance and, if possible, disability insurance, to fund the buyback. In other cases involving deferred payments, management wants protections such as an opportunity to get the stock back free of transfer restrictions in the event of uncured payment defaults and pre-payments out of the proceeds of public offerings.

As in the case with every contractual arrangement, each party must carefully consider the tax consequences associated with the various provisions under negotiation.

CHAPTER 7

FINANCIAL AND ACCOUNTING CONSIDERATIONS

INTRODUCTION

All of the guidance presented in this book cannot make the deal a success if the numbers do not work. Without extensive knowledge of the target's financial affairs, buyers and lenders are likely to be in the dark when making their threshold decision about whether or not to do the deal. The first section of this chapter, "Financial Considerations in Evaluating the Target," identifies the questions that need to be answered to help buyers and lenders in finding hidden treasure, avoiding hidden traps, and understanding the financial and economic picture that the numbers portray.

Accounting for the merger/acquisition/buyout and, specifically, the presentation of the subsequent financial statements may be critical to present and future concerns of buyers and lenders. Using "purchase" accounting often results in a stronger-looking acquisition balance sheet relative to the historical financial information, and a weaker-looking income statement in the future. Using "pooling" accounting can result in opposite effects. These two accounting methods, together with other accounting and financial reporting matters, are discussed in the "Accounting for Mergers and Acquisitions" section of this chapter.

In today's merger and acquisition world, the competition is keener and the pace faster than ever before. Buyers and lenders need more data sooner, more timely and comprehensive analyses of the consequences of proposed terms, a more thorough testing of assumptions, and more projections of the results of a transaction. These requirements have altered the role of the accountant in the due diligence process. No longer is the accountant's role confined to giving advice after the deal has been negotiated. Today the accountant may be the principal financial expert on the due diligence team, participating in every phase of the transaction. The last section of this chapter, "Involvement of Accountants in Mergers and Acquisitions," discusses how investors and lenders can use this resource.

FINANCIAL CONSIDERATIONS IN EVALUATING THE TARGET

What are the buyer's or lender's objectives in reviewing the target's financial and operating information?

In most acquisition transactions, a buyer or lender should evaluate, at a minimum, five principal areas: projected cash flow; the quality and depth of management; overvalued, undervalued, and unrecorded assets and liabilities; the tax structure of the transaction; and items that could be "deal breakers." Deal breakers may include, among other things, inaccurate financial projections, inadequate management information systems, fraudulent conveyance issues on asset-based lending deals, lawsuits, and other unexpected items that require significant outlays of cash or could adversely affect future earnings of the target. A buyer or lender should also obtain information that expands its knowledge of specific areas of the target company. These include: a determination of the adequacy of insurance coverage; a description of existing accounting policies and potential alternatives; a summary of all significant contracts, sources of raw materials, labor conditions, dividend and currency movement restriction and a schedule of key employees, indicating their age, role, salary, location, and potential line of succession.

What sources of information are available to a buyer or lender when evaluating an acquisition or lending transaction?

Sources of information that are generally available to a buyer or lender when evaluating a transaction include:

- Historical financial statements. If the target is a public company, historical financial statements are contained in filings with the Securities and Exchange Commission, such as Forms 8–K, 10–K, 10–Q and proxy materials;
- External and internal auditors' workpapers and management letters;
- Trade publications and other public information;
- Operational and financial management;
- Operating budgets and comparisons to actual performance;
- Cash flow projections and assumptions;
- Prior years' tax returns and revenue agents' reports (federal, state, local and foreign);
- Reports of internal and external consultants;
- Valuation appraisals;
- Contracts and agreements such as leases, compensation and employee benefit agreements, royalty agreements, and previous acquisition agreements;
- Accounting and management information systems;
- Facility tours; and
- Supplier and customer lists.

What assets in a target's balance sheet may be undervalued, and what assets may not be recognized at all?

Financial statements prepared according to GAAP generally measure assets at historical costs or depreciated historical costs. These assets may be carried at amounts below their market or appraised values. Also, certain accounting conventions tend to understate the carrying values of certain assets compared to their market or appraised values, and some valuable assets of a target may not be recognized at all. Assets in a target's balance sheet that typically may be undervalued and assets that may not be recognized at all include:

- Inventories—when the "LIFO" cost convention is used, inventory balances are generally understated in relation to current replacement cost.
- Marketable securities—a marketable securities portfolio is generally reported at cost, which may be below market value.
- Investments in joint ventures and unconsolidated subsidiaries—the "cost" and "equity" conventions may understate these investments in relation to current values.
- Property, plant, and equipment—whether used in revenue-producing activities or held for sale, these assets are carried at depreciated historical cost, which may be below the assets' market or appraised values.
- Computer software—costs of internally developed computer software that is not intended to be sold or leased is written off as incurred and thus may represent an unrecorded asset.
- Net operating loss and tax credit carryforwards—although these may be valuable as offsets to income taxes in the future, they are not recognized as assets until utilized.
- Debt at favorable rates—debt obligations that have a rate of interest below current market rates (technically represents a reduction in a liability).
- Excess pension plan assets—the amount by which the fair value of plan assets exceeds the plan liabilities of a single-employer pension plan is not generally fully reflected in the target's balance sheet.
- Favorable leases—lease obligations for property, plant, and equipment that are below market rates (an unrecorded asset).
- Long-term purchase contracts—product purchase commitments that are below current market prices (an unrecorded asset).
- Intangibles, such as licenses, patents, franchises, trademarks, customer lists, and unpatented technology.

Intangible assets may be acquired from others (as part of a group of assets or as part of an acquired enterprise) or developed internally. Intangibles acquired from others are carried at depreciated historical cost, which may be below fair value; the cost of internally developed intangibles is generally written off as incurred (an unrecorded asset).

What assets in a target's balance sheet may be overvalued?

Examples of assets in a target's balance sheet that may be overvalued include:

- Uncollectable receivables or receivables not currently due that bear no interest or an interest rate that is below current market rates.
- Inventories that are obsolete, slow moving, or otherwise stated above net realizable value.
- Property, plant, and equipment held for sale or used in the business at levels that will not enable recovery of the carrying cost.
- The recorded value of intangible assets may have diminished in relation to current revenue and profitability levels of the target compared to those levels at the date the assets were recorded.
- Investments in consolidated or unconsolidated subsidiaries that may not be realizable at current carrying values. For example, the carrying value of foreign subsidiaries may not be fully realizable due to restrictions on transfer of funds.
- Pension assets in excess of pension obligations recognized in a business combination accounted for as purchase where a subsequent decline in the market value of the assets has occurred.
- Costs of assets currently being constructed that are not recoverable either because the project will not be completed or, if completed, future operations will not be adequate to recover the carrying cost.

What liabilities may not be fully reflected or not reflected at all in the target's balance sheet?

Some contingent liabilities are not required to be recognized in the financial statements of an enterprise under generally accepted accounting principles, while other liabilities may not be fully recognized because the estimate of such liabilities is lower than their potential amount. In addition, some liabilities may arise in connection with the acquisition itself. Examples of liabilities that typically may not be fully reflected or not reflected at all in the target's balance sheet include:

- Obligations related to product warranties and product defects.
- Actual and possible claims or assessments for product liability and environmental liability.
- Pending and threatened litigation.
- Guarantees of indebtedness of others.
- Withdrawal liability from a multi-employer pension plan.
- Unfunded health, life, and welfare obligations of active and retired employees.
- Employment obligations, such as severance, unfunded benefit plans, and incentive contracts.
- Federal, state, and foreign tax deficiencies relating to tax years subject to examination. These include income taxes, personal property taxes, sales taxes, payroll taxes, and excise taxes.
- Obligations for product returns and discounts.
- Obligations under sales, supply, and purchase contracts.

What are the issues a buyer or lender should consider in evaluating the financial affairs of a target corporate division or subsidiary that was not previously accounted for or operated on a "stand-alone" basis?

Three principal issues must be addressed by a buyer or lender in evaluating the financial affairs of a target corporate division or subsidiary that was not previously accounted for or operated on a "stand-alone" basis. These are (1) whether all costs of operating the corporate division or subsidiary are reflected in its historical operating results, (2) whether transactions between the corporate division or subsidiary and its affiliates are valued on an arm's-length basis, and (3) whether the corporate division or subsidiary has the quality and depth of management necessary to operate the stand-alone business successfully.

With respect to operating costs, a corporate division or subsidiary frequently benefits from services provided by its affiliates. In some situations, the corporate division or subsidiary is charged for these services; in other situations, it is not. If a charge is made for the services, the charge may be determined on the basis of what such services would cost if purchased from an unrelated party. Alternatively, the affiliate providing the services may pass on its cost with no markup or the charge may be determined arbitrarily. Services that are frequently provided by affiliates on behalf of a corporate subsidiary or division include: general management, accounting, tax, legal, treasury, benefits administration, internal audit and information processing.

Transactions between affiliates pose another accounting challenge. A corporate division or subsidiary may benefit by being included in certain corporate-wide programs—such as property, casualty and medical insurance programs, pension plans, transportation programs, and advertising programs—for which the charges allocated to the division or subsidiary are less than the costs that they would incur on a "stand-alone" basis.

A corporate division or subsidiary may have other transactions with corporate affiliates. These include product sales, sale or lease of facilities and equipment, and borrowing or lending of funds. In evaluating the financial affairs of a target corporate division or subsidiary, a buyer or lender should consider whether transactions of this nature have been consummated on terms similar to those prevailing with unrelated parties.

Finally, a buyer or lender should consider the quality and depth of management of the corporate division or subsidiary. They need to determine whether the prior success of the division or corporate subsidiary is the result of management of the division or subsidiary, or whether the prior success is directly attributable to management of the corporate parent or an affiliate.

What "red flags" should a buyer or lender look for in reviewing the target's financial statements that could indicate "soft" income or income or loss generated outside normal operations?

Historical trends in the operating results of a target company are a valuable indicator of its ability to achieve future operating goals. Evaluating historical financial information and its relationship to future developments, however, requires identifying and isolating the unusual factors that reduce the comparability of reported results and distort trends. The following "red flags" may be an indication of "soft" income or income or loss generated from outside normal operations:

- Extraordinary and nonrecurring items such as (1) reversals of accounting reserves for bad debts, inventory obsolescence, litigation, self-insurance costs, warranties, and sales discounts and allowances; (2) gains and losses from the sale of productive assets and nonstrategic businesses; (3) litigation and insurance claim recoveries; (4) costs and losses netted against revenues and revenues netted against costs (e.g., nonrecurring cooperative advertising allowances received by a distributor from a franchiser that are netted against advertising expense); (5) barter transactions; (6) pension plan terminations; (7) facility closings and realignments; and (8) significant year-end accounting adjustments (e.g., large adjustments to the year-end inventory accounts resulting from the taking and pricing of an annual physical inventory may indicate that the target's interim period sales margins are unreliable). These items are unusual and generally limited in impact to a specific period of time. Accordingly, financial statements that are affected by extraordinary or nonrecurring items must be carefully analyzed to prevent potentially misleading conclusions about historical data and future results.

- Related party transactions such as compensation, selling, and procurement arrangements between commonly controlled entities or between parent companies and their subsidiaries or divisions. These transactions can reduce the comparability of a company's historical and future results because new management may be able to prospectively eliminate or modify many arrangements that were designed to accomplish the objectives of the prior control group.
- Changes in accounting, which can consist of (1) discretionary changes among alternative accounting methods, such as changes in valuing inventories from LIFO to FIFO and changes in the estimated number of years over which assets are depreciated or amortized; (2) changes in accounting methods required by new professional accounting standards; and (3) changes in management's philosophy with respect to applying accounting principles—i.e., whether the company's approach is conservative or aggressive. Such changes have a direct impact upon the quality of earnings and the comparability of reported results because similar or identical transactions may be accounted for differently in a target company's historical financial statements.

Generally accepted accounting principles specifically require that extraordinary and nonrecurring items, changes in accounting, and transactions with related parties be disclosed in a company's financial statements. The application of these requirements, however, is somewhat subjective because disclosures must be evaluated in light of materiality. Also, the concept of a nonrecurring transaction is difficult to define and may be interpreted differently by accountants. In addition, some related party transactions, such as salaries paid to employees who are related to the ownership group, are not disclosed in financial statements. Furthermore, separate financial statements for divisions and subsidiaries are not always available.

When nonrecurring events or related party transactions are not disclosed in financial statements, a due diligence team will generally identify their presence through comparative reviews of a company's historical income statements, inquiries of management, review of fluctuations in balance sheet reserve accounts, comparisons with other enterprises in similar industries or lines of business, comparisons of actual versus budgeted results, review of workpapers of the target company's auditors, review of agreements and legal correspondence, and other analytical procedures.

ACCOUNTING FOR MERGERS AND ACQUISITIONS

Accounting Methods

What are the principal authoritative accounting pronouncements covering the accounting for mergers and acquisitions?

The principal authoritative accounting pronouncements covering the subject of accounting for mergers and acquisitions (business combinations) is Accounting Principles Board Opinion No. 16, "Accounting for Business Combinations" (APB No. 16). Since its issuance in 1970, APB No. 16 has been the subject of formal interpretations by the Securities and Exchange Commission (SEC), the American Institute of Certified Public Accountants, the Financial Accounting Standards Board (FASB) and, more recently, the Emerging Issues Task Force of the FASB (EITF).

What are the accepted methods of accounting for business combinations and how do they differ?

Two acceptable methods of accounting for business combinations are described in APB No.16: the purchase method and the pooling of interests method. In general, the purchase method accounts for a business combination as the acquisition of one company by another. The purchase price and costs of the acquisition are allocated to all of the identified assets acquired and liabilities assumed, based on their fair values. If the purchase price exceeds the fair value of the purchased company's net assets, the excess is recorded as goodwill. Earnings or losses of the purchased company are included in the acquiring company's financial statements from the closing date of the acquisition.

The pooling of interests method accounts for a business combination as a uniting of ownership interests of two companies by the exchange of voting equity securities. No acquisition is recognized because the combination is accomplished without disbursing resources of the constituents. In pooling accounting, the assets, liabilities, and retained earnings of each company are carried forward at their previous carrying amounts. Operating results of both companies are combined for all periods prior to the closing date, and previously issued financial statements are restated as though the companies had always been combined.

Are these methods alternatives in accounting for the same business combination?

No. In APB No. 16, the Accounting Principles Board concluded that both the purchase method and the pooling of interest method are acceptable in accounting for business combinations, but not as alternatives in accounting for the same business combination. The structure of the business combination transaction (as more fully described below) dictates which accounting method must be used. Also described below are the potential advantages and disadvantages of using each.

Pooling of Interests Method

What are the advantages of using the pooling of interests method?

- Pooling of interests accounting is often preferred if the focus subsequent to the transaction is on the income statement. Income statements for periods subsequent to a pooling of interests are not burdened with additional depreciation, goodwill amortization, and other charges attributable to a purchase price in excess of book value. The higher reportable future income that usually results from application of pooling versus purchase accounting may be of added importance if the objective is a future sale of stock where the sales price is expected to be based on a multiple of reported earnings.

- There are no uncertainties or issues regarding purchase price determination and valuation.
- Prior years' financial statements are restated to reflect the business combination; thus, financial statement year-to-year comparability is not lost.

What are the disadvantages of using the pooling of interests method?

- Assets of the acquired company are not written up to fair value; return on assets and other financial performance measurements may not be comparable with other companies in the same industry.
- A trend of prior increases in earnings may be affected due to restatement of prior years' results to include the combining company.
- The combining company may not have been audited and performance of the audit work necessary to restate the financial statements may not be possible or, if possible, may be costly. Further, if audited, any exception in the reporting company's auditor's report may impact the report of the combined company.

When must the pooling of interests method be used to account for a business combination?

If a business combination meets twelve specific criteria outlined in APB No. 16, it must be accounted for as a pooling of interests. These criteria are broadly classified as pertaining to (1) the attributes of the combining companies, (2) the manner in which the companies are combined, and (3) the absence of planned transactions. All twelve criteria must be met if pooling accounting is to be used. If any one of the criteria is not met, the purchase method of accounting must be used. A brief outline of each of the pooling criteria follows:

Attributes of the Combining Companies

- Neither company can be a subsidiary or division of another company within two years before the plan of combination is initiated.
- Each of the combining companies must be independent of the other combining companies: intercorporate investments in a combining company cannot exceed 10% of outstanding voting common stock.

A business corporation wherein these conditions are met indicates that independent ownership interests are combined entirely to continue previously separate corporations. This avoids combinations of selected assets, operations or ownership interests, which are more like purchases than sharings of risks and rights.

Manner in which the Companies are Combined

- The combination must be effected in a single transaction or completed in accordance with a specific plan within one year after the plan is initiated.
- A corporation must offer and issue only common stock with rights identical to those of the majority of its outstanding voting common stock (the class of stock with voting control) in exchange for substantially all of the voting common stock interest of the other company at the date the plan of combination is consummated ("substantially all" means a minimum of 90%).
- None of the combining companies may change the equity interest of the voting common stock in contemplation of the combination, either within two years before the plan of combination is initiated or between the dates the combination is initiated and consummated; changes in contemplation of the combination may include distributions to stockholders, additional issuances, exchanges, and retirements of securities.
- Each of the combining companies may have acquired shares of its voting common stock (treasury stock) only for purposes other than business combinations, and no

combining company may acquire more than a normal number of shares between the initiation date and the consummation date. Treasury stock acquired for purposes other than business combinations includes shares for stock option and compensation plans and other recurring distributions, provided a systematic pattern of reacquisitions is established at least two years before the plan of combination is initiated.

- The ratio of the interest of an individual common stockholder to that of other common stockholders in a combining company must remain the same as a result of the exchange of stock to effect the combination.
- The voting rights to which the common stock ownership interest in the resulting combined company are entitled must be exercisable by the stockholders; the stockholders can neither be deprived of nor restricted in exercising those rights for a period. The issued shares cannot be transferred, for example, to a voting trust.
- The combination must be resolved at the consummation date, and no provisions of the plan relating to the issue of securities or other conditions may be pending. This precludes the contingent issuance of additional shares.

The essence of a pooling of interests, or "pooling", is that separate shareholder interests lose their identity and all share mutually in the combined rights and risks of the combined entity. The prerequisites to pooling described above relate to the exchange to effect the combination, and they are based upon the premise that mutual sharing is not compatible with alterations of relative voting rights, preferential claims to profits or assets for some shareholder groups, preservation of minority shareholder groups, acquisitions of common stock for assets or debt, and acquisitions of stock for the purpose of exchanging it.

Absence of Planned Transactions. These conditions prohibit the inclusion in the negotiations, either explicitly or by intent, of certain types of transactions after consummation of the transaction. These are prohibited because they are inconsistent with the concept of combining entire shareholder interests.

- The combined company may not agree directly or indirectly to retire or acquire all or part of the common stock issued to effect the combination.
- The combined company may not enter into other financial arrangements for the benefit of the former stockholders of a combining company— such as the guarantee of loans secured by stock issued in the combination—that in effect negates the exchange of equity securities.
- The combined company may not intend or plan to dispose of a significant portion of the assets of the combining companies within two years after combination, other than disposals in the ordinary course of business of the formerly separate companies or disposals in elimination of duplicate facilities or excess capacity.

The SEC staff generally requires that, in order to qualify for pooling accounting, the combining company must be an operating entity with "significant operations" (i.e., something other than nominal). In one case, the SEC stated that a company with little operating activity, but with a substantial asset base (principally natural resource assets whose book values were significantly below fair market values), could not be party to a pooling of interests. The concept is that, in order to qualify for pooling accounting, there must be a combination of operating businesses. The SEC has not defined "little operating activity;" this must be determined on a case-by-case basis.

What are some reasons that preclude a business combination from being accounted for as a pooling of interests?

There are literally hundreds of reasons that preclude a business combination from being accounted for as a pooling of interests. Some of the more common reasons are:

- Sale of significant assets by the combining companies, either prior to consummation of the business combination or subsequent to the business combination. Dispositions occurring within three months prior to the business combination are presumed to be in contemplation of the pooling (and, accordingly, violate the pooling rules).

Dispositions between three and six months prior to the business combination are also presumed to be in contemplation of the pooling if a company cannot substantiate that they were not. Between six months and two years prior to consummation, a disposition is presumed not to be in contemplation of the pooling if a company will represent that fact. The measure of "significance" for this purpose has generally been construed to be the same that is used for a reportable segment in Statement of Financial Accounting Standards No. 14, "Financial Reporting for Segments of a Business Enterprise," i.e., 10% of operating profits, assets, or sales.

- Combination with a new company formed by spinning off a subsidiary, or a new company formed to acquire the spun-off subsidiary. While it is generally understood that the acquisition of a company through a leveraged buyout will not qualify for pooling accounting, the autonomy criterion may also prevent the acquired business from subsequently qualifying for pooling accounting. For example, if the leveraged buyout group's investment vehicle is one of several subsidiaries of a leveraged buyout fund or holding company, an acquired business would fail to satisfy the autonomy criterion. If, however, the leveraged buyout is structured so that the target company is not controlled by another operating entity, i.e., it is not a subsidiary following the leveraged buyout, it can qualify for pooling of interests accounting after two years, provided that all of the other criteria are met.

- Acquisitions of material amounts of treasury shares in relation to the planned combination. Treasury shares are material if they exceed 10% of the shares to be issued in the business combination.

- A contingency arrangement that is based on earnings levels, book values, or stock market prices subsequent to the consummation date. A contingency arrangement that relates to conditions existing at the consummation date, however, would not preclude pooling accounting (e.g., an escrow related to tax returns not yet examined by the IRS).

Does the existence of a standstill agreement preclude a business combination from being accounted for as a pooling of interests?

The FASB's Emerging Issues Task Force has addressed this issue in connection with standstill agreements that prohibit a more-than-10% shareholder from acquiring additional shares for a specified period. The Task Force reached a consensus that pooling accounting would not be precluded if the standstill agreement was not made in contemplation of the combination and was with a less-than-majority shareholder. A standstill agreement made in contemplation of a particular business combination with a more-than-10% shareholder, however, would preclude pooling accounting. Pooling accounting would also be precluded if a standstill agreement with a 10%-or-less shareholder was in contemplation of the combination, if that shareholder and other dissenters aggregated more than 10% of the shares issued in the combination.

Does the granting or exercise of a lock-up option preclude pooling accounting for a subsequent merger between the parties?

Lock-up arrangements take many forms, but most have the same basic structure: an agreement that Company A will acquire all or a specific part of Company B, and that Company A will realize an economic gain if another company buys Company B or the specified part of Company B.

A lock-up structured as an option agreement does not preclude pooling accounting, provided that no consideration is issued or received for the option and the option is not exercised. If the lock-up is structured as a sale of stock, pooling accounting becomes more questionable.

If the business combination plan is initiated after the lock-up purchase, an intercorporate investment of greater than 10% would preclude pooling accounting. A cash purchase of a greater-than-10% interest between initiation and consummation dates would also invalidate pooling treatment. If the lock-up purchase is initiated after the business combination is initiated and the lock-up involves an exchange of voting common stock for voting common stock, however, the exchange of stock interests should not preclude pooling accounting.

The two common types of lock-up options are an option to purchase a prized, highly profitable division, subsidiary, or assets of one entity ("Crown Jewel Option"), and an option to purchase for cash or stock an investment in common stock of one or both of the entities. Provided that no consideration passes hands, the issuance of a Crown Jewel Option will generally not defeat a pooling. Exercising a Crown Jewel Option, however, seems to violate the rule that none of the combining companies can change the equity interest of the voting common stock in contemplation of a combination within two years before the plan of combination is initiated or between the dates that the combination is initiated and consummated, as well as the rule on planned transactions regarding significant dispositions.

The exercise of a lock-up option involving an exchange of equity interests (stock for stock) should not preclude pooling accounting. Exercise of such a lock-up option involving cash, however, will preclude pooling accounting. As an alternative to a lock-up option involving cash, a "rescisionary escrow arrangement" may be used. Under such an arrangement, the lock-up option is exercised and the exchange of stock or assets and cash are placed in escrow. The terms of the escrow require that the exchange be accomplished after one year. In the event that a merger between the parties occurs within the escrow period, the exchange is rescinded prior to such merger. Accordingly, at the date of the business combination, there would have been no exchange for cash, and no alteration of equity interests.

If a buyer is required to account for a business combination using the pooling of interests method, how is this method applied to combine the buyer's and target's financial statements?

In a pooling, the carrying amounts of the assets and liabilities of the constituent companies remain unchanged. The carrying amounts of assets and liabilities of the separate companies are added together to become the assets and liabilities of the combined corporation.

Certain accounting entries are required (or permitted) in a pooling:

- The components of combined stockholders' equity of the surviving corporation may not be the same as the sum of the components of the individual companies. This occurs because a different number of common shares may be issued in exchange for the shares of the combining company, or the par or stated value of the common shares may differ. If the par or stated value of the shares of stock outstanding of the surviving company after the pooling exceeds (or is less than) the total of the capital stock accounts of the constituent companies, the combined additional paid-in capital is reduced (or increased) by the amount of the difference. If the combined paid-in capital account is not sufficient for this purpose, combined retained earnings are reduced by any remaining excess.
- Intercompany accounts and transactions between the separate companies (and the related profits) prior to the combination are eliminated from the combined financial statements.
- If the separate companies have different accounting policies, a change in accounting to conform the methods is permitted. In that case, the accounting change is made by retroactive restatement of the combined financial statements.
- If a pooling is a taxable event and the carrying value of the "acquired" assets is stepped-up for tax purposes, any recognizable tax benefits are recorded as additional paid-in capital. Assuming Statement of Financial Accounting Standards No. 96, "Accounting for Income Taxes," has been implemented, the tax benefits attributable to the increase in tax basis that become recognizable after the combination date are reported as a reduction of income tax expense.

At what date should a buyer that applies the pooling of interests method report combined results?

A buyer that applies the pooling of interests method of accounting for a combination should report results of operations for the fiscal period in which the combination occurs as though the companies had been combined as of the beginning of the period.

Results of operations for that fiscal period thus comprise those of the separate companies combined from the beginning of the period to the date the combination is consummated and those of the combined operations from that date to the end of the period. Previously issued financial statements are restated as though the companies had always been combined.

APB No. 16 does not contain guidelines for recording the combined results of two companies with different fiscal year-ends. Recasting the financial statements of the acquired company to conform its year-end to that of the surviving company could be costly and time-consuming. In such cases, the fiscal year-end of the acquired company may be changed prospectively. The SEC permits the consolidation of two companies with different year-ends as long as the difference is no more than 93 days and that fact is disclosed.

What accounting is required for expenses related to a "pooling"?

All costs incurred to effect a pooling transaction should be recognized as expenses of the combined corporation in determining net income. Such expenses include SEC filing fees, investment banking fees, legal, accounting and consultant fees, and costs incurred in combining and integrating the operations of the previously separate companies, including implementation of efficiencies. One question that frequently arises with regard to pooling expenses is: In which period should the expenses be written off—the period in which the pooling is consummated, or the period in which the expenditure is incurred? In practice, either policy is acceptable, although the predominant practice seems to be to write off such expenditures as they are incurred. The basis for deferring the expenditures until consummation of the business combination is the possibility that the combination may be accounted for as a purchase, in which case the cost will be added to the purchase price. If the expenses associated with the pooling are paid by principal stockholders, such expenses should be accounted for as if the shareholders made a capital contribution to the company, and a like amount should be charged to expense.

Purchase Method

What are the advantages of the purchase method?

- Purchase accounting is often preferred if the focus subsequent to the transaction is on the balance sheet. Assets and liabilities are recognized at their fair values instead of at the acquired company's historical costs. Thus, the post-combination balance sheet *appears* healthier under purchase accounting than under pooling accounting. This may be of added importance if the post-combination balance sheet is a key factor in a lender's decision to finance the acquisition.
- No restatements of prior years' financial statements are required, so sales and earnings trends may show an improvement.

What are the disadvantages of the purchase method?

- Accounting income is exposed to the write-off of additional depreciation, goodwill amortization, and other charges that may adversely affect earnings trends.
- Uncertainties regarding purchase price determination and valuation exist.
- Prior years' financial statements are not restated and, therefore, are not comparable.

When must the purchase method be used to account for a business combination?

The purchase method of accounting is used for any business combination that does not meet all of the conditions for pooling of interests treatment.

How is the purchase price of the target determined under the purchase method?

The purchase method follows principles normally applicable under historical cost accounting to recording acquisitions of assets and issuances of stock. The general principles to apply the historical cost basis of accounting to an acquisition depends on the nature of the transaction:

- If the target is acquired by exchanging cash or other assets, purchase price is the amount of cash disbursed or fair value of other assets distributed.
- If the target is acquired by incurring liabilities, purchase price is the present value of the amounts to be paid.
- If the target is acquired by issuing shares of stock, the value assigned to the stock is the fair value of the consideration received. As a practical matter, in most business combinations it is easier to value the stock exchanged, and this is normally done for convenience.

Cash paid, liabilities incurred, and securities issued comprise the major portion of the purchase price of most acquisitions. Numerous other items, however, must be considered for inclusion in the purchase price. Some of these are:

- Direct expenses, such as finder's and directly related professional fees (legal, investment banking, accounting, appraisal, and environmental consulting).
- Premium or discount on a debt security issued or assumed, imputed to adjust the liability to present value based on current interest rates, if stated rates differ significantly from current market rates.
- A negotiated adjustment to the purchase price related to assumption of a contingent liability such as a lawsuit or tax examination.

Under the purchase method, how should the buyer's cost be allocated to the assets acquired and liabilities assumed?

Under APB No. 16, the buyer's cost is allocated to individual assets and liabilities at their fair market values at the time of acquisition. Independent appraisals may be used in determining the fair value of some assets and liabilities. Subsequent sales of assets may also provide evidence of values.

The following are general guidelines for assigning amounts to individual assets acquired and liabilities assumed:

- Present value determined at appropriate current interest rates:

  Receivables, net of estimated allowances for uncollectibility and collection costs, if necessary.

  Accounts and notes payable, long-term debt, and other claims payable.

  Other liabilities, such as warranty, vacation pay, deferred compensation, unfavorable leases, contracts and commitments, and plant closing expenses incident to the acquisition.

- Current replacement cost:

  Raw materials inventories.

  Plant and equipment, adjusted to remaining economic lives.

- Net realizable value:

  Marketable securities.

  Property and equipment to be sold or to be used temporarily.

- Appraised value:

  Identifiable intangibles.

  Other assets.

- Other:

  Finished goods and merchandise at estimated selling prices less the sum of (1) the cost of disposal and (2) a reasonable profit allowance for the selling effort of the acquiring corporation.

  Work-in-process inventory at estimated selling prices of finished goods less the sum of (1) the cost to complete, (2) the cost of disposal, and (3) a reasonable profit allowance for the completing and selling effort of the acquiring corporation based on profit for similar finished goods.

Previously recorded goodwill of the acquired company is not recognized in the purchase price allocation. If the acquired company sponsors a single-employer defined benefit pension plan, the assignment of the purchase price to the individual assets acquired and liabilities assumed shall include a liability for the

TABLE 7–1
Corporation B Balance Sheet, September 30, 1988

	Carrying Amount	Fair Value
	(in thousands)	
Assets		
Cash	$ 100	$ 100
Accounts receivable, net	300	300
Inventories	600	680
Short-term prepayments	120	100
Land	500	650
Other plant assets, net	1,000	1,250
Patent	80	100
Total assets	$2,700	$3,180
Liabilities and stockholder's equity		
Current liabilities	$ 700	700
Long-term debt	500	480
Capital stock, $5 par	600	
Paid-in capital in excess of par	400	
Retained earnings	500	
Net assets acquired		2,000
Total liabilities and stockholder's equity	$2,700	$3,180

projected benefit obligation in excess of plan assets, or an asset for plan assets in excess of the projected benefit obligation.

The following example illustrates the above principles. Assume that Corporation A acquires Corporation B in a business combination accounted for as a purchase on September 30, 1988. The purchase price is $750,000 cash and 50,000 shares of Corporation A common stock. Transaction costs are $200,000 (unrelated to stock issuance).

The historical carrying amounts and fair values of Corporation B's assets and liabilities on September 30, 1988 are as shown in Table 7–1. The following is the computation of the total purchase price of Corporation B, assuming the fair value of the common stock issued by Corporation A on September 30, 1988 was $20 per share (in thousands):

Purchase price:	
Cash	$ 750
Stock (50,000 shares)	1,000
Out-of-pocket costs	200
Liabilities assumed	1,180
	$3,130
Fair value of assets acquired	3,180
Excess of asset value over purchase price	$ (50)

The purchase price allocation to the acquired assets would have been as shown in Table 7–2. If the fair value of Corporation A common stock on September 30, 1988 was $30 per share, the purchase price would have been computed as follows (in thousands):

Purchase price:	
Cash	$ 750
Stock (50,000 shares)	1,500
Out-of-pocket costs	200
Liabilities assumed	1,180
	$3,630
Fair value of assets acquired	3,180
Excess of purchase price over asset value	$ 450

TABLE 7–2
Purchase Price Allocation Based On $20 Per Share

	Fair Value	Purchase Price Allocation
		(in thousands)
Cash	$ 100	$ 100
Accounts receivable	300	300
Inventories	680	680
Prepaids	100	100
Land	650	634*
Other plant	1,250	1,219*
Patent	100	97*
	$3,180	$3,130

*Discount ($50) was allocated prorata to noncurrent assets (see discussion regarding accounting for the excess of acquired net assets over cost).

TABLE 7–3
Purchase Price Allocation Based On $30 Per Share

	Fair Value	Purchase Price Allocation
	(in thousands)	
Cash	$ 100	$ 100
Accounts receivable	300	300
Inventories	680	680
Prepaids	100	100
Land	650	650
Other plant	1,250	1,250
Patent	100	100
Goodwill		450
	$3,180	$3,630

The purchase price allocation based on $30 per share value would have been as shown in Table 7–3.

What is the appropriate period for amortizing goodwill?

The subject of amortization of goodwill is covered in Accounting Principals Board Opinion No. 17, "Intangible Assets" (APB No. 17). APB No. 17 requires that the recorded costs of intangible assets, including goodwill, be amortized by systematic charges to income over the periods estimated to be benefited, but not to exceed forty years. Goodwill should not be written off in the period of acquisition. No other references are made to a minimum period of amortization in APB No. 17. Any period selected for amortization of goodwill ordinarily is arbitrary. Amortization periods of five to ten years are acceptable in many cases. Amortization periods of less than five years, however, are ordinarily acceptable only on the basis of specific facts related to profitability.

The amount of goodwill reported at the date of acquisition should be evaluated after the acquisition to determine if its value has diminished and, if so, whether it should be completely or partially written off or the amortization period accelerated. Factors to consider include:

- Revenue and profitability levels of the acquired enterprise compared to those levels contemplated at the date of acquisition.

- Projected revenue and profitability levels of the acquired enterprise.
- Management's intentions regarding the future of the acquired enterprise (i.e., whether management intends to discontinue or to sell the operations) .
- Liquidity of the acquired enterprise.
- Projected economic indicators for the industry in which the acquired enterprise operates (e.g., the indicators may point to a down-turn in the industry) .
- The present and expected levels of productivity and utilization of plant facilities.

How should the excess of the value of the acquired net assets over cost be accounted for?

If the sum of the market or appraised values of identifiable assets acquired less liabilities assumed exceeds the cost of the acquired company, the values otherwise assignable to noncurrent assets acquired (except long-term investments and marketable securities) should be reduced by a proportionate amount of the excess to determine the assigned values. If the values of noncurrent assets are reduced to zero, then a deferred credit is recorded on the buyer's balance sheet for the excess of the aggregate assigned value of identifiable assets over cost (sometimes called "negative goodwill") of an acquired company. Negative goodwill is considered a deferred credit rather than an intangible (such as "positive goodwill") and it should not be netted against positive goodwill when reporting those amounts in the financial statements. Negative goodwill is amortized systematically as an increase in reported income over the period estimated to be benefited, but not in excess of forty years. The list of factors discussed above for amortizing goodwill should be considered in determining the amortization period for negative goodwill.

How are the differences between the market or appraised values of specific assets and liabilities and the income tax bases of those assets accounted for?

Statement of Financial Accounting Standards No. 96, "Accounting for Income Taxes," requires, as a general rule, that a deferred tax liability or asset be recognized for the tax consequences of differences between the assigned fair values and the tax bases of assets and liabilities recognized in a business combination. A deferred tax liability or asset is not recognized for a difference between the assigned amount and the tax basis of goodwill, unallocated "negative" goodwill, and leveraged leases. Statement No. 96 contains complexities that could affect the accounting for business combinations. The facts and circumstances of each transaction need to be evaluated.

What is the "allocation period" within which a buyer has to complete the accounting under the purchase method?

The "allocation period" is the period during which the buyer identifies and values the assets acquired and the liabilities assumed. The allocation period ends when the acquiring enterprise is no longer waiting for information that it has arranged to obtain and that is known to be available or obtainable. The existence of a preacquisition contingency for which an asset, liability, or an impairment of an asset cannot be estimated does not, of itself, extend the allocation period. Although the time required varies with circumstances, the allocation period should usually not exceed one year from the consummation of a business combination.

In some business combinations accounted for under the purchase method, the process of allocating the purchase price to the assets acquired and liabilities assumed is not completed before the issuance of the acquiring company's annual or quarterly financial information. For example, if a business combination is consummated at or near the end of the acquiring company's fiscal year or quarter, the acquiring company may not be able to obtain all the data necessary to allocate the purchase price to the net assets acquired prior to issuance of its financial information. A tentative allocation of the purchase price should be made using both appraised values and preliminary estimates. The unallocated portion of the purchase price should be amortized over a period that approximates the amortization period of the assets and liabilities for which preliminary estimates are made. For example, if preliminary estimates are made for a manufacturing facility that has a depreciable life of thirty years, the unallocated portion of the purchase price should be amortized over a thirty-year period. When the necessary data become available, the estimates can be adjusted with a corresponding adjustment to the unallocated portion of the purchase price. The amortization period may also need to be adjusted. The acquiring company's financial statements should indicate that the allocation of purchase price is preliminary.

What are preacquisition contingencies and how should they be considered in the allocation of purchase price?

A contingency is an existing condition, situation, or set of circumstances involving uncertainty as to possible gain or loss to an enterprise that will ultimately be resolved when one or more future events occur or fail to occur. A preacquisition contingency is a contingency of the acquired enterprise that is in existence before consummation of a business combination; it can be a contingent asset, a contingent liability, or a contingent impairment of an asset. Examples of preacquisition contingencies include pending or threatened litigation, obligations relating to product warranties and product defects, actual or possible claims or assessments, such as income tax examinations, assessments by environmental agencies, guarantees of indebtedness of others, and impairment of the carrying amount of productive assets used in the business.

A preacquisition contingency is included in the allocation of purchase price based on an amount determined as follows:

- If the fair value of the preacquisition contingency can be determined during the allocation period, that preacquisition contingency is included in the allocation of purchase price based on that fair value.
- If the fair value cannot be determined during the allocation period, that preacquisition contingency shall be included in the allocation of the purchase price based on the following criteria:

  Information available prior to the end of the allocation period indicates that it is probable that an asset existed, a liability had been incurred, or an asset had been impaired at the consummation of the business combination. Implicit in this condition is that it must be probable that one or more future events will occur confirming the contingency.

The amount of the asset or liability can be reasonably estimated.

Contingencies that arise from the acquisition and that did not exist prior thereto are the buyer's contingencies rather than preacquisition contingencies of the acquired company.

At what date should a buyer who has applied the purchase method report combined results?

The acquisition date of a company ordinarily is the date assets are received and other assets are given or securities are issued. The reported income of the buyer includes operations of the target beginning with the date of acquisition. In a purchase business combination, there is no restatement of prior period financial statements. In certain situations, however, the acquisition date may be "as of" a date earlier than the closing date. These include, for example, situations in which it is the intent of the parties to fix a determinable price as of a specified date other than the closing date or a formula is developed whereby changes in earnings or market price between the specified date and the closing date are considered in the final purchase price. If a date earlier than the closing date is considered appropriate, the following conditions should be met in order for the earlier date to be used as the date on which the buyer includes the results of operations of the target:

- The parties reach a firm purchase agreement that includes specifying the date of acquisition other than the closing date. Effective control of the acquired company (including the risks and rewards of ownership) transfers to the acquiring company as of the specified date.
- The time period between the specified date and the closing date is relatively short.

What are typical forms of contingent consideration in an acquisition, and how should such consideration be included in determining the cost of an acquired company?

A business combination may provide for the issuance of stock or the transfer of cash or other consideration contingent on specified transactions or events in the future. Agreements often provide that a portion of the consideration be placed in escrow and distributed or returned when the specified event has occurred. In general, to the extent that the contingent consideration can be determined at the time of the acquisition, such amount shall be included in determining the cost of the acquired company.

As is often the case, however, the amount of the contingent consideration is not known at the time of the acquisition. As an example, additional consideration may be contingent on maintaining or achieving specified earnings levels in the future. When the contingency is resolved or resolution is probable and additional consideration is payable, the acquiring company shall record the current fair value of the consideration paid as an additional cost of the acquired company. This subsequent recognition of additional cost requires an adjustment to the initial amounts recorded at the date of acquisition. Generally, the amount of goodwill is adjusted for the amount of additional consideration paid.

What accounting is required for expenses related to a "purchase"?

Direct acquisition costs incurred by an acquiring company effecting a business combination accounted for under the purchase method are included as part of the purchase price of the target company. Direct acquisition costs incurred by an acquired company, or its major or controlling shareholders, should generally not be included as part of the cost of the acquired company. Acquisition costs incurred by the acquired company are presumed to be taken into account indirectly by the acquiring company in setting the purchase price. If, however, the acquiring company agrees to reimburse the acquired company's major or controlling shareholders for acquisition costs incurred by them, these costs should be included as part of the purchase price of the acquired company. Direct acquisition costs include fees paid to investment bankers, legal fees, accounting fees, appraisal fees, and other consulting fees.

Fees paid to an investment banker in connection with a business combination accounted for as a purchase when the investment banker is also providing interim financing or debt underwriting services must be allocated between direct costs of the acquisition and debt issue costs.

Other Considerations

What are the disclosure requirements for business combinations?

The disclosures required for a business combination accounted for by either the purchase or pooling of interests method are governed by APB No. 16, as amended, the rules and regulations of the SEC, and the disclosure requirements are as follows:

- APB No. 16

  The disclosure requirements depend on whether the purchase or pooling-of-interests method of accounting is applied to the transaction. For a purchase business combination, the following disclosures are required in the notes to the financial statements of both public and non-public enterprises.

  - Name and a brief description of the acquired enterprise.
  - Method of accounting for the combination–that is, by the purchase method.
  - Period for which results of operations of the acquired enterprise are included in the income statement of the acquiring enterprise.
  - Cost of the acquired enterprise and, if applicable, the number of shares of stock issued or issuable and the amount assigned to the issued and issuable shares.

- Description of the plan for amortization of acquired goodwill, the amortization method, and the amortization period.
- Contingent payments, options, or commitments specified in the acquisition agreement and their proposed accounting treatment.

In addition, notes to the financial statements of the acquiring enterprise for the period in which a purchase business combination occurs should include as supplemental information the following pro forma information (public companies only):

- Results of operations for the current period as though the enterprises had combined at the beginning of the period.
- Results of operations for the immediately preceding period as though the enterprises had combined at the beginning of that period, if comparative financial statements are presented.

The supplemental pro forma information should, at a minimum, disclose revenue, income before extraordinary items, net income, and earnings per share. To present pro forma information, income taxes, interest expense, preferred stock dividends, depreciation and amortization of assets, including goodwill, should be adjusted to their accounting bases recognized in recording the combination. Pro forma presentation of results of operations of periods prior to the combination transaction should be limited to the immediately preceding period.

For business combinations accounted for as pooling of interests, the following disclosures are required in the notes to the financial statements:

- Name and brief description of the enterprises combined, except an enterprise whose name is carried forward to the combined enterprise.
- Method of accounting for the combination—that is, by the pooling of interests method.
- Description and number of shares of stock issued in the business combination.

- Details of the results of operations of the previously separate enterprises for the period before the combination is consummated that are included in the current combined net income. The details should include revenue, extraordinary items, net income, other changes in stockholders' equity, and amount of and manner of accounting for intercompany transactions.
- Description of the nature of adjustments to the net assets of the combined enterprises to adopt the same accounting practices and of the effects of the changes on net income previously reported by the separate enterprises and now presented in comparative financial statements.
- Details of an increase or decrease in retained earnings attributable to a change of the fiscal year of a combining enterprise. The details should include revenue, expenses, extraordinary items, net income, and other changes in stockholders' equity for the period excluded from the reported results of operations.
- Reconciliation of revenue and earnings previously reported by the enterprise that issues the stock to effect the combination with the combined amounts currently presented in financial statements and summaries. The new enterprise formed to effect a combination may instead disclose the earnings of the separate enterprises that comprise combined earnings for prior periods.

In addition, the notes to the financial statements should disclose details of the effects of a pooling business combination consummated before the financial statements are issued, but that are either incomplete as of the date of the financial statements or initiated after that date. The details should include revenue, net income, earnings per share, and the effects of expected changes in accounting methods as if the combination had been consummated at the date of the financial statements.

What is a nonpublic enterprise?

A nonpublic enterprise is an enterprise other than one (a) whose debt or equity securities are traded in a public market, including those traded on a stock exchange or in the over-the-counter market (including securities quoted only locally or regionally), or (b) whose financial statements are filed with a regulatory agency in preparation for the sale of any class of securities.

What is pro forma financial information?

Pro forma financial information reflects the impact on historical financial statements of a particular business combination and its financing as if the transaction had been consummated at an earlier date. Pro forma information ordinarily includes (a) a description of the transaction, the entities involved, and the periods for which the pro forma information is presented, and (b) a columnar presentation of historical condensed balance sheet and income statements, pro forma adjustments, and pro forma results.

Pro forma adjustments to the income statement are computed assuming the transaction was consummated at the beginning of the fiscal year and include adjustments that give effect to events that are (a) directly attributable to the transaction, (b) expected to have a continuing impact on the registrant, and (c) factually supportable. Pro forma adjustments related to the balance sheet are computed assuming the transaction was consummated at the end of the most recent period for which a balance sheet is required and include adjustments that give effect to events that are directly attributable to the transaction and factually supportable whether they have a continuing impact or are nonrecurring.

Typical pro forma income statement adjustments include the elimination of nonrecurring acquisition-related costs (e.g., professional fees, separation bonuses, severance pay), reductions or increases in depreciation due to the step-down or step-up of fixed assets to fair market values, amortization of goodwill, increased interest expense on additional indebtedness, elimination of minority interest, and adjustments to the tax provision. Typical pro forma balance sheet adjustments include the recordation of the additional indebtedness incurred to consummate the transaction, and the revaluation of noncurrent assets to reflect market value, goodwill, and accrued liability adjustments.

CARRYOVER OF PREDECESSOR COST IN LEVERAGED BUYOUTS

What is the significance of the concept of the carryover of historical basis in leveraged buyout transactions?

By definition, a leveraged buyout entails significant new debt used in acquiring the target from the present owners. The LBO lender will be looking at the target's post-acquisition balance sheet to determine whether it reflects sufficient economic health to support the new debt. The lender is usually concerned about the sufficiency of the underlying collateral and with issues concerning fraudulent conveyance and solvency. One of the advantages of the purchase method of accounting, previously discussed in this chapter, is the ability of the purchaser to restate the balance sheet carrying amounts of the target's underlying net assets from a historical basis to fair value.

Recently-issued accounting rules may limit the extent to which full fair values can be recorded in the post-acquisition balance sheet for LBO transactions where a holding company (NEWCO) with no substantive operations is formed to acquire an operating company (OLDCO). The consequences of these rules may be that some portion or all of the historical accounting bases of OLDCO (or the bases of its owners) may have to be carried over to the balance sheet of NEWCO, resulting in reduced asset carrying values and reduced stockholders' equity.

These accounting rules are spelled out in an Emerging Issues Task Force consensus—Issue 86-16, "Carryover of Predecessor Cost in Leveraged Buyouts." The requirements of Emerging Issue 86-16, while complex, need to be understood and carefully considered in planning the structure of each LBO. While the underlying economics of an LBO are not affected by the accounting, the investors' and lenders' perception of an entity's economic health may be affected; a balance sheet with higher asset values and stockholders' equity is obviously viewed more favorably. The concern is that the accounting assumed to be appropriate by investors and lenders in evaluating an LBO may not be acceptable under Emerging Issue 86-16 and, conversely, that the required accounting may become a deal-breaker.

What are the principal provisions of Emerging Issue 86–16?

The EITF's consensus on Emerging Issue 86-16 is currently being reconsidered by the EITF and the SEC. As of early fall 1988, the consensus contains four key principles to be applied in determining the appropriate accounting in NEWCO's financial statements for OLDCO's assets acquired and liabilities assumed, as well as for NEWCO's stockholders' equity. The discussion below presents an overview of these principles; investors and lenders with a need to apply them to a particular transaction should study the consensus in its entirety.

The EITF's consensus provides the following key principles:

- A partial or complete change in accounting basis is appropriate only when there has been a change in control of voting interests; that is, a new controlling investor or group of investors must be established. The condition for a controlling financial interest is generally the ownership of a majority (over 50%) of the voting securities.

    In effecting an LBO transaction, two or more investors acting in concert may combine their interests for purposes of gaining control. The determination of whether two or more investors constitute a control group is a matter of judgment based on the facts and circumstances. If management participates in promoting the LBO and has a voting interest in NEWCO, there is a rebuttable presumption that they are members of the NEWCO control group (resulting in the carryover of their "predecessor basis" to the extent of its voting interest in OLDCO). The presumption applies even though another controlling investor is able to demonstrate voting control by itself (i.e., without consideration of the management voting interest).

Transactions in which either a minority or majority of OLDCO voting interests change hands and no new controlling investor or control group is established should be considered recapitalizations; a change in accounting bases to reflect fair values is not appropriate.

- To distinguish an LBO from other business combinations, the LBO should be effected in a single, highly leveraged transaction or a series of related and anticipated transactions resulting in the acquisition by NEWCO of all previously outstanding voting equity interests of OLDCO; that is, there can be no remaining voting minority interest.

- If a *controlling* shareholder of NEWCO owned a voting interest in OLDCO, the transaction must be accounted for as a step-acquisition to the extent of that controlling shareholder's voting interest in OLDCO. In a step-acquisition, NEWCO controlling shareholders' bases in their prior voting interest in OLDCO—predecessor cost—is carried over to the balance sheet of NEWCO.

- The total consideration paid to *non-controlling* shareholders of NEWCO to acquire their outstanding shares of OLDCO should generally be measured at fair value; however, the fair value of any securities issued by NEWCO should be objectively determinable. To ensure that the fair value of NEWCO securities issued to acquire OLDCO is objectively determinable, fair value should not be used, whether or not the NEWCO securities are publicly traded, unless at least 80 percent of the fair value of consideration paid to acquire OLDCO equity interests from noncontrolling investors of NEWCO are comprised of monetary consideration (cash, debt, and debt-type instruments, such as mandatorily redeemable preferred stock).

If the other provisions of the consensus are met but the 80 percent monetary consideration test is not met, any NEWCO equity securities issued to noncontrolling shareholders to acquire their OLDCO interest should be valued at OLDCO book value.

Exhibit 7–1 illustrates the application of certain provisions of the EITF's consensus.

EXHIBIT 7-1
Application of some EITF Provisions

- OLDCO management and the public owned 20 percent (twenty shares) and 80 percent (eighty shares) of OLDCO, respectively, prior to the LBO.
- NEWCO merges with OLDCO, with OLDCO as the surviving entity.

	OLDCO (book value)	NEWCO			Merger of NEWCO/OLDCO			Fair Value	
		DR	CR	Net Change	DR	CR	NEWCO	OLDCO	NEWCO
				(dollars in thousands)					
Current assets	$16,000	$510 (1) 11,000 (2)	11,510 (3)	$			$16,000	$16,000	$16,000
Investment in OLDCO		98 (1) 11,510 (3) 392 (4)	400 (5)	11,600		11,600 (7)			
Fixed assets	20,000				800 (7)		20,800 (8)	21,000	21,000
Goodwill					800 (7)		800 (9)	1,000	1,000
	$36,000			$11,600			$37,600		
Current liabilities	$15,000			$			$15,000	15,000	15,000
Long-term debt	11,000		11,000 (2)	11,000			22,000	11,000	22,000
Shareholders' equity (100 shares issued and outstanding)	10,000	400 (5)	608 (1) 392 (4)	600 (6)	10,000 (7)		600 (6)	12,000	1,000
	$36,000			$11,600			$37,600		

431

NEWCO adjustments:

(1) Management forms NEWCO and acquired 60.84 shares of NEWCO voting common stock as follows:
- 9.84 shares of NEWCO voting common stock in exchange for .82 shares of OLDCO voting common stock with a fair value of $98,400 ($120,000 per share).
- 51 shares of NEWCO voting common stock for $510,000 cash ($10,000 per share).

(2) NEWCO borrows $11 million from a bank.

(3) NEWCO purchases 95.92 shares of OLDCO voting common stock for $11.51 million ($120,000 per share).

(4) OLDCO public shareholders exchange their remaining 3.26 shares of OLDCO voting common stock with a fair value of $391,600 for 39.16 shares of NEWCO voting common stock.

(5) Reduces management's investment in NEWCO (at a fair value of $608,000) to its basis of $208,000 .

(6) NEWCO equity is valued as follows:

	(000s)
NEWCO voting common stock issued to management for cash (51 shares @$10,000 per share) at fair value	$510
NEWCO voting common stock issued to OLDCO public shareholders at fair value (39.16 shares @$10,000 per share)	$392
NEWCO voting common stock issued to management in exchange for its OLDCO voting common stock at predecessor basis (assumed to be equal to book value) of $2 million (20 OLDCO shares @$100,000 per share) less the 2.302 million (19.18 OLDCO shares @$120,000 per share) cash paid to management for its OLDCO voting common stock	(302)
	$600

Merger of NEWCO/OLDCO:

(7) Eliminate investment in OLDCO and allocate "purchase price."

(8) Fixed assets are value at 80 percent fair value and 20 percent predecessor basis.

80% fair value ($21 million × 80%)		$16,800,000
20% predecessor basis (assumed to be equal to book value) ($20 million × 20%)		4,000,000
		$20,800,000

432

(9) Goodwill, if complete revaluation
% fair value

	$1,000,000
	80%
	$800,000

Method of Acquisition of OLDCO common voting stock:

	OLDCO Shares	Fair Value (000s)	
From Noncontrol group/public shareholders:			
Cash	76.74	$9,208	96%
NEWCO shares	3.26	392	4
	80.00	9,600	100%
From NEWCO Control group/management:			
Cash	19.18	2,302	
NEWCO shares	.82	98	
	20.00	2,400	
	100.00	$12,000	

433

What are the most common situations in which carryover of predecessor basis or OLDCO book value is required?

Based on the provisions of the EITF's consensus, a complete revaluation of NEWCO's net assets at fair value is not appropriate if:

Situations	NEWCO Accounting
No new controlling investor or control group is established (i.e., no change in control of voting interests).	Recapitalization (purchase of treasury stock and the issuance of equity securities).
NEWCO does not purchase all voting equity interests of OLDCO.	OLDCO book value to the extent of the minority interest.
Management participates in promoting the LBO, had a voting interest in OLDCO, has a voting interest in NEWCO, and is a member of the NEWCO control group.	Predecessor basis to the extent of management's voting interest in OLDCO. Predecessor basis refers to a NEWCO controlling shareholder's basis in a prior interest in OLDCO; that is, the original cost of the investment in OLDCO plus earnings (less dividends and any payment received for OLDCO stock) since the date of its acquisition.
NEWCO controlling shareholder owned a voting interest in OLDCO.	Predecessor basis to the extent of management's voting interest in OLDCO.
Monetary consideration is less than 80 % of the total consideration paid to acquire OLDCO voting interests from NEWCO noncontrolling investors.	OLDCO book value to the extent of nonmonetary consideration (i.e., NEWCO equity securities) paid.

This is not intended to be a complete list of situations for which complete revaluation of NEWCO's net assets at fair value is not appropriate.

Securities

How should the fair value or carrying amount of preferred stock issued in business combinations be determined?

The distinctive attributes of preferred stock make some preferred issues similar to debt securities while others are more similar to common stock, with many variations between the extremes. Determining the appropriate carrying value to assign to preferred stock issued in a business combination will be affected by its characteristics.

Even though the principle of recording the fair value of consideration received for stock issued applies to all equity securities, preferred as well as common, the carrying value of preferred securities may be determined in practice on the same basis as debt securities. For example, the carrying value of a nonvoting, nonconvertible preferred stock that lacks characteristics of common stock may be determined by comparing the specified dividend and redemption terms to debt securities with similar terms and market risks.

When is preferred stock issued in a business combination treated as debt?

The SEC requires that preferred stock subject to mandatory redemption by the issuer or subject to redemption based upon an event outside the control of the issuer be excluded from stockholders' equity for purposes of financial statement presentation. The SEC contends that such preferred stock is significantly different from conventional equity capital. Such securities have characteristics similar to debt and should, in the opinion of the SEC, be distinguished from permanent capital. The SEC's rules and regulations are intended to highlight the future cash obligations of these securities through appropriate balance sheet presentation and footnote disclosure. The SEC did not attempt to deal with the conceptual question of whether such securities are debt. The SEC has left the resolution of this question to the FASB. Accordingly, a public company is required to present separately on the face of its balance sheet (a) preferred stock as a liability, if the preferred stock is subject to mandatory redemption requirements or subject to redemption upon an event outside the control of the issuer and (b) preferred stock as equity, if the preferred stock is not redeemable or is redeemable at the option of the issuer.

Nonpublic enterprises have an option for the financial statement presentation of preferred stock subject to mandatory redemption or redemption outside the control of the issuer. They can either follow the SEC presentation requirements or present such preferred stock as a component of total stockholders' equity.

Is convertible or subordinated debt issued in business combinations ever considered equity?

No. Convertible and subordinated debt are never considered equity under generally accepted accounting principles and the rules and regulations of the SEC.

What is the appropriate accounting for issuance costs associated with debt and equity securities?

For debt securities, issuance costs are recorded as intangible assets and amortized as a charge to income over the repayment term of the debt. For equity securities, including preferred stock subject to mandatory redemption or whose redemption is outside the control of the issuer, issuance costs are recorded as a reduction of their recorded value.

Push-Down Accounting

What is push-down accounting?

The previous discussion of the purchase method described the accounting for a business combination required in the Buyer's consolidated financial statements. Push-down accounting is a concept that applies to the separate, stand-alone financial statements of the target.

Push-down accounting refers to the establishment of a new accounting and reporting basis in a target's separate financial statements, resulting from the purchase and substantial change of ownership of its outstanding voting equity securities. The buyer's purchase price is "pushed down" to the target and used to restate the carrying value of its assets and liabilities. For example, if all of a target's voting equity securities are purchased, the assets and liabilities of the target are restated using fair market values so that the excess of the restated amounts of the assets over the restated amounts of the liabilities equals the buyer's purchase price.

In what circumstances should push-down accounting be applied?

The SEC requires the use of push-down accounting by public enterprises with respect to target corporations that are substantially or wholly owned. The SEC stated that when the form of ownership is within the control of the buyer, the basis of accounting for purchased assets and liabilities should be the same regardless of whether the entity continues to exist or is merged into the buyer. The SEC recognized, however, that the existence of outstanding public debt, preferred stock, or a significant minority interest in a subsidiary might impact the buyer's ability to control the form of ownership. As a result, the SEC, although encouraging its use, generally does not insist on the application of push-down accounting in these circumstances.

Push-down accounting is optional for the separate financial statements of a nonpublic target.

In what circumstances should an acquired subsidiary's financial statements reflect the acquirer's debt, interest expense, and allocable issuance costs?

The SEC requires that the buyer's debt, interest expense, and debt issuance costs incurred in connection with or otherwise related to the acquisition should be pushed down to the subsidiary's financial statements if (a) the subsidiary is to assume the buyer's debt, either presently or in a planned transaction in the future; (b) the proceeds of a debt or equity offering of the subsidiary will be used to retire all or part of the buyer's debt; or (c) the subsidiary guarantees or pledges its assets as collateral for the buyer's debt.

Allocation of Purchase Price to Assets to be Sold

An Emerging Issues Task Force consensus (Emerging Issue 87-11) addresses the allocation of purchase price to assets to be sold. What are the principal provisions of Emerging Issue 87-11?

In this emerging issue, the EITF addressed the appropriate accounting for a transaction in which an enterprise (Company A) acquires another enterprise (Company B) in a purchase business combination, financed principally by debt. Company A's intent is to keep the majority of Company B's operations and to sell within one year Subsidiary S, an operating unit. Company A will use the proceeds from the sale to reduce the debt incurred to finance the acquisition of Company B.

The EITF reached a consensus noting that Company A desires to operate and subsequently sell Subsidiary S so as to yield net cash flows from operations, debt service, and sales proceeds equal to the cash flows anticipated by Company A during negotiations for the acquisition of Company B. Consistent with that fact, the objective of the EITF's consensus is that the net cash flows from (1) operations of Subsidiary S from the date of acquisition until the date of sale (the holding period which cannot exceed one year), (2) interest on incremental debt incurred during the holding period to finance the purchase of Subsidiary S, and (3) proceeds from the sale should be considered in the allocation of the purchase price to the assets and liabilities of Subsidiary S. Thus, the earnings or losses of Subsidiary S, interest expense during the holding period on debt incurred to finance the purchase of Subsidiary S, and the difference between the carrying amount of that subsidiary and proceeds from the sale should not affect earnings or losses reported in Company A's consolidated financial statements.

The SEC staff has stated that it will require financial statements and pro forma information that cover the reporting periods in which this accounting is applied to include the following:

- A description of the operations held for sale, a description of the method used to assign amounts to those assets, the expected disposal date, and the method used to account for those assets.
- Disclosure of the operations' profit or loss during the period that has been excluded from the consolidated income statement together with a schedule reconciling that amount to the earnings received or losses funded by the parent that have been accounted for as an adjustment to the carrying amount of the assets (allocated interest cost should be separately identified).
- Disclosure of any gain or loss on the ultimate disposition that has been treated as an adjustment of the original purchase price allocation.

The SEC staff will also expect registrants to continually review the causes for differences between actual and estimated cash flows and the estimate of sales proceeds to determine whether a loss should be reported currently for events that have occurred during the holding period.

INVOLVEMENT OF ACCOUNTANTS IN MERGERS AND ACQUISITIONS

What are the typical assignments given to an outside accountant in the acquisition or lending process?

Outside accountant's assignments include:

- Consulting with investors or lenders early in the decision-making process to evaluate potential tax consequences, deal structures, cash flows, SEC and other regulatory reporting consequences, and economic aspects of a particular industry.
- Participating as a member of the due diligence review team. The accountant is often the principal financial expert on this team. Responsibilities include the evaluation of a target company's historical financial statements to test the key assumptions of the buyer; the identification

of undervalued, overvalued, or unrecorded assets and liabilities; the preparation and assessment of a target company's prospective operating results and cash flows; and the consultation on structuring the transaction.

- Reviewing filings with the SEC (i.e., Forms 8–K, 10–K, and 10–Q, and registration statements, including merger proxies) and monitoring compliance with the SEC's rules and regulations.

- Tax planning with the focus on the target company's potential tax problems, the maximization of tax benefits through the transaction's structure, and after completion of the deal.

- Developing computerized models to project operating results and cash flows under various assumptions. To effectively analyze options, a sensitivity analysis may need to be performed on potential structures analyzing the results of various levels of sales volume and expenditures as well as business mix. This sensitivity analysis may include tax step-up and recapture considerations impacting future tax liabilities, various interest rate and debt servicing assumptions, and assumptions on future disposal of various parts of the acquired business.

- Evaluating the target company's forecasts and projections (see discussion below).

- Valuing the target company's business for purposes of determining and allocating the purchase price for both income tax and accounting purposes.

- Evaluating the adequacy of target company management, computerized systems, and accounting systems and procedures.

- Performing traditional accounting and auditing services, including acquisition and post-acquisition audits.

When should an accountant perform an audit in connection with an acquisition or loan?

An audit of the target company's historical financial statements should generally be performed when:

- The final purchase price or credit approval is dependent upon the carrying value of the target company's net assets or the operating results of the target, as determined in accordance with (GAAP).

- The target company's historical financial statements are required to be included in filings with the SEC.
- The closing of the transaction is more than a few months from the most recent audited financial statements, and the due diligence review noted that significant adjustments may be necessary to the target's interim financial information.
- The target's historical comprehensive statements have been subjected to procedures less in scope than an audit, such as a review or a compilation, and due diligence suggests that net assets or earnings may be overstated.

Forecasts and Projections

Why are forecasts and projections important?

Although historical financial statements provide valuable information, potential buyers and lenders require with increasing frequency information about the future to supplement what they know about the past. Accordingly, the need to obtain and evaluate a target's prospective financial information (forecasts and projections) is becoming common as part of the acquisition and lending decisionmaking processes. Forecasts and projections are particularly relevant to investing in or financing a business acquisition because the ongoing business is likely to have a different operating and financing structure from that of its predecessor. Potential investors and lenders need to see the impact that servicing the acquisition debt will have on prospective cash flows. Changes in operating plans, modifications in the deal, and other variables can be continuously factored into revised forecasts and projections to determine whether the deal works.

What is the distinction between a forecast and a projection, and why is the distinction important?

The use to be made of the prospective financial information determines whether a forecast or a projection is more appropriate, so it is important to understand how they differ. A forecast presents the target's best estimate of expected financial results. It is based on assumptions reflecting conditions that management of the target expects to exist and the course of action it expects to take. A projection, on the other hand, is based on one or more hypothetical assumptions reflecting conditions that management does not necessarily expect to exist and courses of action it does not necessarily expect to take. It presents management's estimate of what would happen if the hypothetical assumptions were to materialize.

A forecast and a projection are presented for different reasons. A forecast presents the financial effect of what management expects to happen, while a projection presents management's answer to the question, "What would happen if . . . ?"

To illustrate, let us say a potential investor is considering buying a restaurant chain and wants to know what earnings and cash flow will look like over the next five years. Management of the business makes various assumptions concerning the key factors of the business and arrives at its best estimates of occupancy costs, equipment purchases, number of meals served each day, the average customer's bill, food and beverage costs, salaries, etc. A presentation of expected earnings and cash flow based on these "best estimate" assumptions is a forecast. Now let us say that the potential investor wants to evaluate the downside risk of not serving the "forecasted" number of meals. Management might assume, hypothetically, that only half of the expected meals will be served each day, and it revises all other assumptions accordingly. A presentation based on the hypothetical volume is a projection.

The distinction is important if the potential investor wants the credibility of the forecast or projection tested by an outside accountant. The outside accountant is restricted by professional standards from reporting on a projection unless the use of the projection is expected to be "limited." In a "limited use" situation, the prospective financial statements are distributed only to those persons who have the opportunity to negotiate directly with the target's management and to challenge and change the terms of a deal. In a "general use" situation, the statements can be distributed to persons who do not have the opportunity to negotiate directly with management. They are considered passive users and typically receive a "take it or leave it" offering.

Forecasts, because they depict what management thinks will happen, are useful in either situation and may therefore receive limited or general distribution. Projections, because they portray "what if" scenarios, are considered useful only to those users who have the opportunity to negotiate directly with management and question the presentation and assumptions. Projections that are accompanied by the report of an outside accountant, therefore, can receive only limited distribution unless, as discussed below, they accompany a forecast. Thus, for example, if a potential investor or lender is issuing an offering memorandum to attract other investors or lenders to participate in the deal ("general distribution"), the prospective financial information included in the memorandum will probably have to take the form of a forecast if it is desired that the report of an outside accountant covering such information be included.

Although projections alone are not appropriate for general use, they may be so used when they accompany forecasts. Such combination presentations may help potential investors and lenders understand the sensitivity to changes in certain key assumptions of the prospective financial information so presented. In the restaurant chain example above, the downside risk projection could be presented in a general use offering memorandum along with the best estimate forecast, and the outside accountant would not be precluded from reporting on both.

What services can an outside accountant perform in reporting on prospective financial statements?

There are three services that an outside accountant can perform when reporting on prospective financial statements for use by one or more third parties—an examination, a compilation, and the application of agreed-upon procedures.

An examination is the highest level of service that an outside accountant can provide for a forecast or a projection. It is similar in many ways to an audit of historical financial statements. When an outside accountant expresses a "clean" opinion as a result of an examination, he does not guarantee that the prospective results will be achieved. In fact, he is precluded from doing so by professional standards, even if he could provide such a guarantee. Those who use the information, however, can be assured that the outside accountant is satisfied that the key factors of the business have been addressed, that the underlying assumptions are suitably supported, and that they provide a reasonable basis for the presentation.

In a compilation, the outside accountant performs limited procedures in much the same way as he does in a compilation of historical financial statements. While a compilation report explicitly disclaims an opinion, potential investors and lenders receive implicit assurance that the information has at least passed a "smell test," and none of the assumptions are obviously inappropriate or substantially out of line.

Finally, the outside accountant may perform selected procedures that have been agreed upon by the parties involved. These agreed-upon procedures may be more or less than the procedures performed in a compilation. The outside accountant's report on an agreed-upon procedures engagement provides assurance only as to the results of the procedures performed, and its distribution is restricted to those parties.

Obviously, each of these services provides a different level of assurance. The decision as to what level of service is needed is based largely on what level of comfort the potential lenders and investors require.

When prospective information is included in a filing with the SEC, two additional limitations are imposed on the services an outside accountant can provide. First, the SEC will not accept compilation reports under any circumstances. Second, the SEC does not permit an accountant to examine prospective information included in a public filing if the accountant helped prepare the information.

Solvency Opinions

What are solvency opinions and who generally requests them?

Solvency opinions are designed to meet the needs of lenders and investment bankers, particularly in highly leveraged transactions. The purpose of the solvency opinion is to help the lender or banker document solvency and enable it to rebut potential fraudulent conveyance claims in case the borrower encounters financial difficulties.

Can outside accountants issue solvency opinions?

No. An outside accountant cannot provide any form of assurance, whether through an examination, review, or application of agreed-upon procedures, that an entity (i) is not insolvent at the time debt is incurred or will not be rendered insolvent thereby; (ii) does not have unreasonably small capital; or (iii) has the ability to pay its debts as they mature. Providing such assurance is precluded because these matters are legal concepts subject to legal definition and varying legal interpretations that are not clearly defined for financial reporting purposes.

What services may an outside accountant provide to assist in solvency determinations?

While outside accountants cannot give any direct assurance as to solvency, they can provide services that may be useful to a company seeking financing. Such services include examination and review of historical information, examination and review of pro forma financial information, and examination and compilation of prospective financial information. Restricted use reports (i.e., agreed-upon procedure reports pursuant to auditing attestation, or prospective financial information standards) may be provided in connection with a financing, but may not speak to matters of solvency.

Comfort Letters

What are comfort letters and who typically requests them?

Under federal securities laws, an underwriter is responsible for carrying out a "reasonable investigation" of financial and nonfinancial data included in registration statements filed with the SEC under the Securities Act of 1933 (the "1933 Act"). As part of this reasonable investigation, letters of assurance regarding financial data (i.e., "comfort letters") are typically requested by underwriters and issued by outside accountants in connection with an underwritten offering of securities under the 1933 Act. Comfort letters may also be requested by underwriters in conjunction with securities offerings not subject to the 1933 Act.

In issuing comfort letters, accountants generally apply selected procedures to financial data not otherwise reported on by the accountant, such as (a) unaudited financial statements, condensed interim financial statements, capsule information, and pro forma financial information; (b) changes in selected financial statement items (e.g., capital stock, long-term debt, net current assets or net assets, net sales, and the total or per-share amounts of net income) during a period subsequent to the date and period of the latest financial statements included in the registration statement; and (c) tables, statistics, and other financial information.

What "comfort" does such a letter provide underwriters?

The assurance outside accountants provide underwriters by way of comfort letters is subject to limitations. First, any procedures performed short of an audit, such as the agreed-upon procedures contemplated in a comfort letter, provide the outside accountant with a basis for expressing, at most, negative assurance (i.e., that nothing came to his attention that indicated that something was wrong). Second, the outside accountant can properly comment in his professional capacity only on matters to which his professional expertise is relevant (e.g., the outside accountant's ability to measure does not make it appropriate for him to give comfort on the square feet in a plant).

In addition, what constitutes a "reasonable investigation" sufficient for an underwriter's purposes has never been authoritatively established. As a result, the underwriter, not the outside accountant, is responsible for the sufficiency of the comfort letter procedures for the underwriter's purposes.

CHAPTER 8

DUE DILIGENCE INQUIRY

INTRODUCTION

The basic function of due diligence, using the term in its broadest sense, is to assess the benefits and the liabilities of a proposed acquisition by inquiring into all relevant aspects of the past, present, and predictable future of the business to be purchased. The term is also used, more narrowly, to describe the duty of care and review to be exercised by officers, directors, underwriters, and others in connection with public offerings of securities.

GETTING STARTED

When does the due diligence process begin?

The due diligence process begins from the moment a buyer senses a possible acquisition opportunity. The buyer then starts to examine the information about the target that is readily available at this early time. This information is usually derived from public documents, ranging from broadly disseminated press reports, recent filings with the Securities and Exchange Commission, to an offering memorandum having been prepared for the consideration of potential buyers.

The initial stage of due diligence review is really the search and screen process and the valuation process described in Chapters 3 and 4. This review seeks to answer the questions: Should we buy this company? And how much should we, and can we, pay for it? It focuses on the company's business operations.

What about appraisals?

A very important part of such a review is the obtaining of appraisals of particular assets which are independently marketable, such as machinery, real property, or inventories. Such appraisals can be key for lenders who intend to determine the amount of their loans on the basis of the value of the assets available as security. Appraisals can also be made of company operations and of assets such as basic patents or trademarks, the value of which may largely be a reflection of the value of the business as a whole. The conduct of appraisals is a specialized area which we do not attempt to cover here. Care should be taken in ordering appraisals to remember that they become material information about the company in themselves, so that the results can either be significant benefits for a buyer or can return to haunt the deal.

At the stage where a sufficient investigation has occurred to arrive at a price for the deal and to tentatively decide to proceed, the buyer should engage attorneys and accountants to conduct a more thorough study of the target. The subject matter of this chapter and, insofar as accountants are concerned, pages 394–402 of Chapter 7, is that study, which might be called the "dirty linen" phase of due diligence, when the buyer is trying to find the things that are potentially bad about the company.

What public records should be checked?

To take a complete look at a company's past and current standing, the due diligence process should search:

- Previous corporate names
- Trade names and other names under which the company may be doing business

Having established possible names for the company to be studied, the acquirer can consult standard company information sources.

The next concern to be satisfied in the due diligence search is basic: the buyer must confirm that the corporation was legally formed (and continues to exist) in the first place. To do so, the buyer will establish the jurisdiction of the company's incorporation and document the company's organization by finding articles of incorporation, including any amendments such as name changes. Articles of Incorporation are public documents which may be obtained (in the form of certified copies) from the Secretary of State of the jurisdiction of incorporation. There should also be obtained, from the same office, evidence of the corporation's continuing status in good standing in the eyes of the state of incorporation. It is also necessary to carefully review the relevant state statutes and corporate minute books to establish that the articles and amendments have been properly adopted and that no action has been taken to dissolve the corporation. An examination of the minute book should also ascertain that the election or appointment of the corporation's directors and officers is duly reflected therein.

Having established that the corporation was indeed duly formed, the buyer's due diligence then examines the company's qualifications to do business in jurisdictions other than its state of incorporation—in other words, in whatever other states or countries it may conduct business. To be thorough in wrapping up this initial due diligence stage, the buyer must seek out good standing certificates and tax certificates from each of the states and foreign jurisdictions in which it operates.

Once corporate formation, qualification, and good standing are established, a search should be made for liens, encumbrances, and judgments that may exist against the company or any of its assets. Sources to be searched in uncovering liens, encumbrances, and judgments include:

- The offices of the Secretary of State of the state where the principal office is located and of other relevant states and, sometimes, County Clerk offices where filings are made to disclose creditors' interests in assets under the Uniform Commercial Code
- All relevant Recorder of Deeds offices
- All relevant courts, including federal, state, and local
- Any special filing jurisdictions for
     patents and trademarks
     copyrights
     bankruptcy
     maritime/aviation assets

Beyond checking basics such as corporate formation and liens, how extensive should the due diligence process be?

How far a buyer wishes to go in the due diligence process depends in part on how much time the buyer has, and how high a cost the buyer is willing to incur. The chief element in both time and cost is staffing. A buyer should also bear in mind that in any acquisition that will require a public offering, the underwriters and their counsel will do an exhaustive due diligence study. In the context of publicly financed acquisitions, any problems and liabilities discovered after the fact could have very adverse consequences and are much better identified early in the process. Therefore, complete due diligence should be done for any target which is to be publicly financed before the acquisition agreement is signed, if at all possible.

What staffing does the due diligence effort typically require?

The acquirer typically draws from sources of expertise available to him both in-house and from retained consultants and advisers. At a minimum, the due diligence team will include financial/accounting and legal personnel. It may also bring in economic consultants, engineers, environmental experts, and a host of other talents.

The thoroughness of due diligence also depends to some extent on what information the seller is willing to give in the form of the representations and warranties to be included in the purchase agreement. At one end of the spectrum, a buyer can choose to rely entirely on the seller's representations and warranties. On the other end of the spectrum, a buyer may wish, or be forced, to perform extensive due diligence, with no post-closing liability being assumed by the seller.

If the buyer decides to rely on representations and warranties, it must nevertheless still conduct at least enough due diligence to be assured that there will be a solvent seller to back the representations and warranties being relied on after the closing!

Moreover, the buyer will find that there are natural limits to the representations and warranties sellers are typically willing to make. Sellers will generally let the buyer rely on specifically scheduled disclosure items in the acquisition agreement and financial statements, but are usually reluctant to let the buyer rely on the entire world of information the seller has provided in trying to sell the company. The seller naturally will not wish to encourage a heavy due diligence effort, although it will frequently, in the course of negotiating reductions in the representations and warranties, insist that the buyer can go out to the plant and kick the tires to his heart's content.

Due diligence is also greatly affected by whether or not the target is a publicly reporting company. If it has outstanding 10Ks and 10Qs on file with the Securities and Exchange Commission, the diligence process can be greatly expedited by examining these, and the agreements, contracts, and other significant company documents which are filed with them as exhibits.

BUYER-SELLER RELATIONSHIP

How can the buyer conduct proper due diligence without harming its relationship with the seller?

The ground rules for due diligence are negotiated by the buyer and seller in the letter of intent or, if there is no letter of intent, in the acquisition agreement. The letter of intent will state the time available for due diligence. The buyer will want a covenant from the seller promising the buyer adequate opportunity to conduct due diligence, and access to its personnel, sites and files. (Refer to the Sample Letter of Intent in Chapter 10.)

The seller, on the other hand, will be concerned about confidentiality, and will often require the prospective buyer to enter into a separate confidentiality agreement. (A sample Confidentiality Agreement is found in Appendix 8B at the end of this chapter.) Therefore, in negotiating the letter of intent, the buyer and seller will discuss at length the way in which material will be handled, the degree of confidentiality that will be given to it, and what will happen to those documents if the deal falls through (often a "burn or return" provision is agreed upon in such an event).

Basic to structuring the due diligence inquiry and obtaining seller cooperation is the due diligence checklist, an outline of which is provided at the end of this chapter. Ideally, this checklist should parallel the structure of the representations and warranties that the buyer will ask the seller to make.

The due diligence checklist provided in Appendix 8A is extremely comprehensive in some areas, and less so in others. Most transactions will show such an "imbalance." In drafting a workable checklist, acquirers should concentrate on areas of particular relevance to the transaction at hand. For example, inquiries regarding the frequency and extent of customer complaints and returned goods would be more relevant to a consumer goods retail business than to a consulting business, while questions regarding environmental violations are obviously more critical in an acquisition in a smokestack industry than in the case of a bank.

Depending on the size of the acquisition, the checklist may or may not reflect a threshold of materiality. For example, a checklist may include only those capital expenditures above $50,000, or set a limit of five years back for certain documents. Acquirers agree to limits of this kind carefully, bearing in mind that any ground given at this point is likely to limit the scope of the seller's representations and warranties in the acquisition agreement.

Remember, the seller's attitude will not be improved by any request of the purchaser for information that requires the seller to create documentation. Thus, to the extent feasible, the checklist should require the seller to produce only documents already in existence. The purchaser should attempt to obtain other data through interviews with the seller's officers or other peaceful means.

TARGET LITIGATION ANALYSIS

Target litigation analysis requires a special procedure, usually conducted by trained litigation analysts. Management or its counsel can ask an attorney who specializes in commercial/corporate litigation to determine the validity of and exposure on existing claims.

How does one begin to analyze existing or potential litigation against a target?

The individual primarily responsible for the litigation risk review must first determine the parameters of the review and identify the litigation or administrative actions that warrant particular scrutiny. The primary reviewer must obtain a schedule of all litigation, pending and threatened, and must arrange to receive copies of all relevant pleadings.

Before reviewing specific cases, the primary reviewer should ascertain what cases the seller *believes* are covered by liability insurance, and then determine what cases, if any, are in fact covered. Because the two do not always coincide, it is critical to review all insurance policies.

The individual responsible for the litigation analysis must have a working knowledge of both the structure of the transaction—e.g., whether it is a stock or asset purchase—and of the corporate and tort law rules concerning successor liability for debts and torts—especially with regard to compensatory and punitive damages. He must then apply these rules to all cases being reviewed.

What general rules govern the buyer's potential liability for the target's debts and torts?

The traditional rule is that where one company sells or otherwise transfers all its assets to another company, the successor is not liable for the debts and tort liabilities of the predecessor. The successor may be liable, however, under the following circumstances: if it has expressly or implicitly agreed to assume liability; if there is a merger or consolidation; if the successor is a "mere continuation" of the predecessor; or if the transaction was fraudulently designed to escape liability.

A further exception exists for labor contracts. If the successor buys the predecessor's assets and keeps its employees, the successor will probably also be bound to recognize and bargain with unions recognized by the predecessor, and to maintain existing employment terms. Existing contracts may also create successorship problems. State law may vary with respect to assumption of debts and liabilities, so the reviewer must be cognizant of the specific statutory or case law that will govern the transaction.

Courts are increasingly likely to find successor liability, particularly with respect to product liability claims, under the "continuity of product line" or "continuity of enterprise" exceptions to the general rule of non-liability. The first of these exceptions applies where the successor acquires a manufacturer in the same product line. The second exception applies where the successor continues the predecessor's business. Faced with the prospect of injured plaintiffs without a remedy, courts are increasingly looking to successors for product-liability damage awards, including in some instances punitive damages. Accordingly, the reviewer must be aware of the current state of the law concerning successor liability for both compensatory and punitive damages.

What about insurance policies and cases being handled by insurance companies?

Every insurance policy must be reviewed to ensure that pending claims for compensatory damages will be covered. What is the deductible? What are the liability limits per occurrence and in total? Are punitive damages excluded by the policy or by state law? For large companies, there may be overlapping policies; all policies must be reviewed to ensure a thorough analysis of what claims will be covered by insurance.

Another consideration when reviewing insurance policies is whether the policies are for "claims incurred" or for "claims made." Coverage under a claims-incurred policy continues after the cancellation or termination of the policy and includes claims that arose during the period of insurance coverage, whether or not those claims are reported to the insurance company during that period. Claims-made policies cover only those claims actually made to the insurance company during the term of the policy.

In addition, under some policies, coverage will continue only if a "tail" is purchased. A "tail" is a special policy purchased to continue coverage that would otherwise be terminated. It is important that the reviewer identify the nature of the seller's policies and determine any potential problems that may result from a failure to give the insurance company notice of claims during the policy period or from a failure to purchase a tail.

Also, cases being handled by insurance companies should be scrutinized. The reviewer should determine if the insurer has undertaken the representation under a "reservation of rights" (i.e., where the insurer agrees to pay for or provide legal representation, without prejudice to its right to later deny coverage), if the insurer has preliminarily denied coverage, or if the damages claimed include punitive or treble damages, which may not be covered.

How does counsel determine whether particular litigation is "material" to the acquiring company in the due diligence context?

Before gathering information through a due-diligence request, counsel must determine what litigation is "material." The materiality determination for litigation, as for other aspects of due diligence, will be relative. A $5 million lawsuit, even if it has merit, may have little significance in the context of a $1 billion deal. On the other hand, even a case with little financial exposure may jeopardize a $20 million deal if the buyer and seller cannot agree on how to handle that case.

When evaluating litigation pending against a mid-sized company, a materiality cut-off point of $250,000 might be reasonable. In addition, certain types of cases might merit close attention, whatever the financial exposure. For example, a product liability case that looks like it might be the first of many should receive close attention, even if the financial exposure on that one case is insignificant.

What material information should the litigator review?

In the due diligence request, counsel should seek a summary of all pending or threatened actions that satisfy the materiality standard that has been established. The summaries should include:

- names and addresses of all parties;
- the nature of the proceedings;
- the date of commencement;
- status;
- relief sought;
- estimated actual cost;
- insurance coverage, if any; and
- any legal opinions rendered concerning those actions.

A summary should also be provided for:

- all civil suits by private individuals or entities;
- suits or investigations by governmental bodies;
- criminal actions involving the target or any of its significant employees;
- tax claims (federal, state and local);
- administrative actions; and
- all investigations.

In addition, counsel should request copies of all material correspondence during the past five years with government agencies such as the Department of Justice, Federal Trade Commission, Equal Employment Opportunity Commission, Environmental Protection Agency, Internal Revenue Service, Occupational Safety and Health Administration, Department of Labor, and any other regulatory agency (either city, state, or federal) to which the seller is subject. If the target itself has subsidiaries, all relevant information should be requested for the subsidiaries as well.

After all this information has been gathered, how is the litigation analysis conducted?

Before the actual analysis begins, the individual in charge of the review must determine who will analyze which claims. Highly specialized claims should be assigned for review to those attorneys in the firm with the most knowledge of the area involved.

The individual reviewer must arrange to receive pleadings and documents concerning any additional relevant claims and to have access to the attorneys representing the target in those matters. Even in an acquisition characterized by cooperation, obtaining all the relevant pleadings may be difficult. This is particularly true if the target is represented by more than one law firm.

The individuals responsible for this aspect of the litigation analysis must establish a particularly good working relationship with the attorneys representing the target company. In some instances, communications with outside counsel should be handled gingerly because that firm may see some portion of its legal work disappearing as a result of the acquisition. More often, with larger target companies, litigation is being handled by several firms around the country; all those firms will have to be consulted.

In some cases, it will be sufficient to review the case file and consult briefly with outside counsel. In other cases, outside counsel will have to become more involved in the analytic process. It will be difficult for the reviewer to approach an unfamiliar case and get its true flavor. The reviewer should be particularly cautious with respect to accepting the representations made by the outside counsel currently handling the case; those representatives may be overly optimistic.

Finally, each pending material case should be systematically evaluated. For litigation being handled on the target's behalf by outside law firms, two major factors should be evaluated, but first, the reviewer should evaluate whether the case is being professionally and capably handled. Even a meritless case can create significant exposure if handled by an inexperienced or incompetent firm or practitioner.

What cases should the litigator consider first?

The reviewer should concentrate on those cases that, if decided against the target, could have an increasingly adverse impact on the target's business operations in general—the "ripple effect." The investigation should also identify and study other known cases involving other companies in the same industry, as these too can trouble the target company's waters. For example, suppose a court decides that a business practice of one company in the industry constitutes a deceptive trade practice or other violation of law. If the target is in the same industry and engages or might engage in the same practice, this can have a significant impact on the future business of the target, even if it is not a party to the litigation in question.

Are there any "hot" topics that recur in litigation analysis?

Two examples of areas of special concern highlight the importance of litigation analysis in due diligence. One potential "hot" area is severance plans. Recent court cases have held that severance plans are "employee welfare benefit plans" and that such plans are subject to the disclosure, reporting, and fiduciary requirements imposed by the Employee Retirement Income Security Act of 1974 (ERISA). For example, in *Adcock v. Firestone Tire & Rubber Co.*, a Tennessee district court held that employees had a contractual right under federal common law to severance benefits established by their employer. This holding is important in the context of mergers and acquisitions because, in at least one case, a court has held that an employer that sells a division or part of its operations as an ongoing business may remain liable under the seller's severance plans to former employees who continue employment in the division after the sale.

A second hot topic is compliance with applicable environmental laws. For example, some states have enacted environmental protection statutes that create a "superlien" on property of those persons liable for pollution. The existence of such far-reaching remedies requires that state and federal environmental laws be considered during due diligence and that the reviewers be familiar with the state of environmental law.

ENVIRONMENTAL EXPOSURE ANALYSIS

Environmental problems are sometimes referred to as the "skeleton in the closet" in a proposed acquisition. Why?

Because environmental problems have the potential to be deal killers. It is sometimes said that there are two kinds of environmental problems to be feared in a proposed acquisition: those that adversely affect the balance sheet, and those that adversely affect the financial projections. Either kind can destroy the economic benefits the buyer hopes to achieve.

What is the difference between a "balance sheet" environmental problem and a "projection" environmental problem?

Balance sheet problems are those that result from liabilities, either disclosed or undisclosed, that the buyer becomes subject to as a result of acquiring the business. Such liabilities typically include the cost of cleaning up a mess caused by the seller or one of the seller's predecessors. It can involve removing contaminated soil or purifying tainted groundwater, and it can cover not only the site purchased by the buyer, but also adjoining properties or remote locations on which hazardous substances generated by the business were dumped. Moreover, under the federal Superfund law, officers, directors and even stockholders can be personally liable for cleanup costs, and the liability of companies which contributed to the pollution of a common dump site are jointly and severally liable for such cleanup costs. Finally, even secured lenders can be liable for such cleanup costs. As a result, the buyer must approach these problems not just from his own point of view; he must also consider how the lender will react. In addition to cleanup costs, a company can be liable to third parties who have become ill or died as a result of drinking contaminated groundwater, or whose property has been contaminated by pollution emanating from the company's facilities.

Projection problems are those which adversely impact on the company's ability to achieve its projected cash flow and earnings goals. They typically arise in situations in which the acquired company has a history of noncompliance with applicable air or water emissions standards. Where the due diligence process discloses such a history of operating problems, the prospective purchaser needs to calculate the cost of bringing the company into compliance and keeping it in compliance. This may involve significant unbudgeted capital costs (to procure needed emissions control equipment) or operating costs higher than anticipated (to ensure that the offending equipment is operated in conformity with applicable environmental standards) or both. In extreme cases, the buyer's diligence may disclose that the company (or a particular plant) cannot be economically operated in compliance with environmental law.

What kinds of acquisitions are most likely to present significant environmental problems?

The classic asset-based LBO, involving a smokestack industry, is the one most likely to present environmental concerns. However, environmental problems are by no means limited to the manufacturing sector. Warehouses, retail businesses, and service companies may own structures which contain asbestos in wall insulation or pipe wrapping; PCB electrical transformers are found in many types of facilities; and underground motor fuel tanks can exist in any business which operates a fleet of trucks or cars. All of these situations are common environmental troublemakers.

What are the principal environmental trouble spots to look for in an acquired company?

Any diligent buyer should work from a comprehensive environmental check list in performing due diligence on a target company, or retain an environmental consultant to do so for him. But the businessman should be sensitive to certain key areas of potential concern:

- Were any toxic or hazardous substances used or generated by the target business? Those most commonly encountered include:

PCBs (used in electrical transformers).

commercial solvents (such as those found in paint thinner and degreasing agents), which are potent carcinogens and which migrate readily into groundwater if spilled.

heavy metals (such as lead, arsenic, cadmium) which are used in various industrial processes and paints.

- Were any hazardous wastes shipped off-site for disposal?
- Are there lagoons or settling ponds which may contain toxic wastes?
- Are there underground tanks which may have leaked and discharged their contents (heating oil, gasoline) into the groundwater?
- Is asbestos present in any structure (as insulation in walls, pipewrapping, or other application)?

Why should the buyer worry about hazardous wastes shipped off the premises?

Because, if they were shipped to a dump which has been declared a federal Superfund site or which may be declared a Superfund site in the future, the buyer will inherit a potential major liability. This liability may flow through to the purchaser even if he purchases assets, rather than stock. Moreover, the purchaser may be liable even though he expressly does not assume the liability, if in fact he intends to continue the same business as his predecessor.

What special problems are posed by Superfund liability?

First, Superfund can pierce the corporate veil. Officers, directors, and even shareholders can be personally liable. Second, cleanup costs can be enormous—well beyond the value of the assets purchased. Third, liabilities of companies which generated wastes dumped in a common site are joint as well as several; every contributor of hazardous waste to that site is theoretically liable for the whole cleanup. And fourth, it can take years before liability is finally determined.

What can the buyer do to protect himself?

A number of things:

• Hire an environmental consulting firm to do an audit of the target company. LBO lenders are tending increasingly to require delivery of such an audit report, showing an essentially clean bill of health, as a condition to lending.
• Make sure that the seller's warranties are broad enough to cover environmental liabilities (i) arising as a result of on-site or off-site pollution, and (ii) all actions causing pollution, whether or not at the time such actions were taken, they were in violation of any law or standard. The latter point is critical because Superfund liability can reach back to actions taken before the adoption of modern environmental protection laws, when the shipment of such wastes by unlicensed carriers to unlicensed sites was not illegal.
• Make sure environmental warranties and any escrows or off-set rights survive as long as possible. It may take years before the pollution is discovered and traced back to the Company.

Are environmental clearances typically required?

Yes. Federal, state, and local permits and consent decrees relating to water quality, air emissions, and hazardous wastes should be checked carefully to make sure they remain effective after closing. In addition, in at least one state—New Jersey—state approval of a cleanup plan or cleanup must be granted or formally waived in connection with the transfer of virtually any kind of industrial or commercial facility in order for the seller to be able effectively to pass title to the buyer.

DO-IT-YOURSELF DUE DILIGENCE

Suppose the seller refuses to produce the requested documentation, but offers access to its files?

If the buyer is faced with a do-it-yourself due diligence process, the buyer must organize an on-site document review effort.

This will typically entail traveling to the entity's corporate headquarters and, depending on the number of sites involved and the nature of the business conducted at each site, other sites as well.

The seller in these circumstances should be willing, at a minimum, to direct the buyer to those employees with knowledge of each subject of inquiry detailed on the checklist or to the relevant files. In this event, the buyer should ask the seller to make a representation that he has been given access to all requested information. The buyer should also ask the seller to provide sufficient personnel and photocopying facilities to make copies of all significant documentation produced by the review effort. If the seller refuses to cooperate, the buyer may have to rent photocopying machines and hire temporary help.

As a courtesy to the seller and to avoid confusion between or among documents, which can vary in format from company to company, the buyer can make two copies, one of which will be retained by the seller.

Throughout the process, the buyer should be sensitive to the stress on his own personnel and on his relationship with the seller. The due diligence effort is a disruption of the ordinary business routine, and may be viewed by the seller as a sign of unwarranted suspicion by the buyer and disregard for the seller's interests. The seller may fear adverse consequences for the conduct or even sale of its business. Indeed, many potential transactions do fall through, usually thanks to the due diligence process, which either alienates the seller, the buyer, or both. Add to these considerations the fact that thorough due diligence increases transaction costs and absorbs the attention of key personnel, and one can see why due diligence can threaten even the healthiest transaction.

ASSESSING INFORMATION

What guidelines should a buyer follow when assessing a seller's assets?

The buyer's examination of the seller's assets occurs both on-site (tire-kicking) and off-site (record-hunting). On-site inquiries may involve discussions with officers and employees and inspections of real property, machinery, equipment, and inventory. With respect to interviews, the investigator seeks to fill in the gaps in the documentation and to ascertain whether there may be areas of potential concern or liability (or definable assets) not identified in the due diligence checklist. Good interview notes will include:

- Time and place of the interview,
- Name and title of the person interviewed,
- Scope of the interview, and
- Significant disclosures made during the interview.

Depending on the size and structure of the transaction and the importance of the specific assets, the buyer may wish to use a real estate appraiser to value any owned real property involved, an engineer to inspect plant and equipment, and an accounting team to review inventory. The accountants should also review the seller's financial statements with respect to these items.

Off-site investigations may include the search of public records and discussions with parties with whom the acquisition target has significant relationships. Among the records that should be reviewed are:

- Records of the Secretary of State (or other responsible official) in each state in which the entity is incorporated or doing business for evidence of incorporation, qualification, and good standing. This is not as critical in an asset sale as it is in a stock sale or merger.
- Relevant records (typically the county recorder of deeds) for (A) recorded copies of title documents for owned real estate and recorded leases for leased real estate together with (B) all mortgages, deeds of trust, or other liens or encumbrances, including tax liens, on any such property.
- Relevant records (typically the Secretary of State or some other central state government office, but sometimes also at the county level) for UCC filings, security agreements, or other liens or encumbrances upon personalty.
- Federal trademark and patent office for evidence of trademarks and patents listed as corporate assets.

• Relevant federal, state, and local courts for evidence of pending lawsuits, orders or judgments to which the business may be subject.

Special care must be taken when discussing the seller's business with third parties. Such discussions may, if correctly conducted, be the source of valuable information. They may also give rise to tensions between buyer and seller if the seller believes that the discussions may be impairing its ability to carry on its business. Discussions with the buyer's lenders may be particularly sensitive in this regard.

Another delicate area is that of standing agreements: if the buyer begins negotiating with parties to existing agreements, requiring that they be assigned to the buyer to remain in effect, this will obviously hurt the seller's business. The seller may even accuse the buyer of violating the buyer's own covenant (typically found in an acquisition agreement) penalizing the seller for any adverse change in the business between the execution of the acquisition agreement (not Letter of Intent), and closing.

How does a buyer perform due diligence when the target is a corporate subsidiary or division?

It is much more difficult to find information about a company discreetly if it is a subsidiary or division as FASB now requires companies to consolidate the financials of all their majority-owned subsidiaries.

DURATION OF DUE DILIGENCE

How long should the due diligence process take?

The due diligence process occurs throughout the acquisition process, which lasts from a few weeks to a year or more. Surprisingly, the due diligence process does not control the pace of the acquisition negotiation in most cases. If the parties are eager to deal, they may substitute extensive warranties for due diligence, or the buyer may have done extensive investigation before making the first offer. Management buyers, who believe they know their own company, may willingly dispense with due diligence, sometimes to their regret.

Several advantages attach to the rapid and efficient conduct of due diligence. The greatest benefit of speedy due diligence is minimal disruption to ongoing business activities and minimal cost (to both parties). Another benefit can be smoother relations between the parties. Revisiting well-fought-over contractual provisions to accommodate a problem turned up by due diligence can inject a major irritant into the negotiation process. Finally, the most valuable result of fast-track due diligence is timely information to the buyer, who can quickly determine whether the acquisition is of interest and, if so, on what terms and conditions.

The buyer can then focus his efforts on determining the appropriate structure for the transaction; the basis for calculation of the purchase price; what representations, warranties and covenants should be negotiated into the contract; and what conditions to closing need to be imposed.

When does the due diligence process properly end?

As important as it is for due diligence to be completed rapidly, the due diligence effort really extends up to, through, and beyond closing. The due diligence, with its panoramic "snapshot" of the condition of the business, may end well in advance of the date of closing. If so, this can give rise to problems. Every deal has its categorical imperative to update or "bring down" the snapshot to the closing date so that the representations and warranties contained in the executed agreement are accurate as of the closing date. This often requires buyer and seller to negotiate an amendment to the agreement at the closing.

The "bring down" factor is one of the reasons that some buyers and sellers prefer not to execute an acquisition agreement providing for a subsequent closing, but instead agree on the terms and conditions of an acquisition and execute this agreement simultaneously with closing the deal.

Does diligence continue to be significant after closing?

Yes. The post-closing significance of the due diligence effort is two-fold.

First, individuals who had hands-on involvement in the due diligence process will have a particularly good insight into the operational areas they studied, and they may be called upon during the initial post-acquisition "re-start-up" period under new ownership to answer questions or provide guidance.

Second, in the event of a claim by the buyer or the seller against the other, the claim's resolution may go back to a due diligence issue, i.e., whether one party disclosed or made available to the other the documents or facts in question. Insofar as the acquisition agreement does not identify all the information the defendant is supposed to know, the due diligence process may be examined to determine where liability lies. For this reason, it is absolutely essential to maintain complete written reports on due diligence results.

APPENDIX 8A
DUE DILIGENCE CHECKLIST[1]

DOCUMENTS

Corporate Documents

Certificate of Incorporation Including All Amendments, Name Changes, Mergers

The CI is particularly helpful in determining what name to search for title to real estate. Special care should be taken not to overlook name variations, e.g., "Rocket Airlines Inc.," "Rocket Air Lines, Inc.," and "Rocket Airlines Corp." These are quite likely to be very separate legal entities. The date and state of

---

[1]Some of the categories in this checklist are from Dan L. Goldwasser, "The Underwritten Offering: Areas of Inquiry" in Securities Regulation (New York: Matthew Bender, 1986), pp. 363–65. All annotations by Lane and Edson, P.C.

incorporation are also critical. There may be different companies with identical names incorporated in different states. (See also Certificates of Good Standing.)

By-laws

Look for change of control provisions. Many by-laws contain "poison pill" provisions designed to place restrictions on changes in control, or to make such changes very expensive to the potential acquiror.

Minutes

Look in particular for information re past acquisitions or mergers and other transactions affecting capital; this will help trace ownership of assets and equity. Make certain the election and appointment of current directors and officers is duly reflected, and that the issuance of all outstanding stock has been properly authorized.

Financial Statements

Develop breakdowns, by location, of assets (land, buildings, equipment, inventory, vehicles, and, if not billed out of a central office, receivables).

Consider whether those provided are adequate for use in possible SEC filings and whether pro forma financials are needed. Examine footnotes as a source of information for more detailed inquiries into existing debt, leases, pensions, related party arrangements, and contingent liabilities.

Engineering Reports

Try to find "as built" drawings, especially if surveys are not available.

Review for environmental problems or other concerns that might require major capital expenditures.

MARKET STUDIES/REPORTS ON COMPANY'S PRODUCT

Key Intangibles

Patents, Trademarks, Tradenames, and Copyrights

These items generally involve "registered" or "filed" rights which can be searched for at the U.S. Patent and Trademark Office and, for copyrights, at the Library of Congress, Washington, D.C. However, such rights may not have been filed, and corporations frequently have other key intangibles that are not filed anywhere, such as trade secrets, especially in companies that deal in high tech, software, etc. Due diligence would call for inquiry as to these other items. Review all related trade secrets, know-how and license agreements.

Licenses

Whether granted by the government, or a private third party, these may be absolutely essential to the ability of a corporation to legally conduct its business. The buyer should ensure that all such necessary licenses are current and in good order and that these licenses will be readily transferable, or remain valid, in the context of the acquisition transaction. It is generally useful to obtain the advice of special counsel or experts in the particular field (e.g., FCC counsel in the case of broadcasting licenses, etc.).

Contracts

Supply and Sales Agreements

Review as to assignability, term and expenditures required. Are they sufficient for the company's business requirements?

Employment and Consulting Agreements

These relate both to current key employees (where the issue is often whether their existing terms are good enough to keep the employees the buyer wishes to retain), and to past employees, where significant past liabilities can be involved.

Leases

Get legal descriptions.

Particular concern as to term and expiration dates renewal rights—rent—special provisions re assignment which may include change of corporate ownership.

License and Franchise Agreements

Look for correspondence re: extension, expansion, disputes, estoppels. Franchise relationships are likely to be stormy. Is there a franchise organization? Note assignment clauses and clauses creating a landlord's lien. Are any prior consents required?

Are these sufficient for the business's requirements?

Loan Agreements

Review terms, intention, and assignability provisions as to any need to refinance or to obtain consents to an acquisition from lenders. Schedules/Exhibits should be reviewed to glean useful information regarding Company's assets and structure.

Shareholder Agreements

Review provisions re their effect on proposed transaction and, if the agreement will survive, its effect on future transactions, i.e., registration rights, antidilution or dissenters' rights.

Agreements with Labor and Management

Obtain and study all agreements for unusual provisions that would unduly constrain management's options. Review benefits, severance, plant closing provisions.

For Labor Agreements

- Is the agreement binding on the buyer? (See Chapter 9.)
- Does the agreement have provisions that restrict the buyer?
- Is the company in compliance with the agreement? Does the agreement expire soon? Will the buyer want it to be reopened? (Notice may be required.) Is a strike likely?
- Are there any grievances that raise general issues of contract interpretation?

For Employment and Consulting Agreements

- Are there golden parachutes?
- Is there excessive compensation? (Compare to current compensation studies by executive search firms such as Heidrick & Struggles, Korn/Ferry, etc., and executive compensation firms such as Hoy Associates.)
- Will the agreements terminate at sale or are they binding on the buyer?

Pension and Profit Sharing Plans: Areas of Concern
- Plan and Trust Document
- Form 5500
  SPD (Summary Plan Description)
  Actuarial Valuation
- Auditor's Report
- Investment Manager Agreements
- Fiduciary Insurance and Bonds
- Investment Contracts
- Investment Policy
- Operational Questions
- Accrued, unfunded liabilities

Welfare Benefit Plans
Be aware that potential liabilities in this area can be very substantial and that valuation of plans requires expert guidance. (See Chapter 9.)

Fiduciary Insurance and Bonds

Insurance Contracts

Multiemployer Plans
These can be a major problem. (See Chapter 9.)

Fringe Benefits

Personnel Handbook or Policy Manual

Executive Compensation (See also Employment and Consulting Agreements)

Deferred Compensation Plan

Stock Option Plans

Supplemental or Excess Pension Plan
- Is the plan exempt from ERISA?
- Will future law affect costs/benefits?

- Are large claims anticipated?
- Are reserves on company books adequate?
- Can the plan be terminated or amended?
- Are any benefits in pay status?
- Are the benefits in effect funded with insurance?

Insurance Policies

Review all policies.

- Do policies cover the areas of risk exposure? (Consider a risk analysis consultant to review this very technical area.)
- What is the deductible?
- What are the liability limits per occurrence? In total?
- Are punitive or treble damages excluded by the policy or by state law?
- Are policies written for "claims incurred" or "claims made?"
- Must a "tail" be purchased to extend coverage?
- Is there a "reservation of rights" clause?

Security Agreements or Other Agreements Giving Other Parties the Right to Acquire Assets of the Company

Review financing statements or other evidence of perfected security interests. Lien searches conducted by professional services engaged in this business are usually the most efficient way of uncovering UCC financing statements of record, but it is also sometimes necessary to check for third party interests recorded against particular assets of the seller, rather than against the name of the seller itself. For example, security interests in assets such as vessels, or aircraft are recorded in special registries (outside of the scope of the usual UCC lien search) against the particular vessel or aircraft itself, rather than against the owning company.

Sales and Product Warranty Agreements

Review for provisions that vary from the description or understanding of such documents that is provided or held by management.

Review for provisions that may be illegal and/or unenforceable.
Review for indemnity obligations of the company.

Selected Correspondence

Useful means of uncovering past problems that may recur.

Acquisition Agreements

Review prior acquisition agreements re surviving provisions, i.e., noncompete clauses, indemnification obligations.

Title Documents to Real Estate and Personal Property

Review title policies and documents creating any encumbrance upon title and deeds/bills of sale by which company acquired assets. If assets were acquired by stock purchase or merger, find evidence of filing of appropriate corporate documents in jurisdiction(s) where assets are located as well as in state(s) of incorporation.

Real Property and Assets Identification

Ask seller to give the complete address (including county) of every facility or piece of real estate owned or leased by the (company), and describe each such facility using the following list of categories (indicate more than one category if appropriate):

- Corporate Offices
- Production, Manufacturing, or Processing Facilities
- Warehouses, Depots, or Storage Facilities
- Distribution Facilities
- Sales Offices
- Repair/Warranty Work Facilities
- Apartments or Other Residential Real Property
- Undeveloped Real Property
- Any Other Facilities

If owned, seller should indicate as "(O)," and provide full legal name in which title is recorded. If leased, seller should indicate as "(L)," and provide full name of lessor.

Seller should indicate whether there is any inventory at any such facility by "(I)."

Seller should indicate whether any goods/products/materials at any such facility are there on consignment from a supplier, as "Supp C."

Ask seller to provide the complete address (including county) of every site not described above where any of the company's assets are located, including every facility of any customer/processor at which the company has raw materials/goods/products /inventory on consignment, and the name of the party in possession of such assets, including any such customer/processor.

Compare actual documents to title insurance. Look for encumbrances, easements, rights of third parties, personal property encumbrances appearing on UCC records which should be checked.

Mortgages

- If significant, request closing binder.
- Notes or other evidence of indebtedness
- IDB or IRB Financing: Request the closing binder. Must review Indenture, etc.

KEY INFORMATION FROM THE COMPANY'S MANAGEMENT

Analysis of Company's Past Operating Performance and Projected Changes in Operations

Relative Profitability of the Company's Various Classes of Products and Business Segments

Ownership of Company's Securities
Trace title of present owners of corporation (if privately held). Review for existing pledges/liens that must be released to permit transaction.

Potential Defaults under Existing Contracts or Potential Litigation
Identify as many as possible and obtain waivers, consents, etc.
  Ask for summary of all pending or threatened legal actions that are material:

  - names and addresses of all parties
  - the nature of the proceedings

- the date of commencement
- current status
- relief sought
- estimated actual cost
- insurance coverage, if any, and
- any legal opinions rendered concerning those actions.

Summaries should also be provided for:

- all civil suits by private individuals or entities
- suits or investigations by governmental bodies
- criminal actions involving the target or any of its significant employees
- tax claims (federal, state, and local)
- administrative actions,
- all investigations, and
- threatened litigation.

Ask for copies of all material correspondence during the past five years with government agencies, e.g.,

- Department of Justice
- Federal Trade Commission
- Securities and Exchange Commission
- Equal Employment Opportunity Commission
- Environmental Protection Agency
- Internal Revenue Service
- Occupational Safety and Health Administration
- Department of Labor
- Public Utility Commissions
- Federal Energy Regulatory Commission

Pending Changes in Laws or Regulations that Might Affect the Company's Business

Review so that risk can be evaluated (also for potential existing noncompliance).

Product Backlogs, Purchasing, Inventory, and Pricing Policies

Pending Negotiations for the Purchase or Disposition of Assets or Liens

The buyer may want to drop real property which it is planning to dispose of into another entity (e.g., affiliated partnership) to avoid gain recognition or provide for means of early investment return to acquiring persons.

KEY INFORMATION
FROM OUTSIDE SOURCES

Market Studies

Product Test Data

Confirmation of Customer Satisfaction from Major Customers

Outstanding Capitalization from the Company's Stock Transfer Agent

Absence of Defaults from the Principal Lenders and Lessors (Landlords)

Absence of Liens or Judgments via Searches of Public Records; Organizing the Lien Search

Whom does one search?

Names of debtors to be searched can be difficult to determine.

- Prior Names—four-month rule regarding after-acquired collateral—cannot rely on creditor
- Fictitious Names or D/B/A
- Continuation Statements

Where Does One Search?

Locations—State and Local Search

- Coordinate between search firm and title company (sometimes not done)
- Consult *Uniform Commercial Code and Related Procedures*, published by Registre, Inc., to determine if state(s) at issue have additional or unusual search requirements
- Lender's/Borrower's Approval

Ordering Search

Letter to Search Firm/Title Company listing names, location, cost and deadline, and request copies of all liens found. Send copy to client, lender's/borrower's counsel.

Reviewing Search

What is your client buying, selling, liening, loaning against?
Is certain equipment, goods, intangibles, supposed to be free and clear? Vital to the business? To the closing? If so, watch for liens upon those items.

- If certain secured debt is remaining in place, one would expect related UCC-1s to show up on the search report.
- If secured debt is to be paid off at closing, the seller must produce UCC-3 or other required forms of releases from the relevant parties.
- What does the appraisal say? What does commitment/finance package say?

Check Report: Names, Jurisdictions. Review UCC-1s sent.

- Debtor
- Secured Party
- Date (five-year rule)
- Description of Collateral

Compare against schedules to be incorporated into loan documents, contracts, bills of sale.

Often, local counsel will need copies of lien searches in order to deliver a priority opinion.

Bringdown of Search

- Telegram or telephone update of lien searches and of corporate good standing.
- Often difficult to get closer than a few days before closing, but every effort should be made to close on the basis of the most recent bringdowns possible.

Assumption of Debt

If secured debt is not to be paid off, get security documents to see if, for example, incurring of acquisition debt, imposition of related liens, merger, change of control or sale of assets is permitted. Are there burdensome covenants? Is prepayment permitted, with or without penalty? See Chapter 4, pages 111–113.

Recognizing the Unusual or the Potential Problem
- Affiliate of Seller named as Secured Party.
- Names of Debtor not exactly right, but "must be" related.
- Bottom line: Detail and curiosity

Patent and Trademark Searches for Possible Infringing Products or Names

Certificates of Good Standing

Title Search/Acquisition of Title Insurance
Appraisal of company owned real property.

APPENDIX 8B
SAMPLE CONFIDENTIALITY
AGREEMENT

STRICTLY PRIVATE AND CONFIDENTIAL

————————— ——, 19——

Acquisition, Inc.

———————————————

———————————————

———————————————

Gentlemen:

In connection with your consideration of a possible transaction with Seller, Inc. (the "Company") or its stockholders, you have requested information concerning the Company so that you may make an evaluation of the Company to undertake negotiations for the purchase of the Company. As a condition to your being furnished such information, you agree to treat any information (including all data, reports, interpretations, forecasts and records) concerning the Company which is furnished to you by or on behalf of the Company and analyses, compilations, studies or other documents, whether prepared by you or others, which contain or reflect such information (herein collectively referred to as the "Evaluation Material") in accordance with the provisions of this letter. The term "Evaluation Material" does not include information which (i) was or becomes generally available to the public other than as a result of a disclosure by you or your directors, officers, employees, agents, or advisors, or (ii) was or becomes available to you on a non-confidential basis from a source other than the Company or their advisors provided that such source is not bound by a confidentiality agreement with the Company,

Buyer Corp.
————————— ——, 19——
page 45

or (iii) was within your possession prior to its being furnished to you by or on behalf of the Company, provided that the source of such information was not bound by a confidentiality agreement with the Company in respect thereof, or (iv) was independently acquired by you as a result of work carried out by an employee of yours to whom no disclosure of such information has been made directly or indirectly.

You hereby agree that the Evaluation Material will not be used by you in any way detrimental to the Company. You also agree that the Evaluation Material will be used solely for the purpose set forth above, and that such information will be kept confidential by you and your advisors for five (5) years provided, however, that (i) any such information may be disclosed to your directors, officers and employees, and representatives of your advisors who need to know such information for the purpose of evaluating any such possible transactions between the Company and you (it being understood that such directors, officers, employees and representatives shall be informed by you of the confidential nature of such information and shall be directed by you to treat such information confidentially and shall assume the same obligations as you under this agreement), and (ii) any disclosure of such information may be made to which the Company consents in writing. You shall be responsible for any breach of this agreement by your agents or employees.

In addition, without the prior written consent of the Company, you will not, and will direct such directors, officers, employees, and representatives not to disclose to any person either the fact that discussions or negotiations are taking place concerning one or more possible transactions between either the Company or its stockholders, on the one hand, and you, on the other hand, or any of the terms, conditions, or other facts with respect to any such possible transactions, including the status thereof. The term "person" as used in this letter shall be broadly interpreted to include without limitation any corporation, company, group, partnership, or individual.

In addition, you hereby acknowledge that you are aware, and that you will advise your directors, officers, employees, agents, and advisors who are informed as to the matters which are the subject

Buyer Corp.
―――――― ――, 19――
page 46

of this letter, that the United States securities laws prohibit any person who has material, non-public information concerning the matters which are the subject of this letter from purchasing or selling securities of a company which may be a party to a transaction of a type contemplated by this letter or from communicating such information to any other person under circumstances in which it is reasonably foreseeable that such person is likely to purchase or sell such securities. You consent that you will not, and you will cause each of the aforementioned persons to not, violate any provisions of the aforementioned laws or the analogous laws of any State.

You hereby acknowledge that the Evaluation Material is being furnished to you in consideration of your agreement (i) that neither you nor any of your affiliates nor related persons under your control will for a period of three (3) years from the date of this letter make any public announcement with respect to or submit any proposal for a transaction between you (or any of your affiliates) and the Company or any of its security holders unless the Company shall have consented in writing in advance to the submission of such proposal, nor will you, directly or indirectly, by purchase or otherwise, through your affiliates or otherwise, alone or with others, acquire, offer to acquire, or agree to acquire, any voting securities or direct or indirect rights or options to acquire any voting securities of the Company, for a period of three (3) years from the date of this letter without such permission, and (ii) that you will indemnify any director, officer, employee, or agent of the Company and any "controlling person" thereof as such term is defined in the Securities Act of 1933, for any liability, damage, or expense arising under federal and state securities laws from an actual or alleged breach of this agreement by you or your directors, officers, employees, representatives, or affiliates. You also agree that the Company shall be entitled to equitable relief, including an injunction, in the event of any breach of the provisions of this paragraph.

In the event that you do not proceed with the transaction which is the subject of this letter within a reasonable time, you shall promptly redeliver to the Company all written material containing or reflecting any information contained in the Evaluation Material (whether prepared by the Company or otherwise) and will

Buyer Corp.
—————— ——, 19——
page 47

not retain any copies, extracts, or other reproductions in whole or in part of such written material. All documents, memoranda, notes, and other writings whatsoever, prepared by you or your advisors based on the information contained in the Evaluation Material shall be destroyed, and such destruction shall be certified in writing to the companies by an authorized officer supervising such destruction.

Although we have endeavored to include in the Evaluation Material information known to us which we believe to be relevant for the purpose of your investigation, you understand that we do not make any representation or warranty as to the accuracy or completeness of the Evaluation Material. You agree that you shall assume full responsibility for all conclusions you derive from the Evaluation Material and that neither the Company nor its representatives shall have any liability to you or any of your representatives resulting from the use of the Evaluation Material supplied by us or our representatives.

In the event you are required by legal process to disclose any of the Evaluation Material, you shall provide us with prompt notice of such requirement so that we may seek a protective order or other appropriate remedy or waive compliance with the provisons of this agreement. In the event that a protective order or other remedy is obtained, you shall use all reasonable efforts to assure that all Evaluation Material disclosed will be covered by such order or other remedy. Whether such protective order or other remedy is obtained or we waive compliance with the provisions of this agreement, you will disclose only that portion of the Evaluation Material which you are legally required to disclose.

This agreement shall be governed by and construed and enforced in accordance with the laws of the State of New York, U.S.A.

Any assignment of this agreement by you without our prior written consent shall be void.

It is further understood and agreed that no failure or delay by the Company in exercising any right, power or privilege hereunder shall operate as a waiver thereof nor shall any single or partial exercise thereof preclude any other or further exercise of any right, power, or privilege.

Buyer Corp.
————— ——, 19——
page 48

If you are in agreement with the foregoing, please so indicate by signing and returning one copy of the letter, whereupon this letter will constitute our agreement with respect to the subject matter hereof.

Very truly yours,

SELLER, INC.

By: —————————

Its: ———————

Confirmed and Agreed to:
BUYER CORP.

By: —————————————
Date: ——————————————

CHAPTER 9

PENSION, LABOR AND COMPENSATION CONCERNS

INTRODUCTION

It is tempting to see in the employee benefit area of the acquisition process only a tangle of complex rules and requirements which should be referred to the experts and otherwise disregarded. Don't do it. Employee benefit plans include almost every kind of commitment that a company can make to its employees, from deferred compensation, medical benefits, vacations, severance pay and stock options, to perks such as cars, rides for the family on the corporate jet, and club memberships. They are so important to company operations, so big a budget item, and offer so many opportunities and pitfalls for both buyer and seller, that they must be properly understood and included in acquisition planning and structuring.

To make this thicket as penetrable as possible, we indicate the general employee benefit objectives of buyers and sellers in acquisition transactions, then outline the principal kinds of plans, and their financial relevance and address the ways in which they impact these objectives. We give particular attention to the employee stock option plan because of its importance as a financing device. We then cover some of the principal issues that arise in acquiring a unionized company.

What are the concerns of a buyer with respect to employee benefit plans?

1. What am I buying? What benefit does each plan provide? What does it cost? What will it cost in future years?

What ongoing liabilities does it involve? Can it be terminated or changed? Does it have assets, and do they exceed or fail to cover its liabilities—that is, is it overfunded or underfunded? Will contemplated company changes, or law changes, alter its costs?

2. Does the price I am paying for the target properly reflect the costs and benefits of these plans?

3. Can employee benefit plans help in financing the acquisition?

4. What benefit structure do I intend to have in the post-acquisition company, and what constraints and opportunities do I have in adapting to this goal the benefit structure I am acquiring?

5. How will the purchased benefit plans affect the rest of my family of companies?

6. Am I organized to take over seller's administrative obligations under the plans?

What are the concerns of a seller?

1. To what extent will I be responsible for plan or personnel charges made by the buyer?

2. Am I protecting the target employees against adverse impacts from the acquisition, or do I care?

3. Do I have continuing liabilities or administrative burdens under any of the plans?

4. Does the price I am receiving properly reflect the costs and benefits of the plans?

How do the concerns of buyer and seller interrelate?

To a certain extent, buyer and seller share complementary concerns that boil down, like many of the issues between them discussed in Chapter 10, to an appropriate allocation of costs or risk between them. The expense of maintaining an elaborate benefit structure, and the increased productivity it may generate, affect the cash flow and thus the value of the company, and logically should be weighed as part of the price calculation (see Chapter 3). For that reason, a seller may decide to include information as to the costs of plans in the financial information initially provided the buyer, so that thereafter when the buyer protests the high costs, the seller can say that these were already factored into the price. Often, however, as discussed below, ongoing plan liabilities are not reflected in financial statements or are based on unstated assumptions which are not examined until a later stage.

An important question in negotiating the allocation of plan responsibilities is whether the price is based on a continuation of seller's past employment practices or assumes that the buyer will carry out significant layoffs or reductions in benefits. The buyer may argue that the target's work force or benefit structure is a problem for which the seller must take responsibility as a condition of sale, and thus that severance obligations should be borne by the seller or the price should be lowered because the buyer is willing to assume these obligations or the political heat and unpleasantness associated with layoffs. The seller's response to this argument is that it will be blamed for layoffs regardless of who does them, and that the buyer will be enjoying the enhanced profits of subsequent operations with reduced labor costs, and thus should bear the cost of layoffs.

Unless the target is obviously over-staffed, the seller, both out of loyalty to its former employees and to minimize its possible future obligations to them as a result of the buyer's actions after the acquisition, will often require that the benefit structure be preserved or not made less favorable for some period of time after the closing, and that the buyer must assume severance obligations. Under such circumstances, the buyer must fully calculate the costs of these requirements and the degree of adaptability of the acquired plans to its present benefit structure.

EMPLOYEE BENEFIT PLANS

What are the main kinds of employee plans?

Most plans fall into one or more of the following categories: defined benefit plans (DBPs), defined contribution plans (DCPs), welfare plans, and executive compensation plans.

What is the difference between a defined benefit plan and a defined contribution plan?

A defined benefit plan is a pension plan which fixes benefits by formula and requires the employer to make contributions to the plan actuarially determined to be adequate to cover the plan's benefit obligations when they fall due. There is some flexibility in the actual contributions based on actuarial methods and assumptions, but the core commitment is a long-term obligation. The commitment cannot be avoided by plan termination unless the plan sponsor and every member of its controlled group is in dire financial distress. Liabilities in excess of assets in a DBP are reflected on the corporate books.

A defined contribution plan, in contrast, requires, at most, a commitment to pay a contribution to a plan for each year in which the plan is in existence. Contributions and earnings on plan assets are allocated to employee accounts. The benefit for each employee is the balance of his or her account at retirement. DCPs can take the form of profit sharing plans or money purchase plans. Profit sharing plans may be with or without salary deferral (the well-known 401(k) plan) and usually have variable contribution levels, so that each year the plan sponsor can determine the level of contributions. Money purchase plans have fixed contribution levels. There are no liabilities to be booked in the financials other than a note as to past and current expense, since a DCP will by definition have assets equal to liabilities.

What are the differences in regulatory controls between DBPs and DCPs?

Both types of plans are subject to elaborate IRS and Employee Retirement Income Security Act (ERISA) rules, which Congress and Treasury seem to change and tighten every year. Department of Labor (DOL) rules impose fiduciary constraints on both pension and other types of benefit plans. Plans are usually "tax-qualified" and thereby receive important tax benefits upon meeting IRS's applicable requirements. ERISA requires extensive reporting and disclosure, both to the government and to plan participants.

DBPs are regulated more extensively than DCPs in a number of respects. ERISA imposes elaborate requirements, including actuarial analysis, to assure that contributions are sufficient to fund benefits and to impose liabilities on the company upon plan termination. DBP benefits are insured by the Pension Benefit Guaranty Corporation (PBGC), established under ERISA, and premiums of up to $50/participant must be paid to PBGC annually. A DBP may fund a maximum benefit of $94,023 (1988 limit), indexed for inflation. DCPs have no PBGC insurance or funding rules, and require no actuarial calculations. DCPs may add up to $30,000 each year, or if less, 25% of compensation (measuring compensation up to $200,000 only) to an individual's account; $7,000 (indexed) of this limit can be deferred through a 401(K) plan.

What is the effect of tax qualification of plans?

The Internal Revenue Code offers important tax incentives to the creation of DBPs and DCPs; plans meeting the Code requirements are "tax qualified." Contributions to fund future benefits in qualified plans are tax deductible (within limits), and plan assets can be accumulated in a separate trust without tax on earnings. The trust is not available to creditors of the sponsor corporation (except plan participants claiming benefits from the plan).

Nonqualified plan costs are also deductible, but generally only when paid to the employee. Nonqualified plans can be funded with "rabbi trusts" but these trusts do not accumulate earnings tax-free and the trust assets are available to satisfy creditor claims. Nonqualified plans can also be funded with insurance.

The IRS qualification rules are designed to require plan coverage to extend throughout the workforce, to impose maximum levels of participation and vesting, and to limit the benefits for highly compensated employees. Despite these elaborate rules, the tax benefits of qualified plans have been viewed as so valuable that plans were adopted despite the IRS burdensome rules until recent years. Now, as tax rates have dropped and plan requirements have grown tighter, there is a movement towards nonqualified plans, which are more flexible.

What are welfare plans? Is "insurance" a misnomer?

In the so-called "welfare plan" area, most employers will provide a medical plan, sick leave, and long-term disability. Dental, prescription drug, vision, accidental death or disability (business travel accident), and life insurance plans are also common. Except for sick leave, benefits in these plans are usually provided through some type of insurance policy. In larger companies, however, the "insurance" component is often little more than a cash management service. These plans are really self-insured, often with a stop-loss insurance package, which protects the company from losses in excess of a maximum amount. Welfare plans can also be funded, in a limited way, through a tax-exempt trust (called "VEBA"). Some employers also provide dependent-care plans, tuition plans, relocation, retraining, and severance plans. All of these plans are subject to ERISA and the Code, but to a lesser degree than are pension plans. Buyer and seller will need to allocate claim liability and policy reserves and work out procedures that ensure a smooth transition with continuous coverage to employees.

What is a "multiemployer plan"?

In a unionized workforce, the employer and other unionized employers often contribute to a multiemployer pension or welfare plan jointly maintained by the union and an employers' association. If pension plans, the plans are usually DBPs. An acquisition can trigger substantial additional liability to these plans for seller, and/or can transfer liability to the buyer. If the buyer plans facility closings or layoffs, it may trigger very large liabilities. In addition, the terms and administration of these plans are typically out of the control of buyer and seller, and information about them can be difficult to obtain. For these reasons they often present problems in an acquisition.

What are executive compensation plans?

A company's executive compensation may involve many other benefit commitments, such as stock option plans, bonus ("incentive compensation") plans, deferred compensation plans, fringe benefits such as club dues, cars, and financial planning, and supplemental pension plans. Remember, when negotiating or providing disclosures under an acquisition or a loan agreement, that references to "employee benefit plans" include these fringe benefits unless they are explicitly excepted out of the contract. Some or all may be provided by an employment contract. Many are subject to ERISA (an insufficiently recognized fact). The tax treatment of many of these benefits has been under congressional attack for many years, and the attacks will probably continue. For example, tax rules for planes, cars, and meals were recently tightened. In an acquisition context, payment on acceleration of these benefits can trigger "golden parachute" taxes (see Chapter 5).

What are current trends in designing benefit programs?

The accepted wisdom in the benefits field is that DBPs are on the wane. DBP plans give rise to fixed and fairly inflexible costs. Their benefit structure is geared to the full career employee—a creature who seems to have disappeared. Every year, new legislation increases the complexity and cost of these plans. As a result, employees and employers have become more interested in DCPs. With a DCP, plan contributions can be flexible, and can be tied to company performance. Benefits are more portable and more easily understood. PBGC has no regulatory role; no actuary is needed. For these reasons, a buyer who values flexibility and ease of administration will usually prefer the DCP. However, in some workforces, especially older or unionized workforces, employees may insist on a DBP, or a DBP may be needed to attract skilled employees.

Sometimes an acquisition represents a major shake up and belt tightening for a target whose benefit programs have grown excessively generous over the years. Major savings can sometimes be achieved in the fringe benefit area. Here the buyer may be able to maintain the basic benefit program and make economizing changes which appear somewhat ancillary. For example, costs of medical plans can be cut (or increases stemmed) with self-insured or minimum premium policies, higher deductibles, second opinion programs, preferred provider options, and employee contributions. The buyer may also wish to convert to a flexible benefit program known as a "Section 125 plan" which permits employees to select their own mix of benefits.

In many cases, the lower-paid employees can receive DCP benefits through matching employer contributions which are (or approximate) benefits under a DBP, while higher-paid employees can receive supplemental benefits through non-qualified programs.

DETERMINING PLAN ASSETS AND LIABILITIES AND THEIR EFFECT ON COMPANY BOOKS

How can a buyer determine the amount of a plan's assets and liabilities?

For defined benefit plans, the best source of information is the latest actuarial valuation of the plan. This document will show the assets and liabilities of the plan and its annual costs (which will probably be different from its accounting expense). The valuation will also show whether assets would exceed liabilities if the plan were terminated. Most important, the valuation will show the assumptions used to calculate these liabilities.

Another source of information about plan value is the employee benefits notes to the company financial statements. These notes will reflect assumptions made by the plan actuaries. The company financials will also show historical and current pension costs. Beginning in 1989, all financials will show unfunded liabilities of plans. However, this information will be based on standardized assumptions and methods and, as with a valuation, may not reflect the plan's true condition.

Plan assets and liabilities are extremely sensitive to interest and other actuarial assumptions. The interest assumption determines the rate at which plan assets will appreciate and, thus the higher the assumed interest rate, the more adequate present assets are to meet projected liabilities. If the interest rate is even 1% off, adequacy of funding can be affected very dramatically: A 1% change in interest rates can result in a 6% change in liabilities. An actuary or an actuarially knowledgeable lawyer may be needed to help extract the true cost and funded status from the valuation, by adjusting the assumptions to the market reality or buyer's intentions, and it is a good idea to get the actuary started early. If the plan is expected to be ongoing, a conservative interest rate may be appropriate. If the buyer intends to terminate the plan, the current rate would be more appropriate. If the rate deemed appropriate by the buyer is higher than the rate used in the plan valuation, from the buyer's point of view the valuation overstates funding obligations. Conversely, the seller may have used relatively high interest rate assumptions, thereby concluding that the plan is overfunded and enabling the seller to minimize funding obligations. In such a case, supposed plan surpluses may be inflated above the amount which could actually be recovered, or may even be nonexistent, and the buyer should resist seller's request for a purchase price increase or other benefit based on the supposed overfunding. Other assumptions can also be very important, including rates of increase in amounts of medical claims, frequency of such claims, changes in size and age of employee work force, and the like.

For defined contribution plans, issues of overfunding and underfunding do not arise. Assets of a DCP will always equal liabilities, by definition, because liabilities are simply the balance of accounts. The buyer should be aware of any contribution commitment imposed by the plan.

Multiemployer plan liabilities are extremely difficult to determine, unless the seller has a trustee on the plan's board of trustees. The seller should be asked to provide its contribution history to the plan and to obtain a withdrawal liability estimate from the plan. Not all plans have this information readily available, and the seller may be reluctant to alert the plan, or the public, to a proposed transaction. A rough estimate can be made from the Schedule B to the Form 5500 (filed annually with the Internal Revenue Service and the Department of Labor). Some plan valuations now routinely include withdrawal liability information. Copies of the Form 5500 and valuation can sometimes be obtained from the Department of Labor, but these are usually not very current.

How are plan assets and liabilities reflected on the corporate books?

The Financial Accounting Standards Board (FASB) recently, for the first time, required recognition of plan liabilities and assets in the financial statement of an employer, rather than in a footnote to the financial statements. FASB Statements No. 87 and 88 are applicable in 1989, although they can be used earlier. These rules require plan liabilities in excess of assets to be reflected on the company books.

Under FAS No. 87, a base liability or asset is recognized equal to cumulative expense less amounts funded. An additional liability for unfunded accumulated benefits is required to be recognized and is generally offset by an intangible asset. Uniform actuarial cost methods and assumptions are required and assumptions are required to be "explicit," meaning individually set forth and determined. Multiemployer plan liabilities do not need to be recognized unless withdrawal liability is "probable." FAS No. 87 also contains elaborate transitional rules which may affect the accounting for a specific plan.

Except in an acquisition, as discussed in the next question, companies with overfunded plans are not permitted by FAS No. 87 to book the excess assets directly on their balance sheet. Even in the absence of an acquisition, however, the excess may be indirectly recognized on the books in some cases because the treatment of pension expense may actually result in a decrease in pension expense or even in pension income if a plan is overfunded.

How are book liabilities for a plan affected by the acquisition of the company?

If an acquisition occurs, the buyer is required to recognize an acquisition asset (or liability) equal to the difference between the acquired projected benefit obligations and the fair value of plan assets. The projected benefit obligation takes into account future salary progression, and is thus typically a higher liability amount than the unfunded accumulated benefits required to be booked when an acquisition is not involved. In all cases an actuary or accountant should be consulted to determine the impact of any proposed transaction on the financial statements of the company.

FAS No. 88 covers employers' accounting for "settlements" and "curtailments" of defined benefit pension plans and for termination benefits, a circumstance which may arise in the mergers and acquisitions situation. FAS No. 88 permits recognition of a gain when there is an irrevocable transfer of liabilities from the employer to another party, for example, by a plan spin-off. The seller may thus be able to recognize a gain by transferring assets and liabilities to the buyer.

Can the seller's other plans (those the buyer isn't acquiring) create liabilities for the buyer?

If the purchased operation is a part of a controlled group of corporations, under IRC Sections 414(b) and (c) and 1563, the buyer must consider the possibility that it will be liable for unfunded benefits and defaulted contribution to plans maintained for parts of the controlled group not being acquired. All members of a controlled group are jointly and severally liable for unfunded DBP liabilities and for unpaid DBP contributions under ERISA Section 4062 and Code Section 412. ERISA Section 4064 may be interpreted to continue that liability for a period of five years after the sale of a member of the controlled group, although this theory is relatively untested. In addition, ERISA Section 4069 provides that if a "principal purpose" of any person entering into any transaction is to evade liability to PBGC, that transaction is treated as null and void. Thus, under these rules, a sale could be ignored and the acquired company could continue to be liable for plan obligations of other members of its former controlled group as if the sale had not taken place.

What IRS requirements are imposed on a control group basis?

The Internal Revenue Code coverage, participation, and benefit tests all operate on a controlled group basis. Any pension or fringe benefit plan (as of 1/1/89) must be tested on a control group basis. The control group rules incorporate Code Section 1563. Essentially these are the 80% parent-sub or brother-sister tests with attribution among corporate family members and principal shareholders of corporations. There is an exception for collectively bargained plans. There is also a separate line of business exception which may allow treatment of benefits differently among the different companies for some purposes. However, the legislative history of the Tax Reform Act of 1986 makes it very clear that a headquarters cannot be a "separate line of business." The parent organization may not have significantly better benefits than the bulk of the controlled organizations. Similarly, a buyer accepting a defined benefit plan for a newly acquired division could find that it must extend that defined benefit plan to all other parts of the operation. A one-year transitional rule permits companies to take at least a year to rationalize their benefit programs when there has been a merger or acquisition.

How does the structure of the acquisition affect the buyer's obligations under the target's employee benefit plans?

When the buyer purchases the stock of the target, it will normally acquire as part of the target all the assets and liabilities of its employee benefit plans, unless other provisions are made in the acquisition agreement. An asset purchase, by contrast, often does not involve the explicit assumption of benefit plan assets and liabilities, although in the benefits area the purity of an asset purchase is frequently eroded by collective bargaining agreements, successorship concepts, and statutory and regulatory definitions of the "employer" liable for benefit costs. Thus the buyer should take great care if it intends not to assume seller's plan obligations.

An example of how a buyer can inadvertently subject himself to the terms of a seller's plan is provided by the *Accardi* case, later reversed on appeal. There, by agreeing to assume the seller's plans, the buyer was held to have assumed the seller's interpretation of those plans as well and could not interpret them by reference to his own benefit programs in an ambiguous situation. The seller was IBM and the court took judicial notice of IBM's policy of extremely generous benefits to apply a generous interpretation of the buyer's assumed plan.

The acquisition structure is very important if the seller contributes to a multiemployer pension plan. A stock sale will not trigger withdrawal liability for the seller, but will transfer it to the buyer in the event that the buyer later ceases contributions to the plan. (Withdrawal liability is calculated as a share of the unfunded vested benefits of the plan. ERISA Section 4201, 29 U.S.C. Section 1381). An asset purchase, unless special agreements are made which meet statutory exceptions (ERISA Section 4204, 29 U.S.C. Section 1384), will trigger withdrawal liability for the seller, but will permit the buyer to start with a clean slate. Purchase of stock in seller's subsidiary may appear more like an asset purchase in some circumstances.

If the purchase involves only a part of a company, it will be necessary to divide plan assets and liabilities in some negotiated manner. This process provides many opportunities for a buyer to increase the amount of assets transferred to it and for a seller to transfer liabilities to the buyer.

PLAN SPLIT-UPS AND PARTIAL TERMINATIONS

If a defined benefit plan covers more than the purchased operations, what techniques can be used to separate the benefit programs?

Unless the seller's entire company is being purchased, the plan will frequently cover employees for more of the seller's operations than those being purchased. Under such circumstances, the buyer and seller have a number of choices.

The buyer or the acquired company could simply hire the employees and place them in whatever benefit program the buyer has in place. The seller would likely, but not necessarily, incur a "partial termination" in the seller's pension plan, vesting all of the transferred participants (Code Section 411(d)). The IRS's current position (but possibly changing) is that for a DBP, there would not be separation of service for the participants, so that the plan may not immediately distribute benefits to the separated participants. (A 401(k) plan may distribute benefits.) Any surplus assets (or liabilities) will be retained by the seller, which has the obligation at the time the employees retire to pay them benefits attributable to their service during the pre-acquisition period. The employees will receive, on retirement, benefits from both the seller's plan (as to their pre-acquisition service) and the buyer's plan (as to the post-acquisition service). The buyer may demand compensation for the loss of the excess assets.

If the buyer and seller do not wish to take the partial termination approach, the plan can be split up and assets and liabilities transferred to the buyer, to the extent attributable to the operations being purchased by the buyer. In a plan split-up there is a great deal of flexibility in the amount of assets and liabilities to be allocated to each party, subject to the restrictions of Section 414(l) of the Code. Obviously, if the plan has excess assets, a key question is who gets the excess and how much of it.

It is very important to consult an actuary and to establish clearly in the acquisition document the assumptions that will be used to divide the plan. It is also very important to establish the treatment of contribution obligations to the plan for periods prior to the closing which may not have been paid to the plan, so these are not double-counted. The liabilities transferred are extremely sensitive to the actuarial assumptions used for the computations, and to the basis on which the allocation is made (such as termination basis, ongoing basis, projected benefit obligation basis), so that seemingly minor differences can have a very major impact. For that reason, the party who gets to select the actuary has a major advantage. Also, the allocation technique should protect the buyer and seller from adverse market performance in the time between signing the agreement and the closing or, if later, the transfer of plan assets.

If the buyer is not going to accept a plan spin-off but has no existing plan, it will have to decide what types of benefit programs, if any, to put in place for the employees. For example, if the buyer decides to set up a new defined benefit plan and provide benefits to the employees under that plan, it must decide whether to credit service prior to the acquisition. If the buyer is beginning the defined benefit plan accruals from the date of closing, and the plan is a salary-based plan, the employees will end up with fewer benefits than if the plan had been based on the employees' initial service dates. In order to avoid a reduction in employee benefits, the buyer can give credit for service from the employee's initial date of employment with the seller, and offset against the benefits any benefit paid out of the seller's plan. By so doing, however, the buyer is assuming liability for projected benefits based on service that was accrued for the prior employer.

Must buyers provide past service credits for the purposes of eligibility and vesting?

The IRS has never issued regulations in this area, which is governed by Code Section 414, but in informal speeches and conversations IRS officials have indicated that an acquisition of assets or stock will create a successorship situation requiring the buyer to provide past service credits (for service with the seller) for purposes of eligibility and vesting.

What practical difficulties arise in a transfer of plan assets?

Paperwork responsibilities need to be clearly defined. Unless assets are transferred to an existing plan, a new trust will be required. During the transitional period, the existing trustee will have to be prevailed upon to serve for two separate plans or a new trustee will have to be appointed. The trustee will be reluctant to collectively invest two different trust accounts, for reasons involving Comptroller of Currency regulations. Valuation poses another serious challenge, especially in a volatile market. It's important to provide that the transferee plan has the right to review the outgoing trustee's allocation of assets and administrative fees in order to ensure a fair allocation.

Another practical question is whether and at what rate interest should be paid between the valuation date and the actual transfer date. If plan assets are to be liquidated, the trustee would normally request a fairly lengthy period of time to liquidate so as to avoid temporary market dips or dumping securities on the market. During this time, the assets should be held in some kind of interest-bearing account. The transferee plan may be willing to accept assets in kind, rather than cash, but the details of this concept can become very complex.

In some situations, the buyer may not be in a position to accept the plan initially. This can create an unusual type of plan, the "multiple employer plan," subject to special application of the Code (and not the same as a "multi-employer plan" discussed above). It is important to begin planning for the plan transfer at the earliest possible date and to have it occur as quickly as possible on or after closing. This goal is frequently not met in practice.

What problems are posed by an acquisition requiring the division of a defined contribution plan?

The main question with a defined contribution plan is whether to terminate the plan (or part of the plan) and vest and distribute accounts to participants, or to transfer accounts in a trust-to-trust transfer to a new defined contribution plan maintained by the buyer.

The seller could hold the participant accounts, but this is usually inconvenient administratively. If the buyer is willing to accept participant accounts, a trust-to-trust transfer is probably the most practical and the most beneficial from the point of view of the participants, because it preserves the tax treatment of the accounts in the plan, rather than forcing them into an IRA tax treatment (resulting in loss of income averaging). However, the transfer of defined contribution accounts could cause problems for the new plan if the old plan is required to have a joint and survivor benefit and the new plan does not. If the accounts in the seller's plan contain considerable employee contributions, recovery of basis rules will come into play. In such cases, it may be better for employees not to merge the seller's plan with a buyer's plan which does not contain employees' contributions, since the blending of different accounts can cause benefits based on employee contributions to be taxable when received under the basis recovery rules.

Only recently has it been clear that a sale of a business is an event which permits distribution of participant accounts in a 401(k) plan.

Other practical problems arise with the valuation of accounts and time lags in accrual of interest on accounts. At some point, accounts need to be liquidated if they are to be transferred, and this may raise valuation issues, particularly in a volatile market. Defined contribution plans will also involve extensive record-keeping questions, and unless a third-party record keeper is used and the contract can be easily transferred, the buyer may face high start-up administrative costs.

If the plan is a salary deferral or employee contribution plan, another problem is a smooth changeover of the employee contributions. On a given day, the buyer will have to cut the pay checks and process a deduction from pay checks for deposit to the plan. The buyer will need to be prepared to implement these deductions.

What fiduciary concerns arise in an acquisition of employee benefit plans?

All plans subject to ERISA have been created and are operated for the benefit of the employees who participate in them, and both buyer and seller must recognize that they assume fiduciary obligations to employees in any transaction involving benefit plans. As discussed below, a quasi-fiduciary level of review is imposed by courts in plan terminations, spin-offs and other situations in which the employer is believed to have a conflict of interest. Particular conflicts of interest can arise inadvertently: for example, an acquisition could turn out to be a prohibited transaction under IRC Section 4975, if the acquired plan has been invested in securities of the buyer.

Naturally, the implementation of the plan transfer, spin-off, or termination will also be subject to fiduciary standards. The buyer should probably obtain fiduciary insurance even before the plan is actually in the buyer's hands and the acquisition contract should clearly specify who has the fiduciary obligations during the transitional period. The practitioner should review the co-fiduciary provisions of ERISA in drafting these provisions.

What reporting obligations to government agencies will be created by the transaction itself?

It is important that the agreement specify who will undertake reporting obligations of the plans arising out of the transaction. Typically, a change in employer is an event that must be reported to the IRS, pursuant to Section 6057 of the Internal Revenue Code. However, this event is generally reported on the annual Form 5500 filed with the IRS, DOL and PBGC. The obligation to file this form will usually be assumed by the post-acquisition company as sponsor of the plan at the time that the form is due; however, because it will address prior periods, it may make sense to require the seller to file the form for all periods prior to the closing. It is helpful to demand that the seller cooperate by providing necessary data for the filings. In addition, if the plan is underfunded, a reportable event notice may need to be filed with the PBGC when the plan changes hands.

If the plan assets are to be transferred, then Form 5310 will have to be filed by both recipient and transferring plan, prior to the actual transfer. If there is a plan termination, the plan as terminated is qualified through the Form 5310. Any new plan adopted by the buyer should be qualified with the IRS by the buyer's filing the appropriate Form 5300, 5301, or 5302.

All filings with the IRS require extensive notification to the plan participants. If the plan is actually terminated, and if it is a defined benefit plan, there are required filings with the PBGC. In the case of partial termination, there will be no IRS filings, except that if the plan should be amended to vest all participants subject to the partial termination; this amendment should be qualified with the IRS. Also if there is a sufficient drop in participants, a partial termination can create a reportable event to the PBGC. Withdrawal of a substantial employer (10%) from a multiple or multiemployer plan can also trigger some reporting obligations.

UNDERFUNDED AND OVERFUNDED PLANS

How are liabilities in underfunded benefit plans divided between buyer and seller?

Underfunding is a problem, as we have mentioned, in defined benefit plans, but not in defined contribution plans, in which benefits equal assets by definition. There are two degrees of underfunding in DBPs. In the worst case, the plan does not have assets sufficient to meet liabilities even if terminated at the measurement date. In the less severe, and in fact normal, case, the plan is underfunded on an ongoing basis and thus has continuing pension costs, but would have assets sufficient to meet liabilities if the plan were terminated.

If a plan is underfunded on a termination basis, under current law it cannot be terminated without funding all benefit commitments, unless the plan sponsor and *all members of the sponsor's control group* are in extreme financial distress. In practice, if the plan is purchased from a seller in distress, the buyer, who is presumably not in extreme financial distress, cannot terminate unless it pays the unfunded benefits. Any plan termination underfunding is a real liability shown on the company books (as of 1989) and should be factored into the value of the acquired entity. The buyer should review carefully with an actuary or an accountant the financial assumptions underlying the booking of the underfunding, because this may differ from the actuarial amount and may not truly reflect the anticipated costs of the plan.

If the plan is fully funded on a termination basis, the buyer can transfer or keep the plan without immediate adverse financial consequences. However, from the buyer's point of view, the future cost of an ongoing plan is not the termination liability, but the difference between the *projected* future benefit obligations and the assets of the plan. Even a plan with sufficient assets on a termination basis will probably create a long-term liability for the buyer, and may create a book liability.

To terminate or continue the plan are not the only options. It may be possible to freeze the plan and thereby curtail future increases in plan liabilities, if this can be done without serious detriment to employee relations. Benefits can be cut prospectively or perhaps replaced to some extent by a DCP. It may also be possible for the buyer or the seller to merge the plan into another, better-funded, plan, thereby eliminating the underfunding of the plan. In such a case, the merged plan could be continued, frozen or terminated.

Generally if a plan is funded on a termination basis, but not on a projected benefit obligations basis, it is considered in good condition. The seller might even seek to get a little additional consideration based on any funding in excess of the termination liabilities. The buyer should be aware of the future costs of the plan, and should consider whether the acquisition provides a good opportunity to shift from a defined benefit to a defined contribution structure.

If the company has a defined benefit plan which is overfunded, in what ways can buyer or seller obtain the benefits of the overfunding?

Any assets of a plan in excess of plan liabilities on a termination basis are corporate assets, but ones which it may be difficult for buyer or seller to get their hands on. Under present law, the owner of such an asset may convert it to cash in one of two ways:

- decrease future funding, which will recover the excess assets over a period of years; or
- terminate the plan and take a reversion of the excess; a reversion is subject to a 10% excise tax unless it is transferred to an ESOP.

Flexibility to change funding has been curtailed by the Omnibus Budget Reconciliation Act of 1987 (OBRA), which imposed a standard range of interest assumptions for funding purposes. OBRA also precludes termination and reversion unless the plan is new or has permitted a reversion for at least 5 years.

The assets can also be realized, but not in cash, through recognition of the excess on the corporate books. Although recognition of the excess assets directly is not permitted under FAS No. 87, recognition may be possible through application of purchase accounting rules or through the "settlement" of benefit liabilities in the plan by the purchase of annuities by the plan.

A less tangible benefit can be realized by passing the excess through to employees in the form of cost of living adjustments or improvements to the benefit formula. Pending law proposals may permit excess assets to be used for retiree medical costs. Another possibility may be to merge an overfunded plan with an underfunded plan, and eliminate the liability in the underfunded plan.

It may be possible to place the surplus assets in an ESOP, using the ESOP as a source of financing and avoiding the 10% tax on a reversion. ESOPs are discussed further below. Plan assets can also be used to purchase employer stock or property, up to 10% of plan assets. This technique is available whether or not there are excess assets. With Department of Labor approval, plan assets, whether or not excess, can also be loaned to the employer.

Legislation has been proposed of two opposing kinds: to permit employers to withdraw excess assets (up to 75%) from ongoing plans, and to increase the tax on reversion to punitive levels.

The seller can in effect realize plan assets by selling them to the buyer. The value of those assets will be a matter of debate — and the seller may have to pay excise tax if the IRS concludes that the purchase price reflects such excess assets.

How can plan funding requirements be adjusted to recover a surplus?

The plan funding requirements are determined by the plan actuary based on a set of assumptions as to interest, inflation, and plan turnover (Code Section 412). Often, the actuary is willing to vary these assumptions so that future contribution obligations are lessened, particularly if the plan is fully funded. Of course, the actuary is required to certify that the assumptions are reasonable in the aggregate and so will not have unlimited flexibility. Sometimes decreased future funding assumptions can be obtained by changing the actuarial method used to calculate funding obligations or even by converting from a smoothing average asset valuation method to a market valuation method.

The actuary might also be able to use an alternative funding method under Code Section 412, which decreases short-term funding costs by amortizing unfunded liabilities under a 5-year period. Another possibility may be to apply to the IRS for a funding waiver under 412(f) of the Internal Revenue Code. However, a funding waiver may be obtained only upon a showing of substantial business hardship for the entire control group and would not be appropriate for all situations.

What are the tax consequences to the seller in a sale of an overfunded plan?

Internal Revenue Code Section 4980 imposes an excise tax on any indirect or direct reversion. IRS officials have informally suggested that IRS may issue regulations saying that the sale of a company with an overfunded plan creates a taxable indirect reversion which imposes the excise tax on the seller. The IRS apparently believes that the sale price includes a payment for the surplus, and the seller has thus received a reversion. Regulations have not been issued on this point.

Section 4980 contains an exception for a surplus placed in an ESOP investing in common stock (as defined in Code Section 409(e)) of the employer.

Why might a buyer prefer not to terminate the plan and receive a reversion of the surplus?

The termination/reversion technique can be cumbersome, complex, and expensive. Several governmental approvals are required. Typically, a new plan, either defined benefit or defined contribution, will be put in place, which is also expensive and obviously entails future pension costs. The lengthy process exacerbates the risk of adverse congressional action (Congress is considering restricting plan reversions in a number of different ways) and also places the surplus at risk in the market. However, market risk can be minimized by hedging techniques.

Recovery of the surplus through a reversion will be under-cut by a 10% nondeductible excise tax (which may be increased to 20% by legislative reforms) and by income tax on the surplus. In addition, if the plan had employee contributions, employees are awarded a part of the surplus under PBGC regulations pursuant to ERISA Section 4044(d)(2).

What are the potential legal restraints on plan termination?

Under ERISA and the Internal Revenue Code, when a plan terminates, surplus assets may only revert to the employer if the plan so provides. OBRA requires the plan provision to have been in place for five years or, if less, the life of the plan. Thus the first potential restraint may be that the plan does not adequately provide for termination and/or a reversion, or did not do so at all relevant times. Even if the plan does provide for termination, if the language is ambiguous and the summary plan description or other plan descriptions distributed to participants suggest that the plan will not be terminated, there could be legal impediments to terminating the plan. Such language ambiguities have been used successfully to block terminations in a number of cases brought by unions and employees, who do not like terminations.

Recently, courts have begun to attack plan termination in somewhat obtuse ways. The *Blessit* case permitted a plan to terminate, but calculated the benefit obligations so that all the surplus had to be applied to benefit payments, and the benefit of the reversion to the employer was virtually eroded. Similarly, the *Tilley* case interpreted accrued benefits in such a way that the plan termination created accelerated benefits for participants. It is not yet known whether the principles of these cases will be followed in the future, but they do present dangers to an employer seeking to terminate a plan.

Another possible restraint on plan termination is a collective bargaining agreement. If the agreement can be interpreted to require the employer to continue the plan, it may prevent a termination. Notice must be given to any unions and to employees in the case of an anticipated plan termination. If the union then protests to the PBGC that the termination is precluded by a collective bargaining agreement, the PBGC will halt or reject the planned termination. In short, unions have a strong weapon for enforcing what they believe to be the provisions of a collectively bargained agreement.

A termination decision may also be invalidated if it is shown to be "arbitrary and capricious." Recent case law interpretation of the arbitrary and capricious standard provides a heightened level of fiduciary scrutiny for plan terminations when the employer has a self-interest in the decision involved. Courts seem unwilling to go so far as to make a decision such as whether to terminate a plan or a fiduciary decision, but they are likely to read some stiff requirements into the arbitrary and capricious standard when there is a substantial plan reversion at stake.

EMPLOYEE STOCK OWNERSHIP PLANS

What is an ESOP?

An ESOP (employee stock ownership plan) is a type of DCP designed to permit the plan to invest in certain employer securities on a leveraged basis. The tax benefits of ESOPs, which flow to the company crediting the plan, to the stockholder contributing stock to it, and to the lender financing the purchase, make them attractive methods to carry out an employee buyout. They are also useful to raise capital, to acquire other companies, to spin off a subsidiary or a division, or as an anti-takeover device. There are, however, some disadvantages to ESOPs, including the need to satisfy the plan trustee, who is an independent fiduciary, and obligations imposed on the company to repurchase the stock under certain circumstances.

An ESOP is only one type of plan owning employer securities: any plan can acquire and hold 10% of its assets in employer stock or real property if certain conditions of ERISA are met (ERISA Section 406). Plans which are "eligible individual account" plans, ERISA Section 407(d), may exceed the 10% limit: these are simply plans which are profit sharing, stock bonus, thrift, savings, ESOP or pre-ERISA money purchase plans which explicitly provide for the holding of employer stock (ERISA Section 407(d)(3)) and which provide for an individual account for each participant with benefits equal to the account plus or less earnings, losses, etc.

Each type of plan has its own set of ERISA and Code rules. An ESOP is a type of individual account plan, called a qualified stock bonus plan, that meets the Code and ERISA ESOP requirements and may therefore enter into an ESOP loan and take advantage of other special ESOP provisions such as higher deductions, higher benefit limits, and special stock transfer and estate tax rules, as well as interest deductions and income exclusions for the lender, all described more fully below. (Two other forms of stock ownership plans, TRASOPs and PAYSOPs, are no longer popular because the tax credits formerly available to them have expired.)

What is the basic structure of an ESOP buyout?

A leveraged ESOP is usually used in an ESOP buyout. A leveraged ESOP is an ESOP which borrows cash to purchase the stock in which it is invested. The shareholders of the target sell all or a portion of their stock to the ESOP, which finances the purchase with a loan from an outside lender or, more commonly, from the target, the target having received a back-to-back loan from the outside lender. The loan is then repaid over time out of target contributions to the plan and perhaps out of dividends and stock appreciation. The securities need not be securities of the plan sponsor, but could be securities of any control group member; as long as if any company stock is publicly offered, the ESOP stock is publicly offered. The loan, if not made by the target, is typically guaranteed by it, and secured by the stock or other assets of the target. Because of special tax treatment, discussed below, the loans are usually obtained at lower than market rates.

How much stock must be held by the ESOP?

There is no required stock holding. However, at least 30% of each class of stock of the target, or 30% of total value of all target stock, must have been sold in the aggregate by all selling stockholders if the selling stockholders are to receive the tax benefits discussed below. In addition, the ESOP must be "primarily," i.e., at least 50%, invested in stock of the target.

What is the tax benefit to the selling stockholder?

No gain is recognized by the selling stockholder on the sale of closely held stock, provided that the 30% ESOP stock ownership test is met and that within one year of the sale, the stockholder reinvests in "qualified replacement property" (Code Section 1042). The replacement property is basically a rollover investment: it must be a security of an operating company, cannot be a government security, may have no more than 25% passive income, and must be issued by an issuer independent of the ESOP sponsor. The replacement property retains the basis of the stock sold to the ESOP, which is usually low, and tax is paid on the deferred gains upon sale of the replacement property. However, there is always the possibility that the next disposition will also be exempt from tax on gain as a result of a gift to a charity, the estate tax rules, another Section 1042 transaction, or a Section 368 reorganization in which the Section 1042 shareholder does not control the replacement property issuer.

The selling stockholders must elect tax-exempt treatment on a timely return and must advise IRS of the qualified replacement property. There are some strings attached: the target is subject to a 10% excise tax if the stock is sold by the ESOP within three years and the ESOP owns less stock than before the non-taxed sale to the ESOP, or owns less than 30% of the total value of stock, unless the ESOP has disposed of the stock due to plan distributions. Another tax, of 50%, applies to any "prohibited allocation" of awards attributed to the transaction, which is an allocation of ESOP benefits to the taxpayer, his relatives, or any 25% shareholder other than a "de minimis" allocation. The target must provide a written consent to both these taxes. (A prohibited allocation also disqualifies the plan with respect to the recipients.)

What about estate planning aspects for selling stockholders?

An ESOP sale is particularly well adapted for stockholders of closely held or family corporations who are considering cashing out their interests.

Special estate tax treatment is available in the form of a deduction of 50% of the proceeds, up to $750,000, of an executor's sale of securities to an ESOP (Code Section 2057). There are some restrictions. The securities must not have been received from a qualified or nonqualified plan (such as an ISO) or as compensation. The sale must take place before the estate tax is due. As with the nonrecognition rule, prohibited allocations trigger an excise tax, to which the ESOP sponsor must consent in writing. The deceased must have owned the securities for a certain period before death. The securities may not be substituted for other securities held in the ESOP and may not be publicly traded.

An executor can also transfer estate tax liability to the ESOP by transferring securities equal in value to the tax. The estate must be eligible for deferred payment of excise tax under Code Section 6166.

Are there any kinds of stockholders who will not receive tax-free rollover benefits?

Yes. Stockholders who are C corporations are ineligible. Also, the tax-free treatment is not available for publicly traded stock. This has the effect of limiting the full tax benefits of ESOP buyouts to situations in which the target is not publicly traded and a substantial amount of its stock is held by individuals, trusts, or S Corporations. In publicly traded situations, the ESOP will still benefit from the other tax advantages and the favorably priced loans.

What are the tax benefits to a lender?

Institutional lenders (banks, insurance companies, investment companies, and the like) can exclude from income taxation 50% of the interest earnings on the loan made by them. Because of these tax benefits, ESOP loans are available at lower than market rates and thus provide cheap financing. The loan may be made either directly to the ESOP to finance the stock purchase or may be made to the target and reloaned by the target to the ESOP on substantially similar terms.

All ESOP loans must be nonrecourse against the ESOP except for the security and may not be payable on demand except in the event of default. If the loan is made to the target, the repayment period may not exceed seven years (including renegotiations). The company and ESOP loan terms must also be substantially similar to each other, in amortization periods and release of collateral, Reg. 1.133–IT, or the ESOP repayment terms must be more rapid, and other rules apply. If the loan is made to the ESOP, a maximum term of 10 years is permitted, unless ESOP shares are allocated to participant accounts, based on pro rata repayment of principal and interest.

From the lender's point of view, a loan to the company is preferable because the lender is then not treated as a fiduciary to the plan and may treat the loan as an ordinary commercial loan. The lender may also be able to impose obligations on the company which cannot be imposed in the loan to the ESOP.

What tax benefits does the target enjoy?

The loan will be repaid through contributions by the target to the ESOP. Such contributions are deductible in their entirety, provided the deduction and benefit limits of Code Sections 415 and 404, which have been eased for ESOPs, are not exceeded. Consequently, the target can in effect deduct not only interest, but also principal repayments on the ESOP acquisition loan.

Code Section 404 limits contributions to 25% for ESOPs (increased from 15% for non-ESOPs) of total compensation (counting only the first $200,000 (indexed) of compensation of each employee). Code Section 415 limits contributions to DCPs allocable to employees to $30,000/year per employee or, if less, 25% of compensation. For ESOPs, if no more than one third of employer contributions are allocated to highly compensated employees, the limit is increased to $60,000 (or, if less, 25% of compensation) *and* excludes interest repayments and reallocated forfeitures of employer securities. For any ESOP, the value of the allocation is based on the contribution allocated, not on the value of the securities released to the employee's account (Treas. Reg. 1.415(6)(g)(5); Code Section 415(c)(6)(A)). As a result of these rules, an ESOP can be "richer" than a non-ESOP plan. Earnings on the securities may also be used to pay the loan, including proceeds of a sale of the securities.

Do these limits tend to make certain types of targets more suitable for ESOPs?

Yes. Basically, an ESOP buyout is most effective for a target such as a manufacturing, service, or retail business which has substantial numbers of employees, and has a relatively high ratio of payroll to acquisition cost. Shareholders of closely held companies receive the maximum tax benefits.

Why did Congress treat ESOPs so generously?

ESOPS are frequently touted as an employee motivational technique. Indeed, this is a basis for Congress' continued favorable treatment of ESOPs. However, the GAO recently concluded that there are no noticeable improvements in productivity in an ESOP-owned company.

Can an ESOP also be of assistance if an overfunded plan is being terminated and assets are reverting to the target?

Yes. The Tax Reform Act of 1986 imposed a 10% excise tax on asset reversions. This tax can be avoided, at least until January 1, 1990, if excess assets are transferred to an ESOP (Code Section 4980(c)(3)). The assets must be transferred directly to the ESOP, and then be used, within 90 days, to purchase target securities. The securities must be allocated to participants over seven years. At least half the active employees in the terminated plan must be ESOP participants. This rule may become permanent if proposed legislation is enacted. The income tax treatment of Section 4980 transfers has not been resolved. However, it offers an additional advantage to accomplishing a buyout through an ESOP if the target also has other overfunded plans which can be combined with the ESOP.

What are the drawbacks of a leveraged ESOP?

An ESOP is a plan subject to ERISA's fiduciary standards. As a result, all transactions between the company and the ESOP are subject to fiduciary rules. The valuation of the stock contributed to the ESOP is a fiduciary issue. All valuations of employer's securities acquired after December 31, 1986, unless readily tradable on an established market, must be made by an independent appraiser. These fiduciary constraints may limit the flexibility in structuring a deal, especially if the ESOP terms are different from those given to other investors. In several cases the DOL has torpedoed ESOP deals or forced changes in them because it viewed the transaction as unfair to the ESOP in relation to the other investors. Blue Bell (which was ultimately successful) and Scott Fetzer are two well-known examples. To allay DOL concerns, independent legal and financial advisors are a practical necessity, even if not a legal prerequisite.

All nonunion employees must be eligible to participate, and stock must be allocated on a nondiscriminatory basis. There will be limits on benefits for highly compensated employees.

The ESOP can restrain or complicate later transactions— for example, the sale of non-ESOP stock at an increased price may call into question the ESOP value of stock allocated to the ESOP.

ESOPs can also raise securities law problems, including registration of the stock held in the ESOP, registration of the company as a result of the distribution of shares from the ESOP, and Section 16 insider trading issues. These are discussed briefly below.

What is the effect of ESOP ownership on voting control by management?

ESOPs necessarily involve a certain sacrifice of control. While shares owned by the ESOP are in hands probably friendly to management, they are not controlled by management. Non-allocated securities are controlled by a trustee, who is imbued with a fiduciary mandate to act in the *sole* interests of plan participants. In some cases, the employer will retain voting and investment control, but in these cases the employer assumes the duty to act for the sole benefit of the plan participants. Even if the employer has taken control, the trustee will not be relieved of responsibility and is required not to follow the employer's directions if they are not in the sole interest of plan participants. DOL advisory letters make it clear that ESOP fiduciaries must obtain (and follow) independent legal and financial advice.

Once securities have been allocated to a participant's account, the participant must be permitted to vote the securities. There are also issues about how securities must be voted when the participant does not respond to the pass-through voting ballot. Should the trustee vote the securities in accordance with the majority rule of the participant votes, may the trustee be subject to direction by the employer, or must the trustee have an independent voting decision? At present, DOL says the trustee must vote in proportion to all other participant directions; IRS says the trustee must not vote at all. Clearly these issues are the more significant, the larger the ESOP holding. (If the ESOP's securities are not "registration type securities" then the voting rights pass-through is only required if the employer stock is not publicly traded and more than 10% of the plan assets consist of securities of the employer—of course the 10% test would always be met for an ESOP because it must be primarily invested in employer stock.) These problems can be especially critical when the employer is sold.

Because of these problems, ESOP ownership of the company sometimes is limited to less than a controlling interest and management may seek, simultaneously with the ESOP acquisition, to increase its holdings in the company.

What happens when the ESOP company is sold?

Fiduciary questions can be especially cumbersome when the company with the ESOP is sold. Later price increases may cast doubt on the fairness of the sale transaction. It is advisable to retain an independent trustee. Finding and educating an independent trustee can cause significant time delays. The trustee, being independent, may not be willing to go along with the deal that has been worked out between buyer and seller, and may have the voting power to block the sale if he does not consider it to be in the interests of plan participants.

Another problem with a leveraged ESOP is that on subsequent sale, the Section 415 limits on plan additions and benefits can restrict the termination of the plan and the allocation of securities to the employee accounts. This may require that the securities be sold by the plan trustee, with attendant fiduciary considerations, and that any net proceeds after the loan is paid be distributed to the employees, perhaps over time. A reversion from an ESOP is not favored by IRS (based on informal discussions) and, therefore, all ESOP assets will have to be distributed to employees.

What types of targets are suitable for ESOPs?

An ESOP is not right for every company. Tax deductions are only of value to a company with taxable income. ESOP debt, like any other debt, can be burdensome. The ESOP must permit employees to put securities acquired from the ESOP back to the company. This can cause a cash drain in later years.

The company compensation levels must be large enough to support the ESOP contributions, or deductions will be lost.

Finally, employees must be willing to accept ESOP benefits in lieu of investments in more diversified and thus safer vehicles. Employees may be reluctant to stake their retirement benefits on company performance, especially if the ESOP replaces a plan with fiduciary controls on plan asset investments.

Does the ESOP impose repurchase obligations on the company?

There are two rules that can impose repurchase obligations on the company. First, an ESOP must provide a put option for any company securities distributed to a participant, unless the shares are readily tradable on an established market (Code Section 409(h)). The put option cannot be terminated even if the loan or the plan is terminated. No other put, call, or buy-sell is permitted, a rule which can impinge on typical corporate control techniques for smaller companies. Another rule which can impinge on control is that an ESOP cannot be required to acquire stock "from a particular security holder at an indefinite time determined upon the happening of an event such as the death of the holder" (Treas. Reg. Section 54.4975–11(a)(7)(i)).

However, if the securities are not publicly traded, a right of first refusal is allowed (Treas. Reg. Section 54.4975–7(b)(9)). Note that stock not publicly traded may only be used in the ESOP if there is no publicly traded stock or if the securities are preferred stock, convertible to traded stock (Code Section 409(l)).

Second, TRA '86 added a requirement that a participant who is age 55 and has 10 years of service be permitted to elect "diversification" of his account in each of the following 5 years. The participant can elect to direct the plan to diversify up to 25% of the account (50% in the last year). The plan must offer three investment options. The plan may distribute the amount to be diversified, thus triggering the put, or may substitute employer securities equal to the diversification with other investments, which may require dispositions of the securities (Code Section 401(a)(28)(B)).

What is the accounting treatment of an ESOP?

The American Institute of Certified Public Accountants, in Statement of Position 76–3, with the surprising title of

"Accounting Practices for Certain Employee Stock Ownership Plans," made several recommendations to FASB. FASB has not yet formally adopted these recommendations. The recommendations are: that the employer records a liability equal to the ESOP obligations, but not include ESOP assets, as long as the employer guarantees the obligation or has a commitment to fund the debt; that the off-setting debt be recorded as a reduction in shareholders' equity, that the liability and reduction of equity are reduced as the ESOP pays down the loan; that ESOP contributions are reported as interest and compensation with dividends charged to retained earnings; and that ESOP-held shares are treated as outstanding for determining earnings per share.

ESOP SECURITIES ISSUES

What is the securities treatment of ESOP stock?

The company stock sold to an ESOP is a security subject to the federal securities laws and to state securities laws. In addition, an ESOP interest may itself be a security if participation in the plan is voluntary or if the participant has a choice whether to invest his own funds in addition to employer funds. If the ESOP interest is a security, the plan must be registered unless an exception applies.

The SEC takes the view that a stock contribution to a plan is not a sale and therefore registration is not required under the Securities Act. Similarly, the distribution of stock to ESOP participants is not a registrable event because it is not a sale. However, where the ESOP purchases the stock or ESOP participants purchase the stock (as occurs with the diversification election) a sale will occur and registration will be required unless an exemption is available. The usual exemptions may or may not be available, depending on the facts of the offering. Note however, that Section 3(a)(2) of the Securities Act, which exempts certain employee benefit plan interests, will typically not apply to ESOPs because the rule is not applicable to plans in which amounts in excess of company contributions are allocated to purchase of company securities. Open market acquisitions and sales are generally exempt under Section 4(1) unless, in the case of sales, the ESOP is an affiliate of the seller (i.e., there is no independent trustee).

The company is almost always exempt from registration under the Exchange Act, under Rule 12h-1(a), 12g-2(H) or 12g-1, at least until significant distributions have been made. Under these rules, an interest held in trust and issued in connection with a qualified plan, an interest in stock bonus, or purchase plans which are not transferable except on death, or accompanying an interest issued solely to fund such plans, and any issuers whose assets are less than $3,000,000, are exempt. Section 12(g) requires registration for issuers with assets in excess of $1,000,000 and securities held by more than 500 persons. For this test, all shares held by one trust are treated as held by one person.

The anti-fraud provisions of the Exchange Act do apply to ESOPs with certain special rules. For example, Rule 10b-13, prohibiting purchases by the offeree during a tender offer, does not apply to ESOP trustee purchases. Similarly, Rule 10b-6, which prohibits purchases of a security which is the object of a distribution, does not apply to purchases by an independent ESOP trustee.

ESOP participants who have pass-through voting rights are entitled to proxies and annual reports under Section 14 of the Exchange Act.

Can ESOP participants encounter insider trading problems?

ESOPs can create problems under Rule 16 which regulates insider trading. Vested ESOP rights create beneficial earnings ownership purposes of the Section 16(a) requirement that beneficial ownership of more than 10% be disclosed. In some cases, ESOPs may be exempt under Rule 16a-8(b) which applies if less than 20% of the trust is owned by officers and directors, or the employer and beneficiary have no right to control ownership, acquisition, or disposition of the securities. An ESOP will not necessarily meet this latter test. If an ESOP owns more than 10% of a security, the ESOP itself must file (Rule 16a-8(c)).

The short-swing trading rules of Section 16b specifically exclude many transactions typical of an ESOP. Rule 16b-3 sets forth specific rules for plans which will be exempt from Code Section 6166, including shareholder approval, disinterested administration, and limits on awards to officers and directors. While shareholder approval may be desirable for Section 16b purposes, it may also be an impediment to plan changes, including plan termination, in the future.

USING NON-ESOP STOCK PLANS

Can a non-leveraged ESOP or other stock plan be used to help with acquisition funding?

A non-leveraged stock plan can invest in any qualifying employer security rather than being limited to Code Section 409(e) common stock. A non-leveraged stock plan can invest in notes, debt, bonds, debentures, preferred stock, or any other marketable securities (ERISA Section 408). As a result, it may be a more flexible funding technique than an ESOP, if there are substantial assets in the plan.

Can a plan own employer stock or real property?

Even if there is no stock bonus or ESOP plan, up to 10% of plan assets may be placed in qualifying employer securities and qualifying employer real property. Qualifying employer securities include debt as well as common stock or preferred stock (ERISA Section 408). Qualifying employer real property is property owned by the plan and leased to the employer plan sponsor or an affiliate, which meets detailed and rigid ERISA requirements: It must be dispersed geographically, suitable for more than one use, purchased at fair market value, and the acquisition must otherwise be consistent with ERISA prudence and diversification standards.

A defined contribution plan that permits participants to

select investment options for their own accounts can permit employees to select company securities as an investment. Some plans encourage the stock investment by, for example, an offer to double the employer's matching contribution if the employee elects to take the match in employer stock. A plan can be structured as an individual account plan which permits participants to invest in employer stock as one of several options, in which case (if DOL rules are met) the employer is relieved from fiduciary concerns as to the investment decision, but obviously loses control over the amount of stock in the ESOP.

PROBLEMS IN ACQUISITIONS OF UNIONIZED COMPANIES

What complications can unionization bring to an acquisition?

If there is a union in place or a collective bargaining agreement, the buyer must examine whether successorship rules under the labor laws will require the buyer to assume the union, i.e., recognize it, or to assume the collective bargaining agreement. In a stock purchase or merger, with the operations continuing, all obligations are assumed, including the obligation to recognize the union and any union contract.

However, if there has been a hiatus in operations, the National Labor Relations Board may find that the buyer is a new entity. In an asset transaction, if a "representative complement" of the union work force is hired, the employer is required to recognize the union and bargain with it. In that circumstance, the employer may be required to keep the terms and conditions of employment static while negotiating a new agreement. Some cases have gone further: in *Fall River Dyeing* the Supreme Court found successorship in an asset sale despite the fact that the buyer acquired only one of the seller's 3 plants, and only after a 7-month shut down.

In both asset and stock transactions, the labor agreement may contain successorship language that requires the seller to require that the buyer agree to assume the union agreement. Technically, of course, if the buyer does not assume the agreement, the seller is the only person liable under the collective bargaining agreement. This nicety can, however, be all too easily eroded in the purchase agreement through general allocations of liability.

What restraints can be caused by the collective bargaining agreement?

As discussed above, the collective bargaining agreement may have to be assumed by a buyer. If so, the agreement will obviously dictate the buyer's compensation programs for union employees. However, it may also restrain the buyer from introducing new technology, from instituting layoffs, from consolidating work forces, from instituting incentive bonuses and productivity plans, and from changing pension and benefit programs, including as mentioned above, terminating plans, changing their nature, and taking a reversion of surplus assets. Moreover, under Code Section 89, if any union employee is eligible for a plan or a plan of the same type, Section 89 discrimination rules apply with respect to both union and nonunion employees, and the terms of the collective bargaining agreement may thus affect the employer's other benefit programs, as other benefits are changed to meet the Section 89 tests.

Does the presence of a union restrain changes in the workforce even if no bargaining agreement exists?

Yes—if the buyer assumes an obligation to recognize and bargain with the union. In practice, this means that the buyer cannot change the economic terms of employment until either an agreement is reached with the union or an "impasse" is reached. At impasse, the employer may implement its last offer. A change in the economic terms during bargaining would be construed by the NLRB as an interference with bargaining.

Are employees entitled to notice of a sale of the company?

Employees represented by unions are entitled to notice of a plant closing, move, a subcontracting, or other major change. They have no right to bargain about the change itself, but they must be given sufficient notice to enable them to effectively bargain about the effects of the change. Federal law and several state statutes now require prior notice of plant closing to employees.

Absent such a major change or a contractual provision, there is no requirement that unions be notified of a company sale. The federal law passed in 1988, requires 60 days notice to employees of mass layoffs or plant closings and applies to employers of over 100 people. Notice to a union can cause confidentiality problems. In some cases, employee morale may be best served by the earliest notification of a plant change, or the employer may find his employees have bolted prematurely. There may be a duty to notify the union if bargaining negotiations which would be affected by the sale are in progress.

Can a merger or acquisition create an unfair labor practice?

If a merger or acquisition is found to be designed to avoid recognition, bargaining, or contractual obligations, it can be an unfair labor practice. This is the so-called "run away shop." The test is whether the action was motivated by anti-union feeling.

If a merger or acquisition will require layoffs, how can the buyer minimize the potential for litigation?

First, buyer and seller should negotiate to reach an agreed severance program and allocate the financial responsibility for the costs of severance.

Second, buyer should establish as neutral a layoff ranking as possible. Seniority is a well-accepted ranking system. If a division, line, or operation is discontinued, that can also provide an objective ranking. If possible, give employees bid rights into remaining jobs.

Third, be prepared to give each employee a clear statement of termination benefits. Be sure to include continued medical coverage, accrued vacation, pension, and severance benefits. Pay earned benefits immediately (except pension).

Fourth, review the proposed terminations for trouble spots— i.e., concentrations of protected groups such as minorities, women, persons age 40 and over, veterans, and handicapped persons. Also beware of "whistle blowers"—state law is becoming increasingly protective of employees and the "at will" employment doctrine has been significantly eroded.

What is the employee role in changing benefit plans?

Any plan required to be maintained by a collective bargaining agreement cannot be eliminated without union consent. Many times, however, the union agreement is quite vague, and in these cases it may be possible to change benefits without breach of contract.

ERISA now requires that unions and employees be given notice of a plan termination. Unions and employees are also entitled to notice of every application to the IRS for a ruling in the plan's qualified status.

Union or no, employees may claim a vested right to continued pension or welfare benefits. As discussed below, most such cases involve medical benefits for retirers. However, any employee who can show a contractual promise of continued benefits, and reliance on that promise, has a potential claim. Thus a buyer should exercise caution in planning benefit changes.

FRINGE BENEFIT PLANS

What liabilities arise when medical plans exist?

Medical plans fall into two basic types, funded and unfunded. If a funded plan is in place, it is funded through a trust and that trust must be terminated or transferred. In these cases, because of strict deductibility rules under Code Section 419A, the buyer should demand representations that the contributions to the plan are deductible.

If the plan is not funded through a trust, then it is either an insured plan or a self-insured plan (also called an "administrative-services only" or ASO) plan. However, the term "insured" can be a bit misleading in that most modern insured plans contain features, such as restrospective rating programs, minimum premium adjustments, or reserves, which essentially adjust the premium cost of the policy to the claim experience under the policy. These features may create unexpected benefits or costs for a buyer.

With medical plans of any type, it is critical to determine exactly what benefits are covered, as of what time, and what will happen if the policy is terminated. If a stand-alone company is purchased, it is probably possible simply to assume the policy. At that point, it is important to determine whether the policy has an excess reserve built up or whether a large retrospective premium assessment is due, and whether buyer or seller is to get the advantage or disadvantage of that reserve or retrospective rating build up. Another key question is whether the premium rates are based on the acquired operations or on the seller's entire workforce. If the latter, a smaller group may be more costly—as will be a higher risk group (older, more hazardous occupation, etc.).

If the operations sold are not a stand-alone company, then it is important to understand how benefits of persons who are severed from the policy will be treated. It is critical to have a clear understanding in the agreement as to who will cover the pre-existing conditions, as to whether the seller will cover all claims incurred up to the closing or only claims filed up to the closing, and who will cover persons who are on sick leave or disability or retired at the time of the closing.

What hidden liabilities should be avoided in medical plans?

The previous answer discussed the problem of experience rating changes that cover future periods but will be assessed retrospectively.

Another area of great concern is benefits for retired employees. The general rule is that retiree medical benefits cannot be modified or eliminated unless the company has clearly stated that those benefits are subject to modification or elimination. In most cases, a court will probably be able to find some ambiguity in the promise made to the employees. Retiree medical costs are footnoted in the financial statements but are not booked. However, FASB is considering a proposal to require recognition of liability for retiree medical benefits on financial statements. The estimates of these costs are variable, subject to health care cost inflation and to problems such as occupational disease in a particular work force. The buyer of an entity that offers retiree medical benefits should attempt either to have the seller retain the retiree medical costs or should factor the cost into the price paid for the company.

Does a severance agreement or policy create potential liability?

Definitely. Recent litigation has created potential severance liability for sellers of divisions and subsidiaries. These cases hold that an employer who has a severance agreement may trigger severance obligations even if the employee continues his employment with the purchasing entity.

Severance obligations are most likely to be triggered if the benefit or salary programs of the buyer are less extensive than those of the seller. However, this is not a necessary precondition to a holding that the seller is liable. Purchase agreements can also contain seemingly innocuous provisions that actually transfer severance liability to buyers (such as by requiring buyers to assume all obligations under benefit plans).

Severance plans are employee benefit plans subject to ERISA that should be contained in a written document and disclosed to participants. In the *Blau* case, the seller was unable to assert as a defense to the severance claim that the terms of the plan did not provide for severance because the seller had not met the ERISA requirements of distributing the plan. Severance is also a situation where courts will apply the doctrine that the arbitrary and capricious standard applied to benefit decisions will be given heightened scrutiny when there is self-interest on the part of the company.

PLANS HOLDING STOCK

What problems arise when a plan assumed by a buyer holds stock of the selling entity?

A plan could hold employer stock in at least two ways. A plan which is invested by a plan trustee may have invested in employer securities. Unless the trustee finds that these securities are not a prudent investment (which is unlikely since that is a requirement for the investment in the first place), there is probably no objection to the plan continuing to hold these securities. If the company is being taken private, and the stock is stock of the acquired company, then the plan trustee will be treated like any other shareholder in that going private transaction. The seller, however, should be alert to the possibility of fiduciary problems or prohibited transaction problems and would probably want to have an independent trustee, or at least an independent appraisal of the transaction before taking any action. In most cases, the plan would be a minority holder and will be forced out by the going private transaction.

Company stock could also be held in an individual account plan in which each employee has been permitted to invest in employer stock. Again, unless the entity is being taken private, the buying entity may have no objection to permitting the employees to continue to hold the employer stock. If the stock is not stock of the sold entity, the selling entity may wish to recover the stock. Because the stock is held in individual accounts, individual employees may have the right to make their own decisions as to whether or not to accept an exchange offer, etc., unless the stock is forced out, or the plan is terminated and liquidated. Under Department of Labor regulations under Section 404 of ERISA, the fiduciary problems should be much less difficult for an individual account plan.

In the case of ESOPs, the sale of the employer stock will destroy the treatment of the plan as an ESOP. This would also be true in a stock bonus plan. More elaborate steps must be taken to remove the stock feature from these plans if that is desired. In the case of an ESOP, the stock ownership must be reduced from the levels acceptable for an ESOP, because the ESOP exception will no longer apply, and the plan will be subjected to the basic prudence and diversification requirements. The ESOP will have to be converted into a profit sharing or defined contribution plan and the stock holdings reduced. If the stock is held in an ESOP suspense account pending payment of a loan secured by the stock, the ESOP trustee will have to make a fiduciary decision as to whether or not to sell or tender the stock.

Also, ERISA's maximum benefit and contribution limits will apply if the stock is distributed to the participant. The stock may have to be sold, the proceeds used to pay the loan, and then the excess distributed to participants.

What happens if the entity being purchased has granted stock options to its employees?

An existing stock option plan must be examined to see whether it can be terminated and whether outstanding options are affected by a change in control of the company. In some cases, plans will provide for acceleration of options in the event of a change in control. Persons who wish to exercise their options will thus have stock which will be subject to whatever terms are generally applicable under the purchase agreement and will have rights of vote and dissent, if applicable.

If the company is taken private, there may be problems in settling out existing stock options. If the options are incentive stock options, care must be taken in modifying them for fear of losing the incentive stock option treatment. Under the Code, a disqualifying disposition of an ISO (a disposition not in accord with Code Section 422A) will create income in the year of the disqualifying disposition. Therefore, if an incentive stock option is cashed out, it will be taxed in the year of the cash out. While it will be taxed at ordinary tax rates, so long as these are the same as capital gains rates, there will be no negative impact on the employee.

Nonqualified stock options are deductible by the employer and this fact may alter the buyer's assessment of whether it wishes to continue the nonqualified stock option program.

In some cases, employers desire to replace the stock option program with a stock appreciation rights plan so as to eliminate equity ownership by employees. This is feasible. A stock appreciation rights plan does create a charge against earnings, unlike stock option plans.

At times, subsidiary employees have been granted stock rights to parent stock. These may well continue to exist after the sale of the subsidiary, and the seller may wish to reach some agreed upon resolution of this problem before the closing.

EFFECT OF CORPORATE STRUCTURE

What effect will corporate structure have on employee benefits?

The Deficit Reduction Act of 1982 basically eliminated the benefit differences between partnerships, Subchapter S corporations, and C corporations. However, there are still a few areas where corporate structure can affect employee benefits.

A Subchapter S corporation may have no more than 35 shareholders, and none of those shareholders may be a trust. Therefore, a Sub S corporation cannot place its stock in a pension plan and typically cannot provide equity rights to employees beyond the first 35. It might be possible to create future option rights that would mature only when the S corporation becomes a C corporation.

Under Section 1372 of the Code, Subchapter S shareholders holding more than 2% of stock are treated as partners in a partnership. A partner cannot take loans from a plan under Section 4975 of the Code. A cafeteria plan may only be provided to employees, not to partners. Other benefits that may be provided only to employees include the exclusion of up to $50,000 of group term life insurance under Section 79 of the Code, the exclusion for accident and health payments under Section 105 of the Code, the exclusion for employer payments to an accident or health plan under Section 106, and the exclusion for meals and lodging furnished for an employer's convenience. However, to the extent a partner functions and is compensated as an employee, he may be treated as an employee.

Factors in determining whether a person is receiving benefits as a partner or as an employee, according to the Deficit Reduction Act of 1984 explanation of Section 707(a) of the Code, include whether the payment is subject to significant entrepreneurial risk, whether the partner status is transitory or continuing, whether the distribution closely follows in time the performance of service, whether the recipient became a partner primarily for tax benefits, and whether his interest in the partnership is small in relation to the allocation. The Section 707 rules, while not directly applicable to the employee benefit area, may be used as some guidance in the benefit area.

CHAPTER 10

NEGOTIATING THE ACQUISITION
AGREEMENT
AND
THE LETTER OF INTENT

INTRODUCTION

The legal centerpiece of any acquisition transaction is the acquisition agreement. It is difficult—if not impossible—to comprehend the negotiation of an acquisition without understanding the rationale underlying the typical provisions of the agreement that makes it possible. Although negotiations begin earlier, with the crafting of the letter of intent, it is the acquisition agreement that is most likely to make or break a deal.

This is not to deny the importance of the letter of intent. Indeed, this chapter begins with a discussion of the purpose and uses of that vital document as it is employed in the acquisition context, and Appendix A of this chapter contains a sample letter of intent. The major portion of this chapter, however, is devoted to the "philosophy" of the acquisition agreement and the most basic negotiation issues it raises. Appendix B of this chapter contains the principal provisions of a typical merger agreement, together with analytical comments discussing the basis for their inclusion, as well as highlighting the alternatives available to the buyer and the seller.

There are numerous issues that must be negotiated in connection with this complex agreement, many of which are purely legal issues. Primarily, the legal points discussed in this chap-

530

ter are those that lawyers bring to their clients as "business" issues, the type of issues that lawyers normally do not resolve. This chapter is not intended to review every conceivable issue which may confront the parties in the negotiation of a merger agreement, but instead to serve as a guide to the major themes of negotiation. It is thus designed to facilitate an understanding of the key points of a negotiation.

The form of agreement analyzed in this chapter is one that would be prepared by a buyer; it is comprehensive and contains many provisions that favor a buyer. Accordingly, many of these provisions may not appear in a document prepared by the seller. Indeed, unless the seller is represented by a total incompetent, there is no way the buyer should expect to get everything that's in this form into the final contract. But from a buyer's perspective, it is a good starting point. In addition, a document used for the acquisition of a public company is likely to be quite different from the form set forth in this chapter. Those differences will be noted, both in the general discussion and, where appropriate, in the context of the agreement itself. Before proceeding further, it would be a good idea to review the Table of Contents of the form agreement at the end of the chapter to become familiar with key provisions of a typical merger agreement.

LETTER OF INTENT

What is a letter of intent?

A letter of intent[1] is a precontractual written instrument which defines the respective preliminary understandings of the parties

---

[1] Also called memorandum of understanding, agreement in principle, letter of understanding, memorandum of intent, gentleman's agreement, etc. Related terms that should not be confused with letters of intent include preliminary agreements, and "option agreements," by which one of the parties gives his definitive consent to the future contract.

about to engage in contractual negotiations. In most cases, such a letter is not intended to have a binding effect except for certain limited provisions. The terms of a typical letter of intent are set forth in Appendix 10A at the back of this chapter. This form can act as a checklist of items that usually appear in such a letter.

What is the purpose of the letter of intent?

The letter of intent crystallizes in writing what up to that point have been oral negotiations between the parties about the basic terms of the transaction. The letter will set forth the proposed structure of the transaction, the price and how it will be paid, the terms of notes or stock to be conveyed as part of the price, and other important, but general, features of the transaction such as special accounting or tax considerations (e.g., will it be a tax-free reorganization or a taxable transaction?).

The letter of intent also sets forth the conditions to consummating the transaction including, among others, the need for regulatory approvals and, most importantly, the completion of due diligence and the execution of a mutually satisfactory acquisition agreement.

Does the letter of intent create a binding legal obligation?

Most letters of intent specifically state that the letter does not create a binding obligation to close the transaction. Because the legal test for the binding character of an agreement is the intent of the parties as determined from all the circumstances, however, the language of reservation typically included in a letter of intent may not be dispositive. For this reason, the parties should take pains to treat the letter, in all possible respects, as a nonbinding memorandum of the terms of a proposed transaction. However, the letter of intent is usually intended to create binding obligations in respect of the provisions governing such things as confidentiality, the bearing of expenses and "no shop" provisions (see discussion below), if any.

If the letter of intent is not binding do you really need one? Why not proceed directly to the contract itself?

Except in rare cases, use of a letter of intent is recommended. First, the letter contains certain provisions that are binding but to which a seller would not agree if there isn't a clear understanding about the basic terms of the deal. For example, the buyer may wish to obtain a "no shop" agreement from the seller, a provision requiring the seller to refrain from negotiating with other parties for a specified period of time in order to give the parties a chance to complete their negotiations and execute a contract.

Second, the parties will have to expend a considerable amount of time and money to complete due diligence and negotiation of a contract. To do so without a clear understanding of the basic terms of the transaction may prove to be a costly error. Thus, the parties may enter into a letter in an attempt to provide an additional level of assurance that negotiations will be successful before incurring the expense of negotiating an acquisition agreement.

Third, although the document is technically not a binding agreement, the execution of the letter often has the effect of creating a moral commitment to use good faith best efforts to consummate the transaction in accordance with the outlined terms. The parties, particularly if they are part of large organizations, become emotionally, and more important, *bureaucratically* committed to getting the deal done. After announcing the execution of the letter of intent, neither party wants to be the one to walk without a very good reason. A carefully drafted letter can be used repeatedly by a party in negotiations to establish initial positions and to rebuff the opposing party's efforts to retake lost ground. If you think the document has no effect, try to change a material term when you negotiate the contract itself without having to give something else up. Such a change puts the party at an immediate negotiating disadvantage.

All this being said, judgment must control the question whether the parties should execute a letter of intent. If negotiations will be difficult and time consuming, the parties may only want to negotiate once. Also, if the agreement can be done quickly, why waste time negotiating a separate letter of intent?

When should the letter of intent be executed?

It usually is executed after the businessmen have completed their basic financial due diligence but before the major legal due diligence is started. This timing reduces the likelihood of incurring substantial expenses before the parties have reached an agreement in principle as to basic business terms.

Many times the buyer and seller will have reached an agreement and set it down in a letter of intent, but make signing the actual agreement conditional on the occurrence of an external event. The problem with this arises when the negotiators fail to make good faith efforts to render the conditions void.

What can happen if buyer and seller have different expectations regarding the letter of intent?

The *Texaco v. Pennzoil* decision highlights the magnitude of problems that can result—in this case, a $10.2 billion judgment—when buyer and seller have a different understanding of their respective obligations arising from the letter of intent. The primary question before the court in the *Pennzoil* case, which rendered a $10.2 billion judgment against Texaco for tortious interference, was whether Pennzoil's agreement with Getty Oil via Gordon Getty, a major shareholder in Getty Oil, was a binding contract.

How can negotiators avoid the "Pennzoil problem?"

When writing up the letter of intent, the parties should define the terms under which it is and is not acceptable to withdraw from negotiations and, in the case of an unacceptable withdrawal, the amount of the liquidated damages, if any. The parties should also agree in advance on their freedom to undertake parallel negotiations, defining the contract as exclusive or nonexclusive. Inclusion of such clauses in the letter of intent may help avert tort liability, as they support the conclusion that the parties did not intend the letter to be a binding agreement in respect of the terms of their transaction.

THE ACQUISITION AGREEMENT

Who usually drafts the agreement?

Customarily, the buyer controls drafting of the agreement. It is a grave mistake to assume that control of the document is not significant. The drafter sets the initial framework of discussions and can regulate the pace of negotiations by controlling the pace of drafting. No matter how many agreements you've worked on, it is always difficult to be certain that an agreement prepared by the opposing party isn't missing some crucial provision or that it doesn't contain the seeds of subsequent legal destruction.

Don't be surprised if the seller tries to wrest control of the documents from the buyer and put it on its word processing system. The process is subtle: "We respect your normal prerogatives as buyer to draft the document, but we had such substantial changes that it just seemed to make more sense to put it on our machines."

It is *very important* for the buyer to protect its customary right to control the drafting of the documents, and the attorneys for the buyer should not be shy about pressing the point and forestalling attempts to usurp control. It is the shortsighted buyer who tries to save legal fees by letting the "other guys" do the drafting. First, the savings in fees are illusory because substantial redrafting will be necessary to make the agreement work from the buyer's perspective. Moreover, the change in the tone of the negotiation and the loss of control over its pace is likely to cost the buyer more in the long run. Every time new sections of the agreement are negotiated, the buyer is left to the less-than-tender mercies of the seller's attorney to draft the changes. Even well-intentioned lawyers may have a hard time sufficiently shedding their adversarial instincts to do complete justice to the buyer's interests.

Notwithstanding the usual rule, when a company is sold in an auction procedure (See pages 576–579 of this chapter), it is customary for the seller to submit the first draft of the contract for comment by the buyer. The buyer submits a bid for the target together with its comments on the draft.

What is the purpose of the acquisition agreement?

The agreement, of course, will set forth almost all of the legal understandings of the buyer and seller about the transaction. It accomplishes four basic goals:

1. It sets forth the structure and terms of the transaction.
2. It should disclose all the important legal, and many of the financial, aspects of the target, as well as pertinent information about the buyer and seller.
3. It obligates both parties to do their best to complete the transaction and obligates the seller not to change the target in any significant way before the deal closes.
4. It governs what happens if, before or after the closing, the parties discover problems that should have been disclosed either in the agreement or before the closing, but were not properly disclosed.

Unlike the typical letter of intent (see pages 532–533) an acquisition agreement is a legally *binding* agreement. Once it is signed, a party that fails to consummate the transaction without a legally acceptable excuse can be liable for damages.

The negotiation of the agreement is, in large part, an effort by the parties to allocate the risk of economic loss attributable to legal (and certain financial) defects in the target that surface before or after the closing. The types of questions which might arise, for example, might be if the parties discover legal problems after the contract is signed (e.g., a major lawsuit against the target, or identification of the main plant site of the target as a toxic waste dump), will the buyer still be required to close the transaction and thus bear the risk of loss, or will the seller suffer the loss because the buyer is not required to close? The same question can be asked if the bright financial prospects of the target are dimmed by a new ruling on import quotas affecting the target's entire industry. Similarly, if after the closing the buyer discovers a liability that existed at the time of the closing but which was not properly disclosed in the agreement, will the buyer suffer the loss, or will it be able to recover damages from the seller? To understand the risks addressed in a typical acquisition agreement, we suggest that you review the representations and warranties section of the sample agreement found at the end of this chapter.

This all sounds beguilingly simple; it is in fact quite complex. That (and not the lawyer's need to bill time) is why acquisition agreements take days, weeks, or even months of negotiation.

What are the buyer and seller really concerned about when negotiating the acquisition document?

Once the parties agree to the key substantive aspects of the transaction (i.e., price and terms), the seller wants to be as certain as possible of at least two things: (1) that the closing will occur as soon as possible after the agreement is signed; and (2) that no post-closing events will require a refund of any of the purchase price.

The buyer's concerns are the converse of the seller's. The buyer would like flexibility to abandon the transaction in the event that it discovers any legal, financial, or business defects in the target. After paying the seller at the closing what the buyer feels is a fair price, the buyer would like to know that he will be compensated penny-for-penny for any economic loss resulting from legal or financial problems that it didn't expect to assume. This is not to be confused with the business risk of operating the target after the closing. General economic downturns, new competition, and failures of management after the closing are pure business risks that any sensible buyer knows it is assuming when it buys a business. But the buyer will seek to protect itself against hidden flaws in the business of the target such as pending litigation, undisclosed liabilities, and environmental problems—to name only a few—that exist at the time of the closing and that causes the target to be worth less than the buyer agreed to pay for it.

It is the extraordinary case where either the buyer or the seller is entirely satisfied with respect to these basic points. Without fail, the buyer will compromise on its flexibility to withdraw from the transaction before the closing. Without this compromise the contract would be an option to acquire the target and not a contract which legally binds the buyer to acquire the target. If the buyer really wants to buy the target, it should be willing to be legally obligated, within reason, to do so.

On the other hand, the seller can never be certain that the transaction will close, simply because there are too many conditions beyond the control of both buyer and seller that must be satisfied before any transaction can close. (These conditions are discussed in greater detail below.) Moreover, although the seller invariably would like to sell the target on an "as is" basis, affording the buyer little or no protection after the closing, the vast majority of private companies are not sold on this basis. Thus, the seller will grudgingly give the buyer a modicum of protection in the event that the target is not what the seller represented it to be.

In this process of risk allocation is there one correct answer? Who should bear the risk of loss associated with undisclosed legal defects in the target discovered after the closing—the buyer, the seller, or both?

At the outset, it is important to understand the basic themes for the negotiation. The seller will say:

> Look, before you sign anything, we'll show you everything we have. Talk to our management, our accountants and our lawyers. Kick the tires to your heart's content. If you discover problems, we'll negotiate a mutually fair resolution in the agreement. Then tell us how much you'll pay on the assumption that any unknown problems are simply your risk of buying and owning the business. Once we close, the business and the risk are yours.

A good buyer's answer is:

> Our contractual arrangements should be structured to provide both of us with strong incentive to unearth problems *before*

the closing. You will have a strong incentive to uncover all the issues only if you share some of the risk of undisclosed problems. Anyway, if after our mutual diligent efforts the target suffers a dollar loss attributable to undiscovered problems, and if the buyer bears the entire risk of loss, we will, in effect, be paying an additional purchase price. In the end we may be paying more than the target is worth. Our price is premised upon the target not having any material undisclosed problems. We're willing to do our share of tire-kicking, but at some point it's absurd for us to absorb a loss that surfaces notwithstanding our extensive due diligence and is so large as to make our price far exceed the value of what we acquired. Surely, you don't want to exact an unfair price under these circumstances.

Reading between the lines the real issue is: What is a fair price for the target? The answer hinges on the assumptions of the parties when the transaction was agreed to. The buyer can either: (1) determine a price based upon assuming the risk, i.e., an "as is" deal, which presumably would be less than the price that would be paid if the seller retains some or all of the risks; or (2) determine a higher price premised on the seller's retention of some part of the risk. The first alternative is more of a riverboat gamble, but it may be acceptable to a buyer comfortable with its knowledge of the target or where the target doesn't engage in activities giving rise to extraordinary liabilities (e.g., violations of environmental laws, products liabilities).

If truth is the equivalent of custom, then alternative 2 is the "right" answer. It is the rule in most sales of private companies that the seller will bear a significant portion of the risk of target defects, and the deal is priced accordingly. The seller, however, does have legitimate concerns about being pestered incessantly about relatively insignificant items that prove not to be true about the target. Everyone knows going into an acquisition that no company is perfect and that in due course blemishes on its legal and financial record will undoubtedly surface. Accordingly, although seller accountability is the general rule, the seller's accountability is usually reduced by limiting the time during which it can be held liable and by requiring the buyer to limit its claims to significant problems. (See the discussion of the *Indemnity* section at pages 564–574 and Article XII in the Model Merger Agreement at the end of this chapter.)

Does the customary practice make sense? Yes: First, an "as is" transaction may force the buyer to reduce the purchase price even though the likelihood of a claim is not substantial. A seller ought to evaluate whether its concern about post-closing hassles is sufficient to justify the trade-off in price that may result from forcing a buyer to price the deal on an "as is" basis. Second, a sharing of the risk between buyer and seller will provide both with a strong incentive to try and discover problems before the agreement is signed or the deal is closed. Thorough investigation by both parties who have a stake in the outcome reduces the likelihood that a claim will arise. Third, if the problem were discovered before the closing, it probably would result in a price adjustment, even to an "as is" deal. Logically, the result should not be different because the problem arises after closing.

This does not mean that every seller should cave in on this issue. In certain circumstances the seller may just prefer the risk of a lower price to the risk of post-closing adversity. Nor should one assume that the pricing will necessarily reflect the risk of an "as is" approach. In the case of a deal-hungry buyer, or a buyer who has confidence in his assessment of the risk of loss attributable to breaches of representations and warranties, the seller may get the best of both worlds—a high price with little or no post-closing risk. This is especially true in a competitive bidding situation. In the end, the allocation of risk will depend more on the bargaining power and negotiating skills of the parties than the niceties of pricing theories.

COMPONENT PARTS OF THE AGREEMENT

What are the major parts of the agreement?

The major segments of a typical agreement are:

- introductory material;
- the price and mechanics of the transfer;
- representations and warranties of the buyer and seller;
- covenants of the buyer and seller;

- conditions to closing;
- indemnification;
- termination procedures and remedies; and
- legal miscellany.

How are the general concerns of the buyer and seller reflected in the acquisition agreement?

The major concerns of the parties are focused on in two sections of the agreement: the *Conditions* section and the *Indemnity* section. The former lists the conditions that must be satisfied before the parties become obligated to close the transaction and thus controls whether the buyer or seller can "walk" from the deal with impunity. The *Indemnity* section establishes the liability, if any, of each party to the other for problems relating to the target which are discovered after the closing. Both sections are generally keyed to two earlier parts of the agreement: the *Representations and Warranties* and the *Covenants*.

In the *Representations and Warranties* section, the parties make statements as of the date of the signing about the legal and financial state of affairs of the target, the seller, and the buyer, including the legal and financial ability of each party to enter into and consummate the transaction. The *Covenants* section contains the parties' agreement to take no action which would change the state of affairs described in the *Representations and Warranties* section. Of course, changes resulting from the ordinary operation of business actions (such as seeking government approvals and other third party consents) which are necessary to consummation of the transaction, and changes (such as certain corporate reorganizations) which are contemplated by the acquisition agreement, are permitted under the Covenants.

The most significant conditions to closing are that the representations and warranties are true on the closing date and that the parties have not breached the covenants. Liabilities under the *Indemnity* section, in turn, arise from breaches of representations, warranties, and covenants.

It is fairly obvious that the fewer the representations, warranties, and covenants of the seller, the less the risk that a closing condition will not be satisfied, and the less the exposure to post-closing indemnity liabilities will be.

Conversely, with broad and detailed representations, warranties and covenants, there is a greater likelihood of a breach that will allow the buyer to "walk," and a greater degree of protection afforded the buyer by the *Indemnity* section.

The impact of this structure on the negotiation is to divide the process into two discrete parts. In the first part, the parties thrust and parry about how much the seller will say about the target in the *Representations and Warranties* section and agree to do (or not do) in the *Covenants* section. This is an important process because the risk of loss from any areas not covered by the seller's statements or covenants falls to the buyer. In the second stage, the parties agree on the consequences if the representations and warranties the seller agrees to make and the covenants it undertakes turn out to be untrue or breached, before or after the closing.

INTRODUCTORY MATERIAL

What is covered in the Introductory Material and Pricing Mechanics of a Transfer?

It is often useful in a legal document to describe the intentions of each of the parties. If set out in the agreement, the parties' intentions may aid in interpreting the agreement in the event of a dispute. Therefore, it has become customary to introduce the agreement with a series of "recitals" that set forth the purpose of, and parties to, the agreement. The legal significance of the introductory material is usually not great, however.

The next sections of the agreement set forth the most significant substantive business points of the agreement, the price, and the mechanics of transfer. This section identifies the structure of the transaction as a stock disposition, an asset disposition, or a merger, and describes the mechanics to be utilized to transfer the property from seller to buyer. The parties may also provide in this section the requirement for a deposit by the buyer, or other security for the buyer's obligations to close.

In the case of an asset acquisition, this section identifies exactly which assets are to be conveyed to and, often more importantly, which liabilities of the seller will be assumed by the buyer. In the case of a merger, these sections contain the consideration per share to be received by the exchanging shareholders, as well as all of the other terms of the merger, including the identity of the surviving corporation, the articles of incorporation and by-laws governing the surviving corporation, the composition of its board of directors, and the names of its officers. For both asset purchases and mergers, this section will, of course, also identify the nature of the consideration to be received by the seller as well as the timing of its payment.

Frequently this section will contain provisions regarding intercompany liabilities, and how they must be satisfied by the surviving company or forgiven by the seller and capitalized as additional equity in the transaction.

For a detailed discussion of business and contract issues relating to pricing, see Chapter 3.

As a part of the purchase price provisions, should the seller require a deposit of some kind?

The value of the seller's right to sue the buyer if the buyer wrongfully fails to close the contract will depend upon the financial responsibility of the buyer. In many cases, the buyer will simply be a "shell" company with no assets, set up specifically and solely for the purpose of the acquisition. Thus, although the seller will have recourse against the shell company, the seller may have no economically meaningful remedy in the event the buyer breaches the agreement. The seller may win the lawsuit, but won't be able to collect damages.

In such circumstances, sellers often insist upon a cash deposit, a cash escrow, or a letter of credit that can serve as security for the buyer's obligations. It is hard for most buyers to argue their way out of such a requirement. This is particularly true where the seller has several creditworthy suitors for the target and where signing with the buyer will cause those potential buyers to lose interest in the deal. However, even if the acquisition company is a shell company, where the buyer has a proven track record of closing deals, and the price is right, it is often possible to avoid the need for a deposit or to delay posting the deposit until some period of time after the signing. For example, a deposit may only have to be posted if the deal hasn't closed by a specified date, or if the buyer hasn't obtained financing commitments by a certain date. (See pages 557–564 for a discussion of financing commitments and conditions to closing.)

At the very least, a seller should try to get a deposit sufficient to cover all of its expenses and to limit the time given to close the contract so that the target is not off the market too long. Also, if the seller has limited remedies, the seller should be expected to try to have similar limitations on its potential liability for failure to close the contract.

REPRESENTATIONS AND WARRANTIES

What is the purpose of the Representations and Warranties section of the agreement?

In this section of the agreement, the seller makes detailed statements about the legal and financial condition of the target, the property to be conveyed, and the ability of the seller to consummate the transaction. The representations and warranties reflect the situation as of the date of the signing of the agreement and, together with the exhibits or schedules (see the discussion of exhibits and schedules below), are intended to disclose all material legal, and many material financial, aspects of the business to the buyer. The seller also gives assurances that the transaction itself will not have adverse effects upon the property to be conveyed. Some of the representations and warranties are not related to the legal condition of the target but serve to provide the buyer information. For example, the seller might represent that it has attached a list of all the major contracts of the target. The buyer makes similar representations and warranties about its legal and financial ability to consummate the transaction and certain other limited representations and warranties.

The buyer should be aware that lenders providing acquisition financing will require the buyer to make extensive representations and warranties about the target as a condition to funding. To the extent that the acquisition agreement does not contain comparable representations from the seller, with appropriate recourse in the event of a breach, the buyer will take on the dual risk of a loan default and any direct loss as a result of the seller's breach. In some cases, it may be more difficult to obtain adequate financing if there are insufficient representations and warranties about the business. The buyer should make every effort to anticipate the representations and warranties which the lenders will require and attempt to obtain coverage for these areas in the acquisition agreement.

What is the role of exhibits or disclosure schedules?

The exhibits are an integral part of the representations and warranties. Each exhibit is usually keyed to a specific representation or warranty and sets forth any exceptions to the statements made in the representation. For example, a representation might provide that there are no undisclosed liabilities of the target "except as set forth on Exhibit A," or state that there is no litigation that might have an adverse effect on the target "except as set forth on Exhibit B." Another representation might state that "except as set forth on Schedule C", there are no contracts of a "material nature," or there are no contracts involving amounts in excess of a fixed sum, say $100,000. Schedule C would contain a list of all the contracts that meet the criteria in the representation, i.e., that are either material or involve dollar amounts above the threshold.

By design, then, the exhibits list all of the items the buyer needs to investigate in its due diligence effort in anticipation of pricing and financing the deal. The exhibits are a critical part of that due diligence; because they require the seller to make statements about all of the pertinent aspects of the target, the schedules comprise a succinct legal and business synopsis of the target.

The use of exceptions to create exhibits might seem odd, but it is merely a practical drafting device. The alternative would be to incorporate each of the target's documents in the acquisition agreement, which would make the agreement unwieldy. The basic contract and the exhibits, because the former contains the terms of the parties' agreement while the latter provides vital information about the target, are a simpler and more practical method.

To ease compliance, the representations and exhibits requested by the buyer should run parallel to the due diligence checklist the buyer gives the seller early in the process. (See Chapter 8, "Due Diligence Inquiry")

Furthermore, the agreement should provide that the information in the exhibits is part of the representations and warranties. The risk of loss attributable to anything disclosed to the buyer on an exhibit will be assumed to be accepted by the buyer, unless the parties specifically agree otherwise. For this reason, the exhibits and all of the documents or matters referred to therein must be reviewed carefully by attorneys and businessmen who are knowledgable about the matters covered. It is a major mistake to assume that the task should be delegated to the most junior person on the project—important nuances are likely to be missed, nuances that can have a significant monetary impact on the acquisition. Thus, for example, each litigation matter should be checked and each contract reviewed, and, if necessary, back-up documents must be provided. Because the review is time consuming, it should not be left to the day before signing. The review process can be greatly facilitated if, as suggested above, the due diligence checklist parallels the order and content of the representations and warranties that are to appear in the agreement.

Time needed to prepare lengthy exhibits can often be used by the seller as an argument to reduce the scope of the representations and warranties. When the seller has prepared the agreement, it will have prepared its exhibits, usually skipping representations and warranties. When the buyer submits proposed changes, including significant "beefing up" of the representations and warranties, the seller will say, "Look, if we want to sign in this milieu, we can't possibly prepare exhibits based on these representations and warranties. We'll have to recirculate questionnaires to all the officers of each member of the target's corporate group (often scattered around the world) and review once again all the pertinent documents (and, of course, there are hundreds of documents) to make sure we don't violate these tighter representations and warranties." Where there is a need to sign quickly, this tactic pressures the buyer's lawyers. His clients will ask "Are we really asking for a lot of unnecessary garbage?" First, the lawyer should be aware of applicable time pressures in preparing the representations and warranties. Having done so, he must be ready to defend the relative importance of the various requests. One way to deal with the problem is to sign the contract, but give the seller additional time to prepare the exhibits. The buyer would reserve the right to abandon the deal if the revised exhibits surface any material problems. A word of caution—don't leave too much time or you'll be getting revised schedules the night before the closing.

Should exhibits be used if the target is, or will become, a public company?

In the event that the target is a public company, or the buyer has intentions to take the target public, the buyer would be well advised to utilize a disclosure statement as opposed to an exhibit or disclosure schedule in order to avoid the public disclosure of information about the target. The utility of a disclosure statement is that it is a separate document which otherwise sets forth all of the items which would be listed in exhibits or schedules to the acquisition agreement. However, since the disclosure statement is a separate document from the acquisition agreement, the target may not be required under the securities laws to file the disclosure statement with the Securities and Exchange Commission.

Just how important are the representations and warranties in an acquisition agreement?

Very. A buyer or seller will be able to back out of the agreement if it discovers that the representations or warranties of the other party are untrue to any material extent; the fewer the items represented to, the less the risk that the other party will be able to back out of the agreement. Also, the seller must indemnify the buyer for problems that surface after the closing only if the seller breached a representation or warranty in the agreement; the fewer the representations and warranties and the narrower their scope, the less the exposure to the seller. For these reasons, a great deal of the negotiation of the agreement centers around the scope of the representations and warranties.

How can a seller narrow the scope of its representations and warranties?

There are several ways in which the seller can attempt to reduce its exposure attributable to representations and warranties. First, the seller may steadfastly refuse to make any representation or warranty about specific items, for example, accounts receivable or the financial condition or liabilities of certain subsidiaries.

Second, the seller may refuse to make representations and warranties about matters not "material" to the transaction or the target, or may attempt to make representations and warranties only to the "best of its knowledge." To protect itself, the seller can seek to insert the word "material," or phrases with the same effect, in every place in the representations that it can. For example, it can state that it is disclosing only "material liabilities," or "material litigation," or that it knows of no violations of law by the company that will have a "material adverse effect" on the company.

What does the term "material" mean when it appears in representations and warranties?

It is often said that materiality is in the eyes of the beholder. Although the courts have defined material information in specific cases (see Chapter 12, "Public Company Acquisitions"), the concept remains vague. Generally, the case law holds that material means important to a normal, prudent investor in determining whether to make the investment. In many contracts the parties agree that a "material" fact must be material to the business of the target and any subsidiaries *taken as a whole.* The purpose of the emphasized language is to assure that the importance of the fact relates to the entire enterprise acquired and not solely to the parent corporation or to a single subsidiary.

In order to reduce the opportunity for disagreement, the parties often set a dollar threshold that defines materiality in particular circumstances. For example, rather than asking for representations about "material contracts," the buyer will substitute a request for disclosure about all contracts involving payments above a specified dollar amount. Similarly, the buyer may request disclosure of all liabilities greater than a certain sum. Use of numbers tends to fine-tune the disclosures and in many ways provides protection for the seller as well. If there is a dollar threshold of, say $100,000, for liabilities, the seller can usually be assured that a $95,000 undisclosed liability should not be deemed "material" in a later dispute.

How and to what degree can the buyer resist the narrowing of the scope of the representations and warranties?

Generally speaking, it is in the buyer's interest to have the broadest possible representations and warranties. However, unreasonable requests for disclosure can threaten a deal. Pressuring the seller of a large, complex target to make comprehensive disclosures may cause the seller to fear that it will inadvertently fail to disclose minor matters, jeopardizing the transaction or leading to unfair liabilities after the closing.

Moreover, anyone buying a business must recognize that no business is more perfect than the human beings that conduct it. Therefore, there are bound to be a variety of problems in connection with the operation or ownership of the business, including litigation, liabilities, or violations of law, which the buyer must accept as part of the package of owning the business. As a result, in most transactions the buyer will permit the seller to limit the scope of the matters that are being represented to those things that are material, individually or in the aggregate, but where appropriate will negotiate over dollar threshold amounts to require more, rather than less, disclosure.

What different motivations might a seller have for narrowing representation and warranties?

For negotiation purposes it is important for the buyer to understand the seller's real concerns. The seller may be concerned simply about the time and expense necessary to uncover a lot of detailed information that in its view shouldn't matter to a buyer or that, under the time pressure of the deal, just can't be obtained. Or the seller may be far more concerned about making representations and warranties that will increase the risk that the buyer will be able to back out of the transaction. Alternatively, the seller's most significant concern may be with post-closing liabilities for breaches of representations, warranties, and covenants in the agreement.

How can a buyer address these different motivations?

Concern about time and expense is legitimate only to the extent that the buyer is asking for truly inconsequential or irrelevant representations or warranties. Remember that the seller's negotiator on these points is likely to be an in-house lawyer or technician more worried about being personally imprecise than about the broad scope of the deal. Where time is truly a critical factor (as opposed to a negotiating point for the parties), the buyer's lawyer should exercise care and use good judgment to pare down the more burdensome, and not critical, representations and warranties.

The buyer should, however, address the more legitimate concerns of the seller. The buyer can address the risks of the deal failing to close or of post-closing liability while still including very broad representations and warranties with low dollar thresholds. The buyer can explain to the seller that it wants very broad, in-depth disclosure of items so that the buyer can determine on its own what is material. Most buyers prefer to determine the materiality of information themselves rather than leaving it up to the lawyers or officers of the seller in the target, whose idea of materiality may differ from the buyer's, and who may not be aware of the buyer's specific concerns about certain legal or financial aspects of the target or the assets to be acquired.

The seller should be assured that extensive disclosures will not increase the risk of a terminated transaction or post-closing liability. The buyer may provide the requisite assurance by agreeing not to terminate the transaction, and that the seller need not indemnify the buyer, except in the event of material breaches of representations, warranties, or covenants. In summation, the buyer must look through the stated position of the seller, determine its real interests and deal creatively with those concerns, rather than simply viewing negotiations as an argument over whether or not the word "material" is going to modify a particular representation or warranty.

What is the purpose of the phrase "best of knowledge" and "ordinary course of business" often found in representations and warranties?

These phrases are simply other ways in which the parties can agree to narrow the scope of the representations and warranties required of the seller. The phrase "ordinary course of business" is usually found in representations and warranties to exclude certain things from the representations. For example, the seller may not be required to disclose supply contracts entered into in the ordinary course of business, or may not be required to disclose liabilities accrued in the ordinary course of business. The definition of "ordinary course of business" will depend upon the normal practice of the specific business being acquired and the industry of which it is a part, including the normal character and size of routine transactions. It can be generally defined not to include business activities that the seller does not engage in on a regular and consistent basis. For greater clarification, the parties could enumerate in the acquisition agreement the seller's ordinary practices. An important point is that any transactions which are extraordinary in nature, price, or size will be included in such representation and warranties.

The phrase "best of knowledge" serves a similar function. A seller may ask that its representation as to litigation be limited to the litigation about which it has knowledge, so that it will not be required to represent and warrant absolutely that there is no material litigation. The seller often argues that the phrase should modify other representations and warranties.

At each juncture the buyer should ask: Is the "best of

knowledge" modification appropriate? Usually it is not, but it is often agreed to in respect of the existence of threatened litigation and infringements by third parties of copyrights and patents. Beyond those few customary areas, the buyer vigorously should resist efforts to base the representations on the knowledge of the seller. Because such a representation and warranty tells the buyer only that the seller is unaware of any problems, it protects the buyer only if problems known to the seller are not disclosed. Thus, "best of knowledge" representations have the effect of allocating to the buyer all the risk of defects no one knows about.

From a "philosophical" perspective, the knowledge of the seller is not pertinent to the key question of the buyer: "Am I getting what I am paying for?" The fact that the seller didn't know that the buyer was overpaying is of little comfort to a buyer who discovers significant defects in its acquisition. Thus, the "knowledge" caveat should be used sparingly unless the buyer is willing to accept a substantial risk in connection with breaches of representations and warranties.

"Best of knowledge" qualifiers may be presented as a compromise to a seller who adamantly refuses to indemnify the buyer for breaches discovered after closing. At the very least, an indemnity should be forthcoming in respect of problems the seller knew about but didn't disclose.

There are other issues in connection with the phrase "best of knowledge." First, whose knowledge are we talking about? Careful sellers will attempt to limit the knowledge to a narrow group of people, such as the executive officers of the target and the executive officers of the seller. Theoretically, the argument will go something like this: "We don't want to be held responsible if one of the loaders on the trucking platform happens to overhear something bad about the target or knows something bad about the target and we didn't seek his information about the transaction." Aside from the fact that any proposition reduced to that level can become absurd, there is some merit to the idea that a large organization ought to be careful about making representations about what "the corporation" knows. Consequently, a buyer accepting a "best of knowledge" representation will often permit the seller to limit the persons whose knowledge will be tested. The buyer ought to be certain that everyone who has material information about the target is included in the selected circle of officers. This will force the seller to quiz the officers whose knowledge will be pertinent for purposes of the agreement.

Another issue is whether the phrase "best of knowledge" implies any obligation of the seller to look into the matter, i.e., does it assume that the knowledge is based upon a reasonable effort to ascertain the existence of any problems. The general answer is that the seller's inquiry would be limited to information already in the seller's possession. A buyer wishing to impose a duty on the seller to make reasonable investigations into the matters represented to the buyer should augment the best of knowledge phrase with the words "after due inquiry."

What if the seller claims to have no knowledge, or ability to get knowledge, about an area that is the subject of a representation or warranty?

In this era of rapidly changing ownership of companies through restructurings and leveraged buy-outs, the seller often has not had a chance to become acquainted with the details of the business it is selling. It is not unusual to hear the seller say, "I really don't know that much about this company, and I don't want to take much risk on these representations and warranties as a result. I don't want to make representations about too many matters or in too much detail."

This may be reasonable from the perspective of the seller, but the buyer should not give the argument much weight. In every transaction the seller will want to reduce its exposure to losses attributable to breaches of representations or warranties. That concern may be heightened by the insecurity of not knowing enough about the target, and possibly not having enough time to become acquainted with the details of the operations of the target. Nevertheless, the knowledge of the seller is not necessarily relevant to a logical allocation of the risks associated with breaches of representations and warranties. As noted above, if the loss due to a breach is absorbed by the buyer, the buyer pays an increased purchase price. The knowledge of the seller should not bear upon the buyer's resolution of the question whether an increased price makes sense.

An appropriate response to the seller might be:

> We certainly understand your concern, but we have even less of a basis for intimate knowledge of the target's operations. The real issue is, who should absorb the risk in the event that there are undisclosed material defects in the business? We have different views, of course, of who should bear the risk, but let's really talk about what matters, not about what each of us knows about the company right now. The agreement between us ought to be structured to provide incentives for both of us to do the best job possible to unearth problems and to increase our knowledge of the Company now, before we close, rather than wait for problems to surface afterwards. Then, if something does surface later, either after we sign or after we close, we need to decide where the risk should reside.

This response addresses the real interest of the parties and will prevent digressions into who knows most about the company or who can know the most about the company.

Sometimes the seller is leery of making legally important statements without being absolutely certain of their truth. It is important for both sides to recognize that the representations and warranties are not a test of the integrity of the parties making them. A party cannot properly be accused of dishonesty if it makes a representation about which it is not certain (provided, of course, that it has no knowledge that the representation is in fact untrue). In order to reduce legal exposure, it makes sense to try to verify the accuracy of the representations and warranties as much as possible. There will always be, however, some degree of uncertainty. But if the parties recognize that the representations are not a test of integrity but a legal device for allocating risk, the process becomes more manageable and less subject to emotional decisionmaking.

When might the knowledge of the parties about the target be relevant?

The traditional format under which the seller assumes the risks associated with breaches of representations and warranties may be attributable to the fact that the seller, rather than the buyer, is in the position to know the most about the target. The seller is the logical candidate for assessing and bearing the risk of loss arising from any breach of the representations and warranties.

There may be unique circumstances, however, where the seller will be in a position to argue persuasively that the buyer has much more knowledge about the target and should be more willing to accept the risk associated with the sale. For example, in a management leveraged buyout (MBO), where management will own the lion's share of the target and has operated the target for several years, it is very possible that management could be persuaded to accept the risk of inaccuracy in the representations and warranties of the target because management is in the best position to assess that risk and make a business decision based upon it. As has been discussed in relation to pricing, the shift of the risk to management is not necessarily fair or logical. If a latent problem causes a loss, the management buyers absorbing the loss are paying an additional purchase price. The fairness of that result has little to do with the state of management's knowledge.

Moreover, this line of reasoning will not apply in most MBOs because a promoter, investment bank, or the lenders, and not the management group, typically end up owning the majority of the equity. They, unlike management, have no basis for certainty with respect to the accuracy of the representations and warranties and should be much less willing to accept the risk that management inadvertently neglected to assess properly the accuracy of the representations and warranties. Although they might be persuaded to rely on management under those circumstances, the logical reason for them not to do so is that the seller controls management during negotiation of the agreement for any other buyer.

Are some representations and warranties more important than others?

Yes. The representations regarding financial statements, litigation, undisclosed liabilities, and taxes are usually the most important. If a buyer is pressed to get indemnities only for what it absolutely needs, it should, at a minimum, argue hard for solid representations and warranties on these subjects. Protection for breaches of the representations on financials should be the last point the buyer concedes; the buyer should make this concession only if it is fully apprised of, and is committed to taking, the associated risk. In general, the audited financial statements represent the best picture of the target as a whole, and many undisclosed material problems will cause that representation to be violated.

COVENANTS

What is the major purpose of the covenants?

The covenants section of the agreement defines the obligations of the parties in respect of their conduct during the period between the signing and the closing. For negotiation purposes, the most significant covenant relates to the obligation of the seller to conduct the business in the ordinary course with such exceptions as are agreed upon by the parties between the time of signing and closing. In the representations and warranties, the seller assures the buyer of the legal characteristics of the target as of the date of the signing of the agreement; in the covenants section, the seller in essence agrees not to do anything to change that picture in any material way, except as necessary in the normal operations of the business.

Any changes other than those which are specifically allowed by the agreement typically can be made only with the consent of the buyer. Under appropriate circumstances it is often necessary to limit the restrictions by requiring the buyer to not "withhold consent unreasonably." This limitation should be sparingly used so as to ensure that it achieves its limited purpose, that is, that in narrow circumstances the seller may be required to take certain actions in order to preserve the business and the buyer should not be allowed to prevent them unless such actions have a material impact on the transaction.

Many attorneys feel that this limitation is never appropriate because, provided that the conditions to closing are fulfilled, the buyer is obligated to purchase the target. The buyer should therefore have control over any extraordinary actions pending closing. That position, however, must be tempered with the following consideration: if there is a specific area of business conduct about which the seller has a great deal of concern, liberalizing the restriction may be the only way to close the gap between the parties. If the phrase "reasonable" consent is troublesome, it is often possible to craft language that more carefully defines the circumstances under which the seller should be permitted to do things not otherwise permitted by the agreement. If the seller is willing to spend the time to come up with such a list, these can be permitted exceptions to the consent process.

CONDITIONS TO CLOSING

What role do the Conditions to Closing play in the acquisition agreement?

The form agreement discussed later in this chapter contains the typical conditions that must be satisfied before the buyer or the seller is obligated to close.

The agreement typically sets forth separate conditions for each of the parties. If a condition to the buyer's obligation to close is not satisfied, the buyer will have the right to terminate the agreement without being liable for damages to the seller. Similarly, if one of the seller's conditions is not satisfied, the seller will not be obligated to close. Under appropriate circumstances a condition might be established that applies to both parties, but that is the unusual case. One mutual condition might be the receipt of certain key governmental consents; another is the absence of litigation or any administrative ruling that precludes the closing. Either party may waive a condition and proceed to close the acquisition notwithstanding the failure of the other party to satisfy each condition.

How do the conditions affect the key concerns of the buyer and seller?

The Conditions to Closing are the first part of the agreement that addresses one of the two major concerns of the parties. The Condition section sets forth the ability of each party to terminate the contract with legal impunity. For example, if any condition is not met by the target or the seller, the buyer will be free to terminate the contract.

The most significant condition is the so-called "bring-down" condition, which makes the buyer's obligation to close contingent upon two facts. The buyer will not be required to close if (1) the seller has breached any of its covenants or (2) any of the representations and warranties of seller and target were not true when made or are not true on the closing date, *as if made on the closing date*. This condition provides an escape for the buyer if the representations and warranties were true on the date of signing but are no longer true as of the closing date, either because of events that occurred after the signing or because breaches were discovered after the signing.

The following example will illustrate the process. On the signing date the seller represents that there is no material litigation involving the target. The condition to closing that the representations and warranties were true when made will allow the buyer to abandon the transaction if it discovers that material litigation existed on the signing date. But what about a lawsuit arising after the signing? Since the representation was true when made, there is no breach of the litigation representation as a result of the post-signing events. Because the bring-down condition obligated the seller to make the same representation as of the closing date, however, the buyer will be able to terminate the agreement if interim events such as new litigation, liabilities, or other post-signing occurrences reduce the value or viability of the target.

In one typical representation, the seller warrants that the target's financial statements, which always predate the signing, represent a true and accurate picture of the target. In a different representation, the seller must state that there has been no material adverse change in the financial condition, operations, or prospects of the target between the date of the financial statements and the date of signing. The "bring-down" condition requires as a condition to closing that the seller extend its representation that there has been no material adverse change through the date of the *closing.*

The effect of the bring-down condition is to assure the buyer that, on the closing date, the target will be the same target, from a legal and financial perspective, that the buyer bargained for in the contract. Because the buyer is not required to close the transaction if any bring-down condition is not satisfied, the condition allocates to the seller the risk of loss attributable to any adverse change during the period between signing and closing. Interim losses probably reduce the value of the target, and the bring-down condition allows the buyer to renegotiate a lower price reflecting the changes.

The form agreement requires a corporate officer to certify that the representations and warranties are accurate in all material respects as of the closing date. Providing this certificate is a condition of closing, but it has another very important effect: it is a restatement of all the representations and warranties as of the closing date.

If the certificate is not accurate, the inaccuracy will constitute a breach of a representation or warranty, and may give rise to liability to the buyer under the Indemnity section of the agreement. In the absence of an officer's certificate, a buyer might be unprotected against certain adverse events occurring between signing and closing. For example, if a material liability arises and is discovered before closing, a closing condition will be unsatisfied, and the buyer can walk from the deal. But if it is not discovered, the parties may close because to their knowledge each closing condition—including the condition that the representation and warranty about undisclosed liabilities is true—was satisfied. Clearly, the buyer needs more than a condition to closing to fully insulate it from undiscovered problems. Requiring the seller to represent that the closing condition is satisfied allows the buyer to treat the seller's failure to satisfy the condition as a breach of the representations. If the buyer is indemnified for losses attributable to such breaches, the buyer, by virtue of the certificate, will be protected against losses resulting from undiscovered problems.

As an aside, it is important that the officer's certificate be made solely on behalf of the corporation and that it not constitute a personal affidavit. Otherwise, the officer might be personally liable to the buyer if the certificate is untrue irrespective of whether the officer is at fault.

The usual bring-down clause also states that representations and warranties that speak as of a specific date in the past need not be restated as of the Closing Date. Be careful!

Certain representations are always limited to a specific date. Occasionally, however, a seller will attempt to limit the applicability of a representation which is not date-specific by adding language like "As of the date hereof. . . ." If the seller were successful in so limiting the representation that the target is not involved in material litigation, for example, the standard bring-down clause would deprive the buyer of the right to walk from the deal in the event material litigation arises after the agreement is signed. (See the discussion of the importance of controlling the drafting on page 535.)

What is a "financing out" condition and when is it appropriate?

The "financing out" condition provides that the buyer need not close if it is unable to finance the transaction. It is a very broad exception to the buyer's obligation to close the deal, and the seller must be very wary of allowing such a condition. The seller may have kept the target off the market for a long period of time and incurred substantial expenses only to find out that the buyer failed to obtain the necessary financing. For these reasons a seller should resist the use of a financing condition or narrow the risk if there must be one.

The seller's initial position should be that if the buyer is confident of the financing, he should be willing to take the risk that the financing will not be available; i.e., there should be no financing out. Next, the seller can attempt to require the buyer to have its financing commitments in place *before* the contract is signed. This strategy limits the seller's risk to those cases where the lenders refuse to consummate the transaction. In addition, the parties will know in advance that the basic transaction is acceptable to the lenders who propose to finance the transaction. Another alternative is to require the buyer to provide financing commitments (or executed loan agreements) within a specified number of days after the contract is signed. After that period, the financing condition falls away. This approach may be preferable to a buyer that doesn't want to incur what can be very costly commitment fees to lenders before it has a contract signed. In addition, the seller should attempt to require the buyer to pay the seller's expenses if the transaction is abandoned because the commitments could not be obtained.

At the very least, the seller should know what the proposed financing structure will be. For example, how much equity will be invested? How much mezzanine and senior debt will be necessary? What are the buyer's assumptions about lender's interest rates and equity demands? With this information, the seller's financial advisors can assist in evaluating the feasibility of the proposed financing. It should go without saying that the buyer should be required in a covenant to use its best efforts to obtain the necessary financing.

Many contracts do not contain a financing out because the buyer is a "shell" company with no assets. Even if the buyer breaches the contract, a lawsuit by the seller will not yield significant damages. For this reason, a seller should investigate the buyer's financial strength and inquire who will stand behind the buyer's contract obligations.

All this being said, the buyer has a strong interest in obtaining a financing out. Often, financing can fall through for reasons beyond the control of the buyer, and it needs protection in such a case. Moreover, in an era of extremely volatile interest rates, a transaction that is financeable when the contract is signed may not be when the time for closing arrives because new rates may place too high a financial burden on the target. The buyer, forced to put more equity in the transaction, may not have the required funds or may no longer find the deal attractive. When all else fails, the buyer should try to obtain a dollar limit on its exposure, in the form of a liquidated damages clause, in the event it refuses to close a deal in which there is no financing out.

This controversial provision generally should be addressed by the seller as early as possible, usually in the letter of intent. The buyer, on the other hand, is better off letting this issue ride until the seller becomes emotionally committed to the deal by signing the letter of intent. Once the letter of intent is signed, the seller also may be bureaucratically (if not legally) committed to selling and may be more amenable to compromise on the point. The parties must approach this problem by crafting a solution that is carefully tailored to the specific concerns of the parties. Compromise can often be reached by adjusting (1) the time within which financing commitments must be provided and (2) the consequences of the buyer's failure to finance the transaction.

One of the conditions to closing for the buyer is that there has been no material adverse change in the financial condition of the target. Who bears the risk if there is a general business downturn or a specific problem in the industry of the target that causes a deterioration in its financial condition, and what if the adverse change will clearly occur, but only after the closing?

The buyer's right to abandon the deal usually does not depend upon the reason for the deterioration in the target's financial condition. Some sellers try to shift to the buyer the risk of general or industry-specific economic reversals: buyers are usually successful in resisting the attempt. The seller's argument is not fatuous, however. The buyer clearly gets the benefit of unanticipated improvements in the financial condition due to such factors because the seller still must close; why not the downside as well?

This issue stems from the signing of a contract binding the parties to close the transaction before they are ready to close. The seller benefits because the buyer is legally obligated to close unless material problems about the company surface. The buyer, on the other hand, has the deal locked up, yet if significant problems arise, the buyer can terminate or renegotiate the acquisition. But from the seller's perspective, it has given up the upside (which should be reflected in the purchase price) but still retains the economic downside until the deal closes. Thus, if the parties' expectations prove untrue because oil is discovered on the property, the buyer gets the benefit. But if a new material lawsuit arises, the buyer can walk. In other words, once the contract is signed, the buyer is the owner, but only if things continue to look good.

It is for this reason that many sellers lately have attempted to shift the date of the transfer of risk from the seller to the buyer to the date the contract is signed. Their theory is: the buyer has to accept a balanced economic deal—it gets both the good and the bad occurring after the signing. So long as (i) the representations and warranties *as of the signing date* are accurate on the closing date and (ii) the seller doesn't breach its covenants concerning the conduct of the business pending closing, the buyer is getting what it bargained for.

The argument has logical appeal, particularly if there will be a great deal of time between the signing and closing, say, on account of the need for regulatory approvals. If the seller is going to push this point, it must also be willing to give up any earnings during the interim period.

Logic notwithstanding, the seller has an uphill battle. This is one of those situations where one custom is worth a thousand arguments. A buyer can be expected to resist strenuously on the grounds that "deals just aren't done this way," "Hey, you still control the operation of the business," or "my price doesn't take into account this type of risk." Because tradition is on the buyer's side, the seller can expect to have to give up something significant to win this point. Where the time span between signing and closing is customarily thirty to sixty days, it may not be worth the fight.

The seller's argument may prove too much. The buyer rarely is expected to assume the risk of other post-signing adverse changes, such as new lawsuits, major undisclosed liabilities, or major uninsured casualty losses. There is no logical basis for distinguishing financial deterioration resulting from a general recession from other types of risks. In any event, in a leveraged buyout the buyer must resist this attempt by the seller, because the buyer may not be able to close its financing in the face of negative events. It does not seem fair to tag the buyer with damages for failing to close in this situation, particularly if the seller knows it is selling in a highly leveraged transaction and if the buyer has obtained financing commitments in advance.

In order to govern events that occur before closing that will harm the financial condition of the company afterwards, the conditions to closing should require that there be no material adverse change in the "prospects" of the target. In the absence of such a provision, the buyer would be obligated to close under these circumstances. The seller often argues that the word "prospects" is too vague. The proper response is to be more specific, not to eliminate the concept and shift the risk to the buyer. Of course, there is no one correct answer as to who should bear the risk of loss associated with clear changes in the prospects of the target, and the buyer may be willing to undertake the risk of adverse events.

What happens if the buyer is aware of a material breach in a representation or warranty and nevertheless proceeds to close?

The buyer would be estopped from asserting a claim for damages based on the material breach because he had notice. Most likely the buyer has negotiated the price accordingly or does not consider the breach of the representation or warranty as substantially altering the basic terms or desirability of the transaction.

INDEMNITY SECTION

Why is there an indemnity section?

The purpose of the indemnification section is to set forth the circumstances under which either party can claim damages or take other remedial action in the event the other party to the agreement has breached a representation or warranty or failed to abide by its covenants. This section usually includes provisions concerning the procedural aspects of indemnity claims and the rights of the parties to take part in any legal proceedings that could give rise to an idemnity claim.

Why is there a need for an indemnity section? Can't the parties simply rely on their general legal rights?

The parties would have the right to collect damages or take other legal action in the event of a breach of a representation or warranty or a specific legal covenant. However, those rights are often vague and do not always comprehend the kinds of recovery to which the parties may feel entitled. For example, it is typical for the indemnity provision to provide specifically that all losses, including reasonable attorney fees and out of pocket expenses, will be recovered by the indemnified party. This is often not the result under general case law. In addition, the indemnification provisions contain specific rules governing the involvement of the indemnifying party in proceedings that could give rise to indemnification claims, as well as specific provisions governing the length of time that the representations and warranties will survive the closing.

The indemnity section also governs items that do not constitute a breach of a representation or warranty because they were specifically disclosed to the buyer at the time of the signing or closing but in respect of which the buyer nevertheless wishes protection. For example, the seller may, in the course of its due diligence, discover that there is a significant potential environmental claim under the federal Superfund laws, or that there is a continuing stream of uninsurable litigation claims attributable to a specific product manufactured by the target. Because the seller disclosed this fact to the buyer, there is no breach of a representation or warranty in connection with these items. However, the indemnification provisions may allocate to the seller the risks associated with disclosed items.

For what period of time is the buyer protected under the indemnity?

This issue is generally expressed in a different way: how long do the representations and warranties "survive" after the closing? Without a specific provision to the contrary, it is not clear that the representations and warranties survive at all. Consequently, the duration of the indemnity is often the subject of substantial negotiation. Theoretically, the statute of limitations applicable to actions for breach of contract could govern the claims under the contract, but in most cases the sellers feel that the statutory period is too long.

The buyer should request a two-year indemnity period. As a fallback position if the seller resists (and it will), the buyer can suggest that the indemnity continue until the buyer receives audited financial statements of the target for a full fiscal year of operations after the acquisition. Because of the time necessary to prepare the target's financials for its first full fiscal year, the buyer may obtain an indemnity period as long as 15 months after the acquisition closes.

One further point: it is important to provide that each party will be indemnified for all breaches discovered during the indemnity period, not merely for losses actually realized during that period. For example, a lawsuit brought by a third party during the period might not be finally resolved by the end of the period. The indemnified party should nevertheless be entitled to recover so long as the claim arose during the survival period.

Should the time limitation for recovering under the agreement apply to all claims under the contract?

The time limitation should not apply to breaches of covenants, which generally involve a willful act, or to willful breaches of representations or warranties. The seller shouldn't be offered reduced exposure for purposeful breaches. Representations and warranties about taxes customarily survive for the full period of limitation under applicable federal, state, or local law.

What is a "basket" and how does it work?

A basket is the dollar amount set forth in the indemnification provision as the loss that must be suffered by the buyer before it can recover damages under the indemnity provisions. In a transaction involving a purchase price of one hundred million dollars it would not be uncommon for the basket amount to be one million dollars or even higher. The buyer is often successful in arguing that the seller should indemnify losses resulting from breaches of covenants or willful breaches of representations and warranties without regard to the basket amount.

The basket closes the gap between the buyer and seller, and permits reasonable negotiation of the post-closing liability issue. The typical argument that the seller will make is,

"You're buying my business, warts and all." The standard buyer's response to this is: "We understand that we are accepting the risks of operating the business on a going forward basis, but we fully expect to get what we paid for without any significant deviation from the target described in the representations and warranties."

Both parties must assume that there will be problems with the business and realize that dollar-for-dollar compensation for imperfections is not realistic. The purchase price should take into account immaterial deviations from the expectations of the parties about the target. However, significant damages flowing from the breach of the representations or warranties may cause the buyer to overpay for the target. The happenstance that the problem arises after the signing or the closing rather than before should not put the buyer in a substantially worse position than if both parties knew of the problem in advance of the closing.

The dollar amount of the basket and the exact mechanics of its operation are often the subject of a great deal of negotiation between the buyer and the seller. It is unwise for the parties, particularly the buyer, to commit to an exact amount early in the negotiation process, since basket flexibility can become a negotiating tool. Seemingly intractable issues can often be resolved by adjusting one feature or another of the basket, including the dollar amount, even when the problematic issue is unrelated to the basket. For example, differences over the representations and warranties can be resolved if the parties negotiate the minimum amount of the claims, the basket amount, how claims are aggregated, or the length of the survival period. Common sense and negotiations experience dictate that the buyer should start *much lower* than it wants to end up.

What are the kinds of issues that most frequently arise in connection with a "basket"?

The first question is the size of the basket. Basket amounts in the range of 1% to 2% of the purchase price are most common, but much larger baskets (in the 4%–5% range) are not unheard of.

The next question about the basket is whether the buyer or the seller should absorb the amount of the basket once the threshold is crossed. For example, if the basket is $1 million and the buyer suffers $1.5 million in damages, is the seller liable for the $500,000 over the basket amount, the full $1.5 million, or for the $500,000 excess plus part of the $1 million? Most often the buyer absorbs the entire amount of the basket (so that in the example the seller would be liable for only $500,000).

There is a cogent argument that buyer and seller ought to split the losses up to the basket amount. The basket provides the *buyer* with incentive to do thorough due diligence, since the basket provision requires the buyer to absorb a significant part of any losses due to breaches of representations and warranties. Splitting liability for the basket amount has the benefit of providing the same incentive to the seller, because if the threshold of the basket is crossed, the seller will be required to pay some part of the initial basket amount. If the basket amount is not split, the buyer may have a legitimate concern that the seller will not be diligent in unearthing problems because it is protected by the basket, especially if the basket amount is large.

Another issue relates to minimum claims. Because the seller does not want to be bothered with small claims—however many of them there might be—the seller often asks for the following additional protection: no claim can be brought if the claim is for less than a specified amount (the "Minimum Amount"). The seller may insist that such claims not even count toward meeting the basket amount. Of course, the buyer should be expected to resist this approach, particularly if the Minimum Amount is significant in light of the size of the target's business. In addition, the buyer will likely request that these smaller claims be subject to the indemnity if they add up to a significant amount in the aggregate.

What is the relationship between the basket amount, the Minimum Amount, and the word "material" when used in connection with representations and warranties?

As discussed above, in order to limit the exposure of the seller for frivolous claims or claims that are appropriately part of the business that is being acquired by the buyer, many of the representations and warranties require disclosure only of material items, or items that are material to the business of the target and its subsidiaries taken as a whole. In the absence of a specific dollar threshold to define what is material, it is unclear exactly how much damage the buyer must incur before it can claim that there has been a breach of a representation containing a materiality limitation. These materiality limitations can create an unfair result for the buyer if there are several legal problems for the target that cause a significant aggregate loss for the buyer but there is no single breach that has a material adverse effect on the business.

The precise effect of the basket amount on all of this is uncertain. It might be argued that the basket amount is a numerical definition of the word "material." Thus, if the basket amount is $1 million, a loss of less than $1 million arising from a breach of a single warranty might not be viewed by a court interpreting the agreement as material to the business as a whole. But what if there are claims in five areas covered by representations and warranties, each of which amounts to $750,000? If the agreement is construed to mean that only a loss of more than $1 million is "material," the buyer will suffer $3.75 million of damage and will have no recourse against the seller. The result is not sensible, but in the absence of any other guidance it is a plausible result. If the parties do not wish the basket amount to be used as a definition of material, they should state so in the agreement.

Can use of a basket and a Minimum Amount provision eliminate the need for including materiality limitations in the representations and warranties?

It is possible to resolve the ambiguity of using the phrase "material" by using the concepts of the basket amount and Minimum Amount in the following manner. A representation or warranty would not be breached unless the resulting loss exceeded the minimum claim amount (say $50,000), and there would be no recovery by the buyer until all of the potential claims add up to the basket amount. This way the seller is assured that relatively minor imperfections in the business will not result either singly or in the aggregate in exposure for indemnity claims, and both parties will have a much better idea of what the expectations surrounding the indemnity provisions are.

The seller must exercise care here. The materiality limitations in the representations and warranties serve another function: they limit the ability of the buyer to terminate the transaction without penalty between the time of signing and closing. If the materiality limitations are eliminated altogether, the buyer could point to a minor legal defect in the business causing a loss equal to the Minimum Amount and say that the representations and warranties were not "true as of the closing date." This problem can be remedied either (i) by leaving the materiality limitations in the agreement solely for this purpose, as is often the case, or (ii) by leaving them out and requiring that potential losses equal the basket amount or some other agreed upon figure before the buyer would be permitted to terminate the transaction.

The latter solution can be very risky for the buyer. The basket amount is frequently the subject of negotiation and manipulation having little or nothing to do with the concept of materiality as incorporated into individual representations or warranties. The buyer may assess the risk of an unknown or undisclosed problem arising after the closing as small because it knows the target or the industry extremely well, or because it has tremendous faith in the management co-participants in the acquisition. It is also conceivable that the buyer may feel that it is getting a bargain price. In this situation, and because of the speculative nature of the losses, the buyer may be willing to agree to a very large basket amount.

On the other hand, the buyer might well feel that if problems actually arise before the closing, it should be free to reevaluate the wisdom of its decision to buy the target long before its losses reach the basket amount. To meet this concern, either a different threshold amount should be established for the Conditions to Closing section, or as is most often the case, the materiality caveats should remain in place in the representations and warranties for purposes of the Conditions to Closing section.

Is the indemnity sufficient protection for the parties, or are escrows or set-off rights necessary?

The indemnity alone is meaningless unless the indemnifying party is creditworthy. The parties should take care to satisfy themselves about the financial strength of indemnifying parties. This is achieved, in part, by the representations and warranties made by the buyer *and its owners* about its and their respective financial condition. Where there are doubts about the ability of the seller to meet its obligations, or where the target has many stockholders, it may be advisable to place a portion of the purchase price in escrow to serve as security for the seller's obligations under the indemnity. Under a typical escrow, which often (but not always) lasts as long as the survival period, the buyer has access to the escrowed funds after it is finally determined that the seller is liable under the indemnity portion of the contract.

Another device that is useful when the seller has a right to receive deferred payments is to give the buyer a right to set off any damages it suffers for breach of the contract against payments due the seller. Is a set-off permissible as a matter of law? Of course, it is legally acceptable and preferable for the parties to define the set-off rights in the agreement. Agreements may permit a set-off either after a final determination of liability or when a loss is suffered despite the fact that the buyer has not yet established the seller's liability. The latter arrangement reverses the normal posture of the parties negotiating a claim for indemnification—normally the indemnifying party has control of the money and the party who has suffered damages must sue to get it. For this reason, an immediate set-off right is fiercely, and usually successfully, fought off by the seller.

In the absence of a specific set-off provision, in most jurisdictions it does not appear that a buyer has the legal right to withhold payments from the seller until there is a final determination of liability under the indemnity. If note payments to the seller are withheld before such a determination, it is probable that a court would grant a summary judgment to the seller and force the buyer to pay principal and interest on the note in accordance with the terms even if the buyer has a separate claim under the contract.

Are there any special concerns of the seller in connection with the indemnity?

Most of the issues for the seller are covered in the preceding text since the basket amounts, survival period, and Minimum Amount are all issues of great concern to both parties. Obviously, the seller will try to avoid any indemnity at all.

In the case of a privately held target, the major thrust of the seller's argument is often to reinforce the basic argument outlined above about who assumes the risk of owning a business with the additional argument that if the target were a public company the representations and warranties would not survive the closing. This argument is more persuasive if there are public securities issued by the target so that it has been regularly filing public reports with the SEC and has a relatively long history of audited financial statements. One major reason for the different treatment of public companies is the impracticality of bringing suits against hundreds or even thousands of stockholders. This burden is not usually present in the sale of a closely held private company. Nevertheless, the apparent willingness of buyers in the public arena to live without indemnities, together with the sale of companies through auction procedures (discussed below), has allowed sellers to avoid indemnities in an increasing number of siuations.

When there are several selling stockholders, the sellers ought to (i) try to limit each stockholder's liability to "several" liability, meaning that one stockholder is not liable if another is unable to satisfy its liabilities under the indemnity, and (ii) be certain that breaches of representations and warranties that are specific to a stockholder, such as a stockholder's failure to have or convey good title to its shares being sold, will not create liability for other stockholders.

The sellers also should argue that there should be a limit on liability. Most buyers will agree to limit liability to the purchase price paid, and some sellers have been successful in arguing for a lower cap on liability, although a lower cap doesn't make much sense.

Finally, the sellers ought to pay close attention to the terms of notes they accept as part of the payment. In order to placate senior lenders, seller notes are often deeply subordinated (see discussion in Chapter 4 at pages 189–191) and contain provisions that limit the ability of the seller to sue if there is a payment default. A buyer should not be permitted to take advantage of this provision to hold back payments (i.e., create a payment default) when there is a potential claim under the indemnity. The subordination provisions are for the benefit of the senior lenders and are not designed to allow the buyer to use the seller's funds to finance indemnity claims; the limitation on the seller's remedies under the note ought not to apply to a constructive set-off by the buyer because of potential indemnity liabilities.

Are there any special items that a buyer is indemnified for even if they are disclosed, such as litigation?

Yes. In the course of due diligence the buyer will often uncover items for which it will either seek a price adjustment or request specific indemnification. Typical examples are unusual litigation that is not insured or reserved for on the balance sheet, and major environmental problems.

What about litigation arising after the closing based on business conducted before the acquisition?

In an asset transaction, the buyer usually does not assume the risk of such litigation and will obtain a specific indemnity against such losses from the seller.

In the case of a merger or stock acquisition, many contracts contain indemnities specifically protecting the buyer against this type of loss. Even in the absence of specific protection, it is at least arguable that such litigation is an unmatured and contingent undisclosed liability that constitutes a breach of the warranty, or an undisclosed liability to which the general indemnity applies.

Before engaging in lengthy negotiation about this issue, the parties should focus on insurance coverage for this type of loss. In this area, the availability of insurance coverage may render the parties' exposure immaterial. In most cases, insurance is on a "claims made" basis; i.e., the insured is protected against losses from claims made during the insurance period. If so, the target's insurance policy will provide protection in the ordinary course, and it would be unfair to expect the seller to cover such losses. It is critical to avoid an insurance coverage gap during which neither the old policy (because it is a "claims made" policy) nor the target's new policy (because it only insures claims based on events occurring during the insurance period) will make good on a legitimate claim. A gap is more likely to arise when the target is part of a conglomerate and coinsured under a single umbrella policy covering all members of the seller's corporate group. In this situation, the target must take out separate policies effective as of the closing date.

What is the purpose of the Termination Section of the agreement?

The Termination Section of the agreement sets forth the circumstances under which the transactions can be terminated by either party and the consequences of the termination. This section normally includes a date by which the closing must occur. If the closing fails to occur by that date as a result of the action or inaction of one party, the party that was capable of closing typically can elect to terminate the contract and sue the other party for breach of contract.

The section also allows a party to terminate if it discovers a material breach by the other of a representation, warranty, or covenant that would cause the bring-down condition to be unsatisfied. (See pages 558–560.) A party should not have to wait until the termination date to terminate if it is clear that it won't be obligated to close in any event.

This section will also set forth any limitation on damages that can be collected by the successful litigant for breach of the contract and any special remedies, such as specific performance, that a nonbreaching party may avail itself of. It is often the case that the requirements for security for the buyer's obligations as well as the condition under which the seller can resort to the security are set forth in this section.

What are the advantages and disadvantages of arbitration provisions in the agreement?

The oft-stated benefits of arbitration—quick and inexpensive resolution of disputes—may make arbitration a satisfactory mechanism by which a party to an acquisition agreement can enforce his rights. However, these benefits, which are not always attained, are sometimes achieved at the cost of a party not being able to appeal an incorrect decision or not having the opportunity to discover facts necessary to prove his claim. Arbitration is best suited for resolution of disputes of little economic consequence or of technical issues, such as valuation of inventory, not readily within the ken of a trial judge. However, even in the latter situation, the parties should consider whether the savings in time and money by arbitration are outweighed by the protections of judicial resolution, particularly where the amounts involved potentially constitute a significant multiple of litigation costs. Where the benefits of arbitration outweigh its disadvantages, the arbitration clause should be drafted to minimize the negative aspects of arbitration.

One factor which contributes to prompt resolution by arbitration is the use of a nonjudicial decisionmaker. An arbitrator's schedule will usually be more open and flexible than that of a court. However, an arbitrator may have biases or lack sufficient knowledge of the law or subject area to reach a proper decision. This disadvantage can be minimized by careful drafting. For example, if the agreement designates arbitration under the rules of the American Arbitration Association, the parties will have to choose an arbitrator from one or more lists of names provided to them. These arbitrators may be unsatisfactory. To avoid this situation, the acquisition agreement can designate another means of choosing an arbitrator, such as having each party choose its own arbitrator, who, in turn, select a third arbitrator.

A second factor which contributes to the speed of arbitration, as well as its lower costs, is the absence of discovery. In certain situations, the lack of discovery may not be a serious disadvantage. For example, if each party has sufficient familiarity with, or access to, the company's books and records, discovery may not be necessary to resolve a dispute concerning those documents. Even if discovery is necessary with regard to a particular issue, arbitration may still be a viable alternative to court. The parties can draft the agreement to allow some discovery but not so much as to make the arbitration process comparable to a judicial one. Furthermore, the extent of discovery can be made subject to decision of the arbitrators.

In drafting an arbitration agreement, the parties should attempt to anticipate all future disputes. If arbitration is broadly required for all disagreements, the parties may be barred from seeking emergency injunctive relief from a court. A narrow arbitration clause, however, may result in requiring counterclaims to be filed in court, thereby compounding, rather than simplifying, resolution of disagreements.

The parties should also draft the arbitration agreement with the controlling law of the relevant jurisdiction in mind. In many jurisdictions for example, absent the parties' agreement to the contrary, only the arbitrators have the power to subpoena witnesses. However, in New York State, the parties themselves have the power to issue subpoenas. Certain jurisdictions, such as California, are less likely than others to limit the scope of the arbitration clause. In those jurisdictions, courts tend to interpret narrow arbitration provisions to require arbitration of issues which the parties neither mentioned nor intended to be arbitrated.

Do the auction procedures that lately have become the rage for selling companies have any effect on the contract negotiation process?

Yes, a significant effect. In the auction process, a seller hires an investment banker to sell the target on a bid basis. The investment banker prepares a "book" describing the target and solicits bids from potential buyers. The buyers receive a form contract and are told that the bid should be accompanied by the form contract together with any changes to it required by the buyer. The buyer is expressly warned that extensive changes will be considered negatively in evaluating the competitive nature of the bid. Often the buyer is offered limited access to the target's management and carefully controlled opportunities for due diligence before the initial bid must be made. Needless to say, the form contract typically provides the buyer no indemnities and only limited representations and warranties. Typically, extensive changes are required to make the contract similar to a typical and *reasonable* buyer's contract.

After the investment banker winnows out unacceptable bids, the seller will deal with only a few serious bidders who are given the chance for more thorough due diligence, often including full, rather than limited, access to management. The seller's representatives will often negotiate the contracts submitted by those bidders in order to finalize the contract before a decision is made. Nevertheless, contract negotiations often continue even after the deal has been awarded to a specific bidder.

How should a buyer respond in this process? There is simply no clear answer. The response will depend entirely upon the strength of the buyer's desire to buy the target and its confidence that it knows the target well enough to take the risk of an "as-is" transaction. Even if the buyer is willing to take such risks, certain points should be addressed in the contract, and the buyer must insist upon the opportunity to do thorough due diligence.

First, the twofold purpose of representations and warranties must be remembered. The representations and warranties not only provide the basis for indemnities but also establish the buyer's right to refuse to close a deal if legal defects are discovered before the closing. The buyer should get representations and warranties ensuring that if the target is not up to legal snuff, the buyer may terminate the contract without penalty.

Second, at a bare minimum the seller should be willing to provide the buyer with indemnity for matters of which it has knowledge.

Third, the same arguments about the unfairness of the buyer "overpaying" apply here. The question is how far to carry the comments provided above.

The bid process often has an intended psychological affect on many buyers. The purchaser's lawyer is likely to hear: "Don't give me the world's most perfect contract. I want the absolute minimum protection I need. *Don't* overlawyer and cause me to get knocked out in the first round." The buyer, who often believes that the contractual protections are overkill by lawyers, gets spooked and doesn't want his lawyers to lose the deal. As noted above, and assuming that (1) the first two points above are accounted for in the contract, (2) the deal is priced on an "as-is" basis, and (3) the buyer is fully informed of the risks, proceeding with a minimum of comments to the seller's contract is not foolhardy.

If additional protection is desired, the buyer might require indemnification for breaches of representations and warranties made regarding the financial statements, undisclosed liabilities, taxes, and litigation. The pill can be made easier for the seller to swallow with generous Minimum Amount and basket provisions.

As a final word, the buyer should not be fooled by the putative formality of the bid procedures and the investment banker's stern admonitions. Most buyers do submit changes to the contract along the lines described above, and in the end the insiders will tell you that the *price* and a credible ability to close, and not the contract terms (provided they are reasonable), will dictate the results in most cases. A buyer which has concerns about the legal aspects of the target or its business should not hesitate to say that it reserves the right to submit further changes after it has been given complete access to management and an opportunity for full due diligence. It is not unusual for the buyer to submit a solid bid and indicate that it would like the opportunity to negotiate the terms of the contract with the seller face-to-face. Typically the buyer would also indicate the several areas where it would require changes.

Another favored approach is to do a relatively extensive mark up and suggest that the contract can be watered down in face-to-face negotiations after due diligence is completed. This approach is constructive because the seller will usually negotiate the contract with the two or three top bidders. Whatever the buyer sends in will be the starting point for negotiation. Even if the buyer is willing to accept only minimum protection, it is important to start ahead of where the buyer wants to end up.

Why have the auction procedures become so popular?

In the case of the sale of a public company, it is generally believed to be the best way of assuring that the highest possible price is obtained. The same sentiment probably drives the seller to use auction methods for sales of divisions or subsidiaries of companies. Also, who can fault a corporate executive for the price he or she agrees to if it was the result of a competitive bid procedure? Finally, with the publicity given the huge profits earned by leveraged buyout experts, a great deal of money is now chasing the same supply of companies being sold. The auction approach in many cases will be the best way to tap these sources of money. Do the auctions succeed in getting the best price? Most people, and certainly investment bankers who run the auctions, would say yes.

The auction process also saves the seller the time and effort of dealing with dozens of potential buyers until the process has reduced the number to a few serious bidders. Sellers must be very careful to supervise the way the investment bankers deal with the bidders. The *seller*, and not the investment banker, should be negotiating the deal, and many buyers are justifiably put off by having to negotiate substantive points through an intermediary. This is especially true where the bidder concedes points in exchange for concessions by the representatives only to have the representative come back and say, "your concessions are acceptable, but my principal has a few problems with some of the other points."

ACQUISITIONS FROM AN AFFILIATED GROUP

Are there any special aspects to be negotiated when the buyer is acquiring the assets of a division or the stock of a subsidiary that is a part of a larger corporate group?

There are numerous issues that arise under such circumstances that should be addressed:

1. Is the buyer getting all of the assets needed to operate the company as a separate business or are some critical assets located elsewhere in the group?
2. Are there any special, advantageous contractual or administrative relationships with the seller that must be continued (for example, supply or purchase contracts), or are there unfavorable ones that must be termi-

nated? This can be a very useful aspect of a transaction for the buyer or the seller. As part of the pricing and as an inducement to complete the transaction, one party can offer a favorable long-term contract to the other. Negotiations over that contract may act as a means for resolving other business issues.

3. Are there administrative services provided to the target by the group that should be continued for a period of time? In many cases the seller's group provides legal, accounting, billing, and other administrative support as well as shared office and warehouse space. Unless replacements will be available at closing, the agreement should contain provisions to continue those services at an agreed upon cost for a specified period of time (often ranging from 30 days to 9 months).

4. Finally, is it clear that the financial information about the target upon which the deal is based takes into account the need to provide for the services or other arrangements described in paragraphs 2 and 3 above?

TRANSACTIONS INVOLVING PUBLIC COMPANIES

Are acquisition agreements different when the target is a public company?

Yes. The acquisition agreement in a public company transaction is very different from the type of agreement used for a privately held target. The differences may be divided into two categories: (a) general differences in format and approach; and (b) certain specific provisions that are frequently found in agreements relating to publicly held companies. Before these differences are discussed, it is useful to understand some of the reasons for the differences.

How does such an agreement differ in general terms?

The basic difference is that the representations and warranties do not survive the closing of the transaction, so that the buyer is given no protection in the event breaches are discovered afterwards. In short, there is no indemnity provision, mainly because an indemnity against hundreds or thousands of shareholders is considered impractical. The buyer therefore must rely on the substantial disclosure required under federal securities laws as the basis for evaluating the legal and financial risks of ownership. It is generally assumed that those disclosures, which if materially inaccurate can give rise to criminal and civil liability on the part of the officers and directors, together with a history of audited financial statements also required under the securities laws, provide a reliable rendition of the legal-financial story of the target.

Because the representations and warranties don't survive anyway, and because of the extensive public disclosures, the representations and warranties tend to be far briefer in a public company deal. They serve more as a means of organizing due diligence. The buyer shouldn't get too carried away, however, with agreeing to gut the representations and warranties. As repeated so often in this chapter, these provisions serve another function—they provide the basis for a buyer terminating the transaction if the representations, warranties and covenants are breached in a material way. Therefore, although much of the detailed disclosures are eliminated, the key concepts must be retained. The key sections that would be retained in a public deal agreement are discussed in the introduction to the form agreement at the end of this chapter.

What are some of the specific provisions that appear in the public deal acquisition agreement?

First, the agreement will contain specific representations and warranties to the effect that the parties have complied with all applicable securities laws and, specifically, that the disclosures made pursuant to those laws are all materially accurate.

Second, the agreement will set forth the specific form of the transaction, e.g., a merger or a tender offer or a combination of the two, and what the responsibilities of the various parties will be for preparing, reviewing and filing the documents that must be filed with the Securities and Exchange Commission.

Finally, the agreement will set forth agreements relating to "lock-up options," bust-up or topping fees, and so-called "fiduciary-out" provisions, all of which are discussed below (see Chapter 12, pages 749–756).

APPENDIX 10A
SAMPLE LETTER OF INTENT

_____ 198_

Target Corporation
Corporate Office Park
New York, New York

Attention: _____
                President

Gentlemen:

This letter of intent sets forth the basic terms and conditions under which Acquisition, Inc. (the "Purchaser") will enter into a definitive merger agreement (the "Merger Agreement") with Target Corporation (the "Company") for the merger of the Purchaser with and into the Company (the "Merger"). It is anticipated that the consummation of the Merger will occur on or before _____,198_, or on such other date to which the parties may agree.

Purchase Price
Pursuant to the Merger Agreement, upon consummation of the Merger, the selling stockholders of the Company will receive in exchange for each share of the Company's common stock and preferred stock (the "Stock") outstanding as of the date of this letter:

(5) _____ Dollars ($_____) in cash; and

(6) One share of preferred stock ("Preferred Stock") of the surviving corporation of the Merger with a liquidation preference in the amount of _____ Dollars (_____) and containing the terms set forth on Exhibit A hereto.

Conditions to Closing

The consummation of the Merger shall be subject to the satisfaction of the following conditions:

(a) the parties shall have received all required approvals and consents from governmental authorities and agencies and third parties;

(b) the Purchaser and the Company shall have executed on or prior to _____, 198__ a definitive Merger Agreement containing mutually acceptable provisions relating to, among other things, representations, warranties, conditions and indemnification;

(c) the truth and accuracy of all representations and warranties and the satisfaction of all conditions;

(d) the consummation of the Merger on or prior to _____, 198__;

(e) Purchaser and certain members of management of the Company designated by Purchaser having entered into mutually satisfactory employment contracts simultaneously with the execution of the Merger Agreement;

(f) since _____, 198__, [date of last audited balance sheet] the business of the Company and its subsidiary shall have been conducted in the ordinary course, and there shall have been no material adverse change in the business, prospects, operations, earnings, assets or financial condition of the Company and its subsidiaries; [and]

(g) Purchaser shall have obtained financing in an amount and upon terms satisfactory to it to consummate the Merger; and]

(h) there shall have been no dividend, redemption or similar distribution, or any stock split, recapitalization or stock issuance of any kind, by the Company since _____, 198__ [date of last audited balance sheet] other than regularly scheduled dividends on the preferred stock.

General

After executing this letter and until _____, 198__, the Company agrees, and shall use its best efforts to cause its officers, directors, employees, agents and stockholders, not to solicit or encourage, directly or indirectly, in any manner any discussion with, or furnish or cause to be furnished any information to, any person other than Purchaser in connection with, or negotiate for or otherwise pursue, the sale of the Stock of the Company or the capital stock of its subsidiaries, all or substantially all of the assets of the Company or its subsidiaries or any portion or all of its business or that of its subsidiaries, or any business combination or merger of the Company or its subsidiaries with any other party. You will promptly inform Purchaser of any inquiries or proposals with respect to the foregoing. [In the event that the agreements in this paragraph are violated by the Company or its officers, directors, employees, agents or stockholders, and Purchaser does not consummate the Merger, then, in addition to other remedies available to Purchaser, Purchaser shall be entitled to receive from the Company all out-of-pocket expenses (including reasonable attorneys' fees and expenses relating to the financing), which Purchaser has incurred.

Neither of the parties to this letter shall disclose to the public or to any third party the existence of this letter or the proposed sale described herein other than with the express prior written consent of the other party, except as may be required by law.

From and after the date hereof, upon reasonable prior notice and during normal business hours, the Company will grant to each of Purchaser and its agents, employees and designees full and complete access to the books and records and personnel of the Company and its subsidiaries. Except as may be required by law or court order, all information so obtained, not otherwise already public, will be held in confidence.

[Except as provided herein,] each party will be responsible for its own expenses in connection with all matters relating to the transaction herein proposed. If this proposed transaction shall not be consummated for any reason other than a violation of the agreement not to solicit other offers or negotiate with other purchasers, neither party will be responsible for any of the other's expenses.

Each party will indemnify, defend and hold harmless the other against the claims of any brokers or finders claiming by, through or under the indemnifying party.

Except for matters relating to (i) the confidentiality of this proposal and the business operations of the Company and its subsidiary, (ii) the agreement not to negotiate with others for or otherwise pursue the sale of the Company or its subsidiary, and (iii) the agreement that each party will bear its own expenses in connection herewith, this letter does not create a binding, legal obligation on any party but merely represents the present intentions of the parties.

In the event that for any reason the definitive Merger Agreement is not executed by _____, 198__, any party may discontinue negotiations and terminate this letter without liability to any other party.

Your signature below shall indicate your agreement with the foregoing letter of intent. We look forward to working with you on this transaction.

Very truly yours,

Acquisition, Inc.

By: _____

Its: Vice President

Agreed to and Accepted
this ____ day of _____, 198__:

Target Corporation

By: _____

Its: _____

APPENDIX 10B

TYPICAL MERGER AGREEMENT AND COMMENTARY

Model Merger Agreement
Table of Contents

ARTICLE I

THE BUSINESS COMBINATION

The following is a discussion of the material items which are usually included in Article I of a merger agreement (the "Agreement"). The Section headings listed below provide the topics frequently covered in this Article.

Article I of the Agreement typically describes (a) how the merger will be accomplished (the "Merger"), (b) identifies which corporation's legal existence will cease and which corporation will be the "Surviving Corporation" in the Merger, and (c) identifies the state laws which will govern the surviving corporation's legal existence. This section also contains the agreement of the parties to meet the corporate legal requirements of the states of incorporation of the respective parties in order to obtain approval of the Merger.

The disappearing corporation frequently commits itself to call a special meeting of stockholders and to use its best efforts to obtain stockholder approval of the Merger. These undertakings tend to be more elaborate where the disappearing corporation is a publicly held corporation and therefore must provide a proxy statement or information statement to its stockholders.

Once the stockholders of the disappearing corporation have approved the Merger and the additional corporate actions and the conditions contained in Articles IX and X of the Agreement are satisfied, the Agreement provides that the articles of merger will be filed in the respective offices of the secretary of state (or comparable authority) of the states in which each corporation is incorporated. The Merger will become effective upon such filing. The effect of the Merger is described by reference to a section of the business corporation laws governing the corporate existence of each corporation involved in the transaction. Some states require the surviving corporation to appoint an agent for service of process if the surviving corporation will no longer be present or resident within the state following consummation of the Merger. This requirement is intended to enable creditors in the state to continue to have recourse against the disappearing corporation. The Merger will have no effect on the rights of creditors or on any liens on the property of either company; liens and debts of the disappearing corporation will become the obligations of the surviving corporation.

The parties stipulate in this Article which corporation's articles and bylaws will apply to the surviving corporation and whether any changes or amendments to these documents will be made upon the consummation of the Merger. The officers and directors of the surviving corporation may also be identified.

In order to preserve structural flexibility, the buyer can suggest the inclusion of language which gives the buyer the right to restructure the transaction for tax, financial, or other reasons. Because a change in the structure of the transaction could have a significant adverse impact on the seller if, for example, the direction of the Merger were to be changed from downstream to upstream, the buyer and seller must reach a resolution which satisfies each of their concerns.

ARTICLE II

CONVERSION AND EXCHANGE OF SHARES

The following discussion pertains to the mechanics of the conversion of shares of the merging corporations and the transfer of the purchase price. The Section headings listed below provide the topics generally covered in this Article.

Section 2.1	Conversion of Shares
Section 2.2	Dissenting Stockholders
Section 2.3	Stock Transfer Books
Section 2.4	Surrender and Exchange of Stock Certificates
Section 2.5	Determination and Payment of Merger Payment

This Article describes the manner in which shares in each of the merging corporations will be converted or, in the case of the surviving corporation, the number of shares that remain outstanding upon consummation of the Merger. It also describes the nature of the cash or securities consideration to be received by each holder of stock of the non-surviving corporation.

Where the disappearing corporation has a diverse group of stockholders, the buyer may wish to consider the potential effects of stockholders' exercise of their dissenters' or appraisal rights under the laws of a particular jurisdiction. In transactions where exercise of dissenters' rights may occur, the buyer should include a provision which describes the effect of the Merger on such stockholders' rights and imposes an obligation upon the seller and target to give the buyer notice of any communications by stockholders with respect to their dissenters' or appraisal rights. The notice obligation is frequently included in the covenant section. The buyer should also attempt to procure for itself the opportunity to direct all negotiations and proceedings concerning these rights.

Also included in this Article is the method of surrender and exchange of stock certificates which enables the stockholders of the disappearing corporation to receive the Merger payment. For a closely held target this may simply involve the seller's surrender of the certificates to the buyer and the buyer's payment to the seller of the agreed-upon Merger consideration. However, in the case of a public target or where the target has a significant number of stockholders, the method for surrender of certificates is somewhat more complicated. The buyer and target will agree that the stock transfer books of the target will be closed as of a particular time, usually the time of the filing of the certificate of merger with the secretary of state, and that stockholders must surrender their certificates to a paying agent which will be responsible for the disbursement of the Merger payment. Typically, the buyer will agree that simultaneously with the consummation of the Merger it will transfer the entire amount of the Merger consideration to an account which will be administered by a paying agent. Funds in the account are then disbursed to the target's stockholders upon the surrender of their stock certificates. See Chapter 5, pages 218–219 for a discussion concerning the timing of the payment of the Merger consideration and the filing of the certificate of merger.

In the event that the target has outstanding preferred stock, options, warrants, or securities convertible into common stock, the buyer should make provision in this Article for the effect that the Merger will have on such securities. The buyer's preeminent concern in dealing with these securities is to extinguish through the Merger, to the extent possible, any right that a third party may have to receive common stock of the surviving corporation and not be subject to any dilution as a result of the exercise or conversion of any such securities. This assures the buyer that it will hold one hundred percent of the common stock of the surviving corporation immediately after the Merger. In certain cases the terms of such securities require the surviving corporation to honor the holder's right to receive common stock; other securities merely fail to provide for their termination in the event of a Merger. The buyer should always attempt to include, as a condition to the buyer's obligation to close the transaction, the agreement of all holders of such securities to surrender their securities for cancellation at the Closing.

ARTICLE III

CLOSING

This Article provides the date, time, and place for the closing of the transaction (the "Closing"). Typically, the parties agree to close the transaction at the offices of the legal counsel for the buyer. Closings generally commence early in the morning so that wire transfers of funds can be accomplished prior to the afternoon close of the Federal wire. The parties further agree that at the Closing the parties will deliver all of the documents and instruments required to be delivered by the acquisition agreement. (The date that the certificate of merger is filed with the appropriate officials governing the Merger is referred to as the "Closing Date.") For a more detailed discussion of the Closing procedures, see Chapter 11.

ARTICLE IV

REPRESENTATIONS AND WARRANTIES OF SELLER AND TARGET

The representations and warranties included in this Article are extremely comprehensive and may, in some instances, be inappropriate in light of the size of the transaction or the nature of the target's business.

In an acquisition of a publicly traded target, it would not be customary to include all of these representations and warranties. As we previously mentioned, the reason for fewer representations and warranties in a public context is that there is usually no one to sue after closing for a misrepresentation or breach of warranty. It is unrealistic for the buyer to expect to recover from thousands of public stockholders. Accordingly, some of the representations and warranties, which are of less importance to the buyer or not directly related to the buyer's ability to terminate the acquisition agreement due to certain adverse changes in the target, are frequently omitted. For example, the following sections in Article IV are typically omitted in the acquisition of a publicly traded target:

Section 4.4	Title to Securities of Target and Subsidiaries
Section 4.9	Solvency
Section 4.10	Debt
Section 4.12	Product and Service Warranties and Reserves
Section 4.13	Reserves for Public Liability and Property Damage Claims
Section 4.18	Intellectual Property
Section 4.19	Assets Necessary to the Business
Section 4.21	Customers and Suppliers
Section 4.22	Competing Lines of Business
Section 4.23	Restrictive Covenants
Section 4.24	Books and Records
Section 4.25	Bank Accounts
Section 4.35	Investment Purpose
Section 4.36	Dealership and Franchises

For further information concerning the acquisition of public securities, see Chapter 12.

The Seller and the Target represent and warrant to Buyer as follows:

Section 4.1. Organization; Subsidiaries and Other Ownership Interests. The Target and the Seller are each corporations duly organized, validly existing and in good standing under the laws of the jurisdiction of their incorporation. Section 4.1 of the disclosure statement of even date herewith delivered to Buyer by Seller (the "Disclosure Statement") sets forth the name of each Person (as defined in Article XII) in which the Target or any other Subsidiary (on a combined basis) owns or has the right to acquire, directly or indirectly, an equity interest or investment of ten percent (10%) or more of the equity capital thereof or having a book value of more than _____ Dollars ($_____) (a "Subsidiary"). Each Subsidiary is duly organized, validly existing and in good standing under the laws of its jurisdiction of incorporation or organization. Each of the Target and the Subsidiaries has the corporate or other necessary power and authority to own and lease its properties and assets and to carry on its business as now being conducted and is duly qualified or licensed to do business as a foreign corporation or other entity and is in good standing in each jurisdiction in which the properties owned or leased by it or the nature of the business conducted by it makes such qualification or licensure necessary except where the failure to be so qualified or licensed and in good standing would not have a Material Adverse Effect. For purposes of this Agreement, the term Material Adverse Effect shall refer to any event which would have a material adverse effect on the financial condition, business, earnings, assets, prospects or condition of the Target and its Subsidiaries taken as a whole. Section 4.1 of the Disclosure Statement sets forth the name of each jurisdiction in which the Target and each Subsidiary is incorporated and is qualified to do business. The Target has delivered to the Buyer true and correct copies of its Certificate of Incorporation and Bylaws and true and correct copies of the certificate of incorporation or comparable charter documents and bylaws of each of the Subsidiaries. Except as set forth in Section 4.1 of the Disclosure Statement, neither the Target nor any Subsidiary owns any equity investment or other interest in any Person other than the equity capital of the Subsidiaries which are owned by the Target or a Subsidiary.

It is customary in acquisition agreements to have the seller and target warrant that the seller, the target, and its subsidiaries are duly organized, and that each is qualified to do business in every jurisdiction in which each is required to qualify. If the seller or the target is not duly organized, the acquisition agreement may not be binding against it since it will not have the authority to execute the document in a corporate capacity. The utility of this representation is often debated in a theoretical context but is rarely heavily negotiated. Underlying the debate is the following question: if the agreement is not binding on the seller or the target, whom do you sue and for what? While the answer is not carved in stone, the buyer could probably sue the person who signed the document in an individual capacity for misrepresentation, although a sizeable recovery is unlikely. More importantly, the buyer would certainly have the right to walk from the deal, and that right is the primary reason the buyer should require this representation.

It is also prudent for the buyer to know that the subsidiaries are duly organized and qualified to do business in order to be assured of the subsidiaries' ability to conduct business or maintain a suit in a particular jurisdiction.

The definition of subsidiaries in this provision is extremely broad as it includes entities in which the target may only have a small equity interest. Depending upon the particular situation, the seller may want to increase the ten percent ownership requirement in order to avoid making representations and warranties about entities with which it may not be overly familiar. In addition, the seller may wish to specifically exclude from this definition entities which are not material to the target.

> *Section 4.2. Authorization.* The execution, delivery and performance of this Agreement and any instruments or agreements contemplated herein to be executed, delivered and performed by Target or Seller (including without limitation [list important agreements to be executed on or before the Closing]) (the "Related Instruments"), and the consummation of the transactions contemplated hereby and thereby, have been duly adopted and approved by the Board of Directors and the Stockholders of the Target and the Board of Directors of the Seller, as the case may be. The Target and the Seller have all requisite power and authority to execute, deliver and perform this Agreement and the Related Instruments, as applicable, and to consummate the transactions contemplated hereby and in the Related Instruments. This Agreement has been and as of the Closing Date, and each of the Related Instruments will be, duly and validly authorized, executed and delivered on behalf of the Seller and the Target. This Agreement is and the Related Instruments will be as of the Closing Date, the valid and binding obligation of the Target and Seller, as applicable, enforceable against the Target or Seller, as the case may be, in accordance with their respective terms.

It is customary for the seller and target to represent to the buyer that the Agreement is properly authorized and enforceable. Certainly, the buyer is entitled to know that the seller and target have taken all the steps which are necessary to authorize the agreement and any documents which are material to the consummation of the transaction (referred to above as the "Related Instruments") in order to ensure that such documents are binding. The Related Instruments might include a non-compete agreement, a separate purchase agreement relating to certain other assets, and other documents containing agreements between the parties which are special to the transaction and therefore are not specifically covered by a stock purchase, asset purchase, or merger agreement.

The most important aspect of this representation relates to enforceability of the agreement and Related Instruments as this will directly affect the buyer's rights under these documents.

A similar issue arises here as was discussed in connection with Section 4.1. What damages would be recoverable by the buyer if the seller breached this representation? If the breach arises because the signatory to the document on behalf of the seller or the target did not have authority to bind that party, the buyer may have a cause of action against the signatory (if the signatory misrepresented his authority) or against the party on whose behalf the signatory executed the document (if such party knew of the misrepresentation, or if the acts of such party created the appearance of authority on the part of the signatory). In addition, the buyer faced with a seller or target who refuses to close the deal because the Agreement was not signed by an authorized agent may be able to force the seller or target to close the transaction if their acts created an appearance of authority, or if they ratified the Agreement after it was signed. Partial performance of the terms of the deal—application for regulatory approval, permitting continued due diligence investigation, or complying with representations requiring the consent of the buyer to certain actions by the target, for example—may provide convincing evidence of such ratification. In any event, the buyer would definitely have the right to refuse to close the transaction.

In a representation by the seller that an agreement is enforceable, the seller may request the inclusion of an exception for certain future events that are beyond its control. For example, a court applying bankruptcy laws or equitable principles may not honor the express terms of the documents if such terms are not in accordance with the principles of bankruptcy or equity. While the seller may have a basis for arguing for the inclusion of this exception, it seems unfair for the buyer to bear this risk. If the documents prove to be unenforceable in some respect against the seller, the buyer should be able, at least, to attempt to recover damages for this misrepresentation, rather than be forced to waive rights in the case of bankruptcy.

Section 4.3. Capitalization of Target and Subsidiaries

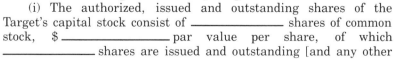

(i) The authorized, issued and outstanding shares of the Target's capital stock consist of _____ shares of common stock, $ _____ par value per share, of which _____ shares are issued and outstanding [and any other shares, such as preferred stock] (the "Company Capital Stock"). The issued and outstanding shares of the Company Capital Stock are duly authorized, validly issued and fully paid and nonassessable and were not issued in violation of the preemptive rights of any person or of any agreement, law or regulation by which the issuer of such shares at the time of issuance was bound. The authorized, issued and outstanding equity capital of each Subsidiary is listed in Section 4.3(i) of the Disclosure Statement. The outstanding shares of, and the outstanding units of equity capital of, the Subsidiaries have been duly authorized, validly issued and are fully paid and non-assessable. Neither the Target nor any Subsidiary has issued any securities, or taken any action or omitted to take any action, giving rise to claims for violation of federal or state securities laws or the securities laws of any other jurisdiction.

(ii) Except as set forth in Section 4.3(ii) of the Disclosure Statement, at the date hereof there is no option, warrant, call, convertible security, arrangement, agreement, or commitment of any character, whether oral or written, relating to any security of, or phantom security interest in, the Target or any Subsidiary, and there are no voting trusts or other agreements or understandings with respect to the voting of the capital stock of the Target or the equity capital of any Subsidiary.

A representation which requires that a seller set forth the capitalization of the target and its subsidiaries is rarely negotiated. Rather, discussions between the buyer and seller generally involve the factual circumstances surrounding the matter being represented. In order for a buyer to understand the effect of its purchase of the capital stock of the target (including the capital stock of the subsidiaries), it must be aware of the capital structure of the target and its subsidiaries.

Section 4.4. Title to Securities of Target and Subsidiaries

(i) Except as set forth in Section 4.4(i) of the Disclosure Statement, the Seller has good and valid title to all of the issued and outstanding shares of the Company Capital Stock free and clear of all claims, liens, mortgages, charges, security interests, encumbrances and other restrictions or limitations of any kind whatsoever (other than pursuant to this Agreement). The Seller is not party to, or bound by, any other agreement, instrument or understanding restricting the transfer of such shares.

(ii) Except as set forth in Section 4.4(ii) of the Disclosure Statement and other than pursuant to this Agreement, the issued and outstanding units of equity capital of each of the Subsidiaries are owned by the Persons listed as owner on Section 4.4(ii) of the Disclosure Statement, in each case free of preemptive rights and free and clear of all claims, liens, mortgages, charges, security interests, encumbrances and other restrictions or limitations of any kind whatsoever.

Generally, a buyer entering into an acquisition agreement is acquiring the entire company. Therefore, it is essential that the buyer know that it is purchasing all of the outstanding capital securities of the target, and that no one can challenge its ownership thereof post-Closing.

Section 4.5. Financial Statements and Projections

(i) Seller has furnished to Buyer true and complete copies of the audited consolidated financial statements (including balance sheets, statements of income, statements of changes in stockholder's equity and statements of changes in financial position) of the Target and its Subsidiaries as of and for the years ended [fill in fiscal year-end for last five years] accompanied by the related opinions of the Target's official independent auditors as of such dates and for such periods (collectively, the "Financial Statements"). The Financial Statements, together with the notes thereto, fairly present the consolidated financial position of the Target and its Subsidiaries at the dates of, and the combined results of the operations and the changes in stockholders' equity and financial position for each of the Target and its Subsidiaries for the periods covered by, such Financial Statements in accordance with generally accepted accounting principles ("GAAP") consistently applied with prior periods except as indicated in the accompanying opinion of the official independent auditors. Seller has furnished to Buyer true and complete copies of the unaudited consolidated and consolidating balance sheets of the Target and its Subsidiaries as at [fill in the date of the most recent quarterly or fiscal period then ended] (the "Most Recent Balance Sheet") and the related consolidated and consolidating statements of income, statements of changes in stockholders' equity and statements of changes in financial position of the Target and its Subsidiaries as of and for the period then ended (collectively, the "Unaudited Financial Statements"). The Unaudited Financial Statements fairly present the financial position of the Target and its Subsidiaries at the date of, and the consolidated results of the operations and the changes in stockholders' equity and financial position for the Target and of its Subsidiaries for the period then ended. Such Unaudited Financial Statements have been prepared in accordance with GAAP consistently applied with prior periods, except that the Unaudited Financial Statements do not contain any or all of the footnotes required by GAAP, are condensed and are subject to year-end adjustments consistent with prior practice.

(ii) Seller has delivered to Buyer true and correct copies of the projected balance sheets of the Target for the fiscal years ending [fill in appropriate information], and the related statements of projected earnings and projected cash flow for the periods then ended (the "Projected Financial Statements"). The Projected Financial Statements are reasonable and mathematically accurate, and the assumptions underlying such projections provide a reasonable basis for such projections. The factual data used to prepare the Projected Financial Statements are true and correct in all material respects.

Generally, the most important representation that a buyer must require of the seller is that the consolidated financial statements of the target fairly present the financial condition of the target in accordance with GAAP. Almost every other representation in an acquisition agreement is in some way related to the financial statements of the target. For example, representations relating to receivables, inventory, real property, and tangible and intangible assets and liabilities concern items which are included on the balance sheet of the target to the extent required by GAAP. Accordingly, while the financial statement representations are somewhat standard in their format, they are vital to the buyer because the buyer has based its entire investment decision on either the overall financial condition of the target or certain financial characteristics of the target such as operating performance or net assets. As a result, the financial statements are usually the basis for fixing the purchase price of the target. Although situations exist where financial statements are less vital to the buyer's investment decision (for example, in the purchase of a start-up company), such statements are usually of critical importance.

The financial statement representation is usually not the subject of intense negotiation. The most frequently negotiated aspects of this representation relate to the kind of financial statements to be included in this representation and the periods to be covered by such financial statements. For example, will the financial statements which are the subject of the representation include balance sheets, operating statements, statements of changes in financial position, and stockholders' equity? Will the seller warrant the accuracy of historical financial statements covering a five-year period? Another area of discussion may relate to specific problems in preparing the financial statements which require the buyer to grant certain exceptions from GAAP. This problem usually arises when the buyer is already aware of the target's accounting problems. However, exceptions from GAAP can have the effect of diminishing the reliability of the financial statements. The determination whether the buyer is entitled to certain financial statements or should accept statements not prepared in accordance with GAAP depends on what information about the target was provided to the buyer prior to striking a deal with the seller, and what the buyer honestly relied on when it made its decision to purchase the target.

In many circumstances, the seller has provided the buyer with projected financial statements of the target. In such cases, if the buyer has relied on them, it is prudent for the buyer to have the seller warrant the reasonableness of the assumptions used in the preparation of the projected financial statements and the accuracy of the financial data underlying such projections. This representation is frequently negotiated and will certainly be more difficult to obtain from the seller than representations regarding the historical financial statements of the target. The reason for this is that projections, no matter how reasonable the assumptions which underlie them, are always the subject of hindsight. For example, a buyer might claim a breach of this representation if, one year after Closing, the target fails to meet its projections. The buyer would argue that the projections were obviously based upon unreasonable assumptions given the post-Closing performance of the target. The decision whether or not this representation should be pursued is, like decisions related to historical financials, largely dependent on the degree of the buyer's reliance on these projections in its decision to buy the target. If the buyer is heavily relying on the projections, which may very well be the case if the target is a company that does not have a long operating history, then this representation should be vigorously pursued. In addition, this representation will commonly be found in loan agreements and lenders will be able to gain some additional comfort from the buyer's right of action back to the seller on this representation.

> ***Section 4.6. Absence of Undisclosed Liabilities.*** As of the date hereof and as of the Closing Date, except as and to the extent reflected, reserved against or otherwise disclosed on the Most Recent Balance Sheet or the notes thereto, or set forth in Section 4.6 of the Disclosure Statement, or otherwise properly disclosed in any other Section of the Disclosure Statement and except for those incurred in the ordinary course of business, the Target and its Subsidiaries did not have and do not have, any indebtedness or liability of any nature, whether accrued, absolute, contingent or otherwise, whether due or to become due, which is in excess of ＿＿＿＿＿ Dollars ($＿＿＿＿＿).

The absence of undisclosed liabilities is by and large a representation which serves as a catch-all for any and all liabilities of the target and its subsidiaries which were not reflected on the Most Recent

Balance Sheet of the target or the notes thereto, or were not otherwise disclosed pursuant to any of the other representations in the acquisition agreement. A smart seller should never agree to this representation without some resistance. To begin with, why should the seller (after having made numerous representations about the target) now be asked to warrant something the buyer may have failed to ask the seller to disclose? The answer is one which relates to a shifting of risk. Who should bear the risk of the buyer's omission? There is no clear answer, except that if the seller has agreed to the concept that it will generally warrant that the Most Recent Balance Sheet includes all liabilities of any kind or nature, then this representation does little more than provide additional comfort for the buyer.

If the seller had not made that general warranty, the buyer should be aware that many liabilities need not be disclosed on a balance sheet of the target prepared in accordance with GAAP. For example, when the amount of a liability cannot be determined because of its nature, like a lawsuit the outcome of which is uncertain, GAAP would not require its disclosure. See Financial Accounting Standards Board Statement No. 5. If the target is subject to off-balance-sheet liabilities, this representation provides the buyer with much more than an additional assurance.

Another aspect of this representation which may be difficult to negotiate with the seller is the period of time to be covered by the representation. A buyer often wants protection against material liabilities beyond the date of the Most Recent Balance Sheet. This may be a problem for the seller since it has no financial statements to rely on for that period. The seller may be able to supply a balance sheet which is current as of the Closing. If this is not possible, and if the buyer fails to persuade the seller to warrant the period after the date of the Most Recent Balance Sheet, the buyer must rely on the covenants (operation of the business in the ordinary course, see Section 6.1 below) or the conditions (material adverse change, see Section 9.6 below) as its way of addressing undisclosed liabilities.

In light of the nature of this representation it would be overreaching not to incorporate an exclusion for minimal undisclosed liabilities. Accordingly, the form of representation set forth above contains a blank amount for such an exclusion. The dollar amount of this exclusion is negotiable and usually depends upon the size of the target and its subsidiaries. For example, in an acquisition of an extremely large company, the buyer would find it extremely difficult to justify an exclusion of only one thousand dollars ($1,000) for undisclosed liabilities.

Section 4.7. Accounts Receivable. Seller has delivered, or shall deliver at Closing, to Buyer a list of all accounts receivable of the Target and its Subsidiaries as at [fill in appropriate date] (the "Accounts Receivable") which list is true, correct and complete in all material respects and sets forth the aging of such Accounts Receivable. All Accounts Receivable of the Target and its Subsidiaries represent sales actually made or services actually performed in the ordinary and usual course of their business consistent with past practice. Since the date of the Most Recent Balance Sheet, (A) no event has occurred that would, under the practices of the Target or the Subsidiary in effect when the Most Recent Balance Sheet was prepared, require a material increase in the ratio of (I) the reserve for uncollectible accounts receivable to (II) the accounts receivable of the Target or the Subsidiary, and (B) there has been no material adverse change in the composition of such Accounts Receivable in terms of aging. There is no contest, claim or right of set-off contained in any written agreement with any account debtor relating to the amount or validity of any Account Receivable, or any other account receivable created after the date of the Most Recent Balance Sheet, other than accounts receivable which do not exceed, in the aggregate, the reserve for uncollected accounts. At the date of the Most Recent Balance Sheet, as of the date hereof and as of the Effective Time of the Merger, all accounts receivable of the Target and the Subsidiary, if any, were, are and will be, respectively, unless previously collected, valid and collectible and there is no contest, claim or right of set-off contained in any written agreement with any maker of an account receivable relating to the amount or validity of such account or any note evidencing the same.

In instances where the Most Recent Balance Sheet reflects a significant amount of receivables, the buyer should require this representation in order to get specific protection that the receivables of the target and its subsidiaries are collectible. A representation with respect to the receivables of the target is sometimes unnecessary depending upon the type of company that is being acquired. For example, if the company that is being acquired entered into a factoring arrangement with respect to all of its receivables, then this representation may be altogether unnecessary or to a great degree simplified. Conversely, the buyer purchasing assets may, in circumstances where the collectibility of the accounts is in doubt, require the seller to guarantee the buyer's ability to collect the receivables.

Section 4.8. Most Recent Inventory. The inventories of the Target and the Subsidiaries on a consolidated basis as reflected on the Most Recent Balance Sheet consist only of items in good condition and saleable or usable in the ordinary course of business, except to the extent of the inventory reserve included on the Most Recent Balance Sheet, which reserve is adequate for such purpose. Such inventories are valued on the Most Recent Balance Sheet at the lower of cost or market in accordance with GAAP.

In the event that the company to be acquired is engaged in manufacturing or is otherwise involved in the distribution of goods whether retail or wholesale, it is extremely important for the buyer to have the seller make a specific representation with respect to the inventory of the target and its subsidiaries. A buyer needs to understand the relationship between the value of the inventory reflected on the Most Recent Balance Sheet and the condition of the inventory. Items which are or may become obsolete should be reserved against on the Most Recent Balance Sheet. In addition, it is important for the buyer to know whether the valuation of inventory on the financial statements reflects its actual value. Accordingly, the seller's representation that inventories are valued at the lower of cost or market in accordance with GAAP will assure the buyer that the inventories are valued in the most conservative fashion. In some cases, the buyer may include a representation that a particular dollar amount is the minimum value of the target's inventories. That type of representation is more common in an asset purchase.

Section 4.9. Solvency. The Seller and each of the Target and its Subsidiaries is on the date hereof, and immediately prior to the Closing Date will be, Solvent. "Solvent" shall mean, in respect of an entity, that (i) the fair value of its property is in excess of the total amount of its debts and (ii) it is able to pay its debts as they mature.

Aside from the obvious pricing implications of acquiring an insolvent corporation, one of the primary purposes of obtaining a solvency representation from a seller regarding the target and its subsidiaries is that lenders providing acquisition debt often require such a representation from the buyer. Especially in leveraged buyouts, one of the principal concerns of lenders is the solvency of the leveraged company because transfers (e.g., security interests granted to lenders) from insolvent companies are voidable as fraudulent conveyances. While the leveraged surviving corporation may certainly be in a more precarious position than the target, this representation provides the initial base from which the buyer will attempt to satisfy its lenders on the solvency issue.

The solvency representation regarding the seller is intended to protect the buyer against the risk of acquiring the target and its subsidiaries in a transaction which could be characterized as a fraudulent conveyance by the seller. A buyer's decision to include the seller in the solvency representation must be based upon the financial condition of the seller, the extent to which the target and its subsidiaries constitute a substantial portion of the seller's assets and the seller's ability to pay its debts as they mature after the sale of the target and its subsidiaries.

> *Section 4.10. Debt.* Set forth in Section 4.10 of the Disclosure Statement is a list of all agreements for incurring of indebtedness for borrowed money and all agreements relating to industrial development bonds to which the Target is a party or grantor, which list is true and correct in all material respects. Except as set forth in Section 4.10 of the Disclosure Statement, none of the obligations pursuant to such agreements are subject to acceleration by reason of the consummation of the transactions contemplated hereby, nor would the execution of this Agreement or the consummation of the transactions contemplated hereby result in any default under such agreements.

This representation serves to break down the debt components of the Most Recent Balance Sheet which relate to debt for money borrowed. It also requires the seller to identify debt items which may be accelerated by reason of the consummation of the transactions contemplated by the Agreement. Because this representation has an information gathering purpose, it is not usually negotiable.

> *Section 4.11. Fairness Opinion.* The Target has received an opinion of [name of independent and nationally recognized investment banker], dated the date hereof, addressed to the Target and has delivered a copy of such opinion to Buyer to the effect that, as of the date of the Agreement, the consideration per share to be received by the holders of the Target's Common Stock in the Merger is fair to the holders of the Target's Common Stock from a financial point of view. The Target believes that it is justified in relying upon such opinion.

The buyer should attempt to include this representation where the target has a significant number of stockholders or is a publicly traded company. The buyer should require the target to obtain a fairness opinion because, after consummation of the Merger, the buyer will succeed to the target's liabilities, including liabilities that may result from stockholder suits against the target or its officers and directors alleging that the Merger price was inadequate. Liabilities could result where stockholders have exercised dissenter's or appraisal rights and sued the target directly or have instituted a derivative suit against officers or directors who are indemnified by the target.

The last sentence of the representation regarding reliance is intended to elicit from the target any facts that might undermine the validity of the opinion, such as facts not disclosed to the investment bankers or knowledge of conflicts of interest that might tend to bias the opinion. Several factors make this reliance representation important. First, investment bankers typically require indemnification in connection with rendering fairness opinions, and the buyer will succeed to any liability of the target to its investment bankers after the Merger. Second, although a target might argue that the buyer is in a position to evaluate the reasonableness of the opinion based on the representations of the target in the Agreement and on its own financial investigation of the target, the buyer is not privy to all the circumstances involving the preparation and delivery of the fairness opinion. Consequently, the buyer should not be reticent about making inquiries into the fairness opinion process and the manner in which the target has attempted to satisfy itself that the opinion rendered is reasonable.

> *Section 4.12. Product and Service Warranties and Reserves.* Except as disclosed in Section 4.12 of the Disclosure Statement, the amount of any and all product warranty claims relating to sales occurring on or prior to the Most Recent Balance Sheet Date shall not exceed the amount of the product warranty reserve included on the Most Recent Balance Sheet which reserve was prepared in accordance with GAAP consistently applied and which the Target believes is adequate in light of any and all circumstances relating to its warranties of which it was aware and the amounts actually paid by it for product warranty claims. The only express warranties, written or oral, including without limitation, [insert warranty], with respect to the products or services sold by the Target and its Subsidiaries are as set forth in Section 4.12 of the Disclosure Statement.

One area that may expose a buyer to tremendous liability is product and service warranties made by the target or any subsidiary. A seller is required under GAAP to have "adequate" reserves on its balance sheet to cover such liabilities, but this standard is a very subjective one. Accordingly, a prudent buyer should have the seller specifically warrant the accuracy of this element of the Most Recent Balance Sheet. In addition, the buyer should be apprised of any and all of the warranties made and reserves held by the target so that the buyer can make its own determination of the adequacy of the target's reserves. In certain situations, a buyer may require specific representations setting forth the annual amount paid in satisfaction of claims under a particular product warranty. Gambling on the law of averages, the buyer may derive some degree of comfort.

Section 4.13. Reserve for Public Liability and Property Damage Claims. The amount of the public liability, property damage and personal injury reserve included on the Most Recent Balance Sheet was prepared in accordance with GAAP consistently applied and the Target reasonably believes such reserve is adequate.

A buyer may be concerned about this type of liability if it is foreseeable that the target or a subsidiary could have exposure above and beyond the limits of its insurance policies. Similar to the product warranty reserve discussed in Section 4.12 above, the adequacy of this reserve is a subjective judgment.

Section 4.14. Insurance. Set forth in Section 4.14 of the Disclosure Statement is a complete and correct schedule of all currently effective insurance policies or binders of insurance or programs of self-insurance which relate to the Target and its Subsidiaries, which insurance is with financially sound and reputable insurance companies, against such casualties, risks and contingencies, and in such types and amounts, as are consistent with customary practices and standards of companies engaged in businesses similar to the Target and its Subsidiaries. The coverage under each such policy and binder is in full force and effect, and no notice of cancellation or nonrenewal with respect to, or disallowance of any claim under, or material increase of premium for, any such policy or binder has been received by the Target or its Subsidiaries, nor to the Seller. Neither the Target, the Seller nor the Subsidiaries has knowledge of any facts or the occurrence of any event which (i) reasonably might form the basis of any claim against the Target or the Subsidiaries relating to the conduct or operations of the business of the Target or the Subsidiaries or any of the assets or properties covered by any of the policies or binders set forth in Section 4.14 of the Disclosure Statement and which will materially increase the insurance premiums payable under any such policy or binder, or (ii) otherwise will materially increase the insurance premiums payable under such policy or binder.

A representation with respect to the insurance policies of the target is important to the buyer in order to safeguard the assets it is buying against a variety of damage claims. Since the buyer may be unaware of what type of insurance should be carried by the target, the seller should warrant that the target has all of the insurance that is customary for the business of the target and its subsidiaries. The seller will not usually quarrel about this part of the representation; what troubles the seller most is the buyer's desire for assurances that the premiums for such insurance will not increase dramatically because of an event or claim that the seller may be aware of. How can the seller be certain what events will increase the premiums? In a clear case—where the seller has recently become aware that its product is carcinogenic, for example—the seller should be aware that its insurance premiums will obviously increase dramatically when this fact comes to the attention of its insurance companies. The buyer should also investigate whether such policies will survive after the acquisition since many policies lapse on a change of control of the target or, in some cases, a buyer may be prudent to include a representation by the seller stating that such policies will survive after the acquisition.

A second important consideration is whether the insurance policies are "claims made" or "claims incurred" policies. The difference between these types of policies is that a "claims made" policy covers only those claims which are made to the insurance company while the policy was in full force and effect, while a "claims incurred" policy covers all claims made at any time, provided that the events giving rise to a liability occurred during the time the policy was in full force and effect.

Lastly, if insurance is an important aspect of the business and a certain portion of the insurance consists of self-insurance, the buyer should factor this in when analyzing the cost of running the business. In the event the buyer wishes to continue to self-insure, the buyer should require the seller's cooperation in obtaining any regulatory approvals necessary to continue to self-insure the operations of the target.

> ***Section 4.15. Real Property Owned or Leased.*** Section 4.15 of the Disclosure Statement sets forth a complete and accurate list or description of all real property (including a general description of fixtures located at such property and specific identification of any such fixtures not owned by the Target or any Subsidiary) which the Target or any Subsidiary owns or leases, has agreed (or has an option) to purchase, sell or lease, or may be obligated to purchase, sell or lease and any title insurance or guarantee policies with respect thereto, specifying in the case of leases, the name of the lessor, licensor or other grantor, the approximate square footage covered thereunder, the basic annual rental and other amounts paid or payable with respect thereto and a summary of the other terms thereof. True copies of all such leases for real property with aggregate annual rental payments (excluding payments to third parties on account of real estate taxes (or increases therein), insurance, operating costs, or common area expenses), individually in excess of _____ Dollars ($_____) (including all amendments thereof and modifications thereto) have been delivered to Buyer prior to the date hereof. Except as set forth in Section 4.15

of the Disclosure Statement, no consent to the consummation of the transactions contemplated by this Agreement is required from the lessor of any such real property.

The scheduling of real property serves to support the buyer's due diligence efforts by identifying each property owned or leased by the target or any subsidiary. In requesting disclosure of leases, consideration should be given to the dollar threshold in annual rental payments which identifies a lease which the target must disclose. For smaller targets, it may be appropriate to include no threshold at all, requiring the disclosure of all leases of real property.

This representation is also designed to elicit disclosure of both (i) obligations for periodic payments or capital commitments which have been incurred by the target or any subsidiary, and (ii) those leases where landlord consents may be required to avoid lease terminations by virtue of the acquisition. Rental commitments and agreements to purchase will have an impact on the cash flow requirements of the target but may not have been apparent to the buyer from a review of the target's financial statements.

The buyer should require the annual lease payment information in order to prepare a cash flow analysis. In addition, this disclosure will aid a buyer who is trying to determine the financeability of the target's and subsidiaries' real estate and the necessity of obtaining appraisals of the real estate to assist its financing efforts.

Section 4.16 Fixed Assets; Leased Assets

(i) Section 4.16(i) of the Disclosure Statement sets forth a complete and accurate list or description of all equipment, machinery, and other items of tangible personal property which the Target or any Subsidiary owns or leases, has agreed (or has an option) to purchase, sell or lease, or may be obligated to purchase, sell or lease having a book value of _____ Dollars ($_____) or more or requiring annual rental payments in excess of _____ Dollars ($_____), specifying in the case of leases, the name of the lessor, licensor or other grantor, the description of the property covered thereby, the basic annual rental and other amounts paid or payable with respect thereto and a summary of the other terms thereof. True copies of all leases for such assets with aggregate rental payments individually in excess of _____ Dollars ($_____) (including all amendments thereto and modifications thereof) have been delivered to Buyer prior to the date hereof. The book value of all such assets owned or leased by the Target and its Subsidiaries not included on such list do not, in the aggregate, exceed _____ Dollars ($_____) at the date hereof.

(ii) Except as set forth in Section 4.16(ii) of the Disclosure Statement, no consent to the consummation of the transactions contemplated by this Agreement is required from the lessor, licensor or other grantor of any such tangible personal property.

As with the representation relating to real estate in Section 4.15, this representation elicits disclosure of each item of tangible personal property owned or leased by the target or any subsidiary that has a value or annual cost in excess of a given dollar threshold. Unlike the real property representation, where the buyer may reasonably request and be interested in information on each piece of real property owned by the target or any subsidiary, requesting disclosure of every item of tangible personal property absent a dollar threshold would impose an unreasonable burden on the seller and would subject the seller to the risk of a misrepresentation in the event an asset were inadvertently omitted.

This risk will motivate the seller to negotiate for a higher dollar threshold. A buyer may determine that it can live with a dollar threshold on the book value of owned assets but must require a lower amount in respect of lease obligations since the latter will have a direct impact on cash flow projections. The buyer, in any event, should base its threshold on the individual value of assets which it deems relevant to any financing that may be necessary for it to finance the purchase price.

Section 4.17. Title and Related Matters

(i) Subject to the exceptions contained in the second sentence of this Section 4.17, the Target or a Subsidiary has, and immediately after giving effect to the transactions contemplated hereby will have, good and marketable title (or, in jurisdictions where title insurance policies insuring good and marketable title are not available, good and indefeasible title, or good and merchantable title or some quality of title substantially equivalent thereto) to or a valid leasehold interest in (a) all of the properties and assets reflected in the Most Recent Balance Sheet or acquired after the date of the appropriate Most Recent Balance Sheet by the Target or a Subsidiary, (b) all properties or assets which are subject to operating leases as defined in Financial Accounting Standards Board Statement No. 13 and are not reflected in the Most Recent Balance Sheet, and (c) all other properties and assets owned or utilized by the Target or any Subsidiary in the conduct of their respective businesses. All properties and assets referred to in the preceding sentence are presently owned or held by the Target or a Subsidiary, and at and immediately after the Closing Date, will be held by the Target or a Subsidiary, free and clear of all title defects or objections, mortgages, liens, pledges, charges, security interests, options to purchase or other encumbrances of any kind or character, except: (v) liens for current taxes not yet due and payable; (w) liens, imperfections of title and easements which do not, either individually or in the aggregate, materially detract from the value of, or interfere with the present use of, the properties subject thereto or affected thereby, or otherwise materially impair the operations of the entity which owns, leases or utilizes such property or materially impair the use of such property by such entity; (x) mortgages and liens securing debt which is reflected as a liability on the Most Recent Balance Sheet; (y) mechanics', carriers', workmen's, repairmen's and other similar liens arising or incurred in the ordinary course of business; and (z) as set forth in Section 4.17(i) of the Disclosure Statement.

(ii) All the plants, structures, facilities, machinery, equipment, automobiles, trucks, tools and other properties and assets owned or leased by the Target and the Subsidiaries, including but not limited to such as are reflected in the Most Recent Balance Sheet or acquired after the respective dates of the Most Recent Balance Sheet by the Target or a Subsidiary are structurally sound with no defects known to Seller and in good operating condition and repair (except for routine immaterial maintenance in the ordinary course of business) and usable in a manner consistent with their current use.

(iii) All leases pursuant to which the Target and the Subsidiaries lease (as lessee) real and/or personal property are valid and enforceable by the Target or a Subsidiary in accordance with their respective terms; other than with respect to property which has been sublet by the Target or the Subsidiaries as noted on Section 4.17(iii) of the Disclosure Statement, the Target or a Subsidiary has been in peaceable possession since the commencement of the original term of each such lease; except for the tenancies in respect of property being sublet, as specified in the second clause of this sentence, there are no tenancies or other possessory interests with respect to any real or personal property owned by the Target or any Subsidiary; all rents due under, or other amounts required to be paid by the terms of, each such lease have been paid; and there is not under any of such leases, to Seller's knowledge, any default (or event which, with the giving of notice, the passage of time or both, would constitute a default), waiver or postponement of any of the Target's or any Subsidiary's obligations thereunder.

(iv) Except as stated in Section 4.17(iv) of the Disclosure Statement, none of the real property owned or leased by the Target or any Subsidiary is subject to any governmental decree or order to be sold and there is no condemnation or eminent domain proceeding pending, or, to the best of Seller's knowledge, threatened, against any real property owned or leased by the Target or any Subsidiary or any part thereof, and neither Target nor any Subsidiary has made a commitment or received any notice, oral or written, of the desire of any public authority or any entity to take or use the real property owned or leased by the Target or any Subsidiary or any part thereof, whether temporarily or permanently, for easements, rights-of-way, or other public or quasi-public purposes, or for any other purpose whatsoever, nor is there any proceeding pending, or threatened in writing or by publication, or, to the best knowledge of the Seller, threatened, which could adversely affect, as to any portion of any parcel of the real property owned or leased by the Target or any Subsidiary, the zoning classification in effect on the date hereof. On the Closing Date, the real property owned or leased by the Target and its Subsidiaries shall be free and clear of any management, leasing, maintenance, security or service obligations other than utilities and except those incurred in the ordinary course of business.

(v) All rights-of-way, easements, licenses, permits and authorizations in any manner related to the location or operation of the business of the Target and the Subsidiaries are in good standing, valid and enforceable in all material respects in accordance with their respective terms. Except as stated in Section 4.17(v) of the Disclosure Statement, neither the Target nor any Subsidiary is in violation of any, and each has complied with all, applicable zoning, building, or other codes, statutes, regulations, ordinances, notices and orders of any governmental agency with respect to the occupancy, use, maintenance, condition and operation of the real property owned or leased by the Target and its Subsidiaries or any material portion of any parcel thereof, and the use of any improvements for all purposes for which the real property owned or leased by the Target and its Subsidiaries is being used on the date hereof will not violate any such code, statute, regulation, ordinance, notice or order. The Target and the Subsidiaries possess and shall maintain in effect all licenses, certificates of occupancy, permits and authorizations required to operate and maintain the real property owned or leased by the Target and its Subsidiaries for all uses for which the real property owned or leased by the Target and its Subsidiaries is operated on the date hereof. Except as stated in Section 4.17(v) of the Disclosure Statement, no equipment installed or located in any part of the real property owned or leased by the Target and its Subsidiaries violates any law, ordinance, order, regulation or requirement of any governmental authority which violation would have an adverse effect on the real property owned or leased by the Target or any Subsidiary or any portion of any parcel thereof.

Title to the property owned by the target and its subsidiaries is important for the purpose of verifying the value and financeability of the assets acquired. It is useful to include within the scope of the title representations assets leased under operating leases as these assets will generally not be disclosed on a balance sheet and may represent significant value if the target's rental payments are below market rates, especially if the target's leasehold interest is mortgageable.

An acquisition lender advancing funds on a secured basis will require the buyer to make extensive representations regarding the quality of its title to the assets securing the loan. The buyer should therefore attempt to obtain as much comfort on the existence of liens and encumbrances from the seller as possible. It is not only important to elicit in the Disclosure Statement all liens which might have an impact on the buyer's ability to obtain sufficient financing, but the buyer must also carefully review the liens disclosed and assess the degree to which the liens impair financeability of the assets of the target and its subsidiaries. Close scrutiny may reveal the existence of liens which limit marketability and prevent the buyer from providing its lender with a first priority security interest. Once these liens have been identified, the buyer may wish to require as its condition to Closing that certain liens be discharged.

As an alternative to having the seller schedule existing liens (as is the approach in the second sentence of paragraph (i)), the buyer could permit an exception for "liens, imperfections of title, and easements which do not, either individually or in the aggregate, materially detract from the value of, or interfere with the present value of, the properties subject thereto or affected thereby, or otherwise materially impair the operations of the entity which owns, leases or utilizes such property or materially impair the use of such property by such entity." In addition, the materiality standard might be made more definite by referring to a lien or imposition in excess of a specified dollar amount. However, while a materiality exception may provide sufficient protection to the buyer vis-a-vis the seller, a lender may find it unacceptable. The buyer employing the exception must be willing to take on the risk that a lender may, through certain loan representations and covenants, require the discharge of liens which are not material to either the seller or the buyer.

The representations in paragraphs (ii) and (iii) are intended to assure the buyer that the assets to be acquired are in good operating condition and that the target's and subsidiaries' leases are enforceable and not in default.

Paragraphs (iv) and (v) attempt to verify that no violations or proceedings exist which might prevent the buyer from using the real estate acquired as it had been used in the past by the target and the subsidiaries. The seller may seek to limit the statement about existing violations by imposing a materiality standard. A buyer might well concede this point; a useful compromise position might be to require the representation that any violation would not result in an award of damages, or require expenditures to remedy the violation, in excess of a specified dollar amount.

Section 4.18. Intellectual Property

(i) Section 4.18(i) of the Disclosure Statement sets forth a complete and accurate list, including, where applicable, the date of registration or expiration, serial or registration number or patent number, of all United States (including the individual states and territories of the United States) and foreign registered trademarks, service marks and trade names; unregistered trademarks, service marks and trade names; trademark, service mark and trade name applications; product designations; designs; unexpired patents; pending and filed patent applications; current and active invention disclosures; inventions on which disclosures are to be prepared; trade secrets; registered copyrights; and unregistered copyrights (collectively, the "Intellectual Property"), which the Target or any Subsidiary owns or licenses, has agreed (or has an option) to purchase, sell or license, or may be obligated to purchase, sell or license. With respect to each of the foregoing items, there is listed on Section 4.18(i) of the Disclosure Statement (a) the extent of the interest of the Target and its Subsidiaries therein; (b) the jurisdictions in or by which each such patent, trademark, service mark, trade name, copyright and license has been registered, filed or issued; (c) each agreement and all other documents evidencing the interest of the Target and its Subsidiaries therein, including, but not limited to, license agreements; (d) the extent of the interest of any third party therein, including, but not limited to, any security interest or licenses; and (e) each agreement and all other documents evidencing the interest of any third party therein.

(ii) Except as set forth in Section 4.18(ii) of the Disclosure Statement, the right, title or interest of the Target and its Subsidiaries in each item of Intellectual Property is free and clear of material adverse Liens.

(iii) Except as set forth in Section 4.18(iii) of the Disclosure Statement, the Target and its Subsidiaries have all right, title and interest in all inventions, trade secrets, proprietary information and have all other intellectual property rights necessary in any material respect for the non-infringing manufacture, use or sale, as the case may be, of all of the products, components of products and services which the Target or any Subsidiary manufactures, uses or sells in their business as currently conducted or which the Target or any Subsidiary contemplated manufacturing, using or selling in connection with the preparation of the Projected Financial Statements.

(iv) Except as set forth in Section 4.18(iv) of the Disclosure Statement, the Target and its Subsidiaries have all right, title and interest in all trademarks, service marks, trade names and product designations necessary for the non-infringing use of all such marks and trade names which the Target or any Subsidiary uses in their business as currently conducted or which the Target or any Subsidiary contemplated using in connection with the preparation of the Projected Financial Statements.

(v) Except as set forth in Section 4.18(v) of the Disclosure Statement, the Target and its Subsidiaries have all right, title and interest in all material copyrights necessary for the non-infringing publication, reproduction, preparation of derivative works, distribution, public performance, public display and importation of all copyrighted works which the Target or any Subsidiary in their business as currently conducted or as contemplated in connection with the preparation of the Projected Financial Statements, publishes, reproduces, prepares or has prepared a derivative of, distributes, publicly performs, publicly displays, or imports.

(vi) Except as set forth in Section 4.18(vi) of the Disclosure Statement, neither the Target nor any of the Subsidiaries has, whether directly, contributorily or by inducement, within any time period as to which liability of the Target or the Subsidiaries is not barred by statute, infringed any patent, trademark, service mark, trade name or copyright or misappropriated any intellectual property of another, or received from another any notice, charge, claim or other assertion in respect thereto or committed any actions of unfair competition.

(vii) Except as set forth in Section 4.18(vii) of the Disclosure Statement, neither the Target nor any of the Subsidiaries has sent or otherwise communicated to another person any notice, charge, claim or other assertion of, or has any knowledge of, present, impending or threatened patent, trademark, service mark, trade name or copyright infringement by such other person, or misappropriation of any intellectual property of the Target or any of the Subsidiaries by such other person or any acts of unfair competition by such other person.

(viii) No product, license, patent, process, method, substance, design, part or other material presently being sold or contemplated to be sold or employed by the Target or any Subsidiary infringes on any rights owned or held by any other person; (b) no claim, litigation or other proceeding is pending or threatened against the Target or any Subsidiary contesting the right of such entity to sell or use any such product, license, patent, process, method, substance, design, part or other material and no such claim is impliedly threatened by an offer to license from a third party under a claim of use; and (c) no patent, formulation, invention, device, application or principle nor any statute, law, rule, regulation, standard or code, exists or is pending or proposed that would have a Material Adverse Effect.

(ix) No filing or recording fees, stamp or transfer taxes or other fees, costs or taxes of any kind are payable by the Target or any Subsidiary in respect of the Intellectual Property and no such filing or recording fees, stamp taxes or other fees, costs or taxes of any kind will be payable by the Target, any Subsidiary or Buyer in connection with the Merger except as set forth in Section 4.18(ix) of the Disclosure Statement.

The intellectual property representation requires the disclosure of all intellectual property which the target or any subsidiary uses in its business and is designed to assure the buyer that the intellectual property, or the target's or its subsidiaries' use thereof, does not infringe upon the rights of third parties. The representation has been drafted to cover any intellectual property rights that may exist or are pending which would adversely impact the target or its subsidiaries. This representation may be extremely important if, for example, the value of the target's business is largely dependent upon its possession of a particular patent or its ability to market its product under a particular trademark.

Subparagraph (ix) is intended to elicit information as to filing or transfer fees that might be incurred in connection with the transaction. Where the target and its subsidiaries have extensive foreign intellectual property holdings, these fees can be of sufficient magnitude that the buyer may desire to attempt to obligate the seller to pay a portion of these costs.

> *Section 4.19. Assets Necessary to the Business.* Except as set forth in Section 4.19 of the Disclosure Statement, the Target and the Subsidiaries collectively own or lease, directly or indirectly, all of the assets and properties, and are parties to all licenses and other agreements, in each case which are presently being used or are reasonably necessary to carry on the businesses and operations of the Target and the Subsidiaries as presently conducted, and none of the stockholders of the Target, the Seller nor any of their affiliates (other than any of the Target and the Subsidiary) owns any assets or properties which are being used to carry on the business or operations of the Target and the Subsidiaries as presently conducted.

Notwithstanding all of the other representations made by the seller about the specific assets, liabilities, and other agreements, rights, and obligations that the target and its subsidiaries may have, a buyer has no way of knowing that it is getting everything that it needs to operate the business of the target and its subsidiaries as presently conducted without this broad representation. This type of representation is critical if the buyer is purchasing a company by means of an asset acquisition or a business which has been operated as a division of another company. If, for example, certain equipment or services necessary to the business of the target or its subsidiaries were provided by the seller or its affiliates, the buyer would be unable to operate the business without replacing such equipment or services, most likely at a cost which far exceeds the cost at which they were provided by the seller or its affiliates.

Section 4.20. Additional Contracts. In addition to the other items set forth in the Disclosure Statement attached hereto pursuant to the other provisions of this Agreement, Section 4.20 of the Disclosure Statement identifies as of the date hereof the following:

(i) each agreement to which the Target or any Subsidiary is a party which involves or may involve aggregate annual future payments (whether in payment of a debt, as a result of a guarantee or indemnification, for goods or services, or otherwise) by the Target or any Subsidiary of _____ Dollars ($_____) or more;

(ii) each outstanding commitment of the Target or any Subsidiary to make capital expenditures, capital additions or capital improvements in excess of _____ Dollars ($_____);

(iii) any contract for the employment of any officer or employee or former officer or employee of the Target or any Subsidiary (other than, with respect to any employee, contracts which are terminable without liability upon notice of 30 days or less and do not provide for any further payments following such termination) pursuant to which payments in excess of _____ Dollars ($_____) may be required to be made at any time following the date hereof;

(iv) any stock option or stock appreciation rights plan or arrangement of the Target or any Subsidiary;

(v) any mortgage or other form of secured indebtedness of the Target or any Subsidiary;

(vi) any unsecured debentures, notes or installment obligations of the Target or any Subsidiary, the unpaid balance of which exceeds _____ Dollars ($_____) in the aggregate except trade payables incurred in the ordinary course of business;

(vii) any guaranty of any obligation of the Target or any Subsidiary for borrowings or otherwise, excluding endorsements made for collection, guaranties made or letters of credit given in the ordinary course of business, and other guaranties which in the aggregate do not exceed _____ Dollars ($_____);

(viii) any agreement of the Target or any Subsidiary, including options, for the purchase, sale, disposition or lease of any of its assets (other than inventory) having a book value of more than _____ Dollars ($_____) for any single asset or _____ Dollars ($_____) in the aggregate or for the sale of inventory other than in the ordinary course of business;

(ix) any contract to which the Target or any Subsidiary is a party pursuant to which the Target or any Subsidiary is or may be obligated to make payments, contingent or otherwise, exceeding _____ Dollars ($_____) in the aggregate, on account of or arising out of the prior acquisition of businesses, or all or substantially all of the assets or stock, of other companies or any division thereof;

(x) any contract with any labor union which the Target or any Subsidiary is a party;

(xi) any contract or proposed contract, including but not limited to assignments, licenses, transfers of exclusive rights, "work for hire" agreements, special commissions, employment contracts, purchase orders, sales orders, mortgages and security agreements, to which the Target or any Subsidiary is a party and which (A) contains a grant or other transfer, whether present, retroactive, prospective, or contingent, by the Target or any Subsidiary, of any rights in any invention, trade secret, proprietary information, trademark, service mark, trade name, copyright, or other intellectual property by whatever name designated, without regard to whether such invention, trade secret, proprietary information, trademark, service mark, trade name, copyright, material object or other intellectual property was in existence at the time such contract was made, or (B) contains a promise made by the Target or by any Subsidiary to pay any lump sum or royalty or other payment or consideration in respect to the acquisition, practice or use of any rights in any invention, trade secret, proprietary information, trademark, service mark, trade name, copyright, material object in which an original work of authorship was first fixed, or other intellectual property by whatever name designated and without regard to whether such lump sum, royalty payment or other consideration was ever made or received;

(xii) any contract with the Seller or any officer, director or employee of the Target or any Subsidiary of the Seller (A) involving at least _____ Dollars ($_____) in aggregate payments over the entire term thereof or more than $_____ Dollars in any twelve month period or (B) the terms of which are not arms-length; or

(xiii) any other contract, agreement or other instrument which the Target or any Subsidiary is a party not entered into in the ordinary course of business which is material to the financial, business, earnings, prospects or condition of the Target or the Subsidiaries and not excluded by reason of the provisions of clauses (i) through (xii), inclusive, of this subsection.

Except as otherwise agreed to by the parties as set forth in Section 4.20 of the Disclosure Statement, true and complete copies of all contracts, agreements and other instruments referred to in Section 4.20 of the Disclosure Statement have heretofore been delivered, or will be delivered at least ten business days prior to Closing, to Buyer by the Seller. All such contracts, agreements and other instruments are enforceable by the Target or the Subsidiaries which is (are) a party thereto in accordance with their terms except as to enforceability thereof may be affected by applicable bankruptcy, reorganization, insolvency, moratorium or other similar laws now or hereafter in effect, or by general equity principles.

This is an information gathering representation which is designed to identify all the important contractual relationships of the target and its subsidiaries. Depending upon the type of deal being negotiated, a seller may be reluctant to make this representation because of the inordinate amount of work required to satisfy the disclosure obligation. The seller may instead tell the buyer that it is welcome to review all the contracts and other agreements at the offices of the seller. However, like any other representation that is founded on access as opposed to identification, the buyer takes responsibility at its own peril. Therefore, a prudent buyer will demand that the seller identify all such documents and, if need be, offer to assist in the seller's preparation of the Disclosure Statement.

The amount of the dollar thresholds in this representation are deal specific and the same considerations previously discussed are appropriate here.

Section 4.21. Customers and Suppliers. Section 4.21 of the Disclosure Statement sets forth (i) a true and correct list of (A) the ten largest customers of the Target and each of the Subsidiaries in terms of sales during the fiscal year ended [fill in date of most recent fiscal year end] and (B) the ten largest customers of the Target and each of the Subsidiaries in terms of sales during the three (3) months ended [fill in the most recent quarter end], showing the approximate total sales to each such customer during the fiscal year ended [fill in date of most recent fiscal year end] and the three (3) months ended [fill in most recent quarter end]; (ii) a true and correct list of (A) the ten largest suppliers of the Target and each of the Subsidiaries in terms of purchases during the fiscal year ended [fill in date of most recent fiscal year end], and (B) the ten largest suppliers of the Target and each of the Subsidiaries on a consolidated basis in terms of purchases during the three (3) months ended [fill in most recent quarter end], showing the approximate total purchases from each such supplier during the fiscal year ended [fill in date of most recent fiscal year end], and the three (3) months ended [fill in most recent quarter end], respectively. Except to the extent set forth in Section 4.21 of the Disclosure Statement, there has not been any material adverse change in the business relationship of the Target or any Subsidiary with any customer or supplier named in the Disclosure Statement. Except for the customers and suppliers named in Section 4.21 of the Disclosure Statement, neither the Target nor any Subsidiary had any customer who accounted for more than 5% of its sales during the period from [insert appropriate period of 12 to 18 months prior to date of Agreement], or any supplier from whom it purchased more than 5% of the goods or services purchased by it during such period.

Depending upon the nature of the target's and the subsidiaries' businesses, the buyer may agree to require disclosure of the largest customers and suppliers on "a consolidated basis." The principal reason for this representation is to identify the dependence of the business on a single or small group of customers or suppliers.

Section 4.22. Competing Lines of Business. Except as set forth on Section 4.22 of the Disclosure Statement, no affiliate of the Seller owns, directly or indirectly, any interest in (excepting not more than 5% stockholdings for investment purposes in securities of publicly held and traded companies), or is an officer, director, employee or consultant of, or otherwise receives remuneration from, any person which is, or is engaged in business as, a competitor, lessor, lessee, customer or supplier of the Target or any Subsidiary.

In certain situations, it may appear unnecessary to require a seller to enter into some sort of non-compete agreement because of the nature of the seller's business. However, it still may be useful for the buyer to assure himself that there are no hidden companies that the seller operates or controls which compete with the target or a subsidiary. The protection afforded by this representation is limited; the seller may be able to adversely affect the business of the target or a subsidiary in light of the seller's inside knowledge or simply because it has greater resources. The buyer should be forewarned that, despite its receipt of this representation, a seller may remain a competitor given the practicalities of a particular situation.

Section 4.23. Restrictive Covenants. Except as set forth in Section 4.23 of the Disclosure Statement, neither Target nor any Subsidiary is a party to any agreement, contract or covenant limiting the freedom of the Target or any Subsidiary from competing in any line of business or with any person or other entity in any geographic area.

A buyer must be aware of agreements which constrain the operation of the target and its subsidiaries. Many buyers purchase targets with the expectation that the business of the target can be expanded geographically. In some cases, the buyer may be relying on this expectation to the point of including such expansion in its projections. Therefore, the buyer should carefully review any agreements which are disclosed as a result of this representation.

Section 4.24. Books and Records
(i) The books of account and other financial records of the Target and its Subsidiaries are in all material respects complete and correct, and have been maintained in accordance with good business practices.

(ii) The minute books of the Target and its Subsidiaries, as previously made available to the Buyer and its counsel, contain accurate records of all meetings and accurately reflect all other material corporate action of the stockholders and directors and any committees of the Board of Directors of the Target and its Subsidiaries.

(iii) The Buyer has been or will be prior to the Closing Date, afforded access to all such records referred to in subparagraphs (i) and (ii) above.

Section 4.25. Bank Accounts.
Section 4.25 of the Disclosure Statement contains a true and correct list of the names of each bank, savings and loan, or other financial institution, in which the Target or its Subsidiaries has an account, including cash contribution accounts, or safe deposit boxes, and the names of all persons authorized to draw thereon or to have access thereto.

Sections 4.24 and 4.25 above are representations which confirm the accuracy of information usually furnished to the buyer in connection with its due diligence efforts.

Section 4.26. Employee Benefit Plans; Labor Relations
(i) The term "Employee Plan" shall mean any pension, retirement, profit-sharing, deferred compensation, bonus or other incentive plan, any medical, vision, dental or other health plan, any life insurance plan, or any other employee benefit plan, including, without limitation, any "employee benefit plan" as defined in Section 3(3) of the Employee Retirement Income Security Act of 1974, as amended ("ERISA") and any employee benefit plan covering any employees of the Target or any Controlled Entity in any foreign country or territory (a "Foreign Plan"), to which the Target or any

Controlled Entity contributes or is a party or is bound and under which employees of the Target or any Controlled Entity are eligible to participate or derive a benefit, except any government-sponsored program or government-required benefit. Section 4.26(i) of the Disclosure Statement lists each Employee Plan and identifies each Employee Plan (other than a Foreign Plan) which, as of the date hereof, is a defined benefit plan as defined in Section 3(35) of ERISA (a "Defined Benefit Plan") or is a multi-employer plan within the meaning of Section 3(37) of ERISA (a "Multi-Employer Plan"). In the case of each Defined Benefit Plan, the unfunded accrued liabilities of such plan as of [insert date], determined on an ongoing plan basis by the actuaries for such plan using the actuarial methods and assumptions used in the latest actuarial valuation of the plan, do not exceed the assets of the plan. Section 4.26(i) of the Disclosure Statement identifies each of the Employee Plans which purports to be a qualified plan under Section 401(a) of the Code (as defined below). In the case of each Multi-Employer Plan, Section 4.26(i) of the Disclosure Statement sets forth the Target or Controlled Entity contributions made to such Plan for the 12 months ended on the last day of its most recent fiscal year. In the case of each Foreign Plan, Section 4.26(i) of the Disclosure Statement sets forth the Target or Controlled Entity contributions made to such Plan for the last plan year ending prior to the date of this Agreement. The Target has delivered, or will deliver prior to the Closing, to Buyer the following documents as in effect on the date hereof: (a) true, correct and complete copies of any Employee Plan, other than a Foreign Plan, including all amendments thereto, which is an employee pension benefit or welfare benefit plan (within the meaning of Sections 3(1) or 3(2) of ERISA), and, in the case of any unwritten Employee Plans, descriptions thereof, (b) with respect to any plans or plan amendments described in the foregoing clause (a), (1) the most recent determination letter issued by the Internal Revenue Service (the "IRS") after September 1, 1974, if any, (2) all trust agreements or other funding agreements, including insurance contracts, (3) with respect to each Defined Benefit Plan, all notices of intent to terminate any such Employee Plan and all notices of reportable events with respect to any such Employee Plan as to which the PBGC has not waived the thirty (30) day notice requirement, (4) the most recent actuarial valuations, annual reports, summary plan descriptions, summaries of material modifications and summary annual reports, if any, and (5) a true, correct and complete summary of the benefits provided under each Foreign Plan, together with the most recent actuarial valuation of financial information relative thereto.

(ii) As of the date hereof:

(a) Each of the Employee Plans that purports to be qualified under Section 401(a) of the Internal Revenue Code of 1954, as amended (the "Code") is qualified as of the Closing Date and any trusts under such plans are exempt from income tax under Section 501(a) of the Code. The retroactive cure period with respect to any plan amendments not yet submitted to the IRS has not expired. The Employee Plans each comply in all material respects with all other applicable laws (including, without limitation, ERISA, the Age Discrimination in Employment Act, the Omnibus Budget Reconciliation Act of 1986, the Consolidated Budget Reconciliation Act of 1986, and the Omnibus Budget Reconciliation Act of 1987) of the United States and any applicable collective bargaining agreement. Other than claims for benefits submitted by participants or beneficiaries or appeals from denial thereof, there is no litigation, legal action, suit, investigation, claim, counterclaim or proceeding pending or threatened against any Employee Plan.

(b) With respect to any Employee Plan, no prohibited transaction (within the meaning of Section 406 of ERISA and/or Section 4975 of the Code) exists which could subject the Target or any Controlled Entity to any material liability or civil penalty assessed pursuant to Section 502(i) of ERISA or a material tax imposed by Section 4975 of the Code. Neither the Seller nor the Target, nor any Controlled Entity, nor any administrator or fiduciary of any Employee Plan (or agent of any of the foregoing) has engaged in any transaction or acted or failed to act in a manner which is likely to subject the Target or any Controlled Entity to any liability for a breach of fiduciary or other duty under ERISA or any other applicable United States law. The transactions contemplated by this Agreement and the Related Instruments will not be, or cause any, prohibited action.

(c) No Defined Benefit Plan has been terminated or partially terminated after September 1, 1974.

(d) No plan termination liability to the Pension Benefit Guaranty Corporation ("PBGC") or withdrawal liability to any Multi-Employer Plan that is material in the aggregate has been or is expected to be incurred with respect to any Employee Plan or with respect to any employee benefit plan sponsored by any entity under common control (within the meaning of Section 414 of the Code) with the Target or a Controlled Entity by reason of any action taken by the Seller, the Target or any Controlled Entity prior to the Closing Date. The PBGC has not instituted, and is not expected to institute, any proceedings to terminate any Employee Plan. Except as described in Section 4.26(ii)(d) of the Disclosure Statement, there has been no reportable event since [insert date] (within the meaning of Section 4043(b) of ERISA and the regulations thereunder) with respect to any Employee Plan, and there exists no condition or set of circumstances which makes the termination of any Employee Plan by the PBGC likely.

(e) As of the date hereof, as to each Employee Benefit Plan, all filings required by ERISA and the Code have been timely filed and all notices and disclosures to participants required by ERISA or the Code have been timely provided.

(iii) Except as indicated in Section 4.26(iii) of the Disclosure Statement, the Target and each Controlled Entity has made full and timely payment of all amounts required under the terms of each of the Employee Plans that are employee pension benefit plans, including the Multi-Employer Plans, to have been paid as contributions to such plans for the last plan year ended prior to the date of this Agreement and all prior plan years. No accumulated funding deficiency (as defined in Section 302 of ERISA and Section 412 of the Code), whether or not waived, exists with respect to any Employee Plan (other than a Foreign Plan) as of the end of such plan year, provided contributions owed with respect to such plan year are timely paid. Further, the Target and each Controlled Entity has made or shall make full and timely payment of or has accrued or shall accrue all amounts which are required under the terms of the Employee Plans to be paid as a contribution to each such Employee Plan that is an employee pension benefit plan with respect to the period from the end of the last plan year ending before the date of this Agreement to the Closing Date in accordance with [insert covenant cross reference] hereof.

(iv) No state of facts exists with respect to a Foreign Plan, the effect of which would have a material adverse effect on the business, assets, earnings, financial condition or prospects of the Target and the Controlled Entities taken as a whole.

(v) All contributions made to or accrued with respect to all Employee Plans are deductible under Section 404 or 162 of the Code. No amounts, nor any assets of any Employee Plan are subject to tax as unrelated business taxable income under Sections 511, 512, or 419A of the Code.

(vi) No facts exist which will result in a material increase in premium costs of Employee Plans for which benefits are insured or a material increase in benefit costs of Employee Plans which provide self insured benefits.

(vii) No Employee Plan provides medical, disability, life, or other benefits to retired former employees.

(viii) Except as described in Section 4.26(v) of the Disclosure Statement, no union has been recognized as a representative of any or all of the Target's or any Subsidiary's employees. There are no agreements with, or pending petitions for recognition of, a labor union or association as the exclusive bargaining agent for any or all of the Target's or any Subsidiary's employees; no such petitions have been pending at any time within two (2) years of the date of this Agreement and, to the best of the Seller's knowledge, there has not been any organizing effort by any union or other group seeking to represent any employees of the Target or any Subsidiary as their exclusive bargaining agent at any time within two (2) years of the date of this Agreement; and there are no labor strikes, work stoppages or other troubles, other than routine grievance matters, now pending, or, to the best of Seller's knowledge, threatened, against the Target or any Subsidiary, nor have there been any such labor strikes, work stoppages or other labor troubles, other than routine grievance matters, at any time within two (2) years of the date of this Agreement.

This particular representation is extremely important in situations in which the target or any subsidiary has a substantial number of employees. Over the past few years, potential liability with respect to employee benefits and related plans has increased dramatically. Therefore, it is important for the buyer to know that the employee plans maintained by the target or any subsidiary are in compliance with existing regulations and are adequately funded. (For a further discussion of employee benefits, see Chapter 9, "Pension, Labor and Compensation Concerns".)

Section 4.27. Litigation. Except as set forth in Section 4.27 of the Disclosure Statement, there is no action, suit, proceeding or investigation pending or, to the best knowledge after due inquiry of Seller and the Target, threatened, which would be likely to have a Material Adverse Effect; there is no reasonable basis known to the Seller or the Target for any such action that may result in any such effect and that is probable of assertion; and the Target, or any Subsidiary is not in default in respect of any judgment, order, writ, injunction or decree of any court or any federal, state, local or other governmental department, commission, board, bureau, agency or instrumentality which would be likely to have a Material Adverse Effect.

Generally, a seller will have no problem disclosing to the buyer the existence of any pending or threatened action against the target or a subsidiary which would have Material Adverse Effect. The part of this representation which is more difficult for the seller to make relates to whether the seller has a reasonable basis to know of any action which may result in a Material Adverse Effect. While there may be no claim pending or action threatened, the buyer wants to know whether the seller, target, or subsidiary has taken any action which would result in a Material Adverse Effect. For example, if immediately prior to the signing of the acquisition agreement the target were to willfully breach a contract essential to its business, the other party to the contract, unaware of the breach, would not yet have filed a claim. Without this particular representation, the seller would not have to disclose this event. Not surprisingly, the seller is often unwilling to evaluate which of its actions may result in a claim which would have a Material Adverse Effect, or make warranties based on its evaluation. The seller may argue that routine corporate actions could result in a Material Adverse Effect, or may express unwillingness to take on liability for the knowledge of each of its directors, officers, and employees. As with other representations, the issue is risk allocation. A smart buyer will soften this representation to appease the seller but will nonetheless seek disclosure, since the seller should be aware of an action taken which would or may constitute a Material Adverse Effect and can always choose to disclose it rather than guess as to its outcome.

Section 4.28. Compliance with Laws

(i) The Target and the Subsidiaries comply with, and have made all filings required pursuant to, all federal, state, municipal or local constitutional provisions, laws, ordinances, rules, regulations and orders in connection with the conduct of their businesses as now conducted.

(ii) The Target and the Subsidiaries have all governmental licenses, permits and authorizations necessary for the conduct of their respective businesses as currently conducted (the "Permits"), and all such Permits are in full force and effect, and no violations exist in respect of any such Permits, and no proceeding is pending or, to the knowledge of the Seller, threatened, to revoke or limit any thereof. Except as otherwise disclosed in Section 4.28(ii) of the Disclosure Statement, all such Permits are set forth on the Disclosure Statement.

(iii) Except as set forth in Section 4.28(iii) of the Disclosure Statement, neither the Target nor any Subsidiary has received notice of violation or of any alleged or potential violation of any such constitutional provisions, laws, ordinances, rules, regulations or orders, cured or not, within the last five years or any injunction or governmental order or decree.

(iv) Except as set forth in Section 4.28(iv) of the Disclosure Statement, there are no present or past Environmental Conditions in any way relating to the business of the Target or any Subsidiary. For purposes of this Agreement, "Environmental Condition" means (a) the introduction into the environment of any pollution, including without limitation any contaminant, irritant, or pollutant or other toxic or hazardous substance (whether or not such pollution constituted at the time thereof a violation of any federal, state or local law, ordinance or governmental rule or regulation) as a result of any spill, discharge, leak, emission, escape, injection, dumping or release of any kind whatsoever of any substance or exposure of any type in any work places or to any medium, including without limitation air, land, surface waters or ground waters, or from any generation, transportation, treatment, discharge, storage or disposal of waste materials, raw materials, hazardous materials, toxic materials or products of any kind or from the storage, use or handling of any hazardous or toxic materials or other substances, as a result of which the Target or any Subsidiary has or may become liable to any person or by reason of which any of the assets of the Target or any Subsidiary may suffer or be subjected to any Lien, or (b) any noncompliance with any federal, state or local environmental law, rule, regulation or order as a result of or in connection with any of the foregoing.

The buyer might limit the representation contained in paragraph (ii) by excepting "any such licenses, permits, and authorizations the failure to obtain which will not have a Material Adverse Effect."

Similarly the buyer might agree to limit the scope of subparagraph (iii) by adding to the five year limitation the phrase "which would be reasonably likely to result in any liability for penalties or damages exceeding _____ Dollars ($____) in the aggregate."

The environmental representation in paragraph (iv) is extremely important in light of the tremendous cost which can be incurred in correcting environmental problems. As a result of significant legislative and judicial developments over the past two decades, unwary buyers may find themselves saddled with obligations to clean up environmental problems caused by their predecessors. Such problems can range from removing asbestos in buildings to expensive groundwater purification programs made necessary by leaks from underground storage tanks.

Section 4.29. Non-Contravention; Consents. Except as set forth in Section 4.29 of the Disclosure Statement, the execution, delivery and performance of this Agreement and the Related Instruments and the consummation of any of the transactions contemplated hereby and thereby by the Seller and the Target do not and will not:

(i) violate any provisions of Seller's or Target's certificate of incorporation or bylaws;

(ii) violate, or result with the passage of time in the violation of, any provision of, or result in the acceleration of or entitle any party to accelerate (whether after the giving of notice or lapse of time or both) any obligation under, or result in the creation or imposition of any lien, charge, pledge, security interest or other encumbrance upon any of the properties of Target or any Subsidiary pursuant to any provision of, any mortgage, lien, lease, agreement, permit, indenture, license, instrument, law, order, arbitration award, judgment or decree to which the Seller, Target or any Subsidiary is a party or by which it or any of its properties are bound, the effect of all of which violations, accelerations, creations and impositions would result, in the aggregate, in subjecting the Target or the Subsidiaries to liabilities in excess of _____ Dollars ($_____);

(iii) violate any law, order, judgment or decree to which the Target or any Subsidiary is subject;

(iv) violate or conflict with any other restriction of any kind or character to which Target or any Subsidiary is subject, or by which any of their assets may be bound, the effect of all of which violations or conflicts would result, in the aggregate, in subjecting Target or the Subsidiaries to aggregate liabilities in excess of _____ Dollars ($_____);

(v) constitute an event permitting termination of an agreement to which Target or any Subsidiary is subject, if in any such circumstance, individually or in the aggregate with all other such events, could have a Material Adverse Effect; or

(vi) require a consent, license, permit, notice, application, qualification, waiver or other action of any kind, authorization, order or approval of, or filing or registration with, any governmental commission, board, regulatory, or administrative agencies or authorities or other regulatory body.

This representation is quite useful in that it clearly lays out the various items that should be of concern to the buyer in its operation of the business after the consummation of the transactions contemplated by the acquisition agreement. The utility of the representation lies in the ability it gives the buyer to address each adverse consequence of the transaction before the deal is closed. For example, many agreements provide for their termination in the event that there is a change of control of the target or a subsidiary, as the case may be. Advance notice of the number and nature of these agreements gives the buyer the opportunity to put replacement contracts in place. In addition, the disclosure of certain consents may prompt the buyer to condition its obligation to close upon the success of the seller in obtaining such consents.

The buyer should give careful consideration to the amount of the dollar thresholds, as items beneath the threshold will not be disclosed and may result in dollar for dollar liability to the surviving corporation.

Section 4.30. Unlawful Payments. Neither the Target nor any Subsidiary, nor to the best of the Target's knowledge any officer or director of the Target nor any officer or director of any Subsidiary, nor any employee, agent or representative, of the Target or any Subsidiary has made, directly or indirectly, with respect to the business of the Target or such Subsidiary, any illegal political contributions, payments from corporate funds not recorded on the books and records of the Target or such Subsidiary, payments from corporate funds that were falsely recorded on the books and records of the Target or such Subsidiary, payments from corporate funds to governmental officials in their individual capacities for the purpose of affecting their action or the action of the government they represent to obtain favorable treatment in securing business or licenses or to obtain special concessions or illegal payments from corporate funds to obtain or retain business.

The purpose of this representation is to identify whether the target or any subsidiary has made any payments which violate laws, such as the Foreign Corrupt Practices Act, or any payments which are not accurately reflected on the target's or subsidiaries' books and records.

In addition, disclosure of these payments might reveal the tenuous nature of certain aspects of the target's or its subsidiaries' business, or the necessity for continuing such payments in order to obtain favorable treatment.

Section 4.31. Brokers and Finders. Neither the Seller, Target, or any Subsidiary nor any stockholder, officer, director or agent of the Seller, the Target or any Subsidiary has incurred on behalf of Seller, the Target or any Subsidiary any liability to any broker, finder or agent for any brokerage fees, finders' fees or commissions with respect to the transactions contemplated by this Agreement, except to [name of broker or finder]. Such fees and commissions will be paid by Seller.

This representation protects the buyer against obligations of the target or any subsidiary to pay certain fees in connection with the acquisition. Buyer and seller may agree to share some of these fees but the buyer certainly doesn't want to be obligated to pay any fees of which it is not aware or which are not included in its calculation of the purchase price. As discussed in Chapter 2, at pages 36–42, these liabilities can be incurred even though no formal written agreement has been executed.

Section 4.32. Absence of Certain Changes or Events. Except as reflected in Section 4.32 of the Disclosure Statement or as specifically set forth herein, since the date of the Most Recent Balance Sheet neither Target nor any Subsidiary has

(i) conducted its business other than in the ordinary course of business;

(ii) issued or sold, or contracted to sell, any of its stock, notes, bonds, or other securities, or any option to purchase the same, or entered into any agreement with respect thereto;

(iii) amended its certificate of incorporation or bylaws;

(iv) had or made any capital expenditures or commitments for the acquisition or construction of any property, plant or equipment in excess of _____ Dollars ($_____) individually and _____ Dollars ($_____) in the aggregate;

(v) entered into any transaction inconsistent in any material respect with the past practices of its business or has conducted its business in any manner materially inconsistent with its past practices;

(vi) incurred (A) any damage, destruction or similar loss in an aggregate amount exceeding _____ Dollars ($_____) and which is covered by insurance or (B) any damage, destruction or loss in an aggregate amount exceeding _____ Dollars ($_____) and which is not covered by insurance;

(vii) suffered any loss or, to the best knowledge of the Seller, Target and the Subsidiaries, any prospective loss, of any dealer, customer, or supplier or altered any contractual arrangement with any dealer or supplier, the loss or alteration of which would (or would, when added to all other such losses or alterations) have a Material Adverse Effect;

(viii) incurred any material liability or obligation (absolute or contingent) or made any material expenditure, other than such as may have been incurred or made in the ordinary course of business and other than capital expenditures described in clause (iv) of this subsection;

(ix) suffered any material adverse change in the business, operations, earnings, properties, liabilities, prospects, assets or financial condition or otherwise of the Target or any Subsidiary and no event which would have Material Adverse Effect has occurred;

(x) declared, set aside or paid any dividend or other distribution (whether in cash, shares, property or any combination thereof) in respect of the capital stock of the Target or any Subsidiary;

(xi) redeemed, repurchased, or otherwise acquired any of its capital stock or securities convertible into or exchangeable for its capital stock or entered into any agreement to do so;

(xii) except as reflected on the Most Recent Balance Sheet and covered by an adequate reserve therefor, made any sale of accounts receivable or any accrual of liabilities not in the ordinary course of business or written off any notes or accounts receivable or portions thereof as uncollectible;

(xiii) purchased or disposed of, or contracted to purchase or dispose of, or granted or received an option to purchase or sell, any properties or assets having a value greater than _____ Dollars ($_____) for any single asset, or greater than _____ Dollars ($_____) in the aggregate;

(xiv) except for normal annual increases or increases resulting from the application of existing formulas under existing plans, agreements or policies relating to employee compensation, made any increase in the rate of compensation payable or to become payable to the Target's or any Subsidiary's officers or employees or any increase in the amounts paid or payable to such officers or employees under any bonus, insurance, pension or other benefit plan, or any arrangements therefor made for or with any of said officers or employees;

(xv) adopted, or amended, any collective bargaining, bonus, profit-sharing, compensation, stock option, pension, retirement, deferred compensation or other plan, agreement, trust, fund or arrangement for the benefit of employees;

(xvi) made any change in any material accounting principle, material accounting procedure or material accounting practice, if any, followed by the Target or any Subsidiary or in the method of applying such principle, procedure or practice [except as required by a change in generally accepted accounting principles in the country of domicile];

(xvii) made any provision for markdowns or shrinkage with respect to inventories other than in the ordinary course of business and consistent with past practices or any write-down of the value of inventory by the Target or any Subsidiary of more than _____ Dollars ($_____) in the aggregate;

(xviii) discharged any lien or paid any obligation or liability (whether absolute, accrued, contingent or otherwise) other than current liabilities shown on the Most Recent Balance Sheet, and current liabilities incurred thereafter;

(xix) mortgaged, pledged or subjected to any lien, except liens specifically excepted from the provisions of Section 4.17 hereof, any properties or assets, real, personal or mixed, tangible or intangible, of Target or any Subsidiary;

(xx) experienced any material shortage of raw materials or supplies;

(xxi) made any gifts or sold, transferred or exchanged any property for less than the fair value thereof; or

(xxii) made or entered into any agreement or understanding to do any of the foregoing.

In order to bring down the financial condition of the target and its subsidiaries from the date of the Most Recent Balance Sheet, the buyer should have the seller represent the lack of certain events since such date. Since there are no financial statements covering the period between the date of the Most Recent Balance Sheet and the Closing Date, it is important for the buyer to understand the operation of the business during this period. In addition, the buyer should require the seller to covenant that it will not breach this representation on or prior to the Closing Date (see Section 6.1). Included in Section 4.32 are representations regarding matters which, although not specifically related to the financial statements, provide vital information about the ongoing business of the target. For example, the representation requires the disclosure of any material shortage of raw materials or supplies. A buyer must, of course, tailor this representation to the business of its target.

> **Section 4.33. Accuracy of Information Furnished.** No representation or warranty by the Seller or Target contained in this Agreement, the Disclosure Statement or in respect of the exhibits, schedules, lists or other documents delivered to Buyer by the Seller and referred to herein, and no statement contained in any certificate furnished or to be furnished by or on behalf of the Seller or Target pursuant hereto, or in connection with the transactions contemplated hereby, contains, or will contain as of the date such representation or warranty is made or such certificate is or will be furnished, any untrue statement of a material fact, or omits, or will omit to state as of the date such representation or warranty is made or such certificate is or will be furnished, any material fact which is necessary to make the statements contained herein or therein not misleading. To the best knowledge of the Seller, the Target and the Subsidiaries, there is no fact which could have a Material Adverse Effect on the Target or any Subsidiary which the Seller has not prior to or on the date hereof disclosed to Buyer in writing.

The buyer will request this representation to provide assurance that the information upon which the buyer has based its evaluation of the target and its subsidiaries is accurate and complete. This representation is typically referred to as a "10b-5 representation" as the language closely parallels Rule 10b-5 promulgated by the Securities and Exchange Commission (the SEC).

Similar to the representation made in Section 4.6 with respect to undisclosed liabilities, the last sentence in this representation shifts to the seller the responsibility of providing any information of which the buyer should be aware. The seller, although typically reluctant to make this representation, may derive some comfort from the fact that it has already told the buyer everything it could possibly know about the target and the subsidiaries in the preceding representations.

Section 4.34. Reports Filed with the Securities and Exchange Commission. Buyer has been furnished with accurate and complete copies of each annual report on Form 10-K that Target has filed with the Securities and Exchange Commission, all other reports or documents, including all amendments and supplements thereto, required to be filed by the Seller pursuant to Section 13(a) or 15(d) of the Securities Exchange Act since the filing of the most recent annual report on Form 10-K and its most recent annual report to its stockholders. Such reports do not contain any material false statements or any misstatements of any material fact and do not omit to state any fact necessary to make the statements set forth therein not misleading in any material respect.

This representation is only applicable to targets which are publicly traded corporations required to file reports with the SEC. The buyer must assure itself that the target has discharged its obligations to file reports with the SEC, and that the statements contained in the target's filings are true and are not misleading. Failure to obtain this representation may expose the buyer to significant post-Closing liabilities, as the target may be the object of stockholders' suits or SEC enforcement actions.

Section 4.35. Investment Purpose. The Seller's acquisition of the [describe securities of Buyer to be purchased by Seller] is made for its own account for investment purposes only and not with a view to the resale or distribution thereof. The Seller agrees that it will not sell, assign or otherwise transfer or pledge the [describe securities of Buyer to be purchased by Seller] or any interest therein except in compliance with the transfer restrictions set forth on such securities.

When the seller has agreed to accept securities of the buyer in partial payment of the purchase price for the acquisition, the buyer should require certain investment representations from the seller. The representations of the seller are intended to provide the basis for characterizing the sale of securities to the seller as a private placement, thereby exempting the securities from registration under the Securities Act of 1933 and applicable state securities laws. However, this representation is not meant to satisfy all the requirements for exemption under the securities laws, especially in cases where there are more than a handful of persons receiving these securities.

Section 4.36. Dealership & Franchises

(i) Section 4.36(i) of the Disclosure Statement contains a list of (a) those franchisees or dealers who or which, as of the date of this Agreement, were authorized by the Seller to operate stores under the name " _____," or other similar name associating such franchisee or dealer with the Seller (the "Franchisees"), (b) those Franchisees whose relationship with the Seller, the Target or any Subsidiary has been terminated within one year prior to the date hereof and (c) those persons who have become Franchisees within one year prior to the date hereof. Such list is true, correct and complete and includes the expiration date of each existing Franchise Agreement. The Seller has given Buyer an opportunity to review true and correct copies of each of the agreements between it, the Target or any Subsidiary and each Franchisee. Except as stated in Section 4.36(i) of the Disclosure Statement, each agreement between the Seller, the Target or any Subsidiary and each Franchisee (A) has been duly and validly authorized, executed and delivered by, and is the valid and binding obligation of, such Franchisee, enforceable against such Franchisee in accordance with its terms, except as may be limited by applicable bankruptcy, reorganization, insolvency, moratorium or other similar laws or by legal or equitable principles relating to or limiting creditors' rights generally, and (B) does not violate any law or regulation applicable thereto, and (C) does not conflict with the provisions of any other agreement.

(ii) Except as set forth in Section 4.36(ii) of the Disclosure Statement, there is not, under any agreement between the Seller, the Target or any Subsidiary and any Franchisee, any existing default or event which with notice or lapse of time, or both, would constitute an event of default and which has or would be reasonably likely to have a Material Adverse Effect. The execution and delivery of this Agreement and the performance of the transactions contemplated hereby will not result in any event of default under any agreement between the Seller, the Target or any Subsidiary and any Franchisee.

(iii) Except as set forth in Section 4.36(iii) of the Disclosure Statement, each Franchisee was offered his, her or its franchise in accordance with all applicable laws and regulations, including, without limitation, the regulations of the Federal Trade Commission, and any state and/or local agencies regulating the sale of franchised businesses. The Seller has not offered any person or entity a franchise since [insert a date eighteen months prior to date of Agreement].

Where the target has entered into franchise or distributorship arrangements in the conduct of its business, the buyer will want to obtain specific disclosures about the terms of these arrangements. This representation is designed to require the seller to disclose the health of its contractual relations with its franchisees and distributors. A statement certifying compliance with Federal Trade Commission (FTC) regulations is important, as the target may be liable for any failure to comply with FTC disclosure requirements.

ARTICLE V

REPRESENTATIONS AND WARRANTIES OF THE BUYER

The Buyer represents and warrants to the Seller and the Target as follows:

Section 5.1. Organization. The Buyer is a corporation duly organized, validly existing and in good standing under the laws of the jurisdiction of its incorporation. The Buyer has delivered to the Seller true and correct copies of its Certificate of Incorporation and Bylaws.

Section 5.2. Authorization. The execution, delivery and performance of this Agreement and any instruments or agreements contemplated herein to be executed, delivered and performed by the Buyer (including without limitation, [list important agreements to be executed by Buyer on or before Closing]) (the "Buyer's Related Instruments"), and the consummation of the transactions contemplated hereby and thereby, have been duly adopted and approved by the Board of Directors and the stockholders, of the Buyer. The Buyer has all requisite power and authority to execute, deliver and perform this Agreement and the Buyer's Related Instruments and to consummate the transactions contemplated hereby and in the Buyer's Related Instruments. This Agreement has been and as of the Closing Date, each of the Buyer's Related Instruments will be, duly and validly authorized, executed and delivered by the Buyer. This

Agreement is and the Buyer's Related Agreements are or will be, as of the Closing Date the valid and binding obligation of, the Buyer, enforceable against the Buyer in accordance with their respective terms.

Section 5.3. Non-Contravention; Consents. Except as set forth in Section 5.3 of the Disclosure Statement, the execution and delivery of this Agreement and the Related Instruments and the consummation of any of the transactions contemplated hereby and thereby by the Buyer do not and will not:

(i) violate any provisions of the Buyer's certificate of incorporation or bylaws;

(ii) violate, or result with the passage of time in the violation of, any provision of, or result in the acceleration of or entitle any party to accelerate (whether after the giving of notice or lapse of time or both) any obligation under, or result in the creation or imposition of any lien, charge, pledge, security interest or other encumbrance upon any of the properties of the Buyer pursuant to any provision of, any mortgage, lien, lease, agreement, permit, indenture, license, instrument, law, order, arbitration award, judgment or decree to which the Buyer is a party or by which it or any of its properties are bound, the effect of all of which violations, accelerations, creations and impositions would result, in the aggregate, in subjecting the Buyer to liabilities in excess of _____ Dollars ($_____);

(iii) violate any law, order, judgment or decree to which the Buyer is subject;

(iv) violate or conflict with any other restriction of any kind or character to which the Buyer is subject, or by which any of their assets may be bound, the effect of all of which violations or conflicts would result, in the aggregate, in subjecting the Buyer to aggregate liabilities in excess of _____ Dollars ($_____); or

(v) require any consent, license, permit, notice, application, qualification, waiver or other action of any kind, authorization, order or approval of, or filing or registration with, any governmental commission, board, regulatory, or administrative agencies or authorities or other regulatory body.

Section 5.4. Litigation. There is no action, suit, proceeding or investigation pending, or, to the best of the Buyer's knowledge, threatened, against or related to the Buyer or its respective properties or business which would be reasonably likely to adversely affect or restrict the Buyer's ability to consummate the transactions contemplated hereby or in the Related Instruments; and there is no reasonable basis known to the Buyer for any such action that may result in such effect and is probable of assertion.

Section 5.5. Brokers and Finders. Neither the Buyer nor any stockholder, officer, director or agent of the Buyer has incurred on behalf of the Buyer any liability to any broker, finder or agent for any brokerage fees, finders' fees or commissions with respect to the transactions contemplated by this Agreement, except to [name of broker or finder], whose fees will be paid by the Buyer.

Section 5.6. Business. The Buyer has not engaged in any activities other than those incident to its organization or as contemplated by the terms of this Agreement.

Section 5.7. Accuracy of Information Furnished. No representation or warranty by the Buyer contained in this Agreement, the Disclosure Statement or in respect of the exhibits, schedules, lists or other documents delivered to Seller by the Buyer and referred to herein, and no statement contained in any certificate furnished or to be furnished by or on behalf of the Buyer pursuant hereto, or in connection with the transactions contemplated hereby, contains, or will contain as of the date such representation or warranty is made or such certificate is or will be furnished, any untrue statement of a material fact, or omits, or will omit to state as of the date such representation or warranty is made or such certificate is or will be furnished, any material fact which is necessary to make the statements contained herein or therein not misleading.

The representations and warranties of the buyer generally parallel the representations made by the seller and target in Article IV. However, there is no need for the buyer, as the acquirer, to make the vast number of representations and warranties required of the seller and target, because it is the businesses and assets of the seller which are being purchased and in respect of which most representations and warranties therefore apply.

In some instances, the buyer may accomplish its acquisition of the target by utilizing a shell company as the acquiror. If properly structured, this strategy may permit the parties to avoid filing a pre-merger notification under the Hart-Scott-Rodino Antitrust Improvements Act of 1974. The representation made in Section 5.6 above regarding the scope of the business of the buyer is useful to the seller in that it assures the seller that there should be few contractual constraints on the shell company to consummate the acquisition.

In circumstances where the buyer is not a shell company, it may be appropriate for the seller to include additional representations about the buyer. For example, a representation relating to the buyer's financial statements and the absence of certain changes or events since the date of such financial statements might assure the seller of the buyer's ability to consummate the transaction.

ARTICLE VI

COVENANTS OF SELLER AND TARGET

> *Section 6.1. Conduct of Business.*   Except as set forth on Section 6.1 of the Disclosure Statement or required to consummate the transactions contemplated hereby, from and after the execution and delivery of this Agreement and until the Closing Date, the Seller shall cause the Target and each of the Subsidiaries (a) to use its best efforts to preserve the respective present business organizations of the Target and the Subsidiaries substantially intact; (b) to maintain in effect all foreign, federal, state and local approvals, permits, licenses, qualifications and authorizations which are required to carry on their respective businesses as now being conducted; (c) to use their best efforts to maintain their respective relationships with and preserve the goodwill of, employees, agents, distributors, franchisees, licensees, customers, suppliers and others having business dealings with them; and (d) without the prior written consent of the Buyer, to take any action which would result in a breach of any of the representations set forth in Section 4.32 hereof.

The "conduct of business" covenant is used by a buyer to ensure that the seller will not do, or cause to be done, anything which would (a) alter the business being purchased, (b) diminish the value of such business to the buyer, or (c) create for the buyer an unanticipated liability or problem with respect to the business it is acquiring. This is important because the buyer has presumably negotiated an acceptable purchase price for the target based on the operations and performance of the business as it presently exists. If the seller were to allow necessary permits or licenses, or business relationships with distributors, employees, or franchisees to lapse, the value of the business could be diminished. If not restricted by such a covenant, the seller could render the buyer's valuation meaningless by taking some action outside of the ordinary course of business which impairs the financial position of the target or the value of the target to the buyer. One issue that often arises is how to define the actions which are in the ordinary course of business. Since most agreements fail to include a definition of this phrase, the buyer should acquaint itself with applicable case law in order to be aware of its usage in the jurisdiction governing the acquisition agreement.

In negotiating this representation, the seller should be certain that, between the signing of the agreement and the Closing Date, it need not obtain the buyer's consent for anything other than items which would not normally occur in the ordinary course of business of the target or its subsidiaries. Subsection (d) incorporates all of the items represented in Section 4.32, and consequently may require the seller to obtain the buyer's consent for actions to be taken by the target or any subsidiary which are extremely important to the continued operation of the business. A seller would likely request that the buyer agree not to unreasonably withhold its consent in order for the seller to take such actions. While this language may seem innocuous, it can in certain circumstances have consequences which the buyer did not intend at the time. As state courts have not consistently interpreted the standard of reasonableness, the buyer may be unable to reconcile its business judgments with local case precedent. A common strategy is for a buyer to require unmodified consent in its first draft, and then, if the seller requests it, add the reasonableness standard as a bargaining point or show of good faith.

> **Section 6.2. Pre-Closing Activities.** Prior to the Closing Date, the Seller shall cause the Target, with the cooperation of the Buyer where appropriate, and the Target shall and shall cause each Subsidiary to use their best efforts to obtain any consent, authorization or approval of, or exemption by, any governmental authority or agency or other third party, including without limitation, their landlords and lenders and those persons (other than the Target or a Subsidiary) who are parties to the agreements described in Section 4.29 of the Disclosure Statement required to be obtained or made by them in connection with the transactions contemplated by this Agreement and the Related Instruments or the taking of any action in connection with the consummation thereof, including without limitation, any consent, authorization or approval necessary to waive any default under any of the agreements described in Section 4.29 of the Disclosure Statement.

Once the buyer is made aware of the various consents necessary to consummate the acquisition by means of the seller's disclosure in Section 4.29, the buyer typically will attempt to require the seller to use its best efforts to obtain such consents. The seller, who has an interest in getting the deal done, should agree to accommodate the buyer, but only to the extent it is reasonable for the seller to do so under the circumstances. It should make clear that "best efforts" do not extend to spending money.

> **Section 6.3. Proposals; Disclosure.** Prior to the Closing Date, the Target and the Seller (i) will not, directly or indirectly, whether through any of their officers, employees, representatives or otherwise, solicit or encourage any written inquiries or proposals for the acquisition of stock, or all or substantially all of the assets or the business or any portion thereof of the Target or any Subsidiary and (ii) will promptly advise the Buyer orally and in writing of any inquiry or proposal for the acquisition of any stock, or all or substantially all of the assets or business or any portion thereof of the Target or any Subsidiary occurring on or after the date hereof.

This covenant is designed (a) to prevent the seller from shopping for a better deal during the period between signing of the acquisition agreement and the Closing Date, and (b) to keep the buyer apprised of any unsolicited inquiries. From the buyer's point of view, the seller has made a commitment to sell to the buyer and should be concentrating all of its efforts toward a Closing with the buyer rather than continuing to court other would-be suitors. In addition, the acquisition agreement represents a binding contract, and the buyer has made a commitment to purchase provided that all conditions to Closing are satisfied. The buyer should have the benefit of having made such a commitment as well as the business risk of a deterioration in the target's business in the ordinary course. One benefit of ownership is the opportunity to sell at a profit. The *Pennzoil v. Texaco* case has highly publicized the fact that this benefit belongs to a potential buyer once a contractual commitment between the seller and buyer has been put in place.

> **Section 6.4. Additional Financial Statements.** Prior to the Closing Date, the Target shall furnish to the Buyer as soon as practicable but in no event later than _____ days after the close of each quarterly period or _____ days after the close of each monthly period (i) for each successive quarterly period ending after the date of the Most Recent Balance Sheet, an unaudited consolidated quarterly balance sheet and related statements of income, stockholders' equity and changes in financial position of the Target and its Subsidiaries and (ii) for each successive monthly period ending after the date of the Most Recent Balance Sheet, an unaudited consolidated monthly balance sheet and related monthly statements of income, stockholders' equity and changes in financial position of

the Target and its Subsidiaries. Such financial statements shall be complete, accurate and correct and present fairly the financial condition of the Target and the Subsidiaries, both individually and taken as a whole, as of the end of each such quarterly or monthly period, as the case may be, and shall present fairly the results of operations for each of the quarterly or monthly periods then ended, in accordance with generally accepted accounting principles consistently applied except for the footnotes thereto, normal year-end adjustments consistent with past practices or as contemplated by this Agreement.

Section 6.5. Additional Summaries of Accounts Receivable. Prior to the Closing Date, the Target will deliver to the Buyer, as soon as practicable but in no event later than _____ days after the close of the appropriate monthly period hereinafter referred to, for each successive monthly period after the date of the Most Recent Balance Sheet a true and correct summary of all accounts receivable of the Target and the Subsidiaries as at the end of each such monthly period.

Sections 6.4 and 6.5 permit the buyer to monitor the operations of the business after the execution of the acquisition agreement by reviewing monthly and quarterly financial statements furnished by the seller. This can be extremely important to the buyer especially if the financial statements reveal a material adverse change in the business. In this event, the buyer would not be obligated to close, since a customary condition to its obligation to close is the absence of any material adverse changes in the business. For a further discussion of material adverse change, see Section 9.6.

Section 6.6. Investigation by Buyer. The Seller and Target shall, and the Target shall cause its Subsidiaries to, afford to the officers and authorized representatives of the Buyer free and full access, during normal business hours and upon reasonable prior notice, to the offices, plants, properties, books and records of the Target and its Subsidiaries in order that the Buyer may have full opportunity to make such investigations of the business, operations, assets, properties and legal and financial condition of the Target and its Subsidiaries as the Buyer deems reasonably necessary or desirable and the officers of the Seller, the Target and its Subsidiaries shall furnish the Buyer with such additional financial and operating data and other information relating to the business operations, assets, properties and legal and financial condition of the Target and its Subsidiaries as the Buyer shall from time to time reasonably request. Prior to the Closing Date, or at all times if this Agreement shall be terminated, the Buyer shall, except as may be otherwise required by applicable law, hold confidential all information obtained pursuant to this Section 6.6 with respect to the Target and its Subsidiaries and, if this Agreement shall be terminated, shall return to the Target and its Subsidiaries all of such information as shall be in documentary form and shall not use any information obtained pursuant to this Section 6.6 in any manner that would have a material adverse consequence to the Target or its Subsidiaries.

The representations, warranties and agreements of the Seller, the Target and its Subsidiaries set forth in this Agreement shall be effective regardless of any investigation that the Buyer has undertaken or failed to undertake.

The "investigation" covenant assures that the seller will cooperate with the buyer by granting access and logistical support for the buyer's due diligence review of the target and its subsidiaries. It is important for the buyer to include the last paragraph of this covenant so that the seller cannot attempt to prevent the buyer from taking action against the seller as a result of a material breach of the seller's or target's representations by alleging that, since the buyer discovered or could have discovered the breach during its investigation of the target and its subsidiaries, the seller should be relieved of any responsibility for such misrepresentations.

Section 6.7. Notification. The Seller shall give prompt notice to the Buyer of (i) any notice of, or other communication received by the Seller, the Target or any Subsidiary subsequent to the date of this Agreement and prior to the Closing Date, relating to a default or event which with notice or lapse of time or both would become a default, or which would cause any warranty or representation of the Seller or the Target to be untrue or misleading in any material respect, under this Agreement, or any other material contract, agreement or instrument to which the Target or any Subsidiary is a party, by which it or any of its property is bound or to which it or any of its property is subject, (ii) any notice or other communication from any third party alleging that the consent of such third party is or may be required in connection with the transactions contemplated by this Agreement, (iii) any material adverse change in the business, operations, earnings, prospects, assets or financial condition of the Target or its Subsidiaries, or (iv) any information received by the Seller or Target prior to the Closing Date relating to the operations of the Buyer which, to the best knowledge of the Seller or Target, constitutes (or would be reasonably likely to constitute) or indicates (or would be reasonably likely to indicate) a breach of any representation, warranty or covenant made by the Buyer herein or in any other document relating to the transactions contemplated hereby.

The "notice" covenant places on the seller the onus of notifying the buyer of any potential material breaches of the seller's representations and warranties. Upon such notification, the buyer has the option of asserting a breach and abandoning the deal on the grounds that the conditions to Closing are not met. However, a buyer does not have a right to walk from the deal if the breach can be cured by the seller prior to the Closing.

Section 6.8. Access to Records. After the Closing, the Buyer shall be entitled to reasonable access to the business and tax records of the Seller relating to the Target and its Subsidiaries for proper business purposes, including the preparation of tax returns. In connection with any such purpose, the Seller agrees to cooperate with the Buyer in the communication of information contained in such records and the handling of examinations, appeals and litigations.

This covenant may be important where many of the records of the target and its subsidiaries are consolidated with those of the seller. It is impossible in such circumstances for the seller to turn over to the buyer such records, since they may also relate to other companies owned by the seller.

Section 6.9. Stockholders Meeting. The Target, acting through its Board of Directors shall, as soon as practicable and in accordance with its Articles of Incorporation and By-Laws and applicable law:

(1) prepare and distribute proxy materials (the "Proxy Statement") in compliance with applicable law for, and duly call, give notice of, convene and hold, a special meeting (the "Special Meeting") of its stockholders as soon as practicable after the date hereof but not later than [insert the date] for the purposes of considering and voting upon this Agreement in accordance with the [name of business code for Target's state of incorporation] Code;

(2) include in the Proxy Statement (as hereinafter defined) the recommendation of the Board that stockholders of the Target vote in favor of the approval and adoption of this Agreement; and

(3) use its best efforts (a) to obtain and furnish the information required to be included by it in the Proxy Statement, (b) to file a preliminary version of the Proxy Statement with the Securities and Exchange Commission ("SEC") not later than [insert number of days] after the receipt by the Target of its audited financial statement for the year ended [insert year], furnish copies thereof to the Buyer and, after consultation with the Buyer, respond promptly to any comments made by the SEC with respect to the Proxy Statement and any preliminary version thereof, (c) to cause the Proxy Statement to be mailed to its stockholders as early as practicable after the date hereof but no later than [insert number of days], and (d) to

obtain the necessary approval of this Agreement by its stockholders. Notwithstanding any consultation with the Buyer in connection with the Proxy Statement, neither the Buyer nor any of its officers, directors, employees or affiliates shall incur any liability to the Target or its stockholders with respect thereto, except with respect to any information contained in the Proxy Statement which any of them has furnished, or confirmed the accuracy of, in writing to the Target.

(4) amend, supplement or revise the Proxy Statement as may from time to time be necessary in order to insure that the Proxy Statement does not contain any statement which, at the time and in the light of the circumstances under which it is made, is false or misleading with respect to any material fact, or omits to state any material fact necessary in order to make the statements therein not false or misleading. Prior to submitting any such amendment, supplement or revision of the Proxy Statement to the stockholders of the Target, such amendment, supplement or revision shall be submitted to the Buyer for its approval. Notwithstanding such approval, neither the Buyer nor any of its officers, directors, employees or affiliates shall incur any liability to the Target or its stockholders with respect thereto, except with respect to any information contained in such amendment, supplement or revision which any of them has furnished, or confirmed the accuracy of, in writing to the Target.

In an acquisition of a target whose equity securities are publicly traded, it is essential that the target comply with all relevant regulations, especially those promulgated by the Securities and Exchange Commission dealing with proxies and required stockholders' meetings. Failure to comply with these regulations can expose the target to stockholder suits or regulatory enforcement actions. The buyer is also desirous of placing an affirmative obligation on the target to solicit proxies and to obtain stockholder approval.

In some circumstances, the buyer may require the seller to deliver a cold comfort letter from the seller's or target's accountants at Closing confirming the financial information in the proxy statement. The purpose of this requirement is to reduce the potential for error in the financial information presented in the proxy statement and thereby reduce the chance that a stockholder may prevail in a suit against the surviving corporation.

Section 6.10. Dissenting Stockholders; Notice. The Target will promptly advise the Buyer of each notice given or demand made by a dissenting Target stockholder pursuant to [cite relevant section of business law in state where Target is incorporated].

No buyer wants to close a transaction in which a large percentage of the target's stockholders are seeking appraisal rights. If such stockholders were to be awarded a price per share in excess of the price paid by the buyer, it could expose the surviving corporation to an inordinate amount of liability. Therefore, as covered in Section 9.10 and the discussion that follows, in order for a buyer to exercise its right not to consummate the transaction pursuant to Section 9.10, it must be aware of any dissenting stockholders of the target.

ARTICLE VII

COVENANT OF THE BUYER

> The Buyer shall give prompt notice to the Seller of (i) any notice of, or other communication received by the Buyer subsequent to the date of this Agreement and prior to the Closing Date, relating to a default or event which with notice or lapse of time or both would become a default, or which would cause any warranty, or representation of the Buyer to be untrue or misleading in any material respect, under this Agreement, or any other material contract, agreement or instrument to which the Buyer is a party, by which it or any of its property is bound or to which it or any of its property is subject, (ii) any notice or other communication from any third party alleging that the consent of such third party is or may be required in connection with the transactions contemplated by this Agreement, or (iii) any information received by the Buyer prior to the Closing Date relating to the operations of the Seller, the Target or its Subsidiaries which, to the best knowledge of the Buyer, constitutes (or would constitute) or indicates (or would indicate) a breach of any representation, warranty or covenant made by the Seller or Target herein or in any other document relating to the transactions contemplated hereby.

Similar to the representations, the seller's covenants usually far outnumber the covenants of the buyer. Typically, a seller would at a minimum require a buyer to give the same "notice" that it is required to give. One useful device (which is advantageous to both buyer and seller) is the requirement that each notify the other in the event that the first party is aware of the other's breach of a particular representation, warranty, or covenant. The utility of this obligation, especially for the seller, is that neither side has a distinct advantage over the other post-Closing by reason of a breach that was known about prior to the Closing. See page 565 of this chapter for a discussion of how the buyer's or seller's knowledge affects each of their respective indemnity obligations under the acquisition agreement.

ARTICLE VIII

COVENANTS OF BUYER, TARGET AND SELLER

Section 8.1. Governmental Filings. The Buyer, the Target and the Seller shall cooperate with each other in filing any necessary applications, reports or other documents with any federal or state agencies, authorities or bodies (domestic and foreign) having jurisdiction with respect to the Merger, and in seeking necessary consultation with and prompt favorable action by any such agencies, authorities or bodies. Without limiting the generality of the foregoing, the Buyer, the Target and the Seller shall as soon as practicable, and in any event within fifteen (15) days, after the date hereof, make the necessary filings under the Hart-Scott-Rodino Antitrust Improvements Act of 1976 (the "Hart-Scott-Rodino Act") and shall cooperate in attempting to secure early termination of the applicable waiting period.

This covenant requires the buyer, target, and seller to work together in making any governmental filing or application. The buyer and the seller should use a general covenant of this type and then specify the particular filings that must be made, i.e., Hart-Scott-Rodino Act filings with respect to a merger, SEC filings, state government filings, etc.

Section 8.2. Publicity. The Buyer, the Target and the Seller will consult with each other before making any public announcements with respect to the Merger or the Related Instruments or the transactions contemplated hereby or thereby, and any public announcements shall be made only at such time and in such manner as the Seller and the Buyer shall mutually agree, except that either party shall be free to make such public announcements as it shall reasonably deem necessary to comply with foreign, federal or state laws.

The buyer and the seller must be aware of each other's plans with respect to publicity surrounding the acquisition of a target so as to be able to coordinate their efforts. It can be extremely harmful to the transaction or one of the parties to the transaction if there are conflicting reports or misleading statements. For example, conflicting reports in the press can disrupt management of the target or may even damage the ongoing business. More importantly, where one or both of the entities involved are public companies, liability can arise from premature press reports which might be alleged to have been made to manipulate the market or mislead stockholders and investors. When possible, the buyer and seller should issue joint press releases or, at least, carefully review releases before they are distributed.

ARTICLE IX

CONDITIONS TO OBLIGATIONS OF THE BUYER

The obligations of the Buyer to consummate this Agreement, and the transactions to be consummated by the Buyer hereunder on the Closing Date, shall be subject to the satisfaction, prior to or concurrently with the Closing, of each of the conditions set forth in this Article IX; such conditions may be waived in writing in whole or in part by the Buyer to the extent permitted by applicable law.

> *Section 9.1. Compliance with Agreement.* The Seller and the Target shall have complied with and performed the terms, conditions, acts, undertakings, covenants and obligations required by this Agreement to be complied with and performed by each of them on or before the Closing Date; and the Buyer shall have received from the Seller at the Closing a certificate, dated the Closing Date and signed by the President or a Vice President of the Seller to such effect.

This condition gives the buyer the opportunity to abandon the acquisition if the seller or the target has failed to perform its obligations under the acquisition agreement. Although this condition is less critical than the bring-down of representations and warranties to the Closing Date which appears in Section 9.2, it provides the buyer a valuable "out" if the seller or the target has breached a covenant which is essential to the buyer's valuation of the target. For example, the duty of the target to endeavor to obtain all regulatory approvals necessary for the transaction would usually arise from a covenant made to the buyer in the acquisition agreement, as would the obligation of the target to conduct business only in the ordinary and usual course. Because failure to perform under these covenants may compromise the value of the target, the buyer must ensure its right to abandon the transaction in these circumstances.

The requirement for an officer's certificate is based upon the belief that prior to any officer's execution of such a certificate, the officer will investigate to ascertain its accuracy, and the certificate can be drafted to include a representation to that effect.

This condition can be drafted without a materiality standard. However, sellers typically demand that the materiality qualifier be incorporated. This position is a reasonable one given the broad language of both the condition itself and the covenants and other agreements to which it refers. Consequently, the buyer should be prepared to accept "performance *in all material respects* of the terms" of the agreement as adequate protection of its interests. A similar qualifier appears in the condition set forth in Section 9.2 below.

> ***Section 9.2. Representations and Warranties True as of Closing Date.*** All representations and warranties of the Seller and the Target set forth in this Agreement shall be true and correct in all material respects on and as of the Closing Date with the same force and effect as though such representations and warranties had been made on and as of the Closing Date and the Buyer shall have received from the Seller at the Closing a certificate, dated the Closing Date and signed by the President or a Vice President of the Seller to such effect.

The importance of this "bring-down" condition was discussed in detail on page 558 of this chapter. A bring-down of the representations and warranties to the Closing Date is, from the buyer's perspective, insurance that the target it acquires is the target for which it bid and upon which it conducted due diligence.

> ***Section 9.3. Third Party Orders and Consents***
> (i) The Seller and the Buyer shall have fully complied with the applicable provisions of the Hart-Scott-Rodino Act and any and all applicable waiting periods thereunder shall have expired, or an opinion, reasonably acceptable to the Buyer, that no such filing is required shall have been delivered to the Buyer.
> (ii) All consents and approvals listed in Section 4.29 of the Disclosure Statement hereto shall have been obtained, and the Seller and the Buyer shall have been furnished with appropriate evidence, reasonably satisfactory to them and their respective counsel, of the granting of such consents and approvals.

This condition enables the buyer to abandon a transaction if all necessary consents are not obtained before Closing. Failure to obtain the consent of the target's lenders, for example, may prejudice the pricing of the acquisition or its financeability because consummation of the transaction may entitle the lenders to accelerate their debts or impose a lien on the property of the target. Failure to obtain necessary governmental consent to an acquisition may preclude the buyer from operating the business of the target as previously operated.

The seller should attempt to limit this condition to governmental consents necessary in order to consummate the transactions contemplated by the acquisition agreement. The seller could reasonably maintain that any debt instruments which are accelerated by their terms should be refinanced by the buyer. If this limitation is accepted, the obligation of the buyer to close the deal should not be conditioned upon the consent of the holders of such debt. Clearly, the buyer and the seller must agree on exactly what consents must be obtained prior to the Closing.

Section 9.4. Corporate Action. The Buyer shall have received:

(i) a copy of the resolution or resolutions duly adopted by the Board of Directors of the Seller and the Target and by the stockholders of the Target authorizing the execution, delivery and performance of this Agreement and the Related Instruments by the Seller and the Target, and authorizing all other necessary or proper corporate action to enable the Seller and the Target to comply with the terms of this Agreement, certified in each case by the Secretary or an Assistant Secretary of the Seller or the Target as the case may be; and

(ii) a certificate of the Secretary or an Assistant Secretary of each of the Seller and the Target, dated the Closing Date, as to the incumbency and signatures of the officers of the Seller and the Target, respectively, executing this Agreement and the Related Instruments and any other documents in connection with the transactions contemplated by this Agreement or the Related Instruments.

A further protection for the Buyer that the acquisition agreement and related documents are properly authorized and delivered is a review of the resolutions authorizing such documents.

Section 9.5. Opinion of the Seller's and Target's Counsel. At the Closing, the Seller shall furnish the Buyer and the banks and/or other financial institutions providing financing for the Merger (the "Acquisition Lenders") with an opinion, dated the Closing Date, of [name of Seller's counsel], in form and substance satisfactory to the Buyer and its counsel and the Acquisition Lenders and counsel to the Acquisition Lenders, to the effect that:

(i) Target (a) is a corporation duly organized, validly existing and in good standing under the laws of its state of incorporation,

(b) is duly qualified or licensed to transact business as a foreign corporation and is in good standing in each jurisdiction in which the properties owned or leased by it or the nature of the business conducted by it makes such qualification or licensing necessary, except in those jurisdictions where the failure to be so qualified or licensed and in good standing will not, individually or in the aggregate, have a Material Adverse Effect, and (c) has full power and authority to carry on its business as it is now being conducted and to own the properties and assets it now owns;

(ii) Target has full power and authority to execute, deliver and perform the Agreement and the Related Instruments and to consummate the transactions contemplated hereby and by the Related Instruments; and the execution, delivery and performance of the Agreement and the Related Instruments and the consummation of the transactions contemplated by the Agreement and the Related Instruments have been duly authorized by all requisite action on the part of the Target;

(iii) the Seller is a corporation duly organized, validly existing and in good standing under the laws of its state of incorporation and has full power and authority to execute, deliver and perform the Agreement and the Related Instruments and to consummate the transactions contemplated by the Agreement and the Related Instruments; and the execution, delivery and performance of the Agreement and the Related Instruments and the consummation of the transactions contemplated by the Agreement and the Related Instruments have been duly authorized by all requisite action on the part of the Seller;

(iv) each of the Subsidiaries (a) is a corporation duly organized, validly existing and in good standing under the laws of its jurisdiction of organization, (b) is duly qualified or licensed to transact business and is in good standing in each jurisdiction in which the properties owned or leased by it or the nature of the business conducted by it makes such qualification or licensing necessary, except in those jurisdictions where the failure to be so qualified or licensed and in good standing will not, individually or in the aggregate, have a Material Adverse Effect and (3) has full power and authority to carry on its business as it is now being conducted and to own the properties and assets it now owns;

(v) the authorized, issued and outstanding equity capital of the Target and each Subsidiary consists solely of (a) in the case of the Target, _____ shares of Common Stock, of which _____ shares are issued and outstanding and _____ shares of Preferred Stock, of which _____ shares are issued and outstanding and (b) in the case of each Subsidiary, as set forth in Section 4.3 of the Disclosure Statement (the "Subsidiary Stock"). All outstanding shares of the Target Common Stock and the Subsidiary Stock have been duly and validly authorized and issued and are fully paid, nonassessable and free of preemptive rights and based upon an examination of the organizational documents, minute books, stock registers and other similar records of the Target, all of such shares are owned of record and beneficially by (x) the Seller, in the case of the Target and (2) as set forth in Section 4.1 of the Disclosure Statement, in the case of each Subsidiary, in each case free and clear of all claims, liens, mortgages, charges, security interests, encumbrances and other restrictions or limitations of any kind whatsoever, and there are no outstanding options, warrants, calls, convertible securities or other rights relating to unissued shares of capital stock of Target or any Subsidiary;

(vi) the Agreement and the Related Instruments have been executed and delivered by each of the Seller and the Target and constitutes the legal, valid and binding obligations of each of the Seller and the Target, enforceable against each in accordance with their respective terms, except (a) as such enforcement may be subject to fraudulent conveyance, bankruptcy, insolvency, reorganization, moratorium or other similar laws now or hereafter in effect, or by legal or equitable principles, relating to or limiting creditors' rights generally and (b) that the remedy of specific performance and injunctive and other forms of equitable relief are subject to certain equitable defenses and to the discretion of the court before which any proceeding therefor may be brought;

(vii) neither the execution, delivery and performance of the Agreement or the Related Instruments by the Seller or the Target, nor the consummation of the transactions contemplated hereby or thereby will violate any provision of the Certificate of Incorporation or Bylaws of the Seller or the Target or of any of the Subsidiaries or, to the best knowledge of such counsel after due inquiry, will violate, conflict with, or constitute a default under, or cause the acceleration of maturity of any debt or obligation pursuant to, or result in the creation or imposition of any security interest, lien or other encumbrance upon any property or assets of the Target or any of the Subsidiaries under, any contract, commitment, agreement, trust, understanding, arrangement or restriction of any kind to which the Target or any of the Subsidiaries is a party or by which the Target or any of the Subsidiaries is bound or violate any statute or law, or any judgment, decree, order, regulation or rule of any court or governmental authority;

(viii) to the best knowledge of such counsel, none of the Target, the Seller nor any Subsidiary is engaged in or threatened with any legal action or other proceeding or has incurred or been charged with or is under investigation with respect to any violation of any law or administrative regulation which if adversely determined might, in such counsel's opinion, materially adversely affect or impair (a) the business or condition, financial or otherwise, of the Target or any of the Subsidiaries except as specifically disclosed in the Agreement or the Disclosure Statement or (b) the ability of the Target and/or the Seller to consummate the transactions contemplated by the Agreement or the Related Instruments;

(ix) no filing, declaration or registration with, or any permit, authorization, license, consent or approval of, any governmental or regulatory authority is required in connection with the execution, delivery and performance of the Agreement or the Related Instruments by the Seller and the Target or the consummation of the transactions contemplated by the Agreement or the Related Instruments, except as expressly disclosed in this Agreement, all of which have been duly and validly obtained;

(x) no facts have come to the attention of such counsel that cause such counsel to believe that any information provided to the Buyer in writing by or on behalf of the Seller or the Target contained any untrue statement of a material fact or omitted to state any material fact necessary to make the statements therein, in light of the circumstances under which they were made, not misleading, except that counsel may also state that it has not independently verified the accuracy, completeness or fairness of such information, and the limitations inherent in the examination made by it and the knowledge available to it are such that it is unable to assume, and does not assume, any responsibility for the accuracy, completeness or fairness of such information.

As to any matter contained in such opinion which involves the laws of a jurisdiction other than the United States or the State of [state in which such counsel is licensed to practice], such counsel may rely upon opinions of local counsel of established reputation reasonably satisfactory to the Buyer, which opinions shall expressly state that they may be relied upon by the Buyer and the Acquisition Lenders. Such counsel may also expressly rely as to matters of fact upon certificates furnished by appropriate officers of the Seller, the Target and any Subsidiary, or appropriate governmental officials.

Typically, the seller and the target will require an opinion from the buyer's counsel (see Section 10.6) which mirrors many of the provisions included in the opinion given by seller's counsel. Although these opinions may be heavily negotiated by the counsel who must render them, they are useful for a variety of reasons. First, legal opinions serve as a due diligence device and force counsel to closely examine the important aspects of the transaction. Second, counsel's reluctance to deliver an opinion regarding a particular issue raises a red flag, permitting the parties to reexamine that aspect of the transaction. Third, the opinion gives the party to which it is addressed legal recourse against counsel delivering the opinion. In this regard, the buyer may be asked to accept the opinion of general counsel to the seller or target. The buyer should resist this request since the buyer's recourse against the general counsel of the target may be tantamount to recourse against the surviving corporation. In contrast, outside counsel's opinion provides recourse against an independent source, one which may be more diligent in its efforts and less biased in its evaluation as a result of its potential liability and relative "distance" from seller's management.

In some circumstances, the buyer may be required to accept the opinion of general counsel with respect to certain matters relating to the law of a jurisdiction where it would be impractical or inordinately expensive to retain outside counsel. In addition, outside counsel frequently relies on a back-up opinion from the general counsel of the target with respect to matters that pertain to the business of the target in general. For example, general counsel would probably provide a back-up opinion with respect to whether the target is qualified as a foreign corporation in each jurisdiction in which the properties owned or leased by it or the nature of the business conducted by it makes such qualification or licensure necessary.

The opinion also may be used as a negotiating tool in the earlier phases of the transaction; counsel's unwillingness to opine that no governmental consent required in connection with the contemplated transactions or to the enforceability of particular documents may cause the parties to revamp the structure of the transaction.

One opinion that counsel is often reluctant to deliver is expressed in clause (x) above. Only rarely will counsel accept such a high level of responsibility. If the acquisition involves a public company, counsel may agree to opine to the accuracy of the proxy statement if counsel oversaw its preparation. Otherwise, despite the buyer's legitimate concern with the accuracy of information provided by the seller, the target, and the subsidiaries, it will not have the comfort of counsel's opinion on the matter. If a party is extremely concerned about the withholding of information or the accuracy thereof, it may be able to persuade the seller's counsel to include clause (x) at the end of its opinion letter without giving it the benefit of being a legal opinion.

> **Section 9.6. No Material Adverse Change.** No material adverse change in the business, operations, earnings, prospects, assets or financial condition of the Target or any Subsidiary and no event which would have such an effect shall have occurred.

As discussed on pages 562–564, a customary condition to the buyer's obligation to close the transaction is that the target has not suffered any adverse change prior to the Closing. The seller should attempt to limit this condition to the target and its subsidiaries taken as a whole since the buyer is not buying the target and its subsidiaries piecemeal. The seller should also focus on the phrase "business, operations, earnings, prospects, assets, or financial condition" because, in some instances, the buyer may not have bargained for a certain earnings stream or the prospects of the target. For example, in a transaction based on the net assets of the target, a seller who has not made any projections as to the growth of the business of the target could argue that the target's "earnings" and "prospects" are irrelevant and should be deleted from this condition since the deal was not priced on a multiple of earnings or discounted cash flow. This appears plausible, since the buyer has based its investment decision only on the value of the net assets. However, most buyers will resist this approach, alleging that future earnings were an important factor in the investment decision.

Conversely, where the buyer has relied on projections, it should specifically include the projections in this condition as a yardstick for measuring the prospects of the target.

What constitutes a material adverse change is unclear and varies from circumstance to circumstance. It's easy to identify an obvious one, like the single line target who has lost the only supplier of raw materials for the manufacture of its product. But the loss of a customer whose purchase of goods from the target constitutes five percent of the target's overall revenues is a less clear-cut situation. The usual vagueness of this condition gives the buyer the opportunity to get out of the deal, even in circumstances where the change is of uncertain harm to the target, because the seller is usually disinclined to bring suit on the basis that no material adverse change has occurred. Of course, the buyer must have some real basis for its belief that a material adverse change has occurred. Usually, the seller and buyer attempt to restructure the transaction in light of any material adverse change.

> **Section 9.7. Litigation.** At the Closing, there shall be no effective injunction, writ or preliminary restraining order or any order of any nature issued by a court or governmental agency of competent jurisdiction restraining or prohibiting the consummation of the transactions provided for herein or any of them or limiting in any manner the Buyer's right to control the Target and the Subsidiaries or any aspect of their businesses or requiring the sale or other disposition of any of the operations of the Target or any Subsidiary or making the consummation of the Merger or the transactions contemplated by this Agreement and the Related

Instruments unduly burdensome to the Target or any Subsidiary, and immediately prior to the Closing Date no proceeding or lawsuit shall have been commenced and be pending or be threatened by any governmental or regulatory agency or any other person with respect to the transactions contemplated by this Agreement or the Related Instruments which the Buyer, in good faith and with the advice of counsel, believes is likely to result in any of the foregoing or which seeks the payment of substantial damages by the Target, any Subsidiary or the Buyer.

The utility of this condition is self-explanatory. It is usually triggered in circumstances in which the acquisition is either unfriendly and a potential suitor has brought suit to enjoin the consummation of the transaction contemplated by the acquisition agreement, or a governmental agency has attempted to enjoin the transaction because of antitrust or other governmental concerns.

Section 9.8. Financing

(i) The Buyer shall have received the financing proceeds pursuant to, and on substantially the same terms and conditions as those contained in, the commitment letter from [name of Acquisition Lender].

(ii) The final documentation of such financing arrangements referred to in the commitment letter from [name of Acquisition Lender] shall in all respects be reasonably satisfactory in form and substance to the Buyer.

The "financing out" is discussed on pages 560–562. The version included here is appropriate if the buyer has obtained financing commitments before signing the acquisition agreement. Another method, which is appropriate if the parties have agreed that the buyer must finance the transaction within a certain period of time, is to build in a provision enabling the parties to terminate the acquisition agreement if commitment letters are not obtained or the deal is not closed by a specific date.

Section 9.9. Title Insurance.

[Insert name of title company], or any other reputable title company reasonably satisfactory to the Buyer (the "Title Company") shall have issued owners', lessees', and mortgagees', title insurance policies (or unconditional commitments therefor) with respect to, and in the amount of the fair market value of, the real property and the leased real property listed in Section

4.15 of the Disclosure Statement and located in the United States, the United States territories and possessions and Canada, on the current edition of the A.L.T.A. Form B, Rev. 1970 (or Loan Policy Form, in the case of mortgagees' title insurance) insuring title, with all standard and general exceptions deleted or endorsed over so as to afford full "extended form coverage," except for the lien of taxes not yet due and payable, and with no further exceptions not reasonably satisfactory to the Buyer. It is hereby agreed that if, in order to delete, or endorse over, standard form or general exceptions so as to afford to owners, lessees or lenders "extended form coverage," the Title Company requires standard form seller's affidavits, the conditions set forth in this Section 9.10 shall be satisfied by an authorized officer of the Seller giving such affidavit. The Buyer shall have received unconditional title insurance commitments reflecting the foregoing matters at least ten (10) days prior to Closing.

This condition provides the buyer comfort that the real property owned or leased by the target is free from defects in title and, consequently, may be used to secure acquisition financing. The seller may demand that this condition be effective only to the extent that Acquisition Lenders require title insurance. On the other hand, the buyer may strengthen the condition to make the existence of a title defect which compromises the business of the target a sufficient basis for abandoning the transaction. To the extent that title insurance is unavailable and the real property is an integral part of the business of the target, this condition gives the buyer the opportunity to renegotiate the price of the acquisition or walk away from the deal.

>   ***Section 9.10. Dissenting Stockholders.*** Holders of not more than [insert percentage] of the Target's Common Stock shall have elected dissenter's rights as provided in Section [ ] of the [business code of Target's state of incorporation] Code, and the Target shall have taken all action with respect to the rights of dissenting stockholders required of it pursuant to such Code.

In an acquisition of a target with numerous stockholders, a buyer should attempt to limit its exposure to liability in the event that the stockholders of the target achieve a higher price for the value of their shares than that paid by the buyer through an appraisal proceeding brought by such stockholders post-Closing. The seller should obviously negotiate a percentage high enough to prevent the buyer from abandoning the deal without good cause, and the buyer should be willing to accept some level of risk. The exact percentage of holders seeking appraisal rights in this condition depends on the circumstance.

ARTICLE X

CONDITIONS TO OBLIGATIONS OF THE SELLER AND TARGET

The obligations of the Seller and the Target to consummate this Agreement, and the transactions to be consummated by the Seller hereunder on the Closing Date, shall be subject to the satisfaction, with the Closing, of each of the conditions set forth in this Article X; which conditions may be waived in writing in whole or in part by the Seller to the extent permitted by applicable law.

Section 10.1. Compliance with Agreement. The Buyer shall have complied with and performed in all material respects the terms, conditions, acts, undertakings, covenants and obligations required by this Agreement to be complied with and performed by it on or before the Closing Date; and the Seller shall have received from the Buyer at the Closing a certificate, dated the Closing Date and signed by the President or a Vice President of the Buyer to such effect.

Section 10.2. Representations and Warranties True as of Closing Date. All representations and warranties of the Buyer set forth in this Agreement shall be true and correct in all material respects on and as of the Closing Date with the same force and effect as though such representations and warranties had been made on and as of the Closing Date and the Seller shall have received from the Buyer at the Closing a certificate, dated the Closing Date and signed by the President or a Vice President of the Buyer to such effect.

Section 10.3. Third Party Orders and Consents
(i) The Seller and the Buyer shall have fully complied with the applicable provisions of the Hart-Scott-Rodino Act and any and all applicable waiting periods thereunder shall have expired, or an opinion, reasonably acceptable to the Seller, that no such filing is required shall have been delivered to the Seller.

(ii) All consents and approvals listed in Section 4.29 of the Disclosure Statement shall have been obtained, and the Seller and the Buyer shall have been furnished with appropriate evidence, reasonably satisfactory to them and their respective counsel, of the granting of such consents and approvals, and such consents and approvals remain in full force and effect on the Closing Date.

Section 10.4. Corporate Action. The Seller shall have received:
(i) a copy of the resolution or resolutions duly adopted by the

Board of Directors of the Buyer and by the stockholders of the Buyer authorizing the execution, delivery and performance of this Agreement and the Related Instruments by the Buyer, and authorizing all other necessary or proper corporate action to enable the Buyer to comply with the terms of this Agreement and the Related Instruments, certified in each case by the Secretary or an Assistant Secretary of the Buyer; and

(ii) a certificate of the Secretary or an Assistant Secretary of the Buyer, dated the Closing Date, as to the incumbency and signatures of the officers of the Buyer executing this Agreement and the Related Instruments and any other documents in connection with the transactions contemplated by this Agreement and the Related Instruments.

Section 10.5. Opinion of the Buyer's Counsel. At the Closing, the Buyer shall furnish the Seller with an opinion, dated the Closing Date, of [name of Buyer's outside counsel], in form and substance reasonably satisfactory to the Seller and its counsel, to the effect that:

(i) The Buyer is a corporation duly organized, validly existing and in good standing under the laws of the state of its incorporation;

(ii) The Buyer has the power and authority to execute, deliver and perform the Agreement and the Related Instruments and to consummate the transactions contemplated by the Agreement and the Related Instruments; and the execution, delivery and performance of the Agreement and the Related Instruments and the consummation of the transactions contemplated by the Agreement and the Related Instruments have been duly authorized by all requisite action on the part of the Buyer;

(iii) This Agreement and the Related Instruments have been executed and delivered by the Buyer and is the legal, valid and binding obligation of the Buyer, enforceable against the Buyer in accordance with their respective terms, except (a) as such enforcement may be subject to fraudulent conveyance, bankruptcy, insolvency, reorganization, moratorium or other similar laws now or hereafter in effect, or by legal or equitable principles, relating to or limiting creditors' rights and (b) that the remedy of specific performance and injunctive and other forms of equitable relief are subject to certain equitable defenses and to the discretion of the court before which any proceeding therefor may be brought;

(iv) neither the execution, delivery and performance of the Agreement and the Related Instruments by the Buyer, nor the consummation of the transactions contemplated by the Agreement and the Related Instruments will violate any provision of the Certificate of Incorporation or Bylaws of the Buyer, or to the best knowledge of such counsel, will violate, conflict with, or constitute a default under, or cause the acceleration of maturity of any debt or obligation pursuant to, or result in the creation or imposition of any security interest, lien or other encumbrance upon any property or assets of the Buyer, any contract, commitment, agreement, trust, understanding, arrangement or restriction of any kind to which the Buyer is a party or by which the Buyer is bound or violate any statute or law, or any judgment, decree, order, regulation or rule of any court or governmental authority;

(v) to the best knowledge of such counsel, the Buyer is not engaged in or threatened with any legal action or other proceeding nor has it incurred or been charged with, nor is it under investigation with respect to, any violation of any law or administrative regulation which if adversely determined might, in such counsel's opinion, materially adversely affect or impair the ability of the Buyer to consummate the transactions contemplated hereby;

(vi) no filing, declaration or registration with, or any permit, authorization, license, consent or approval of, any governmental or regulatory authority is required in connection with the execution, delivery and performance of the Agreement and the Related Instruments by the Buyer or the consummation of the transactions contemplated by the Agreement and the Related Instruments, except as expressly disclosed in the Agreement or the Disclosure Statement, all of which have been duly and validly obtained;

(vii) no facts have come to the attention of such counsel that cause such counsel to believe that any information provided to the Seller in writing by or on behalf of the Buyer contained any untrue statement of a material fact or omitted to state any material fact necessary to make the statements therein, in light of the circumstances under which they were made, not misleading, except that counsel may also state that it has not independently verified the accuracy, completeness or fairness of such information, and the limitations inherent in the examination made by it and the knowledge available to it are such that it is unable to assume, and does not assume, any responsibility for the accuracy, completeness or fairness of such information.

As to any matter contained in such opinion which involves the laws of a jurisdiction other than the United States or the State of [state in which Buyer's counsel is licensed to practice], Buyer's counsel may rely upon opinions of local counsel of established reputation reasonably satisfactory to the Seller, which opinions shall expressly state that they may be relied upon by the Seller. Such counsel may also expressly rely as to matters of fact upon certificates furnished by appropriate officers of the Buyer, or appropriate governmental officials.

Section 10.6. *Litigation.* At the Closing, there shall be no effective injunction, writ or preliminary restraining order or any order of any nature issued by a court or governmental agency of competent jurisdiction restraining or prohibiting the consummation of the transactions provided for herein or any of them or limiting in any manner the Buyer's right to control the Target and the Subsidiaries or any aspect of their businesses or requiring the sale or other disposition of any of the operations of the Target or any Subsidiary or making the consummation of the Merger or the transaction contemplated by this Agreement and the Related Instruments unduly burdensome to the Target or any Subsidiary, and immediately prior to the Closing Date no proceeding or lawsuit shall have been commenced and be pending or be threatened by any governmental or regulatory agency or any other person with respect to the transactions contemplated by this Agreement or the Related Instruments which the Buyer, in good faith and with the advice of counsel, believes is likely to result in any of the foregoing or which seeks the payment of substantial damages by the Target, any Subsidiary or the Buyer.

Sections 10.1 and 10.2 afford the seller the same right to abandon the transaction as the buyer has under Sections 9.1 and 9.2. However, since the buyer enters into fewer and less expansive representations and covenants than the seller, this right is typically less valuable to the seller than it is to the buyer.

Sections 10.3, 10.4, 10.5, and 10.6 conditions are the seller's equivalent of the bring-down, consent, and corporate action legal opinions and litigation conditions given the buyer in Sections 9.3, 9.4, 9.5, and 9.7, respectively.

ARTICLE XI

TAX MATTERS

Section 11.1. Representations, Warranties and Covenants. The Seller and the Target each represents and warrants to the Buyer that:

(i) The Seller, the Target, and each of the Subsidiaries have filed or will file when due all federal, foreign, state, and local tax returns, tax information returns, reports, and estimates for all years and periods (and portions thereof) for which the due date (with extensions) is on or before the Closing Date. All such returns, reports, and estimates were or will be prepared in the manner required by applicable law, and reflect or will reflect the liability for taxes of the Target or the Subsidiary filing same in all material respects and all Taxes (as defined in paragraph (v) of this Section 11.1 hereof) shown thereby to be payable and all assessments received by the Target and any Subsidiary have been paid or will be paid when due.

(ii) Section 11.1(ii) of the Disclosure Statement sets forth all jurisdictions in which the Target and the Subsidiaries have filed or will file income or franchise tax returns for each taxable period, or portion thereof, beginning on [insert date] and ending on or before the Closing Date.

(iii) The Target and each Subsidiary have withheld or will withhold amounts from their respective employees and have filed or will file all federal, foreign, state, and local returns and reports with respect to employee income tax withholding and social security and unemployment Taxes for all periods (or portions thereof) ending on or before the Closing Date, in compliance with the provisions of the Internal Revenue Code of 1986, as amended and currently in effect (the "Code"), and other applicable federal, foreign, state, and local laws.

(iv) The Target and the Subsidiaries have paid, or have provided a sufficient reserve on the Most Recent Balance Sheet for the payment of, all federal, state, local, and foreign Taxes with respect to all periods, or portions thereof, ending on or before the date of the Most Recent Balance Sheet.

(v) "Taxes" or "Tax" means all net income, capital gains, gross income, gross receipts, sales, use, ad valorem, franchise, profits, license, withholding, payroll, employment, excise, severance, stamp, occupation, premium, property, or windfall profit taxes, customs duties, or other taxes, fees, assessments, or charges of any kind whatsoever, together with any interest and any penalties, additions to tax, or additional amounts imposed by any taxing authority ("Taxing Authority") upon the Target or any Subsidiary.

(vi) The consolidated federal income tax returns of the Target through the taxable year ended _____, have been examined by the United States Internal Revenue Service (the "IRS") or closed by applicable statutes of limitations, and any deficiencies or assessments, including interest and penalties thereon, claimed or made as a result of such examinations in respect of the Target and any of the Subsidiaries whose results of operations are includible for such years in the consolidated federal income tax returns of the Target have been paid or provided for.

(vii) Except as set forth in Section 11.1(vii) of the Disclosure Statement, there are no material claims or investigations by any Taxing Authority pending or to the best of the knowledge of Seller threatened against the Target or any Subsidiary for any past due Taxes; and there has been no waiver of any applicable statute of limitations or extension of the time for the assessment of any Tax against the Target or any Subsidiary except as set forth on Section 11.1(vii) of the Disclosure Statement.

(viii) Neither the Target nor any Subsidiary has made, signed, or filed, nor will it make, sign, or file any consent under Section 341(f) of the Code with respect to any taxable period ending on or before the Closing Date.

(ix) No event has occurred or will occur on or prior to the Closing Date that would require indemnification by the Target or any Subsidiary of any tax lessor under any agreements relating to tax leases executed under Section 168(f)(8) of the Internal Revenue Code of 1954 or by Seller as to assets of the Target or any Subsidiary.

(x) Any and all consolidated federal income tax (or similar) agreements executed between the Target or a Subsidiary and the Seller, or any other member of the Seller's consolidated group that relate to any payments or liability therefor by or to the Target or a Subsidiary with respect to its federal income and other Taxes and that are continuing in effect will terminate as of the Closing Date, and notwithstanding any provisions contained in such agreements, and on the Closing Date, the Target and the Subsidiaries shall be relieved of all liability and obligation thereunder.

Section 11.2. Payment of Tax Liabilities

(i) Subject to indemnification by the Seller under Section 11.3(i) hereof, the Target shall pay or cause to be paid at the times required by the relevant Taxing Authority all unpaid separate (unconsolidated) state, local or foreign Tax liabilities, including interest and any penalties thereon, of the Target and any Subsidiary for all periods, or portions thereof, ended on or before the Closing Date.

(ii) The Seller shall pay at the times required by the relevant Taxing Authority all unpaid federal or combined foreign, state or local Tax liabilities, including interest and any penalties thereon, attributable to the Target and the Subsidiaries for all periods, or portions thereof, with respect to which the Target and the Subsidiaries are included in a combined return.

Section 11.3. Indemnification

(i) The Seller agrees to indemnify, defend and hold the Buyer, the Target and the Subsidiaries harmless against and from (a) all unpaid federal or combined foreign, state or local Tax liabilities of the Target and any Subsidiary for all periods, or portions thereof, ended on or before the Closing Date, together with any penalties and interest attributable to such liabilities, and (b) all unpaid separate (unconsolidated) state, local, or foreign Tax liabilities of the Target and any Subsidiary for all periods, or portions thereof, ended on or before the Closing Date, together with any penalties and interest attributable to such liabilities. The amount of the Seller's obligation under this Section 11.3 shall be reduced by the value of any net Tax benefit ("Net Tax Benefit") realized by the Target and/or any Subsidiary by reason of a Tax deduction or loss, basis adjustment, and/or shifting of income, deductions, gains, losses and/or credits. For this purpose, the value of a Net Tax Benefit shall be determined by the accountant of the Target, using reasonable assumptions and methods of valuation.

(ii) The Seller shall indemnify and hold the Buyer, the Target, the Surviving Corporation and each Subsidiary harmless against any loss, liability, damage, or expense (including reasonable attorneys' fees) arising out of or resulting from any inaccuracy or misrepresentation in or breach of any of the warranties, representations, covenants or agreements made by the Seller or the Target in this Article XI.

(iii) The Buyer, the Target, the Surviving Corporation and the Subsidiaries shall indemnify and hold the Seller harmless against any loss, liability, damage or expense (including reasonable attorneys' fees) arising out of or resulting from any inaccuracy or misrepresentation in or breach of any of the warranties, representations, covenants or agreements made by the Buyer in this Article XI.

(iv) The Seller and the Buyer shall satisfy their obligations to each other for indemnification hereunder by check or cash within sixty (60) days after written notice thereof from the other respective party.

(v) The Buyer, the Target and each Subsidiary, on the one hand, and the Seller, on the other hand, hereby agree that in the event a claim is made by one party to this Agreement against the other party, the party making the claim shall furnish to the other party all books, records and other information reasonably requested by such other party that relate to such claims.

Section 11.4. Post Closing Obligations

(i) The Seller shall include the results of operations of the Target and the Subsidiaries for the period ending on the Closing Date in its consolidated federal income tax return and in any consolidated or combined foreign, state, or local income Tax return required to be filed by Seller after the Closing Date; and Seller will pay all federal, state, local, and foreign income Taxes (including interest and penalties relating thereto) due for the periods covered by such returns with respect to the Target and each Subsidiary.

(ii) The Buyer shall cause the Target and the Subsidiaries to include the results of their respective operations in any separate (unconsolidated) state, foreign, or local income Tax return for any taxable year beginning before and ending on or after the Closing Date. Subject to indemnification by the Seller under Section 11.3

hereof, the Buyer shall pay, or cause to be paid, all state, foreign or local income Taxes (including interest and penalties relating thereto) shown as due on any such return with respect to the Target or any Subsidiary.

(iii) All refunds or credits of Taxes paid by the Seller with respect to the Target or the Subsidiaries for periods ending on or prior to the Closing Date shall be the property of the Seller (except for refunds attributable to the carryback of any credits, losses or deductions arising out of the operation of the Target or the Subsidiaries after the Closing Date), and the Buyer shall forward to or reimburse the Seller for such refunds or credits (except as aforesaid) as soon as practicable after receipt thereof. Any refunds or credits of foreign, federal, state, or local income Taxes, paid by the Buyer, the Target, the Surviving Corporation or any Subsidiary in accordance with the provisions of Section 11.4(ii) hereof with respect to the Target or any Subsidiary shall be the property of Buyer, the Targert or the Subsidiary, as the case may be, and the Seller shall forward or reimburse the Buyer, the Target, or the Subsidiary for any such refunds or credits as soon as practicable after receipt thereof.

(iv) Any losses, credits or other Tax items of the Target or a Subsidiary, including, but not limited to, net operating losses, capital losses, business, foreign, and other tax credits (the "Tax Attributes"), which may be attributable to the operation of the business of the Target or a Subsidiary after the Closing Date, including any carry-backs of such Tax Attributes to any period ending on or before the Closing Date, and any refunds of Taxes attributable thereto, shall belong to the Target. To the extent the Tax Attributes are carried back to the Seller's returns under applicable Treasury Regulations, the Seller will file appropriate refund claims upon receipt from the Target of information to be included in such claims. Any refunds attributable to such refund claims received by the Seller shall be received by the Seller solely as agent for the Target and the Seller shall pay over such refunds to the Target immediately upon receipt thereof. The out-of-pocket expenses incurred by the Seller in filing any such refund claim shall be borne by the Target.

(v) To the extent that any election or other action by the Seller or an audit by the IRS or relevant state revenue agency for taxable years ending on or before the Closing Date results in an increase in the federal, state or foreign income Tax liability of the Target or any Subsidiary for a taxable year ending after the Closing Date, the Seller shall promptly pay the amount of such increase to the Buyer, provided, however, that the Seller shall not be required to make such payment until it receives from the Target reasonable evidence that the increased liability of the Target (or a Subsidiary, as the case may be) is due and payable and provided further that in the event that a subsequent audit by the IRS or relevant state revenue agency of the Buyer, the Target or any Subsidiary results in a reduction or elimination of such increase that resulted in any payment made under this paragraph, the Buyer shall promptly refund such payment or portion thereof, as the case may be, together with interest thereon at the prime rate from the date of such payment through the date of such refund.

(vi) If requested by the Buyer, the Seller shall make or cause the Target, with respect to the Subsidiaries, to make a deemed dividend election as of [_____], the first day of the Target's most recent taxable year, pursuant to consolidated return Treas. Regs. 1.1502-32(f)(2) and, with respect to such Subsidiaries, a consent dividend with respect to the period commencing on [_____], the first day of the Target's most recent taxable year, through the Closing Date pursuant to section 565 of the Code. The Seller shall also cause the Target and any Subsidiary, to the extent not inconsistent with the requirements of the preceding sentence, to not have an excess loss account, as defined in Treas. Regs. 1.1502-32(e)(1), in the stock of any domestic subsidiary at the Closing Date.

(vii) At the reasonable request of the Buyer, the Seller will furnish to the Buyer, to the extent prepared or available and without representation or warranty, copies of (i) studies on the earnings and profits of the Target and each Subsidiary made pursuant to Treas. Regs. 1.1502-33 and (ii) computations pursuant to Treas. Regs. 1.1502-32 of actual investment adjustments with respect to the stock of, or any ownership interest in, the Target and each Subsidiary through the Closing Date.

(viii) Subsequent to the filing of the Seller's consolidated federal income tax return which includes the taxable period ending on the Closing Date, the Seller shall determine, under the Seller's policy, consistently applied, and pursuant to Treas. Reg. 1.1502-79, the portion of any net operating loss or capital loss carryover, charitable contribution carryover, or business and other credit carryovers, not availed of in the Seller's consolidated federal income tax returns that are allocable to the Target and each domestic subsidiary of the Target when each such corporation ceased to be a member of Seller's consolidated group.

(ix) In the event that (a) the Target or a Subsidiary pays any separate (unconsolidated) state, local, or foreign tax liability, including interest and penalty thereon, pursuant to Section 11.2(i) hereof and (b) the Target is indemnified against such payment by the Seller under Section 11.3(i) then the Seller shall reimburse the Target or the Subsidiary in the following manner: Any reimbursement payment required to be made by Seller to the Target or a Subsidiary pursuant to this Section 11.4(ix) shall be made no later than thirty (30) days after receipt by the Seller of (x) a notice or demand for payments, (y) a copy of the complete return or report to be filed with the Taxing Authority, and (z) copies of all supporting workpapers or other appropriate assurances showing that the Tax liability less the value of any Net Tax Benefit, as provided in Section 11.3(i), has been correctly computed and apportioned to the Seller.

Section 11.5. Further Assurances and Assistance. From time to time prior to and after the Closing, the Seller and the Buyer will, without further consideration, (i) execute and deliver such documents as the other may reasonably request in order to consummate more effectively the transactions contemplated by this Agreement and (ii) provide such assistance and records as the other may reasonably request in connection with any tax return, tax investigation or audit, judicial or administrative proceeding or other similar matter relating to the Target or any of its Subsidiaries.

There are at least two approaches for dealing with the concerns of the Seller and the Buyer as to who should control the Tax audit. Sections 11.6 and 11.7 are examples of each approach. The first approach is quite straightforward and eliminates any involvement by the Buyer provided that the Seller completely indemnifies the Target from any Tax liability relating thereto. The second approach gives the Buyer the right to control the Tax Contest in situations in which the Buyer has greater exposure than the Seller. The advantages to each of these type of approaches is discussed in connection with the control of proceedings in the indemnity provisions in Article XII on page 677.

Section 11.6. Audit Matters. The Seller will be responsible for and have the right to control, at the Seller's expense, the audit of any Tax return relating to periods ended on or prior to the day of Closing. The Buyer will have the right, directly or through its designated representatives, to approve any settlement, provided, however, that the Seller may settle an audit on any terms by providing the Target with full indemnification against any Tax liability as a result thereof, in form and substance satisfactory to the Buyer.

Section 11.7. Certain Tax Claims for Which Seller May Be Liable

(i) If a claim is made by any Taxing Authority or, if during the course of an examination by a Taxing Authority, it appears that the examining agent will propose adjustments that will result in a claim (a "Proposed Claim") with respect to the Target or a Subsidiary (the "Target Group"), the party to this Agreement that has the legal right to settle or compromise such Proposed Claim under applicable law (the "Controlling Party") shall notify in writing ("Notice") the other party to this Agreement that may incur any liability in respect of such Proposed Claim under this Article XI (the "Noncontrolling

Party") within ten (10) business days of the date of such Proposed Claim. If the Controlling Party is a member of the Target Group, Notice shall be given to the Seller; if the Seller is the Controlling Party, Notice shall be given only to the Target. In the case of any such Proposed Claim, the Controlling Party shall not agree to such Proposed Claim or make payment thereof for at least sixty (60) days (or such shorter period as may be required by applicable law) after the giving of Notice with respect thereto. The Controlling Party need not give Notice of a Proposed Claim if the Controlling Party assumes liability for it. The failure to give Notice as provided hereunder shall not affect a Noncontrolling Party's liabilities under this Article XI unless such failure materially prejudices the ability of the Noncontrolling Party to defend against such Proposed Claim or to seek a refund of amounts paid in regard of such Proposed Claim.

(ii) As to a Tax that would result from a Proposed Claim for which the Controlling Party or the Noncontrolling Party would be solely liable under this Article XI hereof, the party that would be solely liable shall have the right, at its sole cost, to resist the Proposed Claim and if any Tax is paid, to seek the recovery of any such tax ("Tax Contest"). Such party may contest such Tax Contest by any and all appropriate proceedings, whether involving amended tax returns, claims for refund, administrative proceedings, litigation, appeals or otherwise, and in connection therewith, the other party will execute and deliver, or cause to be executed and delivered, to the party conducting the Tax Contest or its designees all instruments (including without limitation powers of attorney) reasonably requested by the party conducting the Tax Contest in order to implement the provisions of this paragraph.

(iii) As to a Tax for which the Noncontrolling Party is liable for a portion hereunder ("Joint Tax"), either the Controlling Party or the Noncontrolling Party shall have the right to institute or maintain a Tax Contest with respect thereto, subject to the provisions of Section 11.7(ii) hereof, as further modified by the following:

(a) If the asserted liability of the Controlling Party hereunder is equal to fifty percent (50%) or more of the Proposed Claim, the Controlling Party may elect to conduct all proceedings of the Tax Contest as to such Joint Tax or to tender the conduct of all proceedings to the Noncontrolling Party.

(b) If the asserted liability of the Controlling Party hereunder is less than fifty percent (50%) of the Proposed Claim, the Controlling Party shall tender the conduct of all proceedings of the Tax Contest to the Noncontrolling Party.

(c) If the conduct of all proceedings of the Tax Contest is tendered to the Noncontrolling Party and it declines to conduct such proceedings, then the Controlling Party (unless it elects to settle or not to contest as provided below) will conduct such proceedings. All costs of the Tax Contest will be shared as between the Controlling Party and the Noncontrolling Party in the ratio in which the Joint Tax is ultimately assessed.

(d) If the party conducting the Tax Contest (the "Manager") wishes to concede a Joint Tax or wishes and is able to compromise a Joint Tax and so notifies the other, the other party must either concede or agree to such compromise, as appropriate, or else agree to bear any portion of the Manager's tax liability in excess of the conceded or compromised amount. The party not wishing to concede or compromise will then assume responsibility for the conduct of the proceedings relating to the Tax Contest, and shall bear all costs of the Tax Contest thereafter incurred.

(iv) The "costs" of a Tax Contest means all out-of-pocket costs incurred by the Manager during the period it is acting as the Manager and any reasonable costs incurred by the other party for other than routine services or materials requested by the Manager in connection with such Tax Contest.

(v) The Target and the Seller will cooperate fully with each other in connection with any audit examinations of the Target by any Taxing Authority or any Tax Contests, including, without limitation, the furnishing or making available of records, books of account, or other materials necessary or helpful for the defense against the assertions of any Taxing Authority as to any income tax returns (consolidated or otherwise) of the Target and the Subsidiaries.

(vi) The Seller shall not agree to a settlement of any such Tax liabilities which would adversely affect any member of the Target Group in any taxable period ending after the Closing Date to any material extent (including, without limitation, the imposition of income tax deficiencies or the reduction of asset basis or cost adjustments) without the Target's prior written consent, which consent shall not be unreasonably withheld, unless the Seller indemnifies the Target Group against the effects of any such settlement. The Target shall not resolve, settle, or contest any tax issue with respect to the Target which would have an adverse material effect on the Seller without the Seller's prior written consent, which consent shall not be unreasonably withheld, unless the Target indemnifies the Seller against the effects of any such settlement.

Many non-tax lawyers merely skim the tax section of an acquisition agreement, since they find it extremely esoteric. While this may be unavoidable, the importance of tax provisions should not be minimized or overlooked. Article XI is used in connection with the acquisition of a target whose federal income tax returns are filed as part of the consolidated tax return of the seller. While pre-Closing federal tax liabilities of the target will be automatically included in the seller's consolidated return, the target will itself have liability to various other taxing authorities for periods prior to the Closing. Therefore, since the target will file a tax return after Closing which covers a portion of the period prior to Closing, the agreement should require the seller to pay any taxes for periods prior to the Closing which may be due to various taxing authorities. This is logical, as the seller reaped the benefits of the target's income during this period. It is also necessary for the seller and the buyer to coordinate the filing of tax returns post-Closing as well as the handling of tax refunds or credits.

When agreeing to indemnify the target for the target's tax liability covering periods prior to the Closing, the seller should require its indemnity obligation to be reduced by the amount of any offsetting tax benefits realized by the target by reason of pre-Closing tax liability. (See Section 11.3(i).) This is at least theoretically a fair result, since the buyer should not be expected to get a windfall from the indemnity provisions. The principal, and fairly valid, argument against such a provision is that the actual determination of an offsetting tax benefit can be quite difficult in practice. Offsetting tax benefits are also discussed on page 672.

The representations and warranties set forth in Section 11.1 assure the buyer that it should not be faced with unanticipated tax liabilities of any kind.

In situations in which the target is not a member of the seller's consolidated group, much of Article XI may be unnecessary, and the buyer should instead require a representation by the seller in Article IV as follows:

> ***Tax Matters.*** For purposes of this Agreement "Taxes" or "Tax" means all net income, capital gains, gross income, gross receipts, sales, use, ad valorem, franchise, profits, license, withholding, payroll, employment, excise, severance, stamp, occupation, premium, property, or windfall profit taxes, customs duties, or other taxes, fees, assessments, or charges of any kind whatsoever, together with any interest and any penalties, additions to tax, or additional amounts imposed by any taxing authority ("Taxing Authority") upon the Target or the Subsidiary.
>
> (i) Except as set forth in Section _____ of the Disclosure Statement, the Target and the Subsidiary have filed or will file when due all federal, foreign, state, and local tax returns, tax information returns, reports, and estimates for all years and periods (and portions thereof) ending on or before the Closing Date for which any such returns, reports or estimates were due. All such returns, reports, and estimates were prepared in the manner required by

applicable law, and all Taxes shown thereby to be payable have been paid when due.

(ii) Section _____ of the Disclosure Statement sets forth all jurisdictions in which the Target and the Subsidiaries have filed or will file income or franchise tax returns for each taxable period, or portion thereof, ending on or before the Closing Date.

(iii) The Target and the Subsidiaries each has withheld or will withhold amounts from its respective employees and has filed or will file all federal, foreign, state, and local returns and reports with respect to employee income tax withholding and social security and unemployment Taxes for all periods (or portions thereof) ending on or before the Closing Date, in compliance with the provisions of the Internal Revenue Code of 1986, as amended and currently in effect (the "Code"), and other applicable federal, foreign, state, and local laws.

(iv) The Target and the Subsidiaries each have paid, or provided a sufficient reserve on the Balance Sheet for the payment of, all federal, state, local, and foreign Taxes with respect to all periods, or portions thereof, ending on or before _____. The amount of any net operating loss for federal income tax purposes shown on the Target's federal income tax returns has been accurately and properly determined in accordance with the Code and other applicable law without giving effect to the transactions contemplated hereby.

(v) The separate and consolidated federal income tax returns of the Target and its Subsidiaries, through the taxable year ended [insert date], have been examined by the United States Internal Revenue Service (the "IRS") or closed by applicable statute of limitations, and any deficiencies or assessments, including interest and penalties thereon, claimed or made as a result of such examinations in respect of the target and any of its Subsidiaries.

(vi) Except as set forth in Section _____ of the Disclosure Statement there are no material claims or investigations by any Taxing Authority pending or, to the best knowledge of the Seller and the Target, threatened, against the Target or the Subsidiaries for any past due Taxes; and there has been no waiver of any applicable statute of limitations or extension of the time for the assessment of any Tax against the Target or the Subsidiaries, except as set forth in Section _____ of the Disclosure Statement.

(vii) Neither the Target nor any Subsidiary has made, signed, or filed, nor will it make, sign, or file any consent under Section 341(f) of the Code with respect to any taxable period ending on or before the Closing Date.

(viii) Except as set forth in Section _____ of the Disclosure Statement, no event has occurred or will occur on or prior to the Closing Date that would require indemnification by the Target or the Subsidiaries of any tax lessor under any agreements relating to tax leases executed under Section 168(f)(8) of the Internal Revenue Code of 1986 as to assets of the Target or its Subsidiaries.

(ix) Neither the Target nor any Subsidiary has ever been, nor is the Target or any Subsidiary currently, a party to any agreement relating to the sharing of any liability for, or payment of, Taxes with any other person or entity.

ARTICLE XII

SURVIVAL OF REPRESENTATIONS; INDEMNIFICATION

Section 12.1. Indemnification by Seller. Notwithstanding any other provision of this Agreement and subject to the terms and conditions of this Article XII, the Seller hereby agrees to indemnify, defend and hold harmless the Buyer, any subsidiary or affiliate thereof (including the Target, the Surviving Corporation and the Subsidiaries) and their respective successors, if any, and their officers, directors and controlling persons (the "Buyer Group"), at any time after the Closing Date, from and against all demands, claims, actions or causes of action, assessments, losses, damages, liabilities, costs and expenses, including without limitation, interest, penalties and attorneys' fees and expenses, which were reasonably incurred by or imposed upon the Buyer Group or any member thereof, net of any insurance proceeds received by any member of the Buyer Group with respect thereto (all such amounts, net of insurance proceeds being hereafter referred to collectively as "Buyer Group Damages"), asserted against, resulting to, imposed upon or incurred by the Buyer Group or any member thereof, directly or indirectly, by reason of or resulting from any misrepresentation, breach of any warranty or nonperformance or breach of any covenant, obligation or agreement of the Seller or the Target or its Subsidiaries contained in or made pursuant to this Agreement, the Disclosure Statement, the Related Instruments or pursuant to any statement, certificate or other document furnished pursuant to this Agreement or the Related Instruments (collectively referred to as the "Indemnity Documents") or any facts or circumstances constituting such a breach. (A claim for indemnification under this Section 12.1 shall be referred to as the "Buyer Group Claims").

Section 12.2. Indemnification by the Surviving Corporation. Notwithstanding any other provision of this Agreement and subject to the terms and conditions of this Article XII, the Surviving Corporation hereby agrees to indemnify, defend and hold harmless the Seller and their respective successors, if any, and their officers, directors and controlling persons (the "Seller Group"), at any time after the Closing Date, from and against all demands, claims, actions, or causes of action, assessments, losses, damages, liabilities, costs and expenses' including, without limitation, interest, penalties and attorneys' fees and expenses, which were reasonably incurred by or imposed upon the Seller Group or any member thereof, net of any insurance proceeds received by any member of the Seller Group with respect thereto (all such amounts, net of insurance proceeds being hereafter referred to collectively as "Seller Group Damages"), asserted against, resulting to, imposed upon or incurred by the Seller Group or any member thereof, directly or indirectly, by reason of or resulting from any misrepresentation, breach of any warranty, or nonperformance or breach of any covenant, obligation or agreement of the Buyer contained in or made pursuant to any Indemnity Document or any facts or circumstances constituting such a breach. (A claim for indemnification under this Section 12.2 shall be referred to as the "Seller Group Claims.")

The Buyer Group Damages and Seller Group Damages take into account any insurance proceeds which are received by the indemnified party in order to reduce the amount of damages that can be recovered by the indemnified party. Another item which arguably should offset the amount of damages that an indemnified party can claim is the amount of any tax benefits that the surviving corporation has enjoyed as a result of such damages. The difficulty of determining the exact amount of the tax benefit that directly resulted from the damages almost always causes the buyer and seller to overlook this potential windfall.

> *Section 12.3. Materiality.* For purposes of determining whether an event described in Section 12.1 or 12.2 has occurred, any requirement in any representation, warranty, covenant or agreement contained in any Indemnity Document that an event or fact be material, meet a certain minimum dollar threshold or have a Material Adverse Effect, which is a condition to such event or fact constituting a misrepresentation or a breach of such warranty, covenant or agreement (a "Materiality Condition"), shall be ignored, if the aggregate Buyer Group Damages or Seller Group Damages, as the case may be, resulting from all such breaches and misrepresentations (determined by ignoring all Materiality Conditions) exceeds the amount of the Basket (as defined in Section 12.5). Notwithstanding the foregoing, an event described in Section 12.1 or 12.2 (other than a claim for indemnification under

Article XI) that would otherwise give rise to a claim for Buyer Group Damages or Seller Group Damages, as the case may be, shall not be deemed to have occurred unless the Buyer Group Damages or Seller Group Damages, as the case may be, resulting from the single misrepresentation or breach of warranty, covenant or agreement that constitute such event exceeds _____ Dollars, provided that for the purposes of this sentence, all claims for Buyer Group Damages or Seller Group Damages, as the case may be, arising out of the same facts or events causing any such breach shall be treated as a single claim.

For a discussion of the purpose of the "materiality" and the "minimum per claim" provisions set forth in Section 12.3, see pages 568–570.

Section 12.4. Survival of Indemnification. The right to make a claim for indemnification under this Agreement shall survive the Closing Date for a period of twenty-four (24) months except that a claim for indemnification under (a) Section 4.4 of this Agreement or based upon any misrepresentation or breach of a warranty which was actually known to be untrue by the indemnifying party when made or asserted or to any willful breach of a covenant, shall continue to survive indefinitely, (b) Article XI shall continue to survive until the latest to occur of (i) the date twenty-four (24) months after the Closing Date, (ii) the expiration date of the statute of limitations applicable to any indemnified liability for Taxes, and extensions or waivers thereof and (iii) ninety (90) days after the final determination of any such Tax liability, including the final administrative and/or judicial determination thereof, and thereafter no party shall have a right to seek indemnification under this Agreement unless a notice of claim setting forth the facts upon which the claim for indemnification is based, and if possible, a reasonable estimate of the amount of the claim, is delivered to the indemnifying party prior to the expiration of the right to make a claim as provided in this Section 12.4. This Section 12.4 shall have no effect upon any other obligation of the parties hereto, whether to be performed before or after the Closing Date. It shall not be a condition to the indemnification with respect to such claim that the loss or liability upon which the claim would be based actually be realized or incurred prior to the date that the indemnifying party is no longer obligated to indemnify the indemnified party pursuant to this Article XII.

As discussed on pages 565–566, the length of time that the seller's indemnification obligations survive the Closing Date is often heavily negotiated, and its outcome is largely dependent upon the nature of the transaction and the strength of the parties' respective bargaining positions. The buyer should require the seller to indemnify the title to the securities to be purchased by it for an indefinite period of time. For indemnification relating to tax liability, the buyer should require the seller to indemnify the surviving corporation until the target can no longer suffer any loss. In some cases, the buyer may require the seller to indemnify certain items, such as on environmental or product liability concern, beyond the general indemnification period.

Section 12.5. Limitation on Claims and Damages

(i) No amount shall be payable in indemnification under this Article XII, unless (a) in the case of the Seller, the aggregate amount of Buyer Group Damages in respect of which the Seller would be liable under this Article XII, or (b) in the case of the Surviving Corporation, the aggregate amount of Seller Group Damages in respect of which the Surviving Corporation would be liable under this Article XII, exceeds in the aggregate _____ Dollars ($_____) (the "Basket"); provided, however, the Basket shall not apply to (a) any Buyer Group Claim or Seller Group Claim, as the case may be, based upon any misrepresentation or breach of a warranty which was actually known to be untrue by the indemnifying party when made or asserted or to any willful breach of a covenant or (b) any claim for indemnity under Article XI. In the event that the Buyer Group Damages or Seller Group Damages exceeds the Basket, the indemnified party shall be entitled to seek indemnification for the full amount of the Buyer Group Damages or Seller Group Damages, as the case may be.

(ii) The maximum amount of Buyer Group Damages for which the Seller may be liable under this Article XII shall be an amount equal to _____ Dollars ($_____).

(iii) A party shall not be liable for Buyer Group Damages or Seller Group Damages, as the case may be, under this Article XII resulting from an event relating to a misrepresentation, breach of any warranty or nonperformance or breach of any covenant by the indemnifying party if the indemnifying party can establish that the party seeking indemnification had actual knowledge on or before the Closing Date of such event.

(iv) In any case where an indemnified party recovers from third parties all or any part of any amount paid to it by an indemnifying party pursuant to this Article XII, such indemnified party shall promptly pay over to the indemnifying party the amount so recovered (after deducting therefrom the full amount of the expenses incurred by it in procuring such recovery and any additional amounts owed to the indemnified party by the indemnifying party under this Agreement), but not in excess of any amount previously so paid by the indemnifying party.

(v) The indemnified party shall be obligated to prosecute diligently and in good faith any claim for Buyer Group Damages or Seller Group Damages, as the case may be, with any applicable insurer prior to collecting or indemnification payment under this Article XII. However, an indemnified party shall be entitled to collect an indemnification payment under this Article XII if such indemnified party has not received reimbursement from an applicable insurer within one year after it has given such insurer written notice of its claim. In such event, the indemnified party shall assign to the indemnifying party its rights against such insurer.

(vi) Except in the case of fraud and other than as set forth in Article XI or Section 12.5(vii) hereof, the indemnification and terms thereof provided for in this Article XII shall be the exclusive remedy available to any indemnified party against any indemnifying party for any damages arising directly or indirectly from any misrepresentation, breach of any warranty or nonperformance or breach of any covenant, obligation or agreement pursuant to the Indemnity Documents.

(vii) Nothing in this Article XII or in Article XI shall be construed to limit the non-monetary equitable remedies of any party hereto in respect of any breach by any other party of any covenant or other agreement of such other party contained in or made pursuant to the Indemnity Documents required to be performed after the Closing Date.

Pages 566–570 explain the importance of the Basket to the seller and the issues relating thereto. The seller, who usually has the most at stake under the indemnification provisions, should require the surviving corporation to pursue collection from an insurance company for the redress of Buyer Group Damages if the insurance policy arguably covers the Buyer Group Damages. In addition, as mentioned on page 565 with respect to the covenants in Section 6.7 and Article VII, the seller should not be liable for any Buyer Group Damages if the buyer was aware of the seller's misrepresentation or breach prior to the Closing Date.

A seller should always attempt to limit its exposure for indemnification. As a practical matter, the seller should not be liable for any amount in excess of the purchase price paid for the target. During negotiations of this ceiling, every argument conceivable is put on the table for consideration. However, its outcome, like that of any other highly controversial provision, rests with the party holding the trump card.

Section 12.6. Claims by Third Parties. The obligations and liabilities of an indemnifying party under any provision of this Agreement with respect to claims relating to third parties shall be subject to the following terms and conditions:

(i) Whenever any indemnified party shall have received notice that a Buyer Group Claim or a Seller Group Claim, as the case may be, has been asserted or threatened against such indemnified party, which, if valid, would subject the indemnifying party to an indemnity obligation under this Agreement, the indemnified party shall promptly notify the indemnifying party of such claim in the manner described in Section 12.4; provided, however, that the failure of the indemnified party to give timely notice hereunder shall not relieve the indemnifying party of its indemnification obligations under this Agreement unless, and only to the extent that, such failure caused the Buyer Group Damages or the Seller Group Damages, as the case may be, for which the indemnifying party is obligated to be greater than they would have been had the indemnified party given timely notice.

(ii) The indemnifying party or its designee will have the right, but not the obligation, to assume the defense of any claim described in Section 12.6(i); provided, however, if there is a reasonable probability that a Buyer Group Claim may materially and adversely affect the Surviving Corporation or any other member of the Buyer Group despite the indemnity of the Seller, the Surviving Corporation or such member of the Buyer Group shall have the right at its option to defend, at its own cost and expense, and to compromise or settle such Buyer Group Claim which compromise or settlement shall be made only with the written consent of the Seller, such consent not to be unreasonably withheld. If the indemnifying party fails to assume the defense of such claim within 15 days after receipt of notice of a claim pursuant to Section 12.6(i), the indemnified party against which such claim has been asserted will (upon delivering notice to such effect to the indemnifying party) have the right to undertake, at the indemnifying party's cost and expense, the defense, compromise or settlement of such claim on behalf of and for the account and risk of the indemnifying party, subject to the right of the indemnifying party to assume the defense of such claim at any time prior to settlement, compromise or final determination thereof and *provided, however,* that the indemnified party shall not enter into any such compromise or settlement without the written consent of the indemnifying party. In the event the indemnified party assumes defense of the claim, the indemnified party will keep the indemnifying party reasonably informed of the progress of any such defense, compromise or settlement. The indemnifying party shall not be liable for any settlement of any action effected without its consent, but if settled with the consent of the indemnifying party or if there be a final judgment beyond review or appeal, for the plaintiff in any such action, the indemnifying party agrees to indemnify and hold harmless an indemnified party from and against any loss or liability by reason of such settlement or judgment. Any party who does not undertake the defense of a claim may, at its own expense, retain such additional attorneys and other advisors as it shall deem necessary, which attorneys and advisors will be permitted by the party undertaking such defense, and its attorneys, to observe the defense of such claim.

(iii) Any member of the Buyer Group shall give the Seller at least thirty (30) days prior written notice before such member shall waive the provisions of any statute of limitations as such provisions may apply to the assessment of taxes payable by the Surviving Corporation or any Subsidiary for any taxable year or period (or portion thereof) ending on or prior to the Closing Date.

An area that can be extremely sensitive is control of a proceeding relating to a claim that is the subject of indemnification. If the indemnifying party refuses to acknowledge its obligation to indemnify a claim, then it should certainly have no right to control the proceeding. However, where the indemnifying party has accepted its obligation to indemnify for a claim, the indemnifying party will probably want to control the proceeding in order to be in command of its own destiny. If the buyer is comfortable with the creditworthiness of the seller, this should not pose a serious threat to the buyer. There are, of course, circumstances in which the buyer may want to control the proceedings notwithstanding the creditworthiness of the seller. For example, if the surviving corporation is temporarily enjoined from conducting its business as a result of the action of a third party, the buyer may feel that the seller will not move quickly enough to resolve the matter.

In some cases, the buyer and seller may have a joint interest in the outcome of a certain proceeding. For example, the proceeding may involve numerous claims against the surviving corporation, only one of which relates to a Buyer Group Claim. One approach that may appease both the seller and buyer in this circumstance is to let the party that has the most to lose control the proceeding.

Section 12.7. Indemnity for Taxes of Indemnified Party.
Each party hereto further agrees that, with respect to payment or indemnity under this Article XII, such payment or indemnity shall include any amount necessary to hold the indemnified party harmless on an after-tax basis from all taxes required to be paid with respect to the receipt of such payment or indemnity under the laws of any Federal, state or local government or taxing authority in the

United States, or under the laws of any foreign government or taxing authority or governmental subdivision of a foreign country.

In circumstances in which the indemnification payment is taxable to the indemnified party, it is common for the seller and buyer to negotiate the inclusion of a tax gross up provision. One difficulty with this concept is that the indemnifying party may be grossing up the indemnified party for taxes that it would have been responsible for had no indemnity been necessary.

> *Section 12.8. Right of Offset.* In the event the Seller should be required to pay monies to the Surviving Corporation pursuant to Section 12.1 or any other indemnification provision of this Agreement, the Surviving Corporation may offset the amount the Seller owes in indemnification against any outstanding principal balance of the [insert title of instrument under which the surviving corporation has continuing payment obligations].

In an acquisition in which the seller has agreed to accept, as part of the purchase price of the target, a note or other instrument that represents a payment obligation of the surviving corporation, the buyer may attempt to satisfy its right to indemnification by the seller by cancelling a portion or all of such payment obligations. A creditworthy seller should resist this provision on several grounds. First, the surviving corporation should have a set-off right only after it has demonstrated, through a final determination from which no appeal can be taken, that the seller is obligated to indemnify the surviving corporation for the Buyer Group Claim. Second, if the seller has sufficient resources, it should be able to choose whether it wants to forgive a portion of the payment obligation or simply pay cash. It is conceivable that the payment obligation may bear an interest rate well in excess of the prevailing market rate. A creditworthy seller should not lose this benefit through an offset provision.

ARTICLE XIII

NON-COMPETE

> The Seller agrees that for the period of three years following the Closing Date (the "Non-Compete Period"), the Seller shall not, without the prior written consent of the Buyer, either directly or indirectly, engage in business of the type presently conducted by the Target or any Subsidiary in the United States or any other jurisdic-

tion in which the Target or any Subsidiary currently conduct business (the "Business"). The Seller may acquire any entity which, directly or indirectly, engages in the Business or any portion thereof (the "Acquired Entity"), if (i) the total assets and gross revenues attributable to or derived from such Business do not exceed [insert percentage] of the total assets and gross revenues of the Acquired Entity and its subsidiaries in the fiscal year immediately preceding the date of acquisition, or (ii) the Seller uses its reasonable efforts to divest itself of the Acquired Entity within a reasonable time (not to exceed six months), subject to receipt of all regulatory approvals. The Seller also agrees that, after the Closing Date, the Seller will not disclose or reveal to any person or an Acquired Entity any trade secret or other confidential or proprietary information relating to the Business, including, without limitation, any financial information relating to Target or any Subsidiary, or any customer lists, unless readily ascertainable from public information, and the Seller confirms that after the Closing Date, such information will constitute the exclusive property of the Target and its Subsidiaries. During the Non-Compete Period, the Seller agrees not to, and to cause its affiliates not to, recruit, directly or indirectly, employees of the Target or any Subsidiary for employment with or as a consultant to the Seller or its affiliates. The Buyer and the Seller hereby agree that of the total cash consideration to be paid to the Seller at Closing, $_____ represents the consideration for the covenants of the Seller contained in this Article XIII.

Covenants not to compete can be difficult to enforce if not structured properly. The difficulty arises from a court's reluctance on public policy grounds to give force to a contractual provision restricting the ability of one of the parties to work freely in any way he chooses, even if the party being restricted has voluntarily agreed and has received consideration to be so bound. Courts have invalidated non-competition provisions (a) which continue for too long a period of time, (b) which are too broad geographically, or (c) which are too indefinite or broad with respect to the restricted activity. Consequently, the buyer must ensure that his non-competition clause is specific with respect to the term (typically one to five years), extends to a limited geographic area, and restricts a specific activity in the industry. For example, a court would probably accept a provision restricting the seller from selling or distributing aluminum baseball bats in the State of California for a period of two years, but would probably not accept a provision restricting the seller from selling or distributing sports equipment anywhere in the world for a period of twenty years. It is, of course, within these extremes that the enforceability of a covenant not to compete is less clear. The buyer must be cognizant of courts' rulings under the state laws that govern the acquisition agreement, and must balance the case law against its need to acquire the target without fear that the seller will acquire or establish a similar business in the same territory and attempt to lure away existing customers of the target.

The seller may also desire to modify clause (ii) above, which requires the seller's divestiture of the Acquired Entity within a reasonable period of time by providing that the seller is only obligated to divest the Acquired Entity "at a price which is economically reasonable in light of the circumstances."

ARTICLE XIV

TERMINATION

Section 14.1. Termination for Failure to Close on Time. This Agreement may be terminated upon two (2) days' written notice (i) by Buyer, on the one hand, or the Seller, on the other hand, at any time after [insert date], or (ii) by the mutual agreement of all parties at any time. In the event of such termination, this Agreement shall be abandoned without any liability or further obligation to any other party to this Agreement unless otherwise stated expressly herein. This Section 14.1 shall not apply in the event of the failure of the transactions contemplated by this Agreement to be consummated as a result of a breach by the Seller, Target or Buyer of a representation, warranty or covenant contained in this Agreement. In such event, the provisions of Section 14.2 hereof shall apply.

Section 14.2. Default; Remedies. This Section shall apply in the event that a party refuses to consummate the transactions contemplated by this Agreement or if any default under, or breach of any representation, warranty or covenant of, this Agreement on the part of a party (the "Defaulting Party") shall have occurred that results in the failure to consummate the transactions contemplated hereby. In such event, the non-Defaulting Party shall be entitled to seek and obtain specific performance pursuant to Section 14.3 or to seek and obtain money damages from the Defaulting Party plus its court costs and reasonable attorneys' fees in connection with the pursuit of its remedies hereunder.

Section 14.3. Specific Performance. In the event that any party shall fail or refuse to consummate the transactions contemplated by this Agreement or if any default under, or breach of, any representation, warranty or covenant of this Agreement on the part of any party (the "Defaulting Party") shall have occurred that results in the failure to consummate the transactions contemplated hereby, then in addition to the other remedies provided in this Article XIV, the non-Defaulting Party may seek to obtain an order of specific performance thereof against the Defaulting Party from a court of competent jurisdiction, provided that it files its request with such court within forty-five (45) days after it became aware of such failure, refusal, default or breach. In addition, the non-Defaulting Party shall be entitled to obtain from the Defaulting Party court costs and reasonable attorneys' fees incurred by it in enforcing its rights hereunder. As a condition to seeking specific performance hereunder, Buyer shall not be required to have tendered the [insert defined term for the total purchase price] but shall be ready, willing and able to do so.

The termination section provides both the mechanism for the termination of, and the remedies available against a non-performing or defaulting party to, the acquisition agreement. In some cases, a seller may want to modify this section to limit liability for a failure to perform the circumstances which are willful. Obviously, there are situations in which the buyer may be disadvantaged by the inclusion of this modifier. Therefore, like other disputed provisions, the outcome rests on the balance of power between seller and buyer.

In an acquisition requiring regulatory approval, the buyer and seller should consider extending the term of the acquisition agreement in Section 14.1 for a certain period of time in case the approval process takes longer than anticipated.

The relief of specific performance afforded the non-defaulting party in Section 14.3 is extremely difficult to enforce in a court of law. If a court can ascertain the amount of monetary damages to award the non-defaulting party, it will not generally grant specific performance.

Special consideration should be given to the termination section in connection with the acquisition of a publicly traded target. For example, an independent committee of the board of directors of the target may determine in light of the circumstances to include a "fiduciary out" for the target. A "fiduciary out" is a unilateral right of the target to terminate the acquisition agreement in the event a more favorable offer for the target is received prior to Closing. The buyer should in this situation and possibly others, require a "break-up" or "topping" fee to compensate the buyer for its damages and out-of-pocket expenses. The following is an example of a "bust-up" fee which covers both buyer and seller:

> ***Damages Upon Default.*** In the event that either Target or
> Buyer shall fail to refuse to consummate the transactions contem-
> plated by this Agreement or if any default under, or breach of any
> representation (other than those contained in Section 3.5 hereof),
> warranty, covenant (other than those contained in ＿＿＿＿＿ hereof)
> or conditions of, this Agreement on the part of the Target or
> Buyer shall have occurred that results in the failure to con-
> summate the transactions contemplated hereby, then (i) if Tar-
> get shall be the defaulting party, Target shall pay to the Buyer
> ＿＿＿＿＿＿ Dollars ($＿＿＿＿＿), or (ii) if the Buyer shall
> be the defaulting party, then the Buyer shall pay to Target
> ＿＿＿＿＿＿ Dollars ($＿＿＿＿＿). In each case such payment
> shall be in consideration of the expenses incurred by and efforts
> expended by and opportunities lost by the nondefaulting party. The
> parties agree that in such circumstances it would be impossible to
> determine the actual damages which any party may suffer and that
> therefore such payments shall be in lieu of any such actual damages
> and shall be full and complete liquidated damages and shall consti-
> tute the sole remedy in the event of such default.

ARTICLE XV

MISCELLANEOUS

Article XV contains provisions which govern the interpretation of the
agreement and the taking of actions thereunder. Although the bulk
of these provisions are generally not negotiated by the parties to the
Agreement, several sections provide valuable rights to both buyer and
seller and may be subject to closer scrutiny by the parties.

> **Section 15.1** *Definitions.*
> **Agreement.** See Article I.
> **Buyer.** See Article I.
> **Closing.** See Article III.
> **Closing Date.** See Article III.
> **Company Capital Stock.** See Section 4.3(i).
> **Disclosure Statement.** See Section 4.1.
> **Financial Statements.** See Section 4.5(i).
> **GAAP.** See Section 4.5(i).
> **Material Adverse Effect.** See Section 4.1(i)
> **Merger.** See Article I.
> **Most Recent Balance Sheet.** See Section 4.5(i).
> **Persons.** First used in Section 4.5(ii) but not defined.
> **Related Instruments.** See Section 4.2.
> **SEC.** Defined in paragraph describing Section 4.33.

Seller. See Article I.
Subsidiary. See Article I.
Target. See Article I.

Section 15.2. Payment of Expenses. Buyer shall pay its own expenses and the Seller and Target shall pay their own expenses incident to preparing for, entering into and carrying out this Agreement and the Related Instruments, except as otherwise provided in this Agreement and the Related Instruments.

Section 15.3. Modifications, Waivers, Agreement. The parties may, by mutual written agreement, make any modification or amendment of this Agreement.

Section 15.4. Assignment. Neither the Buyer, Seller nor Target shall have the authority to assign its rights or obligations under this Agreement without the prior written consent of the other party, except that the Buyer may assign all or any portion of its respective rights hereunder without the prior written consent of the Seller or Target to an entity controlled by, controlling, or under common control with it or to any Acquisition Lender, and the Seller, Target and the Buyer shall execute such documents as are necessary in order to effect such assignments.

Section 15.5. Burden and Benefit

(i) This Agreement shall be binding upon and, to the extent permitted in this Agreement, shall inure to the benefit of, the parties hereto and their respective successors and assigns.

(ii) In the event of a default by the Seller or Target of any of its or their obligations hereunder, the sole and exclusive recourse and remedy of the Buyer shall be against the Seller or Target and its assets and under no circumstances shall any officer, director, stockholder or affiliate of the Seller or Target be liable in law or equity for any obligations of the Seller or Target hereunder.

(iii) In the event of a default by the Buyer of any of its obligations hereunder, the sole and exclusive recourse and remedy of the Seller or Target hereunder shall be against the Buyer and its assets, and under no circumstances shall any officer, director, stockholder or affiliate of the Buyer be liable in law or equity for any obligations of the Buyer hereunder.

(iv) It is the intent of the parties hereto that no third-party beneficiary rights be created or deemed to exist in favor of any person not a party to this Agreement, unless otherwise expressly agreed in writing by the parties.

The buyer and seller may seek to include a provision, often entitled "Burden and Benefit," limiting the rights of the seller in the event of a breach of the agreement to an action against the buyer and not against any officer, director, or controlling stockholder of the buyer. This provision, assuming the entity purchasing the target has elected to do so through a shell or thinly capitalized corporation, generally should insulate the acquiring entity from liability to the seller in the event the deal goes sour.

Section 15.6. Brokers

(i) Each of the Seller and Target represents and warrants to the Buyer that there are no brokers or finders entitled to any brokerage or finder's fee or other commission or fee based upon arrangements made by or on behalf of the Seller or Target in connection with this Agreement or any of the transactions contemplated hereby other than the fee due [insert name of any such entity].

(ii) The Buyer represents and warrants to the Seller and the Target that no broker or finder is entitled to any brokerage or finder's fee or other commission or fee based upon arrangements made by or on behalf of the Buyer in connection with this Agreement or any of the transactions contemplated hereby other than fees payable by it in connection with the financing of this transaction.

Section 15.7. Entire Agreement.

This Agreement and the exhibits, lists and other documents referred to herein contain the entire agreement among the parties hereto with respect to the transactions contemplated hereby and supersede all prior agreements with respect thereto, whether written or oral.

Section 15.8. Governing Law.

This Agreement shall be governed by and construed in accordance with the laws of the State of Delaware.

Section 15.9. Notices.

Any notice, request, instruction or other document to be given hereunder by a party shall be in writing and delivered personally or by facsimile transmission, or by telex, or sent by registered or certified mail, postage prepaid, return receipt requested, addressed as follows:

If to the Seller: [insert name and address of Seller]

with a copy to: [insert name and address of Seller's counsel]

If to Target: [insert name and address of Target]

If to Buyer: [insert name and address of Buyer]

with a copy to: [insert name and address of Buyer's counsel]

If to the Surviving Corporation: [insert name and address of Target post-Closing]

with a copy to: [insert any other desired parties]

or to such other persons or addresses as may be designated in writing by the party to receive such notice. If mailed as aforesaid, ten days after the date of mailing shall be the date notice shall be deemed to have been received.

Section 15.10. Counterparts. This Agreement may be executed in two or more counterparts, each of which shall be an original, but all of which shall constitute but one agreement.

Section 15.11. Rights Cumulative. All rights, powers and privileges conferred hereunder upon the parties, unless otherwise provided, shall be cumulative and shall not be restricted to those given by law. Failure to exercise any power given any party hereunder or to insist upon strict compliance by any other party shall not constitute a waiver of any party's right to demand exact compliance with the terms hereof.

Section 15.12. Severability of Provisions. The parties agree that (i) the provisions of this Agreement shall be severable in the event that any of the provisions hereof are held by a court of competent jurisdiction to be invalid, void or otherwise unenforceable, (ii) such invalid, void or otherwise unenforceable provisions shall be automatically replaced by other provisions which are as similar as possible in terms to such invalid, void or otherwise unenforceable provisions but are valid and enforceable and (iii) the remaining provisions shall remain enforceable to the fullest extent permitted by law.

The provision entitled "Severability," while addressing a purely legal issue, may have great practical impact. The section provides that, in the event particular portions of the document are found invalid, void, or otherwise unenforceable by a court interpreting the agreement, the remaining provisions shall be considered severable from the invalid provisions and shall therefore remain enforceable. This result is of particular concern when the agreement contains ancillary agreements, such as a covenant by the seller not to compete with the buyer after the acquisition. The enforceability of the agreement should not depend on the enforceability of a non-competition agreement, and the severability provision serves to accomplish this end.

Section 15.13. Further Assurance. The Seller, the Target and the Buyer agree that at any time and from time to time after the Closing Date they will execute and deliver to any other party such further instruments or documents as may reasonably be required to give effect to the transactions contemplated hereunder.

Section 15.14. Confidential Information. The Seller, the Target and the Buyer for themselves, their directors, officers, employees, agents, representatives and partners, if any, covenant with each other that they will use all information relating to any other party, the Target or any Subsidiary acquired by any of them pursuant to the provisions of this Agreement or in the course of negotiations with or examinations of any other party only in connection with the transactions contemplated hereby and shall cause all information obtained by them pursuant to this Agreement and such negotiations and examinations, which is not publicly available, to be treated as confidential except as may otherwise be required by law or as may be necessary or appropriate in connection with the enforcement of this Agreement or any instrument or document referred to herein or contemplated hereby. In the event of termination of this Agreement, each party will cause to be delivered to the other all documents, work papers and other material obtained by it from the others, whether so obtained by it from the others, whether so obtained before or after the execution of this Agreement, and each party agrees that it shall not itself use or disclose, directly or indirectly, any information so obtained, or otherwise obtained from the other hereunder or in connection therewith, and will have all such information kept confidential and will not use such information in any way which is detrimental to any other party, provided that (i) any party may use and disclose any such information which has been disclosed publicly (other than by such party or any affiliate of such party in breach of its obligations under this Section 15.14) and (ii) to the extent that any party or any affiliate of a party may become legally compelled to disclose any such information if it shall have used its best efforts, and shall have afforded the other parties the opportunity, to obtain an appropriate protective order, or other satisfactory assurance of confidential treatment, for the information required to be disclosed.

The confidential information section typically requires each party to keep confidential all information obtained in the course of the transaction. Because the target has already been or will shortly thereafter be, the object of an intensive due diligence review when the agreement is signed, the seller is initially more concerned with disclosure issues than the buyer. The seller may take the position that all materials provided to the buyer relating to the target should be returned or destroyed in the event the parties fail to close the transaction.

>   ***Section 15.15. Writings and Disclosures.*** Except as otherwise provided or contemplated herein, each exhibit, schedule, writing or other disclosure described in this Agreement as having been delivered or to be delivered by one party to the other shall be identified by reference to the section of this Agreement to which it relates and shall be signed or initialed on the first page by an officer or legal counsel of the Seller and by an officer or legal counsel of the Buyer and unless so identified and signed or initialed, the party receiving the same shall not be chargeable with notice of its content.

CHAPTER 11

CLOSING

INTRODUCTION

The process described in the preceding chapters culminates in the closing. This chapter discusses the ins and out of that event, which shares many of the characteristics of a multi-course banquet or a symphony performance in that many individual items must be synchronized carefully to produce the long-awaited consummation of the transaction.

THE BASICS OF CLOSING

What is a closing?

A closing is the event through which the parties to a transaction consummate that transaction by the execution and delivery of documentation, and, if applicable, the transfer of funds. Unless funded from internal sources by the buyer, the typical acquisition closing has two major elements: the "acquisition" or "corporate" closing, in which the seller and the buyer effect the merger or the transfer and delivery of the stock or assets pursuant to the acquisition agreement, and the "financial" closing, pursuant to which one or more lenders or other funding parties provide funding for the acquisition to the buyer, as borrower, pursuant to the loan agreement or other financing documentation, a portion of which is remitted to the seller in payment of the purchase price.

Is the acquisition agreement always executed prior to the closing?

Not necessarily. Sometimes the parties will want to simultaneously sign and close the corporate side of the transaction. This most likely occurs where the buyer is financing the transaction internally, where no governmental approvals are required to consummate the transaction, or when the deal must close very quickly after the parties have reached their initial meeting of the minds, for example, to take advantage of a provision of a tax law or to enable a seller to obtain the sales proceeds in time to meet a debt retirement obligation. In some instances, the parties do not intend to simultaneously sign and close, but end up doing so because they fail to reach their basic agreement until the closing date.

If the transaction is at all complex and requires governmental approval or third party financing, the parties will most likely sign a letter of intent, negotiate and execute the acquisition agreement, then proceed to close when the conditions to closing have been met and when the financing is available. Government agencies may require that the parties execute the acquisition agreement prior to consideration of an application for governmental approval. Similarly, lenders may require that the terms of a transaction be established before committing their resources to evaluating the transaction; in particular, they will want to know what representations and warranties are being made by the seller and the remedies available to the buyer in the event of a breach thereof.

Are financing agreements usually handled in the same way?

No. Most financing agreements are entered into at the closing. Prior thereto, however, the borrower and the lenders will have executed a commitment letter, or reached agreement on a term sheet, setting forth the basic terms of the lending arrangements.

How long does a closing take?

The closing process may last for a few hours, or for days or weeks, depending upon how much negotiation is left for the finale and upon the ability of the parties to timely satisfy the conditions to closing. The period immediately prior to the closing is often consumed by final negotiation of the terms and conditions of the operative documents, but this is not always the case. Closings on transactions for which the terms have been negotiated and finalized prior to the closing involve review of documents and confirmation that the conditions to closing have been met, followed by the execution and delivery of documents, and, when appropriate, the funding. The simplest of closings may be effected by an exchange of documents signed in counterpart without convening the parties at a single location.

Can a closing be held if either of the parties has not yet met all the conditions to closing?

Yes. An escrow closing may occur when one or more of the necessary conditions to closing has not been met, but the parties desire to go forward subject to satisfaction of the remaining conditions. In this case, transaction documentation can be executed and entrusted to an escrow agent chosen by the parties, who will break escrow and deliver the documents to the parties upon fulfillment of the outstanding conditions. An arrangement of this nature will require the negotiation and drafting of an escrow agreement among the parties and the agent clearly setting forth the terms upon which the breaking of escrow may occur, and the actions to be taken if those conditions are not fulfilled.

Alternatively, the parties may close if the party for whose benefit the unsatisfied condition was negotiated decides to waive the condition and proceed. In some cases it may be possible for the waiving party to exact some additional concession, such as an increase in the purchase price, or an undertaking from the other party to satisfy the condition after the closing. If the unsatisfied condition is so critical that the deal would unwind were it not to be fulfilled, the prudent path is not to close, since the cost of unwinding a closed transaction or resolving the unsatisfied condition may be much higher than the cost of failing to close.

Who should attend a closing?

Each person responsible for executing a document at the closing should expect to be present at the closing offices, or to be otherwise available, from the time that the closing is scheduled to the time of actual signing. If the signatory officer is also the business person responsible for the transaction, he or she is likely to be engaged throughout the pre-closing and closing process. If, on the other hand, the individual with signing authority is not otherwise involved in the transaction, he or she should be willing and able to remain available in the event that there is a delay in the closing process. Each individual sharing responsibility for the transaction should be on hand to review documents and participate in the negotiation of final changes.

Attorneys for each of the parties to the transaction will typically be required to participate in final negotiations and preparation and review of the closing documents, including, if required, opinions of counsel.

The participation of parties at other locations may also be required, depending on the nature of the transaction. For example, a transaction involving the transfer of assets (rather than stock) will typically require that certain conveyance documents be recorded at the time of closing at the appropriate federal, state, or local recordation offices in the jurisdiction within which that property is located. For multi-state acquisitions involving real and personal property, this may require filings in numerous locations. Further, counsel from each of those jurisdictions may have to render an opinion as to the effectiveness of the conveyances as a condition to closing. If the transaction involves one or more mergers, attorneys or other appropriate persons will have to file merger certificates and other documents at the offices of the Secretary of State of each jurisdiction where filing is required to effectuate such mergers. Finally, if the conveyed assets constitute security for the financing of the transaction, mortgages, UCC-1s, or other types of security documentation will also be recorded, and opinions of local counsel given in connection therewith. The effective coordination of all of these off-site parties is one of the more significant organizational challenges of a transactional closing.

Where should the closing take place?

The closing should be planned for the location most convenient to the parties. In the event that a financing is involved, this is almost always the city in which the lender is located. The offices in which the closing takes place should offer adequate services, space, communications, word processing, and copying, together with sufficient secretarial (and notarial) staff, to complete the transaction documentation and otherwise consummate the deal. These facilities and services are typically found at transactional law firms. Accordingly, the closing is often scheduled to take place at the offices of counsel to one of the parties. In the event that a financing is involved, it is usually held in the offices of the lenders' attorneys.

The buyer should consider seriously having the corporate closing and the financing closing in separate offices, within the same city, of course. Having two locations (or possibly more, if several pieces of large, complex financings are involved) serves a practical purpose of reducing the confusion and tension generated when many people are confined to the same quarters under stressful conditions. It also has tactical significance to the buyer. The most difficult aspect of any closing is the negotiation (and renegotiation) of deal points. Most often, it is in the buyer's best interest to keep the seller and the various lenders physically apart from each other so that the buyer can control the flow of information that each group receives and can broker a consensus on open points of common concern to its best advantage. This can be particularly important in the area of intercreditor relationships. As closing approaches, lenders get increasingly nervous about the risks they are about to take, particularly in a highly leveraged deal, and seek to improve their position by getting more collateral to secure their loans or a piece of the equity, or by imposing tighter post-acquisition covenants. There is a definite "me too" syndrome among lenders; i.e., whatever concession one lender gets, the others will demand for themselves. The buyer has a better chance of neutralizing this syndrome if it can keep the lenders from talking to each other.

How many people should be involved in a closing?

Each party should plan to have staffing adequate to cover all aspects of the transaction from negotiating issues which exist or arise to performing all the mechanical tasks required to complete the transaction. Most of the tasks will be performed by attorneys and other law firm employees. The parties' accountants and various people from the business entities involved in the transaction, particularly the finance department, will also need to be on hand, or easily reachable.

If the transaction will be financed by third parties, it is advisable that the attorneys for the buyer have separate closing teams for the corporate side of the transaction and each major piece of financing. This will be necessary if the closing is split among several physical locations. Each team should consist of the attorneys who have been primarily responsible for that aspect of the transaction since its inception and other attorneys and legal assistants as required. With adequately staffed teams in place to handle the details, the attorney in charge of the entire matter will be freed up to advise his client about the "big picture" and to trouble-shoot different aspects of the transaction where necessary. It is critical, however, that all attorneys and legal assistants involved in the closing be kept informed of changes in the big picture having an impact or potential impact on them. Periodic "all-hands" briefings are a good way to keep everyone abreast of changing events.

What are the phases of a closing?

The typical complex closing has three distinct phases: (i) the pre-closing process; (ii) the closing itself; and (iii) post-closing matters.

PRE-CLOSING

What happens during the pre-closing process?

During the "pre-closing" process: (i) the parties and their counsel distribute closing documents, including drafts of execution documents, for final review and approval prior to the scheduled date of execution and funding; (ii) each party satisfies itself that all conditions to closing have either been satisfied or waived; and (iii) the parties negotiate and resolve any open deal points. The size and complexity of the transaction and the number of open points, including new issues which may arise during this phase, will determine the length of the pre-closing phase. A typical "complex" transaction, i.e., with one or two layers of financing, multi-state collateral, and several third party or governmental consents, can easily involve one or two weeks of "pre-closing" activities.

How do the parties satisfy themselves that the conditions to closing have been satisfied or waived?

With respect to closing conditions which are satisfied through the delivery of documents such as regulatory approvals, landlord waivers, and estoppel certificates and management employment agreements, the parties and their counsel will examine the pertinent documentation and determine whether it comports with the requirements of the acquisition agreement or the relevant financing agreement, as applicable. In some cases, such as legal opinions and officers' certifications as to the accuracy of all representations and warranties as of the closing date, the parties delivering such documents and/or their counsel will have the additional burden of satisfying themselves prior to delivery thereof that the factual and legal matters set forth in those documents are, in fact, true. For example, prior to delivering a legal opinion, counsel will review documents such as UCC lien searches, corporate resolutions, good standing certificates, and officers' certificates as to factual matters, and will verify that certain actions such as the filing of merger documents and the recording of mortgages and UCC financing statements have been completed, in order to satisfy himself that the necessary foundation for issuing the legal opinion exists.

With respect to closing conditions which are not satisfied through the delivery of documents, such as the conditions that there be no pending litigation which threatens to enjoin the consummation of the transaction and that the target shall not have suffered a material adverse change in its business, the parties must resort to a combination of examination and analysis of documents, such as the target's most recently available financial statements, and the other due diligence investigation techniques it employed at the outset of the transaction, to satisfy themselves that these conditions have been met.

To assist in the foregoing process, well in advance of the closing the parties should have prepared one or more closing checklists (see below) which set forth the steps and documentation required for closing. Compliance with the checklist and with the conditions to closing set forth in the basic loan or acquisition documents will increase significantly the likelihood that the requirements for closing are met.

What is a good procedure for a party to follow to ascertain that its representations and warranties are true as of the closing date?

Counsel for each party should periodically confirm with his client that nothing has occurred which makes a representation or warranty of the client untrue. Generally speaking, as soon as any significant event which will make a representation or warranty untrue, such as a loss of a major customer of the seller or the filing of a lawsuit, occurs, the warranting party should inform the other parties of such occurrence so that appropriate waivers or modifications of terms can be negotiated and resolved well in advance of the closing. In addition, *at least two or three days* prior to the closing, counsel should review his client's representations and warranties *line by line* with appropriate employees and representatives of the client. Any facts which deviate from these representations and warranties should be incorporated as exceptions to the client's closing certificate regarding the accuracy of the representations and warranties and be immediately presented to the other relevant parties for their review. If they agree to accept the certificate with such exceptions, they shall be deemed to have waived the condition to closing (although, as discussed in Chapter 10, they may not have waived their claims to indemnification for breach of the representation or warranty).

What other forms do waivers take?

Waivers of conditions to closing may also be made through the acceptance of documents containing terms which differ from the previously negotiated terms, such as legal opinions which take exceptions, make assumptions, or exclude matters not originally contemplated by the parties. Where there is no previously contemplated document into which a waiver may be incorporated, the best course is to create a written waiver for the waiving party to execute.

How much renegotiation of the deal really takes place during the pre-closing phase?

The parties should be prepared for anything and everything. Events such as the filing of a lawsuit or the assessment of a tax deficiency against the seller, a change in the financial condition of the seller, an unresolved personality conflict between the buyer and a key management person, or a demand by lenders that the transaction between the buyer and seller be modified, that additional security be provided, that the buyers raise additional equity, or that the lenders be given an equity kicker can and do happen and may require the parties to renegotiate fundamental business issues. As a result, the buyer and seller should come to the pre-closing phase prepared to compromise where appropriate and to identify what items are non-negotiable for them.

Who has the most leverage in closing week negotiations?

First of all, the convergence of the parties at the various appointed closing offices, added to the resources previously expended by them in getting to this phase of the transaction, creates tremendous momentum and incentives for everyone to close. Therefore, there will be some room for compromise on each party's part. Nevertheless, the parties will not necessarily have equal bargaining strength simply because both of them are fast approaching the finish line. Differences in leverage which developed through the course of prior negotiations are likely to persist during the closing week. However, there are no hard and fast rules about the degree to which the power relationships among the parties will, or will not, change.

For example, it would be logical for the buyer to assume that the sweet image of sales proceeds is dancing in the seller's head, and, as a result, the seller will bend easily to any changes requested by the lenders. But the seller, in fact, may be having second thoughts about its bargain and resist any modifications of the acquisition agreement as a way of trying to force the buyer into a position where it cannot close. Conversely, the buyer may think (or know) that it is buying the target cheaply and, therefore, do whatever it takes to achieve a quick closing. As was the case throughout the entire course of the negotiations of the transaction, each party will have its set of revealed and hidden cards and will have to judge where pressure can be applied effectively on the others.

What is a pre-closing drill?

The pre-closing drill is a dress rehearsal for the closing, preferably held no earlier than three days prior to closing and no later than the night prior to closing. Counsel for the parties conduct the drill; their clients and other persons will be present as needed. Each party puts all of its closing documents out on the closing room table so that the other appropriate parties can satisfy themselves that the conditions to closing embodied in those documents have been met. To the extent feasible, the parties will execute as many documents as possible in order to save time on the closing day and thereby ensure that all conditions to closing will be satisfied early enough in the day to allow any wire transfer of funds or investment of sale proceeds to be completed on the closing day. After review of the closing documents and the closing checklist, the parties will identify tasks which must be completed before, legally and logistically, closing can be effected.

In transactions involving third party financing, lenders and lenders' counsel may require two or more pre-closing drills; i.e., one involving their own financing, one involving review of the corporate side of the transaction, and, if applicable, others involving the other financing pieces of the transaction.

CLOSING

What happens on the closing day itself?

Assuming the parties have conducted a pre-closing drill: (i) the parties and their counsel will review any documents which were revised or newly generated, the parties will execute any previously unexecuted documents, all undated documents will be dated, any required Board of Directors meetings which have not previously been held will be held, and any changed documents or signature pages which must be submitted to local counsel prior to release of their opinions will be transmitted to them; (ii) the parties will recheck all the documents lined up on the closing table against the closing checklists; and (iii) when all counsel are satisfied that all conditions to closing have been satisfied or waived, they will instruct their clients' respective agents to wire funds or file or record documents (simultaneously or in such order as they have agreed), as applicable, and will deem all the documents on the closing table to have been delivered in the sequence set forth in the closing checklist and other governing agreements.

In the case of a transaction involving third party financing, what part of the deal closes first?

Typically, all transactions are deemed to take place simultaneously. Practically speaking, the lenders usually will not release the loan proceeds until they receive confirmation that the corporate portion of the transaction has been completed, i.e., stock certificates or bills of sales have been delivered or merger certificates have been filed, and security and title documents have been properly recorded.

How long does it actually take to close a transaction?

Depending on the complexity of the transaction, the number of things that do not go according to plan or schedule, and the good will, patience, and ingenuity of the parties and their counsel in devising acceptable bridge arrangements, substitutes, or accommodations, the closing phase may be effected within a matter of an hour or two, or may stretch over several days.

On what day should the closing take place?

Preferably any day but a Friday or a day before a holiday. The failure to achieve the closing on the scheduled day prior to a weekend or holiday puts the parties in the awkward position of having to work into or through the non-business day, without the ability to transfer or invest funds prior to the next business day, and with the attendant disruption in the personal lives of all concerned (which can be particularly troublesome for non-professional staff). Depending on the point at which the transaction slipped off schedule, any number of complications may have occurred. Title may have been transferred without funding. Issues of who owns what or who bears the risk of loss may arise. Interest may be claimed on the "lost" or withheld funding by the lender or the seller. Finally, the documents, especially exhibits thereto, even if prepared in an "as of" form, may contain material inaccuracies caused by the passage of time which will require redating, amendment, or waiver in order to close the transaction.

What are some of the most common logistical snafus that can derail a closing?

Some of the biggest headaches result from:

- Unavailability of key business people.
- Failure to have local counsel on stand-by to review last minute document changes.
- Failure to provide local counsel with copies of documents or other items which are conditions to release of their opinions.

- Failure to have precleared Articles of Merger with appropriate jurisdictions.
- Failure to have persons on standby to file or record documents, including merger documents, UCC 1s, mortgages, and terminations of UCC 1s required to be removed off record.
- Failure to have adequate support staff to make last-minute revisions in documents.
- Failure to have conducted the pre-closing drill, including execution of all documents not subject to change.
- Failure to have adequate legal staff at closing headquarters to negotiate final documents, including local counsel legal opinions.
- Failure to obtain proper wiring instructions.
- Failure to ascertain time periods by which wires must be sent or to make arrangements to have banks hold their wires open past normal hours.
- Failure to consummate any pre-closing corporate reorganizations (e.g., mergers of subsidiaries into parent companies, dissolution of defunct subsidiaries, filing of charter amendments) in a timely fashion.
- Failure to have tax counsel review the final terms and documentation to ensure that tax planning objectives have not been adversely affected by last minute restructuring or drafting.
- Failure to obtain required bring-down good standing certificates or other certified documents from appropriate jurisdictions.

Substantially all of the foregoing can be avoided with proper advance planning.

WIRE TRANSFERS

What is a wire transfer of funds?

A wire transfer of funds is payment through a series of debits and credits transmitted via computers. A domestic wire transfer is made through the Federal Reserve System, which is divided into twelve districts throughout the United States, with each district having one main Federal Reserve Bank and a myriad of branch banks. The actual physical transfer of funds takes place on the books of the Federal Reserve Banks and branches. An international wire transfer of funds is payment through a series of debits and credits transmitted directly via telex among correspondent banks.

How is a domestic wire transfer made?

In order to make a wire transfer, both the buyer's and seller's banks must be members of the Federal Reserve System and maintain accounts with a Reserve Bank, or have an account with a member bank. The buyer or lender remitting funds by wire must provide to its bank the name of the seller, the name of the seller's bank and the identity of the account to be credited, and the American Banking Association (ABA) number that identifies the seller's bank in the Federal Reserve System.

Upon the confirmation of customer funds, the originating member bank, or transferor, will notify its Reserve Bank to debit the transferor's account for credit to the member bank transferee. If the transferor and transferee maintain accounts at two separate Reserve Banks, the request for credit will be sent by the transferor's Reserve Bank to the transferee's Reserve Bank for credit to the latter. The transferee's Reserve Bank will then credit the transferee's account.

What does it mean when the originating bank confirms customer funds?

All funds to be remitted must be collected. Thus, a check deposit covering the wire transfer that has not yet cleared will delay or prevent the transfer. Essentially, the remitting bank is protecting itself from exposure on items subject to stop payment orders until final payment is effectuated. This includes certified checks and bank checks. Oftentimes, reference is made to "immediately available funds" or "federal funds," which signifies that the funds for remittance have been collected.

When is final payment of the wire transfer effectuated?

As soon as the transferee receives notice of the credit—i.e., the "Fedwire transfer" from its Federal Reserve Bank—payment is considered final, and, except as described below, the seller has the right to the use of such funds.

Can a transferor revoke the request for a wire transfer of funds once the transferor has notified its Reserve Bank to debit its amount?

The Reserve Bank may cease acting on the wire transfer if the transferor's request for revocation allows the Reserve Bank a reasonable opportunity to comply with the requested revocation. If the request is received too late, the Reserve Bank may ask the transferee's Reserve Bank to ask the transferee to return the funds, if the transferor so desires. However, the Reserve Bank will only be liable for lack of good faith or failure to exercise ordinary care. Therefore, it is not responsible if the transferee refuses to return the funds.

What is the deadline for placing a wire transfer order for funds intended to be received by the seller on the same day?

Although no Reserve Bank will guarantee that it will complete a transfer of funds on the day requested, generally speaking, 3:00 p.m. is the originating bank's deadline. Moreover, the Reserve Bank may, in its discretion, process a wire transfer after its closing hour. This will usually occur in an emergency or when large sums of money are being transferred. The deadline for placing an international wire transfer order is generally 12:30 p.m.

What are the differences between the domestic and international wire transfer of funds?

With an international wire transfer, the ease and security of the Federal Reserve is not available. Hence, the transfer generally takes longer. In addition, with international wire there is a problem of provisional payment. Specifically, the bank which debits the customer's account usually reserves the right to withdraw the credit extended to the corresponding bank, if the customer's account is overdrawn in the process. This may create problems determining when final payment is made.

What are the advantages and disadvantages to a seller in requiring payment through a wire transfer of funds?

Next to actual cash in hand, this is the best way for a seller to assure itself that it will have use of the sale proceeds on the closing day since the Federal Reserve Bank assumes the risk of final payment once the transferor's request is accepted by its Reserve Bank.

One potential disadvantage associated with a wire transfer concerns the nature of the account agreement the seller has with its bank. The seller's bank may not be required to credit the seller's account immediately upon receiving Federal Reserve credit because of the account agreement. Federal law requires that the transferee "promptly" credit the beneficiary's account. However, what "promptly" means is not clearly specified. The seller would be best advised to be familiar with the terms of its bank account agreement. Moreover, the seller could specify in the acquisition agreement that the buyer's duty to deliver funds is completed only when the seller''s individual account has been credited.

Are there any other methods of payment, other than by cash or wire transfer, which would be acceptable to sellers at a closing?

There are three types of bank-issued checks which are virtually risk-free to a seller who accepts them, namely: (a) the certified check; (b) the cashier's check; and (c) the bank check. Each of these checks has some distinguishing feature which differentiates it from the others, but all of them are designed to offer comfort to the recipient that payment will definitely be made by the designated payor bank.

Certified checks are instruments which, upon certification by the payor bank, are not subject to an order to stop payment. Under the Uniform Commercial Code, the certifying bank becomes personally liable for failure to honor the check, and the customer is secondarily liable thereon.

When a bank issues a cashier's check, the bank acts as both the payor and the payee for the amount of the check. As with the certified check, a bank is deemed to have accepted a cashier's check for payment at the moment it is issued. The customer cannot stop payment on it. The seller's only risk of nonpayment is if the issuing bank becomes insolvent before payment can be made. Even in that event, if the bank is a member of the FDIC, the check will be insured up to $100,000.

A bank check does not give a seller the same degree of comfort as either a certified or cashier's check, because, unlike the first two cases, the issuing bank has not accepted the check for payment (i.e., committed to pay the stated amount upon demand) at the moment of issuance. Rather, presentment of the check is required for payment. Despite this difference, the UCC treats bank checks as cash equivalent, and the only instance in which the issuing bank can stop payment is if it is a direct party to the transaction. The only time a customer ordering a bank check can request payment be stopped is in the case of fraud or a theft of the instrument.

POST-CLOSING

What are typical "post-closing" activities?

"Post-closing" tasks typically fall into one of two categories: document distribution and clean-up.

While each of the parties to a closing generally wants to depart the closing table with a complete stack of original closing documents for its file, this is not frequently practical. First, each of the parties has different requirements for closing documents. Some parties should not receive documents that other parties will receive, and some parties need original documents while others need only photocopies.

Further, some documents held or executed at other locations may be available at the time and place of closing only by telecopy, or not at all. Finally, the sheer number and volume of documents may preclude sorting and photocopying of the executed papers swiftly enough to be delivered to the parties prior to their departure from the premises.

At some point, however, each of the participants should receive a complete set of the transaction documents to which it is entitled. In some transactions, the initial distribution of originals and, as available, copies, is followed by the production of a closing binder containing a complete indexed set of documents in one or more volumes. These binders may be velobound or, if the expense is approved by the clients, permanently bound in stitched covers with stamped lettering on the spine. The acquisition documents often are bound separately from the financing documents.

The final document assembly and distribution effort will be much easier if a good closing document checklist was utilized prior to closing. When completed and updated, the checklist may be turned into a closing memorandum (which may double as an index to the closing document binders), with the addition of a brief narrative chronology of the transactions taken prior to, at, and following the closing to complete the transaction. A common closing memorandum can be used even if the acquisition and financing closings occurred at different offices.

The second principal "post-closing" effort is the clean-up process, which involves the finalization or completion of tasks and documents which were not or could not have been completed at or prior to closing. This may include corrections or amendments to ancillary documents, the termination of pension plans, the receipt of consents and approvals not obtainable by closing, the completion and documentation of a closing date audit for balance sheet pricing adjustment purposes, or the receipt of title insurance commitments or policies as of the closing date from jurisdictions with filing delays. In addition, where many real estate parcels in multiple jurisdictions are required to be mortgaged, or collateral is located in foreign countries, completion of recordation of mortgages and perfection of security interests are commonly put aside as post-closing matters, with a deadline for completion of several months after the closing date.

In both cases, individuals responsible for post-closing efforts should strive to complete their tasks as soon as possible before the press of other matters and the passage of time make the wrapping up of these loose ends more difficult than would otherwise have been the case. A post-closing checklist similar in design to the closing checklist described below should be prepared, and adhered to, by the parties responsible for these activities.

PLANNING AIDS

What's the best way to prepare for a closing?

Have your attorney prepare a comprehensive closing checklist well in advance of the closing, in fact, as soon as the deal begins to jell. This checklist should (i) set forth each and every task which must be completed in order for the parties to be legally and logistically ready to consummate the transaction and the date by which such task must be completed; (ii) state, where applicable, the document in which the completion of the task will be embodied; (iii) set forth the name of one or more persons responsible for the task; and (iv) contain a space for status notes. The closing checklist is both a road map and a progress report of the transaction. It can also be a source of embarrassment and a goad to those responsible for producing or reviewing documents whose failure to meet deadlines is documented in the status notes. Finally, it is the basis for the preparation of a closing memorandum for the transaction.

How should one schedule preclosing tasks?

The first concern should be to deal with documents and actions of parties who will either not be at the closing, who have a limited role in the closing, or who are beyond the control of the parties to the transaction. These persons include directors and shareholders whose authorizations are required, governmental agencies without any incentive to expedite review of applications for regulatory approvals, third parties to critical agreements who may prove recalcitrant when asked for consents, estoppel letters, solvency letters, or legal opinions, actuaries who must give up-to-date valuations of pension assets, and persons who are committed to other tasks but need to be on call to file or record mortgages, UCC financing statements, or merger certificates upon a moment's notice. The persons responsible for ensuring that the closing takes place on the appointed day must make an accurate assessment of how long it is likely to take to obtain a required document or to accomplish a necessary task, and, working backward from the expected closing date, attempt to develop a realistic schedule for reaching closing.

Should all the parties use the same closing checklist?

At the very least, by the time the parties arrive for the pre-closing phase, they should be working from the same closing checklist, with the following exceptions. The seller does not need those portions of the checklist dedicated to the financing of the transaction other than items related to the financing in which the seller has a role (e.g., delivery of reliance letters from the seller's counsel to lenders allowing them to rely on such counsel's legal opinion and delivery of the seller's consent to assignments by the buyer to the lenders of the buyer's rights under the acquisition agreement). The seller and the lenders do not need an expansive checklist relating to the tasks associated with the formation and capitalization of the buying group. Moreover, there may be certain tasks or documents, including side letters, which each party wishes to keep confidential within its own group. As a result of the foregoing, each party may have more than one closing checklist, i.e., an expansive one setting forth everything about which it is concerned and other lists, which are abridged versions of the global checklist, to be shared with one or more of the other parties. These latter lists must be developed along with the other parties so that all agree as to what activities will make everyone ready, legally and logistically, to consummate the transaction.

CLOSING MEMORANDUM

Is there one document which sums up the transaction?

Yes. The closing memorandum memorializes the significant activities which comprised the transaction. The sample closing memorandum in Appendix 11A from a very complex transaction, is a good photograph of "the art of M&A."

APPENDIX 11A
MERGER OF TARGET
ACQUISITION CORP.
INTO TARGET CO. INC.
CLOSING MEMORANDUM

DECEMBER 31, 1987
9:00 a.m. Eastern Standard Time

I. GENERAL

This memorandum describes the principal transactions that have occurred in connection with the acquisition (the "Acquisition") of Target Co. Inc., a Delaware corporation ("Target"), by Purchaser Holdings, Inc., a Delaware corporation ("Holdings"). Holdings, Target Acquisition Corp., a Delaware corporation and a wholly owned subsidiary of Holdings ("TAC"), Target and Seller Holdings, Ltd., a Delaware corporation which owns all of the issued and outstanding Stock of Target ("Seller"), have entered into an Agreement of Merger, dated as of October 1, 1987 (the "Agreement"), pursuant to which TAC will be merged into Target pursuant to the Certificate of Merger.

In connection with the capitalization of Holdings to accomplish the Acquisition on the Effective Date, affiliates (the "Investor Shareholders") of Investor Corporation, a Delaware corporation ("IC"), purchased 800,000 shares of the common stock of Holdings for an aggregate amount of $4,000,000. Concurrently, IC loaned $1,000,000 on a recourse basis to certain management personnel at Target (the "Management Shareholders"). The Management Shareholders purchased 200,000 shares of the common stock of Holdings for $1,000,000 and pledged such stock to IC to secure repayment of the loan. TAC then merged into Target.

On the Effective Date, Holdings entered into a Credit Agreement with Lender Bank ("Bank") pursuant to which Holdings obtained a term loan of $40,000,000 and revolving credit loans of up to $10,000,000 (the "Credit Agreement"). Concurrently therewith, Holdings entered into a Bridge Funding Agreement with The Investment Bank Group Inc. ("Investment Bank Group") pursuant to which Holdings obtained a bridge loan of $60,000,000 (the "Bridge Agreement"). Holdings sold warrants for 200,000 shares of its Common Stock (the "Investment Banker Warrants") to Lead Investment Banker Incorporated ("Lead Investment Banker") and its designees for $20,000.

After the Effective Date it is anticipated that Holdings and Lead Investment Banker will enter into a Securities Purchase Agreement (the "Securities Purchase Agreement") pursuant to which Holdings will return the $20,000 to Lead Investment Banker and Lead Investment Banker will return the Investment Banker Warrants to Holdings. Holdings will then sell Warrants for 200,000 shares of its Common Stock to the Purchasers named in the Securities Purchase Agreement (the "Purchasers") for $20,000 (the "Note Purchase Warrants") and deliver to the Purchasers Notes due December 31, 1997, in an aggregate principal amount of $60,000,000 and bearing interest at approximately 14% per annum (the "Note") for which Holdings will receive $60,000,000 cash which it will use to pay off the $60,000,000 bridge loan under the Bridge Agreement.

After the Effective Time and concurrently with the funding of the term loan, the initial revolving loans and the bridge loan, Holdings contributed to TAC the amount of $100,000,000 as a capital contribution. Seller received $100,000,000 cash less the amount of the intercompany loan to be paid after Closing, Series A Preferred Stock of Holdings having a redemption value of $10,000,000 and a Warrant entitling it to purchase 40,000 shares of the common stock of Holdings (the "Seller Warrant").

The Closing occurred on December 31, 1987 (the "Effective Date"), at 9:00 a.m. Eastern Standard Time. The merger was effective on the Effective Date at the time the Certificate of Merger was filed with the Secretary of State of Delaware (the "Effective Time").

All capitalized terms used herein which are not defined herein and which are defined in the Agreement, the Credit Agreement, the Bridge Funding Agreement or the Securities Purchase Agreement have the respective meanings attributed to them in the Agreement, the Credit Agreement, the Bridge Funding Agreement or the Securities Purchase Agreement.

II. TRANSACTIONS PRIOR TO THE CLOSING

The following actions were taken prior to the Closing.

1. On October 1, 1987, the Agreement among Holdings, Target, TAC and Seller was executed and delivered.

2. On October 1, 1987, TAC, Seller and Agent Bank (the "Escrow Agent") entered into an Escrow Agreement pursuant to which TAC deposited with the Escrow Agent One Million Dollars ($1,000,000) pursuant to Section 3.3 of the Agreement.

3. On October 1, 1987, the Board of Directors of each of Holdings and TAC approved the terms of the Merger and the Agreement and the Board of Directors of TAC approved the Escrow Agreement.

4. On October 1, 1987, the Board of Directors of each of Target and Seller approved the terms of the Merger and the Agreement and the Board of Directors of Seller approved the Escrow Agreement.

5. On October 2, 1987, Seller issued a press release announcing the Holdings, Target, Seller and TAC agreement to the terms of the Merger and announcing the execution of the Agreement.

6. On November 16, 1987, Bank delivered to Holdings a commitment letter pursuant to which Bank agreed to provide a $40,000,000 term loan and a $10,000,000 revolving line of credit to facilitate the Acquisition and to provide working capital thereafter.

7. On November 24, 1987, Lead Investment Banker delivered to Holdings a commitment letter pursuant to which Lead Investment Banker undertook to provide a bridge loan for an aggregate amount of $60,000,000.

8. On November 24, 1987, Holdings delivered to Lead Investment Banker a retention letter pursuant to which Holdings retained Lead Investment Banker to sell the Notes and Note Purchaser Warrants.

9. On December 24, 1987, a date at least three business days before the Closing, Seller delivered to TAC pursuant to Section 4.3 of the Agreement a notice setting forth the amount of the Intercompany Loan to be paid immediately after Closing.

10. On December 28, 1987, the Board of Directors and shareholders of Holdings adopted an amendment of the certificate of incorporation of Holdings to authorize the Series A Preferred Stock.

11. On December 28, 1987, Holdings caused to be filed an Amended and Restated Certificate of Incorporation providing for 1,500 shares of Series A Preferred Stock par value $1.00 per share.

12. As of December 30, 1987, the Certificate of Merger was executed by the President of TAC and attested by the Secretary of such corporation and was executed by the President of Target and sealed and attested by the Secretary of such corporation.

13. On December 30, 1987, the Board of Directors of Holding, authorized the issuance of 1,000 shares of Series A Preferred Stock to Seller with the rights designated in the Amended and Restated Certificate of Incorporation of Holdings.

14. On December 30, 1987, Seller, as sole stockholder of Target, consented to the Agreement and Certificate of Merger.

15. On December 30, 1987, Holdings, as sole stockholder of TAC consented to the Agreement and Certificate of Merger.

III. CLOSING DOCUMENTS AND TRANSACTIONS

The following documents were delivered at or prior to the Effective Date, but all such documents are deemed delivered at the Effective Date. All documents are dated as of the Effective Date and delivered in New York, New York, unless otherwise indicated. All transactions in connection with the Closing shall be considered as accomplished concurrently, so that none shall be effective until all are effective. Executed copies (or photocopies, or conformed copies where necessary) of each document will be delivered after the Closing as follows:

one to IC
one to Holdings
one to Seller
one to Target
one to Bank
one to Lead Investment Banker

with photocopies to be distributed as follows:

one to Investment Banker Counsel (IBC)
one to Seller Counsel (SC)
one to Bank counsel (BC)
one to Investor Corporation counsel (ICC)

IV. SCHEDULE OF CLOSING DOCUMENTS

1. Corporate Good Standing, Articles, By-Laws, and Incumbency of Target, Its Subsidiaries, and Seller

1.01. Certificate of Incorporation and all amendments to date of Target certified by the Secretary of State of Delaware on December 3, 1987.

1.02. Certificate of the Secretary of State of Delaware, dated December 3, 1987, certifying that Target is an existing corporation and in good standing under the laws of the State of Delaware.

1.03. Telex from the Secretary of State of Delaware, dated the Effective Date, updating the information described in item 1.02 above.

1.04. Certificates of the Secretaries of State of California and New York dated December 1 and 2, 1987, respectively, certifying that Target is qualified to conduct business and in good standing in such states.

1.05. Telexes or verbal consents from the Secretaries of State of California and New York, dated the Effective Date, updating the information described in item 1.04 above.

1.06. (a)-(b) Articles or Certificates of Incorporation or other organization documents and all amendments to date of the following Subsidiaries of Target ("Subsidiaries") certified by the appropriate authority of the governing jurisdiction:

(a)   New York Target Subsidiary Ltd. (N.Y.)
(b)   Delaware Target Subsidiary, Inc. (Del.)

1.07. (a)-(b) Certificates of the authorities described in item 1.06, certifying that each of the Subsidiaries is an existing corporation and in good standing.

1.08. (a)-(b) Telexes or verbal consents of the authorities described in item 1.06, dated the Effective Date, updating the information set forth in item 1.07 above.

1.09. Certificate of Incorporation and all amendments to date of Seller certified by the Secretary of State of Delaware, dated December 3, 1987.

1.10. Certificate of the Secretary of State of Delaware, dated December 3, 1987, certifying that Seller is an existing corporation and in good standing under the laws of Delaware.

1.11. Telex from the Secretary of State of Delaware, dated the Effective Date, updating the information described in item 1.10 above.

1.12. Certificate of Secretary of Target, dated the Effective Date, as to the Certificates of Incorporation and Bylaws of such corporation, the election, incumbency and signatures of officers of such corporation, and certifying as to the resolutions of the Board of Directors and stockholders of such corporation relating to the transaction pursuant to Section 8.4 of the Agreement.

1.13. Certificate of Secretary of Seller, dated the Effective Date, as to the Certificate of Incorporation and Bylaws of such corporation, the election, incumbency and signatures of officers of such corporation, and certifying as to the resolutions of the Board of Directors of such corporation relating to the transaction pursuant to Section 8.4 of the Agreement.

2. Good Standing, Articles, By-Laws, and Incumbency of Holdings and TAC

2.01. Certificate of Incorporation and all amendments to date of Holdings certified by the Secretary of State of Delaware on December 21, 1987.

2.02. Certificate of the Secretary of State of Delaware, dated December21, 1987 certifying that Holdings is an existing corporation and in good standing under the laws of the State of Delaware.

2.03. Telex of the Secretary of State of Delaware, dated the Effective Date, updating the information set forth in item 2.02 above.

2.04. Certificate of the Secretary of State of each of California and New York, dated December 22, 1987, certifying that Holdings is qualified to conduct business and in good standing in such states.

2.05. Certificate of Incorporation and all amendments to date of TAC certified by the Secretary of State of Delaware on December 10, 1987.

2.06. Certificate of the Secretary of State of Delaware, dated December 21, 1987, certifying that TAC is an existing corporation and in good standing under the laws of the State of Delaware.

2.07. Telex of the Secretary of State of Delaware, dated the Effective Date, updating the information set forth in item 2.06 above.

2.08. Certificate of the Secretary of Holdings, dated the Effective Date, as to the Certificate of Incorporation and Bylaws of such corporation, the election, incumbency and signatures of officers of such corporation and certifying as to the resolutions of the Board of Directors of such corporation relating to the transaction pursuant to Section 9.4 of the Agreement, Sections 5.01(e), (f) and (h) of the Credit Agreement and the Bridge Agreement.

2.09. Certificate of the Secretary of TAC, dated the Effective Date, as to the Certificate of Incorporation and Bylaws of such corporation, the election, incumbency and signatures of officers of such corporation, and certifying as to the resolutions of the Board of Directors and stockholders of such corporation relating to the transaction pursuant to Section 9.4 of the Agreement, Sections 5.01(e), (f) and (h) of the Credit Agreement and the Bridge Agreement.

2.10. Certificate of the Secretary of Target (the Surviving Corporation), dated the Effective Date, certifying as to the resolutions of the Board of Directors of such corporation relating to Sections 5.01(e), (f) and (h) of the Credit Agreement and the Bridge Agreement.

2.11. (a)-(b) Certificates of the Secretaries of the Subsidiaries listed in (a)-(b) of item 1.06 as to the Certificate of Incorporation and Bylaws, the election, incumbency and signatures of officers and certifying as to resolutions of the Board of Directors of such corporations relating to Sections 5.01(e), (f) and (h) of the Credit Agreement.

3. Principal Documents

3.01. Agreement of Merger, dated as of October 1, 1987.

3.02. Certificate of Merger.

3.03. Escrow Agreement, dated October 1, 1987.

3.04. Certificate No.PA-1 evidencing 1,000 shares of Series A Preferred Stock of Holdings.

3.05. Seller Registration Rights Agreement.

3.06. Seller Warrant.

3.07. Credit Agreement, together with Schedules and Exhibits thereto.

3.08. Target Security Agreement, between Bank as Agent and for the Ratable Benefit of Lenders and Target.

3.09. (a)-(b) Subsidiary Security Agreement between Bank as Agent and for the Ratable Benefit of Lenders and each of the Subsidiaries listed in (a)-(b) of item 1.06.

3.10. Holdings Pledge Agreement.

3.11. Certificate No. 8 evidencing 100 shares, constituting all of the issued and outstanding shares of Target together with a stock power duly endorsed in blank.

3.12. Target Pledge Agreement.

3.13. (a)-(b) Certificates evidencing all of the issued and outstanding shares of each of the Subsidiaries listed in item 1.06, together with stock powers or other instruments of transfer duly endorsed in blank.

3.14. Individual Stock Pledge Agreements, executed by each of the Investor Shareholders and Management Shareholders in favor of the Bank.

3.15. Certificates evidencing all of the issued and outstanding common shares of Holdings, together with stock powers from each shareholder duly endorsed in blank.

3.16. Mortgage.

3.17. Joinder Agreement executed by Target.

3.18. Private Placement Memorandum of December, 1987.

3.19. Supplement to the Private Placement Memorandum dated December 30, 1987.

3.20. Bridge Agreement.

3.21. Bridge Notes Indenture.

3.22. Senior Subordinated Bridge Note.

3.23. Bridge Note Registration Rights Agreement.

3.24. Warrants issued by Holdings to Lead Investment Banker.

3.25. Subordinated Pledge Agreement between Holdings and Investment Bank Group.

3.26. Intercreditor Agreement between Bank and Investment Bank Group.

4. Documents Relating to the Escrow Agent

4.01. Joint Written Notice executed by Seller and TAC pursuant to Section 4(a) of the Escrow Agreement to the effect that the Merger has been effected and instructing the Escrow Agent to pay the Escrow Deposit and interest accrued thereon to Target.

4.02. Receipt of Target, dated the Effective Date, for funds received from the Escrow Agent in the amount of $1,025,000.

5. Documents Relating to Compliance with Agreement of Merger

5.01. Certificate of the President of Seller, dated the Effective Date, pursuant to Sections 8.1 and 8.2 of the Agreement and as to compliance with and performance of the Agreement and as to the representations and warranties set forth in the Agreement.

5.02. Certificate of the Vice President of TAC dated the Effective Date, pursuant to Sections 9.1, 9.2 and 9.7 of the Agreement as to compliance and performance of the Agreement; the representations and warranties set forth in the Agreement; and its business, financial conditions and operations.

5.03. Releases executed by each person holding an option to purchase common stock of Target under the Target 1984 Stock Option Plan pursuant to Section 8.9 of the Agreement.

5.04. Certificate No.7 of Target evidencing 1,000 shares of common stock of Target issued to Seller together with such stock transfer tax stamps as may be required.

6. Documents Relating to Compliance with Credit Agreement

6.01 Certificate executed by CEO and CFO of Holdings as to representations and warranties and no event of default pursuant to Section 5.01(d) of the Credit Agreement.

6.02 (a)-(d) UCC-1 Financing Statements covering personal property and appropriate documents for perfecting security interest in U.S. intellectual property as follows:

- (a) Holdings–California Secretary of State; Clerk of Los Angeles County, California; New York Department of State; and City Register of New York City;
- (b) Target–California Secretary of State; Clerk of Los Angeles County, California; New York Department of State; and City Register of New York City;
- (c) New York Target Subsidiary Ltd.–New York Department of State; and City Register of New York City; and
- (d) Delaware Target Subsidiary Inc.–Delaware Secretary of State; Clerk of New Castle County, Delaware.

6.03 Certificate of President of Target to the effect that all indebtedness of Target has been paid or refinanced pursuant to Section 5.01(o) of the Credit Agreement.

6.04 Appointments of CT Corporation System in State of California as agent for service of process executed by CT Corporation, Holdings, Target and the Subsidiaries pursuant to Section 5.01(s) of the Credit Agreement.

6.05 Pro Forma Closing Date Balance Sheet for Holdings and its consolidated Subsidiaries pursuant to Section 5.01(t) of the Credit Agreement.

6.06 Borrowing Base Report, dated not more than two (2) days prior to the Effective Date pursuant to Section 5.01(y) of the Credit Agreement.

6.07 Appraisal of Appraisal Co. as to fair market value and orderly liquidation value of the real and personal property of Target pursuant to Section 5.01(bb) of the Credit Agreement.

6.08 Written undertakings, executed by each of Target and the Subsidiaries pursuant to Section 5.01(dd) of the Credit Agreement.

6.09 Solvency letters from CFO's and accountants for Holdings and Target pursuant to Section 5.01(kk) of the Credit Agreement.

6.10 Bank Credit Audit pursuant to Section 5.01(pp) of the Credit Agreement.

6.11 Certificate of Borrower as to consents pursuant to Section 6.03 of the Credit Agreement.

6.12 Evidence of payment of or indemnification against tax liens: City of New York–$10,000,000, State of New York–$500.00.

7. Consents, Waivers, and Estoppel Certificates of Landlords of Target and Real Estate Matters

7.01. Consent of Lessor Ltd., lessor to New York Target Subsidiary, Ltd. with respect to the facility located at One Main Street, New York, New York.

7.02. Owners' title insurance policy with respect to the California property, dated the Effective Date, pursuant to Section 8.8 of the Agreement.

7.03. Lenders' title insurance policy with respect to the California property.

7.04. Title Insurance Questionnaire.

7.05. Estoppel Certificate.

7.06. Survey.

7.07. Indemnities of Seller to the Title Insurance Company.

7.08. Discharges of Trust Company Mortgages.

7.09. Seller Agreement regarding effluent discharge.

8. Insurance

8.01. Insurance endorsements naming Agent as additional insured or loss payee pursuant to Section 5.01(x) of the Credit Agreement.

9. Documents Relating to Compliance with Bridge Agreement

9.01. Certificate of Vice President of Holdings pursuant to Section 3.1.4 of the Bridge Agreement as to the satisfaction of certain conditions of the Bridge Agreement.

9.02. Warrant Repurchase Letter Agreement, dated the Effective Date, between Holdings and Investment Bank Group.

10. Opinions of Counsel

10.01. Opinion of SC, dated the Effective Date, addressed to Holdings, the Agent, Lead Investment Banker and the Indenture Trustee pursuant to Section 8.5 of the Agreement, Section 5.01 (mm) of the Credit Agreement and Section 3.1.8 of the Bridge Agreement.

10.02. Opinion of ICC, dated the Effective Date, pursuant to Section 9.5 of the Agreement.

10.03. Opinion of ICC, dated the Effective Date, addressed to the Agent pursuant to Section 5.01(c) of the Credit Agreement.

10.04. 0Opinion of ICC, dated the Effective Date, addressed to Lead Investment Banker and the Indenture Trustee pursuant to Section 3.1.7 of the Bridge Agreement.

10.05. Opinion of California Counsel, dated the Effective Date, addressed to the Agent pursuant to Section 5.01(v) of the Credit Agreement.

10.06. Opinion of Copyright Counsel, dated the Effective Date, addressed to the Agent and Holdings as to the trademark and copyright registrations in the United States pursuant to Section 5.01(w) of the Credit Agreement.

10.07. Opinion of BC dated the Effective Date, addressed to the Lenders pursuant to Section 5.01(u) of the Credit Agreement.

11. Documents Relating to IC and Management Shareholders

11.01. Employment Agreement between Target and John Smith, President of Target.

11.02. Powers of Attorney from each Management Shareholder appointing John Smith Attorney-in-fact.

11.03. Recourse Notes in the aggregate of $1,000,000 executed by each of the Management Shareholders (originals delivered to IC).

11.04. Pledge Agreement executed by Management Shareholders in favor of IC.

11.05. Cross Receipt of IC acknowledging receipt of the notes described in 11.03 and by John Smith as Attorney-in-fact for each of the Management Shareholders acknowledging receipt of an aggregate amount of $1,000,000.

11.06. Stockholders Agreement among Holdings, Investor Shareholders and Management Shareholders.

11.07. Agreement for Management Consulting Services between IC and Target.

11.08. IC Intercreditor Agreement by and between IC and Bank.

11.09. Letter as to Recourse Promissory Notes in favor of IC, dated the Effective Date, from IC to counsel for the Management Shareholders.

12. Funding of Holdings and TAC and Merger Payment

12.01. Cross Receipt executed by Holdings acknowledging receipt of $4,000,000, and by the Investor Shareholders acknowledging receipt of Certificate Nos. 1-4 evidencing 800,000 shares of the common stock of Holdings.

12.02. Cross Receipt executed by Holdings acknowledging receipt of $1,000,000, and by the Management Shareholders acknowledging receipt of Certificate Nos. 5-8 evidencing 200,000 shares of the common stock of Holdings.

12.03. Cross Receipt executed by Seller, dated the Effective Date, acknowledging receipt of (a) the Cash Portion of the Merger Payment in the amount of $100,000,000 determined pursuant to Section 3.2(b) of the Merger Agreement; (b) the Warrant; and (c) Certificate No. PA–1 evidencing 1,000 shares of Series A Preferred Stock, and by Holdings acknowledging receipt of (i) $10,000,000 as consideration for the issuance of the Series A Preferred Stock and (ii) a certificate evidencing 1,000 shares of Common Stock of Target.

12.04. Receipt executed by IC acknowledging receipt of $3,000,000 as a structuring fee.

13. Funding of Loan and Sale of Warrants

13.01. Term Note in the amount of $40,000,000 (original delivered to Lender).

13.02. Revolving Note in the amount of $10,000,000 (original delivered to Lender) (only $1,000,000 borrowed at Closing).

13.03. Cross Receipt of Lender acknowledging receipt of the Term Note and the Revolving Note and of Holdings acknowledging receipt of $41,000,000.

13.04. Cross Receipt of Investment Bank Group and Lead Investment Banker acknowledging receipt of the Investment Banker Warrants and Bridge Note and of Holdings acknowledging receipt of $60,000,000.

V. FILING OF CERTIFICATE OF MERGER

When all parties and their counsel were satisfied that the documents described in Section IV above were complete and in order, the Certificate of Merger was filed in the office of the Secretary of State of Delaware, in accordance with the General Corporation Law of the State of Delaware.

CHAPTER 12

PUBLIC COMPANY ACQUISITIONS

INTRODUCTION

This chapter will serve as a guide through the matrix of state and federal law and unique business considerations that so greatly affect a public acquisition. The bulk of the chapter will focus on *friendly*, negotiated transactions involving a target that is a public company.

The last part of the chapter discusses briefly some of the major issues involved in making or defending against a hostile acquisition—i.e., an acquisition where the target's board of directors refuses to cooperate with the buyer and negotiate a sale. That subject, however, is worthy of, and indeed is the subject of, in-depth analysis in several other treatises.

Why are the negotiations for the purchase of a publicly held company very different?

The negotiation of a public deal involves many considerations that are inapplicable to a private setting. First, unlike a sale of a private company, the structure, timing, financing, and negotiation of this type of sale is greatly impacted by the federal securities laws discussed in detail later in this chapter. Because of these laws, the transaction is conducted in a "fishbowl," that is, most material aspects of the transaction quickly become public information. Each decision must be made with an eye on disclosure responsibilities under federal law and its impact on the timing of the transaction.

Second, the board of directors of the target must be ever-mindful of its fiduciary responsibilities under state corporate law to act in the interests of all the shareholders. See the discussion at pages 750–751. The role of the board of directors has been described as that of a "neutral auctioneer" when a decision has been made to sell the target, so that there are constraints on its ability to favor one buyer over another that don't apply to most sales of private companies.

Third, the transaction quickly becomes public knowledge. The existence of an agreement in principle as to price and structure with a successful bidder is most often publicly announced. Moreover, if the sale of a public company is conducted via the auction process described above in Chapter 10 (pages 576–579), there are always statutory and practical delays in closing the transaction that provide ample opportunity for a new bidder to arrive on the scene. The board of directors in fact may be required under state law to provide information to a competing bidder and may no longer be able or required to recommend the agreed-upon transaction once a better, credible offer is on the table. In any event, the stockholders will be free either to vote against the proposed merger with the buyer or to tender their shares into a more desirable tender offer. Thus, the agreement by the board on the behalf of the company can be only of limited value when another bidder appears on the scene with a more favorable bid.

The possible economic consequences for a buyer are dramatic. As a result of the publicity surrounding its offer, the buyer becomes a "stalking horse" to attract other bidders. It will have incurred substantial transaction expenses (legal and accounting fees) and may have laid out significant sums as commitment fees to lenders to arrange for financing. It may have also passed other investment opportunities while pursuing the acquisition of the target. The negotiations often reflect the buyer's need to protect itself against the risks inherent in this scenario.

These considerations cause the buyer to focus particularly on two aspects of the transaction: (1) timing; and (2) so-called "lock-up" arrangements, "topping fees," and "no shop" and other agreements with the target and/or its shareholders, that are designed to decrease the risk of a successful competing bid and to compensate the buyer if it loses to a competing bid. These arrangements are discussed below at pages 753–756.

What form will the acquisition of a public company take?

A public company acquisition is accomplished through a "one-step" or a "two-step" transaction. In the one-step acquisition the buyer organizes an acquisition subsidiary that will merge into the target. Upon consummation of the merger, the stockholders of the target receive cash and, perhaps, other property such as notes, and the stockholders of the acquisition subsidiary receive all the stock of the target. The merger will require the approval of the stockholders of the target; the exact percentage of stockholder approval required will depend upon the articles of incorporation of the target but may be as low as a majority of the voting power of the common stock. To effect the approval, the target will be required to solicit proxies from the stockholders and to vote such proxies at a stockholder's meeting called for the purpose of voting on the transaction. The proxy solicitation must comply with the federal securities laws. See the discussion on pages 735–737.

What is a "two-step" acquisition?

A two step acquisition involves a tender offer followed by a merger. (See the discussion on pages 723–725). In the first step, the buyer organizes an acquisition subsidiary that makes a tender offer for the shares of the target. Usually, the offer is conditioned upon enough shares being tendered to give the buyer sufficient voting power to assure that the second-step merger will be approved. For example, if approval by a majority of the voting stock of the target is required, the offer is conditioned on the buyer obtaining at least a majority of the target stock in the tender offer. In the second step, the buyer obtains stockholder approval, the acquisition subsidiary is merged into the target, the stockholders of the acquisition subsidiary become stockholders of the target, and the original stockholders of the target who did not tender their shares receive cash. If the buyer obtains sufficient stock of the target (90% in Delaware), the merger will not require approval of the target's remaining stockholders (a so-called "short-form" merger).

What are the major advantages and disadvantages of the two-step approach?

Timing is the major advantage. The tender offer can close as early as twenty business days from the date of commencement, and there is no requirement that the tender offer documents be filed with the SEC prior to commencement. At the conclusion of the tender offer, the buyer will have control of the target. This contrasts sharply with a proxy solicitation. The proxy materials must be submitted for review by the SEC; the review will take from ten to thirty days. The materials are rarely sent to shareholders before completion of the SEC review. The shareholder's meeting usually won't occur until at least twenty days (depending upon state law and the bylaws of the target) after the proxy materials are sent out. Twenty days is usually a minimum to assure that the shareholders get the material and have a chance to review it and to submit their proxy. Generally, the time to gain control is 45 to 60 days after the proxy materials are initially submitted to the SEC.

Timing is of great importance to a buyer that wants to minimize the risk that a competing bidder will make an attempt to acquire the company. Timing is also important to the target stockholders—those who tender will be paid sooner in a two-step transaction.

The major disadvantage of the two-step approach relates to financing. For reasons discussed on pages 763–765 it is somewhat more difficult to finance a tender offer then a one-step merger.

In a public transaction is the stock always acquired only through a tender offer or a merger?

No. The buyer may precede his tender offer or the merger with ordinary purchases through the stock market ("open market purchases") or may acquire, or enter into arrangements to acquire, stock from the target or from some of its major stockholders ("lock-up arrangements"). The timing and method of such purchases is affected by the federal securities laws, which preclude certain transactions after a tender offer begins and which may characterize certain open market purchases as tender offers.

In the friendly two-step transaction, at what point do the parties enter into the merger agreement?

The merger agreement is entered into before the tender offer is commenced. There are several reasons. First, if the merger agreement is entered into before commencement of the tender offer is closed, the acquisition subsidiary will be able to utilize certain types of unsecured loans to finance the transaction that would otherwise be unavailable. (See page 765.) Second, there are many agreements relating to expense reimbursement, bust-up fees, lock-up arrangements, etc. (see pages 749–755), that the buyer wants finalized before the expense and risk of a tender offer are incurred. Also, under the target's articles of incorporation the percentage of stockholder votes required for approval of the second-step merger may depend upon board approval prior to the tender offer. The board approval, in turn, may hinge upon the buyer agreeing to make the same payments to all stockholders in the tender offer and the second-step merger. Third, the target board would like to assure fair treatment for all stockholders by binding the buyer to promptly accomplish the merger after the tender offer.

Generally, how long after the closing of the tender offer will the second-step merger occur?

If the parties are Delaware corporations, and the buyer acquires at least 90% of the stock of the target, the merger usually can be accomplished shortly after the tender offer closes. If less stock is acquired, the buyer will have to cause a stockholders' vote to be taken to approve the merger. In almost every case, the buyer will not require any favorable votes from the other stockholders because it will own enough stock to assume approval after the tender offer, so no proxies will be solicited. Nevertheless, the buyer will have to submit an "information statement" (on Schedule 14C) to the SEC and cause it to be distributed to the stockholders. The distribution cannot occur until 10 days after the information statement is sent to the SEC. The stockholders must receive the information statement at least 20 calendar days before the corporate action approving the merger. The result: the minimum waiting period for a merger following a tender offer is 30 days.

In summary, what are the special considerations applicable to a friendly acquisition of a public company?

To understand and negotiate the public company acquisition, the first step is to gain a working understanding of the Williams Act and other basic securities laws that govern the transaction. These include not only the rules on tender offers and mergers but also rules on disclosure of negotiations, insider trading, and certain filings upon the acquisition of 5% or more holdings.

Next, it is critical for buyer and seller to understand the state corporate laws that regulate the behavior of the board of directors of the target. These rules are significant in connection with the agreements that the buyer will seek to negotiate which (i) reduce the flexibility of the board in dealing with other bidders and (ii) make a competing bid less attractive (so-called "bust-up" or "topping" fees, "no shop" provisions, etc.).

Finally, the financing of tender offers is subject to certain unique rules that make its financing somewhat more difficult than the normal financing. The first part of this chapter, dealing with friendly acquisitions, is organized along the lines set forth above. We begin, then, with an analysis of the applicable securities laws.

TENDER OFFER BASICS

What is a tender offer?

A typical or conventional tender offer has been defined as a general, publicized bid by an individual or group to buy shares of a publicly owned company at a price substantially above the current market price (*Hanson Trust*, at 54).

One problem for a company seeking to gain control of a public company through open market purchases of stock is that such purchases may, under certain circumstances, be deemed to constitute a tender offer.

Although the SEC has never adopted a rule defining a tender offer, on November 29, 1979, the SEC proposed the following definition of a tender offer:

> The term "tender offer" includes a "request or invitation for tenders" and means one or more offers to purchase or solicitations of offers to sell securities of a single class, whether or not all or any portion of the securities sought are purchased, which (i) during any 45-day period are directed to more than 10 persons and seek the acquisition of more than 5% of the class of securities, except that offers by a broker (and its customer) or by a dealer made on a national securities exchange at the then current market or made in the over-the-counter market at the then current market shall be excluded if in connection with such offers neither the person making the offers nor such broker or dealer solicits or arranges for the solicitation of any order to sell such securities and such broker or dealer performs only the customary functions of a broker or dealer and receives no more than the broker's usual and customary commission or the dealer's usual and customary mark-up; or (ii) are not otherwise a tender offer under [clause (i)] of this section, but which (A) are disseminated in a widespread manner, (B) provide for a price which represents a premium in excess of the greater of 5% of or $2 above the current market price and (C) do not provide for a meaningful opportunity to negotiate the price and terms.

This proposed rule has been neither adopted nor withdrawn.

As there is no clear definition of the term tender offer, practitioners are well advised to assume that if security holders need the protection of the securities laws and the transaction would constitute a tender offer under the SEC's proposed rule, a court would find the rules governing tender offers applicable.

What are some of the practical considerations in commencing a tender offer?

The first steps in commencing a tender offer are the formation of a team and the creation of a timetable indicating each planned activity and the person responsible for it.

The formation of the team should begin with the retention of a dealer-manager/investment banker and an independent accountant. The dealer-manager and accountant initially will assist in the review of the target company's financials and business and advise as to the desirability of the proposed transaction. The dealer-manager will also be responsible for the solicitation of large stockholders and communications with the financial community and may also assist the buyer in accumulation of a significant stock position prior to the commencement of the actual tender offer.

Experienced lawyers who will prepare the many legal documents required in conjunction with the tender offer are essential members of the team. The lawyers should be familiar with federal and state laws affecting takeovers, antitrust laws, and numerous other areas of the law that may apply to a specific transaction.

Additionally, as litigation is often a by-product of tender offers, the lawyers on a tender offer team should come from a law firm with a strong, experienced litigation department.

Other members of the team will generally include a shareholder solicitation firm that will arrange for delivery of tender offer materials and contact shareholders to solicit their shares, and a depository bank, the function of which will be to receive and pay for tendered securities.

Tender offer teams also usually include a forwarding agent that will receive shares as agent for tendering stockholders and a financial printer with the ability to prepare tender offer documents quickly and provide the confidential treatment necessary to avoid premature disclosure of the proposed transaction.

Should the target company's management be contacted prior to commencement of a tender offer?

The tender offer can be commenced with no prior disclosure to the target company's management. This approach puts significant pressure on the target by allowing it the least amount of time to respond to the offer or develop a workable defense strategy. A tender offeror may also choose to contact the target's management and request a meeting at the same time it makes a public announcement of its intention to commence a tender offer. At this meeting the tender offeror may attempt to obtain the approval and cooperation of the target company's management for the proposed transaction but may also apply additional pressure by indicating that, unless the management of the target company approves the transaction, the tender offer will be made at a lower price. In any event, making a public announcement that a tender offer will be made requires the offeror to proceed with or abandon the offer within five days of such announcement.

When does a tender offer begin?

A tender offer commences at 12:01 a.m. on the date when the first of the following events occurs:

- The bidder publishes a long-form publication of the tender offer, containing required information, in a newspaper or newspapers;
- The bidder publishes a summary advertisement of the tender offer, disclosing certain information, in a newspaper or newspapers;
- The bidder publishes, or sends or gives to shareholders of the target, definitive copies of tender offer materials. (Rule 14d-2(a)).

Also, at 12:01 a.m. on the day the bidder publicly announces certain information: the identity of the bidder, the identity of the target, the amount and class of securities sought, and the price or range of prices being offered—a tender offer will be deemed to have been commenced. An offer, however, will not be deemed to be given to the shareholders on such date if, within five business days of the public announcement the bidder either:

- publicly announces its decision not to proceed with the tender offer, or
- complies with Rule 14d-3(a), which requires the filing and distribution of Schedule 14D-1 and disseminates to shareholders the information required by Rule 14d-6, in which event the commencement date will be deemed to be the date on which the required disclosures are first published, sent or given to shareholders (Rule 14d-2(b)).

In almost all cases, the tender offer is commenced by the use of the summary advertisement, the type so often seen in the financial pages of *The Wall Street Journal*. Copies of the pertinent tender offer materials are sent to the shareholders on the date that the advertisement is published. The date of the commencement is important because it begins the twenty business days that the tender offer must remain open and because certain activities, particularly purchases of shares by the acquiror other than through the offer, are prohibited after the offer is commenced.

What materials are sent to shareholders?

The shareholders receive an "offer to purchase" that sets forth all of the material terms of the offer and a "letter of transmittal" which the shareholder sends back to accept the offer. The contents of the offer to purchase must reflect the requirements of Rule 14d-6. The bidder is also required to publish, send, or give to shareholders notice of a material change in the tender offer materials.

What filings are acquirers of a public company to make?

On the day that the tender offer commences, the buyer must file a Tender Offer Statement on Schedule 14D-1 with the SEC, and hand deliver such Statement to the target and other bidders, and mail a copy of the statement to stock exchanges on which the target's stock is traded or the NASD if the securities are traded over the counter (after having given them telephonic notice of the information required by Rule 14d-2(i) and (ii)).

What information must be included in Schedule 14D-1?

- The name of the target and the address of its principal executive offices; the title and exact amount of the securities being sought; the consideration being offered for the securities; and certain information about the market for such securities, including the stock's current market value.

- The identity and background of the buyer.
- A description (including the appropriate dollar amount) of any contracts, transactions, or negotiations between the buyer and the target and its affiliates which occurred during the three fiscal years of the target preceding the date of filing of the Schedule 14D-1.
- The source and amount of funds or other consideration for the offer and, if any part of such funds will be borrowed, a summary of the loan arrangements.
- The purpose of the tender offer and any plans or proposals that the buyer has to sell or trade assets of the target or change the target's corporate structure, board of directors, management, or operations.
- The number and percentage of shares of the target held by the buyer and a description of any transactions by the buyer involving the target's securities during the 60 days preceding the filing of the Schedule 14D-1.
- Any contracts, arrangements, understandings, or relationships that the buyer has with any person concerning any shares of the target.
- The identities of persons retained, employed, or to be compensated by or on behalf of the buyer to make solicitations or recommendations in connection with the tender offer, and the terms of compensation for such persons.
- The financial statements of the buyer (or its parent(s)), where such financial condition is material to a decision by the target's shareholders whether to tender, sell, or hold shares being sought in the tender offer.
- If material to a decision by a security holder whether to sell, tender, or hold its securities, information concerning arrangements between the buyer and the target company not otherwise disclosed in the Schedule 14D, compliance with regulatory requirements, antitrust laws, margin requirements, and material legal proceedings relating to the tender offer.

The 14D-1 filing usually includes the offer to purchase which contains most of the information required in the schedule.

Do the tender offer materials need to disclose any projections that may have been provided by the target to the acquirer?

The courts that have considered this question have taken different approaches, though generally they have held either that there is no duty to disclose projections in tender offer documents or that there is a duty to disclose only when the projections are substantially certain. Because projections are inherently uncertain, this latter test may in practice result in no duty to disclose financial projections. However, the SEC staff takes the position that the purchaser must disclose any financial projections it receives from the seller in its tender offer documents. As a result, most buyers make some disclosure of projections furnished by the target in the offering materials.

What are the requirements for updating a Schedule 14D-1?

If a material change occurs in the information contained in a Schedule 14D-1, the buyer must file an amendment with the SEC disclosing such change and hand deliver it to the target and other bidders, and mail it to the NASD or the stock exchanges on which the target's shares are traded promptly after the date such tender offer material is first published or sent or given to security holders (Rule 14d-3(b)). Each material amendment also should be the subject of a press release to be issued promptly upon the occurrence of the material change.

Is there a way to avoid filing certain documents with the SEC?

No. However, it is possible to avoid the public disclosure of certain material if it can be demonstrated that the disclosure of such material would be detrimental to the operations of the company and that the disclosure of the material is unnecessary for the protection of investors. A company seeking to avoid the public disclosure of such information must seek an Order of Confidential Treatment from the SEC. Generally, if appropriate grounds for relief are asserted, the SEC will grant confidential treatment of such information for a limited period of time.

How long must a tender offer remain open?

A tender offer must remain open continuously for at least 20 business days. This 20-day period commences upon the date the tender offer is first published, sent, or given to the target company's shareholders (Rule 14e-1(a)). A public announcement that does not constitute commencement of a tender offer under the Williams Act does not trigger the 20-day offering period, although once an offeror has made a public announcement that it intends to commence a tender offer, the tender offer must commence or be abandoned within five days.

Additionally, a tender offer must remain open for a least ten business days following an announced increase or decrease in the tender offer price or in the percentage of securities to be bought (Rule 14e-1(b)).

If a change in the tender offer terms is made and such change is less material than changes related to price or the number of shares sought, the offeror should keep the offer open for five business days to allow dissemination of the new information in a manner reasonably designed to inform shareholders of such changes. If there are less than five days left before the scheduled expiration of the twenty-day period, this will cause the tender offer period to be open longer than twenty business days.

May the offering period be extended?

Yes, but the buyer must announce the extension not later than 9:00 a.m. on the business day following the day on which the tender offer expires, and the announcement must state the approximate amount of securities already purchased (Rule 14e-1(d)).

Once a shareholder tenders his shares may he withdraw them?

Shareholders who tender shares may withdraw them at any time during the tender-offer period unless the shares are actually purchased (Rule 14d-7(a)).

Tendered shares may also be withdrawn at any time after sixty days from the date of the original tender offer if those shares have not yet been purchased by the bidder (Section 14d-5).

When must payment for tendered securities be made?

An offeror must either "promptly" pay the consideration offered or return the tendered securities (Rule 14e-1(c)).

May a bidder make an offer for less than all of the outstanding shares of a target company?

Yes. However, if more shares are tendered than the offeror wishes to purchase, the offeror must purchase the desired amount of shares on a pro rata basis from among those shares tendered.

May an offeror quickly acquire control of the target's board of directors after purchasing shares in the tender offer?

Yes. The tender offeror and the target frequently agree that, after a successful tender offer, the offeror may elect a majority of directors to the board of the target. Such an agreement permits the offeror to obtain control of the target's board of directors without holding a meeting of shareholders. In accordance with Rule 14f–1, ten days before the newly elected directors are permitted to take office, the target company must file with the SEC and transmit to the holders of its voting securities information about such directors that would be required to be provided to shareholders if such persons were nominees for election as directors at a meeting of the target's shareholders.

Must all shareholders in a tender offer be treated equally?

Yes. The same consideration must be paid to all tending shareholders. The offer must be open to all shareholders of the class of securities subject to the offer. However, while the bidder does not need to pay the same type of consideration to each shareholder, it must afford each the opportunity to elect among the types offered. In addition, each shareholder must receive the highest consideration paid to any other shareholder receiving the same type of consideration. Therefore, if the tender price is increased at any time during the period the increased amount must be paid to all tendering shareholders, including those who tendered before the price increase and those whose shares have already been purchased.

It should be noted that the SEC, in promulgating the rules that require all tendering shareholders to be treated equally, appears to be attempting to regulate the substantive fairness of tender offers. The U.S. Supreme Court has held that the Williams Act may not be used for this purpose but only to prevent misrepresentation or non-disclosure. For this reason, the SEC's authority to enforce these rules probably will be challenged in the courts.

What is a short tender?

Short tendering occurs when a shareholder in a partial tender offer tenders more shares than he actually owns in the hope of increasing the number of shares that the bidder actually will accept prorata. A person is prohibited from tendering a security unless at the time of the tender and at the end of the proration period he, or the person on whose behalf he is tendering, owns the security (or an equivalent security). A person is deemed to own a security only to the extent that he has a net long position in such security.

SEC rules also prohibit "hedged tendering." Hedged tendering occurs when a shareholder tenders securities in response to more than one offer or tenders his securities and also sells them in the open market.

May an offeror purchase shares during a tender offer other than pursuant to the tender offer?

No. During a tender offer, the offeror may not directly or indirectly purchase or arrange to purchase, other than pursuant to the tender offer, securities that are the subject of that offer (Rule 10b-13)). This prohibition also includes privately negotiated purchases until the tender offer is concluded or withdrawn.

Purchases made before a public announcement are generally permissible, even if a decision has been made by the purchaser to make the tender offer, but purchase agreements scheduled to close during the offering period are illegal no matter when they are made.

PROXY SOLICITATION DISCLOSURES

What information must be disclosed to stockholders if the form of the acquisition is a merger?

Regulation 14A under the Exchange Act requires that stockholders be provided with a proxy statement that includes the information set forth in Schedule 14A.

Although information is specifically required to be included in the proxy statement if the shareholder meeting to which the proxy statement relates is being held in connection with any merger, consolidation, acquisition, or similar matter and the manner of disclosure thereof varies depending on the level of information available about the parties, such information generally includes the following:

(a) The mailing address and telephone number of the principal executive offices of each party;

(b) A brief discussion of the general nature of the business conducted by each party;

(c) A summary of the material features of the proposed transaction, including: (i) a brief summary of the transaction agreement; (ii) the reason for engaging in the transaction; (iii) an explanation of any material differences in the rights of security holders as a result of the transaction; (iv) a brief statement as to accounting treatment; and (v) federal income tax consequences.

(d) A statement as to the effect of the transaction on dividends in arrears or defaults in the payment of the principal or interest on the securities of any party;

(e) Selected financial data relating to the target company and the acquiror;

(f) If material, such financial information in (e) above on a pro forma basis;

(g) Certain historical and pro forma per share data of the target company and the acquiror;

(h) Detailed pro forma financial information as required by Article 11 of Regulation S-X;

(i) A statement as to the status of any federal or state regulatory approval that must be obtained in connection with the transaction;

(j) Detailed information concerning any report, opinion, or appraisal materially relating to the transaction;

(k) A description of any past, present, or proposed material contracts, arrangements, understandings, relationships, negotiations, or transactions between the target company and other persons and any of their affiliates;

(l) The high and low sale prices of the relevant securities as of the date immediately prior to the public announcement of the transaction;

(m) A statement as to whether representatives of the principal accountants for the current year and for the most recently completed fiscal year are expected to be at the meeting, will have the opportunity to make a statement if they desire to do so and are expected to be available to respond to questions.

Schedule 14A also requires detailed information relating to material changes in the affairs of the company being acquired that have occurred since the end of the latest year for which audited financial statements were included in the latest annual report to security holders.

Any action to be taken with respect to any amendment of the registrant's charter, by-laws, or other documents must be described and the reason for and general effect of such amendment must be disclosed.

The vote required for approval must be described.

What is "going private"?

A Rule 13e-3 transaction is generally known as a "going-private" transaction and arises in situations in which certain of the existing stockholders or affiliates of a public target become stockholders of the entity surviving the acquisition of the target and the target is no longer subject to Section 12(g) or Section 15(d) of the Exchange Act. Because certain stockholders may be on both sides of the transaction, Rule 13e-3 attempts to provide additional disclosures to the public stockholders in order to demonstrate the overall fairness of the transaction. Such disclosures include full blown discussions of any fairness opinions and appraisals obtained in connection with the transaction and statements by the target as to the fairness of the transaction.

Determining whether a particular transaction may constitute a 13e-3 transaction largely depends upon the percentage of stock that the existing stockholders own in the target or the relationship of such affiliates to the target and the percentage ownership that such persons may own in the surviving entity.

When must an acquirer file a Schedule 13D?

The Exchange Act provides for disclosure concerning the accumulation of blocks of voting equity securities if that accumulation might represent a potential change in corporate control regardless of how such securities are accumulated. Any person who beneficially owns 5% or more of the shares of a class of voting equity securities registered under Section 12 of the Exchange Act is required to file a Schedule 13D with the SEC (and each securities exchange on which the securities are traded) containing specified information concerning the filing person. Schedule 13D must be filed with the SEC and sent to the issuer and to each exchange where the security is traded within within ten days after a person acquires 5% or more of an outstanding voting equity security.

This requirement is somewhat relaxed for certain institutional investors whose purchases are made in the ordinary course of their business without the purpose or effect of changing or influencing the control of the issuer and investors that owned their shares prior to the time the company became subject to the Exchange Act. Such investors need only file a Schedule 13G, which is a substantially shorter form than Schedule 13D, 45 days after the end of the calendar year in which the threshold ownership interest was acquired. If, however, such an institutional securityholder changes his intention and decides to influence control of the company, he must file a Schedule 13D within ten days of making that decision. During the ten-day period, the shares already owned may not be voted, and the owner may not buy any additional shares of the target company.

Schedule 13D requires disclosure of ownership of shares that are "beneficially" owned. Shares beneficially owned include not only shares directly owned but all shares with respect to which a person has or shares direct or indirect power to vote or sell. For instance, all shares subject to a shareholders' voting agreement become beneficially owned by each person who is a party to the agreement. The concept of beneficial ownership is especially important in view of the 5% threshold to the filing requirements. Thus, if each member of a group of five persons owns 1% of the shares of a class of a company, that group must file a Schedule 13D or 13G if the group has agreed to vote or dispose of those securities together. Also, a person is deemed to beneficially own any security that he, directly or indirectly, has the right to acquire within 60 days, whether such acquisition is pursuant to a purchase contract, exercise of a warrant or option, or conversion of a convertible security (Rule 13d-3).

Is a written agreement necessary for a group to exist?

No. The existence of a written agreement is not required; circumstantial evidence of an agreement in itself may be enough for a group to be deemed to have been formed.

At what stage of an acquisition is a "group" formed?

The law is not clear. In at least one case the existence of an agreement in principle to act in concert that was substantially similar to the final agreement was sufficient to cause the formation of a group.

Is an agreement to acquire additional shares necessary to form a group?

No. An agreement among the holders of five percent or more of a class of voting stock to act together in the future to further the group's purpose may suffice to form a group regardless of whether acts in furtherance of such agreement (e.g., voting, acquiring stock) occur after the date of the agreement.

Does the management of the Company to be acquired constitute a group subject to Section 13(d)?

Yes. The target's management could be considered a group if it acts as such to acquire shares and if its members own more than five percent of the company. A management group would have to comply with all reporting requirements.

Must members of a group file jointly or may individual members file separately?

A group may file one joint Schedule 13D, or each member may file individually. An individual filing jointly is not responsible for the information concerning other members of the group unless the individual knows or has reason to know that the information pertaining to another group member is inaccurate (Rule 13d-1(f)(1)).

What information is required to be disclosed in a Schedule 13D?

A Schedule 13D filed by an individual must disclose information about the filing person's identity and background. A Schedule 13D filed by a group must disclose the identities and employment of each group member. The filing person or group must disclose the number of shares of the company to be acquired that it beneficially owns; its purpose in acquiring those shares; any plans or proposals to acquire or dispose of shares of the target company; any plans for an extraordinary corporate transaction (such as a merger, reorganization, or liquidation) affecting the target company or any of its subsidiaries; any proposed change in the target's directors or management, in the target's capitalization or dividend policy, or in its business or corporate structure; any past involvement of the individual or group members in violations of state of federal securities laws; the source and amount of funds or other consideration for the acquisition; and any contracts, arrangements, understandings, or relationships that it has with any other person concerning the shares of the company to be acquired.

When must a Schedule 13D be amended?

A Schedule 13D must be amended "promptly" upon the occurrence of any "material change" in the information contained in the original Schedule 13D. While the SEC has not officially defined the terms "promptly" and "material change," Rule 13d-2 provides that the acquisition or disposition of beneficial ownership of one percent of a class of securities is material and requires the amendment of a previously filed Schedule 13D and that the acquisition or disposition of a smaller amount may also require an amendment depending on the surrounding facts and circumstance. Changes in intention regarding the acquisition or disposition of securities also must be disclosed promptly.

The SEC has indicated that "promptly" means immediately when the facts requiring the amendment are important to the market. In a 1985 release the SEC stated:

> Whether an amendment to a Schedule 13D is "prompt" must be judged, at least in part, by the market's sensitivity to the particular change of fact triggering the obligation to amend, and the effect on the market of the filing person's previous disclosures. Although the promptness of an amendment to a Schedule 13D must be judged in light of all the facts and circumstances of a particular situation, [a]ny delay beyond the time the amendment reasonably could have been filed may not be deemed to be [prompt].

What are the remedies for failure to comply with Section 13(d)?

In most cases, both shareholders and target companies may sue for damages for violations of Section 13(d). There are, however, some district court decisions holding that a target does not have an implied right of action under Section 13(d) because the target's shareholders, not the target, were the intended beneficiaries of that section of the statute. The relief given for violations of Section 13(d) generally is equitable rather than compensatory and involves curative disclosure or other injunctive relief rather than damages. This is because the purpose of the law is to provide disclosure, not to prevent takeovers, and once full disclosure is made, prior misleading statements or omissions of material facts usually will not even result in an injunction. Other remedies for Section 13D violations include injunctions designed to prevent voting or further purchases of an issuer's securities until the filer has amended his Schedule 13D to correct any false statements or omissions. Some courts also require a "cooling off" period to provide adequate time for the newly disclosed information to reach the public.

Finally, the SEC may bring an enforcement action that may lead to a rescission or a divestiture order; however, the SEC usually will not take such action while corporate control is being contested.

DISCLOSURE ISSUES

Under what circumstances may a public company deny that it is engaged in merger negotiations?

The Supreme Court, in *Basic Incorporated v. Levinson*, ruled that it is not proper to deny that a company is engaged in merger talks when in fact it is so engaged, even if the talks have not yet resulted in an agreement on the price and structure of a transaction. If inquiries are received, the appropriate response is either "no comment" or a disclosure that negotiations are in fact taking place.

Prior to the *Basic* decision, the court of appeals for the Third Circuit had held that merger proposals and negotiations were not "material" until the parties had reached agreement in principle on the price and structure of a transaction. In *Basic*, the Supreme Court rejected this bright line test and held that the materiality of merger negotiations must be evaluated on a case-by-case basis after considering all relevant facts and circumstances.

When does a company have a duty to disclose merger negotiations?

Generally, the timing of disclosure of material information is at the discretion of the company and will be protected by the business judgment rule. Nevertheless, a company that is the subject of takeover speculation or whose stock is trading erratically typically finds itself pressured by brokers, news services, exchange or NASDAQ officials, securities analysts, and others to voluntarily disclose merger proposals and negotiations. The *Basic* decision probably will accelerate the trend toward voluntary disclosures in these circumstances, although it is still acceptable under certain circumstances for a company to adopt a policy of silence or state that "no comment" will be made with respect to merger proposals or rumors. However, a company may not remain silent where (i) there is an affirmative disclosure rule (such as the tender offer regulations), (ii) the company is about to purchase its own shares in the public market, (iii) a prior public disclosure made by the company is no longer accurate (such as when a company has publicly denied that merger negotiations with a party were occuring), or (iv) rumors that have been circulating concerning the proposed transactions are attributable to a leak from the company. Disclosure may also be appropriate where it is apparent that a leak has occurred, even if the leak is not from the company. In such a situation, consideration should be given to a variety of factors, including the requirements of any agreement with a stock exchange or NASDAQ, the effect of wide price fluctuations on shareholders generally, and the benefits to the market provided by broad dissemination of accurate information. If the company does elect to disclose either the existence or the substance of negotiations, it must take care that its disclosures are neither false nor materially misleading.

It should be noted that if the company refuses to respond to a stock exchange's request for disclosure, or issues a "no comment," it may be subject to disciplinary action by the exchange. This disciplinary action may include public notice of a violation, temporary suspension of trading in the corporation's stock, or delisting. However, the exchanges have a reputation for being "paper tigers" in this area because of their reluctance to enforce these rules. This reluctance is attributed to the competition of "third-market" securities firms that trade listed securities off the exchanges. Moreover, courts have not found a private right of action for violation of exchange rules.

Is management required to disclose inquiries about a possible merger or acquisition?

There is no specific obligation to disclose mere inquiries or contacts made by those interested in acquiring the corporation or its stock.

DIRECTOR RESPONSIBILITIES, LOCKUP ARRANGEMENTS, AND OTHER AGREEMENTS BETWEEN BUYER AND SELLER

What are the primary responsibilities of a corporate board of directors upon receipt of a takeover bid?

The director's primary responsibility is to evaluate and recommend what action a company should take in the event of an offer to acquire the company. The director's conduct in this and other contexts is evaluated under the business judgment rule.

What is the business judgment rule?

The business judgment rule is applied by courts in cases where shareholders have sued directors for violating their fiduciary duties to the corporation. The rule is that the board of directors will be protected unless the shareholders can prove that in making a business decision a director did not act with due care, good faith, and loyalty to the corporation. The business judgment rule protects directors from liability if they act in a manner consistent with their duties of due care and loyalty.

What is a director's duty of due care?

For a director, exercising due care means acting on behalf of the company's stockholders by making informed decisions after obtaining all reasonably available information required to make an intelligent decision and after evaluating all relevant circumstances. Under this standard, his duty is not merely to make the best possible decision for the corporation but to make no decision without careful, informed deliberation. Both the process of decisionmaking as well as the substantive decisions themselves are taken into consideration by courts in evaluating whether a director acted with due care.

The recent Delaware case of *Smith v. Van Gorkom* dealt a blow to the business judgment rule when the Delaware court found that the board of directors of Trans Union, and in particular Trans Union's Chief Executive Officer, Jerome Van Gorkom, were personally liable for actions taken in connection with approving and recommending to shareholders a cash-out merger proposal. The court held that they were not entitled to the protection of the business judgment rule even though Van Gorkom and the other board members may well have been highly qualified to make the decisions they did and had obtained a substantial premium over the market price for the shares of Trans Union.

Nevertheless, the court found that the following actions by the Trans Union board and Van Gorkom evidenced a lack of due care:

- the CEO did not establish a "fair price" for the company's stock;
- the CEO met with the offeror without consulting his directors or any senior management personnel;
- the CEO did not seek the advice of investment bankers or ensure adequate legal counsel;
- copies of the proposed merger agreement were not avail-

able for review by the board of directors at the meeting convened to discuss the merger;

- the CEO did not tell the directors that it was he who had valued the company's stock and suggested the purchase price to the offeror, together with suggestions on how to finance the purchase;
- the directors did not study the merger agreement before voting on it;
- the directors approved the merger agreement based on representations of several members of the management team;
- neither the CEO nor the other directors read the merger agreement before signing and delivering it to the offeror;
- the directors approved amendments to the merger agreement in a meeting convened by the CEO without reviewing the documents or attempting to understand the implications of the amendments;
- the directors did not request that any valuation report/ study be prepared to evaluate the value placed on the company's stock;
- the directors decided to approve the merger without allowing adequate time to consider its adequacy or its repercussions; and
- the company's stockholders were not fully informed of all material facts when the merger was put to a vote.

The unusual element in *Van Gorkom* is that the Court did not concern itself primarily with the ultimate decision (which was arguably a very good one for the shareholders of Trans Union) but instead emphasized the importance of the correct decisionmaking process. Directors must make *informed* decisions and take careful steps to assure they are acting responsibly.

What is the director's duty of loyalty?

A director of a corporation owes a duty of loyalty to act in the best interests of the corporation and its shareholders for which he is a fiduciary. As such, the director is prohibited from entering into a transaction that is tainted by fraud or bad faith, or in which he has a personal interest. If it appears that a director has an interest in a particular corporate transaction, a court often will shift the burden of proof to the director to show that the transaction is fair and serves the best interests of the corporation and its shareholders.

When is it appropriate for a selling company to appoint a special committee of its board of directors to review a proposed transaction?

If there is any question that a majority of the members of the board of directors may have a personal interest in the proposed merger (as where the management directors predominate and will obtain benefits from the merger), an independent special committee of the board should be appointed to handle the negotiation and recommendation of any proposed transaction. A special committee is also appropriate where a proposed transaction is complex enough to require careful study for the board to act responsibly. Having a special committee with adequate authority over the transaction will tend to shift to a plaintiff the burden of showing that the transaction is unfair. This shift will generally preclude the issuance of injunctive relief against a proposed merger.

Which directors are appropriate members of a special committee?

A special committee should consist of independent or disinterested directors. Such directors must not have any financial or personal interest in the proposed transaction that would inhibit their ability to act in an unbiased manner.

What are the benefits of a special committee?

While there is no guarantee that a special commitee will legitimate board action, such a committee may be extremely helpful in, and perhaps essential to, providing directors with the protection of the business judgment rule. It should be noted, however, that courts will closely scrutinize the facts surrounding the actions of the board and that the mere formation of a special committee will not protect the directors from liability for careless actions.

What steps should a special committee take to insure that it is acting responsibly?

The special committee should examine all information about the proposed transaction. This examination must be thorough and members of the special committee should question carefully the persons supplying such information to be sure the information is complete and accurate. The committee should also take care not to act hastily. Recent judicial decisions have indicated that directors who make decisions without adequate deliberation may have difficulty in establishing that they acted with the care necessary to provide the protection of the business judgment rule.

Should a special committee retain independent advisors?

In the context of mergers and acquisitions, the special committee of a board of directors should retain independent legal counsel and financial advisors.

Should a special committee obtain a fairness opinion?

The fairness opinion can be a useful tool both in determining whether to accept an offer and in obtaining the protection of the business judgment rule. In most states, courts ordinarily will not substitute their judgment for that of a board of directors that has acted carefully in approving a transaction. However, when there is a potential or actual conflict of interest in a transaction, courts will also examine the transaction to determine its "intrinsic fairness." Because fairness generally depends on the price to be received by the target company's shareholders, the investment bankers' financial expertise, as reflected in a fairness opinion, can be invaluable to the board. It is, however, necessary for a board of directors to thoroughly question the investment bankers to determine that they have a reasonable basis for their opinion before reliance is justified. However, reliance on a fairness opinion alone may not suffice as proof of the exercise of due care.

What should a fairness opinion say?

A fairness opinion should describe the process the investment bankers used in making their determination that a proposed transaction is fair and should indicate what matters have been investigated and independently verified and what matters the investment banker has not verified independently. The opinion should also describe the fee being paid and all possible conflicts of interest. It is advisable that the investment bankers not accept contingent compensation for the fairness opinion because doing so suggests a lack of independence.

What is the role of counsel to the special committee?

Counsel should advise the members of the special committee about the interpretation of the business judgment rule in the company's jurisdiction of incorporation. In addition, counsel should advise the committee of any potential liability for their actions and the extent to which they may be indemnified or otherwise protected under the company's charter and by-laws and directors and officers liability insurance. Counsel should attend each meeting of the special committee and should prepare or review minutes of each meeting. These minutes should be reviewed for accuracy by each member of the committee. In the event that the proposed transaction may attract other bidders or potential acquirors, counsel to the special committee should be prepared to advise the committee about the legality of various techniques available to the corporation and about the duty of the directors to obtain the best possible price for all shareholders.

Why are these rules concerning the board of directors responsibilities so important?

First, these rules affect timing—the need for the board to act with due care will restrict the board's ability to act quickly on a friendly offer. It will have to appoint a special committee if the transaction involves a management buyout. At the very least, a fairness opinion will have to be obtained, and the investment banker will need several days, at a minimum, to complete the task.

Second, the rules restrict the ability of the board to take action that either eliminates the possibility of a competing bid, so-called "lock-ups," or other arrangements ("bust-up" and "topping fees" and "no shop" clauses) that are designed (in part) to frustrate the efforts of other bidders. These arrangements are among the most negotiated provisions of the public deal.

For reasons outlined above (see pages 721–722), the buyer will seek to minimize the risk of a successful competing bid and will seek to insure that it is compensated if it loses to another bidder. The next several questions deal with these issues in the context of the board's fiduciary responsibilities to the shareholders.

What is a lock-up option?

One mechanism employed by companies to give the favored bidder an edge is a lock-up option. The lock-up agreement may be granted with respect to stock or assets.

In the stock lock-up, the bidder receives an option to purchase authorized but unissued shares. This option aids the bidder in two ways: if the option is exercised he may either vote the shares in favor of the transaction, or, if another bidder wins the contract for the company, he may realize a profit by tendering the stock to the highest bidder. A variation on the lock-up is the reverse lock-up, where stockholders or management agree not to tender their shares to a rival bidder. For the same reason, a buyer also will attempt to obtain options to acquire the stock of stockholders, typically those that have significant holdings. Such options are not subject to scrutiny under the business judgment rule because they are not acts of the board of directors. (See pages 752–753 for a discussion of lock-up arrangements with stockholders.)

Stock lock-up agreements with the target have received mixed results from courts applying the business judgment doctrine. The courts' main concern is that the lock-up may prevent competitive bidding and thereby limit the premiums stockholders would otherwise receive from buyers. Courts are most likely to approve lock-ups granted at the end of the bidding process rather than at the beginning, particularly if there are no other bidders contending for the company.

In the asset lock-up (or "crown jewel" lock-up), the company grants the bidder the option to acquire a particularly attractive asset at a price that may or may not be commensurate with its full market value. Such an option may discourage other bidders if they were also interested in the crown jewel or if the loss of the asset would change considerably the financial position or prospects of the company.

Can directors adopt a lock-up agreement without violating their fiduciary duties?

Yes. A lock-up agreement is not illegal per se. However, court decisions hold a lock-up arrangement generally must advance or stimulate the bidding process, not retard it or cut it off. That is, a board can tilt the playing field towards a bidder if the purpose is to elicit a higher bid from that bidder or to otherwise stimulate the competition.

If the purpose of the lock-up agreement is to completely stifle competitive bidding by definitively preferring one bidder over another, however, the board will likely be found to have breached its duty of loyalty to the shareholders. In *Revlon, Inc. v. MacAndrews & Forbes*, Revlon was faced with a hostile tender offer from Pantry Pride. Having determined that Pantry Pride's initial bid was inadequate, the board advised the shareholders to reject the bid and began the search for a white knight, which it found in Forstmann Little and Co.

Revlon then began negotiating with Forstmann Little to the exclusion of Pantry Pride. It did not invite Pantry Pride to participate in any negotiations, nor did Revlon share financial data with Pantry Pride as it did with Forstmann Little. Eventually, an increased bid from Pantry Pride prompted an increased bid from Forstmann Little that was conditioned upon, among other things, the receipt by Fortsmann Little of a lock-up option to purchase two Revlon divisions at a price substantially lower than the lowest estimate of value established by Revlon's investment banker, plus a "no-shop" provision that prevented Revlon from considering bids from any third party. The board immediately accepted the Forstmann Little offer even though Pantry Pride had increased its bid. The court held that when the focus of the directors changed from keeping the company intact to maximizing the return from a sale of assets, the board assumed the role of auctioneer obligated to obtain the best price for the shareholders. It then determined that by stifling competitive bidding through the lock-up agreement with Forstmann Little, the Revlon Board had violated its duty of loyalty to the company and its shareholders.

Is a lock-up that shuts off the process never permissible?

Cases subsequent to Revlon have indicated clearly that a court will not permit a board to grant a crown-jewel lock-up option to one bidder that would have the effect of cutting other bidders out of the process while bidding is still active. Case law has yet to present the best case for upholding a lock-up. In certain cases, where the lock-up option was defeated, the lock-ups favored an insider group or were designed to favor a friendly bidder instead of one that is hostile to the board. Indeed, a lock-up has been granted even to the lower bidder in certain of the cases. The courts, however, have not addressed a case where the board is well informed and truly disinterested, e.g., where the board knows it may be replaced by any of the bidders, where it otherwise acts consistently with due care, and where the lock-up is deemed necessary to elicit the then highest bid. In such a case, the business judgment of the board logically should be respected, particularly if the company has been shopped to other bidders who have had a chance to evaluate the company. Even in the absence of the latter fact, a strong argument can be advanced that the judgment of a well advised and disinterested board should be respected. The practical problem is that the case probably won't arise unless another higher bid surfaces after the lock-up is granted. Logic notwithstanding, if there is a credible higher bid on the table, it will usually be conditioned on the court's invalidating the lock-up, and a court will be pressed to find a reason to let the shareholders get the highest possible bid.

Will a lock-up agreement subject the bidders to liability for short-swing profits?

A bidder will not be subject to short-swing profits under Section 16(b) of the Exchange Act unless the bidder beneficially owned more than 10% of the target's stock prior to the purchase of the stock pursuant to the lock-up agreement. Once a bidder achieves insider status as a beneficial owner of more than 10% of the stock, all subsequent transactions will be subject to Section 16(b).

What should be considered in purchasing a large block of stock from a stockholder?

One of the most important considerations to a selling stockholder when selling a large block of stock is the duty of due care that such stockholder must exercise, which includes reasonable investigation of the potential purchaser. The courts have imposed liability on a controlling stockholder in circumstances in which such stockholder could reasonably foresee that the person acquiring the shares would engage in activities that would clearly be damaging to the corporation, such as looting, fraud, or gross mismanagement of the corporation. There is no general rule as to how much care one must observe in a particular situation, except in planning an acquisition; a potential seller should fully investigate the potential purchaser's motive, resources, reputation, track record, conflicts of interest and any other material items relevant to the transaction and the corporation.

A second consideration is the duty of loyalty that a controlling stockholder owes to the minority stockholders. This duty generally arises when a controlling stockholder is selling shares at a premium. For example, if a corporation owns a large quantity of a product that is in short supply and could be sold at a premium, a controlling stockholder may have a fiduciary obligation to not sell shares at a premium on the theory that the shareholder's receipt of the premium would constitute a misappropriation of a corporate opportunity (i.e., the stockholder would be appropriating for himself a certain amount of the corporate goodwill). In addition, a few courts have imposed a requirement of "equal opportunity" on a controlling stockholder. This requires a controlling stockholder to offer all of the other stockholders an opportunity to sell the same proportion of their shares as the controlling stockholder. Most courts have refused to apply this principle.

Accordingly, if a block purchase is challenged, the courts will review the particular facts surrounding the purchase to determine its fairness.

What are "bust-up" fees?

It is commonplace for the bidder to enter into agreements with the target to compensate the buyer for potential losses if a new bidder usurps the deal. Because these fees are liabilities of the target, the winning bidder will have to bear the economic cost of the fees. This burden has the effect of increasing the cost of, and thus discouraging, other bids. Another arrangement is for the payment of "bust up" or "topping fees" payable if the transaction is terminated by the target (other than for cause). The fees are designed, at the very least, to reimburse the buyer for all of its out-of-pocket expenses. More often, the arrangements include an additional payment for lost time and opportunity. While the fees can be quite high, in the $20–30 million range, in a large transaction (over $1 billion), usually they are in the range of 1%–5% of the purchase price. The higher percentages apply to smaller to medium size public transactions (i.e., $50 million to $500 million).

The size of the fee must not be so large that it substantially discourages other bidders or it may be struck down by a court as a disguised "lock-up" arrangement. Provided the fee is not excessive, under current case law the fee is very likely to withstand judicial scrutiny if the agreement to pay the fee is viewed as reasonably necessary to attract the bidder or keep it interested in the target in the face of competition. The defensibility of the fee will be enhanced if granted by the target in exchange for a "fiduciary out" clause (discussed below) or if the buyer permits the board to "shop" the company for a period of time, i.e., to try and find other bidders.

What is a "no shop" agreement?

A "no shop" agreement is a provision either in the acquisition contract or in a letter of intent that prohibits the board of directors from soliciting or encouraging other bids. It is always found in private company acquisition agreements and far more often than not in the acquisition agreement for public company transactions.

The buyer always should be expected to request such an agreement at the letter of intent stage, and the seller will usually agree to it if the choice of the bidder is the result of either an auction process or a completed bidding war. When the buyer is the first on the scene, includes members of management, or the buyer is a "white knight" whose bid was solicited to fend off a hostile takeover, however, there are other significant considerations that may indicate that such an agreement should be resisted or that a "fiduciary out" clause should be included in the agreement. Although there is no legal requirement that a company be shopped before a definitive agreement to sell is executed, the courts do not look kindly on no-shop provisions, alone or as part of a package (with lock-ups, etc.), when the effect of such provisions is to frustrate the role of the board as a neutral auctioneer or where they may result in a bargain price to corporate insiders, such as management. (See Chapter 6, on Management Buyouts.) The absence of shopping, coupled with the existence of such provisions, may provide the basis for an argument that the price was not determined fairly, with the result that the transaction could be enjoined by a court at the behest of a competitor or an aggrieved stockholder. In especially egregious situations, members of the board of directors can be subject to personal liability if the price is too low or the board has not performed its duties. (See *Smith v. Van Gorkom.*) When a board is required to defend the process and result as fair to the stockholders, the fact that it has unsuccessfully solicited better offers is telling evidence of the fairness of the transaction.

The buyer, of course, will argue that it needs the no-shop provision to avoid incurring expenses for a deal that doesn't succeed because the board attracts a higher bidder. The response: give the buyer a "bust-up" fee.

Finally, the board must determine whether the bidder will refuse to enter into the transaction without the no-shop clause. If so, and if the board is comfortable with the fairness of the price, the no-shop agreement may be advisable to secure for the shareholders the benefit of a good sale price.

Once the letter of intent stage is passed, the buyer certainly should expect a no-shop clause in the definitive agreement. Otherwise, why sign an agreement? Notwithstanding the clause in the agreement, because of its fiduciary responsibilities the board should avoid agreeing that it may not provide a competing bidder with the same information given to the buyer.

It is worth reiterating that the decision about whether to grant a no-shop agreement falls within the purview of the business judgment of the board of directors. Thus, the timing of the offer, the surrounding circumstances (hostile bidders, management buyers, etc.), other evidence of fairness, and the necessity of the clause to get the best deal for the stockholders all must be considered. There is no hard and fast rule.

What is a "fiduciary out" clause?

A "fiduciary out" clause enables the target to terminate a merger agreement in the event that a more favorable offer is made. In some cases the clause merely allows the board to back out of its obligation to recommend the agreement in the face of a more favorable offer. Although the law is unclear, the latter provision may be unnecessary because the board may have a fiduciary duty to refuse to continue its recommendation if a more favorable offer has been made.

From a buyer's perspective, the insertion of a fiduciary out clause in an agreement may not matter, because if a clearly more favorable bid is made, the chances are great that the stockholders won't approve the buyer's offer or will refuse to tender their shares to the buyer in its tender offer.

INSIDER TRADING

What is an insider?

An insider is an officer, director, or principal shareholder (generally any beneficial owner of more than 10% of the company's equity securities).

An insider may also include any employee who, in the course of his employment, acquires material nonpublic information about a publicly traded corporation. These individuals owe a fiduciary duty to the employer and its security holders not to trade on this information prior to its release and absorption by the market.

In addition, "outsiders" may become "temporary insiders" if they are given information in confidence solely for a corporate purpose. Attorneys, accountants, consultants, investment bankers, financial printers, and underwriters are examples of "temporary insiders" who are involved in a merger or acquisition.

Trading on inside information concerning mergers and acquisitions may be closely scrutinized by the SEC and may result in criminal prosecutions and very substantial civil penalties.

What laws prohibit insider trading?

Most insider trading cases are covered by two rules promulgated by the SEC under authority of the federal securities laws. The first is Rule 10b-5, which prohibits fraudulent or manipulative conduct in connection with the purchase or sale of securities.

The second, Rule 14e-3, prohibits trading on the basis of inside information in the context of a tender offer, whether as an insider or as the "tippee" of an insider. The Insider Trading Sanctions Act of 1984 sets penalties for these violations.

Also, Section 16(b) of the Exchange Act prohibits any officer or director, or any shareholder owning more than 10% of the issuer's stock, from profitting from a purchase and sale or a sale and purchase (a short sale) of securities of the issuer within a six-month period. This is known as the short-swing profit rule. Any profits from such a purchase and sale or sale and purchase must be paid to the issuer. The short-swing profit rule applies whether or not that person was in possession of material inside information.

Must a tender offeror file under Section 16 of the Exchange Act?

Yes. Once a tender offeror becomes a beneficial owner of ten percent of the target's securities, it is an insider for purposes of Section 16 and must file a Form 3 with the SEC within ten days of becoming an insider. The amount and type of ownership interest of the offeror must be disclosed on Form 3. An offeror must file a Form 4 upon any subsequent change in its beneficial ownership of the target securities. The Form 4 must be filed within ten days after the end of any month in which such change in beneficial ownership occurred.

Forms 3 and 4 must be filed with the SEC and the exchange on which the target securities are traded. If the securities are traded on more than one exchange, the target may select the exchange to receive the forms.

Are tender offerors subject to the requirement to disgorge short-swing profits established by Section 16(b) of the Exchange Act?

Yes. All persons required to file Forms 3 and 4 are subject to Section 16(b).

Are there any exemptions from Section 16(b) liability that apply to mergers and acquisitions?

Yes. Under Rule 16b-7 an "insider" is exempt from liability under Section 16(b) if it acquires or disposes of shares pursuant to a merger or consolidation of companies if one of the companies owns 85 percent or more of the combined assets of the other. Rule 16b-7 usually applies to second-stage mergers after completion of a partial tender offer. Also, a transaction that does not follow a typical sale-purchase or purchase-sale sequence may be exempt from the automatic liability provisions of Section 16(b).

"Unorthodox" transactions, such as stock conversions and reclassifications, mergers of a target into a white knight, and other corporate reorganizations, and option transactions, are frequently judged by a pragmatic or subjective test that may enable an insider to avoid liability when the automatic rules of Section 16(b) might otherwise apply. Under this alternate test, liability may be avoided if the insider did not have access to inside information and, in certain cases, if the insider did not have a control relationship with the issuer of the securities.

Private actions are far more common in cases of 16(b) violations than 10b-5 violations. The SEC does not enforce Section 16(b); rather, the statute gives the issuing corporation or a shareholder suing derivatively on behalf of the corporation the right to recover any profit made by an insider from purchases and sales—or sales and purchases—made within six months of each other. Section 16(b) provides for strict liability; that is, it requires that profits be disgorged without regard to whether the insider possesses any material nonpublic information.

What is the "disclose or abstain" rule and how is it applied?

The "disclose or abstain" theory applies when an individual possesses material nonpublic information about a corporation *and* he owes a fiduciary duty to the corporation. The individual must either disclose the information to the market or abstain from trading in securities of the affected company.

In practical terms, the "disclose or abstain" rule means "abstain." To be effective, disclosure of a material development affecting a security must result in dissemination broad enough to inform the entire public trading in that security. Most people cannot adequately disseminate such information themselves and disclosure itself may constitute a breach of fiduciary duty. If the inside information is incomplete or inaccurate, disclosure could be misleading to other investors and result in separate liability under other SEC disclosure rules.

What is the "misappropriation" theory and how is it applied?

The "misappropriation" theory of liability holds that an individual violates the securities laws when he secretly converts information given to him for legitimate business or commercial purposes by trading on the information for his own personal benefit.

For example, in a recent highly publicized case, Dennis Levine, an investment banker who received material information concerning a client and traded in securities of that client on the basis of that information, was found to have violated a duty to his employer and to the client not to use that information for his personal benefit. Under the misappropriation theory, Mr. Levine traded illegally on insider information.

The Supreme Court recently upheld with a 4 to 4 vote the misappropriation theory of liability in a case involving *Wall Street Journal* reporter R. Foster Winans. Winans was charged with, among other offenses, violating the securities laws by misappropriating information from his employer, even though the information was not about his employer and was not used to trade on his employer's securities. In the Winans case, the misappropriated information was the content and timing of publication of Winans' influential "Heard on the Street" column—*about* market information. The tie vote was hailed by SEC enforcement chief Gary Lynch as "an affirmation of our insider trading program. "

Can an insider be convicted of insider trading if he is unaware that information he is trading on is material and confidential?

No. Section 10b-5 has a *scienter* requirement. This means that to be found liable for violating Rule 10b-5 an insider must have either "actual knowledge" of the fraud or omission or have acted with "recklessness and disregard of the truth."

How does Rule 14e-3 operate?

Rule 14e-3(a) prohibits an individual from trading while he possesses material nonpublic information concerning a tender offer if the individual knows or has reason to know that such information is nonpublic and has been obtained, directly or indirectly, from any of the following:

- the entity making the tender offer,
- the corporation that is the subject of the tender offer,
- any persons affiliated with these entities, or
- any person acting on behalf of either entity.

The transfer of such information violates laws against "tipping."

What is "tipping"?

Tipping is the "selective disclosure of material nonpublic information for trading or other personal purposes."

What is a "tipper"?

A "tipper" is a person who, in return for some direct or indirect benefit, provides material nonpublic information to another person who then trades in that security.

What is a "tippee"?

A "tippee" is a person who receives material nonpublic information about a security and then trades in that security. Note that a "tippee" may also become a "tipper" if he or she then divulges the information to another person (who becomes a second- or third-level tippee.)

What laws prohibit "tipping"?

Courts have interpreted Rule 10b-5 to prohibit tipping, although the Rule does not address the issue directly. Rule 14e-3, which supplements Rule 10b-5, does contain an anti-tipping provision that applies in the context of a takeover. However, neither of these Rules contains the term "tipping." The Insider Trading Sanctions Act of 1984 also imposes civil penalties for tipping.

How does 10b-5 treat tipping?

Tipping is only prohibited by Rule 10b-5 if two tests are met: (1) the tipper has breached a duty that he or she owed to the corporation or its shareholders (for example, a fiduciary duty to a company and its shareholders as an officer and director); and (2) the insider will receive a personal benefit, directly or indirectly, from the disclosure.

If the tipper gains no personal benefit—can he still be accused of tipping?

No. Obvious examples of personal benefit include monetary gain or a benefit to the tipper's reputation that might translate into increased future earnings. However, the interpretation of "benefit" is very broad. For example, the Supreme Court has stated that divulging inside information to a relative or friend who then trades and returns a gift or a portion of the proceeds resembles trading by the tipper himself.

Under Rule 10b-5, must a tippee have such a fiduciary relationship with the tipper?

No, the typical tippee has no such relationship. However, if the tippee knows or should have known of the tipper's breach of duty and participates in the violation through silence or inaction, the tippee becomes liable as an aider and abettor if he or she then trades or divulges the information to one who trades.

How does 14e-3 treat "tipping"?

In contrast to Rule 10b-5, Rule 14e-3(d) contains clear anti-tipping provisions in the context of tender offers (although even in Rule 14e-3 the word "tipping" is not used). Rule 14e-3(d) makes it unlawful for certain persons to "communicate material, nonpublic information relating to a tender offer ... under circumstances in which it is reasonably foreseeable that such communication is likely to result in [improper trading or tipping]." This portion of the rule expressly excludes communications "made in good faith to certain individuals."

When are the anti-tipping provisions of Rule 14e-3 triggered?

Rule 14e-3 is triggered when any person has taken a "substantial step" to commence a tender offer, even if the offer never actually begins. A "substantial step" includes:

- the offeror's directors voting on a resolution with respect to the tender offer;
- the offeror's formulation of a plan to make an offer;
- arranging financing for a tender offer;
- authorizing negotiations for a tender offer; and
- directing that tender offer materials be prepared.

What penalties may be imposed for insider trading?

Damages for violation of Rule 10b-5 are limited to actual damages. However, additional charges are usually made in insider trading cases. In general, insider trading may result in criminal penalties of up to $100,000 and five years in jail, or both, if the trading is found to be a willful violation of the Exchange Act or of SEC rules and regulations promulgated under the Act. In addition, the Insider Trading Sanctions Act of 1984 gives the SEC the authority to seek a civil money penalty of up to three times the amount of profit gained or loss avoided by insider trading on a national securities exchange or through a broker or dealer in violation of federal securities laws. Damages are limited to actual damages.

In addition to the civil penalty for insider trading, the SEC may seek ancillary relief, including a court order enjoining the violator from future violations and disgorgement of profits resulting from the illegal trading. The disgorged funds may be paid into an escrow account so that private parties damaged by the insider trading can be compensated for their losses.

If a merger or acquisition involves the issuance of securities to the target's shareholders, may such securities be resold freely or are sales restricted?

Generally, such securities are similar to restricted securities in that Rule 145 under the 1933 Act states that any party to a merger or acquisition transaction receiving securities is deemed to be engaged in a distribution and therefore to be an underwriter.

Because of this "underwriter" status it is necessary to use a Form S-4 registration statement to register securities issued to the target's security holders. This form is basically a wrap around of the proxy statement and permits the shareholders of the target who are non-control persons to sell without restriction. Control persons or "affiliates" must sell, however, either under the registration statement or in accordance with restrictions in Rule 144.

FINANCING THE PUBLIC TRANSACTION

Is the financing of a public company acquisition very different from the financing of the acquisition of a private company?

The financing of a one-step transaction, involving the merger of an acquisition company into the target, is essentially the same as the financing of any other acquisition (see Chapter 4). The financing of a two-step acquisition (a tender offer followed by a merger of the acquisition company into the target) is somewhat different.

How is the financing of a two-step transaction different? Does it have any thing to do with the Federal Reserve margin rules?

The financing of the first step, the tender offer, is subject to Federal Reserve margin rules. These rules generally prohibit lenders, including banks and brokers and others, from making loans secured directly or indirectly by "margin" stock (most publicly-traded stock) if the loan exceeds a specified percentage of the value of the collateral (generally, 50%). For example, if the acquisition subsidiary is going to acquire stock of a target worth $100,000,000 in a tender offer, the maximum secured loan that can be made would be $50,000,000. This means that the other $50,000,000 has to be financed by other than secured loans, e.g., unsecured debt, equity investments, etc. The unsecured loans may be, for example, bridge loans from investment bankers to privately placed debt. Assets of the target are, of course, not available to secure the financing until after the merger. It is important to know that the margin rules apply to *indirectly* secured debt; the substance, not the form, of the transaction will govern the application of the rules. Therefore, if the borrower has no assets other than the target stock and has agreed with the lender not to pledge the stock to any other lender, the loan may be deemed to be indirectly secured by the stock.

If the acquisition subsidiary is a shell corporation can it freely incur unsecured debt and not violate the margin rules?

No. The position of the Federal Reserve is that if lenders make unsecured loans to a shell subsidiary for purposes of a tender offer, the loan will be presumed to be secured by margin stock subject to the 50% of value limitation. There is an important exception to this rule: the presumption does not apply if a merger agreement with the target is signed prior to the closing of the tender offer. Thus, in the case of a friendly two-step transaction, it is important that a merger agreement be signed before the tender offer in order to facilitate the financing of the tender offer. If there is no merger agreement, the amount that can't be financed under the margin rules may have to be financed by preferred or common equity or by loans guaranteed by other parties that have substantial assets.

CONSIDERATIONS APPLICABLE TO HOSTILE ACQUISITIONS

What steps should a board of directors consider after it decides to reject a tender offer?

If the directors determine that it is in the company's best interests to reject a tender offer or defend against a potential tender offer, the directors' duties of due care and loyalty would require that they have taken into account the following kinds of considerations:

- the present and future impact of defenses on the value of the company's stock;
- the ability of the company to pursue a negotiated transaction with friendly bidders (white knights) if the defensive measures are implemented;
- the reasonableness of the defenses in relation to the threat posed.

What does the directors' duty of loyalty require when responding to an unsolicited tender offer?

When considering the response to an unsolicited tender offer, the board of directors of a target corporation owes a duty of loyalty to the corporation's shareholders to adopt defensive measures to defeat a takeover attempt that is contrary to the best interests of the corporation and its shareholders. However, the board must be careful to adopt defensive measures only when motivated by a good faith concern for the welfare of the corporation and its shareholders.

Does it violate the duty of loyalty if a board adopts a defensive tactic in part to retain management control?

No. Defending a corporation against hostile takeovers to maintain control, among other motives, does not violate the duty of loyalty. However, it is improper if a director's *primary* motive for implementing a defensive tactic is to retain control of the company.

On what basis can directors reject an acquisition offer?

There are generally three reasons why an offer can be rejected and defenses implemented: (1) the offer is inadequate (i.e., the director has information that enables him to reasonably determine that the company's outstanding capital stock is worth more than what is being offered); (2) the offer is unfair in that those stockholders not tendering their shares will receive less consideration at a later date (e.g., in the case of a front-end loaded, two-tier offer); or (3) the company determines that it is better served by remaining independent.

Can directors sell their shares of the target company to an acquiror without violating their duty of loyalty?

Directors have the right to deal freely with their shares of stock and to sell them at the best price they can, as long as they act in good faith. "Good faith" means that the director does not misuse confidential information or usurp any corporate opportunity. A director has no duty to disclose his stock dealings to the corporation (except in certain required public filings), nor does he have a duty to offer his shares to the corporation before selling them.

This relative freedom to trade in company stock, as long as it is traded in good faith, applies even when a director of a target corporation decides to sell his shares of stock of the target corporation to a hostile acquiring company. A director of a corporation also has the right to use his company stock to effectuate and promote a third-party takeover of the company.

In *Treadway*, a director of the target corporation failed to disclose to management that he had sold his stock and had subsequently advised a third party of the suitability of making a tender offer. The Court held that he breached no duty to the corporation or its shareholders. Moreover, since he was not a controlling shareholder, he had no duty to account for any premium received from the sale of his stock.

The court also found that he breached no duty by failing to disclose his contacts with the third party and his knowledge of their intention to seek control. Even if the director betrayed the trust placed in him by incumbent management, this fact had no legal significance. Management—as distinct from the corporation—had no legitimate claim to a director's allegiance.

The plaintiff in this case also claimed that two other directors breached the duty of loyalty by placing the third party's interest in obtaining control above any interest of the corporation. However, the Court held that a director does not necessarily breach any duty owed to the corporation by promoting an offer that is likely to result in a change of management, as long as a takeover is not in any way adverse to the best interests of the shareholders. Even if the target company's board of directors, as a whole, determines that the takeover would not be in the best interests of the corporation, each director is "under no duty to follow management blindly. " Instead, each director is under a duty to exercise his own best judgment on the corporation's behalf. Therefore, a director may, in certain circumstances, oppose the majority of the board and support a hostile tender offeror's efforts to win control.

What defenses are commonly adopted against hostile takeovers?

The takeover defenses can be classified generally as restructuring defenses, poison pills, charter and bylaw amendments, and defensive acquisitions. State anti-takeover statutes can also play an important role in defending against a hostile takeover.

RESTRUCTURING DEFENSES

How do recapitalizations work?

A recapitalization substitutes portions of the outstanding capital stock held by the public with cash, debt instruments or securities, or preferred stock. These transactions may increase the percentage of voting stock held by management and employee benefit plans.

There are basically three ways to accomplish a recapitalization:

- through a tender offer for the company's own stock;
- through a transaction such as a merger, where a subsidiary merges into the company when the plan becomes effective; or
- through a reclassification amendment of the company's charter. (This requires shareholder approval and may involve the issuance of options to shareholders to purchase shares of the recapitalized company upon the occurrence of certain events.)

It is also sometimes possible to simply issue large dividends to stockholders by incurring debt to finance such a transaction.

A recapitalization has been likened to a public leveraged buyout because the stockholders who do not sell stock to the company often acquire a much greater percentage of the company's equity. The number of outstanding shares decreases as they are purchased by the company, thereby increasing the percentage holdings of remaining stockholders.

Each type of recapitalization has its advantages and disadvantages. In a tender offer situation, speed is the primary advantage because no stockholder vote or proxy statement is required. The company may also issue securities without filing a registration statement with the SEC because Section 3(a)(9) of the 1933 Act permits the exchange of securities without registration if it only affects existing security holders, and no remuneration is paid for soliciting the exchange.

Recapitalizations have generally withstood court challenges. However, courts will not uphold recapitalizations that appear coercive, i.e., leave the stockholders without a real option to decline participation.

How can a company recapitalize using an Employee Stock Option Plan (ESOP)?

An ESOP may be used as a tool in a recapitalization (see Chapter 9, on Pension, Labor and Compensation Concerns, p. 507). An ESOP purchases stock in the open market or from the company, allowing its employees and management to own part of the company. By borrowing to acquire the shares an ESOP can help finance a recapitalization; it can also purchase shares directly from unrelated parties at a premium, which allows it to purchase shares from a hostile bidder. The disadvantage of ESOP participation is that it can dilute the public's percentage of ownership in the company if the company issues new shares to the ESOP.

An ESOP is managed by trustees who have the duty to act in the best interests of its beneficiaries. If the trustees are also the company's directors, a hostile bidder may assert a conflict of interest by the directors and question their motives for instituting an ESOP during the takeover attempt. The suggestion would be that the directors, as trustees, implemented the ESOP not in the interest of the beneficiaries, but to fend off the bidder.

There may also be a conflict of interest issue when the ESOP is in place before a hostile bid, if the trustees decide to purchase more of the company's stock immediately preceding or during such a bid. However, if the trustees can justify their decisions on the basis of acting in the best interests of all the ESOP's participants and demonstrate the requisite detached judgment, legal challenges can be overcome.

What are some of the concerns involved in a recapitalization?

A company that has undertaken a recapitalization that has caused it to become highly leveraged and/or cash poor may no longer have the financial resources to weather unexpected economic conditions or even to carry on its intended business. The recapitalization plan that engenders such consequences is subject to the Federal fraudulent conveyance and transfer laws, the Federal Bankruptcy Code, and state laws (see Chapter 4, on Financing). Creditors and stockholders alike may contend the company has become insolvent, or no longer able to function with the remaining working capital, or that the company has incurred debts that are beyond its capacity to repay.

Most states impose limitations upon a company's ability to make dividend distributions and to repurchase or redeem its own stock if such transactions would impair the company's capital. These corporation statutes may affect the kind of recapitalization a company might initiate.

How do self-tenders work?

A self-tender is a defensive measure implemented to defeat an unsolicited tender offer or at least to obtain a higher price. The company announces its intentions to repurchase its own outstanding stock, or a portion thereof, to prevent the offeror from acquiring a controlling interest in the company. Self-tenders, like other tender offers, are regulated by the federal securities laws.

In 1986, the SEC adopted an amendment to the tender offer rules to prohibit discriminatory self-tenders. Rule 14l-10 requires that all holders of the same class of stock be treated in the same way, i.e., the same offer must be made to all stockholders whether they are hostile bidders or not. The company is also required to accept all shares tendered to it, including a hostile bidder's shares.

How can open market repurchases dissuade hostile takeovers?

By repurchasing its own shares on the open market without making a formal tender offer, a company can maintain or increase the stock's prices and thereby make the company less attractive to a bidder. Such purchases are often accompanied by sales of assets to finance part of the repurchase if the company's cash flow is not sufficient to effect the purchase.

In implementing a repurchase plan, directors must satisfy the business judgment rule and comply with various other state and federal laws, including, in particular, Rule 10b-18, which regulates the purchase of registered equity securities by an issuer.

Stock repurchases by the company are seldom effective as a defensive tactic if not effected in combination with other techniques, such as stock purchases by management, ESOPs, or other major stockholders, which tend to lock up substantial blocks of stock in friendly hands.

What is the Crown Jewel defense?

The Crown Jewel defense is the sale of particularly attractive assets by the target company to dissuade a bidder from pursuing its takeover attempt. Such sales may also give the company flexibility and resources to fend off a bidder by generating capital and reducing costs. On the other hand, if a bidder is interested in a specific asset, such as a subsidiary, and is willing to acquire the entire company for it, the asset may be very valuable to the company as well, and its sale may be detrimental over the long term.

As discussed earlier, courts will generally view with disfavor an asset or Crown Jewel lock-up that has the effect of discouraging or stopping the bidding process.

How can a master limited partnership be used as a takeover defense?

A company may preserve stockholder value, and even increase stockholder values, by placing crown jewels in a master limited partnership and distributing limited partnership interests to all shareholders. This would make it more difficult for an acquiror to obtain the long-term benefits of such assets. Such a distribution requires substantial disclosures under the federal securities laws.

POISON PILLS

How do shareholders' rights plans/poison pills work?

A poison pill is an increasingly popular defensive tactic that does not require prior stockholder approval. It involves the issuance to stockholders of rights to acquire stock and/or other types of securities of the issuer or acquiror. These rights are not exercisable unless certain triggering events occur (i.e., a takeover attempt) and may be redeemed by the company at a nominal price until the occurrence of such events.

There are two common kinds of poison pills: (1) flip-over and (2) back-end, which may be combined in one defensive plan. Less frequently seen, and not described here are flip-in, convertible preferred stock and voting rights poison pills. The use of poison pills as a defensive measure has generally been upheld by courts, but some plans have been enjoined because of their specific provisions and purposes. In implementing these plans, directors must be able to prove that the measure was adopted in good faith, after reasonable investigation, and is reasonably related to the threat posed.

The primary objective of poison pills is to give management leverage in negotiating bids, to avoid unfair treatment of stockholders (in coercive two-tier takeovers or partial tenders), and to ensure a minimum price in any takeover.

What are flip-over plans?

In this plan each common stockholder receives for each share owned a right to purchase shares of the surviving corporation upon the occurrence of a triggering event. Triggering events are typically the acquisition by a single purchaser or group of a specified amount of stock or the commencement of a tender offer for a specified percentage of the company's stock. Following the occurrence of a triggering event, the company issues certificates to stockholders that allow the latter to exercise and trade their rights. As the rights issuance is in the nature of a dividend, no shareholder approval is required prior to the issuance.

As the rights usually allow the certificate holder to purchase stock of the surviving entity for half price after the merger has been consummated, the effect of the flip-over is to reduce the acquiror's equity. Also, because the rights usually may be redeemed for a nominal amount before the triggering event (and often within a short period of time thereafter), a bidder has an incentive to negotiate with management before a takeover attempt. However, once the rights become nonredeemable, they would adversely affect the company's ability to negotiate with a white knight.

A flip-over plan should also include a provision that a transaction approved by the directors will not result in the stockholders' rights becoming exercisable even though the triggering events have occurred. Such a provision allows the company to seek a white knight.

What are back-end plans?

A back-end plan is similar to a flip-over plan, though its objectives differ. Holders of the company's common stock receive a right for each share owned that entitles them, upon the occurrence of certain triggering events (e.g., a 20% acquisition by a bidder), to exchange each share for a note that matures typically within a short period of time (e.g., one year). Alternatively, the right may be exchanged for cash or preferred stock, or a combination of the three. The value of the right may be fixed at the outset or may be based on a formula based on the highest price per share paid by a bidder during the takeover attempt.

The purpose of the plan is to maximize stockholder value in the event of a merger or business combination by ensuring a minimum acceptable price and to protect stockholders from the adverse effects of a significant minority interest on other bidders even if no merger results. A back-end plan is not designed to prevent a takeover but to ensure a negotiated value for the company and its stockholders.

The plan will usually provide that the rights will not be exercisable if the acquiror, upon reaching a certain level of ownership, offers to purchase the remainder of the outstanding shares at the price set by the plan. The rights are usually redeemable for a specified period of time (e.g., 120 days) to allow a bidder to express his intentions to complete the transaction as specified.

Such a plan will likely be upheld by the courts if: (1) it is not designed to prevent all takeovers; (2) the back-end price is reached with the advice of investment bankers and reflects the realizable value over the plan's life (e.g., one year); (3) the plan is a reasonable response to the threat perceived by the directors, e.g., a possible second-step merger; and (4) the plan is "plausibly related to the goal of shareholder wealth maximization."

CHARTER/BYLAW AMENDMENTS

How do charter and bylaw amendments help companies deter takeovers?

Charter and bylaw amendments will generally not prevent takeover attempts, but they do provide protection from coercive and abusive acquisition tactics. These amendments may also slow down the acquisition process, giving the company's directors more time to react and negotiate.

Any amendments adopted by the stockholders will apply equally to the company's management and any bidder who acquires shares. There is another important consideration in adopting amendments: if the stockholders reject the proposals, the company may seem—and indeed may be—more vulnerable to takeovers by bidders.

What different kinds of defensive charter and bylaw amendments are there?

The most widely used charter and bylaw amendments include: (1) supermajority provisions; (2) fair price provisions; (3) contingent cumulative voting provisions; (4) staggered board provisions; (5) defensive consent requirements; and (6) notice of business and special meetings provisions.

What are supermajority provisions?

A company may adopt a charter amendment to require more than a simple majority (i.e., a supermajority) of its stockholders to approve any merger or business combination. There are several effective variations of this defense, one of which is a requirement that a majority of the disinterested stockholders— i.e., a majority of the minority—approve the transaction. To protect the supermajority provisions, there should be a provision that would require a supermajority to modify the supermajority provisions of the charter.

One of the disadvantages of supermajority provisions is that they apply to friendly as well as hostile takeovers. Therefore, to the extent such provisions may deter hostile bidders, they may also make it more difficult to negotiate a friendly takeover. As a partial cure, such a provision may be coupled with one specifying that a simple majority is sufficient if the directors approve the merger.

What are fair price provisions?

A fair price provision is a variation of a supermajority requirement that would require a specified supermajority to approve a proposed merger unless the bidder pays the minority stockholders a fair price. Usually a fair price means a price that equals or exceeds the highest price paid by the bidder in acquiring shares of the company before the merger. The purpose of this provision is to ensure fairness to stockholders in a two-tier acquisition.

How does contingent cumulative voting work as a defense?

Cumulative voting permits a stockholder to vote the number of shares owned by him multipled by the number of directors being elected; all of a stockholder's potential votes may be added together and cast for a specific director.

Contingent cumulative voting, if coupled with a staggered board of directors (see below), may provide the minority stockholders (who disfavor the merger) with a tool to block or delay the election of a slate of the bidder's directors. For example, a charter amendment may provide that when and if a bidder acquires a certain specified percentage of the company's stock (e.g., 35% or more), cumulative voting goes into effect. In this case, the minority stockholders may be able to elect or retain more directors than if the charter amendment were not in place.

What effect does a staggered board have on a target company?

The election of directors on a staggered basis prevents a bidder from electing a new slate of directors in one meeting of stockholders and thereby gaining immediate control of management. Usually, one-third of the directors are elected each year for a three-year term.

By itself, the staggered board provision would not deter a takeover, but in conjunction with contingent cumulative voting, staggered elections may give a company more flexibility in dealing with unwanted bidders.

How are consent procedures modified?

Many states' corporation laws provide that a majority of stockholders may, without calling a meeting, act by written consent. A company that does not amend its charter to provide otherwise may be susceptible to a bidder acquiring a majority interest and then immediately amending its charter to remove other impediments to control.

To combat this possibility, the company may, by charter amendment, eliminate the written consent provisions entirely or require that all stockholders consent before actions can be approved without a meeting unless state law prohibits the elimination of the consent procedure. Even if the consent procedure cannot be eliminated, a charter amendment or amendment of the company's bylaws that requires stockholders wishing to take action by written consent to notify the directors and request that it establish a record date to determine which stockholders are entitled to sign a consent would also permit the directors a reasonable opportunity to prepare a response and oppose the proposed action, by soliciting proxies, if necessary.

Such an amendment might also contain specified periods for consent revocation and the period of consent validity.

What is a white squire?

To remain independent, the company may determine that its best course of action is to sell a large block of its stock to a friendly investor, a white squire, that the company does not believe is a threat. The obvious danger here is that relations between the white squire and company may take a turn for the worse, and the white squire may decide to acquire control of the company at a later date.

To prevent the white squire from becoming a hostile bidder, companies typically use standstill agreements. A standstill agreement imposes certain limitations on the investor that assure the company that the stock will not find its way to a hostile bidder. Typically, the stock purchase agreement will limit the percentage of stock the white squire may acquire in addition to the shares in question for a specific period of time. It will also contain restrictions on the sale of the minority interest to third parties, which is usually coupled with a right of first refusal by the company. The voting rights relating to the block of shares sold also may be limited.

The directors' decision to enter into such an arrangement and the provisions of the standstill agreement will be evaluated under the business judgment doctrine. These arrangements are generally upheld if the court finds that entrenchment is not their sole or primary purpose.

DEFENSIVE ACQUISITIONS

May a company make an acquisition to avoid being acquired?

The company may combat an unwanted bidder by acquiring other companies or divisions that make it less attractive to the bidder. The company may also acquire assets that may precipitate an antitrust problem for the bidder if the transaction is completed.

The effectiveness of antitrust barriers is mitigated by the fact that government agencies are generally willing to consider curative measures by the bidder before rejecting a merger.

What is the Pac Man strategy of defense?

When a company learns it is the object of a tender offer, it responds by tender offering for the stock of the hostile bidder. The company undertaking the counter tender offer thereby concedes that the business combination is desirable but indicates that it should control the resulting entity. It also concedes certain defenses it might otherwise bring, such as antitrust and other regulatory barriers that concern the legality of the combination.

The disadvantages of the Pac Man defense are that the company's stockholders will not receive any premium (the company may actually give the other company's stockholders a premium); it is very costly; and it may damage the company, even if successful.

When considering the legality of this defense courts will apply the business judgment rule. In *Bendix Corp.*, Martin Marietta countered Bendix's tender offer by tendering for shares of Bendix. As Martin Marietta's majority stockholder, Bendix contended that the company's directors breached their fiduciary duty by disregarding the wishes of their majority stockholder (i.e., Bendix) and purchasing Bendix's stock. The court decided that Martin Marietta's directors owed a fiduciary duty to Bendix's stockholders, not to Bendix as a corporate entity and that Martin Marietta's directors had fulfilled their fiduciary duties because the business rationale spurring them to acquire Bendix was in the best interests of the Bendix stockholders.

An interesting legal question not answered by this case is whether this co-ownership situation would be prohibited by state subsidiary voting provisions. For example, the Delaware statute provides that a subsidiary may not vote the stock of its parent. Therefore, if both companies were deemed to be subsidiaries (and parents) of one another, the majority of each company's stock would be non-voting.

GREENMAIL

What are the costs and benefits of greenmail as a takeover defense?

Bidders sometimes accumulate stock and threaten to initiate a tender offer with the ultimate purpose of reselling those shares to the company at a premium rather than obtaining control of the company. Greenmail is a payment to purchase such stock at a premium.

Paying greenmail is largely ineffective to protect the interests of the target (other greenmailers may surface once the company has succumbed once), discriminatory (other holders of the same class of stock may not share in the premium), and risky to the recipient and the target (there have been stockholder lawsuits with varying degrees of success to recover greenmail payments as corporate assets). Most persuasive of all, Section 5881 of the Internal Revenue Code imposes a 50% excise tax on greenmail payments, payable by the recipient. The tax is imposed not only upon cash payments by the target to purchase the greenmailer's stock, but also other, more disguised payments constituting consideration for the stock, such as reimbursement of the greenmailer's related transaction expenses or purchases of other assets of the greenmailer. It can also be imposed on payments made by related parties, such as a white knight, and thus tends to compel a defeated raider to sell out to an independent holder, such as an arbitrageur rather than to a party controlled by or acting under agreement with the target.

The effect of these developments has been to greatly decrease the incidence of greenmail in recent years.

RELATED STATE LAWS

What provisions of state law limit director and officer liability for defensive measures?

• Charter opt-in provisions authorize corporations to pass a charter or bylaw provision eliminating or reducing the personal liability of directors for money damages. This provision is particularly significant in takeovers, since many shareholder suits against defensive target boards do request money damages.

• Several states have raised the threshold of liability to require more than proof of simple negligence by board members. *Gross negligence*, or *recklessness*, generally must be proved by the plaintiff for personal liability to attach.

• One state (Virginia) has established a money damage "cap" (except in cases of willful misconduct or knowing violation of criminal law or state securities laws), which is the lesser of:

    (a) The monetary limit approved by the stockholders in either the charter or bylaws, and

    (b) The greater of (i) the amount of compensation received by the individual from the corporation during the twelve preceding months and (ii) $100,000.

This provision has been challenged as unconstitutional and is unlikely to be adopted by other states.

• Other provisions protecting directors include: expanded indemnification for derivative suits against the board, expanded provisions permitting corporations to provide benefits other than indemnification, and provisions that permit directors to base their decision to reject an offer on considerations other than price, e.g., the effect of the transaction on the community and other corporate constituencies.

What states have passed antitakeover statutes?

By early 1988, 29 states have passed antitakeover statutes:

Arizona	Mississippi
Connecticut	Missouri
Delaware	Nevada
Florida	New Jersey
Georgia	New York
Hawaii	North Carolina
Illinois	Ohio
Indiana	Oklahoma
Kentucky	Oregon
Louisiana	Pennsylvania
Maine	Utah
Maryland	Virginia
Massachusetts	Washington
Michigan	Wisconsin
Minnesota	

Aren't antitakeover statutes usually overturned?

Court decisions for or against state antitakeover statutes seem to go in cycles. Prior to the 1982 decision of *Edgar v. MITE*, 37 states had antitakeover statutes, all of which were overturned by the decision. Then, in 1987, the *CTS* case reversed the *MITE* decision. By early 1988, 29 states passed antitakeover statutes, the 29th being Delaware.

What are the typical provisions of state antitakeover statutes?

Most recent statutes are patterned after the Indiana Control Share Acquisition Act of 1986. In this and many other statutes, acquirors of over a specified percent (e.g., 20%) of the outstanding stock will only have voting rights if a majority of disinterested shareholders so vote.

Pursuant to the recently adopted Delaware statute, Section 203 of the Delaware General Corporation Law, no acquiror owning more than 15% of a publicly held company's stock can commence any business combination within three years of the stock acquisition unless (a) the directors approve the proposed business combination; (b) the acquiror owned 85% of the stock before the combination was proposed; or (c) the directors approve the combination on or after the date of the combination, and it is authorized at an annual or special stockholders' meeting (but not through written consents) by a vote of at least 66 2/3% of the disinterested shareholders.

Antitakeover statutes apply generally to corporations organized within the state. However, the Massachusetts statute provides that companies not incorporated in the state will still be subjected to the statute's provisions if they have substantial operations therein (e.g., executive offices), the bulk of their work forces or assets within the state, at least 10% of the shares are owned by state residents (excluding brokers or nominees), or 10% of the shareholders reside in the state.

The statutes of Arizona, Ohio, and Minnesota impose a different standard of care on directors in evaluating any business combination. Directors must examine and consider the long-term effects of an offer on the company, its stockholders, the affected community, and other corporate constituencies.

Florida requires an acquiror to pay a statutorily determined fair price for all the shares, unless a majority of disinterested directors or 66 2/3% of the disinterested stockholders decide otherwise. In Pennsylvania control share acquisitions do not require approval by the stockholders, but unhappy stockholders have appraisal rights—a so-called "cash out" option. North Carolina law requires approval by holders of 95% of the voting shares for any combination between the company and a 20% stockholder.

CHAPTER 13

SPECIAL TOPICS RELATING TO TRANSACTIONS WITH INTERNATIONAL ASPECTS

INTRODUCTION

Among the most important lessons that can be learned as a result of the "October Crash" is not to underestimate the growth and importance of the international business community, or the overall impact on the economy of the United States which international market forces and events can have. The growth of offshore currency markets, the availability of international debt financing, the establishment of foreign securities exchanges, and the influx of international merger, acquisition, and other investment activities have made it virtually impossible for large and small businesses alike to ignore the existence of an economically and technologically unified world.

The purpose of this chapter is to give a brief understanding of selected issues that specifically relate to domestic companies acquiring other domestic companies with international components, to direct foreign investment in the United States or direct U.S. investment abroad, or to U.S. companies wishing to finance certain domestic or foreign activities through various international financing techniques. The chapter is divided into tax and non-tax issues, and a distinction is made in each of those areas between issues relating to foreign investment in the United States (inbound transactions) and those relating to U.S. investment overseas (outbound transactions). It must be understood that this chapter is not, nor does it purport to be, a complete statement of every issue which one might encounter in embarking on an inbound or outbound transaction. Rather, we have highlighted some of the concerns which should be raised by businesses or individuals interested in pursuing such activities, and which should be very carefully explored by legal counsel familiar with the U.S. laws which apply, as well as by special counsel located in the foreign country or countries involved.

NON-TAX ISSUES REGARDING FOREIGN INVESTMENT IN THE U.S.

Limitations on Foreign Ownership

Are there any limitations under the U.S. law as to the form of business association in which a foreign person can participate?

Generally, U.S. laws impose no limitations as to the form of business association a foreign person can use to create or conduct a business or own business interests. The type of business association a foreign person decides to use is often dictated by the particular needs of the enterprise and the impact upon that enterprise of federal and state laws— particularly tax laws, which can be an incentive to use one particular structure and a disincentive to use another. Any foreign person would be well advised to check with local counsel on the impact of all relevant tax, business, securities, and related laws prior to deciding on the most favorable form of business association to achieve his specific goals.

Must the parties forming a new corporation (called "incorporators," and not synonymous with stockholders) be citizens of the U.S. and residents of the state of incorporation?

Not necessarily. In the absence of express requirements in state corporation statutes, the incorporators, who are merely legal instruments used to organize a corporation, need not be citizens or residents of the state under whose laws the formation of the corporation is sought. For example, Delaware Corporation Law Section 101(a) states: "Any person, partnership, association, or corporation, singly or jointly with others, and without regard to his or their residence, domicile, or state of incorporation, may incorporate or organize a corporation under this chapter by filing with the Secretary of State a certificate of incorporation which shall be executed, acknowledged, filed, and recorded in accordance with section 103 of this title." The ease and simplicity of corporate formation in the United States may come as a surprise to those accustomed to the formality of certain foreign systems of incorporation.

If everyone owning and operating a corporation which is incorporated under the laws of a state of the United States is a non-U.S. citizen, isn't the corporation foreign?

No. A corporation formed under the laws of any state is, simply, a corporation of that state. However, there still may be restrictions placed on the business activities of such corporation which arise from the fact that its owners are not U.S. citizens (see below), and, of course, there are tax ramifications to such individuals arising from such ownership (see International Tax Considerations, below).

What type of federal restrictions apply to foreign ownership of U.S. businesses?

There are no blanket restrictions on the ownership of U.S. businesses by foreign persons. There are, however, certain federal regulations restricting or limiting foreign ownership in particular industries or in certain circumstances. The following laws control foreign investment and activity in specific industries or circumstances:

• *The Federal Communications Act* bars aliens, foreign governments, certain U.S. corporations controlled by foreign interests, and corporations organized outside the U.S. from possessing a broadcast or common carrier license;

• *The Federal Aviation Act* prohibits any foreign air carrier, or person controlling such an entity, from acquiring "control in any manner whatsoever" of any U.S. entity or enterprise substantially engaged in the aeronautics business;

• *The Mineral Lands Leasing Act of 1920* requires that any corporation applying to the Secretary of the Interior for a federal lease to develop certain natural resources of the United States disclose the identity and citizenship of shareholders owning more than ten percent of its stock, in which case such lease will be granted only if U.S. persons can obtain reciprocal licenses or leases from the home governments of such foreign shareholders;

• *The Shelflands Act* stipulates that offshore leases for the development of energy resources be held only by citizens, nationals, and permanent resident aliens of the U.S., and business associations thereof. However, because the Department of the Interior considers any corporation organized in the U.S. an entity suitable for an award of a lease, foreign possession of leases is possible through incorporation of a U.S. subsidiary;

• *The Merchant Marine Act* restricts the registration and licensing of vessels to those vessels owned, chartered, or leased from the Secretary of Commerce by a U.S. citizen, or a corporation, partnership, or association which is organized in the U.S. and controlled by U.S. citizens; and

• *The Edge Act* limits foreign ownership of corporations chartered by the Federal Reserve Board to engage in international banking and finance.

In addition to the above mentioned U.S. statutes, certain other current legislation has been developed to monitor or control foreign investment in and trade with the United States.

Executive Order 11858 established the Committee on Foreign Investment in the United States in 1975. The mandate of this Committee is to review investments by foreign governments in the U.S. which, in the judgment of the Committee, may have an effect on the national interests of the U.S. The Committee, however, has no power to block or modify investments by foreign governments.

The most recent legislation enacted by Congress which

addresses the foreign acquisition of U.S. enterprises is the Omnibus Trade and Competitiveness Act of 1988. This legislation authorizes the President to suspend or prohibit mergers, acquisitions and takeovers of U.S. entities by "foreign persons," and to seek divestment or other relief in court, if he determines that "the foreign interest exercising control might take action that threatens to impair the national security." The President's determination is not subject to judicial review. The President may take into account in making his determination domestic capacity to meet national defense requirements, among other factors. The President shall commence any investigation within 30 days after notice of the merger, acquisition or takeover, and complete such investigation not later than 45 days from determining to undertake it. Any decision to take action must be announced not later than 15 days after the investigation is completed. The President is directed to issue regulations to carry out this provision.

While this legislation is untried, it could become a significant source of delay for, and possible prohibition of, inbound acquisitions, and will probably cause a lot of touching of bases in Washington before certain major, sensitive acquisitions go forward.

Are there any special federal requirements which apply to U.S. businesses owned or controlled by foreign persons?

Yes, primarily there are disclosure requirements. First, disclosure requirements generally applicable to acquisitions, such as under the Williams Act and Hart-Scott-Rodino Act (See Chapter 10), apply to foreign, as well as U.S., investors. Second, the following federal laws establish specific disclosure requirements for foreign investors:

• *The International Investment and Trade in Services Survey Act of 1976* requires U.S. business enterprises to report to the Department of Commerce, within 45 days, the acquisition of a voting interest of 10 percent or more in such enterprise by one or more foreign persons if such interest was acquired for a price exceeding US $1 million. If the enterprise has annual sales, assets, or net income of greater than $10 million, annual and quarterly financial reporting are also required. In addition to the reporting requirements of foreign investors, the Act also requires reporting by any citizen of the United States who assists or intervenes in the acquisition of a voting interest of at least 10% by a foreign person or who enters into a joint venture with a foreign person to create a U.S. business enterprise;

• *The Foreign Investment in Real Property Tax Act of 1986* granted the Secretary of the Treasury the authority to require reporting by foreign persons holding direct investments in U.S. real property interests having an aggregate fair market value of $450,000 or more. To date, the Secretary has declined to promulgate such an annual reporting requirement;

• *The Agricultural Foreign Investment Disclosure Act* requires a foreign person or entity to file a report within ninety days following the acquisition or transfer of any interest, other than a lien or security interest, in U.S. farming, ranching, or timber land; and

• *The Tax Equity and Fiscal Responsibility Act of 1982* requires domestic and foreign corporations that (i) are controlled by a foreign person and (ii) engage in a trade or business in the United States to file annual information returns.

Must foreign investors be concerned about specific state regulations as well as U.S. federal law when acquiring a U.S. business interest?

In general, states do not restrict foreign investment, except with respect to specific industries, such as banking and insurance. Most states (29 as of early 1988) have passed antitakeover legislation (see Chapter 12, on Public Company Acquisitions). Some states, such as California, Iowa, New Mexico, and Pennsylvania, restrict land ownership with respect to certain types of property, and the exploitation or development of natural resources by foreign investors. A foreign person desiring to acquire a business interest in the United States should seek legal counsel to ensure that there are no special restrictions imposed by the state in which the target business is domiciled, as well as under the federal law.

Do any of the foregoing restrictions apply to U.S. businesses in which foreign persons hold debt rather than equity?

No. In the United States the percentage of equity owned is the exclusive means of measuring the extent of a foreign investor's control of a U.S. corporation. Debt holdings are not considered.

Does federal or state law limit the ability of a U.S. company to guarantee the indebtedness of a foreign affiliate?

There are no federal limitations on the ability of a U.S. company to guarantee foreign indebtedness. Any state limitations on a corporation's ability to guarantee indebtedness would be set forth in the state's corporation statutes, but such limitations are relatively rare. Where limitations do exist under state law, these limitations apply regardless of the nationality of the person on whose behalf the guarantee is given.

Are there legal limitations under U.S. law on the ability of a U.S. company to pledge its assets to a foreign lender?

The power of a corporation to acquire, utilize, and dispose of assets arises from state corporation statutes, and is not dependent upon the identity of other parties to the transaction. For example, Section 122 of the Delaware General Corporation law empowers any Delaware corporation to "sell, convey, lease, exchange, transfer, or otherwise dispose of, or mortgage or pledge, all or any of its property and assets, or any interest therein, wherever situated." U.S. federal law imposes no restriction on the pledge of assets by U.S. individuals or entities.

Does the U.S. impose any restrictions on the amount of dollars which can be paid by a U.S. business to a foreign investor?

There is no limit, under current U.S. law, to the amount of money which can be taken out of the United States by either

U.S. or foreign investors. In fact, it is the lack of such restrictions that has led to the rapid development of large offshore currency markets, such as the Eurodollar market.

Restrictions Imposed by the Acquirer's Home Country

Do most countries have laws that affect their citizens' acquisitions in other countries?

Many industrialized nations impose certain domestic laws and/or additional external investment laws on foreign companies acquired by their citizens. The acquirer must be aware of how these domestic and external investment laws might affect its investment and the operation of the company acquired. Problems may arise when these laws do not conform to the target company's business practices and policies or conflict with the laws of the jurisdiction in which the target is located.

An example of one area of concern is trade policy. Whereas the target company's country may want to increase exports, the parent company's country may wish to restrict imports. In addition to general national trade policy concerns, there may be licensing requirements for imports and exports, and other trade barriers such as quotas and tariffs.

ACQUISITIONS INVOLVING ENTITIES OR ASSETS LOCATED OUTSIDE THE U.S.: NON-TAX ISSUES

Basic Differences

What are the main differences between acquisitions that are confined geographically to the United States and those that are international in whole or in part?

One of the advantages that the United States offers dealmakers is that it is a large, homogeneous area which runs on the same accounting, legal, and cultural principles. A buyer from Washington making an acquisition in Florida, or a company in Arizona selling to a firm in Vermont, negotiate from a great deal of shared knowledge, shared perceptions, and shared business practices. This is not true when a buyer goes abroad, even if only part of a transaction is international. It may seek to find the foreign equivalent of a particular transactional structure in a particular jurisdiction, only to find that there is *no* such equivalent. For example, a buyer of a Japanese corporation may assume it can offer its lenders warrants as part of its financing package. However, warrants are not contractual obligations enforceable against a Japanese corporation. Therefore, the buyer would have to find other devices to give its lender the same or similar economic and legal rights to those embodied in a warrant.

International dealmaking often forces buyers or sellers to learn an entirely different conceptual vocabulary or framework. At a very basic level, they will find that the same words have different meanings in different countries. For example, the French word "directeur" does not mean "director," as in member of the board, but, more generally, an executive. Similarly, the U.S. concept of "antitrust" is practically meaningless in Europe, where antitrust is a situational concept, decided on a case-by-case basis and where, under certain circumstances, acquirers can actually negotiate with European government authorities taking a consensus approach toward maintaining "competition" or toward maintaining a current level of employment or reducing unemployment.

On another front, in some countries an acquirer may find that the seller has the government of its country as a silent partner. Many foreign countries will review substantively the contracts between a seller and a foreign buyer, in some cases to protect its citizens against overreaching by more sophisticated foreign businessmen, in others to ensure that the transaction promotes economic development or other governmental policies.

In the United States a CEO might say, "I'll strike my deal, and then I'll call in the accountants and lawyers." However, that executive is basing his transaction on a great deal of law, tax, and accounting he already knows. However, when dealing in the international arena, managers will need a background on the meaning and reliability of information about the target and country in which it is located. For example, American accounting standards are not universal. In fact, due to generally higher corporate taxes, among other things, Europeans have been accused of playing with reserves in ways to reduce profits (and taxes) in good years. As a result, an income statement of a European company might be virtually meaningless to analysts in the United States.

Finally, an American firm acquiring abroad will encounter a new cultural and ethical framework. Differences in forms of government, legal systems, language, and economic approaches must be considered and generally understood by potential foreign investors. Furthermore, a country's identity is a product of its historical, religious, and social underpinnings, all of which have played a role in the development of that nation's business culture.

Key Areas for the U.S. Acquirer

What are some of the principal issues a U.S. company should know about in connection with the acquisition of a non-U.S. business or a U.S. business with significant foreign assets?

Some of the key areas to focus on are:

- Regulatory requirements and limitations with respect to the acquisition and post-acquisition operations
- Differences in rights accorded to employees
- Sources of overseas financing
- The ability to use foreign assets to support financing from American lenders

Regulatory Constraints

What types of regulatory requirements affect the pre-acquisition stage of a transaction?

The actual purchase of stock or assets and/or any other contractual arrangements between the parties, such as licenses of intellectual property, may require prior foreign government approval or, at minimum, pre-closing, or immediate post-closing, notification. Under the Australian Foreign Takeovers Act, for example, foreign investors acquiring over 15% of an Australian company must notify the Australian Treasury Department for approval, and the Treasury can prohibit any such acquisition it deems would not be in its national interest. In Canada, the recently amended Investment Canada Act requires notification and review of foreign investments in Canadian business where the aggregate value of the target company's assets equals or exceeds $5 million (Cdn.).

Do many countries have local (state or private) ownership requirements for businesses operating within their borders?

Yes, it is common for a government to restrict the percentage of ownership that a foreign investor may hold in a local business. For example, Mexico usually requires that 75% of a company's issued and outstanding stock be held solely by Mexican nationals. Similarly, in nations belonging to the Andean Pact (a regional organization in Latin America), no more than 20% of the capital stock of a company engaged in domestic distribution may be acquired by foreigners.

U.S. and Foreign Laws Affecting U.S. Acquisitions of Foreign Companies/Assets

Are there many restrictions on the form in which one can do business outside the United States?

Generally speaking, one has the same options as those available in the United States, i.e., through a branch or division located in a foreign country, a subsidiary corporation, or a partnership, although it may be necessary to form such corporation or partnership within the foreign country in accordance with local laws. The joint venture is also a popular form of business association. In fact, in some countries, such as most non-market economies, it is the only investment vehicle available to foreigners.

What is the current stance of U.S. antitrust law with regard to foreign acquisitions?

Unless the product manufactured or distributed by the foreign entity enters into the stream of commerce in, or causes a direct anticompetitive effect inside, the United States, U.S. antitrust laws will not apply to the acquisition or to the operations of the entity thereafter. This is true whether the manufacturing or distributing entity is a wholly foreign concern, or a foreign subsidiary of a U.S. corporation. If, however, the product does enter the stream of commerce, or cause an anticompetitive effect, in the United States, then U.S. antitrust laws will apply in the same manner as if the foreign entity was located in the U.S., although, as a practical matter, even where U.S. courts might find that an act overseas is causing an anticompetitive effect within the United States, enforcement may be difficult since the jurisdiction of U.S. courts will usually not reach within the boundaries of another sovereign nation. The Department of Justice has just released a new set of guidelines that deal with these kinds of international antitrust concerns.

What do the new Department of Justice guidelines concerning international antitrust say about U.S. acquisitions of foreign entities?

Early in June 1988, the Department of Justice released draft Antitrust Guidelines for International Operations to replace an earlier Guide issued by the Department 11 years ago.

The Guidelines as proposed in early June 1988 generally follow the Department's 1984 Merger Guidelines and reiterate that the Department's Antitrust Division will seek to prohibit mergers that would create, enhance, or facilitate the exercise of market power. The Guidelines expand the Merger Guidelines's analysis on the treatment of foreign competition, describing four examples of the competitive analysis that the Department would use in mergers involving foreign competitors.

The first case describes an acquisition of a foreign competitor by a U.S. firm. The Guidelines discuss the difficulty in measuring the market power of foreign competitors. Allocating all of a foreign firm's capacity to the U.S. market may be inappropriate if it would have difficulty establishing a reputation for quality or a service and/or distribution network, or if exchange rates are unfavorable. If market share data alone gives a distorted view of the market, the Department will consider qualitative evidence regarding the competitive significance of foreign competitors (e.g., the existence of significant worldwide excess capacity).

The second case discusses how trade restraints such as voluntary export restraints (VER), import quotas, and tariffs affect merger analysis. Foreign competitors will not be excluded from the relevant market solely because their sales into the United States are subject to quotas or VERs, because of the difficulty of assessing the effectiveness and longevity of such restraints and measuring the likely supply responses of competitors not subject to the restraints. However, the competitive significance of a foreign competitor will be discounted in the case of an "effective binding" percentage quota because a reduction in domestic production would lead to a reduction in imports by foreign firms subject to the quota, making collusion among domestic firms more likely. The Guidelines define an "effective" trade restraint as one that cannot be substantially avoided through diversion and arbitrage. A trade restraint is "binding" if firms would sell more than the restraint ceiling if the restraint did not exist. A tariff will be given little significance unless its price level is so prohibitive that imports into the United States would be unprofitable.

The third case involves the acquisition of a foreign potential competitor and is similar to the discussion in the 1977 Guide. The Guidelines note that the merger of a potential competitor will have a significant anticompetitive effect only if: (a) the competitor would enter the market independently in the near future; (b) the market was very highly concentrated; and (c) the foreign competitor was one of only a few firms capable of entering into the U.S. market. Even if the U.S. market was very highly concentrated, eliminating only one of several potential entrants would not have any significant anticompetitive effect. If there are few potential competitors, the Department would consider whether the foreign competitor actually intended to enter the market, past attempts by the competitor to enter the market, and whether independent entry would be profitable.

Finally, the fourth case involves the merger of two foreign firms. The Guidelines note that in evaluating the merger of two foreign firms, the Department would consider the legitimate interest of other nations in determining whether to challenge the transaction. The Department will be more likely to challenge a transaction if the production facilities of the foreign firms are in the United States. If U.S. production facilities constitute a viable business standing alone, the merger might be permitted to go through conditioned on the divestiture of all or a portion of those assets. In addition, the Department may seek the views of the foreign government concerning the impact of various remedies on its national interests.

What are some other examples of U.S. laws that can affect foreign acquisitions?

Of particular concern to an American owner are laws such as the U.S. Foreign Corrupt Practices Act (FCPA), the Anti-Boycott Regulations of the Export Administration Act administered by the U.S. Commerce Department, the Trading with the Enemy Act, and the International Investment and Trade in Services Survey Act of 1976 (IITSSA).

The FCPA requires all U.S. companies to "devise and maintain a system of internal accounting controls sufficient to provide reasonable assurances" that its bookkeeping will adhere to GAAP. It also makes it unlawful for any company "to make use of the mails or any means or instrumentality of interstate commerce corruptly in furtherance of [a payment] . . . while knowing or having reason to know" that the payment will be used to influence a foreign official to assist the company in obtaining or retaining business. The U.S. parent will be responsible for a failure of a foreign subsidiary to comply with these requirements.

The Anti-Boycott Provisions empower the President to issue regulations to prevent U.S. companies engaged in interstate or foreign commerce and their subsidiaries from taking any action intending to comply with a boycott by a foreign country against another country with which the U.S. maintains friendly relations, as long as the company engages in activities in interstate or foreign commerce.

The Trading With the Enemy Act prohibits unlicensed trade between U.S. persons and any individual, partnership, or other body of individuals which is (i) resident within the territory of any nation with which the U.S. is at war or (ii) engaged in business within such territory. Unlicensed trade with corporations incorporated under the laws of an enemy nation is also prohibited, as is unlicensed trade with any party determined to be an ally of a nation with which the U.S. is at war.

The IITSSA requires U.S. companies investing overseas to file certain reports with the Department of Commerce. The filing of reports is mandatory if a U.S. person, including a U.S. corporation, has more than a ten percent ownership interest in a foreign business enterprise and such enterprise has significant assets, sales, or after-tax income. Moreover, there is a proposal which, if adopted, would require a U.S. company that sells service to or purchases services from an unaffiliated foreign person, including legal and accounting services, to file reports.

Are there any future international M&A regulations an acquirer should know about?

The Common Market's main legislative body—the Commission of the European Economic Community—has established a Proposed Regulation on Merger Control, initiated in 1973 and subsequently amended in 1982 and 1984, and still pending. The Proposed Regulation will most likely be adopted when the Common Market becomes an integrated economy. The Proposed Regulation requires prior approval by the Commission of any merger and provides that approval of any transaction that will directly or indirectly enhance the power of a company to hinder effective competition in the Common Market, or a substantial part thereof, will be denied. This supranational body of law operates in concert with, and not in lieu of, the domestic merger laws of each member nation.

The Proposed Regulation defines a "merger" as an act by which a corporation acquires control of one or more corporations. "Control" is defined as the power to determine by contract or right how a corporation shall operate.

FOREIGN EXCHANGE

What are foreign exchange control laws, and how can they impact post-acquisition operations?

Foreign exchange control laws restrict the amount of a country's local currency that can be converted into foreign currencies. These laws can operate either to completely restrict, or partially limit, the ability of a foreign investor to remove any funds from the target's country to his home country ("repatriation") or, if it can withdraw funds, to take its profits in its own currency.

Do foreign exchange control laws include restrictions on repayments of loans to nonlocal parent companies?

Yes, in some cases. For example, Japan's Foreign Exchange Control Law imposes such restrictions for loans above a certain amount. Above this threshold, the loan transaction will require prior Japanese government approval.

In Taiwan, if a subsidiary needs to obtain foreign currency to repay a loan from its foreign parent, the loan agreement itself must be submitted for approval to the Central Bank of China, and only then may the foreign currency be bought.

French regulations require approval from the French exchange control authorities prior to each advance by a foreign company to its French subsidiary or, conversely, for any set off or voluntary prepayment of such loan by the French subsidiary.

Are there any risks involved in doing business in a foreign country because of currency differences between the U.S. parent and a foreign subsidiary or affiliate?

Yes, fluctuating exchange rates pose two types of risk to the investor. First, there is the purely economic risk (i) that a deteriorating exchange rate will require U.S. parent companies to pay more for foreign currency denominated obligations than was originally anticipated when the obligation was approved, or (ii) that a relative increase in the value of a foreign currency will cause U.S. creditors to be repaid a lesser amount in satisfaction of U.S. currency denominated obligations to them. Secondly, there is an accounting risk that the balance sheet, which must express the value of assets and liabilities denominated in a U.S. currency at the exchange rate in place on the balance sheet date, will lose value in the translation from the local currency to U.S. dollars.

How can U.S. owners mitigate the risk inherent to fluctuating exchange rates?

To a large extent, the accounting risk was reduced in 1981 by Statement No. 52 issued by the Financial Accounting Standards Board (FASB), which altered the rule that foreign currency translation gains and losses had to be immediately reported as income. Under Statement No. 52, such gains or losses resulting from the translation of foreign-denominated income statements are now only reflected as an adjustment to stockholders' equity. This change allows a company's lenders or investors to analyze its income statements much more consistently, without worrying as much about the impact of a volatile currency exchange.

In order to alleviate the risk of economic losses due to exchange rate volatility, two forms of hedging contracts have developed: the forward purchase contract and the forward sales contract. Forward purchase contracts are used to protect a U.S. debtor who is obligated to repay a certain amount in a foreign currency at a future date. When the value of the foreign currency rises relative to the U.S. dollar, the debtor will have to spend more dollars to obtain the necessary amount of foreign currency to repay his debt. The forward purchase contract locks up the price at which the debtor may acquire the needed amount of currency at the necessary time for a fixed price which is determined at the time the forward purchase contract is entered into. It is, in effect, a "call" on foreign currency.

Similarly, a U.S. creditor who is afraid that rising exchange rates may cause it to lose the value of its foreign-denominated receivables may hedge against such loss through a forward sales contract. In this case, the creditor contracts to sell the foreign currency to be received at a future date for U.S. dollars at a fixed rate determined at the time the forward contract is entered into. This is a "put" equivalent.

Options to purchase various currencies at a fixed price are available on many foreign and domestic securities exchanges. Currency options are listed on the exchanges at a particular fixed price (the "strike price") in accordance with the length of the option period, which is generally thirty, sixty, or ninety days. The hedging party pays a premium for the ability to purchase the optioned currency at the relevant strike price at any time up to the termination date of the option. If the actual price for one unit of foreign currency exceeds the strike price, the hedging party can exercise its option and receive the currency at a cheaper price per unit. If the actual price never exceeds the strike price for the currency during the option period, the hedging party loses his premium paid for the option, but is not required to take delivery of (or pay for) the actual currency. This feature is the distinguishing factor between forward contracts and options, because forward contracts obligate you to take physical delivery of the currency at an agreed upon date in the future. The degree of certainty of a hedgor's need for a specific amount of foreign currency, plus the difference in the fixed price per unit of foreign currency between forward contracts and options at any given time, will dictate which form of hedging technique will be used.

The foregoing arrangements add to the cost of the overseas investment, and both legal and accounting experts should be consulted with respect to the tax and financial reporting consequences of such hedging methods.

REPATRIATION

After a foreign acquisition, can the investor repatriate profits or investment capital from its business interests located in a foreign country without limitations or restrictions?

As a general proposition, most developing and newly industrialized countries have some form of repatriation restrictions, and some other nations that impose exchange controls also regulate repatriation.

Repatriation restrictions or requirements are usually imposed for the same purposes as exchange controls, i.e., to acquire or retain foreign currency in a country, to monitor foreign investment, and to police potential tax evasion. Many countries regulating repatriations also provide tax incentives for investors to reinvest profits.

Repatriation restrictions are generally accompanied by some form of additional restriction or reporting requirements, such as (i) registration of foreign capital with corresponding restrictions on withdrawal of such capital from the host country; and (ii) notification of amounts of foreign capital invested in the host country. For instance, under Brazil's Profit Remittance Law, registration of foreign investments is required if capital or profit repatriation, royalties, or technical assistance fee remittances are desired. The Central Bank issues a certificate of registration which states the amount of capital brought in—the "registered foreign capital base"—which will determine the subsequent repatriation amounts. Repatriation and remittances are permitted up to a certain percentage of that capital base. Beyond the permitted amounts, a supplementary tax will be imposed. The greater the registered foreign capital base, the higher the remittances and repatriations can be in the foreign currency. If not so registered, the investment will remain in the local currency, and no repatriation will be permitted.

Under Argentina's Foreign Investments Law, even when foreign exchange controls are in force, there is no cap on the amount of profits which may be repatriated by foreign investors, provided the investment has been duly registered at the Foreign

Investments Registry. During a foreign exchange crisis, however, the government is empowered to curtail the ability of foreign investors to freely repatriate profits upon proper notification.

Other Regulatory Concerns

What are some other regulatory concerns involved in a foreign acquisition?

Most other regulations concerning overseas investments can be classified into the following categories: performance requirements, local content regulations, labor requirements, and technology transfer restrictions.

Performance requirements include setting minimum export levels on the one hand and import restrictions on the other. Export level requirements are designed to promote the flow of foreign currency into a country by permitting a foreign person to invest in a particular local enterprise provided a minimum percentage of the finished product manufactured by such enterprise will be exported, rather than distributed locally. Countries may also impose import restrictions, usually expressed as a maximum percentage of the cost of goods produced locally that can be imported, to encourage use of local products and industries.

Local content regulations specify minimum levels of domestic raw materials or component parts to be utilized in manufacturing, limitations on the type of products that can be manufactured in order to encourage local industry, as well as restrictions on product distribution in the country affected and in the world market in order to favor local distributors. Such limitations are often tied to economic incentives, such as government subsidies or tax breaks and, if not imposed by statute, can be negotiated with the host country. Various countries relate local content requirements to specific industries to ensure that local companies do not suffer from the foreign presence.

Countries concerned with unemployment will usually require foreign companies to employ a certain percentage of local labor in unskilled and managerial jobs. Failure by the investor to accede to such demands can cause the host country government to withhold required approval of the acquisition itself. In Mexico, for instance, 90 percent of the employees in any enterprise must be Mexican nationals.

Restrictions on technology transfers usually take the form of limitations on royalty or profit remittances, technical assistance, and payments for transfers of technology, especially between related entities. These regulations are encountered most frequently in the less-developed and newly industrialized nations, though they also exist in any country that desires to promote a particular high technology domestic industry. Technical assistance and royalty payments are frequently subjected to restrictions because they could potentially be used to circumvent dividend remittance regulations, especially to foreign parent companies.

A typical example of such restrictions is the Mexican Law on the Registration and Transfer of Technology and the Use and Exploitation of Patents and Trademarks. This law requires registration of all licensing agreements and prohibits certain agreements that would operate to transfer Mexican intellectual property out of the country.

Another example can be found in Argentina, where a license agreement between a foreign parent company and the local subsidiary requires prior government approval. The approval will be granted if the agreement exhibits the characteristics of an arms length transaction. By contrast, in Brazil, royalty payments between related entities are entirely prohibited when the royalty recipient exercises voting control over the Brazilian subsidiary. Assuming the contract for royalties has received government approval, the subsidiary may only make such payments to the parent's account in Brazil, and must make such payments in cruzados (the Brazilian currency).

Employee Rights

What issues concerning employees should the acquirer be on the look-out for?

First of all, the acquirer should ascertain whether the employees have any rights to approve the proposed acquisition. For example, most workers in Europe have the right to information and consultation when management contemplates major changes or plans. This right emanates from national industry sector collective bargaining agreements that set minimum standards and specific company agreements with employee representatives or trade unions.

Second, the acquirer should familiarize itself with rights of employees with respect to the governance of the enterprise. For example, Europeans have had decades of experience with various forms of so-called "co-determination," imposed by law or won through collective bargaining. Worker participation in management ranges from the right to information, to obligatory consultations, and even to a veto in decisionmaking. The most well-known example of co-determination is found in Germany, where, by law, each company must have two boards, one concerned with operations and the other with more strategic issues. Both boards have employee representatives. In the Netherlands, any company of medium size or larger must consult with its "Works Council" before implementing any decision affecting investments, dismissals, and pensions. The Works Council also has the power to challenge corporate decisions in court if its advice is not followed.

Thirdly, the acquirer should understand the nature of employee benefits afforded in a particular country and take the cost of such benefits into account in evaluating the merits of a potential acquisition. For example, the majority of European workers have, under certain conditions, the right not to be unfairly dismissed. In most European countries, an employee is entitled to redundancy compensation—that is, continued payment even though there may no longer be work for him. Moreover, unemployment compensation rights in the E.C. generally are more substantial than in the U.S. Aside from these legislated rights, an employee can also avail himself of the usual breach of contract remedies, which may include damages and specific performance—forcing the employer to perform on the written contract which is required between the two parties outlining employment terms covering pay scales, work hours, pensions, holidays, and so on. Finally, in several European countries unfair or "abusive" dismissal is actionable, giving the affected employee a claim for damages against the company which dismissed him.

Financing

Once a suitable acquisition of a foreign concern has been identified, how can an acquirer obtain financing for it?

For the most part, the methods of financing an international acquisition will not be very different from those used in a purely domestic deal. The concepts of using bank debt, subordinated debt, the issuance of securities, and securing lenders' interests with a variety of assets can all be used in the international context. How these methods are applied, however, will be impacted by the fact that the acquisition is of a foreign entity or foreign assets.

In considering an international transaction, the potential acquirer may find it necessary to call on a variety of different currencies and to operate within several international jurisdictions. The acquirer must be cognizant that such financial transactions can be affected by regulations imposed by its own government, as well as the governments of the target country, the countries in which investors reside, and the countries in which securities exchanges may be located. Areas of concern will include tax consequences, the ability of investors to repatriate profits, perfecting lenders' security interests, and the like. Similarly, the rules of certain supranational or regional international institutions, such as the United Nations, the GATT, the European Community, or the Organization of American States, may apply.

Happily, there are innovative financing techniques that take into account—and even benefit from—these intercountry peculiarities.

How does an acquirer meet a seller's demand to be paid in a currency that is different from the operating currency of the entity making the payments?

The incompatibility of differing currencies has always ranked high among the classic dilemmas buyers and sellers face when structuring an international transaction.

At the end of the Second World War, many American corporations decided to apply some of their new-found wealth to direct investment in foreign companies, particularly in Europe. To finance these investments, the acquiring corporations found it necessary to come up with large amounts of the functional currency used by the target. To do this, the U.S. entity either had to borrow from unfamiliar banking institutions in the target's home country, which did not always have sufficient funds to meet the purchase price, or go through the cumbersome process of obtaining the necessary funds in U.S. dollars, and converting them into the needed currency, incurring the added expense of an intermediary broker. Since the downfall of the Bretton Woods system in 1971, when the U.S. dollar was taken off the gold standard, potential acquirers have inherited the further difficulty of predicting the rise and fall of fluctuating exchange rates of individual currencies.

It is within this framework that the concept of large offshore international banking markets has developed as an alternative to currency conversion. An example of such a system is the Eurodollar market, that is, the deposit or redeposit of U.S. dollars into a large pool on foreign territory without the conversion of the funds into the local currency. The transaction is recorded by book-entry, and there is no physical importation of the dollars into the foreign country. The pooling entity into which dollars are deposited may be either a foreign branch of a United States banking institution or an independent foreign bank, both of which have become known as "Eurobanks." The Eurobanks can make short, medium, or long term loans for acquisitions or working capital and participate in a wide variety of interbank lending activities. Eurobank deposits also exist for offshore deposits of Japanese yen, French francs, British sterling, and a multitude of other currencies in demand.

Because offshore banking in different currencies has not been heavily regulated by any jurisdiction (for example, Eurobanks are not subject to the same reserve requirements as domestic banks), they are able to have a much higher percentage of bank funds committed to corporate and other loans.

The Eurodollar market has been successful for fostering investment in Europe, but how can the potential acquirer of targets in other parts of the world use offshore markets to finance their acquisitions?

First of all, the Eurocurrency market is not the only site of offshore currency deposits. Another big example of U.S. dollar deposits used for foreign corporate investments is the Asian international currency market, principally located in Singapore and Hong Kong. In Singapore, the government and banking authorities have invented special units of money called Asian Currency Units (ACU's). Banks authorized by the government of Singapore to handle ACU's accept deposits in all foreign currencies to accommodate corporate financing throughout the Orient.

How are interest rates on funds borrowed in the offshore market calculated?

Generally, interest in the Eurocurrency market is tied to the London Interbank Offered Rate (LIBOR), and ACU's are tied to the Singapore Interbank Offered Rate (SIBOR). The interbank offered rate is the interest charged by an offshore depository of a particular currency for funds lent in that currency to another offshore banking facility. This rate is used in international finance in the same way the prime rate is used in the U.S., that is, as a reference rate from which the individual interest rate of a particular loan is created. LIBOR, SIBOR, and other interbank rates can be found listed in many of the world's financial newspapers.

What happens when one bank, whether an onshore or an offshore facility, does not have adequate funds to meet an acquirer's lending needs?

This is the function of the international syndicated loan market, which is particularly useful for onshore banks that must maintain a high ratio of capital reserves to borrowed funds, or banks which do not want to bear the entire risk of a large international loan by themselves.

How do international syndicated loans work?

The principles behind international syndication are generally the same as in a purely domestic syndicated loan, with the added considerations of differing currencies, interest and exchange rates, tax and other government regulatory schemes, supranational currency controls, and the like.

In an international syndication, a group of lenders will pool their funds via a network of selling participations and other agreements, until the required borrowing amount is obtained. There is only one loan agreement between the borrower and the syndication, which is negotiated among the parties to fit the particular needs of the transaction. Funds can flow from either onshore or offshore currency markets.

Typically, the funds borrowed under an international syndicated loan agreement will be subject to five charges to the borrower: (1) interest (which can be tied to an international reference rate such as LIBOR or SIBOR, plus a spread); (2) a management fee, which is paid to the lead bank for arranging and managing the syndication; (3) a commitment fee; (4) an agent's fee, which is usually paid to the lead bank for negotiating the loan and acting as agent on behalf of the other members of the syndication; and (5) any expenses associated with putting together the loan which can include legal and accounting fees, travel costs, and the like.

How do international syndications work mechanically?

There are generally two forms which an international syndication can take. In one, the lenders who are party to the loan agreement commit to lend a stated amount directly to the borrower. The lenders are severally, but not jointly, liable on their lending obligations. Every member of the syndication receives a pro rata portion of the overall receipts from the loan based on its individual commitment of funds.

In the other form of syndication, the lead bank is the only

bank which is bound by a loan agreement to the borrower, and it is solely responsible for the commitment to fund the loan. The lead bank then signs participation or subscription agreements with other lenders who want to participate in the loan as it was negotiated by the lead bank (although, in some cases, it may be necessary for the lead bank to come back to the borrower and ask for amendments which will facilitate the lead bank's finding willing participants). Again, the lead bank will pay the participants their pro rata share of the loan receipts, after deducting whatever management, agent, or subscription fees it may have negotiated.

A very typical situation is where a U.S. company wants to finance the acquisition of another U.S. company which has significant overseas operations. In this case, the lead bank will usually be the primary domestic lender, who may use syndication as a means of bringing in foreign lenders familiar with the business and economic climates of the countries where the target's overseas operations are concentrated. Such syndication will reduce the risk of a U.S. lender which may be otherwise reticent to lend overseas, but there will be a variety of intercreditor issues which will need to be worked out, including the priority of assets securing the acquisition funding.

Are banks the only institutions that can participate in an international loan syndication?

No, recently international syndications have included large scale investors who are willing to take the risk of lending for corporate acquisition or refinancings. Such entities could include insurance companies, pension funds, government-sponsored investment pools, mutual funds, or large corporations. Whether or not a particular entity can participate in a syndicated loan may be governed by national regulations in force in the country where the potential participant is domiciled.

What types of requirements will the syndicating lenders generally ask for from the borrower?

The covenants and representations required by the lenders in an international syndication today are generally not much different from a domestic U.S. syndicator's requirements, although historically the trend has been that loans are unsecured. Today more and more foreign lenders are looking to corporate fixed assets, inventory, and accounts receivable as security for international syndicated loans. Most syndication agreements include, at minimum, a negative pledge clause (where the borrower promises not to encumber any future assets) and a *pari passu* clause, stating that the priority of the lending banks' rights will be *pari passu* (equivalent) as between themselves and other unsecured creditors for the borrower. The loan agreement may also contain financial covenants and other restrictions upon the borrower which are typical in domestic loans.

Are traditional loans the only kind of facilities which can be syndicated?

No, lenders may also wish to use syndication to spread the risk of large letters of credit or guarantees backed by offshore currency deposits, or international commercial paper programs (such as a Euro-CD or Asian Dollar-CD).

Can an acquirer's international merger and acquisition activities be funded by issuing private or public debt securities?

Yes, private or public placements of debt can be effectively utilized by issuers who feel they can attract investors at lower rates than the interbank offered rates, or who desire long-term, fixed-interest debt.

The offshore currency markets have funded individual corporate debt issues in a multitude of currencies, facilitating investment in corporations located all over the world. The most overwhelming example of this has been the Eurobond market, which has been expanding at an astounding rate. The volume of new Eurobond issues has jumped from $25.6 billion (U.S.) in 1981 to $179.9 billion (U.S.) in 1986, although it dropped by almost one-quarter to $135 billion in 1987 due, in part, to the weakness of the U.S. dollar and the October 1987 stock market crash.

Eurobonds can be denominated in any currency, but are issued offshore and are usually structured to be sold outside of the jurisdiction of the nation whose currency is used or where the issuer resides. For example, most countries do not regulate Eurodollar denominated bond issues, and, therefore, careful planning can eliminate many of the regulatory pitfalls which can make the issuance of a bond in one country for distribution in that and other countries undesirable. In the United States, the Securities and Exchange Commission is currently undergoing a review of its policies with respect to unregistered debt issued overseas, but the present policy seems to be that unregistered debt securities may be issued overseas by U.S. issuers, but must not be sold or offered for sale to any U.S. person, or anywhere within the United States, until the passage of a ninety-day "rest abroad" period. The SEC imposes certain requirements on U.S. issuers designed to ensure that no such sales are made during the rest abroad period, including the placement of a restrictive legend on the bond itself.

Offshore bonds are generally issued in bearer form, and many can have provisions that exclude the interest paid thereon from withholding taxes imposed by countries where the bonds are distributed. They may be privately or publicly traded, and often appear on the stock exchanges of the major financial centers from London to Tokyo. Again, the use of international syndicates of underwriters and lending institutions will be instrumental in issuing offshore corporate bonds.

What other types of debt financing are available?

The ability to negotiate lower-interest rates on the part of borrowers, and the need for greater liquidity in offshore currencies on the part of lenders has led to the development of a whole spectrum of international negotiable instruments, the utility of which depends upon the needs and repayment abilities of the borrower.

Negotiable medium or long-term fixed rate notes (FRNs)

are bearer notes evidencing the obligation of the maker of the notes to pay a stated principal amount upon maturity of the note, with periodic payments of interest at a fixed rate. This type of note may be more convenient than conventional bank notes, which usually require the principal to be amortized over the life of the note, rather than deferring payment until maturity. Sale of the FRNs is accomplished through subscription agreements, which provide for investors to buy a note or notes worth a certain stated amount upon fulfillment of various conditions or the making of certain representations and warranties by the issuer. Terms and conditions appear on the reverse of the notes.

Another innovation in the Eurocurrency market is the Euronote, a short-term bearer note evidencing the obligation of the maker to pay the stated principal amount at maturity (generally three to six months). Because of the short term of the notes, Euronote makers can take advantage of lower interest rates in the Eurocurrency markets. The terms and conditions of short-term notes will generally be much less rigorous than those found on FRNs or in bond underwriting agreements.

Suppose an acquirer encounters a group of multinational investors, each of whom desires to lend, and be repaid, with their own currencies rather than offshore funds?

One of the newest innovations in promissory notes is the Medium Term Note (MTN), in which the maker offers a program of notes through one or more agents which place the notes for a commission on a best efforts basis. Initial holders can negotiate the terms of their individual notes to suit such holder's specific repayment requirements with respect to currencies, payment structures or rates of interest. Therefore, using an MTN program a maker may have a series of notes outstanding, each one with a different currency, interest rate calculation, or term. This kind of note program allows an issuer to attract a larger pool of investors by catering to their specific needs at a cost which is often less than a comparable underwriter's fee would be for an underwritten offering.

How can an acquirer obtain the different currencies it needs to meet its obligations to its investors?

It could simply convert the currency generated by the target through a foreign exchange broker for a fee. Another way may be through the use of a swap.

Swaps may be used to exchange currencies or to exchange interest rates or they may combine the two. A Swap Agreement for currencies would be a contract calling for both parties to supply each other with a stated amount of currency at specific intervals. For example, one party might agree to pay the other in Eurodollars or Luxembourg francs in exchange for delivery to it of an equivalent amount of German marks and French francs.

Similarly, the exchanging party may not be a bank, but a large corporation with access to various currencies, perhaps through its own subsidiaries. This corporation may have a Eurobond issue outstanding on which it is obligated to pay a fixed rate of interest. In this case an Interest Rate Swap Agreement may be in order, in which the corporation and another party agree to pay to each other a sum equal to the interest which would have accrued on a specific amount over a specific period of time at the desired rate.

For example, take a company with outstanding loans bearing interest at LIBOR plus 1/4%, payable to one investor in German marks and another investor in French francs, and another company which pays interest in U.S. dollars at a fixed rate (say, 8 1/2%) to its Eurobondholders. A swap could be structured so that the first company receives from the second company a payment in German marks and French francs equal to the interest it must pay its investors in exchange for Eurodollar payments to the second company of the interest which would accrue on the same principal amount at the fixed rate of 8 1/2%. This is a combined Interest Rate and Currency Swap, which meets the first company's requirements for repayment to its investors. So long as the floating rate does not fall significantly below the fixed rate, the foregoing is a good business transaction for the first company.

Swap agreements should generally be for shorter terms

to protect against significant fluctuations in interest rates or currency exchange rates which can throw off the economics of a swap transaction, with periodic rollover provisions allowing for the continuation of the agreement on the same or renegotiated terms of exchange. From a legal point of view, swap agreements are nothing more than international contracts which will be governed under the contract laws of whichever country the parties choose the governing of the contract.

Another financing technique is the conversion of debt for equity, or "debt/equity swap." How does it work and when is its use appropriate?

Debt for equity conversions evolved as one solution to the paucity of foreign exchange available to a debtor country for external debt payments. The conversion allows the debtor country to discharge foreign denominated debt through payments in local currency. Some countries that have formal debt for equity conversion programs are Chile, Mexico, Costa Rica, Ecuador, the Philippines, Brazil, and Argentina.

The basic steps in a debt/equity swap are (i) the foreign commercial bank creditor will either decide to invest in a local business located in the debtor country, or sell its loan asset to a third party investor at a discount; (ii) the bank or the investor then redeems the credit for its designated value in the debtor's local currency, and (iii) the bank or the investor subsequently invests the proceeds in a local enterprise.

The investor generally has one of two reasons for engaging in a swap transaction, i.e., the desire to make a new investment in the debtor country, or the desire to recapitalize an existing subsidiary or affiliate in the debtor country. In both cases, the highly favorable discount rate will substantially reduce the cost of equity to the investor. On the converse side, the debtor country wishes to reduce its external debt and encourage investment in its economy. Moreover, the debtor country can create value for itself, if it can retire its debt at a price below its face value.

Resources derived from such transactions are intended to enhance the debtor country's economy. As a result, certain types of investments, such as those which increase exports of the debtor country, bring new technology into the country, or finance industry expansion or new product development, are given preferential consideration.

Security Interests in Foreign Assets

Can acquirers obtain security interests on the assets of foreign companies to finance acquisitions?

Yes. Today, most foreign countries have the same or analogous concepts to the U.S. regarding security interests on assets to serve as collateral for borrowing.

There are many differences, however, on the types of assets that can be secured, the methods of accomplishing such a transaction, the type of notice required, if any, and to whom notice must be given. Thus, it is imperative that local counsel be enlisted to complete these transactions. In the United Kingdom, the method of securitization is similar to that employed in the U.S. A fixed charge (or mortgage interest) is granted over specific real or leasehold property interests, fixed assets, and goodwill, and a floating charge (or after-acquired property security interest) is granted on accounts receivable and inventory.

France is an example of a country in which securitization becomes more problematic. A *contract hypothecaire* is used to grant a mortgage on real property, while a *nantissement de fonds de commerce* is the French document granting a security interest in tangible or intangible fixed assets. It becomes effective upon the occurrence of a default by the borrower. The *nantissement de fonds de commerce,* however, does not include accounts receivable or inventory, and, while it may be legally possible to cause such items to be included using additional security documents, such a plan may not always be practical, because of the cumbersome nature of perfection. In the case of accounts receivable, perfection requires that notice of the security interest be sent to each account party by a French process server upon establishment of the account. In the case of inventory, the only method of perfecting such an interest is by possession, i.e., a field warehousing arrangement whereby a third party is hired to keep custody of the inventory on behalf of the secured party.

In Japan, civil liens (*sakidori tokken*) and possessory liens (*riyachiken*) are only given by law, and cannot be established by contract or by judicial decree. A Japanese entity may assign rights it has in real property or movable chattels (including inventory) by contract, but, in the case of chattels, in order for such an assignment to be valid against third parties, the secured party must be in possession, and the consent of the assignor must be certified by a notary public or post office. Accounts receivable may be pledged as security in Japan, provided that there is nothing to the contrary contained in the agreement between the original parties establishing the account.

What happens if a country does not permit a floating security interest on after-acquired property?

As previously discussed, in contrast to the customary U.S. practice of obtaining "floating" liens on assets not as yet acquired, many countries do not permit this type of security interest. To include new assets as collateral, the parties must enter into additional security agreements and comply with all formalities imposed by the governing law of the country every time a newly-acquired asset is to be included in the lender's security.

International LBOs

Can the concept of a leveraged buyout be applied in the international context?

Yes, the leveraged management buyout is becoming an accepted acquisition structure in several European nations, particularly in the United Kingdom, France, and the Federal Republic of Germany. It is a useful tool both for large family-owned enterprises which were established after the Second World War and where the owners are now reaching retirement age, and, in the case of countries like France, where privatization of large state-owned conglomerates has occurred, for the divestiture of unrelated businesses, which was not permitted under state ownership.

What would the structure of a leveraged buyout look like, for example, in a management LBO in France?

The structure employed in France would not be vastly different from the structure one would use in the United States, with certain exceptions resulting from the corporate and business laws of France. The financing will usually entail a tripartite structure comprised of (i) senior debt from a traditional lending institution which may or may not be collateralized; (ii) middle-tier financing including subordinated or convertible debt at a higher fixed rate of interest; and (iii) straight equity investment by the managers and other investors. Western European law is, for the most part, sufficiently nonrestrictive to allow creativity in structuring a foreign LBO.

Other than the perfection of security interests, which has already been discussed, are there any other problems which a senior lender seeking security might face?

If shares of the foreign parent company's stock are pledged to a French lender, the lender may not be able to foreclose upon such shares in the event of a default without the prior approval of the French government. In practice this risk has not been an impediment to accepting such pledges of foreign stock.

Can the target company in France guarantee the debt of the foreign parent for acquisition funding?

This sort of upstream guarantee is a problem, because the 1981 French Company Law prohibits a French corporation from advancing moneys, making loans, or facilitating security interests with the intent of aiding a third party to purchase such French corporation's own stock. There is an exemption, however, for loans to employees of the French company. This problem goes away if the LBO is structured as an asset deal, but there are significant tax consequences in the event of an asset transaction, so the potential investor should be very careful in his analysis of which structure to use. In the case of an international LBO, as with all international transactions, consulting with local counsel in the country where the target is located is very important.

INTERNATIONAL TAX CONSIDERATIONS

Introduction

This section covers basic issues that affect the various kinds of acquisition and disposition activities carried on in the United States by foreign nationals and companies ("inbound acquisitions"), and foreign acquisition and disposition activities carried on by U.S. nationals and companies ("outbound acquisitions"). While we will speak generally about the tax laws of many countries, the principal focus of discussion here will be the tax laws of the United States as they apply to transnational relationships.

This section will be divided into three parts:

- a discussion of the general tax rules that apply to inbound and outbound acquisitions;
- a general discussion of the U.S. tax rules that ought to be considered by a foreign person planning to acquire a U.S. business; and
- a general discussion of the U.S. tax rules that ought to be considered by an acquirer planning to acquire a foreign business from a U.S. seller.

This section will not discuss U.S. tax consequences to foreign investors of owning U.S. portfolio investments or U.S. properties unless such holdings are directly related to acquisition of operating businesses. It is assumed that the reader is generally familiar with the basic U.S. federal income tax principles that apply to acquisitions in the domestic context. (See Chapter 5.)

What are the fundamental tax considerations for an acquirer that apply specifically to international acquisitions?

Generally, whether the transaction involves an inbound or an outbound acquisition, the basic rules governing the tax treatment of the parties involved extend above and beyond those that would apply in the domestic context. As a result of these rules, the tax planning in the international context will become more complex.

The most important thing that a buyer or a seller of a business with international components must bear in mind is that at every stage of planning, consideration must be given to the tax rules of each of the countries involved, as well as to the manner in which their tax systems overlap and interact. It is not uncommon to have three or four different tax systems governing parts or all of a single transaction, and this may present both opportunities and traps. Because of the disparities in the tax laws, and because of the existence in many cases of income tax treaties between the countries, it may be possible to structure a transaction so that it results in less overall tax cost than would be the case if the transaction were undertaken in a single country. On the other hand, because there is often overlapping taxing jurisdiction, it is possible, in the absence of careful planning, that the overall tax cost may be greater than if only a single country were involved.

In focusing on the U.S. tax aspects of a transaction, several principles must be borne in mind. First, the United States imposes very different tax rules on individuals and corporations depending upon whether they are classified as "U.S. persons" or "foreign persons" for U.S. tax purposes. For this reason, a determination should be made early in the planning process as to the classification of each of the parties and entities involved in a transaction.

Second, generally speaking, the United States imposes an overall income tax on the worldwide income of individuals who are citizens or residents of the United States and on corporations that are formed in the United States. In contrast, non-resident alien individuals and foreign corporations are not subject to U.S. taxation except on income that is "sourced" in the United States. Therefore, once it is determined whether a party is a U.S. person or a foreign person, each item of income must be analyzed to determine whether it has its source in the United States or outside the United States, i.e., is domestic source income or foreign source income.

Third, foreign persons generally are subject to a gross percentage withholding tax on certain kinds of domestic source passive income. The chief exception to this is in the case of foreign persons that are engaged in a U.S. trade or business (or maintain a U.S. permanent establishment) upon income that is effectively connected with this U.S. trade or business or permanent establishment. In such a case, the foreign person will pay a net income tax on this trade or business income in much the same way that a U.S. person would on its overall income. Additionally, for U.S. non-trade or business income, the taxation will depend on the precise class or category of such income, e.g., dividends, interests, royalties, etc. Therefore, determinations will have to be made as to the characterization of any U.S. source income on a fairly specific basis.

As we will see, there are numerous other very significant issues of U.S. international taxation that will have to be understood and taken into account in undertaking any inbound or outbound acquisition.

Income Tax Treaties

What is the role of income tax treaties in the acquisition process?

Income tax treaties play a major role in structuring international transactions, generally by minimizing the overall tax costs that may be imposed. When a tax treaty is applicable to a particular transaction, it is often useful to review the transaction in light of the treaty before focusing on the laws of the particular countries. In many cases, the treaty becomes the "tax law of the transaction."

Treaty-related tax planning consists of analyzing the alternative structures for the chain of entities, selecting the tax jurisdictions, and defining the sources and classes of income. At each stage, tax treaties may be utilized to avoid double taxation, or, in certain circumstances, triple taxation.

Most tax treaties provide for the reduction or elimination of withholding taxes on portfolio income, such as interest, dividends, and royalties, by the country from which such income is derived (the so-called country of source), and prohibit the country of source from taxing business income of an enterprise resident in the other country, unless the enterprise has a "permanent establishment" in the source country. For example, if a foreign entity is likely to be engaged in business activities in the United States, consideration should be given to placing those activities in an entity which is a resident of a country that has a tax treaty with the U.S., in order to avoid the U.S. taxation of the activity. Furthermore, since most tax treaties provide that capital gains derived by a resident of one country from sources in another contracting country will be exempt from tax by such other country, such a strategy makes even more sense.

What are income tax treaties?

Income tax treaties, or income tax conventions, are international agreements entered into between two or more sovereign nations (and sometimes extended to dependent territories) for the purpose of reducing double taxation on income generated by residents of one of these countries from sources located in the other contracting country. In the United States, an income tax treaty is signed by the Executive Branch (usually by the Secretary of State), and becomes effective, unless modified, after the U.S. Senate ratifies the treaty. As of February 1988, the U.S. had 37 income tax treaties in force.

Under the United States Constitution, treaties are the supreme law of the land and rank equally with any federal statute. If the terms of a treaty conflict with a federal statute, whichever was most recently adopted will generally control. Case law holds, however, that Congress must clearly specify an intent to override a tax treaty for a later-enacted statute to prevail over the treaty. A notable example of a general treaty override is a provision enacted in the Foreign Investment in Real Property Tax Act of 1980, as amended (FIRPTA), which provides that foreign investors will be subject to U.S. taxation upon the disposition of a United States real property interest (which includes equity interests in U.S. real property holding corporations), regardless of any tax treaty that provides to the contrary.

In addition to their role in reducing double taxation, income tax treaties provide, through the "competent authority" mechanism, a means to resolve disputes between two tax jurisdictions that claim the right to tax income that arises in one or both of these countries. Treaties may assist in the prevention of fiscal evasion, for instance, by allowing tax information exchanges between the tax authorities of the contracting countries. Sometimes income tax treaties are used to advance foreign or economic policies of one or both of the countries, for instance, when one of the countries is committed to allow tax breaks for capital investments in preferred industries in the other country.

Can a taxpayer avail itself of a particular tax treaty by incorporating a subsidiary in the treaty country?

Tax treaties ordinarily apply to, and can be invoked by, persons who are residents of the respective treaty countries. Although the definition of a "person" may vary from treaty to treaty, it usually includes individuals, corporations, partnerships, estates, and trusts.

A corporation incorporated in a treaty jurisdiction will in most circumstances be considered a resident of such jurisdiction. Generally speaking, by establishing a corporation resident in a treaty country, investors from another country can subject their investments to the benefits available under that country's tax treaties. However, such so-called "treaty shopping" has, in recent years, been the subject of increasing scrutiny, and restrictions have been imposed by the U.S. Department of Treasury and the Congress. Specific actions taken have included (i) the termination of existing treaties with tax haven jurisdictions; (ii) the renegotiation of existing treaties; (iii) the ratification of new treaties that contain "limitation of benefits" provisions; and (iv) the amendment of the U.S. tax code to allow treaty benefits only to bona fide residents of a treaty country (see the discussion on the branch profits tax at page 832).

Entity Classification

How important is the issue of entity classification in the international context?

The question of whether a particular entity should be classified as a corporation or a pass-through entity (i.e., partnership or trust) for U.S. income tax purposes is of crucial importance in the international context. For inbound transactions, if a pass-through entity is operating a U.S. business, the foreign owner will be subject to regular U.S. income tax at graduated rates. In contrast, if the entity is classified as a corporation, the foreign owner will be subject to a withholding tax on dividend income at a flat rate (30% or reduced treaty rate). Depending upon the application of the branch profits tax, to be discussed later, the overall treatment in these two cases may be quite different. In outbound transactions, if a foreign entity is characterized as a corporation, its U.S. owners may be able to avoid being taxed currently on the income being earned abroad. If, instead, the entity is a pass-through entity, the U.S. owners will be taxed currently under any circumstances. In addition to the above, there are numerous other consequences of the classification of domestic and foreign entities as corporations, trusts, or partnerships.

How does the United States classify an entity that is formed under foreign law?

The Internal Revenue Service has published a list of certain foreign entities and their classification for U.S. tax purposes. With respect to entities not named on this list, the proper classification of a foreign enterprise under U.S. law may occasionally be a mystical task because foreign countries have forms of business entities that do not have U.S. equivalents.

The U.S. classification principles applicable to foreign entities provide that, as a starting point, local law (i.e., foreign law) will determine the legal relationships among the entity and its members, and among the entity, its members and the public at large. When these legal relationships are ascertained, U.S. tax principles will classify an entity as a corporation, a partnership, or a trust. It is generally perceived that the Internal Revenue Service does not apply classification principles to foreign entities in the same manner as it does to U.S. entities. Therefore, caution must be used before assuming that foreign entity would be treated for U.S. tax purposes in a similar manner to its foreign treatment. In addition, one should consider whether a tax treaty prohibits the U.S. from reclassifying the entity for federal tax purposes because of a specific definition in the treaty.

For classification purposes, when is a person considered "foreign"?

A "U.S. person" is either an individual who is a citizen or resident of the United States, a domestic corporation, a domestic partnership, or a domestic trust or estate. A foreign person is a person who is not a U.S. person. Under the above definition, a resident alien individual can be a "U.S. person." Tax treaties may provide different rules.

When does an alien individual become a U.S. resident?

An alien individual is treated as a resident of the United States for a calendar year if such individual satisfies either of the following two tests: (i) the alien is a lawful permanent resident of the United States; or (ii) subject to certain exceptions, the alien is physically present in the United States for 183 days or more during the calendar year, or spends 183 days or more, calculated under a certain formula, in the United States in a 3-year period.

An individual who is a U.S. resident is taxed on his worldwide income regardless of its source, and is entitled to claim deductions and credits against his worldwide income. If a resident alien is subject to foreign taxes on his foreign source income, he or she will be able to claim a foreign tax credit or deduction against his or her U.S. tax liability. Tax treaties may provide "tie breaker" rules in situations in which an individual is treated as a resident by more than one country.

What is a U.S. or a domestic corporation?

Under U.S. principles, all organizations incorporated under the law of the United States or of any State (including the District of Columbia) are treated as domestic corporations for federal tax purposes. For certain purposes, corporations organized in or under the laws of Guam, American Samoa, Northern Mariana Islands, or the Virgin Islands will not be treated as foreign corporations.

What is a dual resident company?

As far as the United States is concerned, a corporation incorpo-rated in the U.S. is a U.S. corporation. This corporation, howev-er, could at the same time be treated by country X as a country X corporation, if country X employed different criteria to deter-mine whether corporations are resident for its tax purposes. In particular, some countries, including the United Kingdom and Australia, treat corporations as domestic corporations if they are managed and controlled therein. Thus, a U.S. corporation that is managed and controlled in one of these jurisdictions can also be a resident of the United Kingdom or Australia under their respective rules. Such companies are referred to as "dual resident companies." Although at one time there could be cer-tain tax advantages in using such dual resident companies in lieu of corporations subject to "domestic" tax in only one coun-try (such as, the deduction of financing costs on the same loan in two jurisdictions), these advantages have been substantially eliminated in 1986.

Can a foreign corporation be treated as a domestic corporation for U.S. tax purposes?

Yes. Code Section 269B provides that if a domestic corporation and a foreign corporation are "stapled entities," the foreign cor-poration will be treated as a domestic corporation. The term "stapled entities" means any group of 2 or more entities if more than 50 percent in value of the beneficial ownership in each such entities consists of stapled interests (i.e., if by reason of form of ownership, restrictions on transfer, or other terms or conditions, in connection with the transfer of one of such inter-ests the other such interests are also transferred or required to be transferred).

More importantly, there are two situations in which an election may be made to treat a foreign corporation as if it were a domestic corporation. One involves an election under Section 1504(d) of the Code to treat certain Canadian or Mexican sub-sidiaries of a U.S. parent as domestic corporations eligible to be included in the parent's consolidated return. The other involves an election under FIRPTA. FIRPTA provides that a foreign corporation holding a United States real property interest may elect to be treated as a domestic corporation (Section 897(i)). FIRPTA and the 897(i) election are discussed in greater detail later in this section.

Are U.S. persons and foreign persons treated alike under U.S. tax rules?

U.S. taxation of U.S. persons and foreign persons differs in a number of significant ways. The most noticeable difference concerns the scope of taxation; while a U.S. person is subject to U.S. taxation on its worldwide income *regardless* of where it was derived (or sourced) and the class of income, the United States will tax a foreign person only on income which has a substantial nexus to the U.S. The nexus is generally defined with reference to a U.S. source or business. Often, the U.S. will not exercise its taxing jurisdiction over certain kinds of U.S.-related income that are generated by foreign persons, due to administrative difficulties concerning collection of the tax from foreign investors.

Would U.S. acquirers of foreign targets be indifferent as to whether they receive foreign or domestic source income?

Source of income (and loss), whether U.S. or foreign, can be a critical factor in determining the U.S. income tax liability of both U.S. and foreign persons. In the case of U.S. taxpayers, foreign source income is often desirable because it increases their ability to offset foreign taxes against U.S. taxes under the foreign tax credit mechanism. On the other hand, if a loss can be sourced in the United States, the U.S. tax liability on domestic source income can be reduced and more foreign tax credits can be claimed against U.S. tax liability on foreign sources. In the case of a foreign taxpayer over whom the United States asserts only a limited taxing authority, foreign source income would likely escape U.S. taxation altogether. Accordingly, in general, there is a strong incentive to convert U.S. source income into foreign source income.

This preference for foreign source income and domestic

source loss was certainly prevalent in tax planning prior to the Tax Reform Act of 1986. By reducing U.S. domestic tax rates from 46% on corporations and 50% on individuals to 34% and 28%, respectively, thus making the U.S. something of a "tax haven" compared to other industrialized countries, as well as tightening the foreign tax credit rules, the 1986 Tax Act has changed the equation very substantially. Therefore, in the current environment, it is important that consideration be given to the applicable foreign tax rates in each case in addition to the regular evolution of the source rules.

How is the source of most investment income determined?

Generally, interest or dividends paid by a U.S. person will be U.S. source income, and therefore subject to a 30% (or lower treaty rate) withholding tax. Exceptions are provided where the U.S. payor meets certain foreign income tests. Rentals or royalties are generally sourced in the U.S. if they are paid for the use of tangible or intangible property which is located in the United States.

Note that U.S. source interest income of a foreign person is not subject to a U.S. withholding tax if it qualifies as "portfolio interest." Generally, among the other requirements for interest to qualify as portfolio interest, the foreign lender must be neither a bank extending an ordinary loan nor a party that is related to the U.S. borrower.

How do you determine the source of gain derived from the sale of stock of a foreign or a U.S. entity?

Income derived by a U.S. resident from the sale of personal property, tangible or intangible, is generally sourced in the United States. Similarly, income derived by a nonresident from the sale of personal property, tangible or intangible, is generally treated as foreign source income. This is called the residence-of-the-seller rule.

Under the residence-of-the-seller rule, when an individual

nonresident who does not have a U.S. office to which the sale is attributed disposes of stock of a domestic corporation, the sale will generate foreign source income, gain, or loss. Similarly, when a U.S. resident individual sells stock in a foreign corporation and the sale is not attributable to a foreign office of the seller, the income, gain, or loss generated by the sale will be U.S.-sourced.

A sale by a U.S. corporation of stock in an 80% owned foreign subsidiary that is engaged in the active conduct of a trade or business which conduct takes place in the foreign country from which the affiliate has derived more than 50% of its gross income for its last three taxable years will be sourced in that foreign country. The practical result of this exception to the residence-of-seller rule is that in such case, this income will be treated for U.S. tax purposes as foreign source income, and the seller will be able to credit foreign taxes against his U.S. tax liability. If this income were treated as U.S. source income, such as in the case of a 50% owned foreign entity, foreign taxes could not be credited against the U.S. tax liability.

Note that for individuals, the definition of the term "U.S. resident" for sourcing purposes does not equal the definition of a "U.S. resident" for other tax purposes. The Code contains an anti-abuse rule that is intended to prevent a U.S. person from claiming to be a nonresident of the United States for income that is sourced in a tax haven country. A tax haven is a sovereign tax jurisdiction which generally imposes only minimal or no tax on income, capital, or estates of nonresidents of such jurisdiction (e.g., the Cayman Islands, the Bahamas, the Channel Islands).

INBOUND ACQUISITIONS

Introduction

An inbound acquisition is an acquisition of a U.S. enterprise by a non–U.S. person. This acquisition may involve financing through loans made by financial institutions resident in either the acquirer's own country or from third country residents or from U.S. financial institutions, or a possible joint venture with

U.S. or foreign equity partners. In debt-financed acquisitions, revenues received from the U.S. enterprise will likely be used to pay off acquisition indebtedness. The acquirers may wish at some point in the future to dispose of the entity or parts thereof in a transaction that will generate a profit over the acquisition price. For these and other reasons, U.S. tax considerations may be important in every stage of the acquisition and disposition process.

This section will discuss the basic U.S. tax consequences applicable to a foreign corporation or a nonresident alien engaged in M&A activities in the U.S., with particular attention to financing the acquisition and planning for eventual disposition.

Basic U.S. Income Tax Principles

What are the basic U.S. income tax principles that determine the overall tax burden on U.S. income and repatriated funds of a foreign investor?

A foreign corporation not engaged in a U.S. trade or business is taxable at a flat rate of 30% (or reduced treaty rate), which is collected by withholding at source, on its U.S. source passive income (such as interest, rents, royalties, dividends, premiums). A foreign corporation engaged in a U.S. trade or business, which does not maintain an office within the United States, is subject to a U.S. net income tax at graduated rates on its U.S. source income that is effectively connected with its conduct of the trade or business in the United States. The latter tax may be referred to as the regular income tax. In addition, a foreign corporation is subject to the branch profits tax (BPT) rules on its "effectively connected earnings and profits," subject to certain adjustments. (The BPT will be discussed on page 832.) If a foreign corporation owns an interest in a partnership (domestic or foreign) engaged in a trade or business in the United States, withholding under the Code may be required on distributions to the corporation. Capital gains, whether short-term or long-term, are not subject to U.S. tax if the foreign corporation is not engaged in a U.S. trade or business, or if the interest disposed of is not a real estate asset subject to FIRPTA.

A nonresident alien individual, not engaged in a U.S. trade or business, will be subject to U.S. tax at the rate of 30% (or reduced treaty rate) on his U.S. source passive income, and at a rate of 30% on net capital gains derived from United States sources provided that he spent 183 days or more in the United States within the taxable year of sale. In addition, if a nonresident alien is engaged in a U.S. trade or business within a taxable year but does not maintain an office in the U.S., then any U.S. source income effectively connected with that trade or business will be subject to U.S. tax at graduated rates. Withholding rules may apply to distributions with respect to partnership interests held by such individual. Like a foreign corporation, if the nonresident alien is careful enough not to fall within the above restrictions, no U.S. tax will be imposed on his U.S. source capital gains.

If a nonresident alien or a foreign corporation engaged in a U.S. trade or business maintains an office in the United States, specified categories of such person's foreign source income are also treated as income effectively connected with a U.S. trade or business.

Tax treaties generally modify the rules described above as they apply to treaty country residents. In particular, tax treaties reduce withholding tax rates and limit taxation of business income to income attributable to a permanent establishment.

What should be clear from the above discussion is that income from operations of the acquired U.S. target will ordinarily be subject to U.S. taxation, even if carried on directly by the foreign acquirer. On the other hand, with proper planning of their U.S. activities, foreign investors may find it relatively easy to avoid U.S. tax on capital gains (other than from the disposition of United States real property interests) derived from the sale of their interest in the U.S. activity.

When is a foreign person treated as engaged in a U.S. trade or business?

Neither the Code nor the regulations thereunder define when a foreign person is engaged in a U.S. trade or business. The determination is generally based on the facts and circumstances of each case and, in particular, on the level of the taxpayer's activities in the U.S. If the U.S. activities of the foreign person are not considerable, continuous, and regular, it will probably be considered as not engaged in a U.S. trade or business. Business activities of an agent in the U.S. will be attributed to its principal. U.S. real estate gains received by a foreign person will be deemed to be income effectively connected with a U.S. trade or business (see discussion of FIRPTA on page 837). Gains from U.S. securities trading activities for the taxpayer's own account are generally not trade or business income.

What issues should an investor consider when undertaking foreign debt financing to acquire a U.S. business?

Foreign financing to acquire U.S. business operations can take many forms. It may take the form of an investment of equity or debt, and it may involve only one foreign lender in a single-lender transaction or many lenders in an offshore public debt offering. Single-lender loans can be made from foreign banks acting in the ordinary course of their business or from foreign non-banking institutions. In addition, loans can be made by foreign shareholders of the corporation. Publicly offered debt obligations may be in bearer form to protect investor anonymity but can also take place in registered form. Among these alternatives one may find various forms of syndicated loans and private debt placements to various investors. In addition, foreign financing may be in the form of short term obligations, such as a Eurocommercial paper, and long term debt. Finally, the debt issued may be in the form of straight debt or in the form of convertible debt or debt with equity features.

An entire chapter could be written on the tax treatment of transnational financing. Very broadly, when a foreign acquirer wishes to raise debt capital outside the U.S., he should consider the following issues:

1. Whether the acquisition indebtedness should be incurred by the U.S. target corporation or by the foreign acquirer. In this regard, the acquirer should weigh the relative

values of the interest deductions in the U.S. and in the foreign jurisdiction.

2. Whether the interest paid to the foreign lender will be free of U.S. withholding tax by virtue of a treaty exemption or a statutory provision (e.g., the "portfolio interest exemption"), or subject to a reduced withholding rate. Note that investors in the Eurobond market generally require that interest payments be free of U.S. withholding tax. Furthermore, consideration should be given to the risk of change of law or treaty termination with respect to U.S. withholding tax liability.

3. Whether a back-to-back loan structure to a U.S. corporation to take advantage of a tax treaty or statutory tax exemption will be respected by the IRS.

4. Whether debt with equity features will be respected as debt for U.S. tax purposes.

Branch Profits Tax

Why should an acquirer be concerned about the Branch Profits Tax?

The issue whether to hold the acquired U.S. business through a U.S. or foreign corporation is often a major consideration in the acquisition process. If a U.S. business is held through a foreign corporation, the foreign corporation may be subject to a second layer of tax in the form of the branch profits tax. If the U.S. business is held through a U.S. corporation, the tax cost may in certain circumstances be substantially reduced.

What is the Branch Profits Tax?

The BPT imposes a second layer of tax on profits of U.S. branches or other U.S. operations of a foreign corporation. The BPT was introduced in 1986 principally to duplicate, in the case of U.S. branches of foreign corporations, the second level of tax on dividends and interest paid by U.S. subsidiaries of foreign corporations.

If one is concerned as to whether the BPT applies to certain U.S. operations, one should focus on these two rules: first, the BPT does not apply to foreign individuals engaged directly or indirectly through foreign partnerships in a trade or business in the U.S., and second, foreign corporations whose U.S. investments or contacts do not amount to a trade or business (or, in the case of a treaty protected corporation, to a U.S. permanent establishment) are not subject to the BPT. Nonetheless, the BPT provisions contain certain anti-treaty shopping rules that will affect even foreign corporations that are not engaged in a trade or business in the U.S. to the extent that they receive dividends or interest from a foreign corporation that is engaged in a trade or business in the U.S. Thus, if an entity is neither a foreign corporation nor engaged (or deemed to be engaged) in a U.S. trade or business, and it does not receive dividends or interest from the U.S. operations of such a corporation, the following discussion will not pertain to its operations.

On the other hand, if one's U.S. operations might be subject to the BPT, the next two questions will provide a short road map on the effects of the BPT on the regular operations of a U.S. branch of a foreign corporation and on the financing of a branch of a foreign corporation.

What are the BPT rules concerning the U.S. operations of a foreign corporation?

Starting in 1987, whenever a foreign corporation operates or acquires an unincorporated business (including a partnership interest) in the U.S., consideration should be given to the BPT consequences of such operation. Remember that under the regular rules, the foreign corporation pays one income tax on its "effectively connected" U.S. trade or business income. The BPT is an additional tax equal to 30% (or a reduced treaty rate) of any foreign corporation's "dividend equivalent amount" for any taxable year in which such corporation is engaged, or deemed to be engaged, in a trade or business in the U.S. A foreign corporation that is subject to the full regular tax rate and the BPT may pay an effective U.S. tax rate of approximately 54% — 34% + 30% × [100 − (100 × 34%)].

The "dividend equivalent amount" includes the "effectively connected earnings and profits" (E&P) of such corporation for the taxable year, as adjusted downwards or upwards to reflect certain increases or decreases in the "U.S. net equity" for the year. In effect, the statute treats a decrease in U.S. net equity as a withdrawal of earnings by the foreign parent, and an increase in U.S. net equity as a contribution of capital to the U.S. branch. The use of the E&P account as the tax base was designed to approximate dividend treatment.

"U.S. net equity" is any money and the aggregate adjusted bases of the foreign corporation's property treated as connected with the conduct of a trade or business in the U.S., less the foreign corporation's liabilities connected with such operation. Investments in business assets will increase the net equity amount and repatriations will decrease such amount, but only to include previous increases of net equity that reduced earnings and profits.

For the BPT to apply to a particular branch of a foreign corporation, such branch must generate "effectively connected" income. Generally, income will be treated as effectively connected if the corporation is engaged in an active business, if the corporation is a partner in a partnership engaged in a U.S. trade or business, or if the corporation invests in U.S. real property with respect to which the foreign corporation has elected under Section 897(d) to be taxed on a net basis, or with respect to a gain from a disposition of a U.S. real property interest (other than interest in a U.S. real property holding corporation). E&P includes certain items not subject to the regular corporate tax, such as tax exempt income. Distributions by the foreign corporation within the taxable year will not reduce E&P for the purposes of the BPT.

If a treaty country corporation earns effectively connected income that is exempt from U.S. tax because such foreign corporation does not maintain a permanent establishment in the U.S., such earnings will not be subject to the BPT, provided that the foreign corporation is a "qualified resident" of the treaty country, as defined on page 836. In addition, BPT rules may be modified in other ways by an applicable tax treaty (see discussion on pages 835–836).

How do the BPT rules affect the financing for a U.S. branch of a foreign corporation?

Generally, if a U.S. branch of a foreign corporation borrows money from a foreign lender, the branch (but in practice, the foreign corporation) will be required to withhold 30% (or reduced treaty rate) of the gross interest paid to the foreign lender. Certain Code provisions, such as the portfolio interest exemption and the bank deposit exemption, may apply to eliminate the withholding requirement. The tax treaties that will determine the lower rate of withholding on interest paid by the U.S. branch will be the treaty between the U.S. and the country of the foreign lender and the treaty between the U.S. and the country of the foreign corporation that maintains the U.S. branch. Section 884, however, curtails treaty benefits in case of treaty shopping (see discussion on page 836). The effect of the withholding requirement can be to increase the cost of borrowing from foreign lenders that do not qualify for an exemption from U.S. taxation and can not obtain complete foreign tax credit benefits in their own country.

Interest expense incurred by the foreign corporation on its worldwide borrowings may be allocated, under a formula, to the U.S. branch beyond the amount of interest actually paid or accrued directly by the branch ("excess interest"). Such excess interest will be deductible by the foreign corporation in computing its U.S. net taxable income for the U.S. branch, but will be treated as paid by the U.S. branch to the foreign owner as if it were a separate lender. As such, unless a specific Code exemption applies, the excess interest will be subject to a 30% (or lower treaty rate) withholding tax imposed on the foreign corporation.

In determining the applicability of a treaty, the excess interest is deemed paid by the branch to the foreign corporation as lender. If the foreign corporation is a "qualified resident" of the treaty country, the excess amount may be subject to lower treaty rates. It is noteworthy that the 30% tax imposed on excess interest allocable to the U.S. branch is levied regardless of whether the excess interest actually resulted in a tax benefit to the U.S. branch. Thus, it is possible that the tax on excess interest will exceed the foreign corporation's U.S. tax benefit from the deduction of excess interest, for instance, in situations where the U.S. branch has net operating losses.

Does the BPT override tax treaties?

Congress intended that the BPT not apply where its application would be inconsistent with an existing U.S. income tax treaty obligation; however, this principle is modified in cases of "treaty shopping." When treaty shopping *is not* involved, (i) a foreign corporation and its shareholders may continue to rely on any benefits provided by an income tax treaty with respect to BPT on earnings, and (ii) a foreign corporation and a third party foreign lender may continue to rely on benefits provided by applicable income tax treaties. When treaty shopping *is* involved, treaty benefits are generally overridden. For instance, unless the actual or deemed creditor or dividend recipient, as the case may be, is a "qualified resident" of a treaty country, the creditor or the dividend recipient cannot claim treaty benefits to reduce the 30% withholding obligation.

It is noteworthy that U.S. shareholders of a treaty shopping corporation or of a non-treaty country corporation may be subject to triple taxation. There are several proposals currently under consideration to eliminate this additional layer of tax on U.S. shareholders.

How can a taxpayer determine whether the foreign corporation in which it holds stock will be treated as engaging in "treaty shopping"?

A foreign corporation will not be considered to be treaty shopping if it is a "qualified resident" of the treaty country at issue. A foreign corporation that is resident in a foreign country will be a qualified resident, unless either (i) more than 50% in value of the foreign corporation's stock is owned by individuals who are neither residents of such country (regardless of whether they are bona-fide residents of another treaty country), nor U.S. citizens or resident aliens, or (ii) 50% or more of the foreign corporation's gross income is used (directly or indirectly) to meet liabilities to persons who are neither residents of that country nor of the U.S. Note that these rules still allow treaty benefits to inure to non-treaty country shareholders, as long as they hold less than 50% of the corporation's stock.

If the foreign corporation fails to qualify under these tests, it will nevertheless be treated as a "qualified resident" if either (i) the foreign corporation's stock is primarily and regularly traded on an established securities exchange in the country in question, or (ii) the foreign corporation is wholly owned (either directly or indirectly) by another corporation organized in the country in which such stock is traded. This may provide an advantage to foreign shareholders of publicly traded treaty country corporations over shareholders of non-treaty or U.S. publicly traded corporations.

What would be the best way to avoid the BPT?

Non-treaty investors and often residents in certain treaty countries will find that operating in the United States through a U.S. corporation is the most attractive way to avoid the BPT. In other words, in an asset acquisition, a foreign corporation will avoid the BPT if it incorporates the branch into a U.S. corporation. The rate of tax on dividends and interest required to be withheld at source by a U.S. subsidiary may be reduced if a treaty country parent corporation is used. If dividends are to be distributed, at least a 5% treaty rate withholding tax will apply. In addition, if the investor is a treaty country resident, he can capitalize the U.S. corporation with indebtedness and receive interest income, sometimes free of U.S. tax, contemporaneously with interest deductions at the corporate level.

FIRPTA

What is FIRPTA?

The Foreign Investment in Real Property Tax Act of 1980, as amended, also known as FIRPTA, was enacted in 1980 to close a number of perceived loopholes that enabled foreign investors to own and dispose of U.S. real properties without incurring U.S. tax on the appreciation of the property, or on the cash flow from the property. Since 1985, FIRPTA overrides all income tax treaties.

FIRPTA applies to *dispositions* of U.S. real property interests (USRPIs). A USRPI generally includes (i) an interest in real estate located in the U.S. or the United States Virgin Islands, or (ii) any interest (other than an interest solely as a creditor) in a domestic corporation, unless it can be established that such corporation was at no time a U.S. real property holding corporation (USRPHC). A domestic corporation is a USRPHC if the fair market value of its USRPIs equals or exceeds 50 percent of its world-wide real estate plus any other trade or business assets. Thus, if the assets disposed of are clearly not USRPIs, or interests in certain pass-through entities that own USRPIs, neither the seller nor the buyer of the assets ought to be concerned about FIRPTA. FIRPTA regulations provide elaborate rules concerning the definition of a USRPI. Because many U.S. corporations own significant amounts of real estate, it will often be difficult to conclude at an early planning stage that a given target is not a USRPHC.

What are the general rules regarding FIRPTA, and how are they enforced?

FIRPTA provides that gain or loss of a nonresident alien individual or a foreign corporation from the disposition of a USRPI will be treated as if the gain or loss was effectively connected with a U.S. trade or business of such person. As such, the gain will be taxed at the regular rates applicable to U.S. citizens and residents, or domestic corporations, as the case may be. Unlike other passive investments, gain recognized in a transaction subject to FIRPTA ought to be reported on a U.S. income tax return. Nonresident alien individuals are also subject to FIRPTA's 21% minimum tax.

FIRPTA compliance is enforced through a withholding system that was implemented in 1984. The Code generally provides that a transferee of a USRPI is required to withhold and pay over to the IRS 10% of the amount realized (i.e., the consideration) on the disposition by the foreign transferor. Partnerships and trusts disposing of real estate are required to withhold 34% of the amount allocable to their foreign partners or foreign beneficiaries. There are several exceptions to the withholding rules which are beyond the scope of this discussion.

FIRPTA applies to dispositions of interests in partnerships holding real estate, and to dispositions of USRPIs by partnerships held by foreigners. Moreover, FIRPTA applies to distributions of USRPIs by foreign corporations to their shareholders, and to capital contributions to foreign corporations. In addition, FIRPTA provisions can override the nonrecognition treatment provided by various other sections of the Code, where necessary to ensure that the gain subject to taxation under FIRPTA is not diminished through transactions such as reorganizations and tax-free liquidations.

Who should be concerned about FIRPTA?

While the FIRPTA provisions may seem to be of little importance in a merger or acquisition that does not involve real estate holding corporations or direct acquisitions of real estate assets, its application is far-reaching. First, as mentioned earlier, the definition of a USRPHC is broad enough to include even a manufacturing company that owns a large plant. A foreign acquirer should take future FIRPTA taxes into account in evaluating a potential acquisition. A domestic as well as a foreign acquirer from a foreign holder is liable as transferee-payor to withhold tax on the consideration paid for the stock if the corporation is a USRPHC and the payee is subject to FIRPTA. Failure to withhold may result in civil and criminal penalties. On the other hand, the foreign transferor (seller) is required to file a U.S. tax return to report his gain from the sale. Finally, if a public offering to refinance a portion of the acquisition indebtedness is contemplated, certain foreign holders (5% or more) will be subject to U.S. tax on the disposition of their holdings if the corporation is a USRPHC; under certain circumstances, the buyer of publicly-traded stock from a 5% or more shareholder will be rquired to withold FIRPTA tax.

Consequently, in any stock acquisition, consideration should be given to the value of the U.S. realty owned by the acquired entity, *vis-a-vis* its other assets, and to the tax status of the seller. If the seller provides a certificate that it is not a foreign person, no withholding will be required. In addition, no withholding is required if a domestic corporation furnishes to the transferee an affidavit stating that it is not and has not been a USRPHC during a certain test period.

What is the Section 897(i) election?

The Section 897(i) election is an election made by a treaty country corporation to be treated as a domestic corporation for FIRPTA purposes. Foreign corporations can make the election under Section 897(i) if they are entitled to nondiscriminatory treatment under a treaty obligation of the United States, even one which is not necessarily an income tax treaty.

There are certain advantages in making the 897(i) election, for example, in a case of a reorganization. The 897(i) election allows flexibility in rearranging a taxpayer's holdings involving the transfer of a USRPI to, or the disposition of a USRPI by, an electing corporation. An electing foreign corporation also is not subject to the limitations which Sections 897(d) and (e) impose on the applicability of nonrecognition provisions to transfers of USRPIs by foreign corporations.

The 897(i) election, however, is not without its disadvantages: (i) in order to qualify for an 897(i) election, the shareholders must start with a "clean slate," which means that taxes which were avoided in the past by means of transfers of stock in the foreign corporation should be paid (plus interest); and (ii) all future dispositions of the stock of the foreign corporation will be subject to FIRPTA taxation.

OUTBOUND ACQUISITIONS

Introduction

In this section we will outline the most prominent features of United States taxation of the foreign activities of U.S. persons. As explained earlier in this chapter, the United States asserts taxing jurisdiction over the worldwide income of its citizens, residents, and corporations. As a general rule, the United States taxes only income received or accrued by U.S. taxpayers.

In the domestic context, with the exception of a group filing a consolidated return or a subchapter S corporation, income earned by a U.S. taxpayer from a controlled corporation is not taxed to the U.S. owner except and to the extent that such earnings are actually distributed to the owner. As we will soon see, the exceptions to the above rules in the international context are so voluminous and complex in U.S. tax law as to suggest that the general rules do not apply at all. As a result of long-standing concerns about the avoidance of U.S. taxes through the expatriation of assets and earnings, there is now a very extensive patchwork of rules under which the United States seeks to tax, or at least take into account, income generated in foreign subsidaries of U.S. persons.

Needless to say, in any transaction involving an acquisition of a foreign business, the primary focus of the tax planner's attention must be the tax laws of the country or countries in which the target does business and holds assets and the country or countries in which its shareholders are located. This is all the more so at a time when income tax rates of most industrialized countries significantly exceed those in the United States. There may in fact be significant opportunities to reduce the impact of foreign taxes through the use of tax treaties and the United States foreign tax credit system. These mechanisms are inherently imperfect, however, and a great deal of attention must be paid to the rules of United States taxation of the international activities of its taxpayers in order to minimize the overall tax costs of U.S. persons engaging in a variety of multinational operations.

Planning the Outbound Acquisition

When planning an outbound acquisition, what information should the purchaser solicit from the seller in order to minimize foreign and domestic tax liabilities?

Today, where an auction process is commonly used to obtain the highest bid for a group of corporations that is for sale, the buyer cannot ignore the tax consequences to the seller resulting from the sale. To obtain a competitive edge over other bidders, the buyer should strive to maximize its own tax benefits without raising the seller's tax costs above its expectations. Alternatively, without sacrificing the purchaser's own goals, it may be possible to structure the offer in a way that reduces the seller's tax costs. With these goals in mind, the purchaser should solicit from the seller the following information:

(i) A precise organizational chart. The chart should describe the Holding Company (assuming that the target is a parent of a group of corporations) and the stock ownership in all the various tiers of the domestic corporations, if any, and of the foreign corporations or entities (the "Group");

(ii) The estimated U.S. and foreign tax bases as of the projected acquisition date that the Holding Company is expected to have in the various domestic and foreign corporations;

(iii) For each of the foreign companies:
A. the taxable year for both foreign and U.S. income tax purposes;
B. the actual and projected earnings and profits by taxable period of such corporation as of the acquisition date computed by the rules set forth in Sections 902 and 964 of the Code;
C. the creditable foreign income taxes paid or accrued during each taxable period ending on or before the acquisition date;
D. the earnings and profits and creditable foreign taxes set forth in subparagraphs B and C accumulated prior to the seller's ownership of the company;
E. all other information—foreign currency gains and losses, tax accounting elections, distributions, utilization of foreign tax credits, etc.—necessary to determine the tax consequences of a later sale of each corporation;
F. the estimated net book value, or pro forma balance sheet, of each foreign company as of the acquisition date; and
G. a listing of the inter-company receivables and payables, if any.

(iv) To the extent feasible, a description of the overall income tax position of the target group and the seller.

Why would one need an organizational chart of the structure of the target?

An organizational chart will describe the precise ownership of the Group and will inform one of the different tax jurisdictions (and income tax treaties) that may affect the acquisition process and the subsequent disposition of the Group or several of its members. One may be aiming to buy a Greek company but may find out that the Greek company is owned by a Spanish holding company, which is in turn owned by a U.S. subsidiary of Holding Company. Therefore, in this scenario the prospective buyer will be required to evaluate the possible tax consequences of the acquisition in Greece, Spain, and the United States.

The organizational chart will also provide information as to whether any of the foreign subsidiaries is, or would be in the purchaser's hands, a "controlled foreign corporation" (CFC). As will be explained shortly, CFC status may have significant U.S. tax consequences to a U.S. shareholder.

Subpart F

What is Subpart F of the Code?

Subpart F (Sections 951-964 of the Code) requires U.S. shareholders of a CFC to include in their U.S. gross income as constructive dividends certain amounts earned by the CFC, regardless of whether such earnings were actually repatriated to the U.S. shareholder. In addition to the "CFC" and "U.S. shareholder" requirements, Subpart F treatment will generally only apply to certain types of income earned by the CFC, which may be broadly termed Subpart F income. Note that a U.S. tax is not imposed on the CFC itself; in fact, if the foreign corporation were itself subject to U.S. taxation, an entirely different set of rules would apply.

What is a CFC?

A controlled foreign corporation, or CFC, is any foreign corporation of which more than 50% of the total combined voting power, or the total value of its stock, is owned directly or indirectly by "United States shareholders" on any day during the taxable year of the foreign corporation. A United States shareholder, in turn, is a U.S. person who owns, or is considered to own under attribution rules, 10% or more of the foreign corporation's voting power. Note that in the definition of U.S. shareholder, unlike the definition of a CFC, voting power, and not stock value, is the sole criterion.

In considering the application of Subpart F, it is important to keep in mind the separate status and consequences of the CFC and the United States shareholder. For example, because of the 10% voting power test, it is very possible to have U.S. persons owning stock in a CFC who are not "United States shareholders" and thus not subject to Subpart F. Additionally, there is much room for structuring flexibility so as to have very substantial U.S. ownership of a foreign corporation without causing it to be characterized as a CFC. One thing to bear in mind in this area is that there may be circumstances in which it will be beneficial for a foreign subsidiary of a U.S. parent to be characterized as a CFC.

How does Subpart F operate?

Subpart F provides that a U.S. shareholder must include in gross income certain classes of the CFC's income as a constructive dividend. Following such an imputation, the basis of the U.S. shareholder's stock in the CFC is increased in order to avoid double taxation when the U.S. shareholder later disposes of the stock of the CFC. An actual distribution of the CFC's earnings subsequent to Subpart F treatment will not be taxable to the U.S. shareholder if it pertains to the previously taxed earnings and profits, and a corresponding reduction in the basis of the stock will take place. Under certain circumstances, the U.S. shareholder may be eligible for the foreign tax credit with respect to foreign taxes paid by the CFC.

As explained in greater detail below, a U.S. shareholder of a CFC is also required to include in gross income its pro-rata share of the foreign corporation's increase in earnings invested in certain U.S. properties.

What classes of CFC income are subject to Subpart F?

Subpart F income includes "insurance income," "foreign base company income," and certain other classes of income subject to specific limited rules (such as international boycott related income, illegal bribes, etc.). If more than 70% of the CFC's gross income is Subpart F income, the full amount of the CFC's gross income will be treated as Subpart F income.

"Insurance income" means income attributable to the issuance of any insurance, reinsurance, or annuity contract in connection with property in, liability arising out of activity in, or in connection with the lives or health of residents of, a country *other* than the country under the laws of which the CFC is created or organized.

"Foreign base company income" includes "foreign personal holding company income," "foreign base company sales income," "foreign base company services income," "foreign base company shipping income," and "foreign base company oil related income" for the taxable year. Foreign personal holding company income consists of interest, dividends, rents, royalties, and other kinds of passive income. Foreign base company sales income generally includes various forms of income derived by the CFC in connection with the sale or purchase of property involving a related party, where the property originated in a country other than that of the CFC and is sold or purchased for use or disposition outside of the country of the CFC. Foreign base company services income generally includes income derived in connection with the performance of various services on behalf of a related person where the services are performed outside the country of the CFC. Foreign base company shipping income includes income from a variety of activities involving the use of aircraft or vessels in foreign commerce. Foreign base company oil related income generally includes income from oil and gas products except where the income is derived in the country from which the oil or gas product was extracted.

What are the rules concerning a CFC's increase in earnings invested in U.S. property?

As a general rule, each U.S. shareholder is required to take into gross income his pro rata share of the CFC's increase in earnings invested in U.S. property for the taxable year. This rule is applicable to all CFC's whether or not they have earned Subpart F income, but to avoid double counting this rule applies only after Subpart F income, if any, has been imputed to the shareholder.

To carve out certain abuses, indirect investments in U.S. property will also be subject to these rules. Under Treasury regulations, any obligation of a U.S. person for which a CFC is a pledgor or guarantor will be considered United States property held by such CFC. If the assets of a CFC serve at any time, even though indirectly, as a security for the performance of an obligation of a United States person, then the CFC will be considered a pledgor or guarantor of that obligation. Consequently, if an acquirer plans to use the stock or assets of foreign subsidiaries as collateral for acquisition indebtedness, it may risk receiving a deemed distribution from the CFCs to the extent of the earnings and profits of the foreign subsidiaries that are used as collateral.

Foreign Tax Credits

What is the foreign tax credit?

A common theme throughout the tax system is that a person should be relieved of the burden resulting from the imposition of tax by more than one jurisdiction on the same income. One example of this principle is the deduction for income taxes paid to states, localities, and foreign governments contained in Section 164 of the Code. In the case of income taxes paid to foreign governments, the Internal Revenue Code provides an alternative to the deduction of the foreign tax from gross income by way of a unilateral tax credit against U.S. tax for the foreign taxes. When the credit works properly, it generally provides a more complete relief from double taxation of income than the deduction. The goal of the foreign tax credit system is to limit the overall rate of tax on foreign source income to the greater of the foreign rate or the U.S. rate. The foreign tax credit is elected by a taxpayer on an annual basis, and is not binding for future years. Because of the various limitations under the foreign tax credit rules, in certain circumstances it may, in fact, be more advantageous for a taxpayer to claim the deduction instead of the credit.

How is the amount of allowable foreign tax credit determined?

The amount of foreign tax credit that may be claimed as a direct credit against U.S. income tax liability is generally determined by applying a fraction to the tentative U.S. tax liability for the year. The numerator of the fraction is the taxable income from foreign sources, and the denominator is worldwide taxable income.

Under the Tax Reform Act of 1986, foreign income and related foreign taxes are divided into nine new categories, or "baskets." Section 904 of the Code contains extensive rules designed to prevent taxpayers from crediting foreign taxes attributable to one basket against U.S. tax liability attributable to another basket. A major effect of the basket rules is to cause many U.S. taxpayers to have excess foreign tax credits that will be difficult or impossible to utilize.

The new baskets are as follows: (i) passive income; (ii) high withholding tax interest; (iii) financial services income; (iv) shipping income; (v) dividends from noncontrolled Section 902 corporations (see below); (vi) dividends from domestic international sales corporations (DISCs); (vii) taxable income attributable to foreign trade income; (viii) foreign sales corporation (FSC) distributions from foreign trade income; and (ix) income subject to an overall basket. There is also a special basket for oil and gas extraction income. In addition, there are rules concerning recharacterization of income, look-through rules for interest, dividends, rents, and royalties paid by CFCs, carryovers and carrybacks, and "high-taxed" income. Needless to say, the proper utilization of the foreign tax credit has been rendered extremely complex after the 1986 Tax Act.

Can a U.S. person obtain a foreign tax credit for foreign taxes paid by a foreign subsidiary?

Under Section 902 of the Code, a U.S. corporation owning 10% or more of the voting stock of a foreign corporation may be entitled to a "deemed paid credit," or indirect credit, for foreign taxes paid by the subsidiary. The deemed paid credit is only available against dividend income received (or deemed received under Subpart F or other provisions) from the foreign subsidiary. The principle underlying this indirect credit is that a U.S. corporation receiving a dividend from a foreign corporation is deemed to have paid the foreign taxes paid or accrued by the foreign corporation on the earnings from which the dividend is distributed.

The deemed paid credit generally works as follows. First, under Section 78 of the Code, a domestic corporation must include in income not only the amount of dividends actually or constructively received, but must also include in income an amount equal to the foreign taxes attributable to such dividend income. This is the so-called "gross-up" provision. Under Section 902, the U.S. corporation is deemed to have paid the same proportion of the income taxes paid by the subsidiary as the dividends received bear to the foreign subsidiary's total earnings. Additionally, if the foreign corporation owns 10% or more of the voting stock of a second foreign corporation, it is deemed to have paid foreign taxes of the subsidiary on the same basis. The same rule goes on for a third tier of subsidiary as well.

Under Section 960 of the Code, similar rules are provided for an indirect foreign tax credit with respect to deemed dividend income from the foreign corporation to the domestic corporate shareholder as a result of Subpart F. Under Section 962, an individual may take advantage of this indirect foreign tax credit by electing to be taxed on Subpart F income as if he were a domestic corporation.

Section 1248

How is a U.S. person treated upon the sale of stock in a foreign corporation?

But for the application of Section 1248 of the Code, a U.S. person will generally recognize capital gain or loss on the sale of stock in a foreign corporation just as it would on the sale of stock in a domestic corporation. Recognizing that this provided an opportunity for the repatriation of foreign earnings at favorable capital gains rates, the U.S. enacted Section 1248 of the Code in 1962. The main purpose and effect of Section 1248 is to recharacterize the gain realized on the sale of stock in the foreign corporation from capital gain to ordinary dividend income to the extent of the selling stockholder's ratable share of the earnings of the foreign corporation accumulated during the period that the stock was owned by the U.S. person. If the selling shareholder is a domestic corporation, then it may claim the benefit of the indirect foreign tax credit with respect to the deemed dividends under Section 902. Where the selling shareholder is an individual, Section 1248 includes a mechanism that indirectly reduces his U.S. tax liability on account of foreign taxes paid by the foreign corporation.

What are the mechanics of Section 1248?

Section 1248 will only apply to a selling shareholder if (i) the shareholder is a U.S. person; (ii) he owned, or is considered to own through specified attribution rules, 10% or more of the voting power in the foreign corporation at any time during the previous five years; (iii) at some point during this five year period when the 10% ownership test was met, the foreign corporation was a CFC. As long as a U.S. person meets those requirements, Section 1248 will apply to all stock that the U.S. person sold in the foreign corporation, even if the stock is nonvoting stock, and even if at the time of the sale he is no longer a 10% shareholder or the corporation is no longer a CFC.

If a U.S. person sells stock in a domestic corporation that was "formed or availed of" principally for the holding of stock in one or more foreign corporations, the domestic holding company will be treated under Section 1248(e) as if it were a foreign corporation.

FOREIGN INVESTMENT COMPANIES AND PASSIVE FOREIGN INVESTMENT COMPANIES

What special tax rules apply on the sale of stock in a foreign investment company?

Upon the sale or exchange of stock in a foreign investment company, a U.S. shareholder is required under Section 1246 of the Code to recognize ordinary income instead of capital gain, to the extent of his share of the company's earnings and profits. A foreign investment company is a foreign corporation that is registered with the Securities and Exchange Commission as a management company or a unit investment trust, or that is engaged primarily in the business of investing or trading in securities, commodities, futures, options, etc. An additional requirement for foreign investment company status is that 50% of the corporation's voting stock or total value be owned by U.S. persons.

Under Section 1247 of the Code, a foreign investment company may allow its shareholders to obtain capital gain treatment on sales of its stock by electing to distribute 90% or more of its income currently.

What is a passive foreign investment company (PFIC)?

In order to deny U.S. taxpayers the tax deferral benefits of holding passive investments in off-shore companies, the Tax Reform Act of 1986 included special rules for the ownership of stock in PFICs, or passive foreign investment companies. Generally, a PFIC is defined as any foreign corporation if 75% or more of its gross income consists of "passive income," or 50% or more of its assets are of a sort that produce passive income.

Passive income specifically does not include bona fide bank and insurance company income. Generally, the rules are designed to look through holding companies to determine whether they are holding passive versus active income producing assets.

How is a U.S. shareholder taxed on the disposition of stock in a PFIC?

Except where the PFIC becomes a "qualified electing fund" (discussed below), the U.S. shareholder is taxed in the following manner. First, an allocation is made of the gain recognized over the shareholder's holding period in the stock. The portion of the gain allocated to the year of actual disposition, or to a period before the company became a PFIC, is simply includible as ordinary income to the shareholder in the year of sale. With respect to the remaining portion of the gain, a special tax is paid in the year of disposition. This special tax is determined by computing the amount of tax that would have been paid during each of the years to which the income was allocated (at the highest tax rates then applicable) and adding to such sums interest on the same basis as for any underpayment of tax.

The above tax provisions apply not only to an outright disposition of stock in a PFIC, but also to an "excess distribution" from a PFIC. An excess distribution is defined as a distribution by the PFIC of an amount during a year exceeding 125% of the average annual distributions during the prior three years.

What are the rules that apply to a qualified electing fund?

As noted above, a shareholder will not be subject to the special tax rules on sales of stock in, or excess distributions by, a PFIC if the entity is a qualified electing fund. Provided the necessary election is made, the PFIC will be a qualifed electing fund. As such, every U.S. shareholder must include in income his pro rata share of the company's ordinary income and net capital gain. The shareholder obtains a corresponding increase in stock basis.

SECTION 367

Do the ordinary rules governing tax-free transactions apply to transfers of stock or assets into or out of the United States?

Because of their potential for being utilized to avoid taxes in the international context, the various provisions of the Code allowing tax-free reorganizations and other tax-free exchanges are subject to limitations under Section 367. Section 367 generally provides that in a variety of situations, tax-free treatment will not be available for transactions unless certain additional requirements are met. Generally, Section 367(a) governs the treatment of "outbound" transactions, i.e., transfers of assets or stock by U.S. persons to a foreign corporation in exchange for stock in a foreign corporation. Section 367(b) governs all other transactions, which are generically referred to as inbound transactions. The latter category in fact includes both transfers into the United States as well as transfers from one foreign entity to another. In the case of outbound transactions the chief concern of the statute is the removal of appreciated property from the U.S. tax jurisdiction prior to their sale. The chief goal of the Section 367(b) rules is to ensure that there will not be avoidance of taxation of shareholders of CFCs under Subpart F and Section 1248.

What kinds of transactions are covered by Section 367?

Subject to numerous exceptions provided in the statute and regulations, Section 367(a) denies nonrecognition treatment to virtually every reorganization or Section 351 transaction by which U.S. shareholders exchange stock in a domestic or foreign corporation for stock in a foreign corporation. Section 367(a) also applies to transfers of assets from domestic corporations to foreign corporations in reorganization transactions as well as tax-free parent subsidiary liquidations where the parent is a foreign corporation.

Section 367(b) deals with special tax consequences when a foreign subsidiary liquidates into a domestic parent, a first tier foreign subsidiary liquidates into a higher tier foreign subsidiary, or a domestic corporation acquires a foreign corporation in a tax-free reorganization. Section 367(b) also covers acquisitions of one foreign corporation by another foreign corporation, and spin-offs of foreign corporations by domestic corporations.

APPENDIX A

THE J.T. SMITH CONSULTANTS CASE

Stanley Foster Reed

I. INTRODUCTION AND HISTORY OF THE CASE*

Some fifteen years ago, when my magazine, *Mergers & Acquisitions* was in its formative years, we started a seminar program in Washington called "Merger Week," which in 1977 was transferred to Northwestern University, where it is still going strong, twice a year.

At that same time, the American Consulting Engineers Council asked us to run a series of merger seminars—local and national—for their members, who were predominantly firms of Registered Professional Engineers. As an RPE myself, I liked the assignment, but we needed a case to illustrate our Wheel of Opportunity and Fit Chart (WOFC) merger-related strategic planning concepts—the pedagogical linchpin of the seminar programs.

The XYZ Consultants case, which appeared in the Fall, 1977 issue of *M&A*, was the result of a collaboration between me and the then-president of ACEC. This case was used not only in the ACEC seminars but at the Northwestern seminars, and at hundreds of one- and two-day and in-house seminars which were attended by executives from manufacturers, insurers, banks, law and accounting firms, governments, academe, etc. It was pedagogically correct to teach from the case because it yielded entries all around the Wheel, it had a high degree of personal and social content, it was in a changing field, it was

---

*See Chapter 2, p. 11

universal in that it could be used anywhere in the world, and people felt comfortable with it because most had some dealings with professional engineers.

In addition, the early Management Buyouts (MBOs) were taking place in that field as a result of the then new ESOP/ESOT (Employees Stock Option Plan/Employees Stock option Trust) legislation. Additionally, it was a good way to teach *process* without getting involved with *product*.

With the name changed from the original case, "XYZ Consultants," to "J.T. Smith Consultants" it has been brought up to date for this book. Here is a step-by-step account of the development of a merger-based strategic plan for J.T. Smith.

II. PRE-WOFC ACTIVITY

A Special Meeting of the Executive Committee of JTS, consisting of the CEO, COO, and VPF (Chief Executive Officer, Chief Operating Officer, and the Vice President—Finance) was called, and the Table, "Strategic Skills & Behaviors," (Exhibit A-1) was reviewed along with the Flow Chart (Exhibit, B-4) to discuss at what level the inquiry might proceed. They opted for an Enterprise Level inquiry and planning program. (To target their Corporate Level or Sector level with only two main divisions, Detroit and New Orleans, seemed unproductive.) While they could have selected one of the smaller profit centers such as Air Conditioning, and at an even lower level the Heat Pump Design Section, they wanted a broad plan even though it was complicated by including New Orleans, whose economy was driven by economic and cultural forces different from their base operations in Detroit.

The additional participants in the WOFC sessions were also selected. In addition to the CEO, COO, and VPF, they were the EXVP (Executive Vice President), the VPS (Vice President—Sales), the VPE (Vice President—Engineering), and the head of the New Orleans office. Seven in all, a good number.

III. THE INTERVIEW PROGRAM

All the participants in the WOFC process were interviewed either one-on-one or in small groups by the VPP (Vice President for Planning), who was not to be a participant but who was to act as Facilitator of the WOFC sessions.

Each was shown the Flow Chart (see Appendix B, Exhibit B-4)

and was handed pads of Opportunity Descriptions (Exhibit A-2), Weakness Analysis sheets (Exhibit A-3), and Strength Analysis sheets (Exhibit A-4), and were assisted in filling some of them out. This process, including the melding of similar opportunities and similar weaknesses and strengths, took about a month prior to the actual WOFC sessions including some inquiry as to the state-of-the-art in some of the more technical Opportunity areas. The strength and weakness analyses were abstracted and gathered into one document called "Descriptions of Potential Variables" (Exhibit A-5).

IV. SITE AND DURATION

It was decided that the WOFC sessions should be held off-site in a secure but convenient location, that it would be 2 1/2 days, and that the program would be as shown on the "WOFC Sessions Schedule" (Exhibit A-6). (See Chapter 2, pages 11–23.)

V. SESSIONS

Evening Session

After the Reception and Dinner, which was attended by the participants, the Facilitator, the Monitor, two board members and six high-level managers, the group was introduced to the WOFC Merger Planning Construct and the rules governing the sessions were outlined. They were:

1. Only the participants could vote in the Delphi.
2. The non-participants could not interrupt the proceedings with observations, but could make their views known during the break periods.
3. Only the highs and the lows were allowed to give their opinions in the discussions without the special permission of the Facilitator.
4. All of the individual scoring was to be anonymous and not to be revealed until the end of the WOFC sessions and then only if the group wished it.
5. Only emergency phone calls were allowed. And the sessions were halted while the participant answered. If any participant left the sessions permanently, they were to start over with a new participant from the observer group.

6. If the company's normal security arrangements for the protection of the company's confidential material were deemed
inadequate, they were to be beefed up for the sessions. Each
participant and observer would sign a confidentiality and non-
disclosure agreement, no documents were to be copied or taken
away without the Facilitator's permission, and no notes were
to be taken by the observers. The Monitor was to make a
record of the proceedings with the aid of a tape-recorder if the
participants so chose.

With those cautions, the participants and the observers were
all handed copies of some 30 Opportunity Sheets similar to Exhibit
A-2 and a copy of SFR's 1977 article "Corporate Growth by Strategic
Planning" from Volume 12 of *Mergers & Acquisitions* magazine for
review that evening.

Second Day, Sessions One and Two

The Opportunities were reviewed one by one, discussed and rerefined
by the group. Where there was no obvious general agreement, they
were put to a vote and the majority ruled for inclusion in or exclusion from the Wheel of Opportunity. Their arguments for exclusion
or inclusion generally paralleled the Fit Chart variables and were
important to discover if any key variable had been missed. (If the participants had wished to, they could have selected the Opportunities
by the Delphi process.) The Wheel was complete at the end of Session
Two. Very few opportunities were rejected as the participants felt that
that was the function of the Fit Chart sessions.

As each opportunity came up for review, it was placed on the
sample wheel which had been chalk-lined on a large blackboard.

Second Day, Session Three

This session was spent in exploring JTS's world potential. (This process had not been covered in the 1977 article.) The interface is the
"Free Form," or "Pure Conglomerate" interface—a new service in a
new geographic territory. While it is possible to generate random
entries, like "manufacturing bicycles in China," probably the best
entry is to look at the growth rates for the new services in present
territories and combine them with the economic growth rates for present lines in new geographic territories.

Second Day, Session Four

This Session focused on a review of Exhibit A-5, "Review of Potential
Variables," which was handed to all participants and the observers.

Each of the 41 variables was taken up in turn and compared to the Strength and Weakness Sheets that had been submitted. (See Exhibits A-3 and A-4 for samples.) There was considerable discussion as to the meaning of each of the variables and its impact on the merger/acquisition decisionmaking process. Some descriptions were modified on the spot, and some were dropped by voice vote. The discussion continued after dinner. The participants were asked to study the variables in Exhibit A-5 that evening and, if they could, prioritize them.

Third Day, Session One

This first session was devoted to a continued discussion of the Description of Potential Variables with the Facilitator abstracting the arguments and finally devising the Final Fifteen as shown on the Fit Chart Tally sheet (Exhibit A-8). This was entered into the computer using Lotus 1,2,3 and sufficient blank copies were run off so that each participant could record his Delphi votes.

Third Day, Sessions Two & Three

The session began with a review of the Delphi process and the rules for voting.

The individual votes were recorded by each person in pencil (to allow for erasure and adjustment before totalling) and were taken off by the Monitor and handed to the Facilitator to administer the Delphi. The Delphi voting was recorded on a large blackboard specially chalk-lined with the necessary 19 columns.

(It takes two people—non-voting, non-participants—to run a Fit Chart Session: a Facilitor—usually an outside consultant or the head of planning—and a Monitor—usually someone from accounting who can add and divide quickly and accurately.)

The Monitor recorded each round, variable by variable and participant by participant on the Master Tally Sheet, and handed it to the Facilitator who then conducted the Delphi. All the voting was secret and anonymous. The Facilitator announced the names of the highs and the lows, but not their scores and not the average. The highs and the lows were then asked to defend their position alternating high and low, variable by variable. At the conclusion of the discussion, the Monitor recorded the *average* on the large Fit Chart that had been chalk-lined on a large blackboard at the front of the room, and at the same time entered the averages on his Master Copy of the Fit Chart.

Here is a condensed transcript of the Delphi discussion and voting variable by variable. (See Exhibit A-8 on pages 892–893.)

Weaknesses/Complements

Round One

Long-Term Cyclical Resistance: The first item, obviously, was a point of contention between the CEO, who gave it zero, and the COO, who gave it his maximum.

The CEO simply stated that he thought there were more important things to worry about than cyclicality, that the firm had learned to live with the business cycle as had their clients, and he liked to go fishing during downturns and "live on my stored up fat." He was joined in his position by the VPF and the VPE. Against them was the COO who allowed that all of them had considerably more stored up fat because of their equity holdings and a solid net worth, that he not only had trouble *personally* in downtimes, he had problems *administratively*. He was joined in his opinion by the EXVP, the VPS, and the New Orleans head who was still trying to recover from an eight-year downturn in the Southwest's economy. But those latter three had not made a sufficient point allocation to gain the floor.

On *Billings Growth*, the CEO also took a determined stand. He said he wanted profit improvement instead. He was alone in his position, as the COO, again the opposition leader, pointed out that J.T. Smith had a long history of highly profitable operation, but they had not grown as they should have.

On *Profit Improvement*, the CEO finally spent some points— amazingly, so did they all. And all gave it a round 100 points simply because they couldn't understand why anyone would want *not* to make more money. Since everyone had voted the same, the discussion centered around the classic relationship between Sales and Profits and the equation S/C $\times$ P/S = ROC. All finally agreed that it *was* like motherhood and apple pie. While it would be nice to increase both sales *and* the rate of profits on those sales, it was rare that one could get both without incurring intolerable levels of risk. Since, historically, they had been well above industry averages on their net margins, and had excess cash not used in the business to finance growth, they decided to go for volume and capital turns.

Effecting *Minimum Market Penetration* was not understood except by the VPS who had just returned from an industrial marketing program and was all turned on about market share, market leadership, and market penetration. But he had trouble explaining it to the group.

Full-Lining provoked the most heated discussion. The CEO and the COO were at odds again, and the group was about evenly divided for and against. The CEO, the New Orleans head, and the VPS made a strong pitch that the industry was heading in that direction and they had better get with it, even if it gave the COO, the EXVP, the VPF and the VPE fits. It was not only a matter of growth, it was a matter of *survival*.

The *Customer Clout* variable was a lead balloon. Few liked the notion of hitting their customers over the head for business or maneuvering them into a position where they had *power* over them. The New Orleans head, voting from his oil-patch perspective, felt that without generating some dependence on the part of their clients, without upping *their* switching costs, that they would likely face a shrinking of sales and profits.

Overhead Reduction was another motherhood and apple pie item that everyone wanted. But how is it effected? Here again the CEO and COO were on opposite sides of the discussion. The former took the position that increased sales would automatically reduce overhead, but the COO and VPF pointed out that it was the *kind* of sales that was important, that adding EE, for instance, might not reduce their overhead but increase it, while a horizontal acquisition—buying a competitor—would probably reduce it substantially.

Reduce Downtime was the only arguable area that the CEO and COO saw eye-to-eye on because it is the "bête noire" of the consulting business. This is another vague item. It was only when it was pointed out that they should apply standard inventory theory to their personnel resources and control downtime that way, and that horizontal mergers automatically reduced inventory carrying costs, that they were able to handle it. They also understood why downtime was not lumped with other overhead items.

The average was 520, showing that the group was certainly conscious of the weaknesses of the company.

Strengths/Supplements

Top Management Fit gave the CEO and the VPE fits. The CEO: "I don't care how we make money. It's the bottom line that should matter to all of us." The VPE: "But Bill, that's what you said about the last two acquisitions outside of our field that we made, and you never had any of them to dinner." "Well, why should I. One guy wore white socks with a business suit and a *black* handkerchief in the breast pocket of a *black* suit." The VPE thus made his point—but the CEO had made it for him.

On *Middle Management Fit*, the VPE took the position that their most valuable asset was their highly trained middle management, all billable bodies who also supervised the jobs, that this "system," developed over many years, was one of the reasons for their superior financial performance, and that any entry not utilizing this asset would probably be a mistake. In opposition, both the CEO and COO opined that it was the managing partners who did the managing, that middle management simply followed orders, and that they were easily replaced. They were joined in their opinion by the head of the New Orleans office. While the ExVP and the FVP agreed with the VPE, neither had allocated enough points to join in the discussion though the Facilitator pointed out their relative position.

On *Staff Skills Fit,* there was considerable discussion of where the "Profit Power" rested in the company, with only the COO taking the position that staff skills were unimportant in rating any potential entry of any kind. His arguments went as follows:

a. In any horizontal merger, we would absorb the *target's* staff.
b. In any vertical acquisition, our staff skills would, in general, be inapplicable.
c. In any service extension, staff skills would, most likely, be inapplicable.
d. In any market extension, not only would we use the target's staff, but probably would recruit there rather than move people from Detroit or New Orleans because, at staff level, they had found a general resistance to relocating.
e. In any free-form extension, the risks were too high to depend on homebodies for the success of any entry. It would have to stand on its own.

On *Salesmen Fit,* five thought it not important that the "project development" people understand the industry, that they were easily recruited, that the target would have its own people, and that all of the "selling" was really done by the principal partners anyway.

On *Customer Fit,* the CEO and FVP both made very high point allocations, with only the VPS and VPE holding the opposite view. The CEO and FVP both felt that their client list was their most valuable resource and discovering what kinds of services their clients might want them to supply seemed a primary pre-acquisition variable. In opposition, the VPS said that he wanted some new customers, that he was tired of soliciting the old. Again, the VPE felt that their continued dependence on their old customers was enervating and that they all needed the stimuli that serving new people would create.

EDP Fit clearly needed exposition and clarification. Did electronic data processing include the CAD equipment? If so, how? Would they eventually interface? Can CAD be extended in CAM (computer-aided-manufacturing) and used in "supervision" jobs to order equipment, or at least as a check on purchased items? How did the equipment and software serve the "project development" people? Could they eventually interface their in-house equipment with a sub-contractor's? With a client's—especially their CAM, MIS (management information systems), and their MRP (materials requirements programs)?

Synergy proved a troublesome variable, with the CEO insisting that any entry must produce "synergistic" results—doing more with less. It was pointed out that the entire Fit Chart was a process to discover synergies and that there was no need for a special category. His answer was that, unless you had a place to enter serendipitous findings—good, but unanticipated benefits of a potential acquisition or entry—they wouldn't be sought after. The COO observed that, from his experience, "barrendipity" was far more common—looking for things that you *know* should be there but are not.

The subtotal of 480 showed that, at least for this first round of the Delphi, the group was somewhat more conscious of their weaknesses than their strengths.

At the end of the round, the average scores of the group were transferred from the Instant Delphi Tally Sheet to the Master Fit Chart on the blackboard for the First Approximation. Since this was the first time that actual numbers had been displayed, there was some general discussion but still no disclosure of the actual individual numerical entries of the participants in the Delphi.

Rounds Two, Three, and Four

(We will now switch from reporting the horizontal spreads to reporting how the vertical values were developed, how the individuals changed their views, and how the list of key variables was shrunk from the Final Fifteen to the Final Nine.)

Complements

The *Long-Term Cyclical Resistance* variable wound up gaining a few points from its opening round score of 79, to a final of 100, with the CEO finally convinced that it was a relatively important phenomenon that should be taken into account in any expansion program. The lone holdout was the VPE who said he needed the points elsewhere.

Billings Growth also increased from an average of 100 points to 120 in the final round, Round Four, with the CEO doing a near-complete about-face in the process, but with the VPE and the New Orleans head reversing their original positive stand.

The *Profit Improvement* variable, after much discussion, was finally eliminated because everyone finally agreed that their problem had never been making money on a job, but getting the job in the first place and staying even with, or growing faster than, the local, national, or world economy.

Effecting *Minimum Market Penetration* was eliminated in the third round as a "textbook variable" more applicable to a manufacturing company with heavy marketing costs than a service organization.

Full-Lining was a consistent winner in the voting with only two last-round hold-outs: the FVP, because of the financial risk of effecting entry into new fields; and the VPE (who managed to allocate it ten points rather than zero in the final round so that he wouldn't have to take the floor and repeat for the fourth time his arguments that "adventuring" in unfamiliar terrains would place the firm's reputation at risk unnecessarily).

Customer Clout was dropped early as something that engineers didn't want to be associated with.

Reduce Overheads got a minimum point score, with the CEO never changing his opinion and eventually convincing the COO that he was right, but never really swaying the FVP, who kept allocating more and more points to it as the others dropped out.

Reduce Downtime made it to the end in spite of the defection of both the CEO and COO, which was offset by a huge allocation by the VPE—a reflection of the miseries of his job in finding things to do for unneeded but valuable employees who could not be riffed.

The Sub-Total of 450 points for Complements, down from 520, meant that over the course of the Delphi, the participants came to be more conscious of their strengths than their weaknesses.

Supplements

On *Top Management Fit*, the CEO did a complete about-face, moving from zero to 300 points as telling arguments were made as to how sensitive the bottom line was to Top Management Fit; the variable showed the most gain, from 100 points to 160 points average.

On *Middle Management Fit*, it gained the most percentage-wise, going from 50 points to 140 with only one holdout at the end, the VPF, who needed his points elsewhere.

Staff Skills Fit lasted through three rounds but was finally dropped due to the growing influence of CAD.

Salesmen Fit was dropped early. First, no one liked the word which was never used in-house, but which had been adopted for the purposes of the WOFC exercise to dramatize and point up the role of marketing; that "project development" was a euphemism that was misleading to planning. The group decided that the partners were the "salesmen" anyway.

Customer Fit had problems, with the CEO dropping his point score in the last round as he needed to bump his Top Management Fit variable; the COO defected too. But the VPS very early saw the errors of his ways and from the second round on voted a solid 300 points for this key variable.

EDP Fit gave the FVP fits. He started out with zero, but in the second round he became the champion of the variable and fought long, hard, and with great asperity for entering fields where their EDP skills could be exploited.

Synergy continued its troubles and, while it lasted through three rounds, the group finally decided that synergy "was a buzzword dreamed up by consultants to part people from their money," and that the whole Fit Chart process was an adventure in matching special talents with special needs, and that was true of *all or any* of the variables.

The averages of the participants' scores had been entered on the blackboard Fit Chart round by round for all to see and discuss, including the rounded numbers for the Final Round.

Third Day, Fourth Session

In rating or scoring the Opportunities, the Facilitator, standing at the blackboard, asked the group to rate the best and the worst of each of the Opportunity entries, variable by variable. The object of the process is to rate each Opportunity *relative to all other Opportunities* and do it variable by variable. For instance:

Long-Term Cyclical Resistance wound up with a final value of 100 points. Obviously, both Detroit and New Orleans have heavily cyclical economies which are reflected in JTS's billings and profit. They, and others which have zero resistance, are scored zero. What's the best? Co-generation in Baltimore, because Baltimore Gas & Electric has stopped all construction of new plants, and EE in China, which does not follow the world economic cycle or at least lags behind it by many years and which desperately needs electrical power which it can get from its tens of thousands of small processing plants that have excess heat, score 100. All the other entries are either at zero or fall somewhere proportionately in between. This same process is repeated for all the other variables.

(The Facilitator has generally done some homework on the major variables, helps the group in the scoring, and points out that if further research on the first five rank-order entries shows any significant differences in proportioning, *so as to change the rank-order*, the Fit Chart will be redone and reissued.)

The Relative Efficiency of each of the Opportunities was then determined by adding the values for each of them horizontally. This yields the *relative risk of entry*. It differentiates each Opportunity from the other by its "fit" with the acquiring company. As such, the number is a proxy for the *relative risk of entry* between the targets and the word "efficiency" has been adopted to describe it. It can be used in pricing an entry by dividing the risk-free rate, or the cost-of-capital of the diversifying company, or its target *hurdle* rate, by that efficiency number. A horizontal integration in Detroit, with an "efficiency" of 750 points out of a possible 1000, yields a 75% efficiency which, with a target hurdle rate or weighted cost of capital of, say 12%, yields a risk-adjusted discount rate of 16% (12/.75). (See Chapter 3, pages 67–68, for a discussion of developing an appropriate discount rate for valuing a potential acquisition's cash flow stream.)

(This method of discovering how "risky" an entry might be, derived from the internal capabilities—or lack of them—of JTS and applied to their special universe of opportunities, is superior to the much-used CAPM (Capital Asset Pricing Model) or models that depend on the "betas" of publicly traded shares in similar industries as descriptive of the "risk" of entry.

It is also better than methods that define a risk-adjusted rate based on historical financial deviations from some mean of the target industry or the target itself. Risk must be defined as coming from the *buyer's* aptitude or the lack of it for operating in the target's area.)

In order to focus JTS's growth efforts on specific targets, the Opportunities are rank-ordered as shown on the Fit Chart and a Strategic Statement, derived from the Fit Chart numbers and rank-orders (Exhibit A-10) developed. In addition, after the rank-orders are determined, the top-ranking candidates' failings—that is where they fail to meet the desired criteria—are flagged. This gives notice to management that the acquisition is short of perfection and pinpoints and *quantifies* the deficiency for all to see. In the case of JTS, it is obvious that the two top-ranked entries fail to meet the cyclical resistance criterion or the billings growth criterion, and only partially fulfill the full-lining objective.

Exhibit A-1
Strategic Skills & Behaviors

	ENTERPRISE	CORPORATE	SECTOR	BUSINESS	PRODUCT	FUNCTION
STRATEGIC FOCUS	Discontinuous	Adaptive	Adaptive	Creative	Creative	Adaptive
COGNITIVE PROCESS	Intuitive	Deductive/ Analytical	Analytical	Analytical	Intuitive	Deductive, Observational
PATTERNS OF DECISION	Autocratic	Small Group	Large Group	Small Group	Individualistic	Individualistic
PROBLEM SOLVING	Creative	Extrapolative	Extrapolative	Extrapolative	Creative/ Extrapolative	Creative
MANAGEMENT	Entrepreneur	Administrator	Administrator	Cooperator	Innovator/ Adaptor	Innovator
RISK-TAKING	High Risk, High-Gain	Familiar Risk	Familiar Risk	Minimum Risk	Limit Risk	Limit Risk
TIME FRAME	Forever	Next Ten Years	Next Five Years	Next Year	Tomorrow	Today
PERFORMANCE MEASURES	Stock Market Price	Return on Capital	Return on Capital	Sales Growth/ Return on Sales	Quality Improvement	Cost- Reduction
REWARD SYSTEM	Stock Appreciation	Stock Appreciation + Cash	Stock/Cash	Cash/ Advancement	Cash/ Advancement	Recognition/ Spot Cash
ACCOUNTABILITY	Stockholders	Board	Corporate Executives	Sector Chiefs	Business Unit Managers	Engineering
FUNCTIONAL GOALS	Position for Change	Achieve "All-Weather" Performance	Strengthen Competitive Position	Build Solid Customer Base	Keep Up with Market Forces	Lower Costs

NOTE: Use this chart to classify opportunities by strategic levels.

EXHIBIT A-2

CONFIDENTIAL

OPPORTUNITY DESCRIPTION
FOR WHEEL OF OPPORTUNITY SESSIONS

INSTRUCTIONS: In filling out the opportunity sheets you should give free rein to your imagination. Please do not fail to submit an entry if your information is incomplete. We need only the kernel of an idea, only a suggestion of truth, only a smidgeon of information to start the entrepreneurial ball to rolling.

Describe the industry:

We should add electrical engineering design and supervision services to the mechanical engineering that has been our forte for many years. All of the characteristics that govern ME bidding and performance are the same for both with the exception that of late the number of criminal indictments for EE bid-rigging and kickback activity is growing at a very high rate compared to ME venal activity which is rare. The checks and balances that we have instituted both at the industry (Society) level and in our own operations are evidently lacking in EE. The industry is badly shaken up right now and this is a good time to enter.

Principal competitors (include market share and growth rates:

There are a number of national firms like Fishbach (formerly Fishbach & Moore) and Dynalectron and hundreds of local--perhaps ten each in the Detroit and New Orleans areas. Some also compete in ME but only marginally.

Customers (to whom do they sell?)

They sell to the same clients that we do.

Suppliers (who supplies them with what?)

EE is not subject to the same environmental problems that ME is so their subcontractors are generally only slave labor peak period suppliers.

How is the product (or process) used?

Same as our ME sevice.

What technical journals exist in the field?

There are too many to name but they are all in our library.

Have you ever been involved in this industry? If so, how?

Yes, I was ten years with an ME/EE firm in a middle management position.

Why do you believe this will be a good entry?

CAD is changing everyone's concepts of how engineering services are being performed. It is during changing times that the scaredy-cats sell out and the confident buy. I believe that we can effect an entry by acquisition at a fairly low multiple of billings.

Specific Candidates (attach any written or printed materials):

The A.J. Hoyt Company, with 40 billable bodies is available here in Detroit and in New Orleans I hear that there are several with superannuated management/owners and no heirs wanting to keep it going. While management buyouts have been around in other industries, they have not yet caught on in New Orleans Engineering.

Session Comments:

We definitely want to look at this area for growth.

Session Action: (check one) ☒ Wheel & Fit   ☐ Internal Growth Plan   ☐ Other
Submitted By: _Yelvata Dew_   Dates: _9/22/86_

Form SFR 1-83

EXHIBIT A-3

WEAKNESS ANALYSIS

INSTRUCTIONS: Please pinpoint those characteristics of your business that are equal or inferior to others.

What is one of your principal weaknesses?

The industry is moving toward "full-lining." Our clients, in seeking to reduce their administrative costs is leaning toward the "engineering conglomerates" who are really functioning as "engineering general contractors" who take on all the engineering responsibilities for a project--ME, EE, EE, FE, etc. While we will lose the distinction as a "boutique," we should gain more because our "development" costs (really our sales costs) should be reduced. One of first areas we should enter is electrical engineering because we are losing billings to the ME/EE firms.

Why do you believe this?

We're losing billings to the full-liners--the industry is moving inexorably in that direction. We are having trouble recruiting. Our CAD skill development is as easily applied to EE as ME (actually more so).

Give a specific example:

On the Porto job we could have done both the ME and the EE work for a substantially less cost to the client and a higher profit to us if we had control of all the engineering work on the project. This is only one job of many. I have also talked to our friends at Ford Motor and they say that if we add EE they will consider giving us both contracts.

Is this weakness management-related, business-related, or industry-related?

It is business-related and an industry trend.

My time frame of reference is: ☐ Short-term (1-2 years)   ☐ Intermediate (2-5 years)
☒ Long-term (5-10 years.)

Session Comments:

Full-lining is a must. The only question was that some of the specialty lines such as environmental engineering are in the higher demand than EE.

Session Action: (check one) ☒ Wheel & Fit   ☐ Organization Development   ☐ Other

Submitted By: _Ybruato Deer_   Date: _9/22/88_

EXHIBIT A-4

STRENGTH ANALYSIS

CONFIDENTIAL

INSTRUCTIONS: Please pinpoint those characteristics of your business that are equal or superior to others.

What is one of your principal strengths?

One of our greatest strengths is our client list. Some of them, like Ford Motor has been a client for fifty years. They pay the rent, educate our children and put food on the table. To ignore their wants and needs is to ignore the reality of economic life. It is a cross-nurturing relationship. Our communications are good. We should learn how to "exploit" that relationship by dicovering what they need in the way of engineering services and acquire in those areas that will fill their needs.

Why do you believe this?

I know that from time to time our clients have hinted that they would be happy if we took over one of our competitors who is a notorious going-in price-cutter who comes out of the job only by outrageous demands for change-orders. And we have had some very strong hints of late that we should add electrical engineering to our mechanical engineering services as so many of our competitors have. Also, our start in CAD is of considerable interest to them.

Give a specific example:

On the Porto job most of the problems were caused be the EE contractor. He was always late or early. He refused to interface with our PERT program and drove us all nuts. I feel that our entry into the EE area will be met with open arms by our clients.

Is this strength management-related, business-related, or industry-related? Explain.

I think that it is certainly business-related and industry-related. But it is the managing partners who have built this strength through many long years of amicable and competent engineering work.

My time frame of reference is: ☒ Short-term (1-2 years)   ☒ Intermediate (2-5 years)
☐ Long-term (5-10 years).

Session Comments:

In the WOFC sessions it was generally agreed that our clients were our greatest asset. There was some concern that we would lose the panache of being a mechanical engineering "boutique" but the general feeling that the rewards were worth the risk. We should go all out to add EE to our work spectrum. (Out of our 100 billable employees, some 20 have EE experience but only one in a lead capacity. We should look for someone with heavy EE job experience to lead the effort. Naturally, he should be of "partner" quality.)

Session Action: (check one) ☒ Wheel & Fit   ☐ Organization Development   ☐ Other

Submitted By: _Yohnatj Deev_   Date: _9/22/88_

EXHIBIT A-5
Descriptions of Potential Variables

Following is a list of variables abstracted from the Strength and Weakness Analysis sheets and converted to COMPLEMENTS and SUPPLEMENTS, along with a suggested legend to be used on the Fit Chart to identify the variable if and when selected.

COMPLEMENTS

A "complement," according to Webster's New Collegiate Dictionary, is "the quantity or number required to make a thing complete." Inherent in the WOFC process is the targeting of industries and their component companies, and their products or services that will offset or "complement" the weaknesses of the company under analysis.

Cyclical Complements

Weakness: Our industry is *cyclical*. It follows the capital spending cycle very closely. Our Detroit-based headquarters operation is especially sensitive to the business cycle and our New Orleans operation is just recovering from the effects of an eight-year downturn in the local oil-patch-based economy.

Complement: enter a countercyclical industry—sometimes called a "defensive" industry such as entertainment, retail food, fast food, automobile parts rebuilding, government-stimulated social programs, and defense spending-driven industries, etc.

Fit Chart Legend: Countercyclical Entry

Weakness: Our industry is *seasonal*. The winter months are especially difficult for us and we must lay off people just as Christmas approaches.

Complement: Enter an industry that has peak activity in the winter.

Fit Chart Legend: Opposite Season Entry

Weakness: The "product life" of our services seems to be short and we are constantly required to update our in-house knowledge about environmental concerns, new physiological constraints in the workplace, restrictive economic constraints on costs, new OSHA and local fire and underwriters codes for hundreds of new materials; all these, and many more, are complicating our operations.

Complement: Find an entry in a "commodity-type" or "assembly-line" operation where we can institutionalize design processes.

Fit Chart Legend: Commodity-Type Entry

Weakness: Sales and backlog seem affected by random factors such as weather, political happenings, fads and fashions in design.

Complement: Increase our involvement with industries affected by random forces and thus decrease the net randomness. This is why insurance companies exist. Do this both by extending our geographic base, and dispersing our services over more industries.

Fit Chart Legend: Effect Dispersive Entries

Weakness: We are too dependent on four or five long-time customers—20% of our customer base provides 80% of our work. While the jobs are bigger and longer-running, like garbage-raised seagulls who die when the town dump is replaced by an incinerator, we have grown too dependent on our larger clients. Some of our best clients are retiring, "going public," or are merging or being acquired. There is no way we're going to keep those accounts when J.T. retires—and maybe before: we could have serious problems in a year or two—especially if some of our prime customers sell out and the new owners start to use their clout on us. Remember, that switching costs for them are quite low.

Complement: Make an entry where the average order is smaller, more frequent, and can be sold by junior people.

Fit Chart Legend: Reduce Customer Clout or, Broaden Client Base.

Entry and Exit Threats

Weakness: We have no proprietary items. Our plans and drawings belong, in general, to the client. While competing defections have been few, we must develop some specialties that defy casual transfer. We must also fear vertical backward competitive entry by our three prime types of customer. ADP, CAD, and other high-tech, computer-aided processes, which can be proprietary, may help us to avoid this threat.

Complement: Raise entry barriers by raising the level of technology and service and continuously lower costs to us and clients.

Fit Chart Legend: Create Entry Barriers

Weakness: We have high barriers to exit. Many of our jobs run over years—especially in the New Orleans office, and our ongoing task-order contract with Ford Motor Company would be hard to end. If we wanted to build in Baltimore, for instance, and shut down New

Orleans which may become only marginally profitable in a year or two, we would have a hell of a time doing it unless we could sell it off to our principal competitor. (The engineering consulting services industry is characterized by non-economic exit barriers—sons carrying on the family name, the panache of being a *registered* Professional Engineer, etc.)

Complement: Effect an entry where exit problems are not so pronounced.

Fit Chart Legend: Lower Exit Barriers

Growth Variables

Weakness: We are in a slow-growth industry with operations in two slow-growth locations. While we have fair market penetration, sales growth has barely kept step with inflation. This is giving us problems in attracting new employees and keeping the old at all levels. While profits, according to trade industry figures, have been above-average, we are investing excess cash flows in things that are foreign to our base business, which has diverted top management's attention away from building our basic business.

Complement: Enter either high-growth (or at least higher-growth) areas either industries or geographic areas.

Fit Chart Legend: Billings Growth Entry

Weakness: While our profits have been above the norm for our industry, it stems more from our long-term relationship with Ford Motor and one or two others. Further, many other areas of professional practice have higher net profit margins than ours, for instance, computer-aided-design (CAD) in which we are only marginally competent. The higher profit may come because of higher risk. Gaining CAD proficiency means a substantial immediate investment not only in equipment, but in training. And, due to the specialized nature of the personnel, much higher-than-normal downtime may result. Both of these factors may temporarily impact our profit stream, but the upside potential does appear to be great.

Complement: Enter higher-margin, higher-markup, higher-profit areas—either geographic or skill-wise.

Fit Chart Legend: Make Higher-Profit Entry

Marketing

Weakness: We are in a fragmented industry with low overall entry barriers and very little potential economies of scale. The learn ing curve has very little slope. Our clients have special industry/area specific needs with only limited transferability to other industries and geographies, and there are few benefits that increases in size alone can wring from our suppliers. And there are some diseconomies of scale; for instance, "QRC" quick reaction capability, keeps our clients happy and the net margins up. *But*, the larger we get, the less quickly can we respond. What we don't know is what the optimum market share should be. (We should not call it the "optimum" market share, but the "minimum" market share to insure survival and continued growth.)

Complement: Attain Minimum Market Share, which in our case, means having at least 100 billable bodies at work which, at $110,000 average yields $11 million minimum. We are billing about three times that in total. We have about 8% of the Detroit, and 6.5% of the New Orleans markets. And each has reached the magic number of 100 billable bodies.

Fit Chart Legend: Attain Minimum Market Share *or* attain critical billing mass.

Weakness: In accordance with classic PIMS (Profit Impact of Marketing Strategy) theory, in neither of our markets have we attained sufficient market share to insure our long-term survival. In other industries, that seems to be at the 35% market penetration figure. We don't know whether that statistic applies to us in our industry in the particular geographical areas we serve, we have the additional problem of defining the relevant market, and getting usable numbers.

Complement: Attain that market share that will allow us to give our customers maximum service, that will optimize our overhead spreads, that will not trigger large capital expenditures for either special buildings, equipment, or, for that matter cause us to move from our present locations.

Fit Chart Legend: Attain Maximum Market Penetration

Weakness: While we have some clients that give us work on a non-competitive basis, we cannot get a premium for it. In other words, we have no "pricing independence" except that our overheads are lower, and thus our net margins higher than the norm for the industry because of a flow of work that we do not have to prepare bids for. Only one or two firms, competing in the mechanical engineering field have this advantage. But it may hold true in other fields that we are considering entering due to the nature of the work, the growth rate, the inexperience of the competition, etc. We should either merge with them and thus compound the advantage or make sure in the event that we make a diversifying entry that either the sector or the target company has a large proportion of such work.

Complement: Attain a higher percentage of non-competitive work either by differentiating ourselves from the competition, by upping the level of QRC, or by other means yet to be discovered.

Fit Chart Legend: Attain Pricing Independence

Weakness: We are entirely dependent on three classes of clients, generally in the heavy industry area, except for the developers who are mostly in mall development. We need to serve other than such architects, developers and turnkey contractors. We need more different *kinds* of clients. For instance, we have no historical restoration work at all, no alteration work, no modernization work, no plant rebuild work, no bridge rebuild work, no co-generation work, no playground or recreation work, no golf courses, country clubs, etc. We need to broaden our client base. (this may infer the opposite of specialization with its supposedly higher net margins.)

Complement: We should try to broaden our client base by entering de novo or by acquiring firms that serve different clients in different markets than we now serve.

Fit Chart Legend: Broaden Client Base

Weakness: The dollar amount of all mechanical engineering consulting work for developers, turnkey contractors and architectural design firms we are contracting with is probably not more than $100 million dollars in each area. If we got it all, we would still not be a BIG company. If we could establish ourself, in say the bridge rehabilitation business, where the market is in the *billions* we would not suffer this restriction. We could go national or international and have some chance of attaining gross revenues in the $500 million to $1 billion level. In other words, while we're scheming and dreaming, let's dream and scheme BIG.

Complement: We should enter only those markets (either by industry or geography) that are truly big and bigger in absolute size than our present markets.

Fit Chart Legend: Enter Larger Markets

Weakness: While we have "salesmen" in both offices, they are really only office workers scanning industry reports and building permit applications and feeding the results to the middle managers who figure the job and then pass the results to the principals of the firm who then do the real selling. All of our *real* marketing is personal and done on golf courses and in the better clubs in the city. We do not advertise and we have never laid out a nickel for a public relations campaign. Being tied to such a restricted marketing methodology, while it has been successful so far, may not survive the retirement or death of our principal partners. If we are to expand by the acquisition route, we should look for firms that get either leads or work by some method other than one-on-one personal contact. (Note that some of our competition have hired public relations firms, have developed traveling exhibits, are writing articles for trade journals, and have junior partners serving on hospital boards and in other public-sector activities. And some are beginning to advertise now that the stigma has gone from this one-time non-professional approach to marketing.)

Complement: We must develop marketing methodologies that do not depend on personal social contact and explore entries into sectors that market by different methods than those we employ.

Fit Chart Legend: Add Marketing Method

Weakness: There are only a limited number of developers, architectural design firms, and turnkey contractors in each of our present market areas. We have a very limited client universe and have developed great dependence on them. We should try, in our diversification program, to enter activities where the number of potential clients is larger.

Complement: Enter industries with a large potential client base.

Fit Chart Legend: Increase Clients by Number

Weakness: Our services are too narrow. While confining ourselves to mechanical engineering services only has some advantages in that, as a "boutique" our clients can more easily focus on our abilities, still, in their attempts to lower their costs of contract negotiation and administration, they are leaning toward broadening their sub-contractors' responsibilities. That this has not yet been sensed by our competition should not deter us from becoming an "engineering conglomerate" or at least a major assembler of engineering services, as there are substantial savings to be realized in marketing, administration, and recruitment.

Complement: Develop a full line of engineering services probably beginning with the addition of electrical engineering services which, in much of the country, are combined with mechanical engineering services. Next add civil engineering, foundation engineering, sanitary engineering, etc. (In the alternative, in the event that such full-lining is too expensive to build due to high prices of target acquisitions, we should consider becoming an assembler or a "bundler" of engineering services—an engineering general contractor.)

Fit Chart Legend: Develop Full-Lining Potential

Weakness: There are some areas of activity that will not support our overhead structure and that will dilute our image as a top-of-the-line mechanical engineering design outfit. However other people are making money at it. "Slave-labor" contracting where design bodies are supplied like Kelly Girls on a daily, weekly, or monthly basis, is an example. While we would not like the name of J.T. Smith to be associated with this kind of activity, we should consider this so-called "second-lining." We could start such an outfit de novo or enter by acquisition and not integrate it into our operations, but operate it as a stand-alone. We constantly run into situations where we are asked to supply such services. We can supply these leads to such a service and from time to time, we ourselves need such services but have refrained from using them due to cultural, non-economic, arbitrary decisions of the firms' founder-owners.

Complement: Create or acquire a "slave-labor" operation and operate it as a stand-alone.

Fit Chart Legend: Make Second-Line Entry

Weakness: The advent of CAD (Computer-Aided Design) might give us some problems. We are only just now entering the area and encountering some resistance from some of the old-line employees. For many, many jobs it is much faster and thus bills out at lower cost to the client. This is, in a very real sense, a "functional competitor" to our standard methods of pencil-on-paper design. With new equipment and new software coming out daily, we must face up to the fact that some of the smaller firms that compete with us don't do any pencil-on-paper work at all. It could be that they will eventually cut price and do us in. Rather than sit back and wait for that guillotine, let us target one of the better shops and again, as in the preceding entry on "slave-labor," operate it separately as a stand-alone and feed it some of our leads and even some of our work that might better be done by CAD.

Complement: Meet potential CAD competition by entering the CAD market with a full-scale entry exclusively engaged in CAD services.

Fit Chart Legend: Effect CAD Entry

Weakness: Due to our association with the automobile companies in Detroit with their years-long resistance to safety, fuel economy, comfort, repairability, and beauty; with the increasing advent of smog-filled cities, ozone problems, greenhouse effect, acid rain, and other pollution problems; with long lines at the gas pump, and huge trade deficits caused by petroleum imports, and our work for the oil and petro-chemical companies in the Gulf, our image as a benefactor of mankind is deteriorating and we are finding it increasingly difficult to recruit the better engineers. We do know that this was a major reason that the third generation of Smiths refuse to join our firm. We should enter—or accelerate or expand our activity if we are presently involved—areas of social responsibility such as retirement housing, environmental engineering, recreation facilities, etc.—doing more that is identified with the public rather than with the private benefit.

Complement: Make an entry that will enhance our image as a community benefactor.

Fit Chart Legend: Improve Social Image

Regulatory & Legal Aspects

Weakness: Our industry, with the exception of the licensing requirements for professional engineer status, is relatively unregulated and has no government subsidy and no government sanctioned monopolistic benefits such as are granted to public utilities. However, one of the most exciting things to come along in many years is the U.S. government's PURPA regulation (Public Utilities Regulation Policies Act) that forces local public utilities to take power generated by industry in so-called co-generation projects usually using waste heat from the process industries. We have had only a peripheral acquaintance with this growing field—generally in the design of heating and air conditioning systems.

Complement: Exploit PURPA potential by entering the co-generation area.

Fit Chart Legend: Exploit PURPA Potential

Weakness: Ours is a fractionated industry with thousands of small shops. Most are poorly managed. Some are heavily niched, either serving special geographic-dependent needs or having a lock on some very large accounts. But this may be changing. Two forces at work are the advent of CAD and communications that will allow us to transmit designs quickly and inexpensively. With a central storage system that can store, literally, millions of proprietary design details that can be recalled any place in the world in minutes, the design of a maharaja's palace can be assembled in Detroit and sent to New Delhi by satellite. CAD is going to allow the concentration of the industry.

Complement: Exploit the concentration potential of our industry.

Fit Chart Legend: Exploit Concentration Potential

Weakness: Unfortunately, we have very little tax shelter available to us out of our operations. But when involved in a merger, acquisition or a buyout—expecially a highly leveraged buyout—there are a number of ways to shelter income that should be explored. For instance, the very generous tax shelter provisions of the ESOP programs should be explored. And acquired assets can be "stepped up" and amortized at rates higher than their true economic rate. Also, it should be noted that the tax attributes of the generation of intellectual properties including Research and Development Limited Partnerships (RDLPs) and tax credits for research have not been explored.

Complement: Exploit Tax Shelter Potential

Fit Chart Legend: Exploit MAB Tax Shelter Potential

Weakness: We have only one patent, no technology that can be transferred for money, no trademarks or copyrights, and very little proprietary technology. We should, if we can, target an entry where we can pick up some protections on our potential income streams.

Complement: Target industries that are characterized by the generation of intellectual property rights (IPR).

Fit Chart Legend: Exploit IPR Potential

Weakness: Our headquarters are in heavily unionized Detroit. We have not completely escaped the long arm of the union and came near losing the election last year, thus escaping ongoing problems in recruitment, training, etc. Our New Orleans operation has not been affected as it is not a strong union town and there is no history of professionals being organized there. We believe that the life of the union will be short-lived here in Detroit. However, our escape was so close, we want to insure that any entry we make is not an entry-point for unionization.

Complement: Explore only those entries in those geographical areas where there is no strong tendency to unionize professionals.

Fit Chart Legend: Non-Union Entry

Operations

Weakness: Only 20 percent of our sales are from the resale of subcontracted services. Some services such as environmental planning, our largest purchase sector, are in short supply and jobs and billings have been held up because of it. *Percentage-wise* they make more money than we do. If we grow by horizontal acquisition, say double our present sales, we will probably double our purchases. We have the problem as to whether that will give us more clout on our suppliers because we're buying more, or less clout because their services are in more demand than ever. The other factor is that in some cases, where we must bid on a job, the premiums that we must pay because of high subcontractor costs have lost us the job.

Complement: We must lower our price-dependence on our subcontractors.

Fit Chart Legend: Develop Supplier Clout

Weakness: We have very little clout on our customers except that we are the archivists for their designs, but they may call for them at will. The fact that we are local, operating in only two non-contiguous locations, and they are, in general, multiplant, multinational, or multiarea operators, gives us very little clout—only the social clout of the principal partners is important. With the present movement in the world, and especially in the United States in this deconglomerating age, toward decentralization, we still have trouble in getting a job in Winston-Salem, N.C. to be run out of Detroit—the Winston-Salem operators want local talent on the job. But that talent is often expensive because it is inexperienced and does not have the CAD-supported data bank that we believe will be important in the future. Further, we should gain clout by emphasizing our skills in what used to be called "supervision" but which is now, because of liability, called "inspection." Such services not only tie the clients to us by making them more dependent on us, such services are very profitable and we should be able to cash in on industry's movement toward the reduction of inhouse supervisory services and the purchase of "inspection" services.

Complement: Develop more services that will cause our clients to increasingly depend on us.

Fit Chart Legend: Develop Client Clout

Weakness: We seem to be locked into an invariate operating cost structure because draftsmen are hard to find and get increasing rates of pay. Scale economies are hard to develop and the slope of our learning curve is not very steep. However, CAD may change all that. The ratio of one professional to five draftsmen, is reduced to one to three where CAD has been introduced and is heading downward. Today, CAD content can run from 20% to 80%, averages about 40% but has been growing about 10% per year. In five years it will *average* 80%. Thus we will unlock the structure and will substantially reduce our costs and get the job out the door faster.

Complement: Develop our CAD skills and resources to reduce operating costs.

Fit Chart Legend: Reduce Direct Costs

Weakness: While reduction of direct costs is important, it is overhead—usually in the form of fixed costs such as rent—that impacts the bottom line and which, in hard times, is the primary reason for engineering business failures. We must learn to operate lean and mean *and* learn how to reduce our indirect costs by expansion of our present activities. One of the best ways of doing this is vertical and horizontal integration and by full-lining. That is the way the competition is going not only in Detroit, but all over the country.

Complement: Use the merger/acquisition process to reduce overhead.

Fit Chart Legend: Reduce Overhead

Weakness: Downtime, that is unbilled bodies, is the curse of the consulting business. While such charges usually go directly to overhead accounts, because they are so important in our business, it is listed separately. (The participants are warned not to double-count.) Downtime seems to decrease as the number of billable bodies goes up, so the reductions in staff that we anticipate from CAD may exacerbate the problem. Probably horizontal merger is the best way to go to reduce downtime. Market extension entries, while not as sensitive to downtime reduction as are pure horizontal mergers, still can be effective absorbers of downtime bodies provided that the job is sufficiently priced to pay for the transportation and maintenance. We should also have a carefully contrived program to absorb downtime in our CAD training program.

Complement: Reduce downtime by emphasizing the Market Intensification Mode.

Fit Chart Legend: Reduce Downtime

Weakness: One of the problems in any program of expansion is the capital it takes to finance it. In our business, the marginal, incremental capital cost to add one more dollar of sales is about 11% for working capital and 13% for fixed capital. (The working capital number has been constant for many years but the fixed capital number is double the historical number because of the CAD revolution which requires very expensive machinery and training which has to be capitalized.) While the numbers are hard to come by, some of our newer personnel claim that our numbers are higher than the competition. Others are not so sure. An educated guess says that the incremental capital cost is a function of size and that the bigger the operation the lower the incremental capital cost due to more rigid billing and collection procedures and more economical purchasing.

Complement: Reduce the marginal, incremental capital costs to add sales dollars.

Fit Chart Legend: Reduce Capital Costs

SUPPLEMENTS

A "supplement" is, according to Webster's New Collegiate Dictionary's first definition, "something that completes or makes an addition [to]." In the WOFC process, I have chosen this word to describe the action that must be taken to exploit basic strengths. Just as a "dietary supplement" adds to the strength and well-being of a person so, in the merger/acquisition area, any entry move must supplement the basic strengths of the organization being planned for. As might be expected, people-strengths are by far the most important, and they are treated first. (Please note that excess resources or under-utilized resources fit better into the Complement side of the Fit Chart because there is something wrong with an operation that has excess machinery, equipment, property, etc. However, experience has shown a very strong tendency to classify as a strength or supplement, any under-utilized resource. In the long run, it does not matter which side it is entered in so long as the participants understand the variable for what it is.)

Strength: We have highly skilled people at the top both at board level and as managers. Two have taken advanced degrees in "engineering management" with a heavy accent on human relations—rare in this industry. With the exception of the Financial V.P., all are registered professional engineers. Their experience, without exception, is in engineering-related enterprise. It is a general feeling that our top management is under-utilized, that they can do more, considerably more, with their talents.

Supplement: We should learn how to exploit our top management skills. But we should insure that it is something they *want* to do and are good at.

Fit Chart Legend: Top Management Fit

Strength: We have a highly skilled, dependable group of middle managers who double as both line (billable bodies) and staff (administrators). Some have spent their entire working lives here. We must ask and answer the question: how important is it that we enter a field of endeavor where their skills and knowledges can be utilized?

Supplement: Learn to exploit our middle management skills.

Fit Chart Legend: Middle Management Fit

Strength: We have a large staff of draftsmen who are, in general, familiar with our work. Some are in school getting their engineering degrees. We must ask and answer the question: how important is it that we enter a field where their skills can be utilized?

Supplement: Learn to exploit our staff skills.
Fit Chart Legend: Staff Skills Fit

Strength: We have a small staff of white collar people which include librarians, bookkeepers, secretaries, typists, and some blue-collar janitorial and service people. We must ask and answer the question: how important is it that we enter a field of endeavor where their skills can be utilized?
Supplement: Learn to exploit our white- and blue-collar skills.
Fit Chart Legend: White- & Blue-Collar Fit

Strength: We have an experienced group of "project development" people who really function as "salesmen" though that word is taboo in the solicitation of professional engineering services. They scan Dodge Reports, building permits, etc. for leads, write them up, and then point the partner principals toward the power that will award the job. The partners do the closing. We must ask the question: how important is it to utilize our present staff of "project development" people in any expansion move?
Supplement: Utilize Project Development Staff.
Fit Chart Legend: Salesmen Fit

Strength: Our customers made us what we are, they pay our rent, educate our children and put food on our table. To ignore their wants and needs is to ignore our very existence. Friction and a modicum of stress are natural components of an economic relationship that has profit as its goal. Old friends are the best because they have learned to cross-nurture and to communicate. And good communications are the stuff of which profitable relationships are made. One of our greatest strengths is our client list. it seems logical that we would first find out what services our present customers want to buy before chasing rainbows looking for the legendary pot of gold at the end.
Supplement: Exploit our present client relationship by entering those areas that synchronize with their needs.
Fit Chart Legend: Customer (Client) Fit

Physical Resources Fit

Strength: We have excellent facilities in both Detroit and New Orleans (we own our Detroit headquarters and have a long-term lease in New Orleans). With the contemplated reduction in staff brought about by CAD, we should have ample room to expand in both locations at minimal expanse. How important is it that we enter a field where we can utilize this resource?

Supplement: Utilize our present physical plant.
Fit Chart Legend: Workplace Fit

Operations Fit

Strength: We are constantly doing work for some of our subcontractors and some of our clients become subcontractors from time to time. We "borrow" men from each other as we "assemble" a job. So we have a kind of de facto vertical integration. The first question to be asked is this: can we wring more profit out of the marketplace if we actually merged operations—or at least the major ones? And the second question is: where is the profit vertically in our industry?

Supplement: Will our operations improve if we integrate vertically?

Fit Chart Legend: Vertical Integration Fit

Strength: Our computer installation is becoming more important each day as our electronic data processing system is expanded to interface and interact with our CAD system. We must answer the question: how important is it that we utilize the machinery, equipment, personnel, software, and communications links that we have developed in any entry?

Supplement: Utilize our present EDP complex.

Fit Chart Legend: EDP Fit

Strength: We have a high level of intelligence in the organization and have been exposed to hundreds of different environments all over the world, even though we are based in Detroit with a branch operation in New Orleans. This exposure and experience has to be of some value. We must look for synergistic situations where $2 + 2 = 5$.

Supplement: Exploit synergistic potential.

Fit Chart Legend: Synergy

N.B. The student will note that there are many, many more variables written up in the laundry list of Fit Chart variables that appeared in the Fall, 1977 issue of *Mergers & Acquisitions*. They include factors such as scale, industrial relations, financing considerations, budgeting, and many different kinds of information flows. However, these concerns have been distributed out to the above variables discussed, or have been arbitrarily dismissed as inapplicable or only remotely applicable to this J.T. Smith case study.

EXHIBIT A-6
WOFC Sessions Schedule for J.T. Smith Consultants

First Day

5:00 Informal Reception

6:00 Dinner

7:30 WOFC Orientation

8:30 Q&A

9:00 Group or individual study period—WOFC material

Second Day

8:00 First Session

Review of Opportunities, discussion and clarification, exclusion of those not clearly understood or of not meeting exclusionary criteria.

10:00 Break

10:15 Second Session

Applying exclusionary criteria and transfer of Opportunities to blackboard Wheel.

12:15 Lunch Break

1:45 Third Session

Exploring world potential by comparing growth rates of Product or Service Extensions with growth rates in new geographic territories to select Free Form entries.

3:00 Break

3:15 Fourth Session

Review and discussion of "Descriptions of Potential Variables"

5:00 Reception

7:00 Dinner

8:30 Private or Group study of notebook material including all Strength and Weakness Sheets

Third Day

8:00 First Session

Continued discussion of strengths & weaknesses, development of Tally Sheet, computer entry of variables.

10:00 Break

10:15 Second Session

Review of Delphi Process and voting rules. First Round of the Delphi.

12:15 Lunch

1:45 Third Session

Completion of Delphi Rounds Two, Three and Four

3:30 Break

3:45 Fourth Session

Vertical distribution of Final Round scores. Horizontal totalling, rank-ordering of target entries and development of The Strategic Statement.

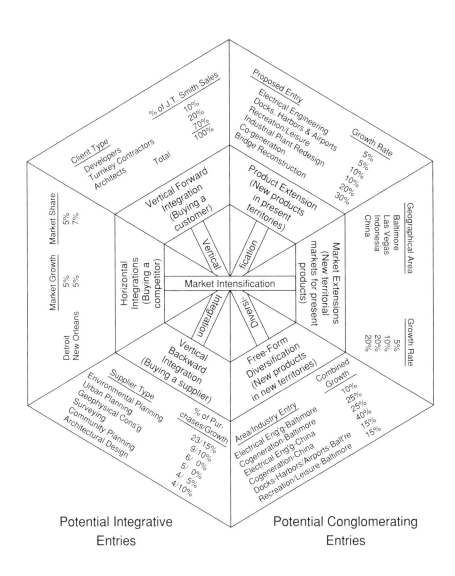

Potential Integrative Entries

Potential Conglomerating Entries

Exhibit A-8
Instant Delphi Tally Sheet for Fit Chart: J.T. Smith Consultants

	Complements								
[Growth Rates in Brackets]	L.T. Cycle Res.	Bill-ings Growth	Profit Improve-ment	Min. Mkt. Pen'n	Full-Lin'g Pot'l	Cust-omer Clout	Reduce Over-Head	Reduce Down-time	Sub-total
ROUND ONE:									
Bill Smith, CHRM & CEO	0	0	100	0	300	0	0	100	500
Tom Jones, Pres. & COO	200	200	100	0	0	0	100	100	700
H. Miller, Ex. VP	150	150	100	0	0	0	0	0	400
H. Teets, VP Sales	100	100	100	200	200	0	0	0	700
W. Clarke, VP Finance	0	100	100	0	0	0	100	100	400
J. Walsh, VP Eng'g	0	50	100	0	0	50	80	70	350
R. Connally, (New Orleans)	100	100	100	0	200	90	0	0	590
Total	550	700	700	200	700	140	280	370	3640
Average	79	100	100	29	100	20	40	53	520
ROUND TWO:									
Bill Smith, CHRM & CEO	0	70	30	0	300	0	0	100	500
Tom Jones, Pres. & COO	200	200	0	0	0	0	100	100	600
H. Miller, Ex. VP	150	150	0	0	100	0	0	0	400
H. Teets, VP Sales	100	100	0	200	300	0	0	0	700
W. Clarke, VP Finance	0	100	110	10	0	0	100	80	400
J. Walsh, VP Eng'g	10	50	0	0	0	0	140	150	350
R. Connally, (New Orleans)	100	100	0	0	70	70	80	60	480
Total	560	770	140	210	770	70	420	490	3430
Average	80	110	20	30	110	10	60	70	490
ROUND THREE:									
Bill Smith, CHRM & CEO	80	100	X	X	300	X	0	0	480
Tom Jones, Pres. & COO	200	240	X	X	100	X	100	0	640
H. Miller, Ex. VP	150	200	X	X	100	X	100	0	550
H. Teets, VP Sales	100	100	X	X	300	X	0	0	500
W. Clarke, VP Finance	0	200	X	X	40	X	200	100	540
J. Walsh, VP Eng'g	0	0	X	X	0	X	90	200	290
R. Connally, (New Orleans)	100	0	X	X	0	X	0	190	290
Total	630	840	X	X	840	X	490	490	3290
Average	90	120	X	X	120	X	70	70	470
ROUND FOUR:									
Bill Smith, CHRM & CEO	100	200	X	X	300	X	0	0	600
Tom Jones, Pres. & COO	200	200	X	X	100	X	0	0	500
H. Miller, Ex. VP	150	200	X	X	100	X	10	40	500
H. Teets, VP Sales	100	40	X	X	300	X	0	0	440
W. Clarke, VP Finance	50	200	X	X	0	X	200	100	550
J. Walsh, VP Eng'g	0	0	X	X	10	X	0	300	310
R. Connally, (New Orleans)	100	0	X	X	100	X	0	50	250
Total	700	840	X	X	910	X	210	490	3150
Average	100	120	X	X	130	X	30	70	450

				Supplements					
Top Mg't Fit	Mid. Mg't Fit	Staff Skills Fit	Sales- men Fit	Cust- omer Fit	EDP Fit	Syn- ergy	Sub- Total	Effic- iency	Rank Order
0	0	100	0	200	0	200	500	1000	---
100	0	0	0	100	100	0	300	1000	---
200	100	100	0	50	50	0	600	1000	---
0	0	110	90	0	0	100	300	1000	---
0	100	180	0	200	0	120	600	1000	---
300	150	100	50	0	50	0	650	1000	---
100	0	110	0	150	50	0	410	1000	---
700	350	700	140	700	350	420	3360	7000	---
100	50	100	20	100	50	60	480	1000	---
0	0	100	X	200	0	200	500	1000	---
300	100	0	X	0	0	0	400	1000	---
200	150	100	X	100	50	0	600	1000	---
0	0	0	X	300	0	0	300	1000	---
0	0	110	X	40	300	150	600	1000	---
300	200	0	X	100	50	0	650	1000	---
40	250	40	X	100	90	0	520	1000	---
840	700	350	X	840	490	350	3570	7000	---
120	100	50	X	120	70	50	510	1000	---
100	0	0	X	200	20	200	520	1000	---
300	60	0	X	0	0	0	360	1000	---
200	200	40	X	10	0	0	450	1000	---
0	200	0	X	300	0	0	500	1000	---
10	0	0	X	0	300	150	460	1000	---
200	10	100	X	300	100	0	710	1000	---
100	360	0	X	100	140	10	710	1000	---
910	830	140	X	910	560	360	3710	7000	---
130	119	20	X	130	80	51	530	1000	---
300	30	X	X	70	0	X	400	1000	---
300	200	X	X	0	0	X	500	1000	---
200	210	X	X	0	90	X	500	1000	---
0	200	X	X	300	60	X	560	1000	---
20	0	X	X	130	300	X	450	1000	---
200	40	X	X	300	150	X	690	1000	----
100	300	X	X	250	100	X	750	1000	---
1120	980	X	X	1050	700	X	3850	7000	---
160	140	X	X	50	100	X	550	1000	

Exhibit A-9
Fit Chart: J.T. Smith Consultants

[Growth Rates in Brackets]	L.T. Cycle Res.	Bill-ings Growth	Profit Improve-ment	Min. Mkt. Pen'n	Full-Lin'g Pot'l	Cust-omer Clout	Reduce Over-Head	Reduce Down-time	Sub-total
COLUMN NUMBER	1	2	3	4	5	6	7	8	9
1st approximation	79	100	100	29	100	20	40	53	520
2nd approximation	80	110	20	30	110	10	60	70	490
3rd approximation	90	120	X	X	120	X	70	70	470
Final	100	120	X	X	130	X	30	70	450
HORIZONTAL INTEGRATION									
Detroit [5%]	0	40	X	X	60	X	30	70	200
New Orleans [5%]	0	40	X	X	60	X	30	70	200
MARKET EXTENSION									
Baltimore [5%]	0	40	X	X	30	X	10	30	110
Las Vegas [10%]	80	80	X	X	30	X	10	30	230
Indonesia [20%]	80	120	X	X	0	X	0	0	200
China [20%]	40	120	X	X	0	X	0	0	160
MARKET INTENSIFICATION MODE									
VERTICAL BACKWARD INTEGRATION									
Environmental planning [15%]	40	40	X	X	0	X	10	10	100
Urban planning [10%]	40	40	X	X	0	X	10	10	100
Geophysical consulting [0%]	0	0	X	X	0	X	0	0	0
Surveying [0%]	0	0	X	X	30	X	20	0	50
Community planning [5%]	40	40	X	X	0	X	10	20	110
Architectural design [10%]	0	0	X	X	130	X	30	70	230
VERTICAL FORWARD INTEGRATION									
Architectural design svcs [5%]	0	0	X	X	130	X	30	70	230
Turnkey contractors [10%]	0	0	X	X	0	X	0	0	0
Developers [10%]	0	0	X	X	0	X	0	0	0
VERTICAL INTEGRATION MODE									
PRODUCT OR SERVICE EXTENSION									
Electrical engineering [5%]	0	0	X	X	130	X	30	70	230
Docks, harbors & airports [5%]	60	0	X	X	60	X	20	60	200
Recreation/leisure [10%]	40	40	X	X	0	X	20	40	140
Plant redesign [15%]	40	30	X	X	60	X	30	70	230
Cogeneration [20%]	100	60	X	X	130	X	10	50	350
Bridge retrofits [30%]	60	120	X	X	60	X	20	40	300
FREE-FORM EXTENSION									
Electrical engineering-Balto.	40	0	X	X	60	X	10	20	130
Cogeneration-Baltimore	100	120	X	X	130	X	0	50	400
Electrical engineering-China	100	60	X	X	0	X	0	0	160
Cogeneration-China	100	120	X	X	0	X	0	0	220
Docks/harbors/airports-Balto.	60	20	X	X	60	X	30	40	210
Recreation/leisure-Balto.	40	60	X	X	60	X	30	40	230
DIVERSIFICATION MODE									

				Supplements					
Top Mg't Fit	Mid. Mg't Fit	Staff Skills Fit	Sales- men Fit	Cust- omer Fit	EDP Fit	Syn- ergy	Sub- Total	Effic- iency	Rank Order
10	11	12	13	14	15	16	17	18	19
100	50	100	20	100	50	60	480	1000	---
120	100	50	0	120	70	50	510	1000	---
130	119	20	X	130	80	51	530	1000	---
160	140	X	X	150	100	X	550	1000	---
160	140	X	X	150	100	X	550	750	1
160	140	X	X	150	100	X	550	750	2
160	70	X	X	0	50	X	280	390	
100	70	X	X	0	50	X	220	450	
40	0	X	X	0	50	X	90	290	
40	0	X	X	0	50	X	90	250	
							Average:	480	
40	35	X	X	50	50	X	175	275	
40	35	X	X	50	50	X	175	275	
0	0	X	X	0	50	X	50	50	
80	35	X	X	100	50	X	265	315	
40	35	X	X	50	50	X	175	285	
[120]	70	X	X	[100]	100	X	390	620	4
[120]	[35]	X	X	100	[100]	X	355	585	5
100	70	X	X	50	100	X	320	320	
100	35	X	X	50	100	X	285	285	
							Average:	334	
[100]	[70]	X	X	150	100	X	420	650	3
150	70	X	X	25	100	X	345	545	
100	70	X	X	50	100	X	320	460	
50	105	X	X	50	100	X	305	535	
50	70	X	X	0	100	X	220	570	
50	70	X	X	0	100	X	220	520	
100	35	X	X	0	50	X	185	315	
50	35	X	X	0	50	X	135	535	
100	35	X	X	0	50	X	185	345	
50	35	X	X	0	50	X	135	355	
100	35	X	X	0	50	X	185	395	
50	35	X	X	0	50	X	135	365	
							Average:	466	

EXHIBIT A-10
The Strategic Statement

The findings of the WOFC Task Group can be summed up as follows:

Our first priority is to expand our operations in the Detroit area which showed an "efficiency" of 75%—i.e., 750 points average out of a possible 1,000. The expansion should be by absorption of competitors. The same thing is true for our New Orleans operation.

At the same time, we should explore immediately the addition of electrical engineering services in our present territories. This also should be by acquisition or merger.

We should also move backward and absorb our architectural design subcontractor or one of their competitors.

Finally, we should move forward and absorb one of the smaller architectural design firms that we now serve.

It is noted that no market extension came in at above the 500 mark which the group decided was the cut-off point for consideration, no matter how attractive a target might appear.

The firm should learn much more about the cogeneration area—especially as it is developing on the east coast. Planning is directed to build a reference library in the area and everyone is asked to keep their eyes and ears open for a possible entry since the profit potential may offset the risk of entry.

APPENDIX B

THE SYSTEMS APPROACH TO GROWTH-BY-ACQUISITION

Stanley Foster Reed

INTRODUCTION

It is well known that the economic performance of firms growing (but not necessarily diversifying) exclusively by the merger/acquisition route, varies widely. Poor post-deal performance can be attributed to many things including chance. But the real reason is lack of structure in the targeting of, the search for, and the evaluation of the "fit" of prospective acquisitions.

Exhibit B-4 of this Appendix B, The Flow Chart, shows a "systems" approach to the merger/acquisition process. Let us examine it, step-by-step. (The steps and circled numbers coincide.)

STEP ONE

The first thing to learn is this: the approach to growth by the M&A route is different at different levels in the organization as the "Strategic Skills & Behaviors" Table, Exhibit A-1 of Appendix A, clearly illustrates. And the first step is to create a systems flow chart for the level that is under study. (Exhibit B-4 has been set up as an Enterprise Level exercise.) It is also at this point that the responsibility for administering the program or programs is laid out in the Business Development Program (BDP) which answers many questions such as: How decentralized is the process to be? Do lower-level people not only search out opportunities but price and negotiate them or do they just search and leave pricing and negotiating to headquarters? In general, the Corporate Strategy Policy Group will have created a "Guide" that will spell out exactly who will be responsible for what at each levels.

STEP ONE-A

Do a financial self-analysis (see Exhibit B-5).

STEP TWO

With the level selected, the BDP is created. Some of the questions that must be asked and answered (without dealing with specific Opportunities) are these:

• What is the *economic* relationship between the level selected and other levels? Is transfer pricing fair? Are shared costs, such as R&D costs properly distributed? Are headquarters costs properly attributed or are they lumped? And what about assigned capital? Has anyone discovered how much capital is in use at the selected level? What are the historical working and fixed capital costs of financing one marginal incremental dollar of sales? What are they today? What value-drivers affect the firm's economic value the most? (See Exhibit B-5, "Sample Financial Analysis Using ALCAR's Value-Planner.") What are the economic *goals* of the parent? Have they been written down? How do they compare with *results*? How *did* they compare? (In other words has planning worked?) What are the values and beliefs that drive the corporate culture which in turn drives M&A decisionmaking? Are they technology driven? Market leader driven? Are they anti-union? Are they concerned with their public image? Do they care *how* they make money?

• Other questions. Is there a *generic strategy* (expressed or unexpressed) at work? For instance, are they committed only to low-price and high-volume items supported by massive advertising as the only way to make money? And what happens to the profits? Can they be reinvested at the Function, Product, Business, Sector or Corporate level? Or do profits flow up to the Enterprise level and are then redistributed downward?

• And compensation? How are executives compensated? Do they share only in the success of their own level or do they share in the overall success of the corporation?

• What *uneconomic* forces are at work? At Bethlehem, wrongly, they cared for only one thing, to make steel–all they could of it. Profit was incidental. (Lately they've learned.)

A formal program (the BDP) to accomplish some specific result or results must be drawn up. It should specify the value-drivers, e.g., target growth rate, and perhaps other, generally exclusionary criteria about the kind of target, its size, location, etc. that the firm does *not* wish to consider under any circumstances. It will name the people in charge of the program and outline their responsibilities; it will refer to a Flow Chart the same as or similar to Exhibit Four. It will (or should) include advice on keeping logs on leads from outside sources, and many other items that are covered in this book. An important input into this process will be a financial self-evaluation (using the ALCAR concepts as shown in Exhibit B-5). This self-evaluation will tell the firm what value-drivers (sales growth, operating profit margin, fixed and working capital requirements, tax rates, and cost of capital) most affect the firm's economic value. For example, if your company's value is sensitive to sales growth, look for companies with a distribution network that can push your current products into new markets.

STEP THREE

After the BDP is on paper, the search for Opportunities begins in general accordance with Exhibit One of this Appendix B, called "Instructions for Inputs to WOFC Sessions." It should be as free-wheeling as possible because the Fit Chart will weed out the off-the-wall ideas. Each Opportunity, whether a specific company to be targeted, or a desirable product line, *or* an interesting industry to target, should be submitted on a separate sheet. (See Exhibit A-2 of Appendix A.)

STEP FOUR

Classify all Opportunity Descriptions by their Entry Level and for this Enterprise Level exercise gather only those which qualify by the criteria recited in the BDP. File all other entry suggestions under the BDP for that particular Level.

STEP FIVE

Create an informal "Consciousness Program" that will create discussion among everyone as to the competitive forces driving the business. Who are we, really? How do we stand in the industry? Start to think about: what do we do well? poorly? and why? Who are we, really, competitively? (At least one person, if not more, should be directed to read Michael Porter's "Competitive Strategy" and lead others in a discussion of how it applies directly to the operation being planned for. Using the ALCAR methodology, the Porter framework can also be linked to the value-drivers which help understanding of the affect of alternative competitive strategies on shareholder value.

STEP SIX

Again following Exhibit B-1 to this Appendix B, record each such strength and weakness on a separate sheet. (See Exhibits A-3 and A-4.) This will inevitably include many items that deal with communications problems, discrimination in promotion, etc. But take them all in—we'll deal with them later.

STEP SEVEN

Before breaking down the S&Ws, we must move up to the Opportunity Sheets that have been accumulated. They must be carefully reviewed and similar notions combined. They must be carefully edited and extended with as much additional competitive informaiton as is readily available. No one person should be allowed to arbitrarily dismiss a suggestion as that is the task of the Fit Chart. (If there are too many to consider within budget or time constraints, it requires a group decision.) Each Opportunity is then classified in one of the six categories and three modes shown on the Flow Chart and described in detail in Chapter Two, and is entered on the Wheel of Opportunity. (See Exhibit A-7 of Appendix A for a typical Wheel.)

STEP SEVEN-A

This step extracts from the Opportunities, those that might better be sent into the Internal Development Program (IDP) than be entered in the Wheel of Opportunity as part of the External Development Program (EDP). (They can be mixed in a Wheel but only those with extensive experience with the WOFC method should try it.) One of the drivers behind the EDP is the necessity to replace mature products and they might better be handled internally than externally once their life-cycle has been identified by the group documenting the Product

Life Cycle of present lines of endeavor. Another source of internal development candidates are obvious entries that can be handled inhouse more expeditiously (which generally means more economically) than they can by being certified into the EDP.

These are then written up in a series of Tasks to do the market analyses, R&D workups, etc., necessary to get them considered for inclusion in the IDP.

STEP EIGHT

The Internal Development Program (IDP), which is usually R&D-based, is created to compete with the External Development Program (EDP) which is M&A-based. The rules for the competition must be spelled out in detail. When properly done, they will stimulate both Programs.

STEP NINE

With the Opportunities split up and certified into either the EDP or the IDP, the next task is to review and classify the Strengths and Weaknesses as they appear on the sheets as shown in sample Exhibits A-3 and A-4. However, these sheets will inevitably contain important observations, suggestions, complaints, etc. which deal not only with general organizational problems but problems specifically affecting the firm's growth. Those strengths and weaknesses that are organizationally-dependent are then certified down to the next step.

STEP NINE-A

There are inevitably produced in any self-analysis program strengths and, especially, weaknesses that deal with how the organization has developed, how it has been designed and how it functions. It is important to separate out those strengths and weaknesses that are generic to *both* the IDP and the EDP. This step treats these organizationally-dependent strengths and weaknesses. Our experience has been that most deal with problems in vertical and horizontal communication, complaints about inequities in compensation between executives in the acquiring and the acquired companies, "sweetheart" deals on transfer pricings, nepotism, rewriting of negative reports, etc. These problems are usually organizational-specific and must be solved if both the IDP and EDP are to proceed successfully. A typical task write-up as submitted on a "Weakness Analysis," is shown as Exhibit B-2 to this Appendix B, and is sent down to the Organization Design/Development Program (ODDP).

STEP NINE-B

Each of the Weaknesses and Strengths are converted respectively to Complements and Supplements and entered on the Fit Chart. (See Appendix A, Exhibit A-4.)

STEP TEN

With a good idea of the merger/acquisition-related strengths and weaknesses and with some notion of organization-related problems, the Organization Design & Development Program (ODDP) is inaugurated whose eventual object will be to create the structure that will assure the success of both the IDP and the EDP (and as some practitioners have discovered, their ongoing operations as well).

STEP ELEVEN

This is the soul, the heart of the EDP because it rates the weaknesses and strengths, now converted to the operating variables, Complements and Supplements, relative to each other. (Read the Case presented in Appendix A to learn how the Delphi process, which rates the variables, works.)

STEP ELEVEN-A

This value is then used to rate each of the Opportunities that had been entered into the Wheel of Opportunity outlined in Step Seven all as explained in detail in Chapter Two and illustrated in Appendix A with special attention to Exhibit A-9. At the conclusion of the WOFC process, a Strategic Statement, (Appendix A, Exhibit A-10) is issued that summarizes the results of the WOFC exercise.

STEP TWELVE

With the target industries defined, and with the priorities defined by the Rank Orders derived from the Fit Chart in hand, with the Organizational Design Development Program in full swing, and with the Internal Development Program well-defined and in place, the External Development Program can begin.

STEP THIRTEEN

The most important thing now is the Search and Screen program as outlined in Chapter Two, pages 23–33, which continually rate target industries and companies against the criteria established by the Fit Chart. The Rank-Order Number One is targeted first and each candidate company that is uncovered is rated against all others *in that category* in the Expert Analysis process.

STEP FOURTEEN

All of the Search and Screen activity and Expert Analysis is brought to focus in an "Industry Situation Analysis" (ISA) which has the following key elements:

a. It will look carefully at the differences between return on capital, or cash flow or other differentiating financial criteria *vertically* in a detailed analysis that answers the question as to "where the money is" in the business. Too often myths abound about certain industries, that one is "more profitable" than the other. But there *are* huge differences in the efficiencies of capital employed at various levels vertically within any one industry, and they must be analyzed to discover at which level to enter.

b. Every industry has a learning curve and the slope of it is extremely important to determine. Can you add the historical quantities produced in a horizontal merger if the operations are not physically integrated? What pricing policy will be followed in future to exploit the slope? Can the slope be steepened? All of this, plus the Expert Analysis feeds into the ISA to help the company come to a go-no-go decision.

c. The analysis will also tot up the evolutionary aspects of the industry and document its past, present, and future economic structure, conduct, and performance. (For an excellent discussion of industry evolution see Michael E. Porter's "Competitive Strategy: Techniques for Analyzing Industries and Competitors" pages 156 to 188, and its Appendix B, "How to Conduct an Industry Analysis.")

STEP FIFTEEN

If the decision is "no-go," the whole file goes to the dead file and you go back to Step Twelve and pick the next highest Rank Order target industry (or company) for expert analysis. (It is not uncommon to have three or four such programs going at once but that depends on many factors including budgets, manpower, size of projected entry, etc.)

If the decision is "go," the hard work begins. A separate file is maintained for each target company which will contain at least the following: credit reports, officer profiles, fact books, annual reports, and any competitive intelligence (In this regard, the book, "Business Competitor Intelligence" by Sammon, Kurland & Spitalnic will tell you where legal and ethical intelligence-gathering ends and immoral and illegal spying begins).

It is followed by contacts with principals, reciprocal site visits and financials gathering.

STEP SIXTEEN

One of the most important aspects of financial analysis of any target is to discover its market posture—both its relative market share and its share relative to its next larger competitor to discover whether it is a market leader or not. This "Target Market Share Analysis" feeds into the financial analysis and is incorporated into the Business Plan for the target.

If there is encouragement to proceed and the information seems to fit the Fit Chart, the financial modeling begins.

One of the most important analytical documents to be generated in the analysis is a financial evaluation including Common-Size, Trended and Industry Comparison analyses. (See Exhibits B-3 and B-5 to this Appendix B.) The evaluation should focus on several key areas: shareholder value and maximum purchase price; pro-forma financial statement analysis, and, most importantly, sensitivity analysis.

The sensistivity analysis tells the buyer which value-drivers affect the seller's value the most. This guides "what-if" analysis, the search for synergies, and the establishment of post-acquisition performance criteria.

No acquisition should ever be attempted without a Business Plan for it. There is no other way to price the acquisition unless you are going to liquidate it and even there the value of the component parts, if to be sold as active businesses, should be sold on the basis of the future stream of earnings that is to be generated. And an integral part of that plan should be an ongoing acquisition program whose potential for success should be impounded in the price.

1. Opportunity Descriptions

    a. When filling out the Opportunity descriptions, make sure that you do not hold back. It will be the job of the Fit Chart to eliminate the off-the-wall notions.

    b. Do not confine your suggested entries to new items alone. Review discontinued operations remembering the "skateboard" effect—its popularity revives about every twelve years. (The vacuum tube effect is similar as the electronics industry now consumes many times the number of vacuum tubes for power uses than were ever used by the industry before the transistor which was designed to replace it.)

    c. Don't worry about duplicating others' ideas. The chances of an exact duplicate is vanishingly small and yours might have a little twist that makes it work.

2. Strength and Weakness Descriptions

    a. S&Ws are often of a subjective nature and to try to separate out those which would apply to an external acquisition and those which would apply to an internal development or to an ongoing organizational problem is a problem. Just let it all hang out.

    b. An underutilized resource is both a weakness—because it is not being used—and a strength because you know how to use it. It can be written up either way but not both.

EXHIBIT B-2

WEAKNESS ANALYSIS

CONFIDENTIAL

INSTRUCTIONS: Please pinpoint those characteristics of your business that are equal or inferior to others.

What is one of your principal weaknesses?

```
Vertical communications between the two top levels at D.I.
```

Why do you believe this?

```
Middle managers are never told when a major change in philosophy or direction is planned.  Problems are
handed up to the top level--really "dumped" on them without any proposed solutions.  Many of the
career people are never asked their opinions about anything.  The field office managers who have
high profit and loss responsibility are never consulted when a job goes bad.
```

Give a specific example:

```
On the Hess job, the output was doubled.  Engineering never told the shop until after the contract was
renegotiated.  We had to go double overtime to get the job out.  If marketing had told us the job was
coming we could have subbed out the high-labor-content portion and even have saved some
money on it.  Purchasing was kept in the dark and we could have bought at mill quantity prices if we
had known.
```

Is this weakness management-related, business-related, or industry-related?

```
Strictly management related.  If we make some aquisitions and don't have a good communications
system in place, we could blow it.  If we can't communicate here where engineering, sales and production
are under one roof, how in the hell will we run something in East Jesus without it getting all screwed up.
```

My time frame of reference is: ☐ Short-term (1-2 years)   ☐ Intermediate (2-5 years)
☒ Long-term (5-10 years.)

Session Comments:

```
A task group, run by J. B. Zorchbeagle will be formed immediately to review the last fifteen jobs where
billings were over $3 million total.  Marketing, Engineering, Production and Field Service will appoint
one top executive each to the Task Group.  They are to bring out a Recommended Order Procedures Guide
in draft form as soon as possible but certainly by June 10, 1985.
```

Session Action: (check one) ☒ Wheel & Fit   ☐ Organization Development   ☐ Other

Submitted By: _____   Date: 9/22/88

Stanley Foster Reed & Associates, 1621 Brookside Road, McLean, Virginia 22101   Form SFR 3-83

EXHIBIT B-3

Assets	Yrs	Actual 19X5	19X6	19X7	Common Size Analysis Total Assets are used as the Balance Sheet common denominator, whereas Sales are used in the Income Statement of J.T. Smith Consultants 19X5	19X6	19X7
CURRENT ASSETS							
Cash & cash equivalents		$2,706	$5,556	$3,322	25.26%	29.62%	18.52%
Work in process		$1,546	$3,122	$3,122	14.43%	16.65%	17.40%
Accounts receivable		$3,396	$4,408	$6,172	31.70%	23.50%	34.40%
Allowance for doubtful accts		($204)	($264)	($270)	−1.90%	−1.41%	−1.50%
Prepaid expenses		$100	$171	$169	0.93%	0.91%	0.94%
Total current assets		$7,544	$12,993	$12,515	70.42%	69.27%	69.75%
PROPERTY, PLANT, & EQUIPMENT							
Equipment, furn & vehicles		$1,266	$2,480	$2,720	$11.82%	13.22%	15.16%
Building		$1,350	$1,350	$1,350	12.60%	7.20%	7.52%
Building improvements		$118	$178	$180	1.10%	0.95%	1.00%
Less: Depreciation		($738)	($1,577)	($1,773)	−6.89%	−8.41%	−9.88%
Total P,P & E		$1,996	$2,431	$2,477	18.63%	12.96%	13.81%
OTHER ASSETS							
Patents/trademarks		$1,200	$1,750	$1,900	11.20%	9.33%	10.59%
Other investments		($27)	$1,582	$1,050	−0.25%	8.43%	5.85%
Total other assets		$1,173	$3,332	$2,950	10.95%	17.76%	16.44%
TOTAL ASSETS							
Liabilities and S/E		$10,713	$18,756	$17,942	100.00%	100.00%	100.00%
CURRENT LIABILITIES							
Payroll payable		$1,092	$1,307	$879	10.09%	7.14%	5.07%
Accounts payable		$270	$900	$863	2.50%	4.92%	4.98%
Accrued payables		$1,841	$178	$199	17.02%	0.97%	1.15%
Total current liab.		$3,203	$2,385	$1,941	29.61%	13.03%	11.19%
LONG TERM LIABILITIES		$845	$936	$497	7.81%	5.11%	2.87%
STOCKHOLDER'S EQUITY		$6,770	$14,989	$14,908	62.58%	81.86%	85.94%
TOTAL LIABILITIES & S/E		$10,818	$18,310	$17,346	100.00%	100.00%	100.00%

	Industry Comparisons Industry norm information below corresponds with J.T. Smith's S.I.C. code.			Trended Analysis All items are expressed as a percentage of the base year, 19X1 of J.T. Smith Consultants.	
19X5	19X6	19X7	19X5	19X6	19X7
			100.00%	205.32%	122.76%
			100.00%	201.94%	201.94%
			100.00%	129.80%	181.74%
			100.00%	−129.41%	−132.35%
			100.00%	171.00%	169.00%
70.0%	69.8%	71.0%	100.00%	172.23%	165.89%
			100.00%	195.89%	214.85%
			100.00%	100.00%	100.00%
			100.00%	150.85%	152.54%
			100.00%	−213.69%	−240.24%
20.5%	20.1%	18.5%	100.00%	121.79%	124.10%
			100.00%	145.83%	158.33%
95.0%	10.1%	10.5%	100.00%	284.06%	251.49%
100.00%	100.00%	100.00%	100.00%	173.28%	165.76%
			100.00%	119.69%	80.49%
			100.00%	333.33%	319.63%
			100.00%	9.67%	10.81%
38.9%	30.8%	26.5%	100.00%	74.32%	60.49%
5.6%	5.0%	5.0%	100.00%	110.77%	58.82%
55.5%	64.2%	68.5%	100.00%	221.40%	220.21%
100.0%	100.0%	100.0%	100.00%	169.16%	160.25%

EXHIBIT B-3 (*Continued*)

Income Statement	Yrs	19X5	19X6	19X7	19X5	19X6	19X7
SALES		$23,494	$34,034	$36,695	100.00%	100.00%	100.00%
COST OF GOODS SOLD:							
Materials		$440	$885	$950	1.87%	2.60%	2.59%
Wages/contract labor		$12,115	$17,001	$17,555	51.57%	49.95%	47.84%
Overhead		$4,105	$6,812	$7,233	17.47%	20.02%	19.71%
TOTAL COST OF GOODS SOLD		$16,660	$24,698	$25,738	70.91%	72.57%	70.14%
GROSS PROFIT		$6,834	$9,336	$10,957	29.09%	27.43%	29.86%
OPERATING EXPENSES							
Advertising/promotion		$605	$900	$1,300	2.58%	2.64%	3.54%
Auto expense		$121	$331	$445	0.52%	0.97%	1.21%
Amortization of patent		$1	$1	$1	0.00%	0.00%	0.00%
Bad debt expense		$130	$128	$89	0.55%	0.38%	0.24%
Collection expense		$2	$16	$3	0.01%	0.05%	0.01%
Commissions		$257	$192	$149	1.09%	0.56%	0.41%
Depreciation-building		$168	$174	$175	0.72%	0.51%	0.48%
Depreciation-machinery		$211	$338	$356	0.90%	0.99%	0.97%
Insurance		$318	$330	$565	1.35%	0.97%	1.54%
Maintenance		$93	$264	$367	0.40%	0.78%	1.00%
Office supplies and expense		$72	$95	$100	0.31%	0.28%	0.27%
Product development		$3	$3	$3	0.01%	0.01%	0.01%
Professional services		$126	$136	$127	0.54%	0.40%	0.35%
Rent		$13	$63	$78	0.06%	0.19%	0.21%
Salaries		$1,322	$1,540	$1,522	5.63%	4.52%	4.15%
Taxes-Local		$172	$281	$282	0.73%	0.83%	0.77%
Telephone		$54	$67	$66	0.23%	0.20%	0.18%
Travel		$960	$1,100	$1,455	4.09%	3.23%	3.97%
Utilities		$33	$106	$145	0.14%	0.31%	0.40%
TOTAL OPERATING EXPENSES		$4,661	$6,065	$7,228	19.84%	17.82%	19.70%
OPERATING INCOME		$2,173	$3,271	$3,279	9.25%	9.61%	10.16%
OTHER INCOME		$181	$425	$455	0.77%	1.25%	1.24%
OTHER EXPENSE:							
Interest expense		$119	$189	$162	0.51%	0.56%	0.44%
Management-building		$3	$0	$0	0.01%	0.00%	0.00%
Profit share & defined benefit		$694	$356	$89	2.95%	1.05%	0.24%
TOTAL OTHER EXPENSE		$816	$545	$251	3.47%	1.60%	0.68%
EXTRAORDINARY ITEMS		($26)	($365)	($860)	−0.11%	−1.07%	−2.34%
NET PROFIT BEFORE TAXES		$1,512	$2,786	$3,073	6.44%	8.19%	8.37%
PROVISION FOR INCOME TAXES		$655	$1,100	$1,155	2.79%	3.23%	3.15%
NET INCOME		$857	$1,686	$1,918	3.65%	4.95%	5.23%

19X5	19X6	19X7	19X5	19X6	19X7
100.00%	100.00%	100.00%	100.00%	144.86%	156.19%
			100.00%	201.14%	215.91%
			100.00%	140.33%	144.90%
			100.00%	165.94%	176.20%
74.5%	74.1%	73.8%	100.00%	148.25%	154.49%
25.5%	25.9%	26.2%	100.00%	136.61%	160.33%
			100.00%	148.76%	214.88%
			100.00%	273.55%	367.77%
			100.00%	100.00%	100.00%
			100.00%	98.46%	68.46%
			100.00%	800.00%	150.00%
			100.00%	74.71%	57.98%
			100.00%	103.57%	104.17%
			100.00%	160.19%	168.72%
			100.00%	103.77%	177.67%
			100.00%	283.87%	394.62%
			100.00%	131.94%	138.89%
			100.00%	100.00%	100.00%
			100.00%	107.94%	100.79%
			100.00%	484.62%	600.00%
			100.00%	116.49%	115.13%
			100.00%	163.37%	163.95%
			100.00%	124.07%	122.22%
			100.00%	114.58%	151.56%
			100.00%	321.21%	439.39%
21.5%	22.0%	21.0%	100.00%	130.12%	155.07%
4.0%	3.9%	5.2%	100.00%	150.53%	171.61%
			100.00%	234.81%	251.38%
			100.00%	158.82%	136.13%
			100.00%	51.30%	12.82%
			100.00%	66.79%	30.76%
4.0%	3.9%	5.2%	100.00%	184.26%	203.24%
1.1%	1.2%	1.2%	100.00%	167.94%	176.34%
2.9%	2.7%	4.0%	100.00%	196.73%	223.80%

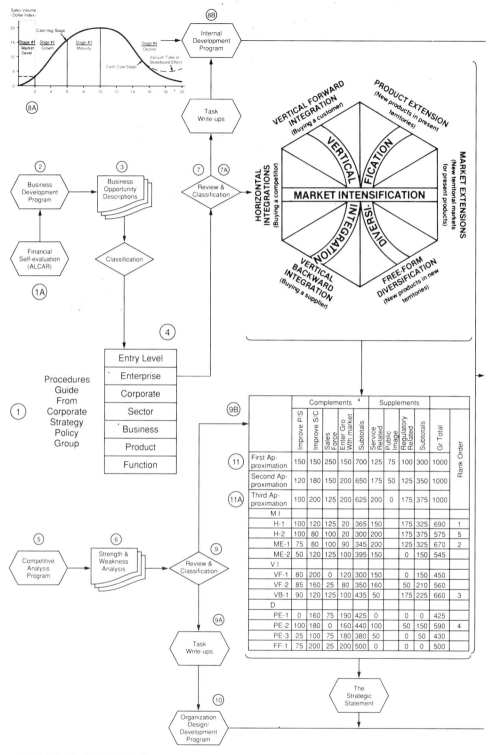

STANLEY FOSTER REED'S SYSTEMS APPROACH

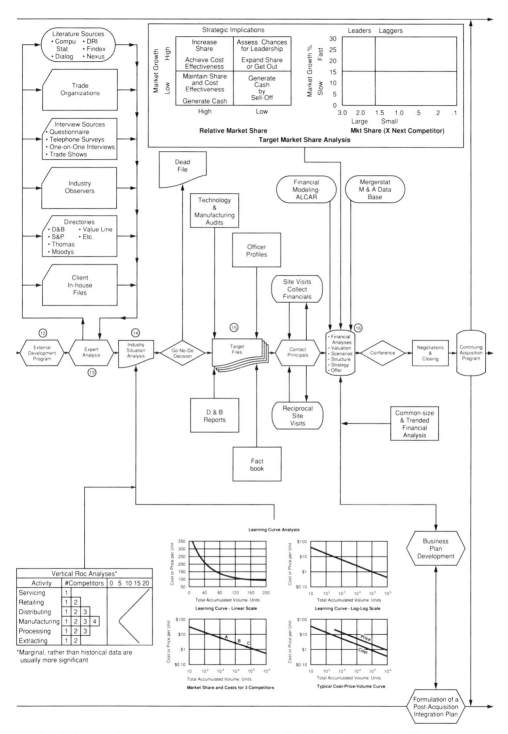

TO CORPORATE GROWTH

Reed Associates McLean, VA 22101
1621 Brookside Rd. Telephone: (703) 534-7771

EXHIBIT B-5

Income Statement for Sample Company

Most Likely Scenario

($ in Millions)	1984	1985	1986	1987	1988	1989	1990
Sales	$1,934.5	$2,032.0	$2,235.2	$2,414.0	$2,558.9	$2,712.4	$2,875.1
Cost of Goods Sold	1,435.2	1,529.9	1,698.8	1,834.7	1,842.4	1,844.4	1,955.1
Gross Profit	499.3	502.1	536.4	579.4	716.5	868.0	920.0
Salary Expense	156.2	169.3	109.5	118.3	125.4	132.9	140.9
Selling Expense	54.3	57.8	55.9	60.4	64.0	67.8	71.9
Administrative Expenses	87.2	93.5	148.2	125.2	251.0	365.7	377.8
Total SG & A Expense	297.7	320.6	313.6	303.8	440.4	566.4	590.6
Other Operating Income	0.5	1.2	0.9	0.9	0.9	0.9	0.9
Depreciation Expense	49.3	55.1	57.5	61.0	64.0	66.1	68.1
Operating Profit	$152.8	$127.6	$166.3	$215.4	$213.1	$236.3	$262.3
Interest Income	0.0	0.0	8.7	20.5	33.0	47.4	64.2
Interest Expense:Sched Debt	N/A	N/A	16.0	16.0	16.0	16.0	16.0
Total Interest Expense	15.4	17.6	16.0	16.0	16.0	16.0	16.0
Less:Interest Capitalized	3.0	3.0	3.0	3.0	3.0	3.0	3.0
Interest Expense	12.4	14.6	13.0	13.0	13.0	13.0	13.0
Gain on Sale of Assets	6.5	7.3	0.0	0.0	0.0	0.0	0.0
Other Non-Operating Income	32.4	36.3	40.2	43.1	45.0	45.0	45.0
Earnings Before Taxes	$179.3	$156.6	$202.2	$266.1	$278.0	$315.7	$358.5
Provision for Income Taxes	67.1	23.4	70.2	92.9	91.8	102.5	114.4
Extraordinary Items	0.0	(2.8)	0.0	0.0	0.0	0.0	0.0
Net Income	$112.2	$130.4	$131.9	$173.2	$186.3	$213.3	$244.1
Preferred Dividends	4.1	4.3	4.5	4.7	5.1	5.1	5.1
Income Available for Common	$108.1	$126.1	$127.4	$168.5	$181.2	$208.2	$239.0
Common Dividends	$12.5	$13.4	$14.1	$57.2	$61.5	$70.4	$80.6

EXHIBIT B-5 (cont.)

Balance Sheet for Sample Company

Most Likely Scenario

($ in Millions)	1984	1985	1986	1987	1988	1989	1990
Cash	$4.3	$17.8	$24.3	$30.0	$34.7	$39.6	$44.8
Marketable Securities	4.1	70.9	166.9	268.2	385.3	522.3	673.1
Accounts Receivable	357.9	397.6	420.4	440.4	456.6	473.8	492.0
Raw Materials	73.0	75.7	78.3	80.7	82.5	84.5	86.7
Work in Progress	182.6	189.2	200.2	209.8	217.7	225.9	234.7
Finished Goods	109.5	113.4	120.5	126.7	131.7	137.1	142.7
Total Inventories	365.1	378.3	399.0	417.2	431.9	447.6	464.1
Other Current Assets	43.7	43.7	43.7	43.7	43.7	43.7	43.7
Total Current Assets	$775.1	$908.3	$1,054.3	$1,199.5	$1,352.2	$1,527.0	$1,717.7
Gross PP&E excl. Int. Cap.	769.8	798.1	844.2	882.7	910.4	934.9	955.6
Cum. Forecast Interest Cap.	N/A	N/A	3.0	5.8	8.4	10.8	13.0
Less:Accum. Depreciation	276.5	269.9	293.7	312.3	329.2	341.2	341.3
Net Property, Plant & Equip	493.3	528.2	553.5	576.1	589.5	604.5	627.4
Goodwill	52.9	46.5	46.5	46.5	46.5	46.5	46.5
Other Intangibles	4.5	3.3	3.3	3.3	3.3	3.3	3.3
Other Assets	22.6	42.3	42.3	42.3	42.3	42.3	42.3
Total Assets	$1,348.4	$1,528.6	$1,699.9	$1,867.7	$2,033.9	$2,223.5	$2,437.2
Accounts Payable	$145.9	$192.7	$221.1	$246.2	$266.5	$288.0	$310.7
Current Portion L-T Debt	12.4	11.8	24.9	25.2	25.9	26.6	27.4
Income Taxes Payable	17.3	17.5	16.4	21.7	21.5	24.0	26.8
Other Current Liabilities	71.6	71.6	71.6	71.6	71.6	71.6	71.6
Total Current Liabilities	$247.2	$293.6	$334.0	$364.7	$385.4	$410.2	$436.5
Total L-T Debt	323.7	335.9	340.0	350.0	360.0	370.0	380.0
Deferred Income Taxes	87.3	98.2	108.9	122.7	136.4	151.5	168.4
Other Liabilities	22.6	14.2	15.0	15.0	15.0	15.0	15.0
Total Liabilities	$680.8	$741.9	$797.9	$852.4	$896.8	$946.7	$999.9
Preferred Stock	37.9	39.4	41.4	43.4	45.4	47.4	49.4
Common Stock and Paid-In Cap	612.4	620.3	620.3	620.3	620.3	620.3	620.3
Retained Earnings	17.3	127.0	240.3	351.7	471.4	609.1	767.6
Total Liabilities and Equity	$1,348.4	$1,528.6	$1,699.9	$1,867.7	$2,033.9	$2,223.5	$2,437.2
Unused Debt Capacity (UDC)	$35.3	$98.6	$153.1	$213.2	$278.3	$355.1	$445.4
UDC plus Mkt. Securities	$39.4	$169.5	$320.1	$481.4	$663.6	$877.4	$1,118.4

EXHIBIT B-5 (cont.)

```
                                      Funds Flow Statement for Sample Company
                                      ----------------------------------------
                                             Most Likely Scenario
                                             --------------------
```

($ in Millions)	1985	1986	1987	1988	1989	1990
Net Income	$130.4	$131.9	$173.2	$186.3	$213.3	$244.1
Depr. Exp. excl. Int. Cap.	55.1	57.5	60.8	63.6	65.5	67.3
Depr. Exp. on Cum. Int. Cap.	N/A	N/A	0.2	0.4	0.6	0.8
Less:Interest Capitalized	3.0	3.0	3.0	3.0	3.0	3.0
Incr. in Deferred Inc. Taxes	10.9	10.7	13.8	13.7	15.2	16.8
Incr. in Other Liabilities	(8.4)	0.8	0.0	0.0	0.0	0.0
Incr. in Debt: Scheduled	12.2	4.1	10.0	10.0	10.0	10.0
Net Bk. Value of Ret. Assets	8.1	20.9	18.3	20.0	20.2	14.0
Incr. in Accounts Payable	46.8	28.4	25.0	20.3	21.5	22.8
Incr. in Curr Port. L-T Debt	(0.6)	13.1	0.3	0.7	0.7	0.7
Incr. in Income Tax Payable	0.2	(1.1)	5.3	(0.3)	2.5	2.8
Proceeds from Sale of Common	7.9	0.0	0.0	0.0	0.0	0.0
Proceeds from Sale of Pf.Stk	1.5	2.0	2.0	2.0	2.0	2.0
Total Sources of Funds	$261.1	$265.3	$306.0	$313.7	$348.5	$378.4
	============	============	============	============	============	============
Fixed Capital Investment	$98.1	$100.7	$98.9	$94.4	$98.2	$102.0
Additions to Goodwill	(6.4)	0.0	0.0	0.0	0.0	0.0
Additions to Intangibles	(1.2)	0.0	0.0	0.0	0.0	0.0
Incr. in Other Assets	19.7	0.0	0.0	0.0	0.0	0.0
Incr. in Cash	13.5	6.5	5.7	4.6	4.9	5.2
Incr. in Mkt Securities	66.8	96.0	101.3	117.1	137.0	150.7
Incr. in Accts Receivable	39.7	22.8	20.0	16.2	17.2	18.2
Incr. in Raw Materials	2.7	2.6	2.3	1.9	2.0	2.1
Incr. in Work in Progress	6.6	11.0	9.7	7.8	8.3	8.8
Incr. in Finished Goods	3.9	7.1	6.2	5.0	5.3	5.7
Total Incr. in Inventories	13.2	20.7	18.2	14.7	15.6	16.6
Preferred Dividends	4.3	4.5	4.7	5.1	5.1	5.1
Common Dividends	13.4	14.1	57.2	61.5	70.4	80.6
Total Uses of Funds	$261.1	$265.3	$306.0	$313.7	$348.5	$378.4
	============	============	============	============	============	============

EXHIBIT B-5 (cont.)

Cash Flow Statement for Sample Company

Most Likely Scenario

($ in Millions)	1985	1986	1987	1988	1989	1990
Sales	$2,032.0	$2,235.2	$2,414.0	$2,558.9	$2,712.4	$2,875.1
Cost of Goods Sold	1,529.9	1,698.8	1,834.7	1,842.4	1,844.4	1,955.1
Gross Profit	502.1	536.4	579.4	716.5	868.0	920.0
Salary Expense	169.3	109.5	118.3	125.4	132.9	140.9
Selling Expense	57.8	55.9	60.4	64.0	67.8	71.9
Administrative Expenses	93.5	148.2	125.2	251.0	365.7	377.8
Total SG & A Expense	320.6	313.6	303.8	440.4	566.4	590.6
Other Operating Income	1.2	0.9	0.9	0.9	0.9	0.9
Depreciation Expense	55.1	57.5	61.0	64.0	66.1	68.1
Operating Profit	127.6	166.3	215.4	213.1	236.3	262.3
Depr. Exp. excl. Int. Cap.	55.1	57.5	60.8	63.6	65.5	67.3
Depr. Exp. on Cum. Int. Cap.	N/A	N/A	0.2	0.4	0.6	0.8
Funds from Opers. Before Tax	182.7	223.7	276.4	277.0	302.4	330.4
Cash Income Taxes	19.5	65.8	85.3	84.3	93.5	103.8
Funds From Opers. After Tax	$163.2	$157.9	$191.2	$192.7	$208.9	$226.6
Increm. Working Cap. Invest.	19.4	22.6	13.6	15.6	13.7	14.4
Fixed Capital Investment	98.1	100.7	98.9	94.4	98.2	102.0
Additions to Goodwill	(6.4)	0.0	0.0	0.0	0.0	0.0
Additions to Intangibles	(1.2)	0.0	0.0	0.0	0.0	0.0
Proceeds (af.tax) Asset Sale	15.4	20.9	18.3	20.0	20.2	14.0
Cash Flow from Operations	$68.7	$55.5	$97.0	$102.7	$117.1	$124.2
Cash Flow from Operations	$68.7	$55.5	$97.0	$102.7	$117.1	$124.2
Interest Expense:Sched Debt	N/A	16.0	16.0	16.0	16.0	16.0
Total Interest Expense	17.6	16.0	16.0	16.0	16.0	16.0
Interest Expense (After Tax)	10.6	9.8	9.8	9.8	9.8	9.8
Non-Operating Inc. (af.tax)	33.5	48.9	63.6	78.0	92.4	109.2
Non-Operating Sources	(8.4)	0.8	0.0	0.0	0.0	0.0
Non-Operating Uses	19.7	0.0	0.0	0.0	0.0	0.0
Proceeds from Sale of Common	7.9	0.0	0.0	0.0	0.0	0.0
Preferred Dividends	4.3	4.5	4.7	5.1	5.1	5.1
Net Cash Provided	$67.1	$91.0	$146.1	$165.8	$194.7	$218.5
Common Dividends	13.4	14.1	57.2	61.5	70.4	80.6
Funding Surplus/(Deficit)	$53.7	$76.9	$89.0	$104.4	$124.3	$138.0
Funding Surplus/(Deficit)	$53.7	$76.9	$89.0	$104.4	$124.3	$138.0
Incr. in Curr Port. L-T Debt	(0.6)	13.1	0.3	0.7	0.7	0.7
Incr. in Debt: Scheduled	12.2	4.1	10.0	10.0	10.0	10.0

EXHIBIT B-5 (cont.)

Cash Analysis Statement for Sample Company

Most Likely Scenario

($ in Millions)	1985	1986	1987	1988	1989	1990
Net Income	$130.4	$131.9	$173.2	$186.3	$213.3	$244.1
Plus: Depr. Exp. excl. Int. Cap.	55.1	57.5	60.8	63.6	65.5	67.3
Depr. Exp. on Cum. Int. Cap.	N/A	N/A	0.2	0.4	0.6	0.8
Extraordinary Items	(2.8)	0.0	0.0	0.0	0.0	0.0
Interest Expense	14.6	13.0	13.0	13.0	13.0	13.0
Provision for Income Taxes	23.4	70.2	92.9	91.8	102.5	114.4
Less: Non-Operating Profit	36.3	48.9	63.6	78.0	92.4	109.2
Gain on Sale of Assets	7.3	0.0	0.0	0.0	0.0	0.0
Cash Income Taxes	19.5	65.8	85.3	84.3	93.5	103.8
Funds From Opers. After Tax	$163.2	$157.9	$191.2	$192.7	$208.9	$226.6
Plus: Incr. in Accounts Payable	46.8	28.4	25.0	20.3	21.5	22.8
Incr. in Income Tax Payable	0.2	(1.1)	5.3	(0.3)	2.5	2.8
Less: Incr. in Cash	13.5	6.5	5.7	4.6	4.9	5.2
Incr. in Accts Receivable	39.7	22.8	20.0	16.2	17.2	18.2
Incr. in Raw Materials	2.7	2.6	2.3	1.9	2.0	2.1
Incr. in Work in Progress	6.6	11.0	9.7	7.8	8.3	8.8
Incr. in Finished Goods	3.9	7.1	6.2	5.0	5.3	5.7
Total Incr. in Inventories	13.2	20.7	18.2	14.7	15.6	16.6
Cash from Operating Cycle	$143.8	$135.4	$177.5	$177.1	$195.2	$212.1
Less: Fixed Capital Investment	98.1	100.7	98.9	94.4	98.2	102.0
Additions to Goodwill	(6.4)	0.0	0.0	0.0	0.0	0.0
Additions to Intangibles	(1.2)	0.0	0.0	0.0	0.0	0.0
Plus: Proceeds (af.tax) Asset Sale	15.4	20.9	18.3	20.0	20.2	14.0
Cash Flow from Operations	$68.7	$55.5	$97.0	$102.7	$117.1	$124.2
Less: Non-Operating Uses	19.7	0.0	0.0	0.0	0.0	0.0
Plus: Non-Operating Sources	(8.4)	0.8	0.0	0.0	0.0	0.0
Non-Operating Inc. (af.tax)	33.5	48.9	63.6	78.0	92.4	109.2
Cash bef.Fin.Cost & Ext.Fin.	$74.1	$105.2	$160.6	$180.7	$209.5	$233.4
Less: Interest Expense (After Tax)	10.6	9.8	9.8	9.8	9.8	9.8
Preferred Dividends	4.3	4.5	4.7	5.1	5.1	5.1
Common Dividends	13.4	14.1	57.2	61.5	70.4	80.6
Cash bef. External Financing	$45.8	$76.9	$89.0	$104.4	$124.3	$138.0
Plus: Incr. in Curr Port. L-T Debt	(0.6)	13.1	0.3	0.7	0.7	0.7
Incr. in Debt: Scheduled	12.2	4.1	10.0	10.0	10.0	10.0
Proceeds from Sale of Pf.Stk	1.5	2.0	2.0	2.0	2.0	2.0
Proceeds from Sale of Common	7.9	0.0	0.0	0.0	0.0	0.0
Incr. in Mkt Securities	$66.8	$96.0	$101.3	$117.1	$137.0	$150.7
Proceeds from Sale of Pf.Stk	1.5	2.0	2.0	2.0	2.0	2.0
Incr. in Mkt Securities	$66.8	$96.0	$101.3	$117.1	$137.0	$150.7

EXHIBIT B-5 (cont.)

Financial Ratios for Sample Company

Most Likely Scenario

	1984	1985	1986	1987	1988	1989	1990
Profit Performance Ratios							
Gross Profit Margin (%)	25.810	24.710	24.000	24.000	28.000	32.000	32.000
Change in Net Income (%)	N/A	16.221	1.153	31.317	7.538	14.497	14.467
Return on Sales (%)	5.800	6.417	5.901	7.175	7.279	7.863	8.491
Return on Equity (%)	17.818	17.449	15.327	17.821	17.063	17.347	17.589
Return on Assets or Inv. (%)	9.022	9.407	8.334	9.796	9.638	10.030	10.417
Return on Net Assets (%)	11.047	11.643	10.372	12.173	11.892	12.299	12.690
Leverage Ratios							
Debt/Equity Ratio (%)	59.393	51.800	47.206	43.064	39.509	36.117	32.911
Debt/Total Capital (%)	37.262	34.124	32.068	30.101	28.320	26.534	24.762
Equity Ratio (%)	46.700	48.888	50.626	52.040	53.674	55.292	56.948
Times Interest Earned	12.448	9.727	13.447	17.442	18.190	20.546	23.221
Activity Ratios							
Days in Receivables	N/A	67.854	66.785	65.072	63.974	62.602	61.307
Days in Payables	N/A	40.391	44.460	46.487	50.781	54.858	55.886
Inventory Turnover	N/A	4.116	4.371	4.496	4.339	4.194	4.289
Fixed Asset Turnover	N/A	3.847	4.038	4.190	4.340	4.487	4.583
Total Asset Turnover	N/A	1.329	1.315	1.292	1.258	1.220	1.180
Liquidity Ratios							
Quick Ratio	1.482	1.656	1.831	2.025	2.274	2.525	2.772
Current Ratio	3.136	3.094	3.156	3.289	3.508	3.723	3.935
Per-Share Data							
Earnings Per Share	8.07	9.41	9.51	12.58	13.52	15.54	17.84
Change in EPS (%)	N/A	16.65	1.03	32.27	7.51	14.91	14.82
Primary EPS	8.07	9.41	9.51	12.58	13.52	15.54	17.84
Fully Diluted EPS	8.07	9.41	9.51	12.58	13.52	15.54	17.84
Dividends Per Share	0.93	1.00	1.05	4.27	4.59	5.25	6.01
Cash Flow per Share	N/A	5.13	4.14	7.24	7.66	8.74	9.27
Book Value Per Share	47.70	56.61	65.20	73.63	82.70	93.14	105.14
Valuation Ratios							
Change in Share. Val./Share	N/A	N/A	7.93	10.12	(0.86)	3.66	3.33
Share. Value per Share (PV)	N/A	N/A	40.11	50.23	49.37	53.03	56.36
Oper. Profit Margin (P) (%)	7.899	6.280	7.439	8.924	8.326	8.712	8.472
Threshold Margin (%)	N/A	7.664	6.325	7.278	8.695	8.118	8.472
Threshold Spread (%)	N/A	(1.384)	1.115	1.646	(0.369)	0.594	0.650
Incremental Profit Margin(%)	N/A	(25.846)	19.035	27.486	(1.638)	15.139	15.971
Increm. Threshold Margin (%)	N/A	2.999	6.774	5.270	4.881	4.639	4.482
Increm. Threshold Spread (%)	N/A	(28.846)	12.261	22.216	(6.519)	10.500	11.490
Value Drivers							
Sales Growth Rate (G) (%)	N/A	5.04	10.00	8.00	6.00	6.00	6.00
Oper. Profit Margin (P) (%)	7.90	6.28	7.44	8.92	8.33	8.71	9.12
Inc. Fixed Cap. Inv. (F) (%)	N/A	44.10	21.30	21.30	21.30	21.30	21.30
Inc. Work. Cap. Inv. (W) (%)	N/A	19.90	11.10	7.62	10.76	8.95	8.86
Cash Income Tax Rate (Tc)(%)	N/A	15.29	39.58	39.58	39.58	39.58	39.58
Discount Rates							
Average Cost of Capital (%)	15.30						
Long-Term Cost of Capital	15.30						
Internal Rate of Return (%)	32.05						

Memo: Avg. Cost of Capital and IRR based on forecast data (1986 to 1990)
      IRR uses Pre-Strat. Resid. Value as investment ($433.673 million)

EXHIBIT B-5 (cont.)

Reconciliation for Sample Company - 1987
Most Likely Scenario
($ in Millions)

	EARNINGS	ADJUSTMENTS	CASH FLOWS
Sales	$2,414.0		
Less: Incr. in Accts Receivable		20.0	
Cash Receipts	1,834.7		$2,394.0
Cost of Goods Sold			
Less: Incr. in Accounts Payable		25.0	
Plus: Total Incr. in Inventories		18.2	
Cash COGS			1,827.8
Gross Profit	$579.4		
Total SG & A Expense	303.8		
Plus: Incr. in Cash		5.7	
Less: Incr. in Income Tax Payable		5.3	
Cash SG & A Expense			304.3
Increm. Working Cap. Invest.		$13.6	
Other Operating Income	0.9		0.9
Depreciation Expense	61.0		
Plus: Depreciation Expense: Funds		61.0	
Depreciation in Other Items		98.9	0.0
Fixed Capital Investment		98.9	98.9
Operating Profit	$215.4		
Interest Income	20.5		
Interest Expense	13.0		
Other Non-Operating Income	43.1		
Earnings Before Taxes	$266.1		
Provision for Income Taxes	92.9		
Less: Incr. in Deferred Inc. Taxes		13.8	
Cash Income Taxes			85.3
Proceeds (af.tax) Asset Sale			18.3
Cash Flow from Operations			$97.0
Net Income	$173.2		

Valuation Summary for Sample Company
Most Likely Scenario
5 Year Forecast
($ in Millions)

Cumulative PV Cash Flows	$315.3
Present Value of Res. Value	437.5
Marketable Securities	70.9
CORPORATE VALUE	$823.7
Less:Mkt Val of Debt	63.0
Less:Unfunded Pension Liabs.	16.7
SHAREHOLDER VALUE (PV)	$744.0
Less:Pre-Strat. Shar. Value	424.9
Value Contrib. by Strategy	$319.1
Share. Value per Share (PV)	$56.36
Current Stock Price	$49.50
Prem/Disc Over/Under Mkt (%)	13.86
Value ROI (%)	180.62
Value ROS (%)	55.79

EXHIBIT B-5 (cont.)

Cash Flows and Shareholder Value for Sample Company

Most Likely Scenario

(Average Cost of Capital (%) = 15.300%)

($ in Millions)

Year	Cash Flow	Pres. Value Cash Flow	Cum. PV Cash Flows	Pres. Value Residual Value	Cum PV CF + PV Residual Value	Increase in Value
1986	$55.5	$48.2	$48.2	$490.1	$538.3	$104.6
1987	97.0	72.9	121.1	550.8	671.8	133.5
1988	102.7	67.0	188.1	472.4	660.5	(11.3)
1989	117.1	66.3	254.4	454.4	708.8	48.3
1990	124.2	60.9	315.3	437.5	752.8	44.0

$319.1
========

Marketable Securities	70.9
CORPORATE VALUE	$823.7
Less:Mkt Val of Debt	63.0
Less:Unfunded Pension Liabs.	16.7
SHAREHOLDER VALUE (PV)	$744.0

========

Share. Value per Share (PV)	$56.36
Current Stock Price	$49.50
Prem/Disc Over/Under Mkt (%)	13.86

Relative Impact of Key Variables on Shareholder Value for Sample Company

Most Likely Scenario

($ in Millions)

A 1% Increase in:	Increases Shareholder Value by:	% Increase
Sales Growth Rate (G)	$0.4	0.054
Operating Profit Margin (P)	8.7	1.163
Increm. Fixed Capital Investment (F)	(1.2)	(0.164)
Increm. Working Capital Investment (W)	(0.5)	(0.074)
Cash Income Tax Rate (Tc)	(2.8)	(0.377)
Residual Value Income Tax Rate (Tr)	(4.0)	(0.543)
Cost of Capital (K)	(4.2)	(0.560)

Profit Margins for Sample Company

Most Likely Scenario

Year	Operating Profit Margin	Threshold Margin	Threshold Spread	Incremental Profit Margin	Incremental Threshold Margin	Incremental Threshold Spread
1986	7.439%	6.325%	1.115%	19.035%	6.774%	12.261%
1987	8.924	7.278	1.646	27.486	5.270	22.216
1988	8.326	8.695	(0.369)	(1.638)	4.881	(6.519)
1989	8.712	8.118	0.594	15.139	4.639	10.500
1990	9.123	8.472	0.650	15.971	4.482	11.490

TABLE OF CASES

Hanson Trust (p. 725)	*Hanson Trust PLC v. ML SCM Corp.*, 774 F.2d 47 (2d Cir. 1985).
Irving Trust (p. 122)	*K.M.C., Inc. v. Irving Trust Co.*, 757 F.2d 752 (6th Cir. 1985).
Kupetz (p. 130)	*Kupetz v. Wolf*, 845 F.2d 842 (9th Cir. 1988).
Martin Marietta (pp. 778-779)	*Martin Marietta Corp. v. Bendix Corp.*, 549 F.Supp. 623 (D. Md. 1982).
Pennzoil (pp. 534, 640)	*Texaco Inc. v. Pennzoil Co.* 729 S.W.2d 768 (Tex. App. 1987), *cert. dism'd*, 108 S. Ct. 1305, 99 L.Ed.2d 686 (1988).
Philadelphia National Bank (p. 52)	*United States v. Philadelphia National Bank, et al.*, 374 U.S. 321, 83 S.Ct. 1715, 10 L.Ed.2d 915 (1963).
Revlon (pp. 750-751)	*Revlon, Inc. v. MacAndrews & Forbes Holdings, Inc.*, 506 A.2d 173 (Del. 1986).
Tilley (p. 506)	*Tilley v. Mead Corp.*, 815 F.2d 989 (4th Cir. 1987).
Treadway (p. 767)	*Treadway Companies, Inc. v. Care Corp.*, 638 F.2d 357 (2d Cir. 1980).
Van Gorkom (pp. 744-745, 755)	*Smith v. Van Gorkom*, 488 A.2d 858 (Del. 1985).

INDEX

Note: When searching for a particular Section or Rule by number, look under the heading "Section" or "Rule" or the name of the applicable statute.

For full citations of cases named in italics, see the Table of Cases, p. 919.